MASTERING
WINDOWS™
NT SERVER 3.51

Mark Minasi
Christa Anderson
Elizabeth Creegan

Second Edition

NETWORK PRESS
SYBEX

San Francisco • Paris • Düsseldorf • Soest

Acquisitions Manager: Kristine Plachy
Developmental Editor: John Read
Editor: James A. Compton
Technical Editor: Howard Crawford
Book Designer: Helen Bruno
Technical Illustrators: Cuong Le and Catalin Dulfu
Desktop Publisher: Deborah Maizels
Production Coordinator: Nathan Johanson
Indexer: Ted Laux
Cover Designer: Archer Design
Cover Photographer: Doug Plummer

This book is dedicated to the management team at Mark Minasi & Company. Without Donna Cook (my company's Marketing Animal), Patrick Campbell (our chief instructor), and Cynthia Dowell (the tireless business manager), I would never have had time to write this book—or many others.

ACKNOWLEDGMENTS

This was an enormous project, and it couldn't have happened without some very important people.

First of all, I want to thank my co-authors Maeve (Elizabeth) Creegan and Christa Anderson. When this project started, Maeve and Christa were both research assistants in my employ, and I envisioned them merely doing some of the spadework needed to get the book underway. I became very busy, however, so I asked them to try their hands at writing some of the chapters. They both performed many times better than I imagined possible, writing some very good stuff indeed. You can see Maeve's hand in Chapters 7, 8, and 10, as well as in the Event Viewer material in Chapter 15. Christa ably penned Chapters 4, 6, 9, and parts of 15, 16, and 17. Their work was so exceptional that it would be criminal not to share authorship with them.

That said, however, a note: I went through all of the text in the book in order to unify the style and voice, as well as check the text for accuracy. For that reason, any errors or oversights are my fault, and my fault only.

Second, I must thank our "silent" co-author, Kris Ashton. Kris knows a million times more about Macs than I do, and wrote Chapter 18.

The folks at SYBEX are always a pleasure to work with. Without the vision of people like Gary Masters and Rudy Langer, these books wouldn't exist. Rudy's untimely passing was a loss to everyone who writes or uses computer books. Our manuscript editors Peter Weverka and Val Potter suffered through a *lot* of text; thanks go to them and to the book's technical editor, Howard Crawford. Thanks also to the SYBEX production team of Dina Quan and Taris Duffié. The editing and production team for this second edition included Jim Compton, Deborah Maizels, Nathan Johanson, Cuong Le, Catalin Dalfu, and Elsie Yim.

My research assistant Leslie McMurrer had the task of converting over 600 pages of data into a format that we could pour into the SYBEX publishing programs, a job kind of like the one Hercules did in the Aegean stables. I cannot thank her enough.

Thanks also to the makers of Presentation Task Force, the best clip art collection around these days, for letting us use some of their icons in this book.

And thanks to the folks at Microsoft for the betas—and for a high-quality product worth writing about!

CONTENTS AT A GLANCE

TABLE OF CONTENTS

17 Using the Remote Access Server 713

INTRODUCTION

In 1986, Microsoft released its first networking product, a tool called MS-NET. It sold mainly in the guise of the IBM PC Network Support Program. The servers were DOS-based, offered minimal security, and, to be honest, provided *awful* performance. But the software had two main effects on the market.

First, the fact that IBM sold a LAN product legitimized the whole industry. That made it possible for others to make a living selling network products. And that led to the second effect: the growth of Novell. Once the idea of a LAN was legitimized, most companies responded by going out and getting the LAN operating system that offered the best bang for the buck. That was an easy decision: NetWare. In the early days of networking, Novell established itself as the performance leader. You could effectively serve about twice as many workstations with Novell NetWare as you could with any of the MS-NET products. So Novell prospered.

As time went on, however, Microsoft got better at building network products. 3Com, wanting to offer a product that was compatible with the IBM PC Network software, licensed MS-NET and resold it as "3+" software. 3Com knew quite a bit about networking, however, and recognized the limitations of MS-NET. So 3Com reworked MS-NET to improve its performance, something that didn't escape Microsoft's attention.

In the 1985–1988 time frame, Microsoft worked on its second generation of networking software, software based on its OS/2 1.0 operating system. (Remember, Microsoft was the main driving force behind OS/2 from 1985 through early 1990.) Seeing the good work that 3Com did with MS-NET, Microsoft worked as partners with 3Com in building this next generation of LAN software, called Microsoft LAN Manager. It was never Microsoft's intention to directly market LAN Manager. Instead, it saw IBM, 3Com, Compaq, and others selling it.

IBM did indeed sell LAN Manager, and it still does in the guise of OS/2 LAN Server. 3Com sold LAN Manager for years as 3+Open, but found little profit in it and got out of the software business, to the chagrin of the businesses who'd invested in the 3+Open software. In late 1990, Compaq announced that it would *not* sell LAN Manager, as it was too complex a product for dealers to explain, sell, and support. Microsoft decided at that moment that if LAN Manager were to be sold, then it would have to do the selling. Microsoft announced on the very same day as the Compaq withdrawal that it would begin selling LAN Manager directly.

LAN Manager in its 1.0 incarnation still wasn't half the product that Novell Net-Ware was, but it was closer. LAN Manager 2.0 started closing the gap, and in fact on some benchmarks LAN Manager outpaced Novell NetWare. Besides, LAN Manager included some administrative and security features that brought it even closer to Novell NetWare in the minds of many network managers. Slowly, LAN Manager gained about a 20 percent share of the network market.

When Microsoft designed LAN Manager, however, it designed the product for the 286 chip. LAN Manager's inherent 286 nature hampered its performance and sales. In contrast, Novell designed its premier products (NetWare 3 and 4) to use the full capabilities of 386 and later processors. Microsoft's breakup with IBM delayed the release of a 386-based product and, in a sense, Microsoft *never* released the 386-based product.

Instead of continuing to climb the ladder of Intel processor capabilities, Microsoft decided to build an operating system that was processor-independent, an operating system that would sit in roughly the same market position as UNIX. It could then be implemented for the 386 and later chips, certainly, but it also could run well on other processors, such as the PowerPC, Alpha, and MIPS chips. Microsoft called this new operating system NT, for "new technology."

In August of 1993, Microsoft released NT Advanced Server in its first incarnation, Microsoft Windows NT Advanced Server version 3.1. NT Advanced Server performed quite well, and network planners started taking a closer look at the new networking product. It was memory-hungry, however, lacked Novell connectivity, and had only the most basic TCP/IP connectivity.

September of 1994 brought a new version, and a new name, Microsoft Windows NT Server version 3.5. Version 3.5 was mainly a "polish" of 3.1; it was less memory-hungry, included Novell and TCP/IP connectivity right in the box, and included Windows for Workgroups versions of the administrative tools so that a network administrator could work from a Workgroups machine rather than an NT machine. To continue the trend, mid-1995 saw the release of version 3.51, which offers some improvements over version 3.5.

Networks in the mid-90s don't just need simple file server capabilities; more and more of them require *client-server* capabilities, and NT Server can actually rival Novell NetWare's attractiveness. Furthermore, NT Server is fairly cheap compared to Novell NetWare, making it even more attractive as a simple file server.

That means that the networks of today often have more than one kind of server software. There are often Novell file servers, NT Server database servers, perhaps a UNIX NFS system around, and of course let's not forget the connections to the old mainframes. But that's a real headache for network managers, who now have to support all these different network operating systems *and* support their *interaction*.

What You'll Learn from This Book

This book is intended to assist a network manager or planner in planning, configuring, installing, running, and repairing networks that include NT Server. Although NT Server is the prime focus of this book, you'll also learn how to make NT Server interoperate with other networks. Throughout the planning of this book, I assumed that only the lucky few had networks composed solely of NT Server servers. (Those of you in that category should count your blessings.)

In this book, I'll expose you to the underlying concepts, and then we'll apply them directly. If there are several ways to get a job done, then I'll try to explain them all, highlighting the ones that cost the least time or money. I'll recommend other sources of information and utilities that will make your job as a network manager a bit more, well, manageable.

Thanks for picking up this book. Now, let's get down to work!

Conventions Used in This Book

In this book, there are a number of things that can be quite complex to have to write out, so I'll use a few conventions that you should be aware of.

x86 vs. RISC

The term *x86*, which is used in this book and in similar books, refers to any machine that uses a processor in the Intel line that includes the 8086, 8088, 80188, 80186, 80286, 80386DX, 80386SL, 80386SX, 80486DX, 80486SX, 80486SL, 80486DX2, Intel DX4, the Pentium, the P54C, or P24T processors.

When I am referring to *client* machines, I could be referring to any of these processors. When I am referring to an NT Server or NT workstation system, I'm referring to one of the 386, 486, or Pentium families of chips.

RISC is short for, as you probably know, *reduced instruction set computing*. As I write this, NT is available for the MIPS R4000 RISC processor in both the workstation and server mode, and for the DEC Alpha. The IBM/Motorola/Apple Power PC chip will see a version of NT soon as well.

All RISC systems must follow a standard called the *Advanced RISC Computer*, or ARC, standard. For that reason, I will generically refer to these three RISC families all as RISC, even though internally they are quite different. That's the good thing about NT: As an architecture-independent operating system, it masks hardware differences.

Assume that the System Is on the C Drive

If you're running NT Server on an x86-based machine, I'll assume that you've installed your operating system in C:\winnt35. That would mean you have a C:\winnt35\system directory, which I'll refer to as the "system" directory, and a C:\winnt35\system32 directory, which I'll refer to as the "system32" directory.

The Text Icons

As you read through the text, you'll see two icons—the Enterprise Networking icon and the NT Server icon—which I'll use to point out items of particular interest.

ENTERPRISE NETWORKING

Enterprise Networking Icon   Much of what NT makes sense for—and one of my main objectives in writing this book—is *enterprise networking*, a term that describes networks built from heterogeneous pieces. Issues specific to connecting NT networks to other NT networks, connecting NT networks to wide area networks

(WANs), or connecting NT networks to other local area networks (LANs) are all marked by the Enterprise Networking icon.

NT Server Icon I originally set out to write a book for people who work mainly with NT Server, rather than NT. I believed, and still believe, that the NT workstation product is of little value in today's world, and it certainly is not a replacement for more common workstation environments like Windows or OS/2. There were books aimed at NT users in general, but no books aimed at NT Server users, at least not until I got finished writing the previous edition of this one. But I found, to my surprise, that most of the power of NT Server was shared by the basic NT workstation product, making this a book of value to users of the NT workstation product after all. For that reason, I attempted to make clear which parts of the text were only relevant to NT Server with the NT Server icon. I want to stress to NT Server administrators that this does not mean that I was waylaid on the path to an NT Server book; nothing could be further from the truth. I have not discussed issues of value only to NT workstation users—issues that were largely irrelevant to NT Server users, such as how to change the wallpaper or where to find really neat NT games. The NT Server icon is there to keep the reader who uses NT's workstation software from wasting his or her time.

In addition, you'll find information highlighted as tips, which look like this:

 Tips are just things that are kind of "aside" information. Often I use them to point out things stumbled upon when researching NT.

"How Do I" Sidebars

NT's *big*. I mean *really* big. A side effect of its bigness is that quite a number of procedures aren't hard to do, or even hard to learn, but they *do* take time. So I decided when writing this that any step-by-step procedure that took me more than 30 seconds to figure out would take *you* more than 30 seconds, too, and for easy reference I pulled these procedures out of the text and placed them in sidebars. Sidebars are marked with the "How Do I" icon.

There's a complete list of "How Do I" sidebars inside the back cover of this book. You'll also find them in the table of contents, listed in italics and beginning with the words *How Do I.*

How to Read This Book

This book is broken into four parts.

The first part, "Getting Acquainted," is an introduction to and overview of the NT Server networking world. In Chapters 1 and 2, I explain why you'd consider using NT Server. I provide an overview of Microsoft networking concepts. Readers who are already familiar with another network, such as Novell NetWare, can use Chapter 2 as a kind of translation device for transferring their Novell-based networking knowledge to Microsoft enterprise networking knowledge. NT Server has a lot of concepts in common with NetWare. Even if you've never set up a network before, Chapter 2 will give you the overview that you need to understand much of the rest of the book.

The second part, "Setting Up NT Server," looks at installing NT Server, and how to use a few tools. It starts with Chapter 3, which explains the ins and outs of installing NT Server. Once your server is installed, you'll want to add other mass storage and fault tolerance, and that's covered in Chapter 4. Chapters 5 and 6 cover two basic tools for viewing and modifying your server's configuration, the NT Registry and the Microsoft System Diagnostics (WINMSD) programs.

The third part, "NT Server Administration," explains how to use the basic tools that all network administrators need. Chapters 7 through 10 explain how to use the User Manager for Domains, the File Manager, the Print Manager, and the Server Manager. These four chapters, taken together, present a kind of basic network administrator's manual.

Chapter 11 starts off the fourth, and more "advanced," part of the book, "Managing NTS in the Enterprise Network." Chapter 11 explains how to control a network and use the User Manager for Domains, the File Manager, the Print Manager, and the Server Manager to administer *multidomain* networks. Chapters 12, 13, and, to an extent, Chapter 18 cover important internetworking topics, including connecting to Novell networks (Chapter 12), TCP/IP and the Internet (Chapter 13), and Macintosh networks (Chapter 18). Chapters 14 and 15 discuss tuning, monitoring, and protecting a network. Chapter 16 introduces the complex and powerful NET command, which can do everything that other administration tools can do without the graphical user interface. It all happens from the command line, which can be useful when you're writing batch files. Chapter 17 shows how to set up and use Remote Access Services (RAS) and extend your network's reach to everywhere the telephone lines go.

Talk Back to Me!

NT is an enormous system. I've worked with it as long as anyone has, but I don't know it all yet, not by a long shot. Got a tip that you'd like me to share with the rest of the world? Send it to me, and I'll acknowledge your help in the next edition of this book. Got a question that I didn't answer? Mail it to me, and I'll do my best to get an answer. Found a (gasp!) error? Again, send it along and I'll acknowledge the help. You can find me either on CompuServe at 71571,264, or on the Internet at mark@smtphost.mmco.com. When I'm out of the country (which is two months a year), I don't pick up my e-mail, so if I don't get back to you immediately, don't be offended—I'll respond as soon as I can. Thanks for reading, and I hope you find this book to be the ultimate NT Server guide!

PART I

Getting Acquainted

NT Server Overview

In many ways, NT Server is a big departure from previous PC-based server products. Those currently managing a Novell NetWare, LAN Server, or LAN Manager LAN will have to understand the ways that NT Server departs from its LAN Manager past in order to get the most from NT Server.

NT Server Capabilities

The NT operating system itself has some quite attractive features, whether it is to be used as a workstation operating system or as a server operating system. Let's take a look at some of the features that make NT Server stand out from the competition.

Architecture Independence

Most operating systems are designed from first conception with a particular target processor in mind. Processor characteristics like word size, page support, big-endian or little-endian storage, and protection modes affect an operating system's design. Powerful but gimmicky features of a processor become integral parts of operating systems, while essential features that the processor doesn't support go by the wayside. For example, look at the pervasive 16-bit nature of many Intel-based operating systems, a nature directly attributable to the 8088 and 80286 processors. The first member of the Intel processor family that PC compatibles have been built around, the 8086, first appeared in 1977. Eight years went by before a 32-bit Intel x86 processor appeared (x86 refers to this family of PC compatible processors: the 8086, 8088, 80188, 80186, 80286, 80386, 80486, and Pentium chips). Even though that 32-bit processor has been available since 1985, it took nearly ten years for 32-bit operating systems to appear.

When Microsoft designed NT, it specifically did *not* implement it on an x86 chip. Microsoft wanted to build something that was independent of any processor's architecture, and it knew that Microsoft programmers knew the x86 architecture intimately and that the programmers' intimate knowledge would inevitably work its way into the design of NT. So, to combat that problem, Microsoft first implemented NT on a RISC chip, the MIPS R4000.

The parts of NT that are machine-specific are all segregated into a relatively small piece of NT (compared to the total size of the operating system) called the Hardware

Abstraction Layer, or HAL. Implementing NT on a new processor type, therefore, mainly involves just writing a new HAL.

What does this mean to a network manager? Well, many LANs have for years used Intel x86-based servers. As the needs of the LANs grew, so (fortunately) did the power of the x86 family of Intel processor chips. These chips steadily grew faster and more powerful. When the average network had about fifteen users, 286-based servers were around. When people started putting a hundred users on a server, 486s could be bought.

Unfortunately, however, since 1991, x86 processors haven't really grown in power as quickly as they previously did. RISC machines that are reasonably priced and that offer pretty high-speed processing have begun to appear. That's why the architecture-independent nature of NT Server is so attractive. The next time you need a bigger server, you needn't buy a PC-compatible machine with all the baggage that PC compatibility weighs a machine down with. Instead, you can buy a simple, fast, streamlined machine designed simply to act as a LAN server and potentially provide decent service to perhaps hundreds of users.

Multiple Processor Support

I just said that CPUs weren't getting faster quite as quickly as they once did. There's more than one way to make a faster computer, however; you can use a faster processor *or* you can just use *more* processors.

Compaq's Systempro was the first well-known PC compatible computer to include multiple processors; nowadays, that would be the Compaq Proliant. IBM likewise offers a multiprocessor PS/2 model 295. There aren't too many multiprocessor PC compatibles, but the RISC world contains a decent number of multiprocessor systems.

NT in its basic form was designed to support up to 32 processors in a PC. NT Server can also split its tasks up among 32 processors. For some reason, however, Microsoft chose to cripple the basic versions of workstation NT and NT Server, shipping Hardware Abstraction Layers (HALs) that support only two and four processors, respectively. If you want to use more than two processors on an NT workstation or four processors on an NT Server machine, then you'll have to bug your hardware vendor for an improved HAL that supports more than those numbers of processors. In any case, however, servers can have up to 32 processors in them, with the right HAL.

Among multiprocessing systems, a computer is said to be a *symmetric* or *asymmetric* multiprocessor. An asymmetric multiprocessor has more than one processor, but each processor has a different, specifically defined job. The early Systempros were asymmetric systems. A symmetric multiprocessing system, in contrast, has processors that can take over for one another without skipping a beat. Each processor has complete access to all hardware, bus, and memory actions. NT and NT Server must have symmetric processor systems in order to use multiprocessor capabilities.

Multithreaded Multitasking

Whether you have more than one processor or just one processor in your system, NT supports multitasking. The multitasking is "true" multitasking in that it is preemptive, time-sliced, priority-driven multitasking. (All that is explained in Chapter 14 on server tuning.)

Multitasking usually means that a single computer can run several different programs. Each program, however, usually is only single-tasking within itself. Consider, for example, how a word processor is built. It picks up keystrokes, then it does something with them, and then it goes on to the next keystroke. Apply that to a *graphical* word processor, and you can see that problems can result.

Suppose you press the Page Down key so the word processor retrieves a page of text either from memory buffers or off the disk and displays a page of text. That can take a bit of time, particularly if the page contains a few graphics, each of which must be retrieved and rendered in a fashion consonant with the abilities of the particular graphics board that you're using. But now suppose you're on page 30 and you want to move to page 33. You just press Page Down three times, and the three Page Down keystrokes go into the keyboard buffer of the word-processing program. Now, because the word-processing program is *single-threaded* (that is, because it does just one thing at a time and in a particular order) it will see the first Page Down key, and it will then retrieve and render the entire page 31. Only after it's through doing that will it look again in the keyboard buffer, see another Page Down, and go through the whole process again for page 32, and then for page 33.

One way to avoid this kind of time-wasting "tunnel vision" is to build the word processor as a group of smaller programs, all of which run simultaneously. There could be a kind of "boss" program that reads the keystrokes, calling the "render the page" routine. That program could interrupt the "render the page" routine when a new keystroke came in, keeping it from wasting time displaying pages that would soon be overwritten on the screen immediately.

NT lets developers create such a program, called a *multithreaded* program. Each of the small independent subprograms is called a *thread*, hence the term "multithreaded."

Multithreading is essential for server-based programs like database servers, which must be able to respond to multiple requests for information from many client sources.

Massive Memory Space

NT programs don't have to worry about running up against some kind of 640K or 16K barrier. The NT architecture can support RAM of up to 4096MB (four *gigabytes*). (Now, where did I put those one-gig SIMMs...?)

I should mention, by the way, that it's not a good idea to put more than 16MB on an ISA (Industry Standard Architecture) bus machine. If your servers are to have more than 16MB, get a PC-based on the Micro Channel Architecture (MCA), Extended Industry Standard Architecture (EISA), or Peripheral Component Interconnect (PCI) bus. Or you could get a RISC machine, where there is no 16MB boundary.

Centralized User Profiles

Each Windows or DOS program seems to need its own configuration file or files, leading to a disk littered with a lot of files with the extensions INI, CNF, or the like. NT centralizes program initialization information with a database of program setup information called *the registry*; part of that database, a user-specific part, is called a *user profile*. NT even allows you to store an NT workstation's profile on a server, making it possible to centrally control the equivalent of CONFIG.SYS and AUTOEXEC.BAT (and Windows.INI) files for a workstation from a central server heaven for support folks.

If your work takes you from workstation to workstation, then you may feel a bit like a Bedouin, with no home. Nomadic computing means that when you log onto a new workstation, you've got to spend time arranging the look of that workstation to your particular tastes. (And, of course, the person who *usually* uses the workstation may not appreciate your "improvements.")

NT improves upon that with the notion of a *profile*. A user profile contains information like

- background colors
- wallpaper
- screen saver preferences
- program manager groups

Under NT, you can create a profile *for an NT workstation*—this is no good for a regular Windows workstation—and then you can tell NT to have that profile follow you around.

As a support person, you'll especially like the fact that you can use a profile to restrict the kinds of things a user can do. You can even make a profile mandatory, moving us one step closer to central control of desktop PCs. The only catch? NT profiles are different from Windows 95 profiles, so the profiles you set up for your NT clients won't work for 95 clients, and vice versa.

Enterprise Networking Features

ENTERPRISE NETWORKING

On top of NT Server's basic operating system features, however, is a wide array of networking capabilities, many of particular value to builders of multi-operating system *enterprise* networks, networks built of large numbers of machines and servers. Enterprise networks have some special needs; here's how NT meets those needs.

Event and Account Logging

When I got started in the computer business, I worked on a mainframe-based system. Like all users on that system, I had an account that kept track of a balance of sort of pseudomoney. Whenever I "logged on to" my mainframe, the account would be debited a bit for every minute that I was on, a bit more for each byte of shared disk storage that I used, and some more for each program I ran on that mainframe.

The other mainframe users and I used to call these accounts "funny money" because, after running a program, you'd get a printout detailing the charges that you engendered by running the program so much for each page printed, so much for the disk space used, and so on. Although it would have a dollar total, no money changed hands. The whole purpose of the "funny money" accounts was to impress upon the mainframe's users that the mainframe was a limited resource and not to waste shared computer resources.

LANs are getting to be more and more like mainframes. They serve hundreds of users in many companies, they're a shared resource, and they cost a lot of money to keep up and running. Eventually, companies will want to assign "funny money" accounts to LAN users as a means of keeping track of who is putting the greatest strain on the system. While this may sound a trifle authoritarian, it's not. Users depend on LANs more and more, and if just a few users make it difficult for others to get *their* jobs done, then there must be a way for network administrators to figure out who's killing the network.

That's what event logging and auditing is all about. Under NT Server, you can keep track of who prints on what printer at what time, who uses what files at what time and for how long, and who's logged onto which server. NT Server provides a great deal of power for keeping track of what's happening on your network.

Remote Access Services

There's always been a need for information workers to be able to take their work home. Once, workers brought a briefcase stuffed with papers home. Then mainframe users dragged home a thermal paper terminal called the "Silent 700." More recently, people with PCs at home dialed up the company LAN via a program like Carbon Copy or PC Anywhere, or perhaps via a more expensive solution like the Shiva NetModem. It's not just office workers who need remote access, either; members of roving salesforces may only physically touch their home bases once a month or so, but they need to exchange data with that home base.

NT Server includes a remote access capability, built right into it. The remote-access software shipped with NT is the *server* end of the software; the client end—the piece that goes on the workstation—is included in the NT workstation software and Windows version 3.11 and later. Microsoft also offers remote-access client software for DOS and earlier versions of Windows; those files can be found in the \CLIENTS\RAS directory of the installation CD-ROM disk.

Domain and Workgroup-Based Administration Features

NT Server includes programs that make it simple to control security on a number of servers.

If your company has just one server, then these features won't be very attractive. But if your firm has a number of servers, then you'll soon find that administering groups of servers can be a real pain in the neck. For example, suppose you want to add a user to the Finance department. There are four servers in Finance. That means that you've got to log onto each one individually and create the same user account on each one; ditto if you've got to delete a user account. With the domain-management capabilities of NT Server, you can make those changes to a whole group of servers with just a few mouse-clicks.

As NT Server is a modern LAN operating system, it goes without saying that you can assign security access rights all the way down to the user and file level; you can say that user X can only read file Y, but user Z can read and write file Y. You can also set files to an "execute-only" privilege level, making it possible for someone to run a program on the server, but *im*possible to copy the program from the server. About the only thing that you can't do with the security features of NT Server is to link them to security programs in the mainframe world, like ACF/2 and RACF, unfortunately.

Fault Tolerance and RAID Support

Part of security involves keeping people from data that they're not supposed to have access to, but an equally big part of security's functions include keeping safe the data that people have entrusted to the network. To that end, NT Server incorporates a number of features that support fault tolerance:

- The database of domain security information resides on a single server called the *domain controller*, but other servers in the domain can act as backup domain controllers, ready to step in as domain controller whenever the primary one goes off-line.

- NT Server supports multiple network cards in a server, so a network card failure won't necessarily bring down a server.

- *Directory replication* makes it possible to designate a directory on a particular server and then create a backup server whose job it is to match, on a minute-by-minute basis, the contents of that directory. This ensures that essential things like logon scripts are available from several sources, making logons quicker.

- *Hot fixes* are a feature on any NT Server whose disk has been formatted under the NTFS file system. NTFS constantly monitors the disk areas that it is using, and if it finds that one has become damaged, then it takes the bad area out of service and moves the data on that area to another, safer area automatically.

- RAID (Redundant Array of Inexpensive Drives) is a six-level method for combining several disk drives into what appears to the system to be a single disk drive. RAID improves upon a single-drive answer in that it offers better speed and data redundancy.

  - Level 0, or *disk striping,* improves speed only. It creates what appears to be one disk out of several separate physical disk drives. Areas that appear to be a cylinder or a track on a logical disk drive are actually spread across two or more physical disk drives. The benefit is realized when accessing data; when reading a block of data, the read operation can actually become several simultaneous separate disk reads of several physical disks.

  - Level 1 is a straightforward *disk mirroring* system. You get two disk drives, and tell NT to make one a mirror image of the other. It's fast and fault-tolerant.

  - Levels 2, 3, and 4 are not supported by NT Server.

  - Level 5 is very much like level 1, in that data is striped across several separate physical drives. It differs, however, in that it adds redundant information called "parity" that allows damaged data to be reconstructed.

The different levels of RAID do not get better as they rise in numbers; they're just different options. The interesting part about NT's RAID support, however, is that it happens in *software,* not hardware. You needn't buy a specialized RAID box to get the benefits of RAID; all you have to do is just buy a bunch of SCSI drives and use the NT Disk Administrator program to RAID-ize them. (You need not use SCSI drives, but they are easier to connect. SCSI drives also support sector remapping, which is another fault-tolerant feature that other drives may not support.)

Relatively Low Price for Server and Client Software

Pricing server products is a difficult thing. On the one hand, network server software equals mainframe operating systems in complexity, so software vendors want to realize the same kind of return that they would from mainframe software. That's not possible, however; no one would pay mainframe software prices for software running on a server with eight workstations. But a *hundred* workstations...?

Server software must be reasonably priced for small LANs. But the very same software runs on large LANs, so how does a LAN software vendor justify charging more money for the very same software, based solely on the number of people using it? Nevertheless, major vendors *do* charge more for server software, depending on the number of users; NetWare can cost from hundreds of dollars to tens of thousands of dollars, depending on the number of users on a server.

Pricing under 3.51 is a mite complex. A copy of NT Server 3.5x costs $700, whether you're upgrading from NT Advanced Server 3.1, upgrading from LAN Manager or Novell, or just buying the NT Server outright. That includes the server, remote access, TCP/IP support, ISDN support, Macintosh support, and software RAID. Upgrading from 3.5 to 3.51 costs $80.

Where things get more complex is in the client pricing. You can either buy a *client license* for each user in order for that user to legally log onto your NT Server domain, or a *connection* license for each server a client—any client—will access. Both licenses ordinarily cost $40 per person or per connection. Client licenses are only $20 for those upgrading from Novell or LAN Manager. Upgraders from NT Advanced Server 3.1 must still buy $40 licenses, *except* that upgraders get the first 250 licenses free.

We'll discuss further ramifications of the two licensing plans a little later in this book, when we get to the installation process.

NDIS Protocol Support

Getting network boards to work with network operating systems has never been a simple thing. Even more difficult has been supporting multiple protocols on a single network card, and most unpleasant of all has been getting multiple protocols to work on multiple network cards.

Novell attacks this problem with its Open Data-Link Interface, or ODI, standard. Microsoft's answer is the Network Driver Interface Specification, or NDIS. Each has its own pluses and minuses, but NDIS 3.0 and later has a terrific feature in its ability to load client software in extended memory, which is quite a plus for those running memory-hungry DOS software.

Protocol Compatibility with Forebears

Obviously, NT Server communicates with its forebears. In particular, LAN Manager 2.2 servers can act as members of NT Server's domains and can assist in some but not all domain control functions.

NetWare Support

Knowing that much of its audience needs to be able to interface with existing Novell NetWare servers, NT Server contains some capabilities to communicate with Novell products. The connectivity isn't perfect, however. You can't unify the domain administration for your Novell NetWare network with the administration for NT Server.

With NT's Client and Gateway Services for NetWare, you can extend Novell services to parts of your network that don't even run Novell software. That's a sneaky way to bend Novell's maximum number of users on each server, but it's a little *too* good: NT makes it tough to carry over Novell security to NT users. (In any case, you can learn all about it in Chapter 11.)

NetBIOS, DLC, and TCP/IP Options

Over the years, a number of network/transport/session protocols have grown up. There is a great variety of these protocols for two reasons. First, some are just products of large computer companies, which want to build their own proprietary protocols and give themselves a competitive advantage. Second, different protocols are built to serve different needs.

NetBEUI was originally built by IBM to quickly zip data around small LANs. It's a really "quick and dirty" protocol in that you cannot easily move NetBEUI data over wide-area networks. NetBEUI is one of the default protocols of NT Server 3.5x. (NWLink is the other.) You'll hear people beat up on NetBEUI for its simplicity, but make no mistake: for a single-segment network, it is *the* fastest transport protocol available.

TCP/IP is a kind of *de facto* standard for building networks composed of many different vendors' products. TCP/IP has until recently not been very popular in the role of LAN protocol, but it *can* serve quite well in that role, and recent improvements to TCP/IP have made it even more attractive on LANs. It is possible to replace NetBEUI with TCP/IP in NT Server.

DLC (Data Link Control) is also known as IEEE 802.2. It's not a complete protocol, so it can't serve in the role of LAN or WAN protocol. But it can provide connectivity to many mainframe gateway products, and to some printers that attach directly to the network, such as any Hewlett-Packard LaserJet with a JetDirect card.

Macintosh Connectivity

Getting Macs and PCs to communicate has always been a bit of a headache. But NT Server makes it very simple. I connected a Mac to my NT Server within fifteen minutes, and it worked the first time.

Under NT Server, you need only create a directory on your server, designate it as a Mac-accessible volume, and start up the Mac Server subsystem.

NT Server has all the ingredients necessary to make it successful in many organizations as an enterprise network server. In the next chapter, we'll look at the network concepts that you'll have to understand in order to work in the Microsoft networking world.

CHAPTER

TWO

2

Microsoft Enterprise Concepts

All networks have their own paradigm and the argot that goes with that. Novell's networks, for example, have always been strongly oriented toward workstation-server architecture. Microsoft's networks grew out of a peer-to-peer network approach, and they show the earmarks of that today.

In this chapter, you'll learn the basic concepts that you'll need in order to plan and manage a Microsoft network.

All of the Microsoft networking products share a whole bunch of scary-sounding terms like SMB, domain, NetBIOS, and the like. In this section, you'll become fluent in "speaking Microsoft."

Types of Networks: Workgroups versus Domains

ENTERPRISE NETWORKING

Microsoft enterprise networking grew out of a circa-1986 product called MS-Net, which was a very simple network that allowed anyone on the network to share resources with anyone else on the network. There were no machines dedicated to the task of providing services; all "servers," therefore, were non-dedicated servers.

That's a nice, simple way to design a network, and it works fine for small offices. Out of that notion grew the idea in Microsoft enterprise networking of a *workgroup*. As LANs became more and more important, however, they also needed facilities for controlling access to network resources—in other words, giving *some* people access to the network printers and disks, and denying access to other people. That kind of selective access control is where *domains* come in. First, though, let's take a look at why we'd worry about workgroups and domains—what are the needs that motivated them?

A Simple Network

To understand why Microsoft networks look as they do, let's go back to 1985, and see how a simple MS-Net network operated. Then we'll see what that network *lacked*, and how NT makes up for those deficiencies.

The whole idea of networks is to share things: share space on a large disk drive, share a particular file on that disk drive, share a printer. Suppose we've got a little office that needs to be able to do some sharing, as you see in Figure 2.1.

FIGURE 2.1:
A simple network

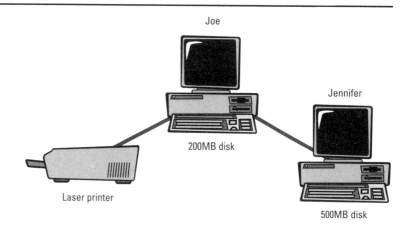

Now, in our simple office, Jennifer's got more storage capacity on her machine than Joe does on his, but Joe's got the office laser printer attached to *his* PC. (It's there because he's bigger than she is, and, as he could carry it to his desk, he got it, rapscallion that he is.) Each PC has an inventory control number, like "DELL05" or "GTW09."

Both Jennifer and Joe work on the office accounting system, so they need to share the accounting files—either that, or they'll have to pass floppies around. Since Jennifer's got more disk space, they put the accounting files on her machine. So, the network problems that we've got to solve are to:

- share Joe's printer with Jennifer, and
- share Jennifer's disk with Joe.

Let's solve their problem with a simplified Microsoft network. With this network, Jennifer just puts her hard disk on the network, and Joe puts his printer on the network.

In a Microsoft network, you start out by naming things. In particular, you've got to give a name to each user (let's use "Joe" and "Jennifer") and also to each PC. We may as well name the PCs with their inventory numbers.

> **TIP** It's a bad idea to name machines after their users, as PCs may get reassigned.

Basically, we get Joe onto Jennifer's disk and Jennifer onto Joe's printer like so:

1. Jennifer says to the networking software (which, again, I haven't named, as there isn't any network exactly like this), "take the \ACCTNG subdirectory on my C: drive and offer it to anyone who wants it. Call it 'ACCNTING.'" ACCNTING is then called, in Microsoft enterprise networking terminology, the *share name* of that drive on Jennifer's machine, and it's the name that others will use to access the drive over the network. In a simple Microsoft network, the command that Jennifer would issue (after loading the basic network software, of course) would be

   ```
   net share accnting=c:\accnting.
   ```

2. Joe then says to the networking software on his PC, "attach me to the ACCNTING drive on Jennifer's machine." Joe doesn't know whether "ACCNTING" is all of Jennifer's drive or just part of it. Joe's networking software then tells him something like, "you're now attached to ACCNTING on Jennifer's machine. It will appear to you as local drive D:."

The actual command that Joe would issue would look like

```
net use d: \\gtw09\accnting.
```

Notice the \\gtw09\accnting term; it's called a *universal naming convention* name, or a "UNC name." The two backslashes are a warning that the name following is a *machine* name, and the backslash after that refers to the *share name* ACCNTING, rather than the directory name.

Now, of course, Joe doesn't *have* a D: on his machine; he's just got network software that takes read and write requests for a mythical (logical) "drive D:" and reformulates those requests into network communication to Jennifer's machine.

3. Joe, meanwhile, runs his network software and tells it to share the printer on his LPT1: port, giving it a name—again, a "share name" of "JOESLASERJET."

4. Jennifer then tells her networking software to attach JOESLASERJET, on Joe's machine, to her LPT1: port, with the command

```
net use lpt1: \\dell05\joeslaserjet
```

From now on, whenever Jennifer tells an application program to print to a LaserJet on LPT1:, the network software will intercept the printed output and direct it over the network to Joe's machine. The networking software on Joe's machine will then print the information on Joe's printer.

What's Wrong with Simple Sharing Solutions?

Nothing is wrong with this network, so long as it never gets bigger. But if it *does* get bigger, then there can be problems like these three:

1. How did we know that Joe's LaserJet was called JoesLaserJet, or that Jennifer's drive was called ACCNTING?

2. What if Jennifer wants Joe to have access to *some* of the files in the shared directory, but not *all* of them?

3. Once the network gets bigger—when other people want to join in—it will have to communicate with other networks. As different networks use different "languages," or, more correctly, *protocols*, how can our one network manage multiple kinds of networks, with their multiple languages/protocols?

The answer to the first question is to have a name server of some kind. The answer to the second question is to install some security features in the system. The answer to the third question is to build a network structure that supports multiple network protocols natively. I'm going to cover all three of these items, as they're crucial to understanding NT Server and Microsoft enterprise networking. But *be warned*: These discussions will start out at a low technical level, but I'll end up getting into some nitty-gritty details, as I don't know where else to put them. If something that you read here doesn't make sense, then go ahead and skip to the next section; once you've finished reading the chapter, then the denser pieces may make sense. You see, the problem is that all the concepts here are interrelated, which makes it difficult to provide a simple top-down explanation of the Microsoft enterprise networking terms.

Browsing and Browse Servers

Years ago, I used the IBM-PC LAN program, the first version of what eventually became NT Server. It was a nice, primitive network operating system much like my Jennifer-and-Joe example. You hooked up to a drive on a server by saying to the PC LAN program, for example, "Attach me to drive E on the machine named AVOCADO." Nice and simple, but it had a major flaw: How did you find out in the first place that the server was named AVOCADO, and that the drive that it was offering was called E? The answer is, *you just had to know the name of the resource before you could use that resource.* There was no "scan the network to find out what's available" feature to the network. (An IBM guy once explained to me that this was "a security feature." Now, why didn't *I* think of that?)

I wanted a kind of "net scan" command, something that would shout to the other systems, "Hey! Whaddya got?" As it turns out, that's not very simple. The whole process of offering services on a network is part of what's known as *name services,* and they're not easy to offer.

Solving the Browse Problem

How would you make a workstation know about every service on the network? There are several approaches.

Static Service Lists

The simplest approach would be to put a file with some kind of services database on every workstation, a kind of "yellow pages" of system capabilities. For example, you might have an ASCII file on every PC that says, "There is a file server on machine BIGPC with a shared disk called BIGDISK, and the computer named PSRV has a shared printer called HP4SI."

This has the advantage of being very fast and very simple to understand. To add a new resource, you would just modify the service list file.

It has the *disadvantage,* however, of being static. Any changes to the system, and some poor fool (that would be *you,* the network administrator) has to go around to all the workstations and update the file. If there were two hundred workstations on your network, then you'd have to actually travel to each workstation and copy that static service list file to that workstation's hard disk. Even worse, this method doesn't take into account the services that were temporarily unavailable, such as a downed server.

This method sounds too primitive to use, but it's not completely useless. In NetWare 3.x, you identify yourself to your desired server via information in NET.CFG. That's a hard-wired server name, and would require a fair amount of editing on every workstation if you wanted to rename an important server—which is why, I suppose, you don't rename servers often in a NetWare world.

Periodic Advertising

Another approach is an occasional broadcast. Every 60 seconds, each resource on NetWare 3.11 tells the rest of the network about itself by shouting, "I'm here!" Novell calls this the Service Advertising Protocol, or SAP. This is another very good idea, and it works great in many cases.

It's not a perfect answer, however. Its problem is that broadcasts take a long time to get around in an enterprise network, and broadcasts clog up the network if that network has a large number of services all advertising. (Imagine if every store in the U.S. were to remind you that it exists *every minute or so*—you'd spend so much time responding to advertising you'd get nothing else done, and your mailbox would be full.) That means that periodic advertising will work on small to medium-size LANs, but on larger networks it would be unworkable. Adding to the problem is the fact that many router systems don't pass broadcast messages, so advertisements may not get from segment to segment.

Name Servers

ENTERPRISE NETWORKING

Yet another approach, and the one used by most enterprise network products, is to assign the task of keeping track of network services to one or more computers, computers called *name servers*. Different parts (usually different geographical parts) of a network each have these name servers, and the name servers update each other's service information periodically. It requires a bit of setting up, but it's one of the most logical ways to keep track of network services.

Microsoft's Answer: Browse Services

Microsoft decided (perhaps rightly) that name servers were hard to set up, and particularly hard to set up in a peer-to-peer network environment where services would be up and down as the day went on, so they developed a different approach.

In Microsoft browse services, there are computers with functions like name servers, but they're called *browse masters* (in some Microsoft literature, they're called *master browsers*, so you may see either term). What's different about the Microsoft browse master concept (by the way, there are also browse backups, machines that back up the browse master) is that there's no one computer fixed as the browse master. Instead, when a computer logs onto the network, it says, "Browse master, I'd like you to add me to your list of browsable computers."

You see a browse list when you're in the Windows for Workgroups or NT File Manager, and click Disk/Connect Network Drive, as you see in Figure 2.2.

FIGURE 2.2:

Sample browse list on Windows NT machine

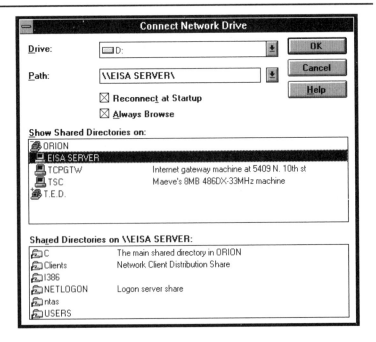

From DOS, you can see a browse list by typing

```
net view or net view \\machinename.
```

Browse Boundaries: Workgroups

Getting back to Joe and Jennifer, the way that Joe knew that Jennifer had a hard disk available for sharing and the way that Jennifer knew about Joe's hard disk was via the browsing information.

But suppose Joe and Jennifer worked in an office with hundreds of workstations. The browse list would be monstrous! (In fact, the browse service has a bit of trouble showing more than fifty "servers," where "server" either means a Windows for Workgroups machine, Windows 95 machine, or any NT machine.) What do we do about that? The answer: a workgroup.

In the simplest kind of Microsoft network, we'd just run Windows for Workgroups or something like that on all our computers, share a few hard disks, share whatever laser printers were around, and that would be fine, except it would make for long browse lists, and an awful lot of things for the browse master to do, particularly if the browse master had to keep track of the comings and goings of dozens of servers. For that reason, Microsoft created the notion of a "workgroup" in Microsoft networking.

When getting started in Microsoft enterprise networking, I had a good bit of trouble understanding the difference between a workgroup and a domain. Part of my confusion about workgroups, as it turned out, came from the fact that there isn't much *to* a workgroup. Here's my definition of a workgroup: *A workgroup is a collection of computers that share resources (printers, disk space, and files) and that share the same browse list.*

In a workgroup, a machine is either a *workstation*, which uses resources but doesn't provide resources, or a *server/workstation*, which both provides resources and uses resources. In a workgroup, there are no machines that function solely as a *server* and only provide resources. Workgroup network software doesn't give you the option to create what's known as a "dedicated server"; instead, it offers only a kind of "workstation/server" combination software.

You may be thinking at the moment, "Wait, what's the big deal with software for a 'dedicated server'? If I want a 'dedicated server,' why don't I just set up that workstation/server software on a machine in a corner somewhere, and then just never use it as a workstation. Wouldn't that be the same as having a 'dedicated server'? What's the difference?" The difference is in the way that dedicated server software is designed versus the way that workstation/server software is designed.

Workstations don't show up on browse lists, as they have nothing to offer. Servers and server/workstations, in contrast, all show up on browse lists. Look back to Figure 2.2, the example browse list, and notice that there are two workgroups, one named ORION and one named T.E.D. The ORION workgroup's list was automatically displayed. To open the T.E.D. browse list, you had to explicitly open it. By only showing the T.E.D. browse list when it's asked for, the browse process gets quicker.

TIP

If you're using Windows for Workgroups, think about disabling file and print sharing on your Windows for Workgroups workstations. The function just makes the browse lists longer, makes browsing take more time, and wastes about 380K of memory. You can disable the sharing either from the Network Setup program, or by changing the FileSharing= and PrinterSharing= settings to NO in the [network] section of a Windows for Workgroups SYSTEM.INI file. The result is that VSERVER.386 isn't loaded, saving the 380K. (While I'm on the subject, you can *improve* network performance at a cost of memory by putting the NumBigBuf= parameter into the [network] section of SYSTEM.INI. Each "BigBuf" is a network buffer, kind of a "cache" for network reads. Each buffer is 4096 bytes in size, and the NumBigBuf= value can range from two to 4096. By default, the system uses one-eighth of free physical memory.

A server program that must also keep an eye out for a local user's needs—that is, a workstation/server program—is mildly distracted from being a server. That means you'll generally be able to serve more users with a machine running *dedicated* server software than you will with a machine running *workstation/server* software.

For best results, you need a piece of software that was designed from the ground up to serve, and only to serve. (That's how Novell beat the pants off Microsoft and IBM back in the late 80s in the network game, and that's why Novell *still* owns most of the network market.)

Which Computers Can Be Workstations or Servers in a Workgroup?

In Microsoft workgroups, some operating environments can act as workstations, some as workstation/servers, and some as dedicated servers. The ones that can only act as workstations are machines running this software:

- Windows 3.x (with Workgroup Connection for MS-DOS clients)
- DOS (with Workgroup Connection for MS-DOS clients)
- LAN Manager Basic/Enhanced 2.2 for MS-DOS and Windows clients
- OS/2 1.x and 2.x (LAN Manager 2.2 for OS/2 clients)

The ones that can act as workstation/servers include these:

- Windows for Workgroups
- Windows 95
- NT Workstation
- NT Server 3.5x (*not* NT Advanced Server 3.1—it can only be part of a domain)
- Workgroup Add-On for MS-DOS

The dedicated servers are:

- Windows for Workgroups 3.11
- NT Server 3.5x

Notice that I did not list NT Advanced Server 3.1. That's because you could not join a simple workgroup with NT Advanced Server 3.1. As a matter of fact, if you *did* join a workgroup with an NT Advanced Server 3.1 machine, then that workgroup would become a *domain* by definition. As of NT Server 3.5, however, that changed; as you'll see in the next chapter, you're asked early in that and later versions of the NT Server installation process whether you want your server to work in a workgroup or a domain.

Security in a Workgroup: "Share-Level" Security

Now, suppose after a while that Joe doesn't want everyone in the world using his laser printer, because the printer has become a popular shared resource, and Joe's system is slowing down as a result. What should he do? There are two possible answers in a workgroup:

- He could hide his laser printer, sharing it but keeping it off the browse list.
- He could put a password on his laser printer.

He can share his printer, but hide it from the browse list, by putting a dollar sign ($) at the end of its name. For example, if I share a printer on my workstation, then the dialog box looks like the one in Figure 2.3 (this is a Windows for Workgroups dialog box).

The default name for this shared printer is HP, as you see in the Share as: field in the figure. If I change that share name to HP$, however, then the share will occur, but the printer won't show up on any browse lists.

That's not exactly great security, but it's a sort of minimum way to keep other people off your printer. The other way to secure the printer would be by putting a password on it. As you can see in the figure, there is a box for entering a password.

FIGURE 2.3:

Sharing printers on a workgroup

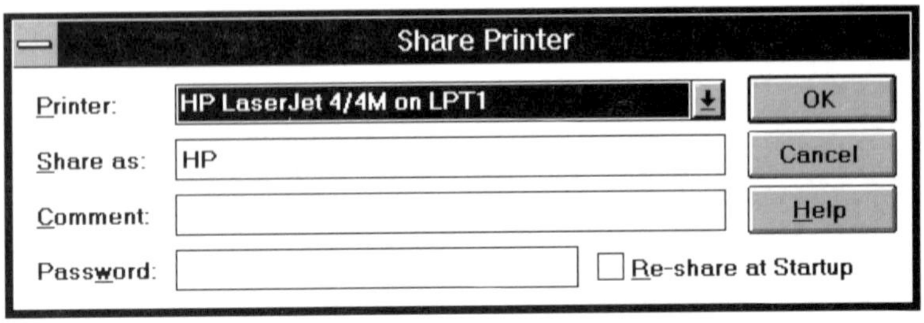

Share Printer		
Printer: HP LaserJet 4/4M on LPT1		OK
Share as: HP		Cancel
Comment:		Help
Password:	☐ Re-share at Startup	

The problem with both of these approaches is that while you can put a password on a printer, it's the same password for *all* of the printer's users. If you wanted to exclude one current user, you could only do it by first changing the password, then finding every one of the other printer's users and telling them the password.

Domains—Improved Workgroups

If you need more intelligent and complete security in a network system, then you need a *domain*. A domain is basically a "super workgroup," a workgroup with centralized control of security.

With a workgroup, your workstation has separate linkages—*shares*, in Microsoft terminology—to each network directory or printer that it uses. Each of those shares can have its own separate password, as you read earlier, but unfortunately each of those shares has one and only one password that every one of its users knows. You can see these relationships in the Figure 2.4.

FIGURE 2.4:
Workgroup security relationships

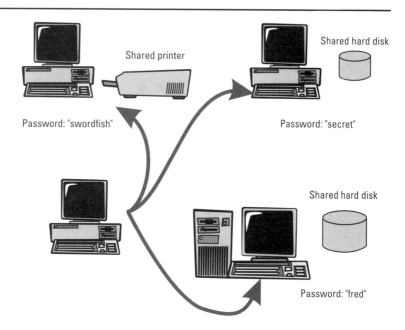

Shared printer

Shared hard disk

Password: "swordfish"

Password: "secret"

Shared hard disk

Password: "fred"

In a domain, all of these relationships between your workstation and the various workstation/server computers do not exist; instead, your system interacts with a computer called the *primary domain controller* or, in some cases, a *backup domain controller.* These controllers are basically the "gatekeepers" of all of the shared items in the domain. A domain controller just keeps a database of security information, and the domain controller then uses that information to validate requests for network resources from workstations. You can see that relationship in the Figure 2.5.

Like a workgroup, a domain is a collection of computers that shares a browse list. Unlike a workgroup, however, all access to domain resources—printers, directories, and the like—is monitored and authorized by one of the computers in that domain. That computer is the primary domain controller that I referred to a paragraph back. Domains offer two main benefits:

- A domain has just one password, and that one password unlocks all of the resources of the domain (the resources that you've got authorization to use, that is).

FIGURE 2.5:

Using the domain controller

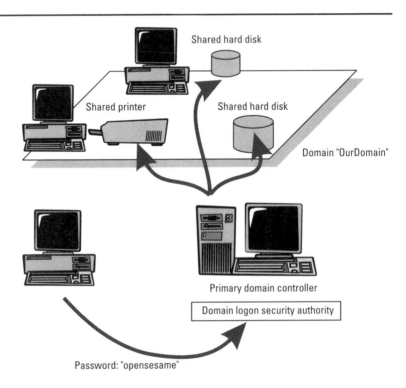

Shared hard disk

Shared printer

Shared hard disk

Domain "OurDomain"

Primary domain controller

Domain logon security authority

Password: "opensesame"

- That password is user-specific. If a network administrator wants to deny a particular person access to the network, all the administrator must do is just delete or disable that person's account. No other users must change passwords in order to continue to use the network.

- As implied by the last point, network administrators can assign specific file and printer access permissions on a user-specific basis.

The notion of a domain is the foundation upon which Microsoft enterprise networks are built. Domains consist of shared resources and the users of those shared resources, so let's look next at those shared resources.

Network Citizens: Users and Machines

The first essential Microsoft enterprise network concept to understand is that Microsoft enterprise networks are composed of *users* and *machines*.

Users in a Microsoft Enterprise Network

A user is just a person who uses the network. Each user has a *user account,* a small database record of information about that user. At minimum, a user account includes information like this:

- User name

- User password

- Use restrictions

The actual meaning of "user account" here is a bit nebulous if your network consists only of simple workgroups; "user account" is a more important piece of information for a user in a domain.

The user account is part of a file called SAM (Security Account Manager) in your primary domain controller's SYSTEM32\CONFIG directory. That file is part of the *registry*, which you'll learn more about in Chapter 5. Basically, the registry is a central database of information about the network system itself, its applications, and its users.

User Rights and Permissions

Every network has its own set of terminology that it uses to describe how it protects its data from its users. In the NT Server world, we talk of rights and permissions.

A *right* is the ability to do a particular thing, like back up data on the file server—a security risk, as whoever's doing the backups could also abscond with them—or log onto the server, whether via the network (not much of a security risk) or locally at the server (a much greater risk). Rights are the difference between administrators and users.

A *permission* is simply a grant of access to a printer, a directory, a file, or some other network resource. There are different levels of access—read-only, execute-only, read/write, and so on—and they can be applied on a file-by-file, user-by-user basis.

Groups

Of course, setting specific permissions for specific users can be tedious and time-consuming. That's why NT Server offers *groups*. Groups let you assign common rights and permissions to collections of users. Examples of groups include:

- Administrators, which have a lot of control over the network
- Users, which have areas over which they have a lot of control, but no control over the administration of the network
- "Enterprise" administrators (Domain Admins), administrators with control over several domains

Those are by no means the only possible groups—they're just examples. For example, suppose you had a single server shared by two departments, the biology researchers and the chemistry researchers. Each user group has an area of its own. Meanwhile, the biology researchers have a common area that they want other biologists to be able to access, but that they don't want chemists to be able to get to. The chemistry researchers, likewise, have a common area of their own that they want to keep biologists from getting into.

Instead of just making all of the researchers "users," you could instead create a group called "Biology" and another called "Chemistry." You'd start off by copying the user rights and permissions from the generic "Users" group into the two new groups, then you could give the "Biology" group access to the shared biology area, and *deny* them access to the shared chemistry area. The "Chemistry" group, similarly, would be granted access to their area and denied access to the biology area.

User Characteristics

We'll mainly be concerned in this book with the *networking* implications of NT, but it's worthwhile taking a quick look at how NT handles users who physically log onto an NT workstation or NT Server.

If you use Windows, then you're accustomed to being able to set your machine's colors, wallpaper, video drivers, and the like. With NT workstations in a domain, however, the notion of "my machine" fades a bit, as the security information on you is, as you recall, kept in a central repository.

Settings on NT machines are either user-specific or machine-specific. The user-specific settings include

- Colors
- Wallpaper
- Mouse settings
- Cursors
- Personal groups
- User name
- Persistent network connections

User names are one of the most important characteristics that the network keeps track of for a user. A user name can be up to 20 characters long. Passwords can actually be 128 characters long, sort of. According to Microsoft Knowledge Base Article Q109927, an NT password can be up to 128 characters long, but the User Manager will only accept passwords of up to 14 characters.

Machines in a Microsoft Enterprise Network

When you log onto a Microsoft enterprise network, the network learns not only who you are, but which machine you're logging on from. Each computer has a computer name; computer names can be no longer than 15 characters, due in part to restrictions imposed by the NetBIOS protocol, covered later in this chapter. Remember:

- User names can be up to 20 characters.

- Passwords can be up to 128 characters, but limitations of the User Manager for Domains cause a practical limit of 14 characters.

- Machine names can be up to 15 characters.

Now let's examine the kinds of cybernetic citizens in a Microsoft network.

Machine Types: Servers, Messengers, Receivers, and Redirectors

In the Microsoft networking world, there are four kinds of capabilities that a server or a workstation can exhibit—redirector, receiver, messenger, or server. These capabilities can appear in combinations. Following is a discussion of each of these network roles.

Redirector   The redirector capability allows software running on your workstation to intercept (redirect) requests for data from network drive letters and printer ports and convert them into network I/O requests. You need a unique user name and machine on the network. A machine running redirector software can request data from a server—that is, it can *initiate* a communication with a server. However, it cannot receive or act upon a *request* from a server. A server can't, so to speak, tap a redirector on the shoulder and hand it a message. You might say that a redirector can talk, but it can't listen.

Receiver   The receiver has redirector capabilities, but can also receive messages forwarded from a computer set up as a messenger. It's an old and basically obsolete type of network citizen, but you'll see references to it now and then.

Messenger   The messenger module sends and receives messages from administrators or from the Alerter service. Messages like print job notification or imminent server shutdown are examples of messages requiring the messenger service. While it sounds a bit circular-defining, the main value of supporting the messenger service is that you can then receive SMB messenger-type blocks from other networked machines. Messenger service is supported via broadcast datagrams. Messenger service uses your user name and your workstation name in the NetBIOS name table, with a hex 03 appended to the end of each name. Messenger service will also support forwarding messages from one workstation to another. In that case, the name will have a hex 05 appended to its NetBIOS name, and that name type is called a *type 5 name*.

Server   Server refers to service that allows a device to accept requests from another computer's redirector. It supports remote procedure calls (RPCs), file and print sharing, and named pipes.

Machine Characteristics

You saw earlier that some characteristics of an NT machine are user-specific, and some are machine-specific. The machine-specific characteristics include the following:

- Initial logon bitmap
- Shared groups
- Network settings, including persistent connections
- Fonts
- Drivers, including video, sound, tape, SCSI, network card, and mouse drivers
- The "services" settings in the Control Panel
- The "system" settings in the Control Panel
- Printer settings

Again, machine names can be up to 15 characters in length. Before going on, let's summarize legal lengths of names and passwords:

Name/Password	Length
User names	Can be up to 20 characters long
Passwords	Can be up to 128 characters long in theory, but 14 characters long in practice
Machine names	Can be 15 characters long

Inter-Domain Security: Trust Relationships

The users in a domain control how they share information via the user rights and permissions of that domain. Again, that information is maintained for that domain by the primary domain controller and its backup domain controllers, in the domain security database.

But suppose you need information in *another* domain? How do you access the resources of that domain?

Inter-Domain Relationships without Trusts

Well, obviously, one way to get to another domain's resources is to just become a user on that domain. Figure 2.6 shows an example of that.

In the figure, you see two domains, one named Andromeda and the other named Cygnus. Both domains are on the same Ethernet. In fact, from the Ethernet's point of view, there aren't two domains here, just one big Ethernet segment with a whole bunch of machines on it. The question of which domain a particular workstation is in is a *software* question, not a hardware question.

FIGURE 2.6:

Becoming a user on another domain

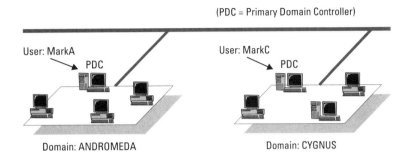

(PDC = Primary Domain Controller)

User: MarkA

PDC

Domain: ANDROMEDA

User: MarkC

PDC

Domain: CYGNUS

What all this means is that there's no reason at all why my workstation can't be a part of two different domains and use two different identities—in the figure, my user ID is MarkC for the Cygnus network, and MarkA for the Andromeda network. What this really means is that there is an entry in the Cygnus security database that recognizes someone named MarkC with some set of rights and permissions, and there's an entry in the Andromeda database that recognizes someone named MarkA with some set of rights and permissions.

More specifically, suppose I log on as MarkC. Now, Cygnus knows MarkC, but Andromeda does not. That means that Andromeda's primary domain controller wouldn't log MarkC onto the Andromeda domain at all, but the Cygnus primary domain controller would accept MarkC's logon.

This underscores an important point: when you log onto a Microsoft enterprise network, you've got to specify which domain you're logging onto. You specify that with your startup parameters. Once I log on as MarkC, I cannot access the resources of Andromeda, but I *can* access the resources of Cygnus.

In the same way, I can use my MarkA account to access resources in Andromeda, but not Cygnus. (By the way, the choice of names MarkA and MarkC is purely arbitrary; I could have had the user names Orca and Delphinus for all it would matter. I just picked MarkA and MarkC to make it easier to remember what each user name did.)

What's wrong with this scenario? Two things. First, it involves administration headaches. If there are five domains in your company, then consider what you'd have to do in order to maintain accounts on the five domains. You'd have to physically travel all over the company to each domain, log onto a workstation on that domain as an administrator, and make whatever changes were required—and you'd have to do it for each domain, *every time* you needed to change a password, user right, or the like. This would, as you'd imagine, get old quickly.

The second problem would be that you couldn't simultaneously access resources from more than one domain. Each account, like MarkA or MarkC, could only access one domain's resources, so to get to the resources of Andromeda while in domain Cygnus, you would have to log off the MarkC account and log back in on the MarkA account. Again, no fun for someone trying to run a network.

Trust Relationships

It would be really convenient to be able to essentially be a part of more than one domain. You can accomplish that with *trust relationships*.

One domain can choose to "trust" another in that it allows users from the trusted domain to access resources in the trusting domain. If Andromeda trusts Cygnus, then Cygnus users can access Andromeda resources, as you can see in the Figure 2.7.

With a trust relationship, the only account that I need is the MarkC account. As Andromeda trusts Cygnus, the primary domain controller for Andromeda extends the normal user rights and permissions to any "visitor" that has been vouched for by the primary domain controller for Cygnus—i.e., by any normal user on the Cygnus domain.

Notice in this example that Cygnus members can access the Andromeda resources, *but the reverse is not true.* If I were a member of the *Andromeda* domain, I would only

---

FIGURE 2.7:

A trust relationship

(PDC = Primary Domain Controller)

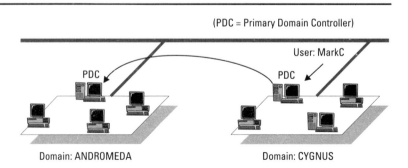

Domain: ANDROMEDA   Domain: CYGNUS

be able to access Andromeda resources. Just because Andromeda trusts Cygnus, that does not imply that Cygnus trusts Andromeda. Each trust relationship is a one-way relationship. That's not to say that you *couldn't* also build a Cygnus-to-Andromeda trust link, but it would require an extra, explicit step.

Network Software: Drivers, Protocols, and Redirectors

The last "basic" that you really have to master in order to be comfortable with NT networking is Microsoft enterprise network software components.

A Network Software Overview

Looking at networks from a high-level point of view, LANs have this basic job: Let the applications programs (WordPerfect, Lotus 1-2-3, Quicken, or whatever) utilize the network hardware to get at data on the network; you see that in Figure 2.8.

FIGURE 2.8:

Application programs utilizing network hardware

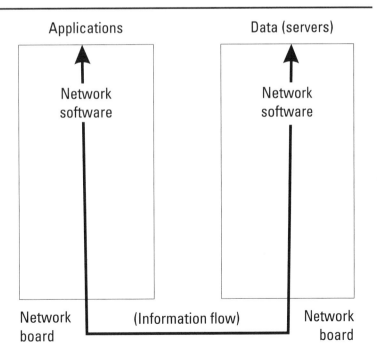

For the application to use data, messages go across network boards and through the network software that runs both in the client and the server machine. The network software can be explained in many ways, but I find it easiest to imagine it in a three-part fashion. The first and easiest piece of software to understand is the network board driver, as you see in Figure 2.9.

FIGURE 2.9:

A network board driver

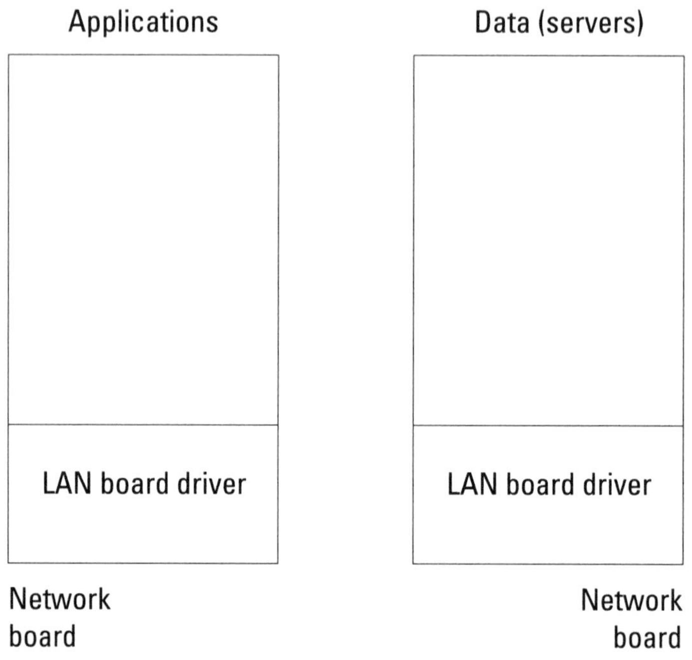

Applications	Data (servers)
LAN board driver	LAN board driver

Network board   Network board

Network Card Drivers

Drivers decouple the network board from the network operating system. For example, suppose you've got a token ring-based network. When you first create your network, you may start off by buying boards from IBM, but you don't want to be locked into IBM or any other vendor, for that matter. And you wonder whether or not a competitor's token ring boards, like the Madge or 3Com token ring boards, will continue to work with your NT Server-based network.

The first place that NT needs compatibility, then, is in the network cards. NT needs the ability to incorporate any kind of network card into its networking system, whether that card is an Ethernet, Token Ring, ARCnet, FDDI (Fiber Distributed Data Interface), or another board, and it must be able to incorporate boards from virtually *any* vendor.

The board driver must know things like which IRQ a LAN board is set at and which I/O address it uses. The board driver must also know how to interface with higher-layer network software. And for some boards, it must know which RAM base address it uses.

Network Redirectors

Up at the top of the network software is the next software piece, the *redirector*. A redirector fools applications into thinking that the application gets data from a local drive, rather than from the network.

For example, consider the case of WordPerfect reading a document from a network drive. From WordPerfect's point of view, there *is* no network. Instead, it knows that one or more disk drives are available with names consisting of a letter and a colon, as in A:, B:, C:, and so on. WordPerfect was not built to accommodate storage devices that don't have names like A: or D:, and so there must be a layer of software placed just below WordPerfect, a layer of software whose job is to present a letter-and-colon face to WordPerfect when supplying data stored on the network. WordPerfect thinks that it is addressing local drives, but its requests for information from drives with names like D: must be *redirected* to network requests, like "Get the data from directory WPFILES on the server named SEYMOUR." The redirector software does that, as you see in Figure 2.10.

In Microsoft networking terms, WordPerfect is accessing data from a share called \\SEYMOUR\WPFILES. If you were to tell WordPerfect that the name of its data drive was \\SEYMOUR\WPFILES, however, it wouldn't work because WordPerfect only recognizes drives names like A:, B:, C:, and the like. Think of the redirector as a drive name translator.

The redirector is only half of a client-server team of software. The redirector is the piece that goes on the client or workstation, and the *file system mounter* is the piece that goes on the server. There are several file system mounters in the network

FIGURE 2.10:

Using the redirector software

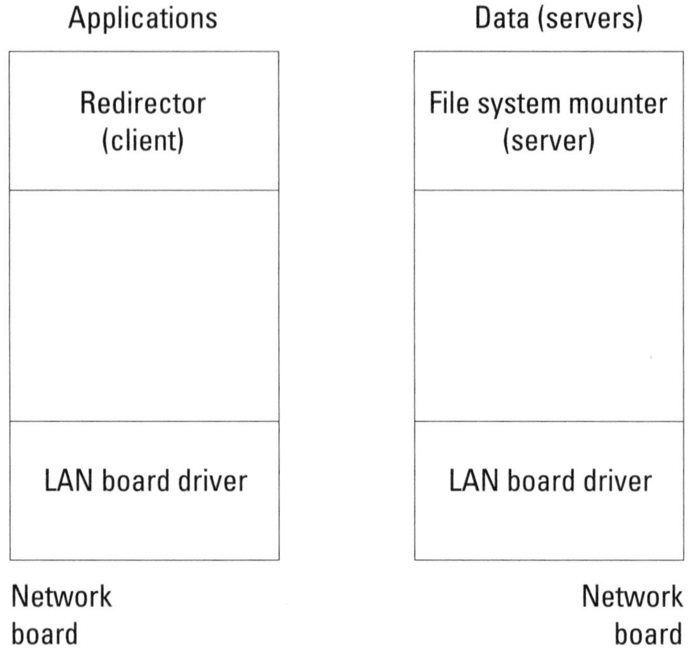

Applications

Data (servers)

Redirector (client)	File system mounter (server)
LAN board driver	LAN board driver

Network board

Network board

world—the best-known are Novell's NetWare File System, UNIX's Network File System, or NFS, and Microsoft's file system mounter, which they usually just call the "server." The redirector on the client and the file system mounter on the server must match, or the client can't use the server's resources.

In the Internet world, servers may run an "NFS server;" workstations must run "NFS client" software. In the Novell world, servers run a program called "NFS.NLM" to support the Novell File System mounter, and workstations run a client program called NET3, NET4, NETX, or the like in order to communicate with the Novell server.

Network Protocols

Third in the trio of network software components is the network protocol. In general, a protocol is just a standardized set of rules invented for the sake of compatibility. For example, when I call you on the phone, we have a protocol that says, "When you hear the phone ring and you pick it up, then *you* should talk first, not me." There's no good reason for why it happens this way—it's just the common agreement in our culture as to how to conduct a phone communication.

I left this middle piece for last, as protocols are the most abstract of the three network software components. You might think of it this way: The board driver keeps the LAN board happy, the redirector keeps the applications happy, and the *transport protocol* glues the two of them together by establishing the rules of the road for network communications. You can see the result of adding the transport protocol to our network software system in Figure 2.11.

Just as we couldn't use the phone without some agreements about how to use it, NT needs a common communications language so that all of the machines on an NT network can talk to one another without confusion. NT also needs to be able to speak the networking languages used by *other* kinds of networks, so it needs to be something of a polyglot. Those networking protocols—"protocol" is a somewhat more accurate term than "language" is here—differ widely because each was originally designed to do different things, and because network protocols were never designed toward being compatible with other kinds of networks.

FIGURE 2.11:
Adding the transport protocol to the network software system

Applications

| Redirector (client) |
| Transport protocol |
| LAN board driver |

Network board

Data (servers)

| File system mounter (server) |
| Transport protocol |
| LAN board driver |

Network board

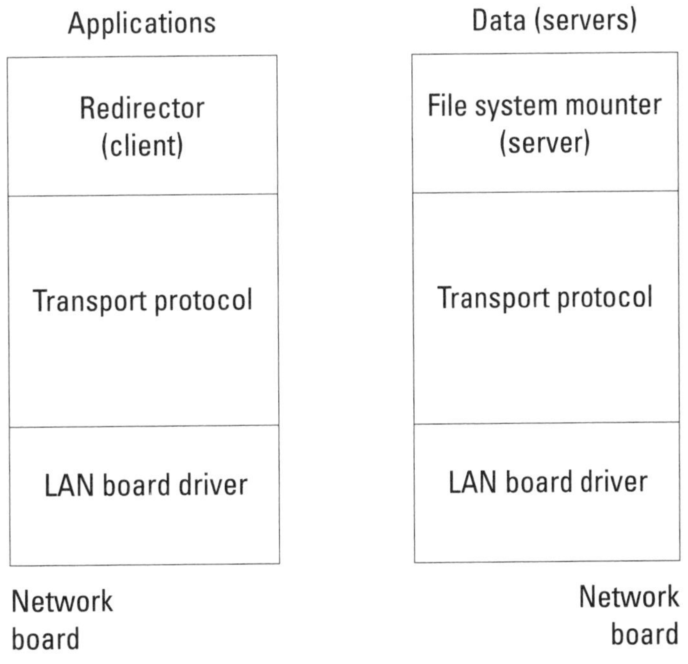

There are a number of transport protocols, unfortunately. Every vendor has its own favorite protocol. On the following pages is a quick overview of the ones you'll run across.

NetBIOS/NetBEUI

Back when IBM first started marketing its PC Network, it needed a basic network protocol stack. IBM had no intention of building large networks, just small workgroups of a few dozen computers or less.

Out of that need grew the Network Basic Input/Output System, or NetBIOS. NetBIOS is just 18 commands that can create, maintain, and use connections between PCs on a network. IBM soon extended NetBIOS with the NetBIOS Extended User Interface, or NetBEUI, basically a refined set of NetBIOS commands. Over time, however, the names NetBEUI and NetBIOS have taken on different meanings.

- NetBEUI refers to the actual transport protocol; it has been implemented in many different ways by different vendors, to the point where it's in some ways the fastest transport protocol around for small networks.

- NetBIOS refers to the actual set of programming commands that the system can use to manipulate the network—the technical term for it is an application program interface, or API.

NetBEUI is the closest thing to a "native" protocol for NT. Unless you tell your system to use another protocol, NetBEUI is one of the protocols that the NT Setup program installs by default—IPX/SPX is the other. NetBEUI should be your protocol of choice for small networks, however, because it's the fastest one around.

TCP/IP (Transmission Control Protocol/Internet Protocol)

The famous "infobahn," the information superhighway, is built atop a protocol created by the U.S. Government over the years—a protocol stack called the *TCP suite*. The TCP suite is a very efficient, easy-to-extend protocol whose main strength has been in *wide* area networking, gluing together dissimilar networks and bringing together similar networks that are separated by distance and low-speed connections. It's one of the best-supported, best-designed internetworking protocols around today.

**ENTERPRISE
NETWORKING**

Traditionally, however, microcomputer networks haven't used TCP/IP as a *local* area network protocol. But that's changing, particularly with the release of the TCP/IP suite in NT Server version 3.5x's 32-bit "turbo" TCP/IP.

DLC (Data Link Control)

Data Link Control is related to an international standard protocol called IEEE 802.2. You'll see it used for two main reasons.

First, many token ring shops use DLC to allow their PC workstations to talk to mainframe gateways. If you use token ring and your CONFIG.SYS contains three device drivers whose names start with DXM, then you're using DLC drivers.

Second, if you've got a laser printer on the network and it's attached *directly* to the network via a JetDirect card, then you'll need to use DLC to control that printer.

IPX/SPX (Internetwork Packet Exchange/Sequenced Packet Exchange)

The most popular local area network type in the world is Novell NetWare. When the Novell folks were building NetWare, they decided to build their own protocol, rather than use an existing protocol. (It's actually based on a Xerox protocol called Xerox Networking Services, or XNS.)

IPX/SPX support came late to NT, but it's here in NT 3.5x as part of the NetWare Compatible Services.

Multiple Transport Stacks

It should be obvious by now that first of all, there is no single best network protocol, and second, you may want to run all four of the protocols described here. You can.

One of the values of the NT networking model is that it supports *multiple* transport protocols, as you see in Figure 2.12.

In the figure, you can see that the client machine has four transport protocols loaded, and the server has one protocol loaded. This could happen if the client machine connected to more than one server—the IPX stack might talk to a Novell server, the DLC stack might allow the workstation to talk to a mainframe gateway, and the TCP/IP stack might talk to an Internet mail router.

43

FIGURE 2.12:

Running multiple transport protocols

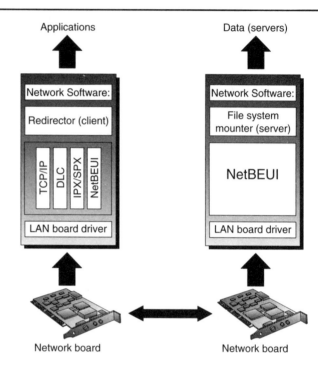

Network Binding Interfaces

But to make all of this *work*, we need a way to attach the network boards to the transport stacks—to *bind* the network transport layer to the LAN board's driver. (The definition of "binding" is to create a software connection between, or essentially "marry," a network card driver and a network transport protocol.) That leads to the need for a very important standard interface—the interface between a LAN board driver and a transport stack. There are two competitors for the title of "world standard binding interface," Microsoft's NDIS and Novell's ODI.

Network Driver Interface Specification (NDIS) version 3.0

Microsoft's standard defines the interface between a network card driver and a protocol stack with an interface called the Network Driver Interface Specification, or NDIS.

NDIS-compliant drivers are easy to find for most network boards, so availability is a strong plus for NDIS. Furthermore, there are NDIS-compatible versions of the NetBEUI, TCP/IP, DLC, and SPX/IPX protocol stacks. NDIS 3.0 drivers are particularly attractive in the DOS/Windows world because they load up in extended memory, away from the precious lower 640K.

Open Data-Link Interface (ODI)

Novell's answer to the binding problem is a different standard, one named the Open Data-Link Interface, or ODI. ODI drivers do not, unfortunately, load high, but they are the easiest drivers to obtain. If a board has any drivers at all, they'll be DOS ODI drivers.

Network Applications Interfaces (APIs)

As you've already read, most applications are unaware of the network or networks that they use. But some, like e-mail or groupware programs, must be cognizant of the network, and exist only *because* of the network. They need to be able to "plug in" and communicate with other programs running on other machines in the network.

Programmers build network-aware programs to be tailored to sets of commands that a network offers to application programs. Those sets of commands are called APIs, or application program interfaces.

Think of an API as being somewhat like the dashboard of a car. Your car's dashboard is the interface that you see, and you learn to use it in order to operate the car. You actually have no idea while you're driving what's under your car's hood—you just push down the accelerator and the car goes faster.

A dashboard consists of just a few "primitive" commands: brake the car, accelerate the car, shift the car's transmission, and so on. There is no command "back the car out of the driveway," and yet you can still back a car out of a driveway by just assembling a number of the primitive commands into the actual action of backing a car out of a driveway. You have, in a sense, built a "program" with your car's API.

There are three APIs that you'll probably come across in the NT enterprise world:

- NetBIOS: A simple set of 18 commands implemented on an NT network. NetBIOS is Microsoft's "native" network API.

- TCP/IP Sockets: The preferred API for working over an internet.

- Novell Sockets: Novell's API.

Getting comfortable with NT networking requires learning a new language—but it's not an impossible language to learn. In this chapter, you've been given the background that you need to "speak NT." In the next chapter, you'll see how to *install* NT.

PART II

Setting Up NT Server

CHAPTER

THREE

3

Installing NT and NT Server

Installing NT Server is simple... *if* you do your homework beforehand. This section provides a step-by-step plan for getting a single server up and running. This section is also of value if you are installing NT on a workstation.

Once you've got your system up and running, you'll learn the steps that NT goes through when booting a server, so that you can recognize how to solve startup problems.

Preparing the Hardware

Despite the fact that NT is a big, complex operating system, you've got a pretty good chance of getting it installed right the first time if you first make sure that you're free of hardware problems. Under DOS, you can have some pretty glaring hardware problems, but DOS will run nonetheless.

The reason why DOS will work—or *appear* to work—on a machine with major hardware problems is simple: DOS isn't really an operating system. It doesn't monitor the hardware, so it never really gets a chance to notice a hardware failure or conflict. DOS basically leaves the problems of hardware control to device drivers and application programs. When some hardware problem arises, it arises while an application program is running, meaning that it's the *DOS application program* that must detect, diagnose, and recover from the hardware failure. Or at least that's the ideal situation.

The reality is, of course, that most DOS programs just crash when hardware problems happen. I just said that DOS program designers should plan for these problems and attempt to avert them in their code, but the fact of the matter is that DOS applications designers shouldn't have to worry about this kind of thing—the operating system should.

Under DOS, a memory failure usually won't show up until you actually try to *use* that memory. Disk failures cause the "abort, retry, fail?" error message, with no real recovery. Interrupt conflicts become mysterious freeze-ups.

You can't afford any of that kind of behavior on your NT server (or workstation, for that matter). For that reason, my strong advice to you is to *test your hardware thoroughly before installing NT.*

Having said that, I've got to admit that it's pretty hard to build any kind of hardware diagnostic program under NT, as a hardware diagnostic must be able to directly access the hardware in order to test it, and one of NT's stated design goals is to make it *impossible* for an application to get to the hardware. Furthermore, most diagnostics require that they be the only thing running in the system, and NT is built out of literally dozens of miniprograms called "threads."

For that reason, I recommend that you run your system through a gamut of specialized DOS-based diagnostics before proceeding with the NT installation. I'll discuss them in more detail a bit later in this chapter.

Getting Ready to Install

First of all, make sure that you have the right hardware for an NT installation. Check the latest Windows NT Hardware Compatibility List for any hardware you are thinking of buying. If it's not on the list, check with the manufacturer to be sure it will work with Windows NT.

CPU   In the Intel x86 world, you'll need a 386-class processor or better, and a 486 is recommended. If you're going to run on a MIPS or Alpha, make sure that you've got the right software for *your* system; NT 3.1 shipped the MIPS and Intel versions in the same box, but later versions don't include Alpha code, for example.

RAM   I strongly recommend that you don't even think about running NT with less than 16MB of RAM. Oddly enough, NT Server seems to need less memory to do *its* job than does the workstation product; my NT Server system has only 16MB and performs superbly for our network, but the workstation product seems sluggish until you put 24MB of RAM on it. NT 3.5 improved the memory situation somewhat, although not by the 50 percent that Microsoft originally promised; it's possible to run an NT 3.5x workstation on a 16MB system comfortably. If you're intending to load SQL Server on an NT Server, then you'd best have about 32MB of RAM.

NT Server needs more RAM if you ask it to do more things. If you're going to load RAS or TCP/IP, then you'll need more memory. NT Server also needs more memory if it will serve more people; see Chapter 14, on tuning, for more information on this.

NT SERVER

Video   You need at least a VGA video board in order to load NT Server. (This surprised me when I first loaded it, as I was used to being able to put low-quality video on a server; after all, nobody's going to use it as a workstation, so who cares what kind of video it's got?) It's chic to buy the fastest turbo-charged PCI video accelerator video board for systems nowadays, but there's no point to doing that for an NT Server installation; a cheap VGA board will be fine.

If you're running an NT *workstation*, in contrast, then by all means invest in better video. Microsoft has expended a great amount of programming effort in two video drivers: the basic VGA driver and the S3 driver. One of NT version 3.5's top-ten features is a newer, improved S3 video driver.

As video accelerators go, the S3-based systems are definitely not the fastest boards around. For better speed, you could look to an ATI or Matrox video system. On the other hand, think twice before straying from S3-based systems. S3 boards are the ones that will always get the most solid, debugged drivers among the video accelerator bunch, and they'll likely get the *earliest* drivers when beta versions of new software arrive. The S3 systems also tend to be cheaper than the other accelerators.

CD-ROM   You definitely want a CD-ROM for the server, if you're loading NT Server. As you'll read later in this book, there are number of pieces of software in the NT package that you can't get to from the floppies—they're only on the CD-ROM. Additionally, you've only got to do one NT floppy installation before you'll be convinced that CD-ROM installs are the way to go.

What about CD-ROMs on workstations? I'd still think about getting at least a cheap double-spin CD-ROM. Software has gotten so huge that even *games* are shipping on CD-ROMs. Terrific, inexpensive databases are available on CD-ROM; for example, you can buy twelve months' worth of *PC Magazine* on CD-ROM for about $20! Think of the time saved with just one literature search, and the CD-ROM drive starts to look like a bargain. (NT troubleshooters will want to subscribe to Microsoft's TechNet service, a complete set of all Microsoft literature on supporting their applications and environments.) There's a fantastic trove of goodies out there…but you can't get to them if you don't have a CD-ROM.

If you decide to buy a CD-ROM, then be sure that it uses a SCSI interface card, not a proprietary interface; the proprietary CD-ROM interface cards aren't generally supported by NT.

A last, somewhat esoteric but important point about CD-ROMs under NT: Not only must they be SCSI-based, they must also support the newer SCSI-II interface, as NT requires that a feature called *SCSI parity* be enabled in order for the installation to go well.

Tape Drive   It is essential that any enterprise server have a tape backup unit. I use the Colorado PowerTape, a Tandberg 4100 SCSI-II compatible drive, and it suits the backup job just fine. The tape subsystem should be SCSI-based.

Hard Disk   If you want to support large drive sizes *and* low-level device multi-tasking, then you'd do well to choose some kind of SCSI-based hard disk. NT has exceptionally good support of SCSI host adapters, so you can choose from a large number of possible adapters. (It would be a good idea to consult the *Hardware Compatibility List*, available from Microsoft, before buying a SCSI host adapter.)

Any machine running NT Server should have some kind of advanced 32-bit bus—such as EISA, Micro Channel, or PCI—that supports bus mastering. (The lack of bus mastering means that VESA slots are not all that good an idea.) It's a good idea to stay with a big name SCSI vendor, like Adaptec. Its 1542C 16-bit adapter is probably the most popular SCSI host adapter among NT users. Its 32-bit EISA cousin, the 2742T, is a mite pricey—about $300—but quite a performer, and serves as two SCSI controllers on a single board. I would strongly recommend that you avoid the somewhat cheaper Ultrastor controllers. My experience with Ultrastor has been that they're slow to deliver drivers, difficult to get in touch with for technical support, and tend to completely abandon any controller that isn't their latest and greatest.

Another reason to buy SCSI-based storage systems is fault tolerance: disk mirroring and RAID pretty much *require* SCSI disk subsystems in order to work. You can create a mirrored set of non-SCSI drives, but the drives may not have sector-remapping capability (which is an important part of any fault-tolerance scheme), so I would not recommend it.

Mice and Serial Ports   This is pretty straightforward, but one word of advice: get PS/2-type or InPort mice. You'll need a port for your mouse, a serial port to attach your uninterruptible power supply (UPS) to, and a serial port for a modem to support the Remote Access Services (RAS). If the mouse is a serial mouse, then the system requires three serial ports, which gets problematic—you can't really have more than two serial ports on most PC compatible systems.

Once you've got the hardware together, you have to test it.

Testing Memory

An awful lot of people think that the short ten-second memory test that systems go through every time they are turned on actually *does* something. (Now, if you believed *that*, then you probably think that those buttons next to the "Don't Walk" signs on the street corners actually do something.) The quick power-on RAM test is just a quick "are you there?" kind of inventory of memory.

The problem with this approach is that many memory errors are not absolute errors, errors that will essentially "sit still" and let you find them. Some memory errors appear because of addressing logic problems: change a bit at address X, and bits change at address Y. Other memory errors occur because the memory modules are just a trifle different in terms of their access speeds from other memory modules in the system. A third group can appear from differences in electrical characteristics between memories on a motherboard versus memories on a high-speed expansion card.

In any case, thorough memory testing is a step that shouldn't be skipped. To that end, here's a few suggestions:

- Use either Checkit, from Touchstone software, or QAPlus, from DiagSoft. They're the only two programs I've ever looked at that can find those pesky odd errors.

- Run these tests in their "slow" mode. By default, they run a quick test, but you don't want a quick test—you want all of the various tests, like "walking bit," "checkerboard," "address line," and whatever your package supports.

- Run the tests from DOS, and do *not* load a memory manager before you do.

- If you're using an ARC (Advanced RISC Computer) machine, then ask your vendor for a recommendation on a stringent memory tester.

Don't be surprised if a memory test takes up to eight hours; that's possible, on a 32MB system.

Testing Disks

You'll find that NT relies heavily upon *paging* data out to disk. "Paging" is a process wherein disk space is used as a "stand in" for memory space. Whenever data is paged from RAM to disk, the operating system assumes that the data will remain safe and sound out on the disk. When NT reloads the data from disk to RAM, it doesn't even check it to see that the data is undamaged. That means that you'll need a 100-percent reliable disk to support NT.

As with memory, disks often show problems only under certain circumstances. It would be nice if you could just write out some simple bit of data, like the word "testing," all over the disk, then go back and read the disk to be sure that the word "testing" was still on it, but a test like that would only find the grossest of disk errors. DOS's SCANDISK is a tester of this variety, useful only in the most disk-damaged situations.

Instead, you need a *pattern tester* for your disk drive. There is one that I can recommend: SpinRite 3.1 from Gibson Research. SpinRite is a high-quality disk tester.

Now, there are two disadvantages to disk testing: the time involved, and the fact that all the good ones are DOS-based. It can literally take *days* to do a thorough test on a disk. Running SpinRite on a 1700MB disk took *three days,* but when it was done, SpinRite had found some errors on the disk that hadn't been found by the manufacturer, the low-level format program, or the DOS FORMAT program.

NT SERVER

The DOS heritage of these programs means that the only disk system that they recognize is the FAT file system, *arrgh!* That implies that when you get a new server, you should temporarily put DOS on it, format its disk to a FAT format, install NT Server, and convert the FAT format to NTFS format.

Here's a case where those of you installing an NT workstation system will have it better, as you'll probably stay with the FAT file system for an NT workstation.

You may be scowling right now because of the work that I'm setting out for you; *don't.* Believe me, I've seen a number of client network problems boil down to flaky memory or flaky disks. You really only need to test RAM once, when you first install it. Disks really should be tested once a year.

Preparing the Data

If you're converting your server from some other operating system to NT Server, then you'll first have to protect the data on your server's disk.

If this is a brand-new server, then there's really nothing to do in the way of backup. If not, however, here's a few strategies.

Backing Up to Another Machine

If you have another computer around with enough mass storage to hold your server's data, then you can run some kind of peer-to-peer LAN, like Windows for Workgroups, share that machine's drive, and then just copy the whole drive over with an XCOPY /S command. Then, once you get NT Server up, you can connect the NT Server machine easily to the Windows for Workgroups machine, and XCOPY back.

Temporarily Installing the Tape to Another Machine

Suppose you're currently using some lower-level FAT-based server system, like LANtastic or Windows for Workgroups, and you're going to change over to NT Server. You run a DOS-based tape backup program, put the tape drive away, and install NT Server. In the process, you format your server to the New Technology File System (NTFS). Then you try to restore the data to the server.

And that's when the problem becomes evident.

You see, just about every backup program saves data in different ways. Say you have a program—let's call it SB, for Simple Backup—that shipped with the tape drive. It's a DOS-based program, so it ran fine when you were backing up the disk, but *now it won't run under NT*. Why? Two reasons. First, it probably directly controls the tape drive, and NT absolutely forbids DOS programs (or NT applications programs, for that matter) to directly manipulate hardware; try to run the program, and it would crash. Second, the tape restore program *might* work by directly writing data to the disk, and that would not only be intercepted by NT, it would fail even if NT didn't stop the restore program—after all, this disk is now formatted in NTFS, not FAT.

What about going at it the other way? Just boot the server from a DOS floppy and run the restore program. That'll work, won't it? Unfortunately, it won't work. Remember, the disk is now formatted under NTFS, and a DOS program couldn't recognize the C drive anyway.

Well, NT comes with a tape backup program. Won't it read my DOS backups? No. Emphatically *no*. The NT backup program uses its own "Microsoft Backup Format" to write tapes, a format that, so far as I know, is unique in the industry. ("How many Microsoft programmers does it take to change a light bulb?" "None; they just declare darkness a Microsoft standard.")

So what's the answer? One approach is to just take the tape drive out of the server, install it in another computer, and use Windows for Workgroups or something like that to share the hard disk of the soon-to-be NT Server machine, then do the backup over the peer-to-peer network onto the tape. Then set up the server, reconnect it to the Windows for Workgroups machine, and then restore from the Windows for Workgroups machine. Cumbersome, but it'll work.

Setting Up the Server for FAT, Restore and Convert

This last approach takes a bit more time, but it's simpler, and truthfully it's the one that I've used. The best way to restore your backups may be to restore your backups to a FAT volume and then convert the volume to NTFS. Read the "How Do I" sidebar to find out how.

One of the morals of the story is: Backups look different on different operating systems. I found that out a few years ago when using a portable Bernoulli box.

The Bernoulli is a 90MB cartridge storage device (they have them in 150MB and larger now, but the one I worked with was a 90) whose most interesting feature was that it could be hooked up to a parallel port via a converter built by the Iomega people, makers of the Bernoulli box. The Bernoulli box really uses a SCSI interface, but the Iomega parallel port converter faked the box out into thinking that the parallel port was a SCSI port.

Anyway, you could do backups easily, if not quickly, via the parallel port with the Bernoulli box. A few of my systems, however, already had SCSI ports built right

How Do I Convert a FAT Volume to an NTFS Volume?

1. Do the backup under DOS, a FAT-based backup.

2. Install NT Server, but don't reformat the disk to NTFS.

3. Reboot under DOS, from a floppy.

4. Run the tape restore program and restore the files.

5. Boot the server, and run the FAT-to-NTFS conversion program to make the server's disk NTFS.

After you've done the conversion, run NTBACKUP *immediately* and get a first backup of the new disk format.

into them, so I tried hooking the Bernoulli right into the SCSI port. It worked, but not with the Iomega software; I ended up using some generic SCSI removable cartridge hard disk formatting software. I was able to back up, and back up much more quickly than via the parallel port, but the resulting cartridges couldn't be read when the Bernoulli was attached via the parallel port. So be careful when backing up!

Backups If You're Converting from LAN Manager

One more thought: Microsoft distributed SyTOS, a tape backup program, with its LAN Manager 2.2 product. The version of SyTOS that came with LAN Manager won't run under NT, but the NTBackup program *can* read SyTOS-formatted tapes, *if you get the version of NT Server that is the LAN Manager upgrade*. Even better, the upgrade is less than half the list price of NT Server.

Further, the LAN Manager Upgrade package has a utility to convert from the HPFS and HPFS386 formats used by LAN Manager to NTFS *in situ*, so you may never need those backups at all.

Setting Up the LAN Card

Next, get your network card set up properly. If you're just installing the network card now, then be careful that the things that you do right now don't get you in trouble later. Now's the time to be sure that:

- Your system doesn't have any interrupt (IRQ) or input/output (I/O) address conflicts.

- You've written down any settings that you've made to the system.

- The card works in a stand-alone mode.

The first step is to find acceptable interrupts and input/output addresses.

Setting an Interrupt

Interrupts are how your LAN card tells the CPU that the CPU must pay attention to the LAN card, *now*! Why does the LAN card have the right to bug the CPU like that? Well, mainly because the LAN card has only a limited amount of buffer space, and if the CPU doesn't come to get this data quickly, then *more* data will come into the LAN card, knocking the current data right out of the LAN card's buffers and off to data heaven.

Your system can support up to 16 different devices interrupting your CPU. Each one of those interrupts is more properly called a "hardware interrupt" or an "IRQ level." In general, you can only have one hardware device on a given IRQ level. I say "in general" because it *is possible* to share IRQs on a machine with a Micro Channel, EISA, or PCI bus architecture. EISAs and PCIs, however, usually coexist with older ISA bus slots, making interrupt sharing impractical in most cases.

You can see common IRQ settings in Table 3.1.

Part of setting up a LAN board involves setting an IRQ level for that board. You set a board's IRQ either by moving a switch or jumper on the card, in the case of older cards, or by running a setup program, in most modern LAN boards. For example, in the case of Intel EtherExpress LAN boards, you run a program called SoftSet, which is shipped with the EtherExpress board. It examines your system and attempts to find a good IRQ (and I/O address, for that matter) for your system. It then

TABLE 3.1: Common IRQ Settings

IRQ Level	Common Usage	Comments
0	Timer	Hard-wired on motherboard; impossible to change.
1	Keyboard	Hard-wired on motherboard, impossible to change.
2	Cascade from IRQ9	May or may not be available, depending on how the motherboard is designed. Best to avoid if possible. Some old VGAs may use this for "autoswitching". Disable the feature, if present.
3	COM2 or COM4	
4	COM1 or COM3	
5	LPT2	Most of us don't use a second parallel port, and so can use this for something else. It is safe to use this if you have a "virtual" LPT2, as in the case of a network connection.
6	Floppy disk controller	
7	LPT1	
8	Real-time clock	Hard-wired on motherboard, impossible to change.
9	Cascade to IRQ2	Wired directly to IRQ2, so this does not exist as a separate interrupt. Sometimes when you set a board to IRQ2, you have to tell the software that you set it to IRQ9 to make it work.
10	Unused	
11	Unused	
12	PS/2, InPort mouse	
13	Math coprocessor	Used to signal detected errors in coprocessor.
14	Hard disk controller	
15	Unused	

suggests these settings, and you can either accept them or reject them; if you reject the settings, then you can directly enter the ones that you desire.

These software setup programs are a great improvement over the LAN boards of just a few years ago, which required interminable DIP switch flipping and jumper-setting. The process that I described for the Intel board is similar to what I've seen on the SMC Elite cards, NE2000-based boards (although you must set a jumper to enable configuration), and the 3Com 3C509 cards.

But let's get down to work. Which interrupt is the right one to choose?

A lot of people buy themselves grief by putting their network cards on IRQ2. Don't do it. IRQ2 was available back on the 8-bit PC/XT type designs, but it serves a valuable role in modern PCs.

The PC/XT systems had a single interrupt controller: an Intel 8259 chip. The 8259 could support up to eight interrupt channels, and the original PC/XT systems hardwired channels 0 and 1 to the system timer (a clock circuit that goes "tick" every 15 milliseconds) and the 8042 keyboard controller.

The system was wired with those interrupts because IBM wanted to make sure that the keyboard and the timer had high priorities. You see, with an 8259, when two interrupts occur at the same time, the one with the lower number gets priority.

Interrupts 3 and 4 went to COM2 and COM1, respectively; the idea was that COM2 would support a modem and COM1 would support a printer, and so the modem would have slightly higher priority.

TIP   To this day, it's a good idea to use COM2 for higher-speed communications.

Interrupts 5, 6, and 7 were assigned to the hard disk controller, the floppy disk controller, and the parallel port.

In 1984, the first 16-bit PC compatible system was released—the IBM AT. The proliferation of add-in devices on the market made it clear that eight interrupt levels just wasn't enough. So IBM decided to add another 8259. The problem was that just slapping the extra 8259 onto the motherboard might present some backward compatibility problems, so IBM decided to kind of slip the extra 8259 in "via the back door." How they did this is illustrated in Figure 3.1.

The way they did it was to take the new IRQs 8 through 15 and route them through IRQ 9, then connect IRQ 9 to IRQ 2. Result: whenever IRQ 8 through 15 is triggered, IRQ 9 goes off, which makes IRQ 2 look like *it* went off. The PC's BIOS then knows that whenever IRQ 2 appears, that *really* means to check the second 8259 to find out which IRQ *really* triggered. By the way, they also freed up IRQ 5; it's no longer needed by your AT or later hard disk controller.

FIGURE 3.1:

Extra 8259 on the IBM AT

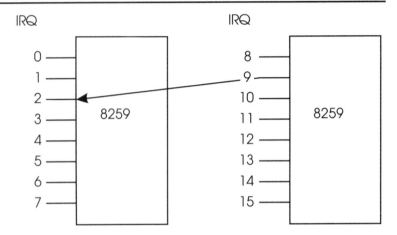

This implies a few things:

- Don't use IRQ 2, as it's already got a job: it's the gateway to IRQs 8 through 15.

- If you *do* use IRQ 2, then you may have to tell the NT software that you've got your network card set to IRQ 9. IRQ 9 and IRQ 2 are electrically equal under this system, as they're tied together.

- Because interrupts 8 through 15 slide into the architecture via IRQ 2, they essentially "inherit" IRQ 2's priority level. That means that IRQs 8 through 15 are of higher priority than IRQs 3 through 7.

- Don't use IRQ 9, as it has a cascade responsibility.

- Safe IRQs are 5, 10, 11, and 15; avoid the others. You'll probably need to use these IRQs for the following hardware:

  - Sound cards. If it's an 8-bit card, then your only option is IRQ5 for the sound card.

  - LAN boards (as we've already discussed).

  - SCSI host adapters (although an Adaptec 2742 can actually forgo interrupts, needing only a DMA channel).

TIP

Whatever you set your boards to, *write it down*! You'll need the information later. I tape an envelope to the side of my computers. Each time I install a board (or modify an existing board), I get a new piece of paper and write down all the configuration information on the board. For example, I might note "Intel EtherExpress 16 card installed 10 July 1994 by Mark Minasi; no EPROM on board, shared memory disabled, IRQ 10 used, I/O address 310 set."

Setting an I/O Address

IRQs are a mite scarce, so they're the things that you'll worry about most of the time. But LAN boards also require that you set their *input/output address*, or I/O address; it's sometimes called the "port address." I/O addresses are generally three digit numbers. For LAN cards they're typically a range starting at either 300 hex or 310 hex.

A LAN board's input/output address is the electrical "location" of the LAN board, from the CPU's point of view. When the CPU wants to send data to a LAN card, it doesn't issue an instruction that says, "Send this data to the EtherExpress board," because the computer's hardware has no idea what an EtherExpress board *is*. Instead, every device—keyboard, video adapter, parallel port, whatever—gets a numerical address between 0 and 1023 called its *input/output address*. The value is usually expressed in hex, so it ends up being the range from 000–3FF in hex. (A discussion of hexadecimal is beyond the scope of this book, but many other sources cover hex.) Just as the postal carrier would be confused if there were two houses at 25 Main Street, a PC system can't function properly if there is more than one device at a given I/O address; hence, part of your installation job is to ensure that you don't set the LAN card to the same I/O address as another board.

In general, I/O addresses won't give you too much trouble, but once in a while... On one of my systems, I had a video accelerator that used I/O addresses around 300 hex. My newly installed board, which also was set to 300 hex, didn't work. My clue to the problem was that the video display showed some very odd colors when first booting up. I checked the video accelerator's settings, and *voilà!* the problem became apparent. I then changed the Ethernet card's address, and the problem went away.

In any case, the I/O address is another thing that you've got to be sure to write down in that envelope attached to your computer. For those of you working for larger companies, an envelope taped to the side of a computer isn't a practical answer, of course, but why not build a small database of PC information? Keep it on your system, and key it to an ID number that you can affix to a PC by engraving it on the side of the case or with some kind of hard-to-remove stickers.

For those Network cards that use memory-mapped buffering, it is important to use a RAM base address that is not being used by another device in your system to avoid conflicts. Check the documentation that came with your other adapter cards, especially your SCSI controller card, for a RAM address it might be using.

Stand-Alone Card Tests

Now that the card is installed, it's a good idea to test the card and the LAN cable before going any further. The four kinds of tests that you'd do on most networks include:

- An on-board diagnostic
- A local loopback test
- A "network live" loopback test
- A sender/responder test

These four tests are usually encapsulated in a diagnostics diskette that you'd get with the LAN board. The first, an on-board diagnostic, is a simple test of the circuitry on the board. Many of the modern boards have a "reset and check out" feature on their chips, so this program just wakes that feature up. If the chips check out okay, then this step is successfully completed.

That first test can be a useful check of whether or not you've set the IRQ to a conflicting level, or perhaps placed any on-board RAM overlapping other RAM.

The second test, a local loopback test, is one wherein you put a loopback connector (exactly what a loopback connector *is* varies with LAN variety) on your network board. The loopback connector causes any outgoing transmissions from the LAN board to be "looped back" to the LAN board. The loopback test then sends some data out from the LAN card, and listens for the same data to be received by the LAN card. If that data *isn't* received by the LAN card, then there's something wrong with the transmitter or the receiver logic of the network card.

Notice that for the first two tests, you haven't even connected your system to the network yet. In the third test, "network live" loopback test, you do the loopback test again, but this time you do it while connected to the network. The board should pass again.

The final test, sender/responder test, involves two computers, a sender and a responder. The responder's job is to echo back anything that it receives; for example, if Paul's machine is the responder and Jeff's machine is the sender, then any messages that Jeff's machine sends to Paul's machine should cause Paul's machine to send the same message back to Jeff's machine.

To make a computer a responder (and any computer can be a responder; you needn't use a server) you've got to run a program that makes it into a responder. But that's where the problem arises. The responder software is packaged on the same disk as the diagnostic software that comes with the network board and, unfortunately, the responder software usually will only run on network boards made by the company that wrote the diagnostic software. So, for example, if you've got an Ethernet that is a mixture of 3Com, SMC, and Intel LAN boards, and you want to test a computer with new 3Com Ethernet board, then you'll have to search for another computer that has a 3Com board in order to run the responder software on that computer.

Once you're certain that the hardware is all installed, you're ready to start installing NT or NT Server.

Running the NT Install Program

Next, you'll start up the Setup program. My examples assume that you're installing from the CD-ROM. Floppy installation looks about the same, but is more tedious.

You pop the "Setup Boot Disk" into drive A and reboot. NT then runs NTDE-TECT.COM, which figures out what kind of hardware you have on your system. You'll see a message that says "Windows NT Setup/Setup is inspecting your computer's hardware configuration."

Next, you'll see the following on a blue screen with white letters:

`Windows NT Setup`

And on the bottom of the screen:

`Setup is loading files (Windows NT Executive)...`

You're then prompted to insert Setup Disk number 2 and press Enter. You'll see some messages on the bottom of the screen about what's loading.

Setup then turns the screen to 50-line mode, announcing how much system memory you have and that the NT kernel is loading. The screen shifts back to normal mode, and the "Welcome to Setup" message appears. Pressing Enter continues the process.

Express or Custom Installation?

As with all Microsoft installation programs, NT Setup offers both Express and Custom options. In general, I recommend Custom, because the Express installation is basically Custom with a bunch of settings predefined with defaults. You're only going to install your server software once or twice per machine, so take the time and do Custom. You choose Custom by pressing **C**.

Scanning for SCSI Adapters

Next, Setup auto-detects any SCSI adapters in your system. Your adapter should be auto-detected properly—I've installed systems with four different SCSI adapters, and they all installed correctly. If the adapter wasn't recognized, then you have a chance to punch it in directly, or if it's not on the list of adapters that NT has built-in support for, then you can tell NT to use a device support disk at this point.

If your adapter is on the NT compatibility list and wasn't recognized, then I recommend that you *not* hand-configure the SCSI adapter by pressing S. Instead, I recommend that you exit Setup (press F3) and go back and recheck that the SCSI adapter is installed correctly. In the SCSI host adapter scanning process, you'll have to insert the third (and final, if you're doing a CD-ROM installation) diskette.

Once the adapter (or adapters) is recognized by NT Setup, press Enter to continue.

CD-ROM or Floppy Installation?

Now you tell NT whether you'll install from floppy or CD-ROM; press Enter to indicate that you'll install from CD-ROM, or A to install from floppies.

Hardware Configuration

NT Setup then tells you what it thinks that you have in terms of:

- Basic PC type
- Video system
- Mouse
- Keyboard
- Country layout for keyboard

This list is usually correct, except for the video. The NT Setup program at this point always starts you off with basic VGA, leaving the video configuration to a later point in the setup. The NT designers reasoned that if you choose a super VGA type, then you may choose wrong. If you choose wrong, however, then the system won't be bootable, requiring you to reinstall from the ground up. In contrast, if you choose VGA, then VGA drivers work on just about any video board around. They may not exploit the full resolution or color depth of most boards, but they *do* work. Then, once you've got the system up and running with the VGA drivers, you can install the super VGA drivers. If, after installing the new drivers, your system doesn't work, then you can always load the "last known good" configuration, as you'll see in Chapter 15.

Actually, even if you *do* mess up when picking a video type, NT 3.5x resolves the problem by including an option on the Operating System Picker called Windows NT 3.51 [VGA mode]; no matter how badly you've bollixed up the video, you can always reboot and choose the VGA option. Then, once you've booted, you can adjust your video driver to something more appropriate.

When you're satisfied that the list matches your configuration, highlight "The above list matches my computer" and press Enter.

At this point, if you're installing the NT *workstation* operating system, and you intend to coexist with DOS, or if you're installing an NT Server on top of an existing DOS machine, then you may see a message telling you that you are using the Delete Sentry or Delete Tracking features of Undelete under DOS. NT does not recognize that feature (it doesn't have either Delete Sentry or Delete Tracking) and so NT may end up reporting different amounts of free space than DOS does.

What this means in English is that NT may think that you don't have as much free space on your disk as DOS reported before you got started. Unless you're going to reformat the partition, this may make it impossible for NT to install on your system. If that's the case, then reboot under DOS, disable the Delete Sentry system, and destroy the \SENTRY directory. (This will defeat the Delete Sentry feature, but that may be necessary in order to get NT to load.)

Choosing an NT Partition

Next, NT Setup will show you the partitions on your system and ask you which one you want to install NT on. You can delete partitions with this option, but, as always, be aware that you're permanently destroying data if you do that. (You *did* back up before you started doing this, didn't you?)

> **TIP**
>
> If you're converting a server from Novell NetWare, you must delete the existing NetWare partition before proceeding; NT can't simply convert an existing NetWare partition to an NT partition. Again, that would destroy data on your partition, so don't do it unless you've backed up to a backup format that can be restored under NT, as discussed earlier in this chapter.

Picking Your Drive

Select the partition that you want to install NT on, and press Enter. You'll next choose how you want to format the partition, if you want to format it at all. Your choices are:

- Leave current file system and data alone
- Wipe the disk, formatting to a FAT system
- Wipe the disk, formatting to an NTFS system

- Convert an existing FAT system to NTFS

- Convert an existing HPFS/HPFS386 system to NTFS (LAN Manager upgrade for NT Server only)

FAT or NTFS Disk Partitioning Options

Of the FAT or NTFS disk partitioning options, which should you use?

The File Allocation Table file system has only one advantage, but it's a compelling one: It's the file system that DOS uses. If you're moving from a FAT-based workstation (which is likely), or a FAT-based server (which is unlikely), then you may want to be able to boot from a DOS floppy and read the hard disk. That's possible if you leave the disk in a FAT format. Moving to NTFS makes it impossible to boot from a DOS floppy and still be able to read the hard disk (a security feature of NTFS).

The main features that NTFS offers include:

- Directories that are automatically sorted.

- Support of upper- and lowercase letters in names.

- Support of Unicode in file names.

- Allows permissions to be set on directories and files.

- Multiple "forks" in files—subfiles that essentially "branch off" from a file. (The closest analogy would be to the data fork and resource fork in the Macintosh file system.)

- Faster access to large (over $1/2$ megabyte) sequential access files.

- Faster access to all random access files.

- File and directory names can be up to 254 characters long.

- Long names are automatically converted to the 8+3 naming convention when accessed by a DOS workstation.

- Macintosh compatibility: You cannot share volumes with Mac clients on an NT network unless the host disk partition has been formatted to NTFS.

- NTFS uses the disk space more sparingly than does FAT. Under FAT, the minimum size that a file *actually* uses on disk is 2048 bytes, and as disk partitions get larger, that minimum size also gets larger. On the 1700MB disk I use on my server, that minimum size would be *32768* bytes! Under NTFS, that same hard disk—and any hard disk, in fact—supports files so that no file actually takes more than 512 bytes of space. The final release default allocation unit size is based on the disk size: 512 bytes if less than 512MB, 1024 bytes if 512MB to 1GB, 2048 bytes if 1GB to 2GB, and 4096 bytes if the hard drive is greater than 2GB.

NT SERVER

I'll discuss all of this in more detail later, in Chapter 4 on the Disk Administrator, but as I said earlier, it's just plain crazy to use NT Server with any disk format other than NTFS. If you do, you lose most of the security options, a good bit of performance, and some of the disk space currently wasted by the FAT file system for its clusters. The FAT and HPFS conversion routines both have worked without a hitch for me, so long as there's enough free space on the hard disk. Make sure there's about 100MB free before proceeding.

For an NT workstation, you may want to stay with the FAT file system so that you can dual-boot to DOS, because DOS can't read or write a disk partition formatted to the NTFS format.

CHKDSK in Disguise

NT Setup then runs a special version of CHKDSK to make sure that the file system is clean. This test is *not* a disk media test like the old Novell COMPSURF, so, as I've said earlier in this chapter, the onus is on you to make sure that you've got a reliable disk before beginning the installation process. This CHKDSK-like program runs if you're not formatting the partition; if you're formatting, then you'll see a message to that effect, and the Setup program will format the hard disk. Then, unbelievably, Setup will run the CHKDSK program on your just-formatted disk (*grrr…*).

Which Directory Do I Put It On?

After CHKDSK, choose the directory that you'll install the NT files to. \winnt, the recommended directory, is fine. NT Setup will then copy a bunch of files, just enough to boot the system, to your hard disk. If you're installing from floppies, then you'll get a minor workout. These files are mainly just enough to get the graphical portion of Setup running, although a number of help files get installed in the process. These help files are for things that aren't necessary until the system's up and running (Mail, Schedule+, and so on).

Even with a triple-spin CD-ROM, the copying takes about ten minutes, so be patient until you get a message like:

```
Setup has successfully configured your computer for Windows NT.
To continue Setup, your computer must be restarted. Remove any
floppies from drive A: and press Enter.
```

Pop out the Installation disk and reboot the computer. It then boots a kind of mini-NT into a graphical Setup program.

TIP   If you told the Setup program to use NTFS, then you'll be confused when Setup reboots and displays a message that says "Check in file system on C: ... the type of the file system is FAT." Don't worry about it; you won't see NT say that you have an NTFS volume until you're done with the installation.

Entering Graphical Setup

As the system reboots, you first see NTDETECT's announcement; NTDETECT runs every time you boot NT. You then get a black screen with white letters telling you to press the spacebar now to return to the "Last Known Good" menu. That's really not relevant here, as you don't yet *have* a Last Known Good menu. (That'll be explained in the troubleshooting section.) Then the screen turns blue, meaning that the NT kernel has loaded, and then the graphical portion loads.

Per Connection or Per Seat?

Next, your licensing choices will appear. NT Server 3.51 is a little different from NT Server 3.5, and one of those differences lies in the licensing choice you have for the software. After you've rebooted to the graphical portion of Setup, 3.5 users will notice an addition to the installation process: the licensing screen.

In this dialog box, you'll be presented with two licensing options: per connection and per seat. The implications of these two options may not be immediately clear, so here's what your choices are:

- Per-*seat* licensing means that you need a license for every workstation that will ever log onto the domain. This is the kind of licensing that came by default with previous versions of NT Server. Per-seat licensing has a few advantages. First, it's easy to understand: you count the number of workstations that log onto the domain, and you've got the number of licenses that you need. Second, you don't have to worry about the number of servers in the domain: whether you've got one server in the domain or six, per-seat licensing requires that you have one license for each workstation that logs into the domain.

- Per-*connect* licensing means that you need a license for every simultaneous NT Server connection. If user Ignatz logs onto server RAMSES, that uses up one license. If he then logs onto server ISIS to get to the printer (without leaving his user directory on RAMSES), then that uses up another license. If Ignatz connects to six servers, then he uses up six licenses.

Why might per-connect licensing be a good idea? First, it works well for offices with staff that's on the road a lot. In Mark Minasi and Company, for example, much of the staff is on the road at any given time, teaching. When they're on the road, they're not logging into any servers, so I could save on licenses if I knew that I had only two NT Servers and five users in the office at any given time (for a total number of ten required licenses, just to be safe), even if I had a staff of 25. (As it happens, everyone's in the office and logging onto the servers most Fridays, so the per seat licensing was easier, but you can see how this might have worked.) The other situation in which per-connect licensing might be handy is if not everyone in your office gets their own workstation. If more than one person will be using a workstation, it's easier to keep your licensing honest if you think in terms of server accesses rather than warmed chairs.

Think about your needs before choosing a licensing method. You get one shot at changing the licensing style from Per Server to Per Seat, using the Licensing icon in the Control Panel. After that, or if you originally specified Per Seat licensing, you'll have to reinstall to legally change it.

Personalizing Your Copy of NT

As with many products these days, you personalize your copy of NT or NT Server by entering your name, company name, and product number. Enter those and click the Continue button; you'll be asked to verify it, so click Continue again. Be sure to put the correct product number in your server. If you must make one up or leave it blank, then your server won't be able to communicate with any other NT Server machine with the same product number.

Domain Controller or Server

Recall from the last chapter that an NT domain differs from a workgroup in that a domain has a master security database, and that security database is used to approve or reject requests for data or other resources on the network. In a simple NT network, all of the burden of security verification is shouldered by an NT Server machine acting as the primary domain controller. The workload of verifying requests can be shared, however, amongst a number of NT servers by making them backup domain controllers.

NT Server machines do not *have* to be domain controllers, however; they can simply act as servers. The Setup dialog box labeled Windows NT Server Security Role lets you choose which part this server will play in your domain.

The first NT server that you install in a domain *must* be a domain controller; in fact, it becomes by default the primary domain controller. The second should be a backup domain controller, as it's just about impossible to reinstall a primary domain controller, should you need to, without a backup domain controller to stand in for the primary while you're reinstalling the primary. But I recommend that you keep the number of domain controllers to a minimum, probably no more than one for every 100 users. Designate other servers as just "Server," rather than "Domain Controller."

You can't change this machine's status from server to domain controller without reinstalling NT Server.

Choosing a Computer Name

You'll next have to give your computer a name by which it is recognized on the network. It can be up to fifteen characters, and the name can include spaces. A few suggestions here:

- Don't put spaces in your computer's name. It causes some trouble accessing this computer via Windows for Workgroups, and even if you're not using Windows for Workgroups, the presence of a space in the name means that whenever you do a command-line reference to the computer name, you have to surround it with quotes. All in all, spaces make for some annoyance, so avoid them.

- Don't name a computer based on the person who uses it; that person may move from computer to computer. And even if that's not true, you'll still find it confusing, for example, to have a user Meredith and a computer named Meredith. Some network commands refer to machines, and others refer to users. Giving users and machines different names helps keep the differences straight.

Once you've entered the machine name, click Continue, and then confirm it.

Watch Your Language!

Setup will next ask for a language; enter the appropriate one. NT out of the box assumes English, probably correctly. If you're running NT in French or Chinese, you'll need a different edition of NT.

Customizing the Setup

The next dialog box will ask if you want to:

- **Set up Windows components**   Unless you've got a reason not to, you may as well install all of the NT components, with the possible exception of the stupid system sounds, wallpaper, and screen savers. Keep at least one screen saver, however, for security purposes.

- **Set up network**   You've got no real choice here for NT Server; servers aren't too useful without network cards. If you chose earlier to make this machine a

Domain Controller rather than a Server, then the "Set up network" item is actually checked and grayed out, as you *must* set up a network card.

- **Set up local printers** As with Windows, you need printer drivers (although for NT Server, they end up doing very little, unless you have NT workstations).

- **Set up applications on the hard disk(s)** You can probably skip this one for NT Server, as you won't be running DOS or Windows applications right on the server; in fact, you probably won't be running too many applications of any kind on the server. For NT workstations, however, it's probably a good idea to acquaint NT with the Windows and DOS programs already on the system.

  It should be obvious, but I'll mention anyway. If you've just formatted the disk, then there is no point in checking "Set up applications on the hard disk(s)," as there aren't any.

Once you've made the choices, click Continue.

Choosing Windows Components

If you selected "Install selected Windows components," you'll get a dialog box allowing you to choose which components to install. What you install here is a matter of choice, but in general I find bitmaps, sounds, and screen savers a waste of CPU power, memory, and disk space. (This *is*, however, a matter of opinion.) It's always a good idea to install readme files, unless you've previously installed this version of NT, and so already know what the readme files say.

Setting Up Local Printers

If you told Setup to install local printers, then you'll get to choose which printers are attached to your machine. Name the printer, and once again, give it a useful name. For example, "Tom" is not a particularly good name. Giving the name "HP4" to a Hewlett-Packard LaserJet 4 is a bit better, and the name "SalesHP4" is even better. Then choose the printer type, and specify which interface it's attached to.

Notice that this only sets up *local* printers. One of the truly amazing things about NT workstations in combination with an NT Server is that you don't need printer drivers on the workstation. But if you are using any other type of workstation, such as Windows for Workgroups, you need to have the print driver(s) on the workstation. The single printer driver on the server can serve as the printer driver for all workstations attached to it, so there's no need to install printer drivers on the workstation.

Setting Up Network Cards

Next, you've got to set up your network card. One of NT's really nifty features is an "auto-detect" system that is right most of the time. You see a dialog box called Network Adapter Card Detection, click Continue, and the vast majority of the time, the "auto-detect" system will figure out which network card you have without trouble.

If, on the other hand, Setup can't detect your network, card, or, in rare instances, it locks up when it tries to detect your network card, then rerun Setup, choose Do Not Detect, and directly choose the network card. If the driver for the card isn't on the NT setup disks, then you're probably out of luck. There's not a huge market for NT LAN card drivers, so you probably won't find them on the driver disk that came with your LAN card. (That may change with time, however.) As I suggested a few pages back, it's a good idea to buy one of the top twenty or so LAN cards because it's easy to find drivers for those cards. And if you want to be pretty much *sure* that your NT drivers are good, consider this: Much of Microsoft uses the Intel Ether-Express 16 LAN boards. Guess which drivers are likely to be the most stable under NT?

Once Setup has detected your LAN card, you'll click Continue to set up the card. One thing that Setup is *not* good at is figuring out things like which IRQ, I/O address, or RAM addresses your card uses, but that won't be a problem for you if you took my advice earlier in this chapter and documented those things. Enter those values, click Continue, and NT will move on to the main installation process.

Next, you'll select the protocols that you'll use on the server. NetBEUI is kind of *de rigeur*, and IPX/SPX is fine to connect Novell.

If you choose TCP/IP, then you'll be prompted for installation options. I'd just select Connectivity Utilities and Simple TCP/IP Services for the moment, and look to Chapter 13 for more details on using TCP/IP features.

> **TIP** At this point, NT Setup will start reading the CD-ROM drive. Now and then, it seems not to see the CD-ROM, instructing you to insert it in the CD-ROM drive. Don't fret at that; just remove and reinsert the CD-ROM disk, and click OK on the dialog box.

Adjusting the Network Settings with Control Panel

Once the bulk of NT has been transferred to the hard disk, you'll be presented with a formidable-looking set of options in a dialog box labeled Network Settings. You needn't worry that you must get this right the first time or all is lost, as you can get to this dialog box any time you want by opening the Control Panel and double-clicking on the Network icon. You cannot adjust most of these items; if you click on an item like Computer Browser and then click Configure…, then you'll get this message: "Cannot configure the software component." You'll see that message on all but a few of the items in the Installed Network Software list box. The exceptions follow.

RPC Name Service Provider

You can specify a particular name service provider other than the default NT Name Service Provider, but you'll only do this if you're running particular server products, and the installation programs there will make this adjustment automatically.

Server

NT SERVER

This is a fairly important setting, particularly for NT Server. This dialog box directs the system how to divert memory and CPU power among the programs and systems running on the PC.

The default setting, Balance, is fine for an NT workstation. But for an NT Server, you should set the radio button to Maximize Throughput for File Sharing if its function will primarily be file serving, or Maximize Throughput for Network Applications if it acts as the server in some client-server application.

The check box at the bottom, Make Browser Broadcasts to LAN Manager 2.x Clients, should just be labeled LAN Manager 2.x clients present on network. You should select this check box if you still have LAN Manager servers on your network. (A LAN Manager server is a "LAN Manager client" from the point of view of NT Server, as it can't participate in domain security.)

Leave the Bindings... button alone for the moment; we'll examine it later in Chapter 14, on tuning. Click OK.

If you've selected TCP/IP or IPX/SPX protocols, then Setup will prompt you for information about those protocols. To see how to answer those questions, see Chapters 12 (Novell) and 13 (TCP/IP). Once you're through with that, you'll see the message "Setup is starting the network..."

Setting Up Domain and Administrator Accounts

NT SERVER

The next dialog box will vary depending on whether you chose Server or Domain Controller in the earlier Windows NT Server Security Role dialog box.

Installing in an Existing Domain

If you're just installing an NT Server machine in an existing domain, then you'll see a dialog box labeled Domain/Workgroup Settings. You'll have the choice to either join an existing workgroup or become a member of an existing domain.

Remember that NT is massively security-conscious. As a result, not just any NT workstation or server can be part of an NT domain; instead, it has to be *granted* access to the domain by the Primary Domain Controller. That happens one of two ways:

- An administrator of the domain can create a machine account with the Server Manager (this topic is covered in Chapter 10) before installing the new server.

- The Setup program gives an administrator the option to create a machine account right here in the Domain/Workgroup Settings dialog box.

This can be a bit confusing (at least it threw *me* when I first started working with NT), so let's look at what's going on in some more detail. Most kinds of workstations can just jump right onto an NT domain without any kind of prior notice. For example, DOS, Windows, OS/2, or Windows for Workgroups machines can just "appear" on an NT domain without the permission of the NT Primary Domain Controller, *save* for the fact that whoever is logging onto the NT domain must be a user with a valid network account created with the User Manager for Domains (see Chapter 7).

In contrast, an NT domain won't even *talk* to an NT workstation or server to whom it has not "been properly introduced." Now, in general, you introduce a machine to a domain by first logging onto the domain as an administrator, then running the Server Manager. In the Server Manager, you can tell the domain to expect to hear from a new machine called, say, Ignatz. Then, when you're installing your next NT machine—workstation or server—you just name that machine Ignatz. The domain says, "Oh, *you're* Ignatz! We've been expecting you!" And all is well.

The problem with that approach is, of course, you'll end up nine times out of ten forgetting to run the Server Manager before installing NT, forcing yourself to abort an NT installation in midstream or to run around looking for an already-working NT machine from which to run the Server Manager. For that reason, Microsoft decided to make your life easier and just put a tiny piece of the Server Manager in the Setup program. If you are installing NT, *and* if you are an administrator (you must verify this by entering the user name for your administrative account and password), then you can create the machine account right then and there, in the Setup program.

In the section of the dialog box labeled Create Computer Account in Domain, you're prompted for a User Name and a Password. It kind of looks like you're being prompted to create a new user in this dialog box, but you're not; this is the user name and password of your administrative account, the administrative account that you'll use to create the new *machine* account on the NT domain.

Once that's all plugged in, press OK.

Installing in a New Domain

By contrast, if you're creating a new domain, then there's no one to inform that you're going to be part of that domain. In that case, you don't get the Domain/Workgroup Settings dialog box; instead, you get the Domain Settings dialog box.

If you indicated that you would be a domain controller, then Setup gives you the opportunity at this point to either specify an existing domain to be a part of, or to report the name of a new domain that you want Setup to create.

The Domain Settings dialog box allows you to name the domain that the NT Server will control, or to name an existing domain that the NT Server will be a member of. You indicate "Computer Role," which can either be as a Primary Domain Controller or as a Backup Domain Controller.

Now, if your computer is to be a Primary Domain Controller, that implies you're creating a whole new domain. You then enter the new domain's name and press Enter. If, on the other hand, you want the computer to be a Backup Domain Controller, then you've got to create a machine account in an *existing* domain—after all, you can't have a Backup Domain Controller until you have a Primary Domain Controller. As when you add a simple Server, you've got to create a machine account for this new NT machine in the domain, and so you can enter the name and password of someone with administrator privileges, or you could have created the machine account beforehand with the Server Manager.

TIP

If you are reinstalling a Primary Domain Controller, then it's very important to read the section "Reinstalling NT Server" at the end of this chapter. If you simply try to reinstall your PDC as a PDC, and specify your current domain name as a *new* domain name, then you'll create a host of problems.

Whatever you're going to call your domain, *this* is where you name (and create) it. If you change the name from Networks in the Control Panel, you'll have to re-establish all the trust relationships and re-enter the domain name for all the clients. It's not so bad, but it's easier if you stick with the name you choose at installation. Given that fact, give some thought to how you name domains. While you can get away with it, don't put spaces or periods in your domain names.

For some people, the domain names will be obvious: Shipping or Marketing. If you have many domains within a particular organizational function—for example, if you have ten domains within the Marketing department—then you can do one of two things:

- Give them names like Marketing01 through Marketing10. After all, you've got 15 letters to work with.

- Find different instances of a group. For example, you could name the marketing domains after colors (Red, Green, Blue, Yellow), name the research domains after constellations (Bigdipper, Orion, Cygnus, Libra), or name the top executives' domains after precious metals (Gold, Platinum, Iridium, Silver).

Why do it that way? If you've got a lot of domains, then it can get tedious to look at Marketing01, Marketing02, Marketing03, and so on, as the domain names all look the same on first glance. Using a group of names that are related in some way makes it easy to identify what group a domain is affiliated with, and the different members of that group are more easily distinguished from one another.

Next, you'll be prompted to set the password for the mandatory Administrator account. This is the Administrator account for *this* computer, not the domain administrator. As always, don't pick obvious passwords, and keep the passwords secure. If, on the other hand, you work in a place where you don't particularly care about security, then you can omit a password—but I don't recommend it. If your data is worth the $700 you spent to put the NT Server software on your file server, then it's worth protecting. Administrators can do *anything* to a workstation or server.

Setting Virtual Memory

Windows NT essentially requires page file support for virtual memory, no matter *how* much RAM you've got. For now, accept the default settings unless they'll use up too much hard disk space. We'll take up virtual memory optimization in Chapter 14, on tuning.

Setting Up Applications

The next dialog box asks where to look for applications to migrate over to NT program groups. The migration process translates INI information into your system's registry, adding DOS PIFs as necessary. The process will prompt you about any programs that it is unsure of; respond to the dialog boxes and tell Setup which programs to convert to NT. Setup will create a personal group called Applications (Common) to contain them.

Setting the Time Zone

NT next must know what time zone you're in. It even knows when Daylight Savings Time takes effect!

Creating the Emergency Repair Disk

I mentioned the important emergency repair disk before; this is where you create it. Just put a floppy that you don't mind zapping into the A drive, and Setup will format it and create an emergency repair disk. This isn't a *bootable* disk, it's just a disk that contains the data necessary to reconstruct a configuration if your NT system is no longer able to boot.

The formatting part of the program seems to run the drive pretty hard. You may find that the format process gets a bit noisy after about 75 percent, but don't worry about it. If the floppy is bad, then you'll get a chance to insert a different floppy.

Incidentally, you can create a new, up-to-date emergency repair disk any time after installation by using NT Server's repair disk utility, RDISK.EXE, which is in the SYSTEM32 directory. This handy little program will not only create the new repair disk, it will also update the system repair information stored on the hard disk.

That's all there is to it. Reboot, and the system comes right up.

Upgrading to 3.51

Running the upgrade is a lot like running the installation, except that it's simpler and offers you fewer options—for example, you don't get to repartition the hard disk or choose an installation drive if you're upgrading. Full installations of NT Server 3.51 do allow you to do these things; it's just the upgrade that's different.

Upgrading Steps

If you're upgrading, the process goes something like this:

1. Insert the upgrade CD in the drive. For the purposes of the upgrade, it doesn't matter whether the drive is local or only accessible from the network. Move to the \I386 directory on the CD.

2. From the command prompt, type `winnt /b` to tell the system that you want to do a floppyless install.

3. A dialog box will appear, asking you for the location of the upgrade files. If it didn't guess right (i.e., if it doesn't list the \I386 directory on the CD-ROM), then type the correct path. By default, the upgrade program will copy the files to your local hard disk. If you don't want it to, click the Options... button and de-select that option. Click OK once you've set the file location.

4. If the upgrade program copies the installation files to your hard disk, it will need 51MB of free space on the disk to do the install (this is more than the actual operation files will require). If you don't have that much free space, the installation program will alert you and let you pause the upgrade while you free up some space on the hard disk. Once you've got enough free space on the drive (if you're copying the files locally) and have indicated the location of the upgrade files, the upgrade program will copy the files to your hard disk.

5. After it's finished copying the installation files (this takes a while, so be patient), you'll need to restart the computer. (If you can't restart right at that moment, you can cancel out of this dialog box rather than restarting immediately. When you restart, choose the Installation/Upgrade option from the startup menu.)

6. You'll move to the Windows NT Setup blue screen. From here, the upgrade should proceed like a normal installation (express or custom, hardware detection, etc.), with the following caveats:

   - You don't have a choice of installing from the floppy or CD-ROM— you're installing from the local hard disk.

   - You don't get to change your partition information or file system.

   - CHKDSK doesn't run.

After the upgrade program has finished checking out your hard disk and copying files needed to boot the system to the boot drive, it'll prompt you to remove any floppies from Drive A: and then press Enter to reboot. From here, upgrading 3.5 to 3.51 looks a lot like installing 3.51 new, as described in the previous pages.

Cautions About the Upgrade Process

I'd like to issue a couple of cautions about the upgrade. First, upgrading will only work if you have previously installed 3.5, and second, if the upgrade doesn't work, you may destroy your previous installation and have to start over.

You Must Have 3.5 in Place

The upgrade software only works if you have a previously installed copy of NT Server 3.5. If you try to run the upgrade software on a machine that doesn't have version 3.5 installed, the program will let you waste time copying files until you get to the first re-boot. This is annoying. Ergo, if you bought both an upgrade version for the older server and a full-blown version for the new server, don't get the CDs mixed up.

Files That Don't Get Copied Can Corrupt a Previous Installation

Sometimes, when you're copying files from the \I386 directory on the local hard disk to the boot area, some files don't make it. NT Server will complain that it couldn't get to the files and request that you make sure that the CD or floppy is properly in the drive. (My reaction at this point was to mutter, "Of course it's prop-erly in the drive, you idiot. You're copying files from the local hard disk, and if the hard disk *isn't* in the drive, there's not much I can do about it.") Your choices at this point are to press Enter to retry the copy, Escape to ignore the file, or F3 to cancel the installation. If pressing Enter a few times doesn't do the trick, you can tell the upgrade to skip copying that file and just get on with it.

This doesn't matter with some files, but it *really* matters with others. For example, if the file COURBD.TTF doesn't copy, this is not the end of the world—that's just a TrueType font. Lack of Courier Bold won't keep your operating system from run-ning. If the file that won't copy is something vital, however (such as NTDLL.DLL), then not copying that file will prevent the upgraded operating system from running and you won't be able to get to your previous installation of 3.5 because you overwrote it with the bad upgrade. When you try to restart the second time during the upgrade, everything will look fine until you get to the blue Startup… screen, at which point the system will freeze, you'll see a message that it couldn't find the file that it needed, and you'll need to do a cold reboot even to begin to repair the installation.

The bottom line here is that, if you tell the upgrade (or installation) program to skip files, be very sure that you know what you're skipping. Knowing which files are vital and which aren't takes some experience, but as a general rule I'd say that procedure files, such as .EXEs and .DLLs, are not optional. Information or otherwise expendable files like .HLPs, .TTFs or .TXTs can probably wait for you to copy them.

What's Next?

But you're not done yet, not by a good bit. Network installations will vary from location to location, but common remaining tasks include the following items. If an item is followed by a chapter subject, then you can read about it there; otherwise, I'll cover it in the remainder of this chapter.

- Finish setting up Windows apps on a workstation
- Create users (see "User Manager for Domains" in Chapter 7)
- Set the policy for the Guest account (see "User Manager for Domains" in Chapter 7)
- Make whatever modifications are necessary to user rights (Chapter 7)
- Install, interface, and configure a UPS
- Install optional modules, like Mac support, TCP/IP, DLC, or Remote Access Services (see Chapters 18, 13, and 17, respectively)
- Tuning (see Chapters 14)
- Install fault tolerant features (see Chapter 4)
- Create a directory structure and share it (see Chapter 8)
- Install tape drivers
- Set up scheduled events (see Chapter 10)
- Install extra printer drivers (see Chapter 9)
- Share printers (see Chapter 9)

- Set default printer (see Chapter 9)
- Establish links to and from trusted domains (see Chapter 11, Cross-Domain Management)

While I'd like to cover every detail of a complete installation in this chapter, I feel that some of the larger issues should stay in their own chapters. In the next few sections, we'll take a look at some of the simpler setups you'll do to move your server installation further along.

Migrating Windows Applications

For some reason, even though Setup promises to migrate your Windows applications over to your NT setup, it doesn't do it. That means you've got to sort of lead it by the nose. This section explains how.

Not Every Windows Program Will Run

Understand right off that not every Windows program will run. In particular, say good-bye to programs like the following:

- Undelete
- Fax
- System utility

Those will, in general, not work under NT.

Moving the Fonts

Even though the Event Log shows that the Registry was updated with font information, NT seems unaware of your old Windows fonts. Fixing that is a snap.

1. Open the Control Panel.
2. Open the Fonts applet. You'll see a dialog box like the one in Figure 3.2.
3. Click the Add... button. You'll see a dialog box like the on in Figure 3.3.

FIGURE 3.2:

Fonts dialog box

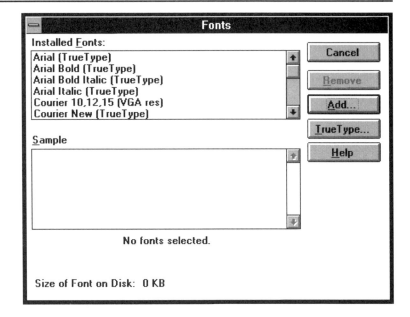

FIGURE 3.3:

Adding fonts with the Add Fonts dialog box

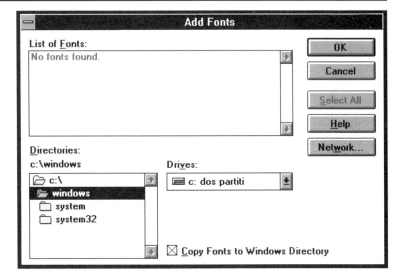

4. Uncheck Copy Fonts to Windows Directory—no sense in having two copies of a font on your already-overworked hard disk—and click the C:\windows\system directory.

5. After a minute or two of disk activity, you'll see your fonts appear. Select them all (just click on the top one, then scroll down to the bottom font, press the Shift key, and click the bottom item), and click OK. You'll soon see a dialog box like the one in Figure 3.4.

FIGURE 3.4:

Control Panel asking for an already-recognized font

That's just telling you that you asked for a font that is already recognized by the system. That's okay; just click OK and keep going. You'll see a bunch of these dialog boxes, but just keep clicking OK until you're done.

6. After the last "Remove this font and reinstall" dialog box, click Close on the Fonts dialog box, and close up the Control Panel. Your fonts are now restored.

In short, read the "How Do I" sidebar for a quick summation.

Getting Your Apps Back

For some reason, migrated Windows apps don't get migrated properly. The result: You'll probably experience problems getting your Windows apps to run on an NT workstation. My suggestions for fixing this are:

- Make sure that the applications' directories are on the path.

- You may have to copy the applications' INI files to the C:\Winnt35 directory, or whatever directory you've put NT in.

- In many cases, you simply have to reinstall the application.

How Do I Get My Old Fonts Back?

1. Open the Control Panel.

2. Open the Fonts applet and click the Add… button. Uncheck Copy Fonts to Windows Directory and click the C:\windows\system directory.

3. After a minute or two of disk activity, you'll see your fonts appear. Select them all (just click on the top one, then scroll down to the bottom font, press the Shift key, and click the bottom item), and click OK. You'll see dialog boxes telling you that a copy of this font is already on the system, but just click OK and keep going.

After the last "Remove this font and reinstall" dialog box, just click Close on the Fonts dialog box, and close up the Control Panel. Your fonts are now restored.

Believe me, reinstalling seems to be the best method. I know, it's bad news, but there doesn't seem any way around it. Funny thing—install OS/2 2.x on a system, and it effortlessly moves your Windows applications over to its desktop. Odd that IBM can do with *its* operating system what Microsoft couldn't do with *its own*.

Choosing and Installing an Uninterruptible Power Supply

One of the most important parts of server security is *power* security. Once, backup power supplies were tremendously expensive, but that's not true any more. You can buy a cheap, basic standby power supply (SPS) for around $200. Better yet, that cheap SPS can alert NT when the power's going down. But let's take a moment and look at what kinds of power protection devices you should invest in.

The Problem with Electrical Outlets

Power coming in from your outlets is of a high quality, but it's not high quality enough to trust your server to it. For example, on my sites (three commercially zoned buildings), we experience about three or four outages per year. They're not *long* outages—usually just a minute or two—but that's quite enough to shut down the servers and sometimes damage data.

Power problems come in three main types:

- **Surges and spikes** Transient noise appearing on the power line that can permanently damage your electronic components.

- **Voltage variation** The power coming out of the wall is supposed to be 120 volts in North America, 240 volts in the U.K. and Ireland, and 220 throughout continental Europe. (EEC members will note how delicately I sidestepped the "Is the U.K. part of Europe?" question.) Usually too *little* voltage is the problem, but sometimes you get too much voltage. In any case, neither is desirable.

- **Outages** Whether they last for a second or a day, a power outage will crash a server, which can spell disaster for an application server.

You've heard of surge protectors, and perhaps some of you *use* them. But I recommend that you avoid them, as they are really only rated to catch one surge. After that, they're not reliable. (Honest, it's true—surprising, though, isn't it?) Worse yet, there's no way to find out if that surge has *already happened*! Furthermore, surge protectors are of no value whatsoever for low voltage or outage situations.

What, then, is the best answer for power protection? Some combination of a *power conditioner* and a battery-backed power supply.

Power Conditioners for Protecting Data

Between a surge protector and a backup power supply is a device called a *power conditioner*. A power conditioner does all the things that a surge protector does, including filtering and isolating line noise, and it does more besides. Rather than relying on the nonreusable components found in surge protectors, the power conditioner uses the inductance of its transformer to filter out line noise. Additionally, most power conditioners will boost up undervoltage so that your machine can continue to work through brownouts.

Which power conditioner is right for you? The one that I use is Tripplite's LC1800. I've seen it in mail-order ads for as little as $200, and I've used mine for many years.

The LC1800 even shows you your incoming voltage via some LEDs on its front panel. *Do not* plug your laser printer into a power conditioner, as most power conditioners are only rated for a few amps; laser printers, in contrast, draw up to 15 amps. If you *do* want to use a power conditioner for a laser printer, then make sure that the power conditioner is one of the more expensive models that provide sufficient amperage to keep the laser going.

Backup Power Supplies

In addition to protection from short power irregularities, you may need backup power. I have lived in a number of places in the northeastern U.S. where summer lightning storms kill the power for just a second—enough to erase your memory and make the digital clocks blink. Total loss of power can only be remedied with battery-based systems. Such systems are in the $200 to $1200 range and up. There are two types of backup power systems, *standby power supplies* (SPS) and *uninterruptible power supplies* (UPS). Figure 3.5 illustrates the differences between them.

SPS's   SPS's charge their batteries while watching the current level. If the power drops, the SPS activates itself and supplies power until its batteries run down.

The key difference between a good SPS and a not-so-good SPS appears when the power goes out. When that happens, the SPS must quickly figure out that power's going down, and must start supplying power from the battery just as quickly. A fast power switch must occur here, and it's important to find out what that switching time *is* for whatever model SPS you're thinking of buying. The speed is rated in milliseconds (ms); 4 ms or under is fine. 8 ms—the speed of some SPS's—is not fast enough in my experience.

UPS's   The other kind of battery backup device is a UPS. It is a superior design, but you'll pay for that superiority. A UPS constantly runs power from the line

FIGURE 3.5:

How UPS's and SPS's work

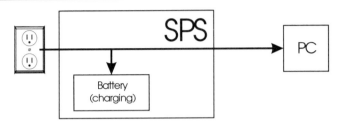

When power is normal, an SPS passes current through to the PC, spikes and all, while siphoning off a bit of the power in order to keep the battery charged.

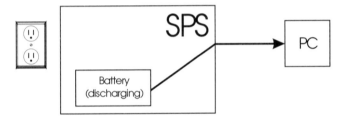

When the power is interrupted, the SPS supplies power to the PC from the battery, for as long as the battery lasts. The SPS must also sense the power-down condition and get the battery on-line quickly enough for the PC to continue to work uninterrupted.

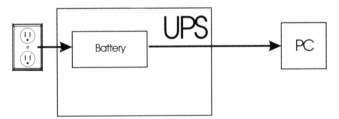

A UPS sends power from the socket right into the battery, then takes the power out of the battery and gives it to the PC. Benefits: constant surge protection and zero switching time.

current to a battery, then from the battery to the PC. This is superior to an SPS because no switching time is involved. Also, this means that any surges affect the battery charging mechanism, not the computer. A UPS also serves in the role of a surge suppresser and a voltage regulator.

A UPS or SPS must convert DC current from a battery to AC for the PC. AC is supposed to look like a sine wave. Cheaper UPS and SPS models produce square waves. See Figure 3.6 for a comparison of the two. Square waves are bad because they include high-frequency harmonics that can appear as EMI or RFI to the computer. Also, some peripherals (printers in particular) can't handle square wave AC. So, when examining UPS's, ask whether they use square wave or sine wave. Some produce a pseudo-sine wave. It has the "stairstep" look of a square wave, but fewer harmonic problems.

FIGURE 3.6:
UPS AC waveforms

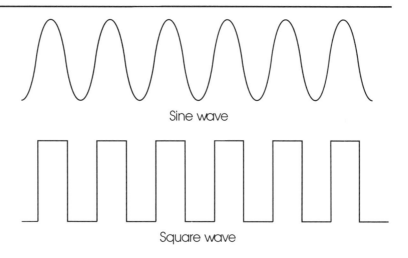

Sine wave

Square wave

Ordinarily, the purpose of a UPS is to allow you enough time to save whatever you're doing and shut down gracefully. If you are in an area where the power may disappear for hours, and may do it regularly, then you should look for the ability to attach external batteries to the UPS so that you can run the PC for longer periods.

Remember that a sine-wave UPS is the only way to really eliminate most power problems. The reason *everyone* doesn't have one is the high cost.

A decent compromise can be found in a fast (4 ms) square-wave SPS. I know, I said square waves are bad for your peripherals, but consider this: How often will the SPS actually be doing anything? Not very often. Remember, it only supplies power when the line voltage drops out, which is not a common occurrence. The brief minute or two each month of square-wave power that your peripherals end up getting won't kill them. And you'll save a pile over a UPS.

On the other hand, remember that a UPS is *always* on line, and so must produce sine-wave output. But UPS's have the benefit that they provide surge protection by breaking down and reassembling the power, and SPS's *do not* provide this protection: You must still worry about surge protection when you buy an SPS, but not if you buy a UPS. So make the choice that your budget allows.

Whether you buy an SPS or UPS, however, be sure to look for a backup power supply with a serial port.

Serial port? Yes, a serial port. NT and NT Server can monitor a signal from a serial-port-equipped UPS/SPS. When power fails, the operating system is informed by the backup power supply of that occurrence, and the operating system does a graceful shutdown in the battery time remaining. Table 3.2 summarizes what we've seen about power problems and solutions.

Notice that the combination of a power conditioner and an SPS would provide all the power protection that you need. Recognizing that, one firm—American Power Conversion—has made a device that combines an SPS with a power conditioner. Called the Smart-UPS (okay, so even *they* don't understand the difference between a UPS and an SPS), they range from a 400-watt model, which can be obtained by mail order for about $350, on up to 1800-watt models. I use Smart-UPS 400s in my office, and have had very good luck with them. (Of course, they've got the serial port connection.)

TABLE 3.2: Power Problems and Solutions

Protection Method	Remedies Surges?	Remedies Low Voltage?	Remedies Outages?
Power Conditioner	✓	✓	
SPS			✓
UPS	✓	✓	✓

Interfacing the UPS/SPS

NT in both its server and workstation configuration is designed to be able to control a UPS/SPS, and to act on information from the UPS/SPS. NT expects two kinds of signals *from* the UPS/SPS ("power failed" and "battery low"), and can provide one signal *back* to the UPS/SPS ("remote UPS shutdown").

- **Power failed** This signal comes from the UPS/SPS to the NT machine. When this signal is activated by the UPS/SPS, it means that the input power has failed, and that the NT machine is now running on battery power.

- **Battery low** Some UPS/SPS systems can only signal that the power has failed, leaving NT to guess how much battery life is left on the UPS/SPS. Others can signal that about two minutes of battery life is left. If you have such a UPS/SPS, then NT can recognize the "battery low" signal.

- **Remote UPS shutdown** If your power backup device is an SPS rather than a UPS, it may sometimes be desirable to temporarily disable the battery. NT will do this if it senses extremely erratic signals from the "power failed" or "battery about to fail" signal. If that happens, NT instructs the SPS to shut down its inverter, a part of the SPS circuitry, so that all the SPS will do is to charge the battery and provide power off the mains. This is the signal *from the PC* to the SPS.

If you have a UPS/SPS with a serial port, then you should get a cable built for that UPS/SPS from its manufacturer. The manufacturer can also probably give you guidance as to how to set the UPS service settings.

TIP   If your UPS/SPS manufacturer does not sell a cable for interfacing with NT Server, buy the cable for Microsoft LAN Manager; the interfacing is the same, except that the third parameter is not referred to as "remote UPS shutdown" in LAN Manager documentation, but rather as "inverter shutdown."

Configuring a UPS

To configure your UPS, get the correctly wired cable from your UPS/SPS manufac-turer, and hook it up to a serial port on the server and to the one on the back of the UPS/SPS. Then, in NT, start up the Control Panel and choose UPS. You'll see a screen like the one in Figure 3.7.

This is a setup screen for an SPS that supports all three features. Notice first that next to the three options—Power failure signal, Low battery …, and Remote UPS Shutdown (interesting capitalization, Microsoft; whatsamatter, no editors on staff?)—there are radio buttons for Negative or Positive.

Negative or Positive refers to the kind of signal from the UPS/SPS. There is no real standard for using a serial port to interface a UPS/SPS with a PC, and there are 25 different control lines on a serial port. Furthermore, each one of those 25 lines can either display negative voltages or positive voltages. The purpose of these radio buttons is to inform NT of what a signal means. You see, on one UPS, a negative sig-nal might mean "We're losin' power, Captain! Better evacuate while we still can!" *or* it might mean, "All is well." Where do you get this information? Well, the best source is, again, the manufacturer. Failing that, however, you can just try the com-binations until the system works. Or you can do what I ended up doing: working with a breakout box.

FIGURE 3.7:

Configuring the UPS

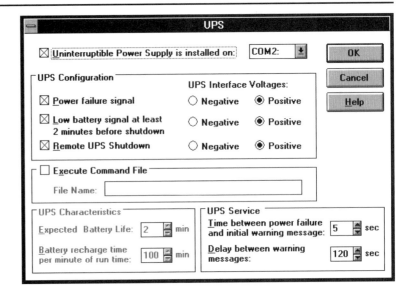

Breakout Boxes

Now, to do this involves a bit of experience with a data communications test device called a *breakout box*. If you don't know what they are or how to use them, I'm afraid that an explanation is a bit beyond the scope of this book. There *are*, however, many good sources on the subject, one of them by me: *The Complete PC Upgrade and Maintenance Guide* (Sybex, 1995). This discussion assumes that you've worked a bit with serial ports, but even if you're not an expert, you may find it useful anyway.

Serial ports use either a 9-pin or 25-pin connector. Every UPS/SPS system that I've ever worked on used the 9-pin, so I'll assume that we're working from one of those. Most breakout boxes are equipped with 25-pin connectors, so get one of the 25 to 9 converters, and plug the breakout box into the port on the back of the UPS.

Turn the UPS on. On the breakout box, you'll see LEDs up to 25 different signal lines (depending on how well designed the breakout box is), but you should be noticing the ones labeled as follows:

- CD or DCD (carrier detect)
- CTS (clear to send)
- RTS (request to send)
- DTR (data terminal ready)
- DSR (data set ready)
- RX (receive data)
- TX (send data)

NT expects three signals on these lines:

- **Power failed**   This must appear to the PC on its CTS line.
- **Low battery**   This must appear to the PC on its DCD line.
- **Remote UPS shutdown**   These signals will be provided from the PC on its DTR line.

Breakout boxes display the status of a serial port's 25 lines with LEDs. Some breakout boxes' LEDs glow whether the line is positive or negative; those breakout boxes won't be of any help to you. The LEDs on better-designed breakout boxes glow either red or green depending on whether the line is positive or negative; that's the kind of breakout box that you want.

With the breakout box connected, unplug the UPS/SPS. You'll see one of the LEDs change color. That line is the Power failed line; it should connect to the CTS line on the PC serial interface. Leave the UPS/SPS unplugged until it runs out of power. A bit before the batteries run down all the way, you'll see another one of the LEDs change color. That's the Low battery connection; that line should connect with the DCD line on the PC serial interface. You may not see any LED change color before the UPS/SPS fails. If so, that means that your UPS/SPS does not support the Low battery signal. There really is no reliable way to detect which line to use for the Remote UPS shutdown.

Before you start playing around with a UPS and a breakout box, however, let me stress that this is a time-consuming project, inasmuch as your hard work won't really pay off until you take the information that you've just gained and construct a cable to connect your PC and your UPS/SPS.

What Does the UPS Service Do When Power Fails?

When the Power failure signal is asserted to the PC, then the NT machine sends a broadcast to all users like the one in Figure 3.8.

Your workstation only gets this message if you've enabled the Messenger service, or run the WinPopup program or an equivalent. This message gets rebroadcasted every x seconds, where x is set in the UPS dialog box that you saw in Figure 3.7. You can also specify a delay between the Power failure signal and the first message, although I'm not sure why you would want to do this; after all, the sooner people

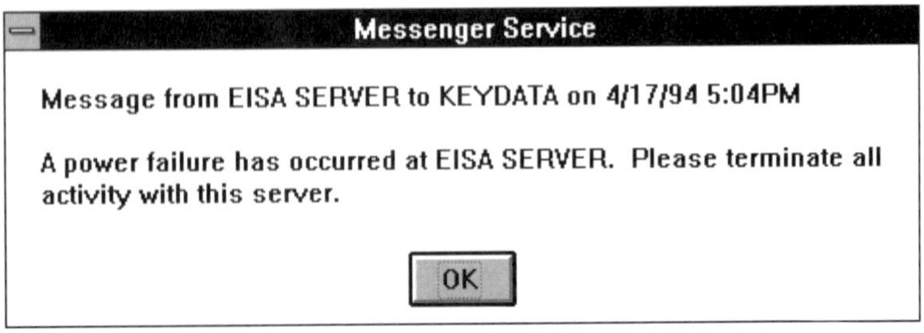

FIGURE 3.8:
NT broadcast concerning power failure

Messenger Service

Message from EISA SERVER to KEYDATA on 4/17/94 5:04PM

A power failure has occurred at EISA SERVER. Please terminate all activity with this server.

OK

know that there was a power failure at the server, the sooner they can save their work to another drive or shut down their application. At this point, however, the Server service is paused, and new users cannot attach to the server.

If power is restored before the batteries fail, then the UPS service sends out an "all clear" message like the one in Figure 3.9.

FIGURE 3.9:
NT's power restoration message

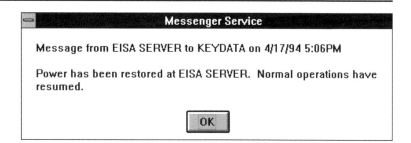

Two fields are relevant if your UPS/SPS does not support the Battery low signal:

- Battery recharge time
- Expected battery life

Both of these fields are basically "guesses" of how much time you have before the system fails. Use the manufacturer's suggested values, but be darn sure to test them, which brings me to the next subject.

Testing the UPS Service

Whether you have a UPS/SPS that supports Low battery or not, you should do a scheduled test of the UPS/SPS. How do you do it? Simple. First, be sure to do it after hours. Second, send a network broadcast to everyone warning them that the server will be going down because of a planned power outage, and that they should log off *immediately*!

The "How Do I" sidebar explains how to notify everyone of the imminent server shutdown.

How Do I Send a Broadcast Message to the Entire Network?

1. Start the Server Manager.

2. Click on the primary domain controller.

3. From the menu, select Computer/Send Message...

4. Fill in the message and click OK.

Make sure that you're on a workstation, either Windows with WinPopup, or an NT workstation. Then go to the UPS/SPS and pull out its power plug. Let it run until the server loses power altogether. Check the following:

- Did your workstation get a message about the power failure?

- Did you get a message every two minutes, or however far apart you set the messages?

- Did you get a final "The UPS service is about to perform final shutdown" message?

- How long was the server able to run with the UPS?

If necessary, go back and adjust the UPS service software if you don't have low battery support and your guesses were wrong about how much time you had on the battery.

Setting up the UPS is a bit of a pain, but once you get it done, write down what you did, so that you can redo it quickly if you ever reinstall.

Installing Tape Drivers

Most servers will have a backup device of some kind, and there's a good chance that it'll be a tape drive. It would be smartest to use a SCSI tape drive, as they are supported by the most backup software.

While the beauty of SCSI is supposed to be that it is "plug and play," you will still need a driver for your tape drive, so it wouldn't be a bad idea to look at the current Hardware Compatibility List that Microsoft publishes before purchasing a tape drive. (There is a copy of the list in the NT Server box, but it's also on CompuServe, TechNet, and a number of other sources.)

I use a Tandberg model 4100 and have had very good luck with it; it's packaged by Colorado Memory Systems as a "PowerTape." As with many tape drive manufacturers, however, Colorado falsifies the tape's capacity, claiming that it is a "2GB tape drive." It is actually a 1.2GB tape, but with the data compression software included with the tape, you can store 2GB of data. I say this is falsification for these reasons:

- Not all data *can* be compressed.
- The compression and backup software that gives this "2GB" tape its supposed 2GB capacity is *DOS* software, and so doesn't run under NT or OS/2.

It's a good idea to look closely when buying a tape drive, as this blatant lying about tape capacities seems to be business-as-usual in the tape business. For example, every single tape on the market that advertises itself as a "250MB" tape drive is actually a 120MB drive that assumes a 2-to-1 compression ratio. I mean, optimism has its *place*, but... And even worse, the NT Backup program doesn't compress.

You install the tape drive just as you'd install any SCSI device. When you power up your system, your SCSI BIOS will probably list the SCSI devices that it finds on the SCSI bus. The tape drive should show up. Now, if the tape drive *doesn't* appear on the list, then you've probably installed the tape drive wrong; go back and get the physical installation straightened out before going any further.

Then, once the drive is recognized on the SCSI bus, you have to install an NT driver for it. Here's how to do it.

1. Start NT Setup.
2. Click on Options and then Add/Remove Tape Devices... You'll see a dialog box like the one in Figure 3.10.

Don't panic when you don't see your tape drive in the box; that's normal. For some reason, Microsoft did not include auto-detect on tape drives. You're pretty much on your own here.

FIGURE 3.10:

Tape Device Setup dialog box

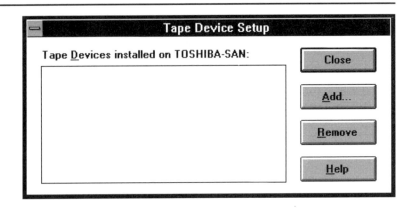

3. Click Add..., and you'll see a dialog box like the one in Figure 3.11.

4. Browse through the model numbers to see if you can find a tape drive that matches yours. If you can't find an exact match, try something close to it. Again, using my Tandberg as an example, when I turn my system on, I see the following report from my SCSI BIOS:

```
SCSI ID #0 - FUJITSU M2652S-512    -Drive C: (80h)
SCSI ID #1 - MAXTOR 7290-SCSI      -Drive D: (81h)
SCSI ID #2 - TANDBERG TDC 4100
SCSI ID #3 - MAXTOR 7290-SCSI      -Drive 82h
SCSI ID #5 - NEC   CD-ROM DRIVE:841
```

I see from my device number 2 that I have a Tandberg 4100, which unfortunately does not match any option. The closest option was the one you see, the Tandberg 3660, 3820, 4120, 4220 option. I tried that option for my 4100, and it worked. Later, Microsoft agreed in a Knowledge Base article that the 4100 would work with the other Tandberg drivers.

FIGURE 3.11:

Select Tape Device Option dialog box

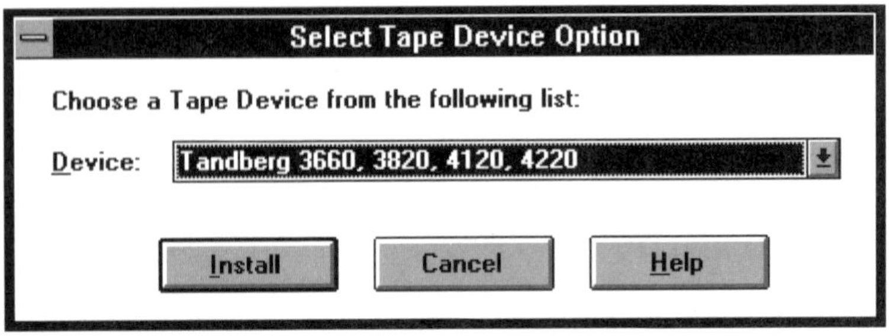

5. Once you have the driver set up, you have to restart your server.

6. After restart, you'll be able to use the NTBACKUP program.

The "How Do I" sidebar gives a brief rundown on installing an NT Server tape driver.

How Do I Install an NT Server Tape Driver?

1. Start NT Setup.

2. Click on Options, and then Add/Remove Tape Devices.... You'll see a dialog box like the one in Figure 3.10.

3. Don't panic when you don't see your tape drive in the box; that's normal. For some reason, Microsoft did not include auto-detect on tape drives. You're pretty much on your own here. Click Add....

4. Browse through the model numbers to see if you can find a tape drive that matches yours. If you can't find an exact match, try something close to it.

Once you have the driver set up, you have to restart your server. After restart, you'll be able to use the NTBACKUP program.

Installing Client Software

The ideal clients for an NT-based network are probably either NT workstations, Windows 95 workstations, or Windows for Workgroups workstations. Many of us, however, don't use those operating systems on our workstations. In this section, we'll look at how you install software to accommodate workstations running DOS, Windows(3.1x), or OS/2.

The Network Client Administrator

Network Client
Administrator

Set up NT, and you'll find a group called "Network Administration." A simple NT installation will put two icons in that group: the Network Client Administrator (NCA) and the License Manager.

The NCA simplifies the task of setting up DOS and Windows clients. The NT 3.5x CD-ROM contains a subdirectory called CLIENTS that contains all of the client code needed to attach DOS or OS/2 clients, as well as *all* of the code needed to install Windows for Workgroups.

Note: even though all the installation files for WfW are on the NT disk, that *doesn't* mean that you can install WfW willy-nilly on every workstation; you've still got to have a license for every one of your workstations before you can install WfW.

> **TIP**
>
> For those people who've already got WfW, then a directory on the CD-ROM entitled CLIENTS\WFW\UPDATE contains about a half-dozen files that update the redirector code in your existing WfW setup. Copy all the files except NET.EXE (NDIS.386, NETAPI.DLL, NWNBLINK.386, VNETSUP.386, and VREDIR.386) to your WINDOWS\SYSTEM directory, copy the NET.EXE file to your WINDOWS directory, and you'll get faster response to your network requests.

Anyway, the NCA automates the process of putting DOS/Windows client software on an existing machine, or the process of installing Windows for Workgroups from a network.

It does that by first building a simple NIC driver, transport protocol, and redirector onto a floppy disk. Then it puts an AUTOEXEC.BAT file on the disk that connects the new workstation to the CLIENTS directory. The other commands in the batch file run a setup program that loads the network client on the workstation's hard disk.

The first time you start up the NCA, it'll ask you how to set up the CLIENTS directory. It needs to know where to find the client software—will you leave it on the CD-ROM, or should NCA copy the client software to a directory on the server? I always copy it to the hard disk on the server, as there's no guarantee that your original setup CD-ROM disk will be sitting in the server's CD-ROM drive when you need it to be. If you allow the NCA to copy the client software to the server's hard disk, the NCA will create a directory called CLIENTS and will share it; then it'll copy about 49MB of data to that directory.

Then you'll see a dialog box like Figure 3.12.

This confirms that there is a directory with the client software, and where it is. Click OK, and you'll see Figure 3.13.

Basically, all you've got to do is tell the NCA whether to prepare a 5.25" diskette or a 3.5" diskette, whether to set up DOS/Windows client software or a whole new Windows for Workgroups installation, and what kind of network board is in *the workstation*; this isn't asking what kind of board is in the server. After that, you'll see a dialog box like the one in Figure 3.14.

FIGURE 3.13:

Installing the Network Client
software (step 2)

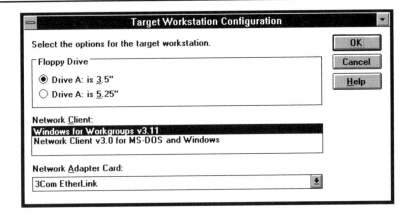

FIGURE 3.14:

Installing the Network Client
software (step 3)

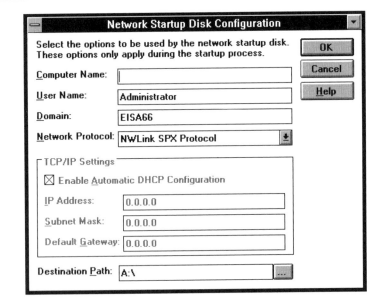

The Computer Name, User Name, Domain, and Destination Path fields are self-explanatory. But note the Network Protocol field: this is pretty dumb.

You get three options: TCP/IP, NWLink (IPX/SPX), and NetBEUI. Sounds good, right? It isn't. You see, there are two kinds of NDIS drivers around, NDIS version 2.0 and NDIS version 3.0. The NWLink and TCP/IP stacks will both run only on top of NDIS 3.0 drivers; they won't run atop the older NDIS 2.0 drivers. NetBEUI will run atop either 2.0 or 3.0.

During the initial boot and setup, however, your workstation *must* run the NDIS 2.0 drivers, as simple DOS requires them. The initial boot-the-system-and-get-the-rest-of-the-drivers-from-the-server part of the process *must* occur atop NDIS 2.0 drivers.

Which means that you've got to use NetBEUI to get started. Unfortunately, however, the default protocol is NWLink. Use it, and the system boots fine until you get to trying to hook up to the server, and you'll get an Error 53, telling you that the network doesn't exist. So, the bottom line is: select NetBEUI for the network protocol.

Click OK, and the NCA then creates the diskette.

In addition to the protocol goofup, it's worth noting a couple of other stupid things that the NCA does that you should be aware of.

First, it requires that you create a DOS bootable floppy and then put that floppy in your server's drive so that the NCA can set it up. This is something of a pain, as you've got to go find a DOS workstation and do a format a:/s on that system.

Second, you've got to modify PROTOCOL.INI yourself with Notepad or some other editor, filling in the IRQ, I/O address, and the like information. I don't know why NCA doesn't just activate the Notepad automatically, but it doesn't, so you've got to start up Notepad and then modify the PROTOCOL.INI file that you'll find in the NET directory of the floppy that you just created.

Third, if the name of the server to which the client connects has a space in it (like "EISA SERVER"), then NCA is not smart enough to put the name of the server in quotes in the AUTOEXEC.BAT, as is required by workstations for the name to make any sense. You must modify the startup file by hand.

NCA is a good program. Although it needs more work, even with its flaws, it simplifies the network client setup process.

Setting Up a DOS Workstation

To set up a DOS workstation, get The Workgroup Connection for DOS from Microsoft. They'll send it to you for shipping charges, or you can download it from CompuServe or Microsoft's Internet site. It all fits on a single 1.2MB or 1.44MB disk, which you put in drive A on your DOS workstation. You change your default drive to drive A and type **SETUP**.

You get the usual Microsoft "Welcome to Setup for Workgroup Connection" screen. Press Enter to continue.

Where is DOS?

Setup will then confirm the location of DOS on your workstation. You needn't put the files in the DOS directory, but by default that's where Setup wants them. I use a directory called WGC (Workgroup Connection) to hold my files.

How Should I Set Up?

Next, you'll be offered a number of setup options:

- **Computer and workgroup name**   Enter the domain name for the workgroup name, same as before. You'll have to hand-edit the setup to insert a user name, or else Setup uses the machine name as the user name.

- **Install Mail**   The Workgroup Connection includes a simple DOS-based mail client for Microsoft Mail users. Install it if you use Microsoft Mail.

- **Redirector**   You can choose to load either the Basic redirector or the Full redirector. Most people can get by just fine with the Basic. If you plan to run a client-server application that requires the named pipes interface in order to work, then load the Full redirector. In any case, you can always change your mind later if you don't make the right choice initially.

- **Pop-up key**   Once you've loaded the Workgroup Connection, it remains accessible from inside applications with the pop-up key. That key is usually Alt-N, but you can change that here.

- **Startup option** This controls how much of the network software you want to load automatically.

- **Path** Same as the earlier question.

- **Network card** This is important. Select this, and you'll see an option that says "Edit settings for network card driver." This is the place that you set the IRQ level, I/O address, and whatever other options exist for your network card.

- **Protocol Driver** For most people, this will be NetBEUI, but if you had a non-standard protocol, then you'd specify it here. DOS-based TCP/IP drivers are not shipped with the Workgroup Connection, so TCP/IP or DLC are not options here. You'd need a different protocol disk from another vendor to load it here. Whatever protocol you use, it must be NDIS-compatible.

When all the option settings are correct, click "The listed options are correct" box. The software will be copied from the floppy. When it is finished you will see the message "Workgroup Connection is now installed on your computer."

After that, just press Enter, and you'll get a "you're now ready" screen. Pop the Workgroup Connection Setup disk out of drive A and press Enter. The system will reboot with the Workgroup Connection drivers.

Hooking Up

When you reboot, you'll see messages telling you that you've loaded network software. For instance, my system says:

```
Microsoft Protocol Manager version 2.1
Microsoft Workgroups Driver version 1.0
Copyright (C) Microsoft Corporation 1992
Transport Hooks Enabled

Intel EtherExpress(TM) 16 Ethernet adapter NDIS Driver, version
2.23 920821.
Copyright 1990, 1991, 1992 Intel Corporation. All Rights Reserved.

C:\>net start
Microsoft Netbind version 2.1
Microsoft NetBEUI version 2.2
Type your user name, or press ENTER if it is MARK:
```

Before we press Enter, let's take a look at how the system has gotten this far. My CONFIG.SYS contains the following lines:

```
device=C:\WGC\PROTMAN.DOS /I:C:\WGC
device=c:\WGC\WORKGRP.SYS
device=c:\WGC\EXP16.DOS
```

These lines load the NDIS 2.0 drivers that let the network get going:

- PROTMAN.DOS is a small driver that basically just tells the other network drivers where to find PROTOCOL.INI, a setup file for the network.

- WORKGRP.SYS supplies binding routines for NetBEUI, which hasn't loaded yet.

- EXP16.DOS is the NDIS 2.0 real mode driver for the EtherExpress 16 board.

PROTOCOL.INI File   Looking at the PROTOCOL.INI file, we see

```
[network.setup]
version=0x3100
netcard=ms$ee16,1,MS$EE16
transport=ms$netbeui,MS$NETBEUI
lana0=ms$ee16,1,ms$netbeui

[MS$EE16]
IOCHRDY=Late
IOADDRESS=0x300
DriverName=EXP16$
IRQ=11
TRANSCEIVER=Thin Net (BNC/COAX)

[protman]
DriverName=PROTMAN$
PRIORITY=MS$NETBEUI

[MS$NETBEUI]
DriverName=netbeui$
SESSIONS=6
NCBS=12
BINDINGS=MS$EE16
LANABASE=0
```

Basically, the DOS software reads this INI file from the top to the bottom. The [network.setup] section contains lines that reference two other sections: the net-card=ms$ee16,1,MS$EE16 says "look in the section [MS$EE16] to find out about the network card." The line transport=ms$netbeui... describes the transport software, and points to the [MS$NETBEUI] section. You originally set up the net-card information and the transport information with the Workgroup Connection Setup program, but here is where you'd change it.

The main thing to see here—that is, the main thing that you'll ever think about changing—is the section specific to your board. The section pertinent to my Ether-Express board is the [MS$EE16] section. Note the references to IRQ and I/O address; if you've got to change those on your board, then make the corresponding changes here.

You won't usually change the information in [MS$NETBEUI]; in fact, I've never had reason to play with it. Note the line BINDINGS=MS$EE16; translated, it means "use the NetBEUI protocol stack on top of the EtherExpress 16 board," as it would be possible to have several protocols and network boards supported. If you've got a NetWare installation, then you'd see an IPX/SPX section here as well.

The section labeled [protman] tells the system which protocol has higher priority over the other protocol. Sometimes, the installation programs for Microsoft network client software take a mental holiday and goof up the PROTOCOL.INI; in particular, I always experience trouble with the SMC 8216 Elite 16 Ultra board. As a result, I've learned how to take a PROTOCOL.INI from *one* NIC and convert it into a PROTOCOL.INI file for another kind of NIC. The heart of making these changes lies in correctly identifying the NIC type, and telling PROTOCOL.INI where to find the driver. For that purpose, I've kind of collected all of the dependencies within PROTOCOL.INI in Figure 3.15.

If you wanted to change this PROTOCOL.INI file from one that handles an SMC8000 card to an Intel EtherExpress board, for example, then you'd change all the SMC800X references to EE$16 (although you could probably make up any name), and then you'd change the DriverName= line to EXP16, as EXP16.DOS is the name of the NDIS driver for the EtherExpress 16.

FIGURE 3.15:

PROTOCOL.INI dependencies

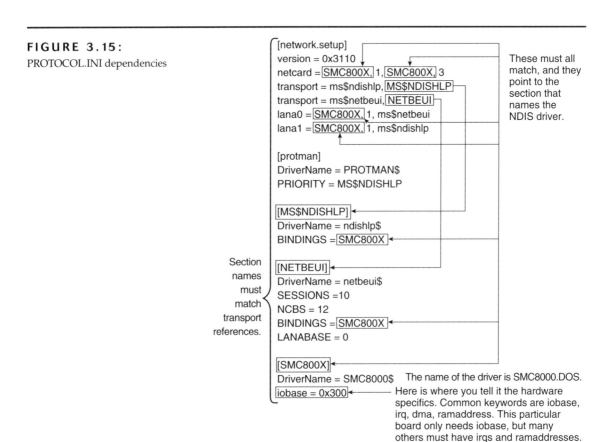

SYSTEM.INI File   The other file that the Setup changed was SYSTEM.INI. Now, you certainly have heard of SYSTEM.INI if you use Windows, but this was a setup for DOS, not Windows. So what's SYSTEM.INI doing here? Basically, it's because the Workgroup Connection was originally built with Windows for Workgroups version 3.1, and Microsoft hasn't changed all that much about it since. Because the

Workgroup Connection was originally intended for Windows workstations, it seemed logical to put the network information in SYSTEM.INI. So if you install the Workgroup Connection in your Windows directory, then that information will go in your SYSTEM.INI. If, on the other hand, you install the Workgroup Connection in another directory, then the Setup program for Workgroup Connection will create a SYSTEM.INI solely to store network information. Mine looks like this:

```
[network]
computername=TOSHIBA-SAN
lanroot=C:\WGC
autostart=basic
dospophotkey=N
username=MARK
workgroup=ORION
reconnect=yes

[Password Lists]
MARK=C:\WGC\MARK.PWL
```

Notice the [Password Lists] section. That doesn't appear until after the first time that you log on. The first time that you log on, you'll be asked for a password.

TIP   This password does not have to be your NT Server password, but you'll find working with the system easiest if you use the same password.

You'll find a section called [network drivers], and it's the last link in the chain that you'll need to get your NDIS 2.0 drivers running. The `netcard=` parameter must also point to the NDIS 2.0 driver. You may not find a section like that in SYSTEM.INI, but don't worry about it; whether or not you need it is determined by the DOS client software that you use. When I installed the Workgroup Connection, I ended up with a SYSTEM.INI that looked like this:

```
[network]
computername=TOSHIBA-SAN
lanroot=C:\WGC
```

```
autostart=basic
dospophotkey=N
username=MARK
workgroup=ORION
reconnect=yes

[Password Lists]
MARK=C:\WGC\MARK.PWL
```

The password is then encrypted and stored in a file with the extension PWL. As my user name is Mark, I have a password file named MARK.PWL. You should understand these things about password files:

- What does this password file do?

- How do I log onto NT Server resources?

- How can multiple users share a DOS workstation under the Workgroup Connection?

What Does the Password File Do?

The password file contains the encrypted versions of any passwords that you use to connect to system printers, drives, or the like. You'd need a lot of passwords if you are using a workgroup rather than a domain, as you read in Chapter 2.

The persistent connections information is stored in a file called CONNECT.DAT, which resides in the same directory as PROTOCOL.INI and SYSTEM.INI. It is a binary file, so you can't edit it. You can, however, list your persistent connections by typing:

```
net use /persistent:list
```

You can clear persistent connections with this command:

```
net use /persistent:clear
```

If you are sharing this DOS computer with other DOS users, then you should understand that there is only one CONNECT.DAT.

How Do I Log onto NT Server Resources from the Workgroup Connection?

 Given that your NT domain does not use share-level security, how do you get to a domain resource? Simple: just attach to it. For example, in the case of my Orion domain, I can attach to the C drive on the primary domain controller, calling it H, by typing

```
net use h: "\\eisa server\c"
```

Now is when it matters whether I've made my Workgroup Connection password the same as my domain password. If I've used a different password for Workgroup Connection than for my domain, I'll get this message:

```
The password is invalid for \\EISA SERVER\C.
Type the password for \\EISA SERVER\C:
```

This is confusing the first time you see this, because there *is* no password for a domain resource. What's really happening here is that your DOS workstation requested a domain resource, waking up the domain security system. The domain security system tried to verify your logon by asking the Workgroup Connection for your domain password. The Workgroup Connection has no idea what a domain password *is*, so it just handed the domain security system whatever password you gave the Workgroup Connection. The domain security system is smart enough not to reject the logon out of hand. Instead, it sends a message to the Workgroup Connection that looks like "There is a password on this resource—please supply it," as if the C drive on the \\EISA server were a share-level workgroup resource. *Now* you should type in your domain password, and you'll get this response:

```
The command completed successfully.
```

Because the Workgroup Connection thinks that you've just entered a share-level password, it stores a copy (encrypted) in your PWL file. In the future, you can simply logon with your Workgroup Connection password, and you'll be logged right into your persistent domain connections, as your domain password is entered for you automatically when you log onto the Workgroup Connection.

> **TIP**
>
> Once you've connected to *one* domain resource, you can get to any others without a password. Once the domain security system is satisfied that you're a valid domain member, you can get to anything that you can normally get to.

How Can Multiple Users Share a DOS Workstation under the Workgroup Connection?

When your system boots, and the redirector starts, you'll see the opening message:

```
Type your user name, or press ENTER if it is xxxxx:
```

The *xxxxx* you see here is the default user name that you entered when installing the Workgroup Connection. (You can change that name at any time by editing SYSTEM.INI's username= line.)

If you press Enter, then Workgroup Connection will use the PWL file associated with the default name. If, on the other hand, you enter some other name—Jane, for example—then the Workgroup Connection looks for a line in the [password lists] section of SYSTEM.INI for the PWL file that corresponds to that user. By default, it's a PWL file with that user's name—JANE.PWL, in my example.

If, on the other hand, there is no password reference for that user, then she'll be prompted for a password, and will be asked to reenter the password to confirm it. The Workgroup Connection then uses that password to create another PWL file, and another entry goes into SYSTEM.INI's [password lists] section.

The separate password files are nice, but there's one flaw in the way that the Workgroup Connection separates users: you see, it keeps separate *password* files, but not separate *connection* files. All users on a given machine have the same persistent connections, whether they like it or not. There is only one CONNECT.DAT.

NET.EXE   Now that we've seen how we got to the NET START command, let's do something useful with the network. You use the command-line interface NET.EXE to manipulate your network connections, and it's covered in detail in Chapter 16. Here's a quick "survival guide" to NET, until then.

- *net use d: servername\resourcename* connects you to resource *resourcename* on server *servername*, assigning device name *d:*. Consider this example:

  net use e: \\ourserver\c Attaches a server named *ourserver*'s C drive to your system, with the local name E:.

  net use lpt1: \\ourserver\hplaser Attaches a printer named *hplaser*, attached to server *ourserver*, to your LPT1 printer port. Any printing that you do to LPT1 will automatically be redirected to the network shared printers.

- *net use d: /delete* disconnects you from a resource.

- *net view servername* shows you the available resources on server *servername* (don't forget the \\ before the server name).

- *net logoff* disconnects you from network resources. It does not unload the network redirector from memory.

- *net stop* unloads the network redirector from memory, if possible. It does not unload the NDIS drivers from memory.

For more details, consult Chapter 16.

Setting Up a Windows Workstation

Before saying anything else, let me just say this: If you're using Windows as your client operating system, and NT Server is your server platform, *strongly consider* moving to Windows for Workgroups. Its integration with NT Server is excellent, and its upgrade price (around $40 per workstation) is reasonable.

Reasonable, perhaps, but even *one* dollar per workstation makes for an expensive upgrade if you're upgrading 10,000 workstations. Many of us can't yet afford Windows for Workgroups, but for us there's still a way to attach to regular old Windows 3.11. (Windows 95 does not have a "workgroups" version; it comes with the network interface built in no matter what.)

The ideal way to set up Windows to communicate with NT Server is just to set it up with the LAN Manager options. That works best if you've got some kind of redirector already loaded (like the Workgroup Connection) when you install Windows, as the Windows Setup program will then sense the network connection, and will load the drivers accordingly.

Run the Windows Setup program, and you'll see the screen that describes what kind of hardware attached to your system. Under Network, you'll either see Microsoft LAN Manager (version 2.1 Basic), something similar, or No network installed. Change the value to Microsoft Network (or 100% compatible).

When working under Windows with NT Server, you should log into the network and make your network connections *before* you enter Windows. Windows 3.11 really doesn't include any new network support except for three main things:

- There is a Network applet inside the Control Panel. It sets whether you want your connections to be persistent or not.

- The File Manager gets a new menu item, Network Connections. It works like the NET command line in that you must know the UNC name of the resource that you want to connect to, as you can see in Figure 3.16. In the figure, the Browse button is grayed out because I haven't enabled LAN Manager Broadcasts on my server.

- The Print Manager gets two items on its Options menu, Network Settings... and Network Connections.... Network Connections lets you connect to a network printer, and Network Settings controls how your print jobs are sent to the server and how you see the print queue.

FIGURE 3.16:

Network Connections dialog box

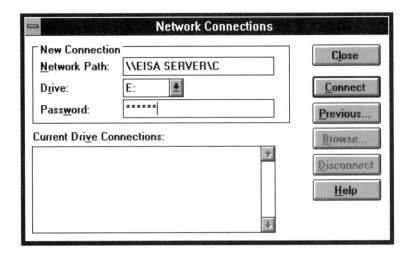

Windows 3.11 is largely network-unaware, so don't expect to see big differences once you've installed network support. Sharing drives and printers works fine, however, once you have the Workgroup Connection loaded under DOS before loading Windows.

The License Manager

OK, you've installed all of these clients and they're merrily accessing the servers in your domain. Ah, but have you *licensed* all those users? If so, how have you organized it so that you can keep track of new and outdated users?

Licensing can be a pain to administer, and the bigger the network the harder it becomes. To help you do it, NTS 3.51 comes with a new tool: the License Manager. This tool can monitor licensing not just on the local machine but on NT Servers in other domains with which the domain you're starting from has a trust relationship, so you can monitor the entire network without trotting from server to server.

When you install NTS, its icon will automatically go into the Network Administration program group. Click it, and you'll see a dialog box like the one shown in Figure 3.17.

FIGURE 3.17:

Opening screen of License Manager

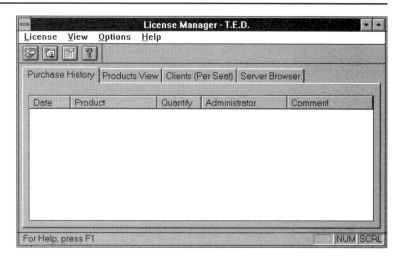

Microsoft went to a lot of work to create some very good help files for the License Manager, so there's not much to be said that they didn't say already. Just to review, however, here's the basics of the License Manager and how you can use it to inventory software licenses. This isn't all there is to this tool, but it's the essentials to get you started.

Purchase History

Click on this tab, and you'll see a record of all the software licenses that you've purchased and entered into this database. (If you don't enter them, this database can't help you—it only knows what you tell it.) You'll also enter new per-seat licenses and change the domain to administer here.

Products View

From this tab, you can view product information either for the entire network or for a selected domain. Select the Per Seat or Per Server tab as needed to get information about:

- which products are licensed properly (and which are not)
- which products are at their license limit

From here, you can also add or delete per-seat licenses or view the properties of a particular license.

Per Seat Administration

Click on this tab to access information about the clients who have accessed a particular product (such as NTS) throughout the domain or entire network. From here, you can see the number of licenses already used, those still available, and the dates on which all the licenses were last accessed.

Server Browser

From the Server Browser tab, you can access other domains to see their licensing information, add and delete per-server client licenses for servers and products, and add new per-seat licenses for the entire enterprise.

Setting Up an OS/2 Workstation

Begrudgingly, Microsoft offers a way for OS/2 2.x clients to attach to an NT domain. There's no graphical interface for the NT Server client software. The installation is straightforward.

The OS/2 NT client setup (actually called the OS/2 LAN Manager Setup on the diskettes) comes on four disks. As always, you just put the first disk in drive A, change to that drive, type **Setup**, and press Enter.

Where Am I From? Where Do I Go?

The Setup asks you where to install from, and where to install to. The default directory is C:\LANMAN, which I use without any trouble.

Next, you'll be prompted to insert a number of diskettes. Setup will give you a running status of how many more files to go.

After disk 3 ("OS/2 Workstation Disk 2") loads, you'll get a list of LAN boards, and you must tell the Setup program which one you have—no auto-detect functions here. (Get the further impression that Microsoft didn't want to write this software?) If your LAN board isn't in this list, then all you need is an OS/2 NDIS driver for your board. IBM keeps track of who makes those things, so you might check with either IBM OS/2 technical support or look on the OS/2 forums on CompuServe.

One very positive feature is that this setup procedure includes both the expected NetBEUI protocol *and* a Microsoft implementation of TCP/IP for OS/2.

Once you've selected both board drivers and protocols, you move on to configuring the software. You'll notice that nowhere are you asked about your board's IRQ or I/O address. You'll have to hand-edit PROTOCOL.INI (yes, there's one of those here also) to add that information, unfortunately. (Microsoft must have *really* hated writing this program!)

TCP/IP Settings

If you've chosen to load TCP/IP drivers, then you have to fill in the basic three things that any TCP/IP installation needs: IP address, subnet mask, and default gateway. We'll discuss TCP/IP in greater detail in Chapter 13, but for the moment, here are a few suggestions on how to fill in these numbers:

- **IP address** You *must* get this from your local network administrator. I know, when people say, "Get this from your local LAN administrator," it's kind of a nice way of saying, "Go take a walk." But I *mean* it this time. You see, IP addresses are part of an international system of network addresses. Once you get a real, live IP address, then your computer will have an address unique in all the world. (Well, that's only if your IP address is registered with the Network Information Clearinghouse—but most internets *are*, nowadays.)

- **Subnet mask** Ditto.

- **Default gateway** Ditto again, *but* if your network administrator has no idea what to put in here, just leave it blank. If your internet is not part of *the* Internet, then you may not *have* a default gateway. You can always edit this and change it later.

Workstation Settings

Next, Setup will ask you for the computer name, the user name, and the domain to work in. It will even give you a chance to name other domains to monitor. You can choose to load the network popup, which is a very good idea, and to load the Messenger service. Although Setup doesn't make this clear, you must load the Messenger service for the network popup to work properly. NetBIOS 3.0 support is unnecessary unless you have a particular application that requires it.

After that, you press Enter, and you'll be prompted to insert the fourth and final disk, the OS/2 Drivers 1 disk. Once it loads everything that it needs, you'll see Saving LAN Manager configuration… and the final screen.

Tweaking PROTOCOL.INI

Once you press Enter at the final screen, you'll return to the OS/2 command prompt. The next thing to do is to take the OS/2 Drivers 1 disk out of drive A and put it and the other disks away, and then look at PROTOCOL.INI. It is in the C:\LANMAN directory.

The PROTOCOL.INI file contains the TCP/IP information that you've entered, as well as any hardware information about the LAN card. Oddly enough, it seems not to require IRQ information, although there is a line that says IOADDRESS=0x0300, implying that it must know the I/O address. I have actually added an interrupt line to my PROTOCOL.INI, using the DOS PROTOCOL.INI as a model, and received an error message, so I guess there's no need for the OS/2 LAN drivers to know interrupts.

Once you reboot, you'll see (I hope) LAN drivers load, and a window will appear with STARTUP.CMD in it, starting your network services. From here on in, the commands are the same as in DOS, so turn to Chapter 16 for more on the NET command.

Common Installation Problems

Most installations of NT Server (or NT workstation, for that matter) are pretty trouble-free. But here's a look at some of the more common problems and questions that *do* arise.

Incorrect Hardware

If you can't get *anywhere*, did you make sure that you have "regulation" NT hardware? Check back in this chapter to ensure that you have the right hardware, and that it's configured correctly. Remember that interrupt conflicts that never gave you trouble under DOS stick out like a sore thumb under NT!

Image Can't Be Relocated, No Fixup Information

NT requires that 600K of memory be free in the low 1MB of RAM space. While most computers have 640K of conventional memory, a few either have only 500K of conventional memory, or—in the case of some high-performance server computers like the Compaq System Pro XL—have no conventional memory at all. Now, if you *do* have an XL, you can run its EISA configuration program and set the memory on the motherboard from "linear" to "640K Compaq compatible." That'll solve the problem on that machine.

How Do I Remote-Boot NT?

Most PC operating systems will support remote boot. NT, however, does not, at least not now.

"Boot couldn't find NTLDR. Please insert another disk."

One of the essential files to boot NT, a file that you can't hope to start up without, is the NT loader program NTLDR. It *must* appear in the root directory, and that's where you can get in trouble.

You see, on hard disks formatted with the FAT file system, you are limited to 512 files in the root directory. While that's an unusual number of files to see in a root, there are people who have that many files in their root.

It's particularly easy to accumulate files in the root if you had disk problems and ran CHDKSK/F under DOS or OS/2 before installing NT. The result is potentially hundreds of files with names like FILE0000.CHK. Having 512 of these files means that you can't put any more files on your root, including NTLDR.

You'll see this problem crop up if your system is unable to perform the reboot that happens about one third of the way through the installation process.

The fix is simple: Clean out some files from your root directory, and do the installation over. If you don't want to do the whole installation over, then read the "How Do I" sidebar.

TIP If you're expanding NTLDR from floppies, it is called NTLDR.$ on floppy disk 2.

Setting Up DLLs

Anyone who's ever set up an application server under LAN Manager knows the LIBPATH command. LIBPATH is a command somewhat like the familiar PATH command, except that it allows LAN Manager (which runs atop OS/2 1.3) to find

How Do I Fix the System after It Can't Find NTLDR?

1. Boot the system with a DOS-bootable floppy.

2. Eliminate unnecessary files in the root directory.

3. In the \I386 directory of the NT setup CD-ROM (or disk 2 of the setup floppies—*not* the CD-ROM Installation disk), you'll see NTLDR._. It is the compressed version of NTLDR. (I understand why Microsoft compressed the files on the *floppies,* but why the CD-ROM version? There's plenty of space on that CD-ROM disk.)

4. Expand the file onto your root directory either using the EXPAND program from MS-DOS 6.0, Windows 3.1, or Windows for Workgroups. For example, if the NTLDR._ file were on the CD-ROM, and the CD-ROM was on drive D, then the command would look like this:

```
expand d:\i386\ntldr._ c:\ntldr.
```

You should be able to continue with Setup now.

dynamic link libraries (DLLs) in particular. The logical question is, how do applications server programs under NT find DLLs?

The answer is surprisingly simple. DLLs are located via the PATH statement under NT.

DoubleSpace and Stacker Support

How do I get my PC, which uses a disk compression routine like DoubleSpace or Stacker, to run those routines with NT?

I once put that question to a "highly placed member of the NT development staff." (I can't be more specific because I appreciate his candor, and wouldn't want to get him in trouble.) His answer? With a sly grin, he responded, "DoubleSpace? That piece of … Currently, we do not anticipate supporting disk compression routines."

If you currently have data on a DoubleSpaced drive, then you should back that data up, remove DoubleSpace (or just reformat the drive), and then install NT.

Where Do I Load ANSI.SYS?

Problem: I have DOS programs that require ANSI.SYS, but I can't get them to run under NT.

There is a file in your SYSTEM32 directory called CONFIG.NT that tells NT how to run DOS sessions. Add this line to CONFIG.NT:

```
device=c:\winnt35\system32\ansi.sys
```

Alternatively, you can say:

```
device=%systemroot%\system32\ansi.sys
```

Then start up a command-line session by starting the COMMAND.COM that comes with DOS 5.0. (Gotta search around for that one...)

While it *is* a pain having to find a copy of DOS 5.0's COMMAND.COM, it *is* pretty neat that you can change this CONFIG.NT file and see its effects without having to reboot.

Must My RISC Computer Be FAT-Based?

The FAT file system has its problems, but it's your *only option* if you're using a RISC-based system, at least for your boot partition.

Answer: Create a small FAT partition that contains your boot files, and format most of the hard disk as NTFS, so that you can keep the data files secure on the NTFS partition.

Microsoft claims that you can actually make this boot partition only about 1MB in size, and the only files that *must* be on that partition are HAL.DLL and OS-LOADER.EXE.

Another problem that some RISC machines (MIPS machines, in this case) may show is that the MIPS machines must have an R4000 chip that is version 2.0 or later.

Installing NT on Workstations over the Network with WINNT.EXE

Not every system on your network will be equipped with a CD-ROM, and a floppy installation of NT is something that involves more patience than *I* have. That's why it's nice that Microsoft included a capability to install NT from a CD-ROM on the network.

Now, IBM included a capability like that in OS/2, something called the Central Installation and Distribution (CID) facility, but it was amazingly painful to work with. That's why I was so surprised about the network installation option for NT. Here's how it works.

Step 1: Create a Shared Directory with the Setup Files

A network-based installation of Windows NT requires a directory on a server. (What *kind* of server? I'll cover that in a minute.) That server must contain the NT setup files. You create that in one of two ways: Either share the CD-ROM directory with the installation files, or just XCOPY the files from the CD-ROM to a directory on the server. For those running Intel servers, all you need do is to copy the files from the \I386 directory on the CD-ROM to a directory on an already-running server, then share that directory.

A few notes on preparing this shared directory:

- Make sure you have something else to do while this step is going on. It takes a while to transfer about 30MB of data from the CD-ROM. You may get messages indicating that Setup cannot read certain files, like LANMANNT.BMP or SFM*.*. (I put in the *.*—any file like that counts.) Tell the program to just ignore those files. For some reason, INITIAL.INF tells Setup to look for NT Server files.

- Again, once the drive is set up, don't forget to share it.

- Strangely enough, you can use any kind of network—Novell, Banyan, or whatever—that you like to kick off this process. You must be running NT when you do this Setup command, but once you've created that shared directory, then you need not create it again.

Step 2: Set Up the Workstation

Next, go to the computer that you're going to install NT on, and boot DOS and your workstation redirector. Again, this can be Novell, a Microsoft Network, Banyan VINES, or whatever. Just make sure that it will be possible for your DOS workstation to attach to that directory with the shared NT files.

Step 3: Get a Floppy Ready

Make sure that you have another floppy around to give Setup when it wants to create the Emergency Repair Floppy.

Step 4: Attach to the Shared Drive

Now go to the machine that you'll be installing NT on. Load whatever software you need to attach to the shared directory. For example, if I'd created a directory on my server called NTFILES, then I would attach my DOS workstations to that directory as, for example, their E drive.

Step 5: Run WINNT.EXE

Once you've attached to the shared directory, log onto it (make it the default drive and directory), type **winnt /b**, and press Enter. Notice that if you just type "winnt," then you'll have to let WINNT create three boot floppies that it uses to start up the installation procedure. Starting the process with the /b option does the whole operation without any floppies. (I know, you've wondering, "Why is the cumbersome floppy version of WINNT the default?" I just don't know. I stumbled on the /b option one day, and I've used it since.)

Where Are the Files?

It seems something of a dumb question, but WINNT wants to know where the NT files are. ("Probably on the drive that *you're* in, dummy," I'd like to tell it.) Tell it the drive name, and press Enter.

Then it will copy a bunch of files—just enough to get a mini-redirector going—onto the floppy. It'll take a minute or two to copy the files over.

Fill Up the Hard Disk Too

Then WINNT copies (and decompresses) the majority of the NT files to your local hard disk. This, too, takes a bit of time.

Although the process of copying to the hard disk seems a bit tedious, it may actually be faster than installing from a CD-ROM, as there's a good chance that your LAN is faster than your CD-ROM at transferring data.

Step 6: Reboot

Once the files have all copied, WINNT will prompt you to press Enter to reboot. Unlike most setup programs, however, this one warns you to *keep* the floppy in drive A when you boot.

Step 7: NT Setup

Once your system has booted, it will look as if you're in the normal first screens of Windows NT Setup. You will need another floppy, as you must prepare an emergency boot floppy. It needn't be a blank floppy, as the Setup program will zap whatever is on the floppy.

Express or Custom Setup?

Much like the normal Setup, you have to choose whether you want to do an Express or a Custom setup. As I said earlier in this chapter, I recommend Custom always, as you never know what Express assumes, and besides, you often learn some interesting things about a program when you put the installation program in "custom" mode.

From here on in, it looks very much like the normal Setup.

- It checks for SCSI devices.
- It shows you what kind of hardware it thinks your system has.
- It issues any warnings about an undelete sentry or tracker.
- It asks if you want to install NT in the same directory as Windows.
- Depending on how you answer the previous question, it prompts you for a partition to load NT onto, and whether or not to reformat it to another file system.
- It runs CHKDSK to test your disk for problems.

Then Setup goes through its copying process again, still in text mode, much the same as normal NT Setup. Finally, it prompts you to remove the floppy from A and let it reboot.

After the penultimate boot, NT Setup continues running the normal course. You respond to these requests:

- Your name and company
- The "computer name" for your PC
- The language that you want NT to use
- What components to set up
- What printers and network cards to support

Then, NT Setup goes through what looks a lot like the file-copying operation that you'd expect if you were doing a normal Setup, but it goes by very quickly. I imagine that all it's really doing is seeing if the files are there at all, rather than copying them; after all, the earlier part of the install operation did the copying.

Setup then offers to add you to a domain. As always, it prompts you for the floppy to use for the Emergency Repair Disk. You'll also be prompted to restart the computer. Once you do, you'll have installed NT via WINNT.EXE!

By the way, this only works if you're putting NT on a system that currently has a FAT file system.

Reinstalling NT Server

Once you get your NT Server up and running, you'll probably never have to reinstall it. But, if you *do*…

Recall that an NT domain keeps track of the particular machines in the domain that run NT or NT Server. This is part of the security that is so integral to the design of NT. A side effect of this security is that you can't simply reinstall NT on a workstation, server, or domain controller, and expect it to work. NT reasons something like this: "Well, you *say* that you're a machine named PSERVER01, and I know a machine named PSERVER01, but how do I know that *you're* that computer?"

NT internally creates passwords that you never see, and the primary domain controller uses these passwords to verify that a machine is, indeed, who it says it is. As a result, if you reinstall NT or NT Server on a machine that's already running NT or NT Server, and you give the machine the same name that it was previously using, then you'll get a message that looks like "No domain controller was available to validate your logon."

That means that there is a *very* specific way to reinstall NT or NT Server on a computer. It takes just three steps:

1. Shut down the computer that you're going to reinstall NT or NT Server on.

2. Log onto your domain as an administrator, run the Server Manager, and delete the to-be-reinstalled computer from the domain.

3. Reinstall NT on the computer, specifying that you are not *upgrading* but rather are *replacing* the NT software on the machine. In the process of reinstallation, you'll be given the chance to create a new machine account on the domain. Take that opportunity, and you'll be back up and running.

Don't ignore this! In the course of writing this book, I reinstalled NT Server a number of times. I had thought that I understood how the system worked fairly well, but I *didn't* understand the reinstallation procedure. Worse yet, I only had one domain controller on my network for quite some time. That's why it surprised me when the following happened.

One of my networks had been based on Windows for Workgroups prior to using NT Server. As I was previously using Windows for Workgroups, I didn't have a domain, I had a workgroup—a workgroup somewhat facetiously named "Us." In my other office, we had a workgroup named "NextGeneration." When I first installed NT Server, I frankly expected to spend several days on it. After all, I've installed a pile of networks—IBM PC LAN, LAN Manager 1.x and 2.x, Novell 2.15, 3.11, LAN-tastic, PC-Office, PC-Net, and a number of others. (If you've never heard of some of the aforementioned networks, don't worry about it—no one else has either.) I learned the hard way that you have to set aside *at least* a day or two the first time that you install a server.

That's why installing NT Server the first time was such a pleasure. The whole installation took me about two hours, including all the ancillary stuff. Of course, I just converted my workgroup "Us" to a new domain named "Us."

By the next time I installed NT Server—*re*installed it on that same server machine—we had an ISDN bridge in place between the LANs in the two buildings. Since the workgroup in the other building ("NextGeneration") would interact with our workgroup, "Us" seemed like a silly name. Casting around for domain names, I picked a constellation name, figuring that many constellations are easy to spell. (Well, okay, except for Sagittarius, Cassiopeia, and Ophiuchi.) If necessary, I figured, we could name machines in the domain after stars in the constellation.

So, this time, I installed NT Server with a new domain name, "Orion"—a nice, easy-to-spell name. Knowing that all the workstations would run into trouble because they were set up to log onto a domain named "Us," I went to all the workstations in the office and reset their logon domain to "Orion." I was able to do this because, as you probably surmised, I did this work after hours, just as *you* probably have to do just about *all* work on *your* server after hours.

The *next* time I reinstalled NT Server, however, I was merely reinstalling the primary domain controller for "Orion," so when installing the server software (after hours, again), I just typed in "Orion" as the domain name. I didn't go to the workstations and make any changes, as it didn't seem that I'd changed anything.

Hoo boy. *Big* mistake.

The DOS and Windows for Workgroups workstations were quite happy, logging on and emitting no complaints. But two things were quite wrong:

- The NT workstations all complained that "a domain controller could not be found," refusing to let me get to any server resources.

- The domains that we previously trusted, and that trusted us, wouldn't talk to us any more.

After a little thought, the answer dawned on me. *I had created a completely new domain.* A new domain named "Orion," to be sure, but a new domain nonetheless. I mean, suppose you're a foreign domain that trusts another domain named Orion? Some domain named Orion says, "Here I am," but the foreign domain has to ask itself, "Yeah, this guy *says* he's Orion, but how do I know?"

NT uses not merely *names* to identify objects—names like Orion—but also internal security ID numbers, or SIDs, as Microsoft calls them. When you reinstall a primary domain controller, you create new security ID numbers, even if you use an old name.

Each domain needs a primary domain controller. Primary domain controllers *must* be computers running NT Server. But in my domain—as in many domains in the real world—there is only one NT Server, so when you take the server down and reinstall it, you kind of create a vacuum. When the server's running again, it says, "I'm the primary domain controller of Orion," and the NT machines on the network say, "Okay, but you're not the primary domain controller of the Orion that *we* know."

What's the answer? Two possibilities:

- If you only have one NT Server in your domain, then you have to do a silly workaround where you first tell your NT workstations that they are no longer part of a domain named Orion—they are, instead, part of a *workgroup* named Orion. Reboot, and then tell the workstation that you've changed your mind again, that it is now part of a domain after all—a domain named Orion. Then all will be well.

- That first answer sounds like a bit of work, and it is. A better answer requires that you have another NT Server in your domain. Just promote the other NT Server and make it primary domain controller, demote the one that you're going to reinstall, then reinstall the server, promote it to primary domain controller, and demote the alternate NT Server machine. The moral of the story seems to be: If you're going to reinstall your NT Server software, make sure that you have more than one domain controller on your network.

Creating an NT Boot Disk

Those of you who've had to support DOS in the past (and those who haven't, spare us the condescending grins, okay?) know that an essential support tool is the boot floppy.

A boot floppy is just a floppy diskette that contains a minimum operating system that you use to get a faulty system started. Is it possible, then, to create a boot disk for NT Server? Not completely. NT Server is so large that there wouldn't be a prayer of getting it running simply from a floppy.

Sometimes, however, you can lose an important boot file, and that can keep it from booting. For example, I recently added two SCSI hard drives to my server. Either some sort of power glitch occurred, or perhaps NT doesn't like you adding drives, or… I'm not sure what caused it, but when I turned the system on and tried to boot, I got this message:

```
error 08: error opening NTDETECT.COM
```

Now, NTDETECT.COM is the first program that NT loads, and this error message indicated that NT couldn't load it, so the server would not boot. As it turned out, the only file damaged on the server was NTDETECT.COM, so it would have been nice to have a floppy around that contained NTDETECT.COM. That boot floppy would get the server started in the boot process; after that, the hard disk could take over.

One good answer—and the one that I eventually used—was the Emergency Repair Floppy. But each Emergency Boot Floppy is specific to a particular NT machine, and this bootable NT floppy is generic.

Given that bit of information, the "How Do I" sidebar explains how to create a generic NT boot floppy.

How Do I Create a Generic NT Boot Floppy?

1. Format a floppy under either NT File Manager or from a command line under NT. *Do not use a DOS-formatted floppy, or this won't work.*

A DOS-formatted floppy looks for the DOS boot files IO.SYS and MSDOS.SYS; an NT-formatted floppy looks for the NT boot file NTLDR. (From File Manager, just click Disk, then Format Disk.)

You're going to copy a bunch of files from the root directory of your server to the floppy in the A drive. The files are hidden, however, so you've got to tell the File Manager to show you hidden files.

2. To do that, click View, then By File Type, and check the box that says Show Hidden/System Files.

3. Looking in your server's root directory, copy the following files from the server's root to the floppy disk:

- NTLDR
- NTDETECT.COM
- BOOT.INI
- NTBOOTDD.SYS, if your server boots from a SCSI hard disk; if not, then you probably won't have this file in the root, and don't need to copy it

Once finished, you'll have a floppy that can essentially "jump start" your system.

CHAPTER

FOUR

RAID for Speedier, Safer Disks

4

Disk
Administrator

Disks on servers are different from disks on workstations.

Server disks must be faster, more reliable, and larger than their workstation-based cousins. How do you achieve those goals of speed, reliability, and size? Well, there's always the *simple* answer: spend more money for a drive with more of those three characteristics. But the past few years have yielded another solution: A group of mediocre drives can band together and, acting in concert, can provide speed, capacity, and high fault tolerance. The process of doing that is called *redundant array of inexpensive drives*, or RAID. Until recently, putting a RAID on your server required buying an expensive RAID system (the *drives* are "inexpensive," but the entire RAID subsystem *isn't*, unfortunately). However, NT changes that with the Disk Administrator. With the Disk Administrator, you can take a bunch of hard disks and "roll your own" RAID system.

The Disk Administrator offers a lot of options, and this chapter explains what your organization and protection options are and how you can use the Disk Administrator to best arrange your data for your particular situation.

While you'll set up the initial disk partitioning when you install NT Server, you can use the Disk Administrator (it is found in the Administrative Tools program group) to make changes to your disk setup after you've installed NT. With the Disk Administrator, you can:

- Create and delete partitions on a hard disk and make logical drives.
- Get status information concerning these items:
  - The disk partition sizes,
  - The amount of free space left on a disk for making partitions,
  - Volume labels, their drive-letter assignment, file system type, and size.
- Alter drive-letter assignments.
- Create, delete, and repair mirror sets.
- Create and delete stripe sets and regenerate missing or failed members of stripe sets with parity.

Don't recognize some of these terms? Hang on, they're defined in the section below.

Disk Administrator Terminology

Before we get into the discussion of how you can use the Disk Administrator to arrange and protect your data, you need to know some of the terms that we'll be tossing around. These terms will be explained further in due course, but this section introduces them to you.

SLED

An acronym for *single large expensive drive*, SLED just means that you put your data on one very large, very (I hope) reliable drive. SLED is currently the most popular method of arranging data for two reasons:

- It's simple. You only have to buy one disk and store your data on it.
- Dedicated RAID hardware has been expensive in the past.

RAID

"Apply a shot of RAID, and all those nasty data problems will be gone!" No, it's not really a household product. RAID, which stands for *redundant array of inexpensive drives*, is a method of protecting your data by combining smaller, less expensive drives together in such a way that your data redundancy and therefore security is increased. There are six kinds of RAID implementation, each of which works in a different way and has different applications. NT Server can handle levels 0, 1, and 5. We'll talk about exactly what those levels are later in this chapter.

Free Space

This sounds like an obvious term—"free space on a disk is just space that's free, right?" It's not. Free space is space on the disk that is *not part of a partition*. That means it's not committed to be a simple logical drive, a volume set, a mirror set, or a stripe set. You can convert free space to anything else. In the Disk Administrator, it is indicated with diagonal striping.

Notice here that free space refers to *uncommitted* space, space that is not part of any drive letter. *Free space does not refer to unused areas within established drives.*

Physical Drives vs. Logical Partitions

Physical drives are not usually important in the Disk Administrator, but it's worthwhile getting the distinction between physical drives and logical drives or partitions clear. A *physical drive* is that contraption of plastic and metal that you inserted in your server's case or have stacked up next to it. Physical drives have numbers assigned to them that you cannot change, such as 0, 1, 2, 3… you get the idea. You cannot change the size of a physical drive. In order to use it, you must do a *low-level* format or a *physical* format, two synonymous terms for a software preparation that all hard drives must undergo before an operating system can use them. There is no way in NT to do that, as formatting is usually handled by directly executing a program on the disk drive controller. Consult the documentation on your disk controller to see how to do a low-level format on your drive. The size to which it is low-level formatted is the size that it will always be.

Note, by the way, that if you're putting a number of hard disks on a PC, then the PC may boot up only recognizing two of those drives. Don't worry about that; what you're seeing is a limitation of the DOS-based BIOS on the SCSI host adapter. Once you've booted NT, it will be able to see however many drives you've attached to your system. Similarly, DOS and BIOS have a lot of trouble seeing more than 1GB on a hard disk, so you may be told by the installation program that you only have 1GB on your hard disk, even if you have a larger disk. The installation program is misinformed because it's still relying on your PC's BIOS, which can't usually see more than 1GB. Once NT is up and running, however, it will see all of your hard disk.

In contrast to a physical drive, a *logical partition* is a volume set, logical drive, primary partition, or anything else in the Disk Administrator that is assigned a drive *letter*. You can change drive-letter assignments and adjust the sizes of logical partitions, as they have no physical presence. A logical partition can be part or all of a physical drive, or even (in the case of volume sets, mirror sets, and stripe sets) extend across more than one physical drive.

Partitions

A *partition* is a portion of a hard disk that is set up to act like a separate physical hard disk, rather like splitting a single physical hard disk into several logical drives. Partitions are referred to as either *primary* or *extended* partitions.

Primary Partitions   A primary partition is a portion of a physical hard disk that has been marked as bootable by an operating system (like Windows NT). Primary partitions cannot be broken down into sub-partitions, and there can only be up to four partitions per disk. You might, for example, partition your hard disk so that one primary partition is running Windows NT and another part is running OS/2. In the Disk Administrator, a primary partition is indicated with a dark purple stripe across the top. The exact colors you see will vary depending on your video card's capabilities. The legend at the bottom of the screen will tell you the status of your drives. They also can be changed by the user according to the user's preference.

Extended Partitions   An extended partition, on the other hand, is created from free space on the disk. Extended partitions can be broken down into smaller logical drives. You can only have one extended partition per hard disk, but you don't have to have a primary partition to have an extended one. In the Disk Administrator display, an extended partition is striped and labeled just like free space. The only way that you can tell a free space area from an extended partition is by clicking on the area. In the status bar below the color legend, you'll see a description of exactly what the area that you selected is.

Once you've established an extended partition, you can convert it to a logical drive.

Logical Drive

A *logical drive* is a partition on one disk that behaves as an entity unto itself. You can divide an extended partition into as many logical drives as you like, with only two limitations:

- NT Server only supports 24 fixed-disk drive letters (25 if you don't have a second floppy drive).

- There is a minimum size for each logical partition. This shouldn't be much of a limitation, however, because the minimum size is 2MB. That's not much bigger than a floppy disk's capacity.

Logical drives are indicated in the Disk Manager display with a royal blue stripe. (I'm sorry the book's not in color, so we can't show stripe colors. You'll have to take my word for it.)

Volume Set

A *volume set* is a drive or portion of a drive that has been combined with space on another physical drive to make one large volume. You can assign a drive letter to a volume set and format it like a logical drive, but a volume set can extend across two or more physical disks, while a logical drive is restricted to one physical disk.

Why use a volume set rather than a logical drive? The ability to extend across more than one disk is the answer. Since volume sets are not limited to one physical disk, you can make a quite large volume set out of a bunch of tiny little pieces of free space (defined below). Therefore, you can use your disk space as efficiently as possible. It's much easier to figure out how to fit 30MB of data into a 35MB volume set than it is to fit it into two 10MB logical drives and one 15MB. What if you need to resize a volume set? You can make a volume set larger by *extending* it if more free space becomes available, but you cannot make it smaller unless you delete it and create a new one.

That's worth repeating: You can enlarge a volume set without damaging the data on it, but you cannot *reduce* a volume set without destroying it and rebuilding it altogether.

Volume sets do not protect your data; they only give you more efficient use of your available drive space. If something happens to one of the hard disks used in a volume set, that volume set is dead. Since the more hard disks you have, the more likely it is that one will fail at any given time, be sure to back up volume sets regularly.

In the Disk Administrator display, a volume set is indicated with a yellow stripe across the top of the area in it.

Mirror Set

Disk mirroring helps protect your data by storing a copy of all your data onto an identically sized area of free space on another disk. The original and the copy together are called a *mirror set*. If anything happens to your original data, you still have the identical copy on the other half of the mirror set. Mirror sets are not very space-efficient, as every piece of data that you record has an identical twin on the other half of the mirror set. You need exactly twice as much storage space as you have data. The Disk Administrator displays mirror sets with a magenta stripe across the top.

Stripe Set

For data protection, or to decrease your disks' read time, you can select areas of free space on your disks (three or more if you want parity, two or more if not) and combine them into a *stripe set*. Data stored in a stripe set is written in chunks of a certain size, called *stripes*. A stripe set is assigned a drive letter and, once formatted, behaves as a drive.

Once you have the stripe set established, every time you write to the drive letter that represents the set, your data is written in stripes across all the members of the stripe set. In other words, not all your data ends up in one place. Even if there's room for an entire file in one of the areas in the set, the data won't all be written there. If you've established a stripe set *with parity*, then parity information is written to the disks along with the data. Parity information is always stored separately from the data to which it corresponds. That way, if something happens to the disk with the original data, the parity information will still be all right, and the data can be reconstructed from the parity information. Obviously, a stripe set without parity cannot be reconstructed if the disk with the original data on it fails, since the data only exists in one place in the stripe set.

The Hazards of Striping without Parity

And there's the rub. Since the stripe set, although spread out over a number of disks, acts as one drive, all the parts of the stripe set must be working for the data to be accessible. If one member of a stripe set without parity information becomes inaccessible for whatever reason, all the data in the stripe set is lost.

You can see, therefore, how striping without parity actually increases your failure risk. While it's true that the more disks you have, the less likely it is that *all* of them will fail at the same time, the flip side of this is that the more disks you have, the more likely it is that *one* of them will fail at any given time. In a situation in which one disk failure brings down the entire system, having more disks actually increases your vulnerability to hardware failures. As with volume sets, you must back up non-parity stripe sets regularly.

All stripe sets, whether with parity or without, are shown in light green in the Disk Administrator. You can tell what kind of stripe set a particular one is by clicking on it and looking at the status bar below the color legend.

Before Using the Disk Administrator...

The Disk Administrator is very easy to use and can be fun to play around with. (When experimenting with it for this chapter, my assistant Christa spent a couple of hours creating and deleting logical partitions and cackling, "The power is mine, all mine!") This is fine, so long as you keep a couple of things in mind:

- You can make any changes you like in the Disk Administrator, adding, adjusting, or deleting partitions, and the changes will not take effect until you save them.

- Once you *do* save them, the changes will take effect as soon as you shut down the system and restart.

- If you save a change, the system will want to shut down and reboot when you exit the Disk Administrator. If you're not in a position where you can reboot, press Ctrl-Esc to switch to the Program Manager.

- If you add a new physical disk to your system, it should automatically show up in the Disk Administrator after you reboot. If it doesn't, then something was wrong with the installation.

- Deleting a partition of any kind will destroy any data saved there.

- If you intend to experiment with a partition or drive on which you have data, back it up before doing anything else.

Keeping It All Together with SLED

Even if it's partitioned into smaller logical drives, most of us use SLED, or a single large expensive drive, as the arrangement for our data storage. Why SLED? Essentially, SLED is so popular because it's easy. You buy a large disk from a trusted manufacturer, slap it in, save your data there, perform regular backups, and you're good to go. Using SLED is like buying all your stock in one giant company with an excellent track record. It's dependable, but if it goes, you're sunk—time to haul out the backups. (Pity that you can't haul out the backup *money* when it comes to stock losses.)

Using Logical Drives to Divide Information

Even if you rely on the SLED model for your data storage, you may want to divide that single large physical drive into smaller logical ones. You could, for example, keep all the accounting information on logical drive C, the engineering information on logical drive D, the personnel information on logical drive E, and so on.

Creating an Extended Partition

To create a logical drive, you must first take free space and convert it to an extended partition. Open the Disk Administrator so that you see the screen shown in Figure 4.1.

Notice that my example screen shows four drives on my server. Drive 0 is taken up entirely with a large NTFS partition where I put my data, and drives 1 through 3 are 276MB hard disks that I'll use for my examples. Click on the free space, and then choose Create Extended Partition from the Partition drop-down menu. When you have done so, you'll see a dialog box like the one in Figure 4.2, asking how big you want to make the extended partition.

Select the size that you want (you don't have to use up all the free space available) and click OK.

FIGURE 4.1:

Disk Administrator window

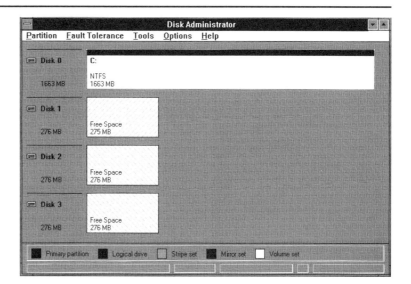

FIGURE 4.2:

Create Extended Partition dialog box

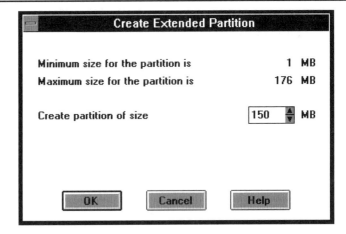

Converting the Extended Partition to a Logical Drive

Once you've created the extended partition, you're ready to create a logical drive. To do so, click on the area of the extended partition to select it, and then select Create... from the Partition drop-down menu. When you do, you'll see a dialog box that looks like the one in Figure 4.3.

Type in the size of the logical drive that you want to create, or press Enter to select the default option and take all the available space. Once you've pressed OK, your logical drive is set up.

When you exit the Disk Administrator, you'll see a dialog box like the one in Figure 4.4. Click Yes to save. Disk Administrator will confirm that it made the changes with the dialog box in Figure 4.5.

When you quit the Disk Administrator, you'll see a dialog box like Figure 4.6, advising you that the changes that you have made require restarting your computer. Click OK and the system will shut down and restart automatically.

FIGURE 4.3:
Create Logical Drive dialog box

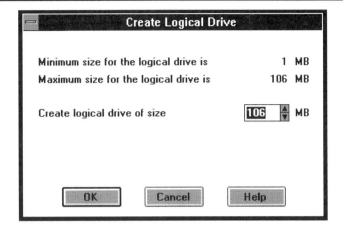

FIGURE 4.4:
Confirm configuration changes
dialog box

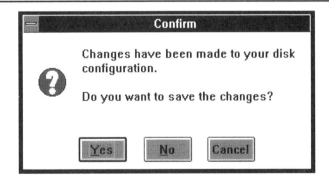

FIGURE 4.5:
A dialog box confirming your
configuration

FIGURE 4.6:

The dialog box asking you to restart your computer

> **TIP**
>
> If you don't want to shut down now, you can press Ctrl-Esc to switch to the Program Manager. However, the changes have still been made, and, once you shut down and restart the system, the repartitioning will take effect.

Formatting the New Drive

Before you can store data on the new drive, you've got to format it. In previous versions of NT Server, you could only format disks from the command prompt—kind of silly for a graphical operating system. In 3.51, you have a new drop-down menu in the main menu, called "Tools." The Tools menu contains four disk administration tools, one of which is Format. (The others are Label, Drive Letter, and CD-ROM Drive Letter—they're for assigning drive letters and labels, and they're pretty self-explanatory.)

To format, you must first create a partition or logical drive; you can't format free space. Click on the partition to be formatted to select it, and choose Commit Changes Now from the Partition menu. When the partition information has been stored, keep the partition highlighted and choose Format... from the Tools menu.

In the Format dialog box, choose the file system that you want to use on the partition. NT Advanced Server 3.1 lets you format disks with HPFS (the OS/2 file system); but since version 3.5, NT Server has offered only the choices of FAT and NTFS. It's not much of a loss, as anywhere that HPFS made sense NTFS made more sense because of the security it offers. For best security, make all of your partitions NTFS. The only exception to this is that it may be a good idea to keep the boot partition FAT, so you can boot from a DOS system floppy if necessary; and any partitions that you need to be available if you boot from DOS must use the FAT system as well.

(DOS doesn't recognize NTFS partitions.) Please note: that's "*if* you boot from DOS"; DOS machines connected to the server can access data in an NTFS partition without any problem.

If you're formatting a partition or logical drive, you can check Quick Format to tell NT Server not to scan the disk for bad sectors. If the section you're formatting is a fault-tolerant volume such as a mirror set or stripe set with parity, then this is not an option.

Click the OK button to start the format. A dialog box will appear, asking you to confirm the format; click OK again and the format operation will begin. A dialog box will show you the progress of the format. Be warned: although the dialog box has a Cancel button, canceling the format won't necessarily restore the partition to its original condition.

If you're addicted to the MS-DOS command line, you can still use it to format disks. To do so, open a command prompt and type `format` *driveletter:* `/fs:`*filesystem*, where *driveletter* is, of course, the drive letter of the logical drive, and *filesystem* is either "FAT" or "NTFS." For example, to format a newly-created drive E: as NTFS, you'd type "`format e: /fs:ntfs`."

If you open the File Manager and try to access the new drive letter before you format it, you'll get a nastygram like the one shown in Figure 4.7.

FIGURE 4.7:
"Can't access drive" error message

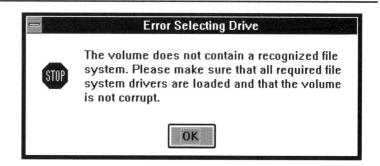

Here, in a nutshell, are the steps for creating a logical drive:

How Do I Create a Logical Drive?

Take the following steps to create a logical drive:

1. Open the Disk Administrator and select an area of free space.

2. From the Partition menu, select Create Extended... and choose the size of extended partition that you want to make.

3. Having selected the extended partition that you just made, select Create... from the Partition menu, and choose the size of logical drive that you want to make.

4. You'll see the new logical drive shown in royal blue. Open the Partition menu and choose Commit Changes Now for the changes to take effect.

5. Format the drive to NTFS or FAT, using the Format... option from the Tools menu.

You can now use the logical drive letter like you would any other.

Use the Most Recent Drivers!

If you experience strange problems with the Disk Administrator, make sure that you've got the most recent drivers. For example, if your NT server has an EIDE (Enhanced Integrated Drive Electronics) drive controller for which you're using the DOS drivers, you may notice problems with the Disk Administrator. First of all, any time you've opened the Disk Administrator, when you exit, the system will demand that you reboot even if you didn't do anything. Second, the EIDE hard disk won't hold a partition no matter what you try. What's going on?

It appears that the two sides of the problem have their root in the same difficulty: the EIDE disk won't hold a partition, so every time you run the Disk Administrator, it perceives changes whether you personally made them or not. There is a happy ending to the story, however—when we called the EIDE controller manufacturer and had them send us the NT 3.51 drivers, the problems went away.

Other Disk Administrator problems may also be caused by obsolete driver software.

Deleting a Logical Drive

Deleting a logical drive will destroy all the data on it, so back up before you do anything drastic. The next "How Do I" sidebar explains how to delete a logical drive.

How Do I Delete a Logical Drive?

To delete a logical drive:

1. Select the drive in the Disk Administrator and choose Delete from the Partition drop-down menu.

2. A message like the one below appears:

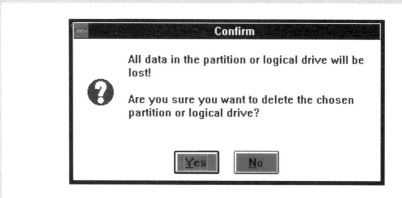

3. Yes is the default. Once you've confirmed, the logical partition will be deleted and will become an empty extended partition. If you want to convert the extended partition to free space, you must delete it as well.

When you exit the Disk Administrator, you'll be prompted to confirm your changes. Once you've confirmed, click OK to restart the system or press Ctrl-Esc to go to the Program Manager.

Using Space Efficiently

Even if you're a devoted SLED aficionado, you may one day be faced with space restrictions that force you to get another drive. In that event, you'll want to use the space on that new drive as efficiently as possible.

Volume Sets to Get the Most Out of Existing Disks

How can you use disk space efficiently? Well, keeping the drives separate from each other clearly isn't the way. Unused space is more efficient if combined because, even if you have a total of 40MB of unused data space on the two drives, you can't fit one 35MB chunk of data in it if 25MB is on one disk and 15MB is on the other. If you want to get as much data squeezed onto your disks as possible, therefore, you can combine the two (or more) disks into a volume set, as seen in Figure 4.8.

FIGURE 4.8:

How a volume set works

In this figure, 65MB of free space is available, but no more than 20MB of this sapce is contiguous. To get the most efficient use of this space, you could combine it in a volume set, so that all of the data is considered in one large chunk. Once this free space has been made into a volume set, you could store a 65MB chunk of data in it, even though the largest contiguous space is only 20MB in size.

Cautions about Volume Sets

Don't forget that volume sets have one big drawback: They span more than one physical disk and are dependent on all of those disks to function. If one disk turns belly-up and dies, then the rest of your volume set becomes inaccessible. If you try to read or write to a dead volume set, you'll get a message like the one in Figure 4.9. And then you'll see a dialog box like the one in Figure 4.10.

FIGURE 4.9:
System Process – Lost Delayed-Write Data message box

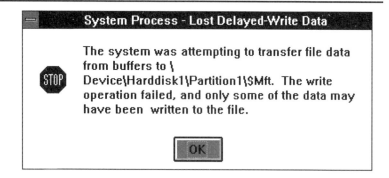

System Process - Lost Delayed-Write Data

The system was attempting to transfer file data from buffers to \ Device\Harddisk1\Partition1\$Mft. The write operation failed, and only some of the data may have been written to the file.

OK

FIGURE 4.10:
Error Copying File dialog box

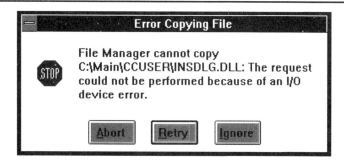

Error Copying File

File Manager cannot copy C:\Main\CCUSER\INSDLG.DLL: The request could not be performed because of an I/O device error.

Abort   Retry   Ignore

Here's a case where the user interface folks were out to lunch. It would have been easier and clearer to just put up a dialog box at this point that said, "One of your drives isn't working. You can no longer access data on drive X." This is just another reason why frequent backups are essential.

TIP

If you accidentally switch off an externally mounted drive that's part of a volume set and get messages like the ones in Figures 4.9 and 4.10 when you try to write to or read from that drive, just reboot and the volume set will recover without any problems.

Creating a Volume Set

To create a volume set, back up any data on your disks, make sure that there is free space on them, and follow these steps:

1. Open the Disk Administrator in the Administrative Tools program group.

2. Select one or more areas of free space on your hard disk(s) by clicking on the first one and then Ctrl-clicking on the others to select them all at once—just like selecting more than one file at a time in the File Manager. This is demonstrated in Figure 4.11.

FIGURE 4.11:

Selecting free space on hard disks

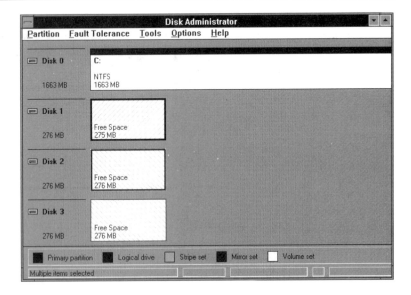

3. Go to the Partition menu and choose Create Volume Set. When you've done this, you'll see the dialog box in Figure 4.12 displaying the minimum and maximum sizes for the volume set.

FIGURE 4.12:

Create Volume Set dialog box

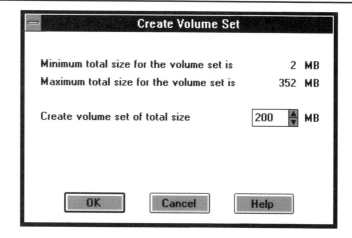

4. In the box, type the size of the volume set that you want to create. Obviously, the size must be somewhere between the minimum and the maximum sizes available, here, 2MB and 352MB, respectively. When you've entered the proper size (200MB, in this case), click OK.

You'll return to the Disk Administrator display and see the members of the volume set shown in yellow. In Figure 4.13, drive G is the volume set.

The display in Figure 4.13 shows a 200MB volume set on two disks that already have primary partitions. As you can see, there is still free space left on the disks that could be used for something else. When creating a volume set, you don't have to use all the available space. If you select a size smaller than the maximum, the Disk Administrator divides the size you chose roughly equally across all the partitions that you selected to be part of the volume set, so that all the partitions in the volume set are approximately the same size (so far as possible).

FIGURE 4.13:

The volume set

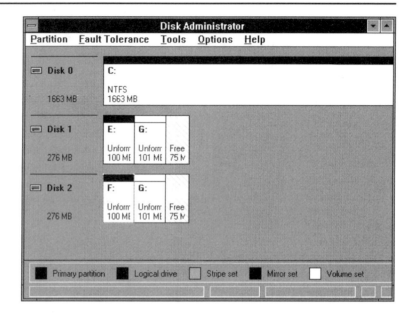

When you exit the Disk Administrator, you'll be prompted to save your changes and shut down the system, as we've discussed in earlier sections. Shut down and restart, and the volume set will be created.

Formatting the Volume Set

After you've restarted the system, format the disk either from the Tools menu or from the command line with the following command:

```
format x: /fs:filesystem
```

where x is the appropriate drive letter and *filesystem* is the type of file system (NTFS or FAT) to which you want to format that drive. Formatting may take a while, depending on the size of the set you've created.

Read the "How Do I" sidebar to review how to create a volume set.

How Do I Create a Volume Set?

To create a volume set, do the following:

1. Open the Disk Administrator and select all the areas of free space that you want to include in the set.

2. From the Partition menu, choose Create Volume Set.

3. Choose the size of the set that you want and click OK. You can choose any size that is within the maximum and minimum parameters.

4. Exit the Disk Administrator. You'll be prompted to reboot the system.

When you return to the Disk Administrator, the new volume set will appear in yellow. It will have a drive letter, but won't yet be formatted.

5. To finish, you'll have to format the new logical drive, using either the command prompt or the Format... command in the Tools menu. To format from the command prompt, open a DOS window and type `format driveletter: /fs:filesystem` where *driveletter* is, of course, the drive letter of the logical drive, and *filesystem* is either "FAT" or "NTFS." For example, to format a newly-created drive E: as NTFS, you'd type `format e: /fs:ntfs`.

Deleting a Volume Set

Ultimately, you may want to reorganize the data on your disks, or you might start having problems with one of your disks and need to replace it. If one of these situations is the case, you'll need to delete the volume set.

TIP Deleting the volume set will permanently delete all the information that was in it, so back up any data in the set before deleting it. The next "How Do I" sidebar explains how to delete a volume set.

Enlarging a Volume Set

If it turns out that your volume set is smaller than you need it to be, it's not necessary to delete it and re-create it from scratch. Instead, you can *extend* it by adding areas of free space to its volume. The process described in the next sidebar also applies to extending existing primary partitions to make their area bigger. (Once you extend them, however, they show up in the Disk Administrator color-coded as volume sets.)

You cannot use the instructions in the "How Do I" sidebar to make volume sets *smaller*. To do that, you must delete the volume set and create it again.

There are three limitations on extending volume sets:

- Again, you cannot use this procedure to make a volume set smaller. To do that, you need to delete the volume set and create a new one.

- You cannot extend a volume set when working with the partition with the system files on it. The Disk Administrator will not let you add free space to this partition.

- You cannot combine two volume sets or add a logical drive to a volume set.

Non-Parity Disk Striping to Increase Throughput

Another way to get more bang for your disk-buying buck is with disk striping without parity, also known as RAID level 0. When you create a stripe set from free space on your disks, each member of the stripe set is divided into stripes. Then, when you write data to the stripe set, the data is distributed over the stripes. A file could have its beginning recorded onto stripe 1 on member 1, more data recorded onto stripe 2

How Do I Delete a Volume Set?

To delete a volume set:

1. Go to the Disk Administrator.

2. Click on the volume set that you want to delete to select it. It will become outlined in black:

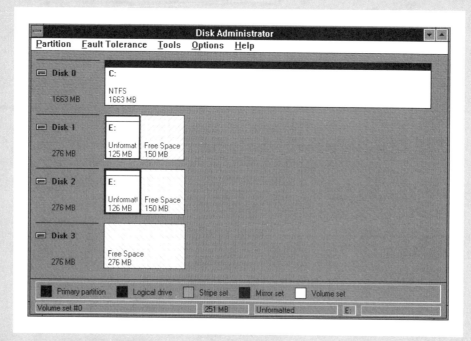

3. From the Partition menu, select Delete.

A message box like the following tells you that all data in that set will be lost. The message box asks you to confirm the action before continuing.

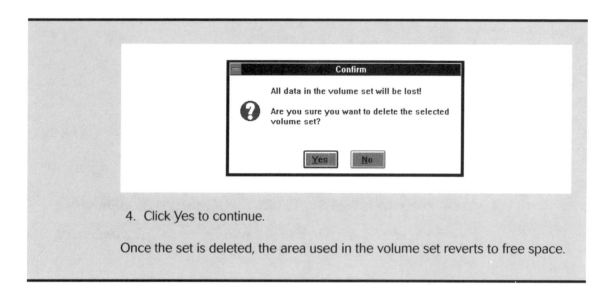

Confirm

All data in the volume set will be lost!

Are you sure you want to delete the selected volume set?

Yes   No

4. Click Yes to continue.

Once the set is deleted, the area used in the volume set reverts to free space.

of member 2, and the rest on stripe 3 of member 3, for example. If you're saving data to a stripe set, a file is never stored on only one member, even if there is room on that member for the entire file. Conceptually, striping looks something like Figure 4.14.

FIGURE 4.14:

Stripe set without parity

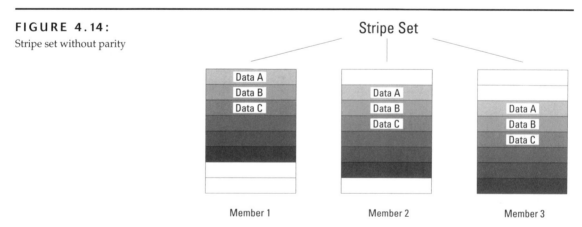

Stripe Set

Member 1   Member 2   Member 3

Different data files are represented here by different shades of gray. As you can see, an entire data file is never all put onto one member of the stripe set. This improves read time. For example, if Data A is called for, the disk controllers on all three members of the set can read the data. With a SLED data arrangement, only one of the members could read the data.

If you take free space on your disks and combine them into one stripe set with its own drive letter, then the seek-and-write time to that drive will be improved, since the system can read and write to more than one disk at a time. To do striping without parity information included, you need a minimum of 3 disks to a maximum of 32.

How Do I Extend a Volume Set?

To extend a volume set:

1. From the Disk Administrator, select an existing volume set or primary partition that has been formatted (one that is not part of a mirror set or stripe set) and has one or more areas of free space. The volume set *must* have been previously formatted to extend it.

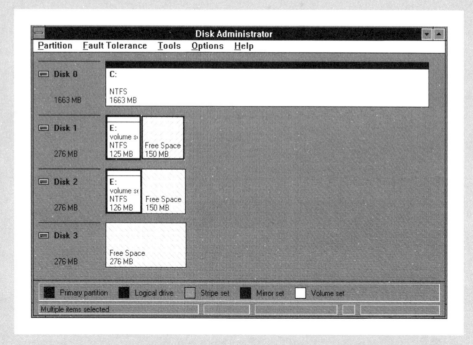

2. Go to the Partition menu and select Extend Volume Set. As you did when you created the volume set, you'll see a dialog box showing the minimum and maximum sizes for the volume set:

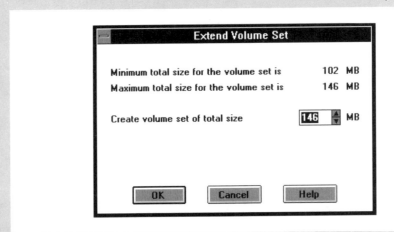

Extend Volume Set

Minimum total size for the volume set is   102 MB

Maximum total size for the volume set is   146 MB

Create volume set of total size   146 MB

OK   Cancel   Help

3. Enter the size of the volume set that you want, and click OK.

The volume set is now the larger size that you specified, and all the area in it will have the same drive letter. The free space that you added is automatically formatted to the same file system as the rest of the volume set.

Creating a Stripe Set

Creating a stripe set without parity is quite simple. Just follow the steps in the "How Do I" sidebar.

Deleting a Stripe Set

If anything happens to any member disk of your non-parity stripe set, all the data in the set is lost. Not only can you not get the data back (except through backups), but you can't use the disks that are part of the stripe set until you delete the stripe set and establish a new one. If the disk is dead, you'll have to delete the stripe set and start over. How to do that is explained in the sidebar.

How Do I Create a Stripe Set without Parity?

To create a stripe set without parity:

1. In the Disk Administrator, select two or more areas of free space on from 2 to 32 hard disks. (Note that, without parity, you need a minimum of only 2 disks, not 3.) To do this, click on the free space on the hard disk and then Ctrl-click on the others, as though you were selecting more than one file in the File Manager.

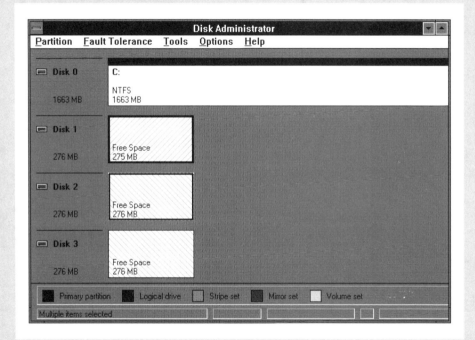

2. From the Partition drop-down menu, choose Create Stripe Set. You'll see a dialog box that displays the minimum and maximum stripe sizes:

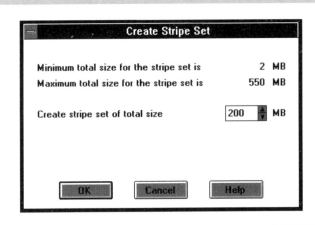

3. Choose the size stripe you want, and click OK.

The Disk Administrator will now equally divide the total size of the stripe you selected among the available disks, and then assign a single drive letter to this set. If you selected a size that could not be divided equally among the number of disks involved in the stripe set, the Disk Administrator will round to the nearest number. When you exit, the system will reboot to implement the change unless you press Ctrl-Esc.

The stripe set is now created, but not formatted, as you can see from this picture:

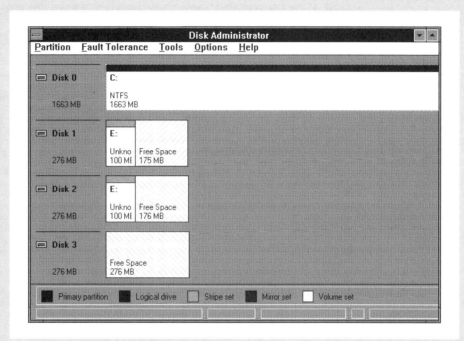

4. To format the stripe set, either choose Format... from the Tools menu or open a command prompt and type

```
format driveletter: /fs:filesystem
```

where *driveletter* is, of course, the drive letter of the logical drive, and *filesystem* is either FAT or NTFS. For example, to format a newly created drive E as NTFS, you would type

```
format e: /fs:ntfs
```

When you're done, the stripe set will show up like this:

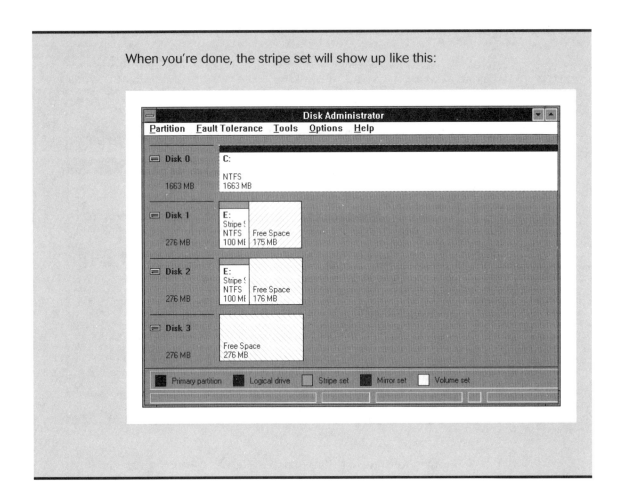

Protecting Your Data

Using your disk space efficiently and improving data throughput are important, but they don't do anything to protect your data's integrity. If you want to do that, NT Server offers you two methods: disk mirroring and disk striping.

How Do I Delete a Stripe Set?

To delete a stripe set:

1. In the Disk Administrator, select the stripe that you want to delete, as you see in this graphic:

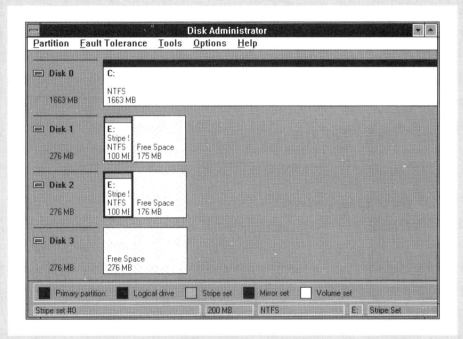

2. From the Partition drop-down menu, select Delete.

You'll see a message box advising you that this action will delete all the data.

The box asks you to confirm that you want to delete:

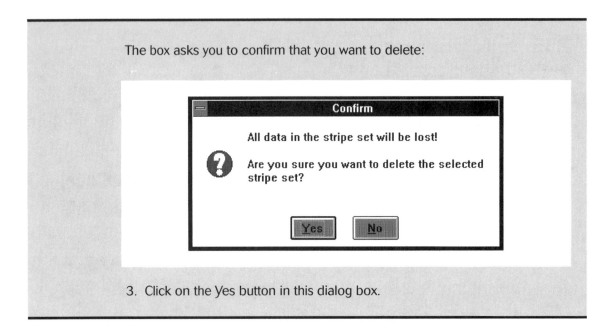

3. Click on the Yes button in this dialog box.

Disk Mirroring

If you have more than one disk, you can *mirror* a partition on one onto free space on another. This means that you'll keep an exact copy of one partition on another disk. Once you have established this relationship between the two disk areas, called a *mirror set* (mirror sets were explained earlier in this chapter), every time that you write data to disk a duplicate of that data is written to the free space on the other half of the mirror set. Disk mirroring is equivalent to RAID level 1.

How well does disk mirroring perform? Data must be written to both drives in the mirror set, but it suffers no performance lag since each disk can do its own writing. In addition, mirrored drives are fast when it comes to reads, as data can be pulled from both halves of the mirror set at once.

Mirroring and Duplexing   If you've ever heard or read anything about disk mirroring, you've probably also heard the term *disk duplexing*. Disk duplexing is much the same as disk mirroring, except that duplexing generally refers to mirroring information on disks that each have their own disk controller, so that the data is not vulnerable to controller failures. When NT Server talks about disk mirroring, it is referring to both duplexing and mirroring, as seen in Figure 4.15.

FIGURE 4.15:

Disk mirroring vs. disk duplexing

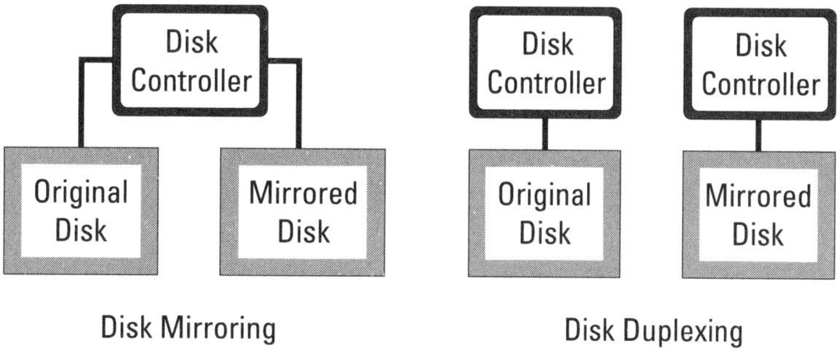

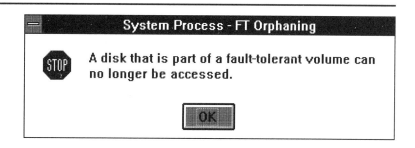

Establishing a Mirror Set

You can mirror a drive's data without affecting that drive's accessibility while you do it. See the sidebar to find out how.

Breaking a Mirror Set

If something unrecoverable—like hardware damage—happens to half of the mirror set, you need to break the mirror set to get to the good data that you've backed up. It will be pretty apparent when something's gone wrong. You'll see a message like the one shown in Figure 4.16 when you try to write to the mirrored drives if one of the disks isn't working. Kind of looks more like a fortune cookie fortune than a system message, doesn't it? You can still use the drive, but the benefits of mirroring will be suspended.

FIGURE 4.16:

System Process – FT Orphaning message box

How Do I Set Up a Mirror Set?

To set up a mirror set:

1. Click on the partition that you want to maintain a copy of (such as the primary partition).

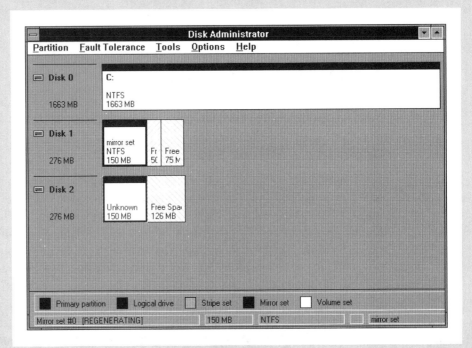

2. By pressing Ctrl and clicking at the same time, choose the free space on another disk that you want to make the other half of the set.

This area must be the same size as or larger than the partition or drive that you are mirroring. If you select an area of free space that is too small, the system will complain to you that "The free space you have chosen is not large enough to mirror the partition you have chosen."

3. From the Fault Tolerance drop-down menu, select Establish Mirror.

Once you've done this, you have established the mirror set. The Disk Administrator now establishes an equal-sized partition in the free space to be the mirror, and assigns the drive letter to the mirror set. Now, whenever you save a file to that drive letter, two copies of the file will be saved.

4. Format the new logical drive. You do that either with the Format... command in the Tools menu or by opening a command prompt and typing

```
format driveletter: /fs:filesystem
```

where *driveletter* is, of course, the drive letter of the logical drive, and *filesystem* is either FAT or NTFS. For example, to format a newly created drive E as NTFS, you would type

```
format e: /fs:ntfs
```

How Do I Break a Mirror Set?

To break a mirror set:

1. Open the Disk Administrator and select the mirror set that you want to break. When you open the Disk Administrator, you'll see a message like this, telling you that something is different:

Disk Administrator

Disk Administrator has determined that one or more disks have been removed from your computer since Disk Administrator was last run, or that one or more disks are off-line.

Configuration information about the missing disk(s) will be retained.

OK

2. From the Fault Tolerance menu, select Break Mirror. You'll then see a message like this one:

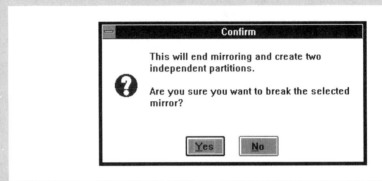

3. Click on Yes to break the mirror set.

Breaking a mirror set does not affect the information inside it. Still, as always before doing anything drastic with the drive that holds your data, it's a good idea to back up first.

If you break a mirror set when nothing's wrong with it, then each half becomes a primary partition with its own drive letter. The original partition keeps its original drive letter, while the backup partition gets the next one available.

Recovering Data from a Mirror Set

Once you've broken the mirror set so that you can get to the good data, the good half of the mirror set will be assigned the drive letter that belonged to the now-defunct mirror set. The half that crashed is now called an *orphan* and is, in effect, set aside by the fault-tolerance driver so that no one will attempt to write to that part of the disk. When you reboot, the dead disk disappears, as in Figure 4.17.

At this point, you take the good half of the old mirror set and establish a new relationship with another partition, as discussed earlier in "Establishing a Mirror Set." When you restart the computer, the data from the good partition is copied to its new

FIGURE 4.17:

Recovering data from a mirror set

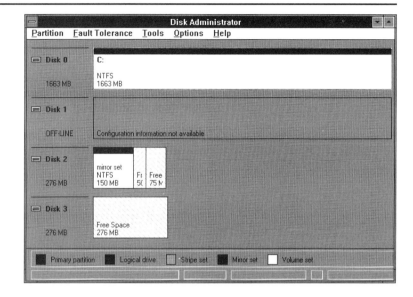

partner. While the regeneration process is going on, the type on the new half of the mirror set will show in red. However, it doesn't take long to regenerate mirrored material and the process takes place in the background anyway—you don't have to wait for it to finish to use the computer.

To review how to repair a broken mirror set, read the sidebar.

How Do I Repair a Broken Mirror Set?

To repair a broken mirror set:

1. Open the Disk Administrator and select the good half of the mirror set and an area of free space the same size or larger than the area to be mirrored.

2. Choose Establish Mirror... from the Fault Tolerance menu.

The new mirror set will be displayed in magenta.

Mirroring Considerations

As you're deciding whether or not to protect your data by mirroring it, keep these things in mind:

- Mirroring to drives run from the same drive controller does not protect your data from drive controller failure. If there's any kind of controller failure, you won't be able to get to the backup copy of your data unless you are mirroring to a disk run from a separate controller.

- For higher disk read performance and greater fault tolerance, use a separate disk controller for each half of a mirror set.

- Disk mirroring effectively cuts your available disk space in half. Don't forget that when you're figuring out how much drive space you have on the server.

- Disk mirroring has a low initial cost, since you must purchase only one extra drive to achieve fault tolerance, but it costs more in the long-term due to the amount of room your redundant information takes up.

- Disk mirroring will slow down writes, as the data must be written in two places every time, but will speed up reads, as the I/O controller has two places to read information from. For multiuser environments (like the network you're using NT Server for), it gets the best performance of all the RAID levels.

Disk Striping, the Slow but Steady Method

In addition to disk mirroring, NT Server gives you the option of using level 5 RAID, also known as *disk striping with parity*. Disk striping with parity differs from regular disk striping in the following ways:

- Although data lost from a stripe set without parity is unrecoverable, data from a parity stripe set can usually be recovered. ("Usually" because if someone puts a bullet through every one of your disks, then all the parity information in the world won't help you.) If more than one disk of the 2 to 32 hard disk drives fails, you will not be able to recover your data.

- Regular disk striping improves data read and write speeds. Striping with parity slows down writes, but improves access speed.

How It Works

Every time you write data to disk, the data is written across all the striped disks in the array, just as it is with regular disk striping (RAID level 0). In addition, however, parity information for your data is also written to disk, always on a separate disk from the one where the data it corresponds to is written. That way, if anything happens to one of the disks in the array, the data on that disk can be reconstructed from the parity information on the other disks.

Level 5 RAID differs from level 4, which also uses parity information to protect data, in that the parity information in level 5 RAID is distributed across all the disks in the array, rather than being kept on a specific disk dedicated to parity information. This makes RAID level 5 faster than 4, as it can perform more than one write operation at a time. This is shown in Figure 4.18.

If you think about it, writing parity information every time that you save a document can turn into quite a space-and-time waster. Take, for example, the document I'm writing this book on. If I've protected my data with level 5 RAID so that parity information is stored to disk every time that this file is saved, does that mean that there is parity information for every incarnation of this document from the time I began writing? If so, how can all the parity information and data fit on the disks?

FIGURE 4.18:
Disk striping with parity information

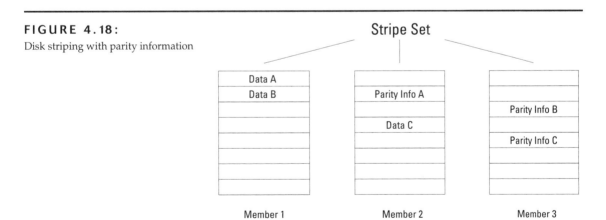

As you can see, no single member of the stripe set keeps all the original data or all the parity information. Instead, the data and the parity information are distributed throughout the stripe set, so that if one member disk fails, the information can be reconstructed from the other members of the stripe set.

The answer is, of course, that it doesn't, and this is what produces the performance degradation that's unavoidable in striped disk writes. Every time a document is saved to disk, the parity information for that document must be updated to reflect its current status, so that you don't keep backup parity information for every version of that document that you've ever saved.

Updating the Parity Information

There are two ways to update the parity information. First, since the parity information is the XOR (exclusive OR) of the data, the system could recalculate the XOR each time data is written to disk. This would require accessing each disk in the stripe set, however, because the data is distributed across all the disks in the array, and that takes time.

What is an *XOR?* On a *very* simplistic level, the XOR, or *exclusive OR arithmetic*, is a function that takes two one-bit inputs and produces a single bit output. The result is 1 if the two inputs are different, or 0 if the two inputs are the same. More specifically:

0 XOR 0 = 0

1 XOR 0 = 1

0 XOR 1 = 1

1 XOR 1 = 0

When you're XORing two numbers with more than one bit, just match the bits up and XOR them individually. For example, 1101010 XOR 0101000 equals 1000010. The result you get from this function is the parity information from which the original data can be recalculated.

A more efficient way of recalculating the parity information, and the one that NT Server uses, is to read the old data to be overwritten and XOR it with the new data to determine the differences. This process produces a *bit mask* that has a 1 in the position of every bit that has been changed. This bit mask can then be XORed with the old parity information to see where *its* differences lie, and from this the new parity information can be calculated. This seems convoluted, but this second process only requires two reads and two XOR computations, rather than one of each for every drive in the array.

Establishing a Stripe Set with Parity

To create a stripe set with parity, follow these steps:

1. In the Disk Administrator, select three or more areas of free space on from 3 to 32 hard disks (the exact number is determined by your hardware configuration—NT Server can handle up to 32 separate physical disks but your hardware setup may not be able to). To select the free space areas, click on the free space on the first hard disk and then Ctrl-click on the others, the same way that you select more than one file in the File Manager.

As you can see in Figure 4.19, the areas of free space that you select don't have to be equal in size because the Disk Administrator will distribute the available space evenly, adjusting the size of the stripe set as necessary.

2. From the Fault Tolerance Menu, choose Create Stripe Set With Parity. You'll then see a dialog box that displays the minimum and maximum sizes for the stripe set with parity, like the one in Figure 4.20.

3. Choose the size stripe you want and press OK.

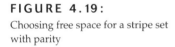

FIGURE 4.19:

Choosing free space for a stripe set with parity

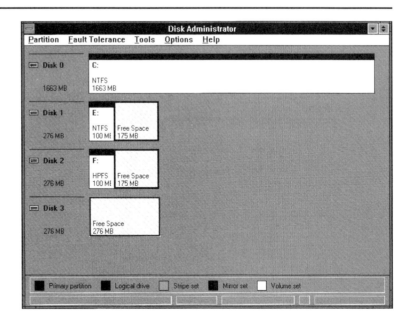

FIGURE 4.20:

Create Stripe Set With Parity
dialog box

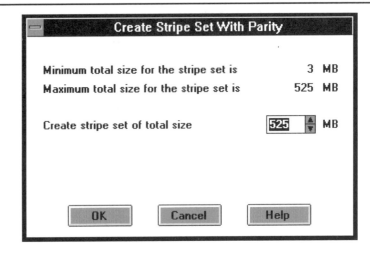

The Disk Administrator will now equally divide the total size of the stripe you se-lected among the available disks, and then assign a single drive letter to this set, as you see in Figure 4.21. In the case of this figure, the stripe set has been assigned letter D.

FIGURE 4.21:

Disk Administrator after creating
stripe set with parity

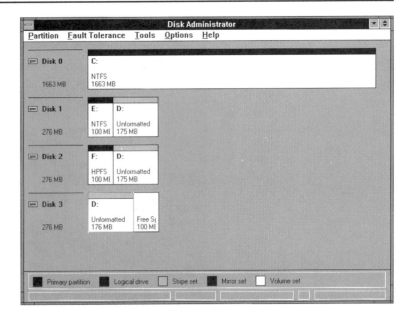

If you selected a size that could not be divided equally among the number of disks involved in the stripe set, the Disk Administrator will round down the size to the nearest number evenly divisible by the number of disks in the stripe set.

Once you've created the stripe set and try to exit the Disk Administrator, you'll see the usual dialog box telling you that the changes that you have made require you to restart your system, and asking you to click OK to begin shutdown.

When you restart, rebooting takes a little longer than normal, and when you reach the blue screen telling you what file system each of the drives on your system is using, the system will tell you that it cannot determine the file system type of the stripe set's drive letter—not that it is RAW, as you've seen before, but that it can't determine it. This may look worrisome, but it's just due to the fact that the system has to initialize the stripe set. Wait for the drive activity on the stripe set drives to subside (by watching drive LEDs or by listening for drive activity), and then format the new partition. If you don't format first, you'll get an error message like the one in Figure 4.22. One you've formatted, everything should be ready to go.

To recap, the sidebar on the following page explains how to stripe with parity.

FIGURE 4.22:
Error Selecting Drive message box

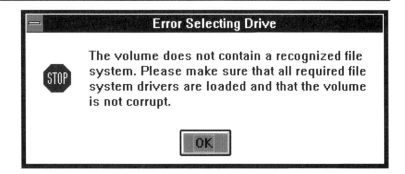

Retrieving Data from a Failed Stripe Set

If there's an unrecoverable error to part of a striped set with parity, you can regenerate the information stored there from the parity information stored on the rest of the set. You can even do this if one of the member disks has been low-level formatted.

How Do I Create a Stripe Set with Parity?

To create a stripe set with parity:

1. Open the Disk Administrator and select areas of free space on at least three physical disks.

2. Pull down the Fault Tolerance menu and select Create Stripe Set With Parity.

3. Fill in the size that you want the stripe set to be, and click OK.

The system will reboot upon your confirmation, and the stripe set will be initialized. As always, you have to format it from the command line before you can use the drive.

How do you know when something's wrong? If you attempt to write to a stripe set and see an error message like the one in Figure 4.23, it's a bad sign.

To recover the data, put a new disk in place and reboot so the system can see the new disk. Next, go to the Disk Administrator and select the stripe set that you want to fix and the new piece of free space that is at least equal in size to the other members of the set. Choose Regenerate from the Fault Tolerance menu, quit the Disk Administrator and restart the computer.

FIGURE 4.23:

Error message while writing a stripe set

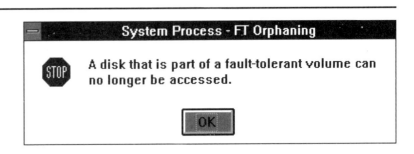

When you restart the computer, the fault-tolerance driver will collect the information from the stripes on the other member disks and then re-create it onto the new member of the stripe set. If you open the Disk Administrator while it is doing this, you'll see the text on the part being regenerated displayed in red. Although the regeneration process may take a while, it doesn't conflict with your ability to use the server. You don't need to keep the Disk Administrator open—the restoration process works in the background, and you can access the information in the stripe set.

Once the stripe set is fixed, you'll need to reassign it a new drive letter and restart the computer. The failed portion of the original stripe set is set aside as unusable, and is called an *orphan*. In the Disk Administrator, the failed disk will look as shown in Figure 4.24.

FIGURE 4.24:

A failed disk in Disk Administrator

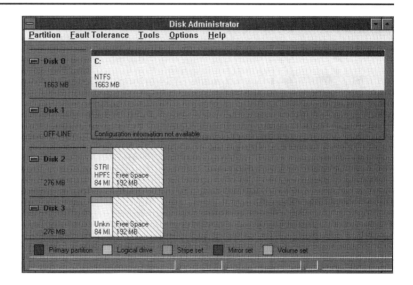

The next sidebar reviews how to regenerate a failed stripe set.

How Do I Regenerate a Failed Stripe Set?

To regenerate a failed stripe set:

1. Put a new disk in place and reboot the system.

2. After you've logged on, go to the Disk Administrator and select both the stripe set that you need to fix and an area of free space at least equal in size to the other members of the set.

3. Choose Regenerate from the Fault Tolerance menu.

The system will shut down, and the regeneration process will take place in the background after it restarts. The regeneration process doesn't affect your ability to use the computer or access the information being regenerated.

TIP

When you're regenerating an NTFS stripe set with parity, make sure that you have a new disk in the system. When a disk goes bad and you're trying to regenerate its data onto a new one, NT Server will not gray out the Regenerate option even if you don't have a new disk in yet to put the data on. Instead, it will tell you that the stripe set with that number has been recovered, but when you reboot and check the Disk Administrator, you'll see that the stripe set is still listed as "Recoverable."

Deleting a Stripe Set

Deleting a stripe set is quite simple. It is explained in the next "How Do I" sidebar.

How Do I Delete a Stripe Set?

To delete a stripe set:

1. In the Disk Administrator, select the stripe that you want to delete.

2. From the Partition drop-down menu, select Delete. You'll see a message advising you that this action will delete all the data and asking you to confirm that you want to do this.

3. Click on the Yes button in this dialog box.

Don't forget that deleting a stripe set destroys the data in it—even the parity information!

Things to Remember about Disk Striping with Parity

Keep these things is mind when it comes to disk striping with parity:

- When you first set up the stripe set and reboot, the rebooting process will take longer than it normally does, as the system must initialize the stripe set before it can be used.

- Striping with parity has a greater initial cost than disk mirroring does (it requires a minimum of three disks, rather than two) but allows you to get more use out of your disk space.

- Although you can access the information in a stripe set even after one of the members has failed, you should regenerate the set as quickly as possible. NT Server striping cannot cope with more than one error in the set, so you're sunk if anything happens to the unregenerated stripe set.

- Striping with parity places greater demands on your system than disk mirroring, so you may get better performance from your system if you add 2MB of RAM to the system minimum of 16MB.

- If you have fewer than three physical hard disks on your server, you cannot make stripe sets with parity. The option in the Fault Tolerance menu will be grayed out.

Working with NTFS

NTFS is the filing system especially designed for use with Windows NT and NT Server. It's significantly different from the FAT system that you're used to if you've been working with DOS:

- NTFS supports file names up to 256 characters long (including spaces and periods), with multiple extensions; FAT supports 8-character file names with 3-character extensions.

- NTFS is designed for system security (i.e., setting file permissions); FAT is not. (You can, however, restrict access to directories even when using FAT.) To learn how file permissions work, see Chapter 8, "Using the File Manager."

- NTFS preserves upper- and lowercase file names (although it does not distinguish between upper- and lowercase when searching for file names); of course, FAT does not.

- FAT is not equipped to deal with the stripe sets, volume sets, and mirror sets, so any of these partitions will be invisible to anyone trying to read them from DOS.

- NTFS keeps a log of activities in order to be able to restore the disk after a power failure or other interruptions.

In short, Table 4.1 gives you an at-a-glance comparison of NTFS and FAT.

TABLE 4.1: File System Comparisons

	NTFS	FAT
File Name Length	256 characters	8 + 3 characters
File Attributes	Extended	Limited
Associated Operating System	NT *and* NT Server	DOS
Organization	Tree structure	Centrally located menu
Multidisk Drives?	Yes	No
Software RAID Support?	Yes	No

NTFS Naming Conventions

NTFS file names can be up to 256 characters long with the extension, including spaces and separating periods. You can use any upper- or lowercase character in an NTFS file name except the following characters, which have special significance to NT:

?   "   /   \   <   >   * | :

Even though NTFS supports long file names, it maintains its compatibility with DOS by automatically generating a conventional FAT file name for every file. The process doesn't work in reverse, however, so don't save a file when working with an application that doesn't support long file names—it will save the file to the FAT name and erase all memory of the NTFS file name. The data won't be erased, however; only the descriptive file name will be affected.

When converting a long file name to the FAT format, NT Server does the following:

- Removes spaces

- Removes periods, all except the last one that is followed by a character—this period is assumed to herald the beginning of the file extension

- Removes any characters not allowed in DOS names and converts them to underscores

- Converts the name to six characters, with a tilde (~) and a number attached to the end

- Truncates the extension to three characters

Given how NT Server converts NTFS file names to FAT conventions, you may want to keep in mind how the conversions are made when using long file names, so that your file names make sense in both FAT and NTFS. For example, you could name a file PRSNLLET-Personal letters file.SAM, so that the shortened name would be PRSNLLET.SAM.

File Forking and Extended Attributes

Two of the things that make NTFS extra easy to work with are its ability to use file forking and extended attributes.

File forking is a term that up to now has only been used in the Mac world, so don't be surprised if it sounds unfamiliar. Essentially it's an association, so that if one file gets opened another one, associated with the first, gets opened too. AmiPro, a Windows word processor, saves files with a .SAM extension. Due to file association, if you open a .SAM file from the File Manager, a copy of the AmiPro program will open to support it. Under true file forking, each Ami document would contain a small program that would tell NT to start up Ami. That would allow an Ami document to have *any* extension, instead of requiring the .SAM extension.

Like file forking, *extended attributes* is a concept that sounds much trickier than it is. If you're familiar with DOS, then you're familiar with file attributes. You can attach an attribute to a file to say that it has been modified since the last backup, that this file should be read-only, or that the file should be a hidden or system file. You do this by setting the *archive bit* on that file to whatever you like.

FAT's attributes are limited, however. You can say that a file should be read-only, but you can't identify that file as the last CONFIG.SYS that you got to work properly on your machine. NTFS, on the other hand, allows you to tack extended attributes onto file names to give you a more complete description of what a file is for. Essentially, in combination with its ability to handle 256-character file names, NTFS's extended attributes give your system a somewhat more Mac-like feel. You're no longer dependent on FAT's 8+3 naming conventions or limited attributes.

Long Names on Floppies

NT's NTFS support sort of slops over into floppies. You can't format a floppy to NTFS format—if you try, you'll get the error message "Cannot lock current drive"—but you *can* create files with long names on a floppy.

NT keeps two names for floppy files, the long name that you originally assigned, and a truncated 8+3 name. The long name is disguised as a directory entry with meaningless information inside it, and so DOS ignores it. DOS *does* see the shorter 8+3 name, however, making it possible for you to work with files that have long names under NT but short names under DOS.

CHAPTER

FIVE

The Registry Database

5

If you've ever been a DOS and Windows user, let me ask you a question. (If you've never been one, then just try not to smirk, okay?) Wouldn't it be neat if you could keep old combinations of CONFIG.SYS/AUTOEXEC.BAT files, combinations that you could name "configuration that I'm *sure* works," "test configuration with those crufty TCP/IP drivers," and the like? Then wouldn't it be neat to be able to store not just CONFIG.SYS and AUTOEXEC.BAT, but configuration files for *all* of your applications, your WIN.INI files, and SYSTEM.INI files?

Better yet, how about if you could smoosh together all of those configuration files into one nicely organized database, with a unified editor for all of the files? And, while we're at it, why not set up the editor so that whenever one of these initialization files gets updated, it's done so that the database can't be damaged, even by a power failure in the middle of the update process?

I'd say that it sounds pretty nifty.

Which is why you've just gotta like NT's Registry.

What Is the Registry?

The Registry is a hierarchical database of settings, much like INI files, describing your user account, the hardware of the server machine, and your applications. Knowing how to work with it is an important key to being able to tune and control your NT servers and NT workstations.

Now, editing the Registry is likely the part that you *won't* like about NT. It's not documented with the pile of manuals that come with NT Server, but it's referred to in many of the Microsoft help files, and in bug fix reports. You're just supposed to *understand* phrases like the following:

> "You can ... force a computer to be a Browse Master by opening HKEY_LO-CAL_MACHINE\SYSTEM\CurrentControlSet\Services\Browser\Parameters, and creating an IsDomainMasterBrowser value, defining it as type REG_SZ, and specifying the text TRUE for the value of the string."

Registry Terminology

What did that last paragraph mean? To get a first insight, let's look at the Registry. You see it by running the program REGEDT32.EXE (it's in the C:\WINNT35\SYSTEM32 directory), or by accessing it through WINMSD.EXE. An initial screen like the one in Figure 5.1 appears.

FIGURE 5.1:

Registry Editor dialog box

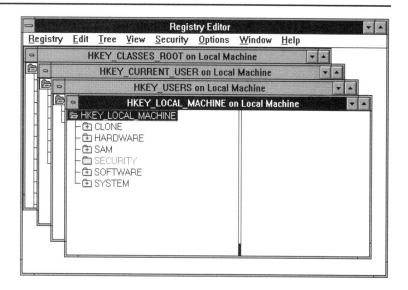

The terms to know in order to understand the Registry are subtree, key, value, data type, and hive. All are explained below.

It's easy to accidentally blast some important data with the Registry Editor, so it might be a good idea at this point to put the Editor in *read-only* mode by clicking on Options, then Read Only Mode. You can always reverse the read-only state whenever necessary in the same way.

Subtrees

The Registry stores all information about a computer and its users by dividing them up into four *subtrees*. These subtrees provide a rough division of the kinds of Registry information:

Subtree	Description
HKEY_LOCAL_MACHINE	Contains information about the hardware currently installed in the machine, and programs and systems running on the machine. You'll do most of your work in this subtree.
HKEY_CLASSES_ROOT	Holds the file associations, information that tells the system "whenever the user double-clicks on a file with the extension BMP in the File Manager, start up PBRUSH.EXE to view this file." It also contains the OLE registration database, the old REG.DAT from Windows 3.x. This is actually a redundant subtree, as all of the information in this subtree is found in the HKEY_LOCAL_MACHINE subtree.
HKEY_USERS	Contains two user profiles, a DEFAULT profile used for someone logging in who hasn't logged in before, and a profile with a name like S-228372162…, which is the profile of a user already known to the system. The long number starting with the *S* is the Security ID of the user.
HKEY_CURRENT_USER	Contains the user profile for the person currently logged onto the NT Server machine.

Sometimes there is conflicting information in these subtrees. For example, data in HKEY_CURRENT_USER may include some of the same parameters as HKEY_LOCAL_MACHINE; in that case, HKEY_CURRENT_USER takes precedence.

Registry Keys

In the Figure 5.1, you saw the Registry Editor display four cascaded windows, one for each subtree. HKEY_LOCAL_MACHINE was is the front; you can see the other three subtrees' windows behind it. HKEY_LOCAL_MACHINE's window has a right and left pane to it. The left-hand pane, a tree structure of folder icons, looks kind of like a screen from the File Manager.

In the File Manager, those folders represent subdirectories. Here, however, they separate information into sections, kind of in the same way that old Windows INI files have sections whose names are surrounded by square brackets, names like [386enh], [network], [boot], and the like. Referring back to the HKEY_LOCAL_MACHINE screen in Figure 5.1, let's compare this to an INI file. If this were an INI file, then the name of its sections would be [hardware], [sam], [security], [software], and [system]. Each of those folders or sections are actually called *keys* in the Registry.

But here's where the analogy to INI files fails: You can have keys within keys, called *subkeys* (and sub-subkeys, and sub-sub-subkeys, and so on). I've opened the SYSTEM key, and you can see that it contains subkeys named Clone, ControlSet001, ControlSet002, CurrentControlSet, Select, and Setup, and that CurrentControlSet is further subkeyed into Control and Services.

Notice, by the way, the key called CurrentControlSet. It's very important. Almost every time that you modify your system's configuration, you'll be doing it with a subkey within the CurrentControlSet subkey.

Key Naming Conventions

The tree of keys gets pretty big as you drill down through the many layers. CurrentControlSet, for example, has dozens of subkeys, and each of *those* subkeys can have subkeys. Identifying a given subkey is important, so Microsoft has adopted a naming convention that looks just like directory trees. CurrentControlSet's fully specified name would be, then, HKEY_LOCAL_MACHINE\SYSTEM\CurrentControlSet. In this book, however, I'll just call it CurrentControlSet, or else the key names will get too long to fit on a single line.

Value Entries, Names, Values, and Data Types

If I drill down through CurrentControlSet, I'll find a subkey named Services, and within Services, there will be many subkeys. In Figure 5.2, you can see some of the subkeys of CurrentControlSet\Services.

FIGURE 5.2:

Subkeys of
CurrentControlSet\Services

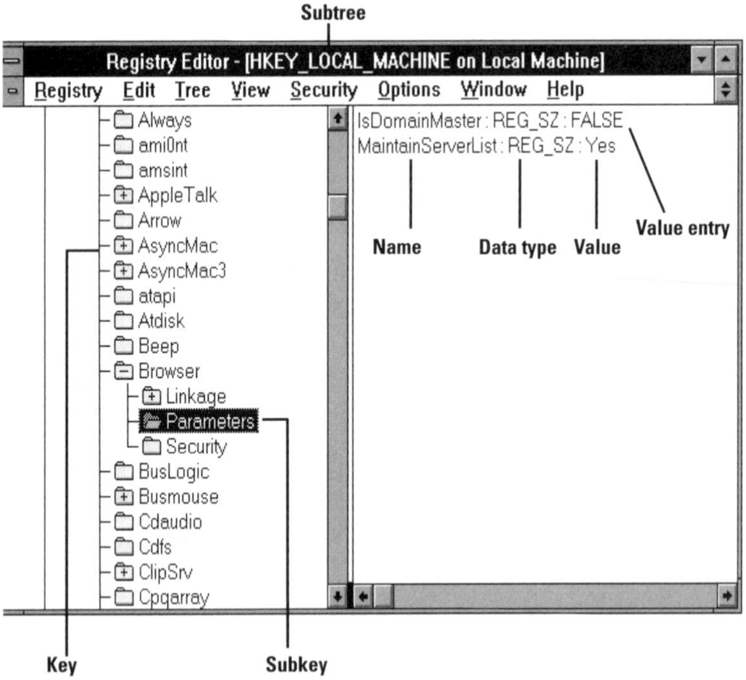

One of those keys, Browser, contains subkeys named Linkage, Parameters, and Security. Once we get to Parameters, however, you can see that it's the end of the line—no subkeys from there. Just to quickly review Registry navigation, the key that we're looking at now is in HKEY_LOCAL_MACHINE\SYSTEM\CurrentControlSet\Services\Browser\Parameters.

In the right-hand pane, you see two lines:

```
IsDomainMaster : REG_SZ : False
MaintainServerList : REG_SZ : Yes
```

This is how the registry describes what would be, in the old INI-type files, something like this:

```
IsDomainMasterBrowser=No
MaintainServerList=Yes
```

Each line like IsDomainMaster:REG_SZ:Yes is called a *value entry*. The three parts are called a *name*, *data type*, and *value*, respectively. In this example, IsDomainMaster is the *name*, REG_SZ is the *data type*, and Yes is the *value*.

Microsoft notes that each value entry cannot exceed about 1MB in size. It's hard to imagine one that size, but it's worth mentioning.

What is that REG_SZ stuff? It's an identifier to the Registry of what *kind* of data to expect: numbers, messages, yes/no values, and the like. There are five data types in the Registry Editor (although others could be defined later):

Data Type	Description
REG_BINARY	Refers to raw binary data. Data of this type usually doesn't make sense when you look at it with the Registry Editor. Binary data shows up in hardware setup information. If there is an alternative way to enter this data other than via the Registry Editor—and I'll discuss that in a page or two—then do it that way. Editing binary data can get you in trouble if you don't know what you're doing. The data is usually represented in hex for simplicity's sake.

Data Type	Description
REG_DWORD	Is another binary data type, but it is 4 bytes long.
REG_EXPAND_SZ	Is a character string of variable size. Often the information can be understood by humans, like path statements or messages. It is "expandable" in that it may contain information that will change at run time, like %username%—a system batch variable that will be of different sizes for different people's names.
REG_MULTI_SZ	Is another string type, but it allows you to enter a number of parameters on this one value entry. The parameters are separated by binary zeroes (nulls).
REG_SZ	Is a simple string.

Working with the Registry: An Example

Enough talking. Let's try modifying something with the Registry Editor. Before we do, however, I have to underscore a point: You must be *very* careful when working with the Registry Editor. It is very easy to render your system totally unusable with the Registry Editor. At least until you figure out what you're doing, it's probably best to stick to the book. In any case, you edit your Registry at your own risk.

That's not just boilerplate. Don't get mad at *me* if you blow up your server because you didn't pay attention. In any case, if you *do* mess up your Registry Editor, you can always reboot the server and wait for the message that says "Press spacebar now to restore Last Known Good menu." That's NT-ese for "Press the spacebar and I'll restore the last control set that booted well for you." Unfortunately, however, that doesn't restore the entire Registry, just the control set; fortunately, the control set is a *lot* of the Registry.

In any case, let's try something out, something relatively harmless: Let's change the background color of your desktop. This won't work if you've got a bitmap loaded, so remove any bitmaps on your desktop. (Go to the Control Panel and open the Desktop applet, then choose None under Wallpaper.) Then change your Desktop's background color to medium gray with these steps:

1. Open the Registry Editor. From the Program Manager, click File and then Run.

2. In the Command Line field, type **REGEDT32** and press Enter.

3. Click Window, and choose HKEY_CURRENT_USER on Local Machine. Maximize that window and you'll see a screen similar to the one in Figure 5.3.

FIGURE 5.3:

Registry Editor—
[HKEY_CURRENT_USER on Local Machine] dialog box

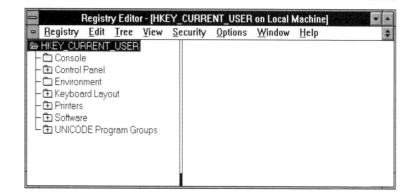

4. We're going to modify the value entry in HKEY_CURRENT_USER\Control Panel\Colors. Double-click on the Control Panel key, and you'll see the key's folder icon open up. Double-click on the key named Colors and you'll see a screen like the one in Figure 5.4.

On the left pane, you still the see the Registry structure. On the right you see the value entries in the Colors subkey.

FIGURE 5.4:

Control Panel—Colors

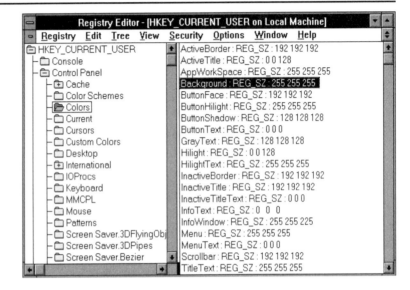

5. Double-click on Background and you'll see a screen like the one in Figure 5.5.

6. Highlight the three numbers and replace them with the value **128**. Click OK, and close up the Registry Editor.

7. Close down all of your running programs and log off.

8. Log back on under your normal user name. You will see a medium gray background.

How Do You Find Registry Keys?

How did I know that I had to go to HKEY_CURRENT_USER\Control Panel\Colors to modify my screen background? Partly by guesswork. I knew that things like desktop colors weren't global to the system, because if you and I both use the same NT machine, you can have wallpaper, color, and sounds that are completely different from my wallpaper, color, and sounds. So HKEY_CURRENT_USER seemed like the right place to look. Once I saw the Control Panel key, it was simple.

FIGURE 5.5:

String Editor dialog box

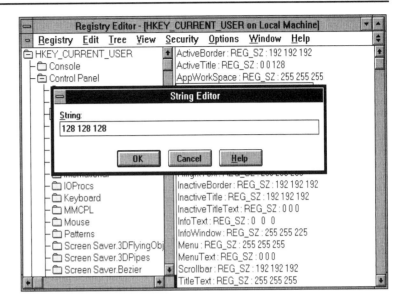

If you have the Windows NT Resource Kit from Microsoft—and if you don't, then *get it!*—then you'll find 150 pages detailing each and every key. (That, by the way, is why there isn't a complete key guide in this book. First of all, there wasn't anything that I could add to what's in the Resource Kit; second of all, Microsoft has already published the Kit; and third of all, 150 pages directly lifted from someone else's publication is a pretty serious copyright violation, and I don't think it was possible to "paraphrase" 150 pages of reference material.) Additionally, the Registry keys are documented in an on-line help file.

If you do *not* have the Resource Kit, you can download the Registry key help file from the WINNT forum on CompuServe.

Let's see how to find something tougher, however. Let's find out where the user-definable settings for the File Manager are. In File Manager, you can click on Options/Confirmation, and control what the File Manager will and won't require confirmations for. Where does all that reside?

The key (no pun intended) to finding something is in the View/Find Key command in the Registry Editor. I'll start looking in HKEY_LOCAL_MACHINE, for no other reason than a lot of things are in there. First I click on the root of the subtree (the folder labeled HKEY_LOCAL_MACHINE), and then I choose View/Find Key. I get a dialog box like the one you see in Figure 5.6.

FIGURE 5.6:

Registry Editor—Find dialog box

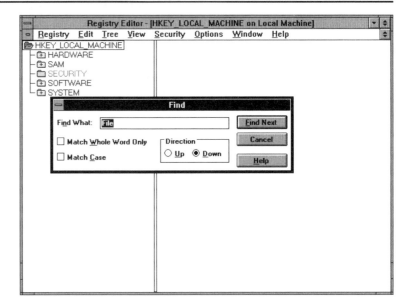

I enter **File** and uncheck the Match Whole Word Only criterion. The word *file* appears a few times, but not in reference to the File Manager. The first interesting-looking match is to something called SOFTWARE\Microsoft\WindowsNT\CurrentVersion\File Manager (your first match may be different, as your system won't be identical to mine). Opening that key shows only one subkey, called AddOns, as you see in Figure 5.7.

That's only relevant to some reference to Mail, so keep clicking Find Next. A couple of items later, you'll see another reference to something relevant to the File Manager. That next matching key is still in SOFTWARE\Microsoft\Windows NT\CurrentVersion, but the subkey name is now IniFileMapping\Winfile.INI; it could look something like Figure 5.8.

FIGURE 5.7:

Registry Editor—Finding the
AddOns subkey

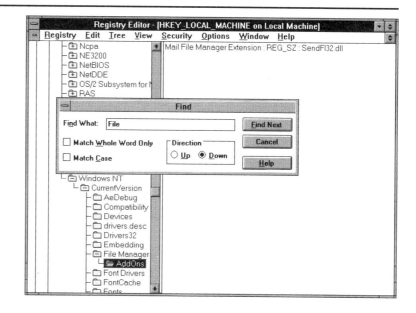

FIGURE 5.8:

Registry Editor—Winfile.INI

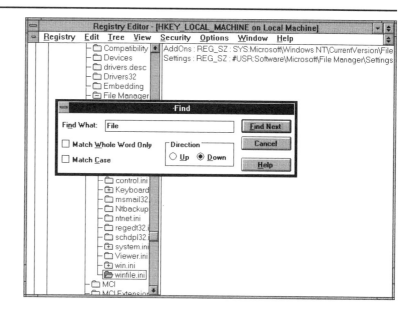

On the right-hand pane is a reference to Settings. It refers us to #USR:Software\Microsoft\File Manager\Settings.

Now, that *looks* like a key reference, but there *is* no Software\Microsoft\File Manager\Settings in HKEY_LOCAL_HARDWARE. Notice the #USR:; it indicates that the subkey is in a user settings file. (You'll meet them when we discuss *hives* later in this chapter.) Bring that window up, and you'll see a screen somewhat like the one in Figure 5.9.

Aha! Now, *that* looks like the File Manager settings! From the looks of the value entries, it looks like 0=unselected and 1=selected.

Using Find Key, you can poke around the Registry and figure out where keys are. But it's time for some more cautions....

FIGURE 5.9:

Registry Editor—Settings

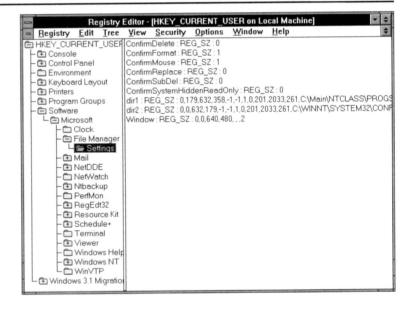

Cautions about Editing the Registry

If you're just learning about the Registry, then you're probably eager to wade right in and modify a value entry. Before you do, however, let me just talk a bit about using caution in manipulating the Registry.

The vast majority of Registry items correspond to some setting in the Control Panel, Server Manager, User Manager for Domains, or the like. For example, you just saw how we could change screen colors or File Manager confirmation options directly via the Registry Editor.

I only picked those examples, however, because they were fairly illustrative and simple to understand. In general, *don't use the Registry to modify a value that can be modified otherwise.*

For example, take the background color, which I set to (128, 128, 128). How did I know what those color values meant? Because they're the same as Windows 3.x color values. Color values in Windows are expressed as number triplets. Each number is an integer between 0 and 255. If I'd entered a value greater than 255, the Registry Editor would neither have known nor cared that I was punching in an illegal color value. Now, in the case of colors, that probably wouldn't crash the system. In the case of *other* items, however, you could easily render your system unusable. For example, I'm running NT Server on a system with just a single 486 processor, so the Registry reflects that, noting in one of the Hardware keys that NT is running a "uniprocessor" mode. Altering that to a multiprocessor mode wouldn't be a very good idea.

Why, then, am I bothering to tell you about the Registry Editor? Three reasons.

First, there are settings—important settings—that can only be altered via the Registry Editor, so there's no getting around the fact that an NT expert must have some proficiency with the Editor.

Second, you can use the Registry Editor to change system value entries on *remote* computers. To use a very simple example, if I'm at location A and I wanted to change the background color on the server at location B, I'd have to physically travel to location B in order to run the Control Panel on the NT machine at location B. Instead, I can just start up the Registry Editor, choose Registry/Select Computer, and edit the Registry of the remote computer. (This assumes that you are running NT Server and that you have the security access to change the registry of the remote computer—that is, you're a member of the Administrators group on that computer.)

Third, there is a program that comes with the Resource Kit called REGINI.EXE that allows you to write scripts to modify Registries. Such a tool is quite powerful; in theory, you could write a REGINI script to completely reconfigure an NT setup. Again, however, before you start messing with that program, *please* be sure that you have developed some proficiency with the Registry. I've explained some of the kinds of mischief that you can cause working by hand with the Registry Editor; imagine what kinds of *automated* disasters you could start at 66 MHz with a bad REGINI script!

Hives in the Registry

The Registry is partly contained in a set of files called the *hives*. Hives are binary files, so there's no way to look at them without a special editor of some kind (the Registry Editor, in fact). They are, however, an easy way to load or back up a sizable part of the Registry.

Most, although not all, of the Registry is stored in hive files. They're not hidden, system, or read-only, but then you can't really do anything with the Registry Editor without Administrator privilege, so I guess there's no need in making it difficult to get to these files, as you can't do anything with them unless you are an Administrator anyway.

The hive files are in \WINNT35\SYSTEM32\CONFIG directory. You can see the hive 01files that correspond to parts of the subtree in the Table 5.1. You can always find out what files correspond to Registry keys by looking in HKEY_LOCAL_MACHINE\SOFTWARE\Microsoft\Windows NT\CurrentVersion.

Table 5.1 needs a few notes to clarify it. First, about the HKEY_CLASSES_ROOT subtree: It is copied from HKEY_LOCAL_MACHINE\SOFTWARE\Classes at boot time. The file exists for the use of 16-bit Windows applications. While you're logged onto NT, however, the two keys are linked; if you make a change to one, then the change is reflected in the other.

TABLE 5.1: Hive Files

Subtree/Key	File Name
HKEY_LOCAL_MACHINE\SAM	SAM (primary) and SAM.LOG (backup)
HKEY_LOCAL_MACHINE\SECURITY	SECURITY (primary) and SECURITY.LOG (backup)
HKEY_LOCAL_MACHINE\SOFTWARE	SOFTWARE (primary) and SOFTWARE.LOG (backup)
HKEY_LOCAL_MACHINE\SYSTEM	SYSTEM (primary) and SYSTEM.ALT (backup)
HKEY_USERS\DEFAULT	DEFAULT (primary) and DEFAULT.LOG (backup)
HKEY_USERS\Security ID	xxxxxnnn, xxxxnnn.LOG
HKEY_CURRENT_USER	USER### *or* ADMIN### (primary), USER###.LOG, ADMIN###.LOG (backups); ###=system ID for user
HKEY_CLASSES_ROOT	(Created from current control set at boot time)

The reference to HKEY_USERS\Security ID is to the strange-looking keys that you'll see under HKEY_USERS; for example, on my workstation, I have a subtree that looks like the one in Figure 5.10.

FIGURE 5.10:
HKEY_USERS dialog box

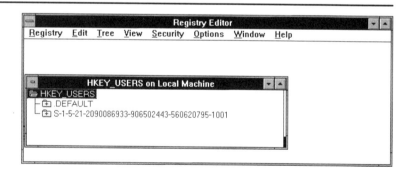

There are two keys: DEFAULT is just a default user environment. It is stored in a hive file called DEFAULT in the \WINNT35\SYSTEM32\CONFIG directory; actually, it's a *profile*, a special hive file that keeps track of user preferences. The second, S-1-5-21-2090086933-906502443-560620795-1001, is the internal Windows NT security ID for my supervisor account. Unless you knew that my user name is MarkS

(Mark in Supervisor mode), you would have no way of knowing that the profile that created that key was called MARKS000. If I look in \WINNT35\SYSTEM32\CONFIG on my machine, then I see a directory like the one in Figure 5.11.

FIGURE 5.11:

File Manager for
c:\winnt35\system32\config

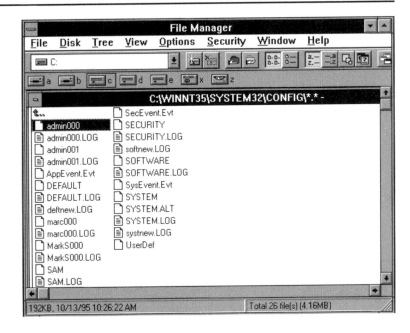

Marc000 refers to my nonsupervisor account, and ADMIN000 refers to the Administrator account. You can see the user profiles on your system by looking at the subkeys of \HKEY_LOCAL_MACHINE\SOFTWARE\Microsoft\WindowsNT\CurrentVersion\ProfileList. User profiles on my system are shown in Figure 5.12.

One question remains about the user profiles, however. Why do all the files have a paired file with the extension LOG? Read on.

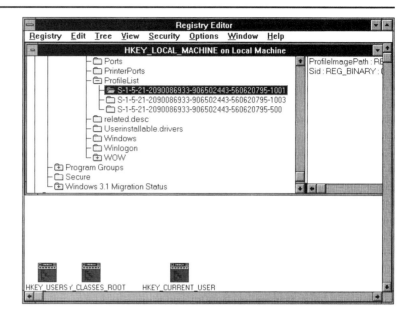

FIGURE 5.12:
User profiles

Fault Tolerance in the Registry

Notice that every hive file has another file with the same name but the extension LOG. That's really useful, because NT Server and, for that matter, NT workstations use LOG files to protect the Registry during updates.

Whenever a hive file is to be changed, the change is first written into its LOG file. The LOG file isn't actually a backup file; it's more a journal of changes to the primary file. Once the description of the change to the hive file is complete, the journal file is written to disk. When I say "written to disk" here, I *mean* written to disk; often a disk write ends up hanging around in the disk cache for a while, but this write is "flushed" to disk. Then the system makes the changes to the hive file based on the information in the journal file. If the system crashes during the hive write operation, there's enough information in the journal file to "roll back" the hive to its previous position.

The exception to this procedure comes with the SYSTEM hive. The SYSTEM hive is really important, as it contains the CurrentControlSet. For that reason, the backup file for SYSTEM, SYSTEM.ALT, is a complete backup of SYSTEM. If one file is damaged, the system can use the other to boot.

Notice that HKEY_LOCAL_MACHINE\HARDWARE does not have a hive. That's because the key is rebuilt each time you boot, so that NT can adapt itself to changes in computer hardware. The program NTDETECT.COM, which runs at boot time, gathers the information that NT needs to create HKEY_LOCAL_MACHINE\HARDWARE.

Confused about where all the keys come from? You'll find a recap in Table 5.2. It's similar to Table 5.1, but it's more specific about how the keys are built at boot time.

TABLE 5.2: Construction of Keys at Boot Time

Key	How Constructed at Boot Time
HKEY_LOCAL_MACHINE:	
HARDWARE	NTDETECT.COM
SAM	SAM hive file
SECURITY	SECURITY hive file
SOFTWARE	SOFTWARE hive file
SYSTEM	SYSTEM hive file
HKEY_CLASSES_ROOT	SYSTEM hive file, Classes subkey
HKEY_USERS_DEFAULT	DEFAULT hive file
HKEY_USERS\Sxxx	username000 hive file
HKEY_CURRENT_USER	username000 hive file

Remote Registry Modification

You can modify another computer's Registry—perhaps to repair it or to do some simple kind of remote maintenance—by loading that computer's hive. You do that with the Registry Editor by using the Load Hive or Unload Hive commands.

You can only load or unload the hives for HKEY_USERS and HKEY_LOCAL_MACHINE. The Load Hive option only appears if you're selected one of those two subtrees; Unload Hive is only available if you've selected a subkey of one of those two subtrees.

Why specifically would you load a hive, or a remote registry?

First of all, you might load a hive in order to get to a user's profile. Suppose a user has set up all of his or her colors as black on black, making understanding the screen impossible? You could load the hive that corresponds to that user, modify it, and then unload it.

Second, you can use the remote feature to view basically *anything* on a remote system. Suppose you want to do something as simple as changing screen colors. You'd do that on a local system by running the Control Panel, but the Control Panel won't work for remote systems. Answer: Load the Registry remotely.

You could load and save hive files to a floppy disk, walk the floppy over to a malfunctioning machine, and load the hive onto the machine's hard disk, potentially repairing a system problem. This isn't possible if you're using NTFS, unless you have multiple copies of NT on your system, something most of us don't have; but if you have an NT workstation running a FAT file system, then you can always boot from DOS and replace the hive files under DOS, then reboot under NT.

When you boot under NT, you see the reference to a "known good menu." That's because NT keeps track of not only the current control set, it also keeps the *previous* control set. That way, if you messed up your system, you can always roll back to the previous configuration. Those control sets are kept in the same key as the CurrentControlSet. Within HKEY_LOCAL_MACHINE\SYSTEM\Select\Current, \Default, \Failed, and \LastKnownGood are numbers indicating which of the two kept control sets are failed, current, good, and the like.

Backing Up and Restoring a Registry

The Resource Kit includes two useful utilities. REGREST.EXE allows you to restore a registry file.

I should note that the best way to restore registries is through the NTBACKUP program. Using a tape drive is the simplest way to put a registry back on your system. Only use REGBACK/REGREST if you don't have a tape drive.

The REGBACK.EXE program allows you to back up a registry file; the REGREST.EXE restores it.

CHAPTER

SIX

Monitoring Your System with WINMSD

6

WINMSD

If you want nuts-and-bolts information about the hardware on your NT Server server, you *could* go to the documentation for all your hardware and read all the notes you made about changes to the default configurations. Even the most dedicated record keeper won't have information about everything, however, and NT Server keeps information about your system that you might never have known you had. To get a more complete idea of the picture, then, you can check with WINMSD, the Windows NT diagnostics.

WINMSD is in the Administrative Tools group, under the name Windows NT Diagnostics.

Before we get into the details of WINMSD, let me make clear that this is not a terribly powerful tool. It won't solve a *lot* of problems. Its main value is that it allows you to take a quick "bird's-eye" view of a system, something of considerable use if you've been called in to look at a problem on a server that you've not looked at before.

Once you have the icon in the Program Manager, you're ready to view your configuration information. Double-click on the icon, and you'll see a screen that looks like the one in Figure 6.1.

FIGURE 6.1:
Opening WINMSD screen

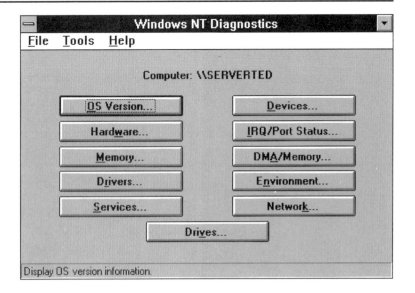

Each button on this screen connects you with different information about your hardware. If you place the mouse cursor on a button and hold the mouse button down, a message appears in the lower-left part of the screen telling you what that button is for. In Figure 6.1, the message is "Display OS version information."

TIP WINMSD only offers you information—you can't use it to change anything. (You'll notice that if you click in the text boxes and try to type.) To make changes, you need the Control Panel or the Registry Editor (accessible from the Tools menu, as we'll discuss later). All that you can do from WINMSD is view information, or select and copy it to paste into place if you modify the Registry Editor.

Let's discuss the information that WINMSD offers you.

WINMSD System Information

First of all, WINMSD provides you with information about your system: what operating system you're using, the memory you have available, what hardware is in place, and so on. Push the OS Version... button and you'll get a screen like the one in Figure 6.2.

OS Version Information

Most of the information on the OS Version screen is self-explanatory. From here, you can see the installation date, who this copy of NT Server is registered to (as defined during the installation process), the version number, what CSD is installed (CSD stands for *Corrective Service Diskettes*, the program patches released by Microsoft now and then to fix known NT bugs), and the system root directory.

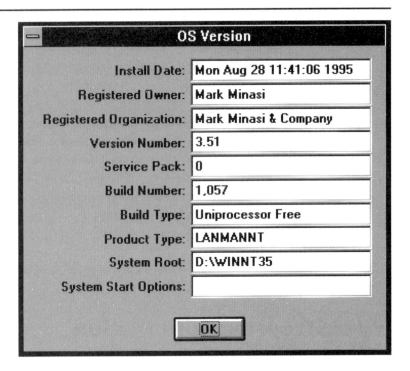

The build type and build number refer to sub-versions of the main version. The process of writing code is an ongoing one, but there comes a point at which someone at Microsoft (or any software company) has to say, "Okay, that's enough modifications." When that happens, the current version of the code gets labeled with a build number and set aside. That doesn't mean that the current version is the final version that goes out the door as version 3.5 (or whatever), but it's a step along the way. The build type and build number are a way of keeping track of modifications.

The information on the OS Version screen really can't be changed without reinstalling NT Server, but since the only point of this dialog box is to remind you of when you installed NT, where you installed it, and to whom it's registered, that doesn't really matter. What *is* important is the CSD number. As time goes on, you'll find that Microsoft releases CSDs, also called "service packs," to fix errors great and small. Get the CSDs and apply them, as they're important. WINMSD can help because you can quickly see whether or not the latest CSDs have been applied to the machine that you're working on. I spent many an hour trying to fix something on a client's NT server only to realize that the client hadn't installed the latest service pack. Eventually I wised up, and ran WINMSD first thing to find out the latest service pack.

Hardware Information

The Hardware opening screen is shown in Figure 6.3. This screen is a little more obscure than the OS Version screen, but not by much. You see here information about your system BIOS (Basic Input/Output System) and video BIOS, your video resolution, and your CPU type. With the possible exception of the BIOS dates, you probably knew all this already.

The page size is perhaps a little trickier; it's the amount of data that can be passed back and forth when NT Server or NT is using virtual memory—in this case, 4KB. What is virtual memory? In order to get more work out of the system RAM than it could provide on its own, NT Server uses a special file on your hard disk called a

FIGURE 6.3:

Hardware opening screen

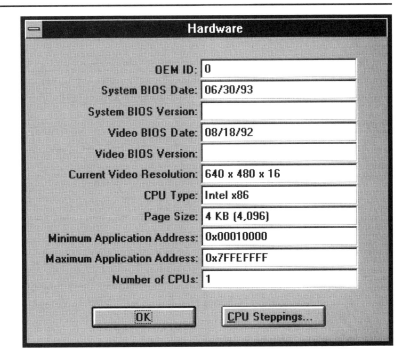

virtual memory *paging file*, or *swap file*. When NT Server is demanding more of the system memory than it can really give, it will keep some of the program code and other information in RAM, and put some of it in the paging file on the hard disk. When that information is required, NT Server pulls it out of virtual memory (swapping other information into the paging file if necessary). The end result is that you get more bang for your RAM buck.

The minimum and maximum application addresses are the beginning and ending points for the memory that applications can access. These addresses are written in hex, if you're wondering where the letters in the number came from—letters A through F are legitimate hexadecimal numerals. Applications can't touch any memory addresses above or below this range.

If you click on CPU Steppings…, the button at the bottom of the screen, you see a screen that looks like Figure 6.4. This screen tells you the kind of CPU that is in this machine. The version number that you see indicates the capabilities of that CPU. For example, one version of the 386 CPU could not do math functions properly, and you could identify it by this number. There are 32 spaces here because NT Server can support machines with up to 32 CPUs.

FIGURE 6.4:

CPU Stepping screen

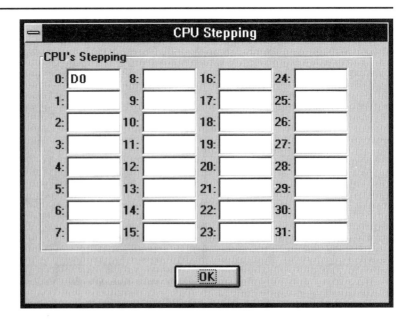

Most of the information in the opening Hardware screen (see Figure 6.3) is related to your system's physical attributes, and therefore cannot be changed (without changing, for example, your BIOS and reinstalling NT Server). Users with administrative privileges can change the paging information during installation, or they can change the paging information from the System icon in the Control Panel. You can change the video resolution from Windows NT Setup, found in the Main program group.

Memory Information

As you'd probably guess from the title, the Memory screen gives you information about your system's memory—how much it has, and how much is still available. As you can see from Figure 6.5, this server has 16MB of RAM on board (of which about 1MB is currently unused) and a 37MB paging file (of which 16MB is currently unused). You can also see where your system's paging file is located (in this case on C:\pagefile.sys) and how big it is (27MB).

The Memory Load Index (the bar at the bottom of the screen) is a measure of how much of your system's memory is being used. Up to 50, the bar shows green; between 50 and 75, it shows yellow; and then comes red. You can use this status bar

FIGURE 6.5:

Memory use screen

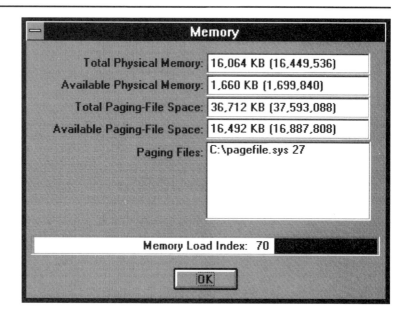

215

to get an idea of how much of your system resources are in use. Keep in mind that loading a program utilizes much more memory than *keeping* it in memory. Loading Micrografx's Designer 4.0 drawing program, for example, puts you into the red almost without fail, but keeping it open requires a lot less memory.

Drivers Information

The Driver List screen, shown in Figure 6.6, gives you a list of all the drivers that are available on the system and what their status is. (You start or stop them from the Services program in the Control Panel.)

If you double-click on one of these drivers or select one and click on Driver Details, you'll see a screen like Figure 6.7. Here, you can get more details about the drivers:

- **Service Type:** Tells you whether the driver works on hardware (Kernel Driver) or on the operating system (File System driver).
- **Start Type:** Tells you when the driver starts:

    Boot   Begins at computer bootup. Applies to drivers for hardware without which the computer cannot function, such as disk drives.

FIGURE 6.6:

Opening Drivers List screen

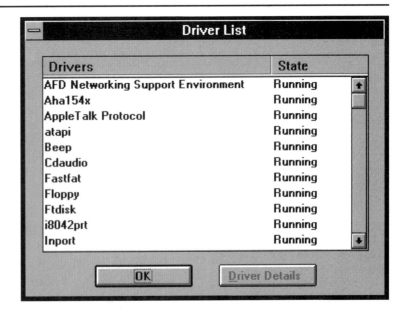

FIGURE 6.7:

Display Driver screen

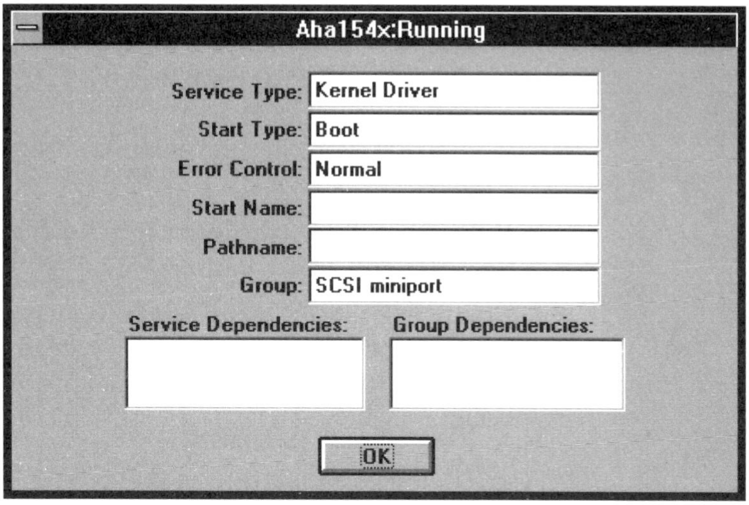

System   Begins when the operating system starts up. Applies to devices that are critical for the operation of the operating system, such as display drivers like ET4000.

Automatic   Begins when the operating system has begun, like the system drivers, but is not crucial to the operation of the operating system. The Net-BIOS interface is one example of such a driver.

Demand   Begins when started by the user or a dependent device. For example, by default the Datagram Receiver is set up to begin on demand. Microsoft refers to this kind of startup as Manual in the Devices dialog box, and I wish that they'd stuck to calling this kind of startup either Manual or Demand, so as to avoid confusion.

Disabled   These drivers cannot be started by a user, but the system can start them. This is why you may see drivers that are running but are listed disabled—that threw me for a loop the first time I noticed it. The FastFAT is one example of such a driver.

- **Error Control:** Tells you what kind of error control the drivers have. The level of error control determines what happens to the system startup if a given driver fails. The types of error control are:

    Critical   Doesn't start up the system.

217

Severe Switches to the Last Known Good setup, or, if already using that setup, continues on.

Normal Continues startup, but displays an error message stating that the driver did not load.

Ignore Doesn't halt the system or display an error message, just skips that driver.

- **Pathname:** Tells you the path where the driver is found (for some system drivers and all demand drivers).

- **Group:** Tells you the group that the drivers are associated with (SCSI miniport, video, etc.). The group that they are in determines their load order, as, for example, the boot file system loads before video, and SCSI miniports load before each of these.

Users with administrative privileges can add device drivers to the system from the Drivers icon in the Control Panel, or adjust their startup time or error control from the Devices icon. Be careful about adjusting these things, however. If you change a Boot or System driver to a different time, you could keep your system from working.

Services Information

In the screen in Figure 6.8, you can see the status of each of the services that are available on the system. Double-clicking on one of these services gets you a screen like the one in Figure 6.9, which provides more details about how that service is set up.

The screen in Figure 6.9 gives you details about the service configuration that are similar to the ones you saw about the driver configuration:

- **Service Type:** This can be either a Shared Process (interconnected with others on the network) or an Own Process (centered in the server or workstation on which it resides).

- **Start Type:** Either Automatic or On Demand (i.e., set to "Manual" in the Services dialog in the Control Panel and the user is responsible for starting it). Once again, it would have been less confusing if Microsoft could have stuck with either "Manual" or "Demand."

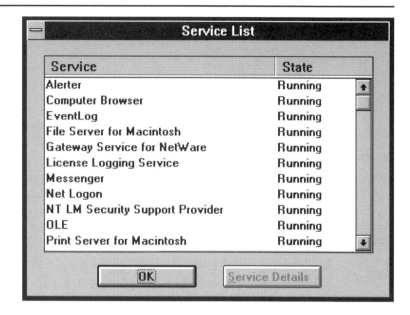

FIGURE 6.8:

Opening Service List screen

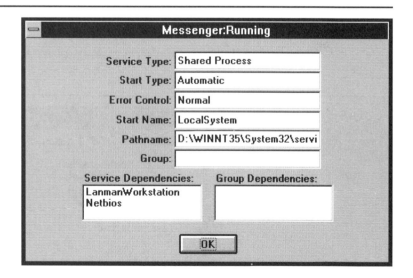

FIGURE 6.9:

Display Service screen

- **Error Control:** For all services this is set to Normal by default, meaning that if the service can't start NT Server will notify you, but the absence of this service won't affect the running of the system.

- **Start Name:** This is the account name that starts the service. By default, Local-System will be the account name, but some things (such as directory replication) may require you to put another account name on the job.

- **Pathname:** This is the path where the service's program can be found. By default, all service executable files are found in the SYSTEM32 subdirectory of your NT Server directory (WINNT35, if you kept the name that the installation program suggested).

- **Group:** Specifies the groups you belong to. Groups are covered in Chapter 7.

Users with administrative privileges can adjust the Services settings or start or stop services from the Services icon in the Control Panel.

Devices Information

The Devices screen in Figure 6.10 shows you all the devices that are present on the computer that you're working on. If you double-click on one of the items in the list or select it and click on the Display... button, you'll see a screen that looks like Figure 6.11. The information in this screen is useful if you plan to set up more hardware on your system and want to make sure that the two devices don't conflict.

You could adjust these settings by reinstalling your hardware and adjusting the IRQ and DMA settings, but in most cases that isn't necessary. This dialog box (like the

FIGURE 6.10:

Opening Devices screen

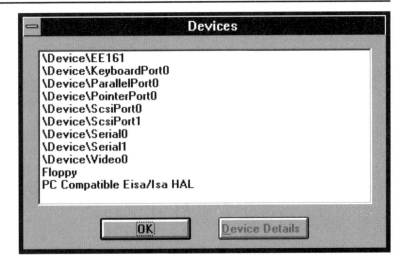

FIGURE 6.11:

Display... screen of the
Devices dialog box

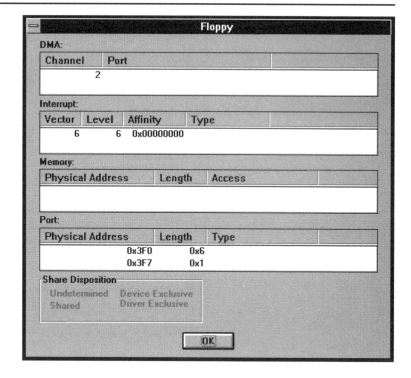

FIGURE 6.11:

Display... screen of the
Devices dialog box

ones that show the IRQs and DMA channels in use) are really for information purposes only.

DMA/Memory Status Information

The DMA/Memory status screen shows you the location and size of fixed blocks
of memory, and reports which devices are using direct memory access (DMA)
ports. The report looks like the one in Figure 6.12.

Only two devices use DMA channels on this machine: the floppy uses channel 2,
and the SCSI host adapter uses channel 7. The Memory section in the lower half of
the screen displays fixed blocks of memory, the areas of physical memory that must
not be moved by the operating system. Those areas are rare, and they typically are
buffers for peripherals. The areas displayed by WINMSD here are the video memory buffer, the video BIOS, and the SCSI BIOS on this system.

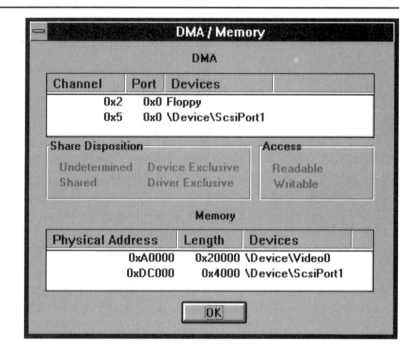

Environment Information

Every computer has information that is specific only to itself: what command interpreter it is using, what its home drive is, and the like. That information is stored in NT in the *environment*, an area of memory storing configuration-specific information. The Environment information screen is shown in Figure 6.13.

This screen provides information about the computer and the person using it: the directory in which NT or NT Server is set up, the domain the user belongs to, the computer name, and so on. This information varies depending on who is doing the looking. While the information shown here applies to the Administrator account, some of it will be different if another person logs in to check, depending on that person's user profile.

Users with administrative privileges can change this information from the System icon in the Control Panel.

FIGURE 6.13:

Environment information screen

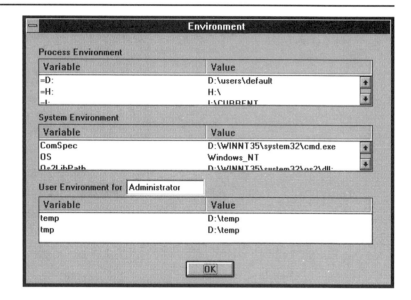

WINMSD Disk Information

Using WINMSD, you can get information about any drive connected to the server or workstation that you are working from. Whether the drives are remote (located on another computer) or local, accessing the information is done in the same way. Click the Drives button on the opening WINMSD screen to display the Drive Information screen shown in Figure 6.14.

This window is a list of every drive on the server. This list includes drive letters, not necessarily physical drives—although drive C refers here to one complete physical drive, the drive E that you see at the bottom of the list is actually a volume set that extends over two physical drives, but has only one drive letter. Drives that you access through the network also show up in this list. (For more information about logical drives versus physical drives, see Chapter 4.)

If you select one of the drives in the list and click the Details button or double-click, you'll see a screen like the one in Figure 6.15. This is the Details window for drive C. As you can see, the space information about the drives is pretty straightforward—

FIGURE 6.14:

Opening screen of the Drive
Information window

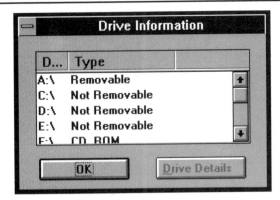

this is information about how the disk was formatted, how much space is available on the drive, and the type of file system used.

The file system information refers to what file system is on that drive and how it is configured. As you can see in the figure, this drive is formatted to NTFS, and so file names on this drive can be up to 255 characters long, including spaces and periods (that's what Maximum Component Length means). The maximum component length of a FAT drive is 12; of an HPFS drive, 254.

The flags used depends on the file system in place:

- **NTFS** Under NTFS, the case of file names is preserved (so that a file called AdvanceSales does not become advancesales or ADVANCESALES) and file names are case-sensitive (that is, AdvanceSales and ADVANCESales are two different files). Unicode—code like ASCII, but capable of using characters other than the standard alphabet—is stored on the disk. The presence of Unicode means that you could write NT applications to display using Chinese ideograms or Russian characters, rather than just using the characters found in the English alphabet. You can't do that without Unicode.

- **HPFS** If the disk is formatted to HPFS (the OS/2 file system), then case in file names is preserved, but file names are not case-sensitive—Advanced-Sales does not change to advancesales or ADVANCESALES, but HPFS cannot distinguish between the two file names. Unicode is not stored on the disk.

FIGURE 6.15:

FIGURE 6.15:

Details screen of the Drives window

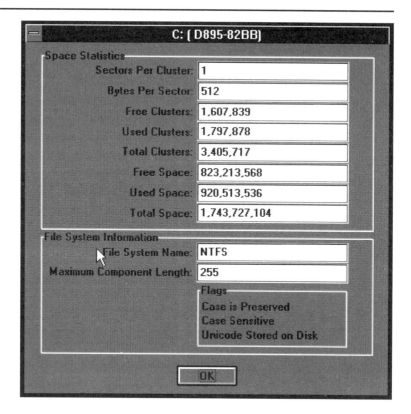

- **FAT** If the disk is formatted to FAT, then the file system does not preserve case in file names and cannot tell the difference between file names with different cases. To a FAT drive, SCARAB.DOC is the same file as scarab.doc or Scarab.Doc. Unicode is not stored on the disk.

Although WINMSD will display CD-ROM or remote drives that your machine is connected to and will display details about these drives, you cannot view details about floppy drives with the Details button.

To change the information shown here, you would use the Disk Administrator to change a drive size (or create a new logical drive) or else format a drive to a different file system.

IRQ, DMA, and Port Information

IRQ, DMA, and Port information windows, which you can get by clicking buttons on the WINMSD screen, give you information about what interrupts, memory accesses, and ports your system is using. You can't change anything with these dialog boxes, but they can help you resolve interrupt conflicts or memory errors.

IRQ/Port Status

If you click on the IRQ/Port Status button, you'll see a screen that looks like the one in Figure 6.16. From this screen, you can see what interrupts are in use, what addresses they have, and what devices are using them. Clicking on any of the entries in the list highlights the relevant information in the space below. For example, Interrupt 3 is always used by COM1 (a serial port) and is not shared with the network.

FIGURE 6.16:

Interrupts/Ports screen

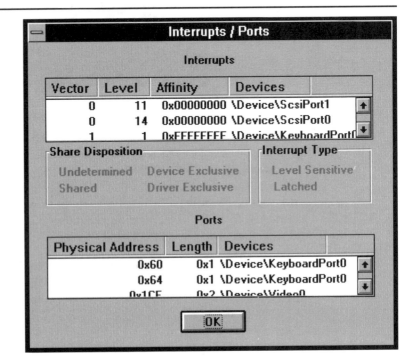

The Ports part of the screen tells you what input/output addresses are used by which devices. In this example, you see that the keyboard controller uses addresses 60 and 64 hex. What would you use this information for? It can serve as a partial guide to current port addresses on your computer, so that you don't install a new device that causes a port conflict.

Network Statistics

Click the Network button on the opening WINMSD screen and you'll get a big dialog box like the one in Figure 6.17. There's not space here to catalog all of the information in this window, but following are a few of the high points.

Network info for This is a nice summary of your machine's name, your user name, logon information, and the like.

FIGURE 6.17:
Network information dialog box

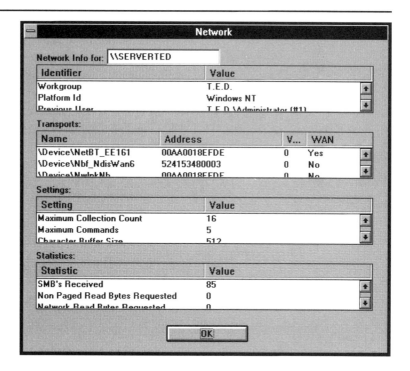

Transports   The Transports window is a nice, convenient way to find out which transport layers you're running. In theory, if you were running a TCP/IP stack, then this would be a quick way to find out what IP address you were using.

Settings   There are dozens of settings that you can use to tune an NT Server installation. This window shows you their current values. The interesting part of this window is that it can give you ideas about what kinds of things you can control with NT Server—ideas about things that you might not have known you could do. (The important ones are covered in the book, by the way, so you don't have to do any digging.)

Statistics   As the network works, statistical monitors in each computer keep track of how many bytes have been transmitted or received, how many errors occurred, and the like. This section reports those values.

The System Window

The System window reports the names and priorities of programs (processes) running in the computer, as well as printer status and active fonts. Processes, printers, and fonts seem an odd troika of "system" information to report, but perhaps this part of WINMSD is a "work in progress."

Accessing Tools from WINMSD

While you can't change anything from WINMSD itself, you can access some of the tools that allow you to change things. If you click on the Tools menu, you'll notice that you can access the Event Viewer, Disk Administrator, and Registry Editor without having to close down WINMSD. The use of these tools is dealt with extensively elsewhere in this book, so I'll just mention that you *can* get there from here and have done with it.

The only tool really relevant to this chapter is the WINMSD report. If you generate this report, all of your WINMSD information will be collected in one file for you:

all the information about each drive, each device, each service, and so on. On a typical server, the report will come to about forty pages of information. You can keep track of changes that you make to your system with this report, as each time you generate it the system will give the new report an individual name—old copies don't get overwritten.

PART III

NT Server Administration

CHAPTER

SEVEN

User Management

7

User Manager
for Domains

As an NT Server administrator, you'll rely on a few major tools to get the administrative job done:

- The User Manager for Domains creates user accounts and defines what kinds of things users can do, as well as oversees relationships between domains.

- The Server Manager lets you control what services run and what resources are shared in any of the server machines in your network. The File Manager and the Control Panel can also do some of the Server Manager's job, but only on the particular computer that you're working at; Server Manager lets you reach out and control any server on your network.

- The Print Manager controls printer access and print queues.

In the next few chapters, you'll learn how to use these tools to do your job more quickly and easily. The first, and in many ways most important, of the tools is the User Manager for Domains. (After all, networks without users are really simple to maintain, but they're not worth much.)

Introducing the User Manager for Domains

In Windows NT Server, the User Manager for Domains is the primary administrative tool for managing user accounts, groups, and security policies for domains and computers on the network.

Domains are the basic units of security and administration in an NT Server network. Recall from Chapter 2 that a domain is a collection of computers that share a common security database and browse list. Servers on the domain share security policies and all account information. In a domain with more than one server, one of the servers functions as the primary domain controller (sometimes just "domain controller"). The domain controller authenticates domain logons and maintains the master security database (which contains all user account, group, and security policy information). All other backup domain controllers in the domain have a copy of the master security database.

The absolute minimum requirement for a domain (a true bare-bones domain, as it were) is one machine running NT Server and acting as a domain controller; recall from Chapter 3 that it's possible (although not very bright) to install an NT Server machine as a mere workgroup member, forgoing any domain leadership. Optional components of a domain include additional servers, running either NT Server or LAN Manager 2.x, and other workstations (running NT, Windows for Workgroups, and DOS).

User Manager for Domains provides the network administrator with the means to:

- Create, modify, and delete user accounts in the domain
- Define a user's desktop environment and network connections
- Assign logon scripts to user accounts
- Manage groups and group membership within the accounts in a domain
- Manage trust relationships between different domains in the network
- Manage a domain's security policies

If you are an administrator, then all of the User Manager for Domains' features are available to you. If you are a member of the Account Operators group, then you won't be able to use some of the User Manager for Domains' capabilities; you can manage most user accounts, but you cannot implement any of the security policies. As a user, you can only look at the User Manager for Domains; you can't make any changes with it.

When you open User Manager for Domains, you will see a list of all of the accounts in the domain, followed by a list of the groups defined in the domain. The user and group information displayed initially is the information for the domain where your user account is located (your home domain), and the name of the domain appears in the title bar. This can be seen in Figure 7.1.

To view users and groups from other trusted domains, use the Select Domain command under the User menu. In the resulting dialog box, as seen in Figure 7.2, select or type in the name of the domain whose accounts you wish to view.

You can also use this command to view the accounts on individual computers that maintain their own security databases (that is, workstations running Windows NT). To do this, type in the computer name preceded by two backslashes (*computer-name*) in place of the domain name. If the computer name happens to be a server

FIGURE 7.1:

User Manager for Domains

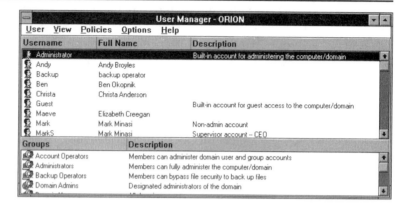

FIGURE 7.2:

Select Domain dialog box

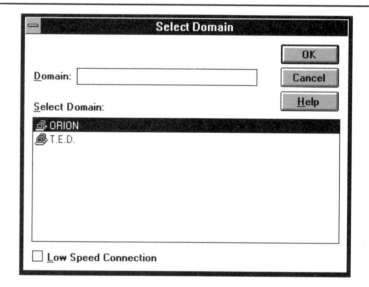

running NT Server or a domain controller, the domain information is displayed instead. If you want to, you can open multiple instances of User Manager for Domains, each with a different domain's data.

If the domain or computer you choose happens to communicate with your computer through a connection that has relatively low transmissions rates, select Low Speed Connection in the Options menu (or in the Select Domain dialog box). This option disables the producing and displaying of lists of user accounts and groups in the User Manager for Domains window (which can take a long time across a low-speed link). Although the option is disabled, you can still create or manage users accounts and local groups using the New User, New Local Group, Copy, Delete, Rename, and Properties commands. Under the Low Speed Connection option, global groups can't be created or copied, but global group membership can still be managed somewhat indirectly by managing the group memberships of individual users. Global and local groups are explained in detail in Chapter 11.

Lists of users and groups can be sorted by either user name or by full name with the options in the View menu. Bear in mind that View menu commands are unavailable if Low Speed Connection is selected. Any changes made to any account or group while in User Manager for Domains are automatically updated in the view. Other changes, such as an administrator adding an account in your domain from a different, trusted domain, are updated at fixed intervals. If necessary, use the Refresh command to get the latest information for the domain.

To view and manage the properties of any of the displayed user accounts or groups, simply double-click on the name of the account or group (alternately, you can select the entry and then choose Properties in the User menu). You'll see the User Properties dialog box, as shown in Figure 7.3.

FIGURE 7.3:

User Properties dialog box

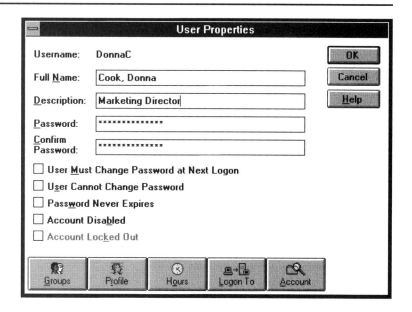

Certain shared characteristics of a collection of accounts (instead of just a single account) can also be examined and managed by selecting all of those user accounts, then choosing Properties.

Creating User Accounts

In NT Server, a user account contains information such as the user name, password, group membership, and rights and privileges the user has for accessing resources on the network. These details are described in Table 7.1.

User accounts, when first created, are automatically assigned a security identifier (SID), which is a unique number that identifies that account in NT Server's security system. SIDs are never reused; when an account is deleted, its SID is deleted with it. Each new account always has a different, unique number, even if the user name and other information is the same as an old account. This way, the new account

TABLE 7.1: Information in a User Account

Part of User Account	Description
Username	A unique name the user types when logging on. One suggestion is to use a combination of first and last names, such as "Janed" for Jane Doherty.
Password	The user's secret password for logging onto his or her account.
Full name	The user's full name.
Logon hours	The hours during which the user is allowed to log on and access network services.
Logon workstations	The computer names of the NT workstations that the user is allowed to work from. (By default, the user can work from any workstation.)
Expiration date	A future date when the user account automatically becomes disabled.
Home directory	A directory on the server that is private to the user; the user controls access to this directory.
Logon script	A batch or executable file that runs automatically when the user logs on.
Profile	A file containing a record of the user's Desktop environment (program groups, network connections, screen colors, settings determining what aspects of the environment the user can change) on NT workstations.
Account type	The particular type of account that the user account is; i.e., a local or global account.

cannot have any of the previous rights and permissions of the old account, and security is preserved.

Creating new user accounts in NT Server is fairly easy. Under the User menu, choose the New User option. You'll see the dialog box shown in Figure 7.4.

To begin, type in a unique user name in the Username box (as suggested in the Table 7.1, one option is a combination of the user's first and last name). This name can have up to 20 characters, either upper- or lowercase, with the exception of the following:

```
"  /  \  [  ]  ;  :  |  =  ,  +  *  ?  <  >
```

Blanks are okay, but I'd avoid them, as they necessitate surrounding user names with quotes when executing commands.

In the Full Name and Description boxes, type in the user's full name and a short description of the user or of the user account. Both of these entries are optional, but recommended. Establish a standard for entering full names (last name first, for example), because the viewing options in User Manager for Domains allow you to sort user accounts by the users' full names instead of their user names.

Next, type a password in both the Password and Confirm Password boxes. Passwords are case-sensitive, and their attributes are determined under the Account Policy, which I'll cover a bit later in the section on managing security. After you've entered and confirmed a password, select or clear the check boxes that determine whether or not the user can or must change the password at the next logon. If you don't want anyone using the new account just yet, check the Account Disabled box. All of the options in this series of check boxes are described in Table 7.2.

TABLE 7.2: Password and Account Options for Creating New User Accounts

Option	Default	Description
User Must Change Password at Next Logon	On	Forces the user to change passwords the next time he or she logs on; this value is set to No afterwards.
User Cannot Change Password	Off	If checked, prevents the user from changing the account's password. This is useful for shared accounts.
Password Never Expires	Off	If checked, the user account ignores the password expiration policy, and the password for the account never expires. This is useful for accounts that represent services (such as the Replicator account) and accounts for which you want a permanent password (such as the Guest account).
Account Disabled	Off	If checked, the account is disabled and no one can log on to it until it is enabled (it is not, however, removed from the database). This is useful for accounts that are used as templates.

At the bottom of the New User dialog box are five buttons: Groups, Profile, Hours, Logon From, and Account. Here is where you define the properties of the user account.

Assigning Groups

Selecting the Groups button allows you to specify which groups the new user account will have membership in. NT Server has a number of useful predefined groups, and I'll explain them in more detail a bit later in this chapter in the section "Managing Groups." Group membership is shown in the Group Memberships dialog box, seen in Figure 7.5. You can click the Groups button to open this dialog box.

FIGURE 7.5:

Group Memberships dialog box

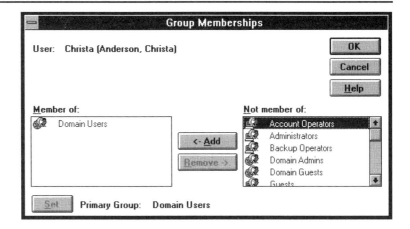

The dialog box displays which groups the user is or isn't a member of. Note the icons next to the group names:

- A globe behind two faces indicates a global group.
- A computer terminal behind two faces indicates a local group.

Again, sorry to appear to be ducking the explanations of global and local groups, but the whole discussion of global and local groups is completely incomprehensible until you understand how to manage multiple domains under NT; hence locals and globals are covered in Chapter 11. To quickly summarize the differences, however, global groups are groups that are accessible to the entire network, while local groups are local to the domain they're defined in.

To give new group memberships to the user account, select those groups from the Not Member of box, then choose the Add button or drag the group icon(s) to the Member of box. To remove membership in any group from the user account, select the desired groups from the Member of box and click on the Remove button or drag the icon(s) to the Not member of box.

User accounts must be a member of at least one group, referred to as the *primary group*, which is used when the user logs on to NT Services for Macintosh or runs POSIX applications. Primary groups must be global groups, and they cannot be removed. A different global group can be designated as the primary group, if desired; to do this, select a global group out of the Member of box, then choose the Set button beneath the Member of frame. When you're finished configuring the group membership, choose OK.

Setting the User's Environment

If you wish, you can define the user environment for each user account. You can give the account a *user profile* or a *logon script*, or specify where the user's home directory will be. You can use logon scripts and home directories for any kind of user, but user profiles work only for NT workstations.

None of these parameters need to be defined when creating a new user account; you can leave them out now, and add them later if you decide that assigning them will aid your network management.

User profiles, logon scripts, and home directories will be discussed in more detail in the upcoming section on defining user environments. In brief, a user profile is a file containing desktop and program settings, while a logon script is a batch file set to run whenever a user logs on. A home directory is a directory whose permissions are set to allow only one person access. You can put home directories anywhere you like, but it's probably most logical to put them in the C:\USERS directory of one of your servers. The home directory can be used as a location for user programs as well as a storage area for a user's private data.

On an NT workstation, a home directory becomes the user's default directory for File Open and Save As dialog boxes, for the command prompt, and for those applications that don't have a predefined working directory. Home directories can be located on an NT Server machine or on an NT workstation.

To specify where a user's profile, logon script, and home directory are located, choose the Profile button in the New User dialog box (see Figure 7.4). You'll see the User Environment Profile dialog box shown in Figure 7.6.

Under User Profile Path, type in the full network path (including the file name) for the user's profile. For example, you could type \\eisa server\profiles\andy.usr. To specify a logon script, type simply the name of the batch file (this file, incidentally, must be placed in the directory WINNT\SYSTEM32\REPL\IMPORT\SCRIPTS).

Home directories can have either a local path or a network path. If you are administering a user account on an NT workstation, specify a local path for the home directory by typing in the path (including the drive letter). For an account in a

FIGURE 7.6:

User Environment Profile dialog box

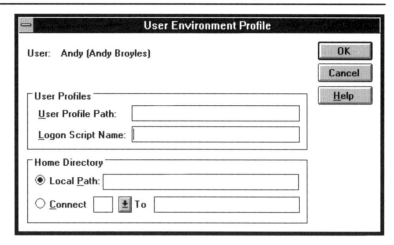

domain, choose a network directory instead: Select the Connect button, pick a drive letter, and type in a network path.

Permissible Logon Hours and Locations

By selecting the Hours button in the New User dialog box (see Figure 7.4), you can specify the days and hours during which a particular user can access the network. Similarly, choosing the Logon From button lets you limit the workstations where a user can log on.

Logon Hours By default, a user can connect to the network all hours of all days of the week, but circumstances may exist that require user access to be restricted. Additionally, if a user doesn't have any need to work outside normal office hours, adjusting this scale could prevent an intruder from using that user's account after those hours. To change the default settings, select the Hours button. You'll get the Logon Hours dialog box shown in Figure 7.7.

To administer the hours during which the user account is allowed to access the network, select the hours by dragging the cursor over a particular block of hours. Conversely, you can select all the hours of a certain day by clicking on that day's button, or you can choose certain hours across all seven days by selecting a button on the top of an hours column. Then choose either the Allow or Disallow button to grant

FIGURE 7.7:

The Logon Hours dialog box

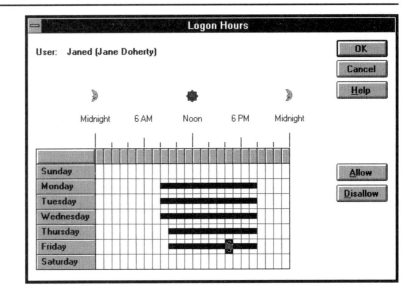

or deny access to the network at those selected hours. Filled boxes indicate the hours when the user is authorized to connect to the network; empty ones indicate the time when access is denied. When done, choose OK.

Depending upon which option is chosen under the Account Policy (described later in this chapter), a user connected to the network when the logon hours are exceeded is either forcefully disconnected from all server connections at the specified time, or allowed to stay connected (but with no new connections allowed). Workstations running NT will receive a message warning of the impending disconnection a few minutes before the time expires; if the user is allowed to stay connected, warning messages appear every ten minutes beyond the expiration time.

In contrast, non-NT workstations are sometimes unaffected by the logon hours constraints. If you try to log on outside your allowed hours from a DOS, Windows, OS/2, or Windows for Workgroups workstation, you won't be logged on. But if you were *already* logged on, then…

I admit that I find this a bit confusing, but here's what I've found about logon hours:

- First of all, if you try to log onto your domain outside your acceptable logon hours, you don't get logged in, period.

- If you exceed your acceptable logon hours, *and* the box labeled "Forcibly disconnect remote users from server when logon hours expire" (it's in the User Manager for Domains; click Policies, then Account...) is checked, will you be disconnected? It depends:
    - If you're running an NT workstation, definitely yes. You get a five-minute warning, then you're logged off.
    - If you're running DOS, it seems that you don't get logged off.
    - If you're running Windows for Workgroups with the improved redirector, then it seems that you're disconnected from your devices, but you get no logoff message.
    - If the Administrator has changed your hours while you're logged on, then nothing happens until you next log on. If you try to attach to new network devices, then you'll get a network error 2241, which indicates that you've tried to log on outside of your logon hours.

This complex situation leads to a common question: "How can I boot everyone off the server at 2 AM so that the scheduled backup can occur?" That's simple. Just write a batch file with these commands:

```
Net pause server
Net send * The server is going down in 5 minutes for maintenance.
... use a command to wait for five minutes ...
Net stop server
```

The pause command keeps anyone new from logging on. The send command sends a message to everyone running the messenger service and a network pop-up. The stop command shuts down the server, disconnecting everyone.

Logon Locations   When you select the Logon From button in the New User window (see Figure 7.4), you get the Logon Workstations dialog box shown in Figure 7.8. This dialog box allows you to manage at which workstations this particular user can log on to the domain's servers. As with the logon times, the default is no restrictions; a user is allowed to log on at any workstation on the network.

If you want to restrict the user's choice of workstations where he or she can log onto the network, select the User May Log On To These Workstations button and type in the computer names (without preceding backslashes) of the allowed workstations. Up to eight workstations can be specified. For example, if the machines that

FIGURE 7.8:

Logon Workstations dialog box

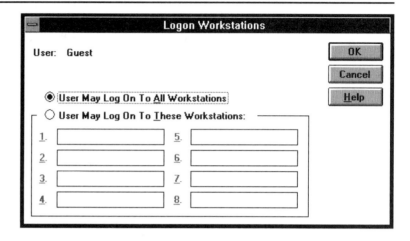

I regularly log onto are called SDG90 and LAPDOG, then I just punch those names in, again with no preceding backslashes.

This feature works for all workstation types.

Account Duration and Type

When creating or managing a user account, you can set the account to expire after a certain time period. If you have a summer intern or other temporary personnel, you don't want them to be able to log onto the network beyond the time that they're authorized to. Setting an account to expire will avoid this problem. Click the Account button in the New User dialog box to display the Account Information dialog box shown in Figure 7.9.

FIGURE 7.9:

Account Information dialog box

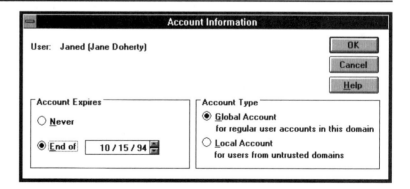

An account with an expiration date becomes disabled (not deleted) at the end of the specified day in the Account Expires box. If the user happens to be logged on, the session is not terminated, but no new connections can be made, and once the user logs off, he or she can't log back on.

Global and Local Accounts

In addition to setting an account expiration date, you can also set whether the user account in question is a *global account* or a *local account* (don't confuse these with global and local *groups*).

Global accounts, the default setting, are normal user accounts in the user's home domain. These accounts can be used not only in the home domain, but also in any domain that has a trust relationship (more on trust relationships shortly) with the home domain.

Local user accounts, on the other hand, are accounts provided in a particular domain for a user whose global user account is not in a trusted domain (i.e., an untrusted NT Server domain or a LAN Manager 2.x domain). A local account can't be used to log on interactively at an NT workstation or an NT Server server, but, like other accounts, it can access NT and NT Server computers over the network, can be placed in local and global groups, and can be assigned rights and permissions. If a user from an untrusted domain (either NT Server or LAN Manager 2.x) needs access to other NT Server domains, that user needs to have a local account on each of those other domains, since local accounts from one domain (the user's home domain) can't be used in other trusting domains.

When you've finished selecting the desired account options, choose Add, choose Close, and then choose OK. Then, choose OK in the New User dialog box to create the new user account with the properties you've just specified. The new account will now appear in the list of users on the current domain shown in the User Manager for Domains window.

How Do I Create a User Account in a Domain?

Open User Manager for Domains. Under the User menu, select New User. In the New User dialog box:

1. Type in a user name and the user's full name.

2. Type in a description of the user or account (optional).

3. Type in a password in the Password and Confirm Password boxes. Select the password's characteristics from the options presented. Choose whether or not the account will be disabled.

4. Using the Groups, Profile, Hours, Logon From, and Account buttons, do the following: set the user's group membership; user profile, logon script, and/or home directory; hours which the network will be available to the user; from which workstations the user is allowed to log on; and account characteristics (expiration date and account type).

5. When you're done configuring the account as described in step 4, choose Add.

Managing User Accounts

Once a user account has been created, you can look at and modify the properties of that account by either double-clicking on that account or by highlighting the account and choosing Properties from the User menu. You'll see the User Properties dialog box, as shown in Figure 7.10.

Anyone logged on as an administrator or as a member of the Account Operators local group (more on groups shortly) can then reconfigure the account's properties, following the same procedures as are used for creating a new user account.

Copying Accounts

Instead of creating each user account on your network individually, you can also copy existing user accounts. The primary advantage of creating user accounts this

FIGURE 7.10:

User Properties dialog box

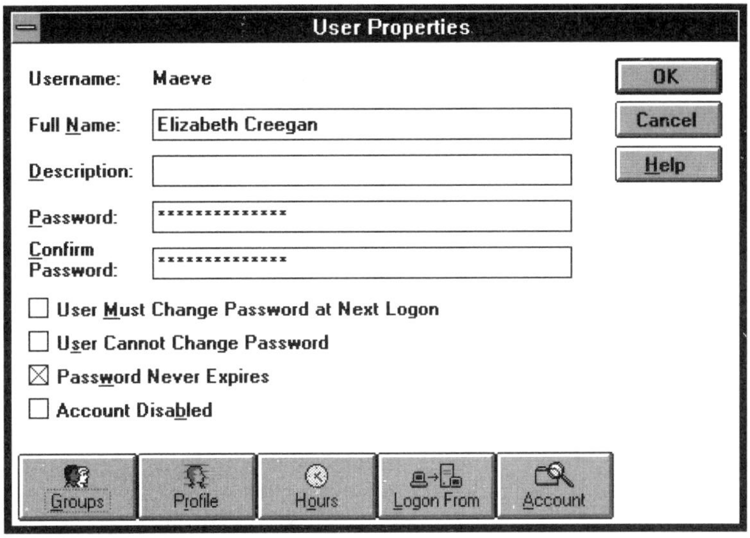

way is that all of the original user account's properties (including group member-ships) are copied over to the new user account, thus speeding up administrative chores. If you have a large network, you might want to create one or more template accounts containing specific properties shared by groups of users. For greater secu-rity, keep the template accounts disabled so that no one can actually log on to them.

To copy an existing user account, select the account from the list of user accounts in the User Manager for Domains window, then choose Copy from the User menu. You'll see the Copy dialog box shown in Figure 7.11.

The copy retains all of the information from the original, except for the username, full name, and password, which you must provide. Configure the new account, making changes to names and properties as needed, then choose Add. When done, select Close.

Note that the original user's user rights, as defined by the User Rights command under the Policy menu, are not copied from one user account to another. If the newly copied accounts must have certain rights, you must grant them separately. Granting rights to a group and putting accounts in that group is the best way to manage rights for multiple users.

FIGURE 7.11:

Copying an existing user account

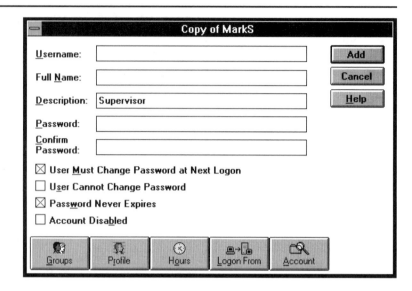

All user accounts, including the built-in ones, can be renamed by choosing the Rename command in the User menu. Renamed accounts retain their original security identifier (SID), and thereby keep all of their original properties, rights, and permissions.

Managing Properties for More than One Account

You can manage several user account properties for more than one account at the same time. To do this, first select two or more user accounts. You can select a number of accounts either individually with the mouse from the currently displayed list of users, or (if you have a significant number of user accounts) you can select all members of a particular group within the domain with the Select Users command in the User menu. You'll see the Select Users dialog box shown in Figure 7.12.

You'll notice that the Select Users command is actually more of a Select Group command; by choosing a group on the domain, you are selecting all of the users who are members of that group. The Select Users option is cumulative; if you first select Administrators, and then select Backup Operators, all members who are either in the Administrators group or the Backup Operators group are selected. (The Deselect button lets you take groups off of the selected list.) Note that when you choose

FIGURE 7.12:

The Select Users dialog box

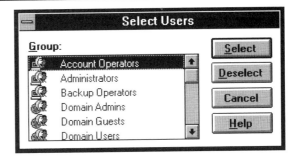

a group using the Select Users command, only members from the local domain are chosen. For example, if you select a local group (which can contain both users from the home domain as well as users from other, trusted domains), any changes that are made won't affect members from the trusted domains.

After you've selected the user accounts, close the Select Users dialog box and then choose Properties under the User menu. Figure 7.13 is the screen you will see next.

As with a single user account, you can select any of the buttons at the bottom of the dialog box to make certain modifications to all of the selected accounts.

FIGURE 7.13:

Modifying the properties of a group of user accounts

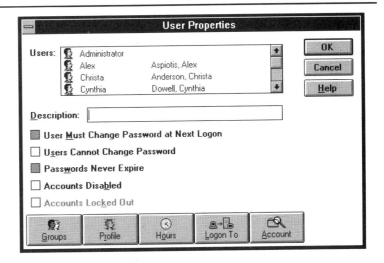

For example, let's say you want to modify the group membership for the selected user accounts. By choosing the Groups button, you will see the group memberships that each of the selected accounts have in common (as listed in the All Are Members Of box). You can see this in Figure 7.14.

FIGURE 7.14:

Modifying the group membership of selected users

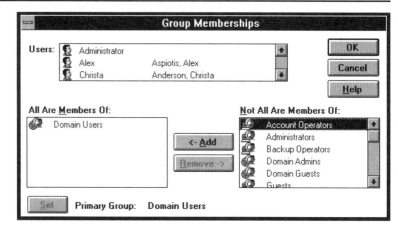

How Do I Ensure that a Selected List of Users Are Not Members of a Particular Group in the Domain?

To make sure of this:

1. Select the users in the User Manager for Domains window.

2. From the User menu, choose Properties.

3. In the User Properties dialog box, choose Groups. Add the particular group from the Not Member Of box to the Member Of box.

4. Choose OK to save the change.

5. In the User Properties dialog box, choose Groups again.

6. Select the group in the Member Of box and choose Remove.

You can then add or remove group membership from the selection of users by high-lighting the groups and choosing the Add or Remove buttons.

One more example of how handy multiple user selection can be involves the creation of new groups. If you have two existing groups and you wish to create a third group containing all of the users in the first two groups, you can use the Select Users command to select all of those user accounts, then choose New Local Group to place them in a new group.

Deleting User Accounts

There are three ways to rescind a user's ability to log onto the network with his or her account: by disabling the account, by restricting the access hours, and by deleting the account.

As mentioned earlier, a disabled account continues to exist on the server, but no one can access it. Even so, it (and with it, its properties) can be copied, it appears on lists of user accounts, and it can be restored to enabled status at any time. A deleted account, on the other hand, is completely removed from the system, vanishes from user account lists, and cannot be recovered or restored.

A new user account can be created with the same name and properties as a deleted account, but it will receive a different, unique security identifier (SID). Because internal processes in NT refer to a user account's SID rather than its user name, none of the rights or permissions granted to the deleted user account will transfer to any new account that has the same name as the old.

As a measure against inadvertent, hasty, and perhaps regretted deletions of user accounts, you might choose to first disable unused accounts, then periodically remove those disabled accounts. Incidentally, NT Server prevents the deletion of the built-in Administrator and Guest accounts.

To delete one or more user accounts, select the account or accounts from the list in the opening window of User Manager for Domains. Then, under the User menu, choose Delete. Confirmation boxes will appear to remind you of your choice and ask if you want to continue. Select OK to proceed.

Configuring the User Environment

NT SERVER

A Windows NT Server network provides administrators with the ability to not only define a user's desktop environment, restricting it if necessary, but also to store the information on the server, so that regardless of which workstation the user logs on to, his or her desktop settings stay the same. This information is administered under the Profile section of a user's account; there you can specify the placement of an account's user profile, logon script, and home directory. All profile information is optional; you need to decide for yourself whether your network structure can benefit from its use. Note that, unfortunately, most of this workstation control is only possible for users with NT workstations; none of the profile capabilities apply to Windows 3.x users.

User Profiles

User profiles, which can only be used on NT workstations, are files stored on the server that contain information on a user's desktop settings, specifically such items as network connections, program groups, window sizes and positions, screen appearance, and any information saved by the Save Settings On Exit commands in Program Manager, File Manager, and Print Manager. The information stored in a user profile can be seen in Table 7.3.

TABLE 7.3: Information Stored in a User Profile

Source	Values Saved in the User Profile
Program Manager	All user-defined settings, including personal program groups and their properties, program items and their properties, and settings saved by the Save Settings On Exit and Save Settings Now commands
File Manager	All user-defined settings, including network connections and anything saved by the Save Settings On Exit command
Command prompt	All user-defined settings, including fonts, colors, settings for the screen size buffer, and window position
Print Manager	Network printer connections and anything saved by the Save Settings on Exit command

TABLE 7.3: Information Stored in a User Profile (continued)

Source	Values Saved in the User Profile
Control Panel options	All settings for the Color, Mouse, Desktop, Cursor, Keyboard, International, and Sound options; entries in the User Environment Variables box under the System option
Accessories	All user-specific applications settings affecting the users NT environment (includes settings for Calculator, Cardfile, Clock, Notepad, Paintbrush, and Terminal)
Third-party applications written for NT	Any settings the application is designed to track on a per-user basis
Online Help bookmarks	Any bookmarks a user places in the NT Help system

All NT workstations automatically maintain a local user profile, where the settings any user of that workstation happens to make while logged on are kept. However, these local profiles are computer-dependent; a user's settings are only available at that one workstation, not at any other he or she might use.

Specific user profiles defined and assigned to a user account in NT Server are stored on the server, and are available across the network. These profiles provide several benefits over local profiles:

- They allow a user to have the same desktop environment at any computer on the network, keeping all preferences and settings regardless of which workstation the user is sitting at.

- An administrator can create one user profile for a set of users who perform similar tasks.

- A user's access to parts of the system can be limited, enhancing network security. For example, an administrator can disable Program Manager's Run command, preventing some or all changes to program groups and items, or deny the ability to add or remove network connections.

- The administrative workload can be reduced because an administrator can add a new application or resource to a number of users all at once (provided they share the same mandatory profile).

User profiles are either personal profiles (saved with a .USR extension) or mandatory profiles (saved with a .MAN extension). Personal profiles can be permanently changed by their users because, whether done consciously or not, changes are saved every time users alter their desktop environment settings. Mandatory profiles, however, cannot be permanently changed by a user; a user can modify settings during one logon session, but the settings revert back to the mandatory profile the next time the user logs on. With mandatory profiles, an administrator can restrict users' abilities at their own workstations, as well as easily update the environments of many users at one time.

User profiles are created using the User Profile Editor, but in some circumstances, a user profile can be created by other means. If you assign a mandatory user profile to a user account, you *must* manually create (using the User Profile Editor) a mandatory profile of that name in the specified location or else the user will be unable to log on. However, if you assign a personal user profile to a user account, you have two choices:

- You can create the profile using the User Profile Editor and put it in the directory you specify in the User Profile path.

- You can simply not create the profile. At the user's first logon to his or her account, the system copies the default local profile from the logon computer and saves it under the specified file name and directory. This allows a manager to assign many personal profiles without having to create each one individually with the User Profile Editor. If you choose to do this, make sure that the path for the user profile is one that's accessible to the user's account (it should be shared on the network, and the file and directory permissions should not restrict access to it).

Creating a Profile Using the User Profile Editor

Since creating a user profile involves altering Control Panel settings and arranging windows, it's a handy idea to create a separate Profile Administrator account with Administrator privileges for this purpose to avoid constantly changing your regular administrator account.

To create the profile, first log on as an administrator, and then configure the desktop environment of the computer you're on so it conforms exactly to the user profile you are creating. Set all desired user-specific options, as defined in Table 7.3.

Then, start the User Profile Editor in the Administrative Tools group. You'll see the dialog box shown in Figure 7.15.

To assign the profile to a user, select the Browse button (...) on the right of the Permitted to Use Profile box to get the User Browser list. Select the Show Users button, highlight the user name, select Add, and add the name of the individual user you want to assign the profile to. This action gives the particular user the necessary read and write access to the profile.

Personal profiles should be assigned to individual users; mandatory profiles can be assigned either to users or to global groups. (Contrary to what the NT Server manuals say, you can't assign a mandatory profile to a local group—Microsoft acknowledges this as a documentation error.)

Set the rest of the User Profile Editor options as you see fit. These options are explained in Table 7.4.

FIGURE 7.15:

The User Profile Editor

257

TABLE 7.4: Options in the User Profile Editor

Option	Performs this Action
Program Manager Settings	
Disable Run In File Menu*	Disables the Run command in Program Manager, preventing users from directly running programs other than those in the available program groups.
Disable Save Settings Menu Item and Never Save Settings	Disables the Save Settings On Exit and Save Settings Now commands of the Program Manager Options menu.
Show Common Program Groups	Displays the common program groups in Program Manager. Clear this option to hide common program groups from a user of this profile.
StartUp Group	Defines which group is the StartUp group for the user.
Program Group Settings	
Program Group settings	Controls the user's ability to make changes to personal program groups. Users cannot change locked program groups or their program items. Unlocked program groups can remain completely accessible, or you can limit the kind of modifications the user can make under the For Unlocked Groups, Allow User To: option.
Allow User to Connect/Remove Connections in Print Manager	Controls the user's ability to connect to, and disconnect from, network printers in Print Manager.

* Checking this option does not prevent users from starting programs from within other programs by running File Manager or the command prompt or by changing program item command lines to run other programs. Use the other security features in NT Server to restrict access, if necessary.

Finally, choose the Save As File command under the User Profile Editor's File menu, as in Figure 7.16. In the Save File as Type box, choose Per-User Profile or Mandatory Profile. Per-user profiles are saved with the .USR extension, while mandatory profiles use the .MAN extension. Choose a path in the Directories box. If you want to save the profile to a shared directory that you aren't connected to already, use the Network button to make the connection.

Type in the desired name for the file. Your best bet is to give profiles a file name that's the same as the user name of the assigned user (for example, the user JaneD's profile would be JANED.USR). Then choose the OK button. The user profile will

FIGURE 7.16:

Save As dialog box

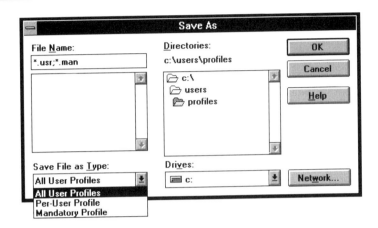

then be saved with both the option settings in the User Profile Editor and the user-specific information from the current desktop configuration.

When you create user profiles, have on hand hardware and software information for the user's workstation. Windows arranged for a VGA display won't look the same on super VGA, and putting an application in a user's startup group won't be useful if that user doesn't have or can't access the software in question.

Changing a User Profile

Changes to a user profile are made whenever the user logs on and alters any of the saved settings, such as in Program Manager and Control Panel; they are saved to the file when the user logs off. Alternately, you can change an existing user profile with the User Profile Editor, although changes are limited to the options presented in the User Profile Editor. For example, you can't create personal program groups, change window sizes, or change screen colors.

To change a user profile:

1. Start the User Profile Editor.

2. Choose Open from the File menu and select the user profile you want to modify.

3. Set the options as described above for creating a user profile.

4. Save the profile as a file, as described above.

Note: If you're modifying a personal user profile that's already assigned to a user, save the profile under a different file name. Otherwise, if the user happens to be logged on, your modified version of the profile will be overwritten by the old version (which is still being used) as soon as the user logs off. After saving the new profile under a different name, you can then change the user profile path for the user account in User Manager for Domains.

When you assign user profiles, make sure that they're accessible by the user accounts. The system won't be able to load a profile if any of the following conditions exist:

- The profile does not exist (i.e., the file is missing).
- The path or share does not exist.
- The permissions of the path or share do not allow you to connect to it.
- The permissions on the profile do not allow you to read the file.
- The user does not have access to the data inside the profile (this is set in the User Profile Editor's Permitted To Use field).

Not being able to find a profile isn't as critical a problem with personal profiles as it is with mandatory profiles; if NT can't find a user's personal profile, then the default profile is loaded instead, but if the mandatory profile is unavailable, then the user won't be able to log on.

For NT workstations, mandatory profiles provide an easy way to restrict access and add network resources to many users at once, but their inability to maintain the desktop environment preferences of users might steer you towards personal user profiles instead. If you choose to assign personal profiles instead of mandatory ones, then giving users access to new resources by editing their profiles no longer becomes practical—the administrator has to change each personal profile individually. And what about a network with DOS workstations? A mixed network containing both NT and DOS workstations can't take full advantage of the user profile features. In both of these cases, it would be more practical to use *logon scripts*.

Logon Scripts

A logon script is simply a batch file (.BAT or .CMD file name extension) or an executable program (.EXE extension). Logon scripts are set to run automatically whenever a user logs on, and the same script can be assigned to one or many user accounts. Unlike user profiles, logon scripts work on computers running either NT, Windows 95, or MS-DOS. Logon scripts are used to configure users' working environments by making network connections and starting applications.

Logon scripts aren't as versatile as user profiles, but you'll want to use logon scripts in the following situations:

- The network includes users with MS-DOS/Windows workstations (user profiles only work on NT workstations).

- You want to manage only part of the users' environments (for example, network connections), without managing or controlling the entire environment.

- You have an NT network using only personal (not mandatory) profiles, and you want to create common network connections for multiple users without having to individually modify each profile.

- You have LAN Manager 2.x running on your network, and you want to keep the logon scripts you made for that system.

Logon scripts are also easier to create and maintain than user profiles; depending on your network situation, they might be the better choice.

Whenever a user logs on, the server authenticating the logon looks for the logon script by following the server's logon script path (the default path is WINNT35\SYSTEM32\REPL\IMPORT\SCRIPTS). If you place your logon script there, you only have to type in the name of the script itself in the logon script path name box. If the logon script happens to be located in a subdirectory of the logon script path, include that relative path when you type in the name. The entire logon script path can be changed in Server Manager, under Directory Replication. Consult Chapter 10, on server management, for the procedure.

If your domain has more than one NT Server server, any one of them may authorize a user's log on attempt, so copies of logon scripts for every user in the domain should exist on each of the servers in the domain. Using the Directory Replicator service is the best way to ensure this.

Creating a Logon Script

To create a logon script, simply create a batch file. This file can contain any NT command. For example, you could have a batch file containing the following two lines:

```
@echo off
net time "\\eisa server" /set /yes
```

This logon script synchronizes each workstation's clocks with that of the primary server in the domain (which, in this case, is the computer \\eisa server). As far as I'm concerned, all logon scripts should start with the time synchronization command NET TIME.

Keep your logon scripts short if your network uses Windows and Windows for Workgroups machines. When a Windows 3.x user who's been assigned a logon script logs on, the machine starts a virtual DOS session in which to execute the script. This session typically lasts only about 30 seconds and isn't configurable. If the script takes longer than that, it will quit and the user will get a system integrity violation error. This is especially a problem for remote users working over slow links (for example, using RAS or through a TCP/IP gateway over async modem lines). At worst case, you can disable script operation for users with the following procedure:

1. In Control Panel, choose the Network icon.
2. Choose the Networks button.
3. In the Other Networks In Use box, select Microsoft LAN Manager.
4. Choose the Settings… option.
5. Clear the Logon to LAN Manager Domain check box.

Using the Logon Script Variables

There are several wildcards you can use as you write your logon script. These are listed in Table 7.5. (Note that these script variables only work for people with NT workstations.)

If you are typing up a logon script for multiple users who, for example, are not all in the same domain, then you can type %USERDOMAIN% instead of an actual domain name in a command, and the system will automatically insert the specific user's domain when it executes the logon script.

TABLE 7.5: Logon Script Variables

Parameter	Description
%HOMEDRIVE%	A user's local workstation drive letter connected to the user's home directory
%HOMEPATH%	The full path name of the user's home directory
%HOMESHARE%	The share name containing the user's home directory
%OS%	The operating system of the user's workstation
%PROCESSOR%	The processor type (such as 80486) of the user's workstation
%USERDOMAIN%	The domain containing the user's account
%USERNAME%	The user name of the user

In addition to the logon scripts, these wildcards can also be used in other situations, such as when specifying application path names in Program Manager, or when assigning user profiles and home directories to a number of users at once. One note about using %USERNAME% to create home directories and user profiles file names: Don't use the wildcard when assigning home directories that are on a FAT volume if at least one of the selected user accounts has a user name longer than 8 (or 8+3) characters. On NTFS volumes, this limit doesn't apply, and you can use the wildcards regardless of name length.

Home Directories

Home directories are directories, on a server, that are assigned to particular user accounts; they are accessible to the user, and the user has access control over his or her directory. To provide a home directory service for a network user, you need to do two things:

- Create a directory that only the user can get to, and

- Assign a particular logical drive letter for that directory to that user.

If the user's home directory is located on a computer other than his or her own workstation, then a connection is automatically made to the home directory every time the user logs on.

NT users and non-NT users of a network must get home directories differently. Creating and using home directories is easy for NT users, and not-so-easy for non-NT users.

Building Home Directories for NT Users

A home directory, when assigned, becomes an NT user's default directory for File Open and Save As dialog boxes, for the command prompt, and for those applications that don't have a predefined working directory. Home directories can be located on an NT Server machine or on an NT workstation.

You'll typically put the home directories for your users into the directory USERS on one of your NT servers. The User Manager for Domains can handle the directory setup, save for one thing: when it tries to create and share the user home directories, it will fail *unless* you first share the USERS directory.

This is just one of those NT oddities that you've got to learn to live with, so before starting to create users, share the USERS directory. Give the group EVERYONE access with change control.

Now the business of creating a home directory can be a bit of a chore. You've got to create a subdirectory under the USERS directory, then set its directory permissions so that only one user can see it, and then tell the User Manager for Domains where that directory is. (Directory permissions are explained in the next chapter.) Here's where the User Manager for Domains can make setting up home directories easier.

Home directories aid user management; since many or all of a user's files end up in the home directory, an administrator can more readily back up user files and delete user accounts.

How Do I Assign Personal Profiles, Logon Scripts, and Home Directories to a Group of Users?

To assign these items to a group of users:

1. In User Manager for Domains, select the user accounts to which you want to add the profiles. You can do this either manually or by using the Select Users command from the User menu.

2. From the User menu, choose Properties.

3. Select the Profiles button. Using the wildcards, type in the paths of the profiles, logon scripts, and home directories.

For example, let's say you want to do the following:

- Give each user a personal profile, to be stored on the existing directory PROFILES on a server named MARS,

- Give each user the logon script WINNT\SYSTEM32\REPL\ IMPORT\SCRIPTS\startntc.bat, and

- Connect each user to a home directory located at \\mars\users,

you would type in the information illustrated in the following graphic.

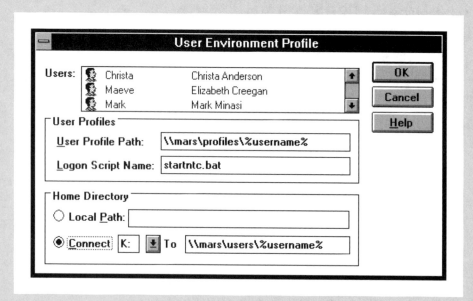

This procedure will do the following:

- Assign to all of the selected user accounts a personal profile using their own username as a filename,
- Set the logon script startntc.bat to start when each user logs on, and
- Create directories with the same name as their user name in the specified path.

For example, the user whose user name is Maeve will have a profile named MAEVE.USR and will be assigned a home directory called MAEVE, which will connect to K: when she logs on. Remember to make sure that the permissions on the directories containing the user profiles and the home directories allow the user to access them.

Creating Home Directories for Non-NT Users

The User Manager for Domains will still create home directories for non-NT users, but those users won't get hooked up to those directories unless you put this command in their logon script (or just execute it once from their workstation):

```
net use driveletter: /home
```

where "driveletter:" is, of course, a logical drive letter from D: to Z:.

NT Server has three built-in global groups: Domain Admins, Domain Users, and Domain Guests.

Domain Admins. By placing a user account into this global group, you provide administrative-level abilities to that user. Members of Domain Admins can administer the home domain, the workstations of the domain, and any other trusted domains that have added the Domain Admins global group to their own Administrators local group. By default, the built-in Domain Admins global group is a member of both the domain's Administrators local group and the Administrators local groups for every NT workstation in the domain. The built-in Administrator user account for the domain is automatically a member of the Domain Admins global group.

Domain Users. Members of the Domain Users global group have normal user access to, and abilities for, both the domain itself and for any NT workstation in the domain. This group contains all domain user accounts, and is by default a member of the Users local groups both for the domain and for every Windows NT workstation on the domain.

Domain Guests. This allows guest accounts to access resources across domain boundaries, if they've been allowed that by the domain administrators.

Managing Groups

NT SERVER

In NT Server, a user group is a set of users who have identical network rights. Placing your domain's user accounts in groups not only simplifies general (as well as security) management, but also makes it easier and faster to grant multiple users access to a network resource. Additionally, to give a right or permission to all of the users in a single group, all you have to do is grant that permission or right to the group.

Creating and Deleting Groups

To create a new local group, select New Local Group under the User menu. You'll see the dialog box shown in Figure 7.17.

FIGURE 7.17:

New Local Group dialog box

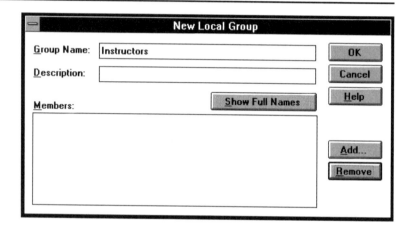

Type in the name of the local group you wish to create (in this example, we're creating a group called Instructors). Include a description of the group, if you want.

Select the Add… button to add members to the group. You will see the Add Users and Groups dialog box in Figure 7.18.

In the Add Users and Groups dialog box, select a name or global group from the desired domain list, and choose the Add button to place them in the Add Names list. (Remember, a local group can contain both users and global groups from trusted domains as well as from the local domain.) Alternately, you can type the user names into the Add Names list; make sure you separate them with a semicolon. When you've collected all of the names in the Add Names list, choose OK.

The names you chose will appear in the Members box of the New Local Group dialog box. (To see their full names, choose the Show Full Names option.) To remove a name from the list, just highlight it and click on the Remove button. When your new local group's membership is to your satisfaction, select OK. The new group will now appear in User Manager for Domains list of groups.

FIGURE 7.18:

Adding accounts to the new local group

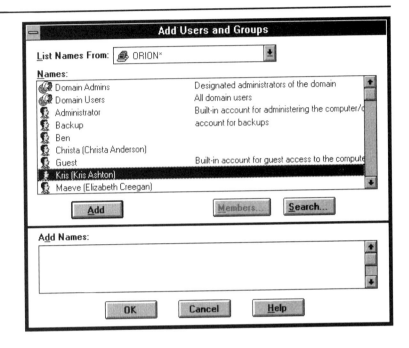

Creating a Global Group

Creating a new global group is just as easy. Under the User menu, choose New Global Group. In the New Global Group dialog box, as seen in Figure 7.19, type in a name and description for the new group. In this example, the new global group is called ResearchAssistants.

A global group can only contain user accounts from the domain where it is created, so the Not Members box will contain only those accounts on the current domain. To give any user on the list group membership, select one of the entries in the Not Members list and click on the Add button. When finished, choose OK; the new global group will be visible in the User Manager for Domains group list.

You can change any user's or group's membership in another group by displaying that group's Properties (in the User Manager for Domains window, either select the group and choose Properties under the User menu or double-click on that group). The dialog boxes for Group Properties are identical to those for New Groups, and you can add and remove members using the same procedures described above.

FIGURE 7.19:

New Global Group dialog box

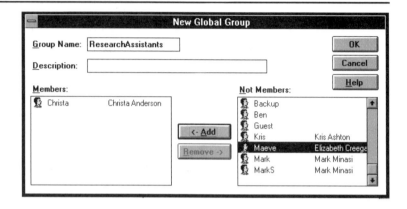

Deleting groups is accomplished by selecting the group in the User Manager for Domains window and choosing Delete (in the User menu). The same cautions about deleting user accounts apply to deleting groups as well, since groups also have their own unique security identifier (SID). Before allowing you to delete a group, NT Server prompts you with a reminder message, as in Figure 7.20. Deleting a group removes only that group from NT Server; all user accounts and groups within the deleted group are unaffected.

FIGURE 7.20:

Warning message for deleting a group

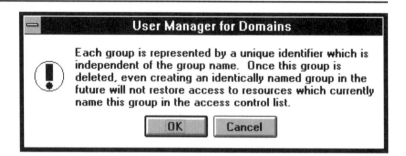

Predefined Groups

A number of predefined groups, both local and global, are built into NT Server to aid network administration and management. The local groups are described in the following pages.

Administrators   Not surprisingly, this is the most powerful group. Members of the Administrators local group have more control over the domain than any other users, and they are granted all of the rights necessary to manage the overall configuration of the domain and the domain's servers. Incidentally, users in the Administrators group do not automatically have access to every file in the domain. If the file's permissions do not grant access to Administrators, then the members of the Administrator's group cannot access the file. If it becomes necessary, however, an administrator can take ownership of such a file and thus have access to it. If he or she does, the event is recorded in the security log (provided that auditing of files has been activated) and the administrator does not have the ability to give ownership back to the original owner (or to anyone else, for that matter).

Within the Administrators group is a built-in Administrator user account that cannot be deleted. By default, the Domain Admins global group is also a member of the Administrators group, but it can be removed.

Given that it's possible for the Administrator account to be disabled, it might be wise to create a backup administrator account to be used in case of emergency.

Server Operators   The Server Operators local group has all of the rights needed to manage the domain's servers. Members of the Server Operators group can create, manage, and delete printer shares at servers; create, manage, and delete network shares at servers; back up and restore files on servers; format a server's fixed disk; lock and unlock servers; and change the system time. In addition, Server Operators can log on to the network from the domain's servers as well as shut down the servers.

Account Operators   Members of the Account Operators local group are allowed to use User Manager for Domains to create user accounts and groups for the domain, and to modify or delete most of the domain's user accounts and groups.

An Account Operator cannot modify or delete the following groups: Administrators, Domain Admins, Account Operators, Backup Operators, Print Operators, and Server Operators. Likewise, members of this group cannot modify or delete user accounts of administrators. They cannot administer the security policies, but they can use Server Manager to add computers to a domain, log on at servers, and shut down servers.

Print Operators   Members of this group can create, manage, and delete printer shares for an NT Server server. Additionally, they can log on at and shut down servers.

Backup Operators   The Backup Operators local group provides its members the rights necessary to back up directories and files from a server and to restore directories and files to a server. Like the Print Operators, they can also log on at and shut down servers.

Everyone   Everyone is not actually a group, and it doesn't appear in the User Management list, but you can assign rights and permissions to it. Anyone having a user account in the domain—this includes all local and remote users—is automatically a member of the Everyone local group. Not only are members of this group allowed to connect over the network to a domain's servers, but they are also granted the advanced right to change directories and travel through a directory tree which they may not have permissions on. Members of the Everyone group also have the right to lock the server, but won't be able to unless they've been granted the right to log on locally at the server.

Users   Members of the group simply called Users have only minimal rights at servers running NT Server. They are granted the right to create and manage local groups, but unless they have access to the User Manager for Domains tool (such as by being allowed to log on locally at the server), they won't be able to perform this task. Members of the Users group do possess certain rights at their local NT workstations.

Guests   This is NT Server's built-in local group for occasional or one-time users to log on. Members of this group are granted very limited abilities. Guests have no rights at NT Server servers, but they do possess certain rights at their own individual workstations. The built-in Guest user account is automatically a member of the Guests group.

Note: The Guest account should never be disabled, because a number of services must actually log on to the network before executing, and the Guest account is often automatically used for this purpose. Disabling the Guest account may prevent certain applications from running. In the same consideration, you might want to leave the password blank on the Guest account.

Replicator   This local group, different from the others, supports directory replication functions. The only member of a domain's Replicator local group should be a single domain user account, which is used to log on the Replicator services of the domain controller and of the other servers in the domain. User accounts of actual users should *not* be added to this group at all. (Wondering what you'd use this group for? It's instrumental to directory replication, which we'll discuss in Chapter 10.)

Table 7.6 summarizes user rights (more on user rights in the next section) and the special abilities granted to NT Server predefined local groups.

TABLE 7.6 :   Rights and Special Abilities Granted to NT Server's Predefined Local Groups

User Rights	Members Can Also
Group: Administrators	
Log on locally	Create, manage user accounts
Access this computer from the network	Create, manage global groups
Take ownership of files	Assign user rights
Manage auditing and security log	Lock the server
Change the system time	Override the server's lock
Shut down the system	Format server's hard disk
Force shutdown from a remote system	Create common groups
Back up files, directories	Keep a local profile
	Share, stop sharing directories
	Share, stop sharing printers

TABLE 7.6: Rights and Special Abilities Granted to NT Server's Predefined Local Groups (continued)

User Rights	Members Can Also
Group: Server Operators	
Log on locally	Lock server
Change system time	Override server's lock
Shut down system	Format server's hard disk
Force shutdown from remote system	Create common groups
Back up files, directories	Keep local profile
Restore files, directories	Share, stop sharing directories
	Share, stop sharing printers
Group: Account Operators [1]	
Log on locally	Create and manage user accounts, global groups, and local groups
Shut down the system	Keep local profile
Group: Print Operators	
Log on locally	Keep local profile
Shut down system	Share, stop printers
Group: Backup Operators	
Log on locally	Keep a local profile
Shut down system	
Back up files, directories	
Restore files, directories	
Group: Everyone	
Access this computer from network	Lock the server [2]

TABLE 7.6: Rights and Special Abilities Granted to NT Server's Predefined Local Groups (continued)

User Rights	Members Can Also
Group: Users	
(None)	Create and manage local groups[3]
Group: Guests	
(None)	(None)

1. Account operators cannot modify administrator accounts, the Domain Admins global group, or the local group's Administrators, Server Operators, Account Operators, Print Operators, and Backup Operators.

2. In order to actually lock the server, the member of the group must have the right to log on locally at the server.

3. In order to actually create and manager local groups, the user must either have the right to log on locally at the server, or must have access to the User Manager for Domains tool.

NT SERVER

NT Server only has two built-in global groups, Domain Admins and Domain Users:

- **Domain Admins** By placing a user account into this global group, you provide administrative-level abilities to that user. Members of Domain Admins can administer the home domain, the workstations of the domain, and any other trusted domains that have added the Domain Admins global group to their own Administrators local group. By default, the built-in Domain Admins global group is a member of both the domain's Administrators local group and the Administrators local groups for every NT workstation in the domain. The built-in Administrator user account for the domain is automatically a member of the Domain Admins global group.

- **Domain Users** Members of the Domain Users global group have normal user access to, and abilities for, both the domain itself and for any NT workstation in the domain. This group contains all domain user accounts, and is by default a member of the Users local groups for both the domain and for every Windows NT workstation on the domain.

Built-In Special Groups   In addition to the built-in local and global groups, there are a few special groups which appear now and again when viewing certain lists of groups:

- INTERACTIVE: Anyone using the computer locally.
- NETWORK: All users connected over the network to a computer.
- SYSTEM: The operating system.
- CREATOR OWNER: The creator and/or owner of subdirectories, files, and print jobs.

Incidentally, the INTERACTIVE and NETWORK groups combined form the Everyone local group.

Managing Security Policies

The User Manager for Domains is part of a trio of programs that provides network security options in NT Server. While the File Manager and the Print Manager control specific access to files, directories, and printers, User Manager for Domains gives the administrator the ability to assign system-wide rights and to determine what the auditing policies of the network will be.

In User Manager for Domains, an administrator can manage the following security policies:

- Account, which controls the characteristics of passwords for all user accounts
- User Rights, which determines which user or group is assigned particular system rights
- Audit, in which the kinds of security events to be logged are defined
- Trust Relationships, which establishes how other domains on the network interact with the local domain

Password Characteristics

Under the Account policy, you can set and adjust the password characteristics for all user accounts in the domain. From the Policies menu, choose Account. You'll see the Account Policy dialog box, as in Figure 7.21.

FIGURE 7.21:

Account Policy dialog box

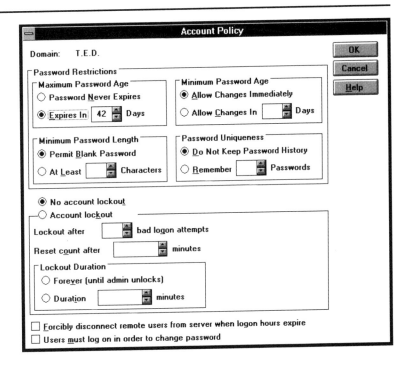

Make your selections for the following options:

- **Maximum Password Age** This option sets the time period in which a password can be used before the system requires the user to pick a new one.

- **Minimum Password Age** The value set here is the time that a password has to be used before the user is allowed to change it again. If you allow changes to the password to be made immediately, make sure you choose Do Not Keep Password History in the Password Uniqueness box.

- **Minimum Password Length**   This option defines the fewest number of characters a user's password can contain.

- **Password Uniqueness**   Here you can specify the number of new passwords that must be used before a user can employ an old password. If you choose a value here, you must specify a password age value under Minimum Password Age.

- **Account lockout**   will prevent anyone from logging into the account after a certain number of failed attempts:

    - **Lockout after "x' bad logon attempts**   This value defines how many times the user can attempt to log in.

    - **Reset count after "x' minutes**   This setting defines the time in which the count of bad logon attempts will start over. For example, suppose you have a reset count of two minutes and three logon attempts. If you mistype two, by waiting two minutes after the second attempt, you'll have three tries again.

    - **Lockout Duration**   This setting determines whether the administrator must unlock the account manually or the user may try again after a certain period.

The option Forcibly Disconnect Remote Users From Server When Logon Hours Expire is tied in to the available logon hours you specified when you created the user account. If it's selected, the user is disconnected from all connections to any of the domain's servers once the logon hours expire.

Not selecting this option enables the user to stay connected once the logon hours expire, but no new connections will be permitted. Checking "User must log on in order to change password" permits the user to change her password after demonstrating that she knows it already.

User Rights and Object Permissions

User access to network resources—files, directories, devices—in NT Server is controlled in two ways: by assigning *rights* to a user which grant or deny access to certain objects (e.g., the ability to log onto a server), and by assigning *permissions* to objects which specify who is allowed to use them and under what conditions (e.g., granting read access for a directory to a particular user).

Consider the groups Users, Administrators, and the others. What makes Administrators different from Users? Well, Administrators can log on right at the server; Users can't. Administrators can create users and back up files; Users can't. Administrators are different from Users in that they have rights that Users don't have. The central thing to remember here is that the very thing that separates one group in NT from another is largely the rights that groups have. You control who gets which rights via the User Manager for Domains.

Rights generally authorize a user to perform certain system tasks. For example, the average user can't just sit down at an NT Server and log on right at the server. The question "Can I log on locally at a server?" is an example of a right. "Can I back up data, or restore data?" "Can I modify printer options on a shared printer?" These are also user rights. User rights can be assigned separately to a single user, but for security organization reasons it's better to put the user into a group and define which rights are granted to the group. You manage user rights in User Manager for Domains.

Permissions, on the other hand, apply to specific objects such as files, directories, and printers. "Can I change files in the LOTUS directory on the BIGMACHINE server?" is an example of a permission. Permissions are set by the creator or owner of an object. Permissions regulate which users can have access to the object and in what fashion.

> **TIP**
>
> You can only set permissions on particular files on an NTFS volume. Directory and file permissions are administered in File Manager; printer permissions are regulated in Print Manager.

As a rule, user rights take precedence over object permissions. For example, let's look at a user who is a member of the built-in Backup Operators group. By virtue of his or her membership in that group, the user has the right to back up the servers in the user's domain. This requires the ability to see and read all directories and files on the servers, including those whose creators and owners have specifically denied read permission to members of the Backup Operators group; thus the right to perform backups overrides the permissions set on the files and directories.

There are two types of user rights: regular user rights and advanced user rights. NT Server's built-in groups have certain rights already assigned to them; you can also create new groups and assign a custom set of user rights to those groups. As I've said before, security management will be much easier if all user rights are assigned through groups instead of being granted to individual users.

To look at or change the rights granted to a user or group, select the domain where the particular user or group resides (if they are not in the local domain), then choose User Rights from the Policies menu. You'll see the User Rights Policy dialog box, as seen in Figure 7.22.

Check the arrow box next to the currently displayed user right to see the entire list of regular user rights. Clicking on any one of the rights shows the groups and users who currently have been granted that particular right. In the figure, you can see that the right "Access this computer from network" has been granted to the Administrators and Everyone groups.

The regular rights used in NT Server are:

- **Access this computer from network** Allows a user to connect over the network to a computer.

- **Add workstations to domain** Make machines domain members.

FIGURE 7.22:
User Rights Policy dialog box

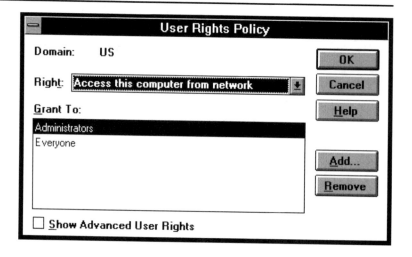

- **Back up files and directories** Allows a user to back up files and directories. As mentioned earlier, this right supersedes file and directory permissions.

- **Change the system time** Grants a user the right to set the time for the internal clock of a computer.

- **Force shutdown from a remote system** Note that, although presented as an option, this right is not currently implemented by NT Server.

- **Load and unload device drivers** Users can add drivers to the system or remove them.

- **Log on locally** Allows a user to log on locally at the server computer itself.

- **Manage auditing and security log** Gives a user the right to specify what types of events and resource access are to be audited. Also allows viewing and clearing of the security log.

- **Restore files and directories** Allows user to restore files and directories. This right supersedes file and directory permissions.

- **Shut down the system** Grants user the right to shut down Windows NT.

- **Take ownership of files or other objects** Lets a user take ownership of files, directories, and other objects that are owned by other users.

The advanced rights in NT Server are summarized in Table 7.7. These rights are added to the rights list when you click the Show Advanced User Rights option, located at the bottom of the User Rights Policy dialog box.

Most of the advanced rights are useful only to programmers writing applications to run on Windows NT, and most are not granted to a group or user. However, two of the advanced rights—Bypass traverse checking and Log on as a service—might be useful to some domain administrators. Bypass traverse checking is granted by default to the Everyone group in NT Server.

In general, I find that the only user right that I ever end up granting is to log on to the server locally; now and then, a user needs that ability.

TABLE 7.7: Advanced User Rights

Advanced User Right	Meaning
Act as part of the operating system	Users can act as a trusted part of the operating system; some subsystems have this privilege granted to them.
Bypass traverse checking	Users can traverse a directory tree even if the user has no other rights to access that directory; denies access to users in POSIX applications.
Create a pagefile	Users can create a pagefile.
Create a token object	Users can create access tokens. Only the Local Security Authority can have this privilege.
Create permanent shared objects	Users can create special permanent objects used in NT.
Debug programs	Users can debug applications.
Generate security audits	Users can generate audit-log entries.
Increase quotas	Users can increase object quotas (each object has a quota assigned to it).
Increase scheduling priority	Users can boost the scheduling priority of a process.
Lock pages in memory	Users can lock pages in memory to prevent them from being paged out into backing store (such as PAGEFILE.SYS).
Log on as a batch job	Users can log onto the system as a batch queue facility.
Log on as a service	Users can perform security services (the user that performs replication logs on as a service).
Modify firmware environment values	Users can modify system environment variables (but not user environment variables).
Profile single process	Users can use Windows NT profiling capabilities to observe a process.
Profile system performance	Users can use Windows NT profiling capabilities to observe the system.
Replace a process level token	Users can modify a process's access token.

Security Event Auditing

NT Server maintains three event logs to which entries are added in the background—the System log, the Applications log, and the Security log. You can set up security auditing of a number of events on NT Server in User Manager for Domains to help track user access to various parts of the system. To enable security auditing, pull down the Policies menu and select Audit. You will see the dialog box in Figure 7.23.

FIGURE 7.23:

Audit Policy dialog box

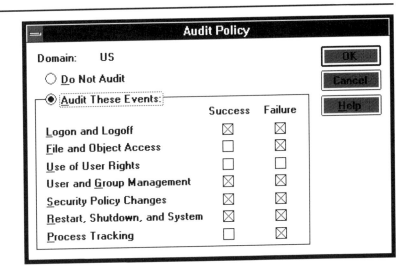

As you can see, the Audit Policy dialog box gives you a choice whether or not to activate auditing, followed by a list of the types of security events you can audit. The default setting is Do Not Audit; with this option selected, all of the Audit These Events options are grayed out. If you choose to activate auditing, the information about a selected event is stored as an entry in the computer's Security log when the event takes place. This log, along with the System and Application logs, can then be viewed with the Event Viewer.

Table 7.8 describes the auditing options you can select.

TABLE 7.8: Security Auditing Options

Events to Audit	Description
Logon and Logoff	Tracks user logons, logoffs, and the creating and breaking of connections to servers.
File and Object Access	Tracks access to a directory or file that has been selected for auditing under File Manager; tracks print jobs sent to printers that have been set for auditing under Print Manager.
Use of User Rights	Notes when users make use of a user right (except those associated with logons and logoffs).
User and Group Management	Tracks changes in user accounts or groups (creations, changes, deletions); notes if user accounts are renamed, disabled, or enabled; tracks setting or changing passwords.
Security Policy Changes	Tracks changes made to the User Rights, Audit, or Trust Relationship policies.
Restart, Shutdown, and System	Tracks when the computer is shut down or restarted; tracks the filling up of the audit log and the discarding of audit entries if the audit log is already full.
Process Tracking	Records detailed tracking information for program activation, some types of handle duplication, indirect object accesses, and process exit.

It's important to keep in mind that all of the event logs are limited in size. The default size for each of the logs is 512K, and the default overwrite settings allow events older than seven days to be discarded from the logs as needed. When managing the auditing policy in User Manager for Domains, choose your events to audit carefully—you may find that you get what you ask for, sometimes in great abundance. For example, auditing successful File and Object Accesses can generate a tremendous amount of security log entries. A reasonably simple process, such as opening an application, opening a single file within that application, editing and saving that file, and exiting the application can produce more than 60 log events. A couple of users on a system can generate 200 log entries in less than two minutes. Auditing successful Process Tracking events can produce similar results.

If your network requires that you monitor events that closely, make sure you choose appropriate log size and overwrite settings. You can change these settings for the Security log (and for the other two logs, for that matter) in the Event Viewer.

Summary: The User Manager for Domains

That's not all that the User Manager for Domains can do. I haven't covered trust relationships and local and global groups but, again, I *will* cover those things in Chapter 11.

Notice that the User Manager does more than just manage users; it is, in some way, the Security Manager for NT—but just a *part* of the Security Manager role. Before leaving the User Manager for Domains let's review what it does. It lets you:

- Create, destroy, and modify network user accounts
- Assign and remove user rights
- Create, destroy, and modify groups
- Control what users go in which groups
- Assign and remove rights to and from groups
- Create and destroy trust relationships

The User Manager is a powerful tool that you'll find yourself using quite frequently. Get to know it, and you'll be able to get your network administration chores done more quickly.

CHAPTER

EIGHT

Using the File Manager

8

File Manager

If you've ever worked with Microsoft Windows, then you've seen the File Manager. It's an application that lets you organize and work with files and directories. It's the basic tool for viewing, organizing, and connecting to directories and files.

For a network administrator, however, the File Manager is also a simple graphical front-end for controlling disk, directory, and file permissions.

Tasks that are performed through File Manager include:

- Displaying and navigating through directories and files
- Creating and removing directories
- Moving, copying, and deleting files
- Determining file attributes
- Maintaining floppy disks
- Connecting to directories shared on the network
- Sharing directories
- Securing files and directories

I realize that many of you already know how to use the *Windows* File Manager, and so the part of this chapter that covers how to move, copy, and erase files and directories will be a bit of a yawn. I included the information for people who have never worked with Windows before. If you *do* already know how to work the File Manager for disk and file management, then just skip to the section entitled "Network Connections in the File Manager."

Introducing the File Manager Display

When you double-click on the File Manager icon for the first time, the directory tree and the contents of the current directory for the local volume appear. If you choose Save Settings on Exit in the Options menu, the information displayed in subsequent openings of File Manager will be that for the last drive administered. You can see this in Figure 8.1.

FIGURE 8.1:

The File Manager window

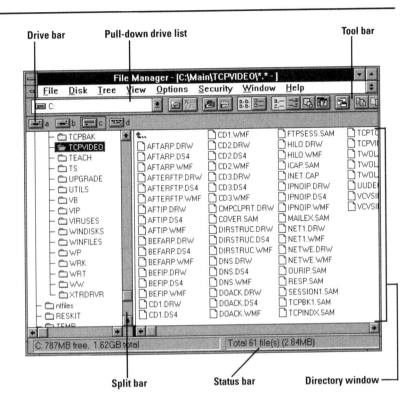

The title bar gives the current drive and directory path, followed by either the drive's volume label (if local) or the network name (if remote). Beneath the title bar is the menu bar. Right below the menu bar are the toolbar, which contains the pull-down drive list, and the drive bar with its selection of drive icons. (By the way, you can quickly select a drive for display by pressing Ctrl and the drive's letter; for example, you'd select the H drive by pressing Ctrl-H.) Positioned along the bottom of the window is the status bar, which lists disk information for the currently selected drive.

To change the currently selected drive, click on the appropriate icon in the drive bar or choose the drive from the drive list on the left side of the tool bar.

You can configure the tool bar to your own satisfaction by opening the Options menu and choosing Customize Toolbar. Conversely, if you don't need the tool, drive, or status bars, you can switch them off by selecting the appropriate commands in the Options menu.

The predominant component of the File Manager display is the directory window. The directory window shows the directory and file information for the current drive in two panes: on the left is the drive's directory tree, and on the right are the contents of the currently selected directory. The two sides are separated by the split bar, which can be adjusted to either side by dragging it with the mouse or by choosing Split under the View menu and using the arrow keys to move it left or right. Further options in the View menu let you select whether or not to display the directory tree only, the contents of the directory, or both.

Viewing Directories

The directory tree shows how the directories on the drive are structured. At the top of the list is the root directory. Located next to the root directory is the file system name for the drive, i.e., NTFS, HPFS, or FAT. For example, Figure 8.2 shows an NTFS volume.

Branching beneath the root directory, forming the rest of the directory tree, are the other directories and subdirectories on the disk. Directories are represented by small file folder icons. Shared directories are depicted as a folder being held by a hand, while the directory currently in use is shown as an open folder.

FIGURE 8.2:

The directory window for an NTFS volume

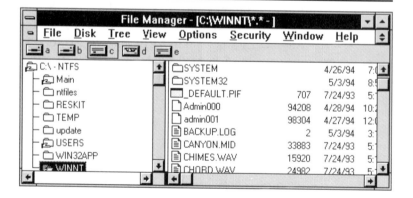

In the directory tree, directory icons are connected by lines to the directory level above them. Double-clicking on any directory expands that directory branch one level downward, displaying that directory's subdirectories.

Within the Tree menu are options you can choose to determine how the directories in view should be displayed:

Option	Use
Expand One Level	Displays the next directory level down for the selected directory.
Expand Branch	Lets you view just the subdirectories of a single selected directory.
Collapse Branch	Displays the current directory.
Expand All	Displays the entire directory tree. Be aware that a complex directory tree may take some time to generate. Pressing the Esc key stops the process and gives you a partial directory tree.
Indicate Expandable Branches	Lets you see which directories contain subdirectories. Any directory that has unexpanded subdirectories is then marked with a plus sign (+). When expanded, the plus sign changes to a minus sign, indicating that the directory is expanded and can now be collapsed. This is demonstrated in the dialog box in Figure 8.3. Not unexpectedly, File Manager takes longer to create the directory tree when the Indicate Expandable Branches choice is selected.

When you select a directory in the directory tree, the contents of that directory are displayed on the right side. To see the contents of a different directory, simply click on it in the directory tree. You can use the directional keys on the keyboard (the ↑, ↓, Page Up, Page Down, Home, and End keys) to step through the tree and contents list.

FIGURE 8.3:

A directory tree showing expandable branches

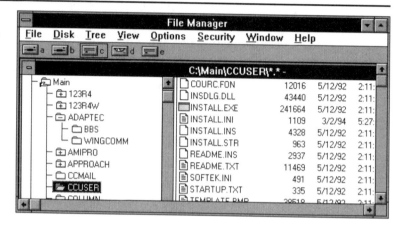

Viewing the Contents of a Directory

When the Tree and Directory option in the View menu is marked, the File Manager displays the contents list of the currently selected directory in the right pane of the directory window.

At the top of the list is an "up icon," a little arrow pointing upwards. Double-clicking on this arrow takes you up a level in the directory tree, as in Figure 8.4.

FIGURE 8.4:

Directories and files in the contents list

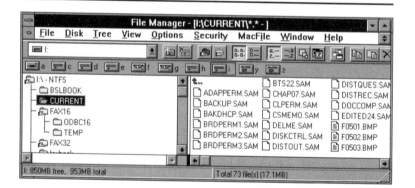

Files in the contents list of the File Manager directory window can be displayed in a variety of ways. From the View menu, you can choose Name to see simply the name of the files, or All File Details, which include the file's size, last modification date and time, its attributes, and the truncated version of the name for MS-DOS. If you prefer, you can pick which specific details you want displayed by choosing Partial Details. If you want to see all files of a particular type, choose By File Type and use the asterisk wildcard to define which types of files you want to see. Hidden and system files are also displayed when the Show Hidden/System Files check box is selected. In addition to choosing which file details you want to see, you can determine whether the contents list is sorted by name, type, size, or date by choosing the appropriate option in the View menu.

In File Manager, you can open as many directory windows as you need, either for displaying the contents of a different directory on the drive, or for viewing another drive. A new window is opened when you select New Window from the Window menu, or when you double-click on any of the drive icons. New directory windows inherit their display options from the current window. If you've opened more than one window for the same drive and directory, a number appears in the title bar to let you know there's more than one instance of that window.

Multiple directory windows can be arranged in three different ways—by cascading them, tiling them horizontally, or by tiling them vertically. You can choose which way you prefer by selecting the desired option under the Window menu. Directory windows can also be minimized to appear as icons, and can be organized by choosing the Arrange Icons command.

File and directory management occurs only in the currently selected window (the active window). To make a window the active window, you can:

- Click anywhere on the window,
- Select the window from the list displayed at the bottom of the pulled-down Window menu, or
- Hit Ctrl-F6 or Ctrl-Tab until the window you want has been selected.

You can close any open window except the last one—in File Manager, at least one window is always displayed. Active windows can be closed by choosing Close under the File menu, or by double-clicking on the window's Control-menu box in the upper-left corner.

Information in open directory windows is updated automatically in most cases. To update manually, click the drive icon for the current drive, or choose Refresh from the Window menu.

Incidentally, you can change the font used for the directory windows by choosing Font from the Options menu. In the resulting font box, select the font that you want, the desired style (bold, italic, etc.), and the size. Changes to the font affect all directory windows.

Selecting Directories and Files

Before a directory or file can be managed, it must first be selected. When selected, directory and file names appear highlighted in the directory window. There are several ways to select directories and files in File Manager; they are summarized here:

To Select	Selection Techniques
A single directory or file	*With the mouse:* Click on the name of the directory or file you want to select. *With the keyboard:* Hit Tab to move the cursor to the contents list, then use the ↑ and ↓ keys to select the directory or file.
Two or more items in sequence	*With the mouse:* Click on the first file or directory. Then hold down the Shift key while you click on the last item in the group. *With the keyboard:* From the contents list, use the arrow keys to select the first item. Then hold down the Shift key while selecting the remaining items using the arrow keys.
Two or more items not in sequence	*With the mouse:* Hold down the Ctrl key while clicking on each item. *With the keyboard:* From the contents list, use the arrow keys to select the first item. Press and release Shift-F8. Use the arrow keys to move to each item and use the spacebar to select it. Press Shift-F8 again when done.

To Select	Selection Techniques
More than one group of directories or files	*With the mouse:* Select the first sequential group of items. Hold down Ctrl while clicking on the first item in the next group. Hold down Ctrl and the Shift key while clicking on the last item in the second group. *With the keyboard:* Select the first group using the Shift-F8 method, then use the arrow keys to move to the first item in the second group and repeat the process. Press Shift-F8 again when all items are selected.
All files in a directory	*With the keyboard:* Press Ctrl+/ (slash). (There is no mouse technique for selecting all files.)

In addition, you can select all files of a particular file type (or all files having other similarities in name) by choosing the Select Files command in the File menu and using the asterisk wildcard to specify a set of files, as in Figure 8.5.

FIGURE 8.5:
Select Files dialog box

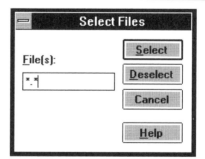

Managing Directories, Files, and Disks

In the process of setting up a server, you'll be creating directories and subdirectories as well as managing a large number of files. Creating directories is easy. To create a new directory (or subdirectory) anywhere on the volume, first select the directory you want the new directory to be placed within, then pull down the File menu and choose Create Directory. You'll see the Create Directory dialog box, as shown in Figure 8.6. Type in the name of the directory, and choose OK. Recall that you can use names of up to 255 characters even on FAT volumes with NT version 3.5 or later.

FIGURE 8.6:

Create Directory dialog box

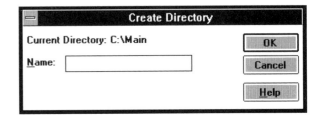

Moving and Copying Files and Directories

To move or copy files or directories, you can either drag the files to their new locations with the mouse (to make copies, hold the Ctrl button down while dragging), or you can use the Select Files command in the File menu to select all of the files (or directories) you want to move or copy. Then choose the appropriate command (Move or Copy) from the File menu.

If you're working with a drive formatted to use NTFS, there are a few things to keep in mind when you move or copy files and directories. First, files and directories can't be moved or copied unless you have permission to do so. Second, when you copy files or directories, their original security permissions, auditing parameters, and ownership information is not retained and transferred—they will inherit new permissions from the directory in which they've been copied. For a file, if the new directory does not specify permissions for files, then only the file's owner (the person who copied the file) will have permission to access the file.

When files and directories are copied or moved from NTFS volumes to drives formatted using HPFS or the FAT file system, all permissions are discarded, as neither file system supports NTFS file and directory security. Permissions and other security features available for NTFS volumes will be discussed later in this chapter.

To rename any directory, subdirectory, or file, select it in the directory window, choose the Rename command under the File menu, and type in the new name.

Naming Conventions in NTFS

On an NTFS volume, files and directories can be given names that are longer than DOS's standard 8+3 characters. NTFS supports file names that are up to 255 characters in length (including any extensions), as long as the following characters are not used:

```
? " / \ < > * | :
```

Names created using NTFS can be upper- or lowercase, and they retain whatever case they were typed in as, but are not case-sensitive.

> **TIP**   The NT Server default for displaying files and directories on FAT drives is all lowercase. You can alter this by changing the choices in the dialog box for Font, under the Options menu.

For DOS users, in which long names are not supported, NT provides name-mapping. Long file and directory names are truncated by the following procedure to create DOS-type names:

- Any spaces in the long name are removed.

- Characters not allowed in DOS names are changed to underscores (_).

- The name is truncated to its first six characters (if there's a period within the first six characters, then it's truncated to those characters before the period).

- A tilde (~) and a sequential number are added to the characters (if the number exceeds nine, then the name is truncated to the first five characters).

- The long name is checked for any periods followed by characters; if some are found, then the last of those periods and the first three characters following that period are used as the file name extension for the short name.

For example, if a file on an NTFS volume has been given the name

```
Proofs - Proofs list from Apr94 through May94.sam
```

it will be truncated to

```
proofs~1.sam
```

Bear in mind that if you use a file that has a long NTFS name in an application that doesn't support long file names and you save the file, the long file name will be lost and the saved file will have only the short name.

Viewing Properties and Attributes

You can check the properties and attributes of any file or directory in File Manager by selecting the directory or file, then choosing the Properties option in the File menu. You'll see the Properties dialog box, as in Figure 8.7. Directory properties include the name, path, last change date, and its attributes.

File properties, in addition to those for directories, include these properties: the file's current version number, copyright information, size, and network information, such as who is currently using the file. This can be seen in Figure 8.8. The four attributes are read-only, archive, hidden, and system. They are defined in Table 8.1.

TABLE 8.1: File Attributes

Attribute	Description
Read Only	File can be read, but not written to. Prevents a file from being changed.
Archive	Identifies a file that has been modified since it was last backed up.
Hidden	The file does not appear in directory listings from the command prompt; it is hidden from directory lists in File Manager unless the Show Hidden/System Files check box (choose the View menu, then By File Type) is selected.
System	Identifies a file as a system file. As with hidden files, system files appear in a directory window only if the Show Hidden/System Files check box is selected.

These attributes help NT Server identify the file and control the type of activity that can be performed with the file. File attributes appear in the directory window when the All File Details option under the View menu is selected. If a selected file has version information, a company name, and other comments attached to it, these also appear in the file's properties, within the Version Information box.

FIGURE 8.7:

Viewing directory properties

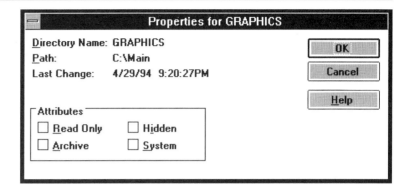

FIGURE 8.8:

Viewing file properties

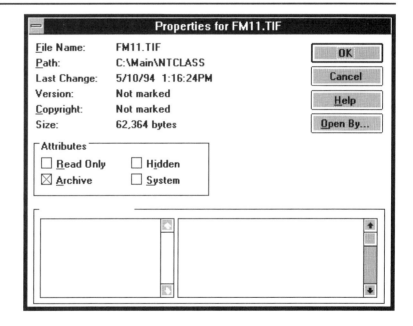

To view a file's network properties, choose the Open By... button in the properties box. You'll see the Network Properties dialog box, as in Figure 8.9. Here you can see the total number of users working with the file, the total number of locks on the file, the users that have the file open, the type of access each user has on the file, and the individual locks that users have on the file. In addition, NT Server's identification number for the file is listed under File ID.

FIGURE 8.9:

A file's network properties

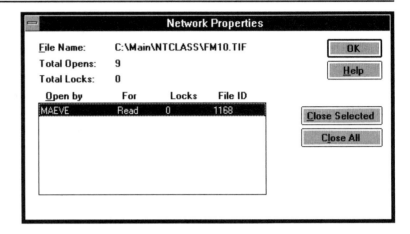

You can stop the use of a file by one or more users by selecting the users from the list and choosing the Close Selected button. Choosing the Close All button stops the use of that particular shared file by everyone. If you remove a file from sharing while users are still connected to it, those users may lose their data, so don't do it without warning those users. (On the other hand, suddenly disconnecting people from their data can be an effective way to find out who in the company owns an assault rifle.)

Searching for Files

The Search command under the File menu lets you scan all or part of the directory tree for a particular file or for files of a certain type. You can subsequently print, copy, move, rename, or delete the files. To search for a file, select the directory from which you want to start the search, then choose Search. You'll see the Search dialog box, as in Figure 8.10. Type the name of the file or directory in the box—you can use the asterisk wildcard to look for a group of files or directories with similar names or extensions. By default, File Manager searches the directory specified in the Start From box and all of the subdirectories within it; you can prevent this by clearing the Search All Subdirectories box.

You can continue File Manager tasks while the search continues in the background by choosing the Hide button, as in Figure 8.11. When the search is complete, the Search Results window will appear.

FIGURE 8.10:

Search dialog box

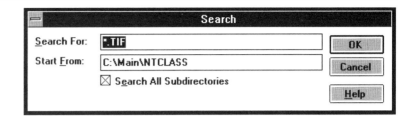

FIGURE 8.11:

Search in progress

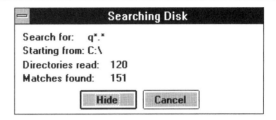

Deleting Directories and Files

To delete any directories or files, select them in the directory window, then either hit the Delete button on the keyboard or choose Delete from the File menu and type in the name of the file or directory you want to delete, as shown in Figure 8.12. If the name contains spaces, then you have to enclose the entire name in quotation marks. You'll be prompted for confirmation prior to the deletion, as in Figure 8.13, unless you have switched the Confirmation option off in the Options menu.

Deleted files and directories cannot be recovered, and, on an NTFS volume, you must have permission to delete the files or directories before the action can proceed.

FIGURE 8.12:

Delete dialog box

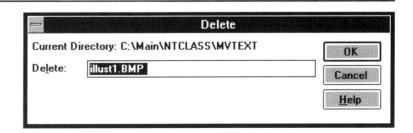

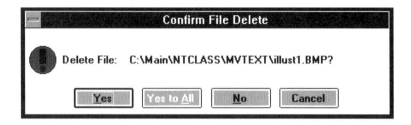

Associating Files with Applications

Files are associated with specific applications through their file name extension and the application's file type. Once you associate a file with an application, you can:

- Double-click on any file with the same file name extension in the directory window to start the application and load that particular file

- Print the file while in File Manager (provided the application supports printing)

A single file extension can be associated with only one application. However, one application can be associated with several different file types. For example, files with the extensions .BMP, .PCX, and .TIF can be associated with the same graphics application, but you couldn't associate .BMP files with two different graphics programs.

To create or change a file association, first select the file in the directory window that has the extension you want to associate. Then, from the File menu, choose Associate. You'll see the Associate dialog box, as shown in Figure 8.14. If there's a current association already for that file type, it is displayed in the Associate With list; if not, then None will be selected.

To make the association, select the desired application from the Associate With list. If the application isn't listed, then either type in the name of the application, or use the Browse button to search for the program name. Selecting a program name in the Browse dialog box and choosing the OK button places that program name and its path in the Associated With list.

FIGURE 8.14:

Associate dialog box

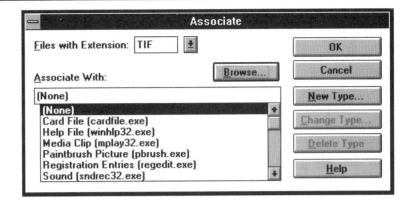

If you need to, you can also create and define your own file types and associate them as required with your applications.

Starting Applications from File Manager

Applications can be started from File Manager by several ways:

- Double-click on the application's file name in the directory window.

- Select the application and choose Open from the File menu (you can do this by simply hitting the Enter key).

- Select the application and choose Run from the File menu, then type in the application name, as in Figure 8.15.

FIGURE 8.15:

Starting an application with the Run command

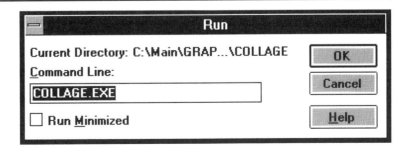

You can also run an application using a particular data file if both are visible in the directory window—just drag the icon for the data file on top of the icon for the program file.

The Minimize On Use command in the Options menu reduces File Manager to an icon each time you start an application. If you choose to start an application using the Run command, you can set that application itself to run minimized by choosing the Run Minimized button.

Disk Maintenance

The Disk menu contains commands that allow you to format and copy floppy disks, as well as make system disks and assign a label to any available disk. (As I observed in Chapter 4, you can't format a hard disk from the File Manager, unfortunately.) When you copy floppy disks, remember that you can't recover the information on the destination disk if it is accidentally overwritten, so check your paths and disks carefully. Floppy disks are formatted using the FAT file system.

You can perform other activities in File Manager while the formatting or copying takes place; just choose the Hide button in the dialog box (see Figure 8.16) to move it out of the way.

To assign a label to a disk, simply click on the drive icon for the drive whose label you want to change, then type in a new label. Labels on NTFS disks can contain up to 32 characters; FAT disks can have labels containing up to 11 characters.

FIGURE 8.16:

Formatting in progress

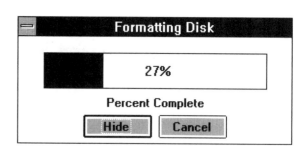

File Compression

Are things feeling cramped yet in that 1.2 GB drive on the server? It never fails—the more disk space you have, the more you seem to need. In the interests of freeing up more space on the server without forcing you to use tape archives for everything or buy larger disks, NT Server 3.51 offers a file compression utility. File compression won't solve all of your space crunch worries, but it may buy you some time to think about the best way to get more storage space.

Using compression tools in NT Server 3.51's File Manager, you can compress either individual files or entire directories. The process for each is similar.

Compressing a Single File

The course manuals and books that we produce at my company are kept on one of the file servers. As you'd expect, the file for an 800-page book is pretty hefty (nearly 2MB just for the *text*, and another 31MB for the pictures); and when you've got a dozen books and all their pictures stored on the server, things can get pretty crowded. The books are each stored in their own directories according to subject, so I can't compress them all at once, but I *could* compress each book's text file so that it's taking up less room on the server. To do that, I'd perform the following procedure.

1. Open the File Manager, move to the directory containing the file that I want to compress, and select the file.

2. I can compress the file in either of two ways: choose Compress… from the File menu, or, as shown in Figure 8.17, open the file's Properties dialog box (accessible from the File menu), check the Compression box in the Attributes section, and click OK to exit.

3. In either case, the compression takes place immediately. When I deselect the file in the File Manager listing, I can see that it's listed in blue rather than black.

You can't see the effects of compression from the main windows in the File Manager; you have to open the file's Properties dialog box to show the effects. Select the file, choose Properties… from the File menu, and you'll see a dialog box like the one in Figure 8.18. If you're used to consulting the Properties dialog, you'll notice that there's a new entry in this box—unless a file is compressed, there's no compression information listed here at all.

FIGURE 8.17:

Enabling the Compression attribute

FIGURE 8.18:

Properties dialog box for a compressed file

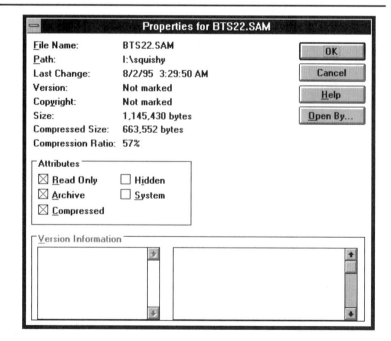

To expand a file back to its original size, select the file and either choose Uncompress... from the File menu or open the Properties dialog and uncheck the Compression attribute. The file will return to its normal size.

Compressing a Directory

Compressing a directory works much like compressing a single file, except that you can choose whether or not to compress all files within the directory. To compress an entire directory, select the directory and either select Compress... from the File menu or check it in the directory's Properties dialog box, as you can see in Figure 8.19.

FIGURE 8.19:

Enabling a directory's Compression attribute

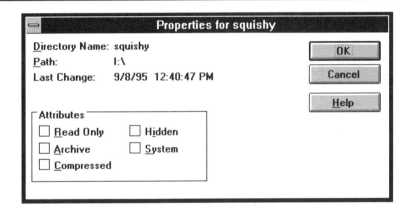

When you click Compress... or set the compression attribute, NT Server will ask whether you want to compress all the files in the directory or not, using a dialog box like the one shown in Figure 8.20. If you click the OK button, each file will be

FIGURE 8.20:

Compress all files in directory?

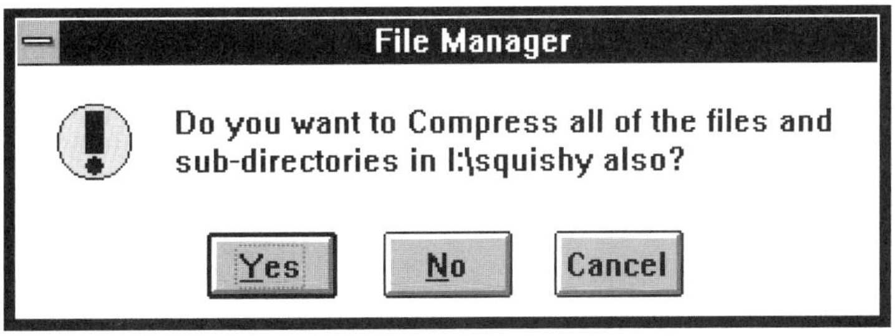

individually compressed—this doesn't work anything like the compression routines that package a bunch of files together into one. If you choose "No," then the files within the directory won't be compressed.

It takes NT Server a little longer to compress a number of files than it does just one, so while it's compressing the files you'll see a dialog box such as the one shown in Figure 8.21.

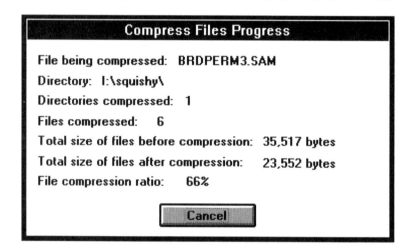

Even when compressing a directory containing several biggish files, the operation doesn't take long. When you're done, you can open either the Properties dialog box for files within the compressed directory or Properties for the folder itself to check out the rate of compression.

File Compression Tips

File compression is a new utility with NT Server 3.51, so keep a few things in mind when you're getting used to it.

- The compressed file size and compression ratio are shown in the compressed item's Properties dialog box, not the main screen of the File Manager.

- If you move files or directories to an NTFS partition, they'll take on the compression attributes of the directory that you move them to. For example, if you move a compressed file to an uncompressed directory, that file will no longer be compressed. Move a full-size file into a compressed directory, and it'll be compressed in its new location.

- You can't recompress a file already compressed in the File Manager. You could try to recompress a file or directory already compressed with another utility, but it probably won't do much.

Network Connections in the File Manager

Anyone can browse a network's domains, computers, and workgroups to look for shared resources, which include directories and files. In addition to its basic file management and security duties, File Manager gives administrators the capability to share directories. Users can then connect to those shared directories over the network and access the information within.

Connecting to Network Resources

To view a network's shared resources, pull down the Disk menu and choose Connect Network Drive or click the Connect Drive button on the toolbar. You'll see the dialog box in Figure 8.22. In this dialog box, the network's domains, workgroups, computers, and shared directories are organized in a tree structure. For example, in the dialog box in the figure, you see that the highest level of organization is the network itself, which in this case is Microsoft Windows Network. If you had the Client and Gateway Services for NetWare (CSNW) installed—you'll learn about it in

FIGURE 8.22:

Connect Network Drive dialog box

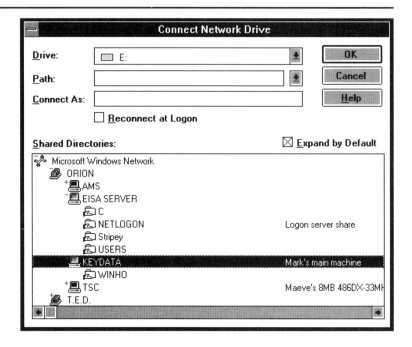

Chapter 12—you'd see Novell Network as another network option. Within the network, there are domains; here, you can see two of them, ORION and T.E.D. Within the ORION domain, there are servers, and you can see servers AMS, EISA SERVER, KEYDATA, and TSC in the figure. Finally, within servers there are available directories, and EISA SERVER offers shared directories called C, NETLOGON, Stripey, and USERS.

Double-clicking on any of the networks, domains, workgroups, or computers in the list expands the tree further, displaying any shared directories. Choosing a network name displays available domains and workgroups in that network; choosing a domain or workgroup name displays available computers in that group; and choosing an individual computer displays any available shared directories that computer might have.

To connect to a shared resource on the network, first choose a drive letter in the Drive box (the next sequentially available letter is given as a default). Then select the shared directory in the Shared Directories box. When you select the directory, its path appears in the Path box. Choosing OK then connects you to that directory. Alternately, you can make the connection by double-clicking on the shared directory in the network tree.

If you want to connect to the shared directory whenever you log on, click the Reconnect at Logon box. Then choose OK. Or, you can simply double-click on the directory in the Shared Directories box to connect to it using the default drive letter.

When the new connection is made, File Manager opens a new window displaying the newly connected drive's directory and file information. You can switch this feature off before making any connections by pulling down the Options menu and deselecting the Open New Window On Connect command.

Network users logged on as members of the Administrators, Server Operators, or Backup Operators groups can connect to a server's administrative root shares, i.e., *servername*\c$, to access a server's directories from a remote workstation. These administrative shares are not displayed in the Shared Directories box in the Connect Network Drive dialog box.

Sharing Drives and Directories

Most servers on networks function as repositories for files and directories that must be accessible to the network's users. Files and directories on a server running NT Server must first be *shared* in order for network users to access them.

Shared directories act like another hard disk that's available to users on the network. Once a directory is shared, users can connect to it from their own workstations and access the files in that directory over the network. When a directory on the server is shared, everything in it is shared—the directory, its files, its subdirectories, and the contents of the subdirectories. Some restrictions can be placed on shared directories; they apply only if the directory and its contents are accessed over the network (not locally).

> **TIP**
>
> You should use NTFS as the file system for your NT Servers, as its features provide superior security, performance, and reliability for file sharing. The contents of shared directories, when no special share restrictions have been set on them, are available to all users on the network. On an NTFS partition, you can block access to different parts of that shared directory by setting individual permissions on the directory's contents. The levels of security can be applied differently for files and directories—for each object on an NTFS volume, you can specify which users and groups can access the file, and what level of access each user or group is allowed to have. These file and directory permissions determine the access regardless of whether the information is accessed locally—that is, if you're sitting right at the server—or over the network. The security features on NTFS volumes also allow you to audit file and directory access. All of this provides additional security on top of that specified by the share permissions.

When you share a directory, you have to provide a *share name* for it. This is the name that network users will use to refer to the directory. It doesn't have to be the same name as the shared directory itself, and the same directory can be shared several times with different share names.

Users see the shared directory when they use the Connect Network Drive command in the Disk menu of File Manager from either NT workstations or Windows for Workgroups machines. It appears in the network tree as the share name appended to the computer name of the server. For example, a shared directory named Applications on a server named Polaris will show up as POLARIS\APPLICATIONS in the tree. The user can make a connection to the shared directory by assigning a drive letter to that shared directory at their workstation.

Sharing a Directory

You should share a directory when the directory's contents need to be available to users on the network. Note that the Server service must be running before you can share a directory, but it's usually started by default on NT Server machines. If you have to start it up, then you can start the Server service by using the Services option in the Control Panel.

Before sharing a directory on an NTFS volume, you should set individual permissions on that directory and its contents. Members of the Administrators local group, for example, should be granted Full Control so that all of the administrators of the domain can administer the directory and its files in the future.

To share a directory, you must be logged on as a member of the Administrators or Server Operators groups. Administrators can share directories on the server from remote computers by first connecting to the administrative share, C$, and then following these steps:

1. Select the desired directory in the File Manager window.

2. From the Disk menu, choose Share As. You'll see the New Share dialog box, as in Figure 8.23.

3. Fill in the share name and path. The default share name is the directory's own name; you can type in a different share name, if desired.

4. Set the user limit on the shared directory (the default is no limit).

5. If needed, select the Permissions button and set share permissions on the directory.

6. Choose OK. The directory will now appear in the directory tree with the Shared Directory icon.

Keep in mind that if your shared directory is to be accessed by MS-DOS users (running Windows for Workgroups, for example), you need to assign a share name that

FIGURE 8.23:
New Share dialog box

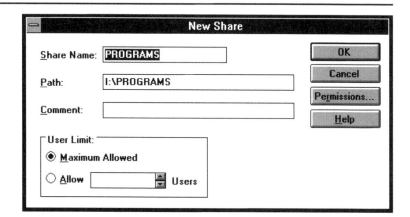

follows the DOS convention of 8+3 characters, or else the DOS users won't be able to access the share. (NT will remind you of this when you try to share the directory.) Now, that's a *share name*—your DOS workstations won't care what the directory name is, just the share name. For example, if you had a directory on an NT server called "really big directory," then of course the name "really big directory" would give DOS fits—*if* DOS saw it. What DOS sees is the share name, so you can just give it the share name "big" or something like that. Then the local NTFS name can be long and descriptive, but the share name can be of a type that won't upset DOS machines. For NT users, the share name can have up to 12 characters. Although NTFS provides name mapping for files and directories, it can't do this for share names.

If you need to share an already shared directory under a different name, select the directory in File Manager's window and choose the Share As command in the Disk menu. Instead of the New Share dialog box, you'll get the Shared Directories box. In this case, select the New Share button from that box to create the new share from the shared directory.

You can share a directory and have it remain invisible to network users by giving it a share name that ends with a dollar sign (for example, APPS2$). Although it doesn't appear in lists of shared directories in the Connect Network Drive dialog box, users can connect to the share by typing its name (including the $) in the path box. Anyone who knows the name of the hidden share can make the connection to it, but if they don't have Read or higher access to the share, they will not be able to view or modify the directory's contents.

How Do I Keep Users from Logging onto the Server's Root Directory?

Given that C$ is an administrative share that you're not supposed to get rid of, how you can you keep users from logging onto the server's root directory?

The share permissions of C$ are set and cannot be modified, but they don't give full access to all users on the network. Only users who are members of the Administrators, Server Operators, and Backup Operators groups can access the server's root from a remote location. Other users cannot connect to C$ without specifying a password.

Stopping Directory Sharing

Users who are members of the Administrators and Server Operators groups can stop sharing a directory. Check who is using the directory before you stop sharing it; if you stop sharing while users are still connected, those users may lose their data.

You should not stop sharing those administrative shares created by the system—for example, c$ or print$. Administrative shares that are inadvertently deleted are re-created automatically the next time the Server service is started.

To stop sharing a directory:

1. Click on the drive icon for the drive that the shared directory is on.

2. From the Disk menu, choose Stop Sharing. You'll see the Stop Sharing dialog box, as in Figure 8.24.

3. In the dialog box, select the directories that you want to stop sharing. If you highlighted a directory before choosing the Stop Sharing command, the names of the shared directories corresponding to that directory will already be selected.

4. Choose OK.

FIGURE 8.24:

Removing a directory from shared status

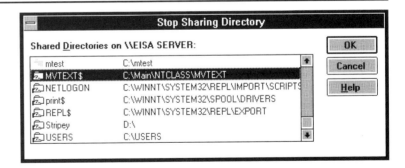

Changing Share Properties

To change the share properties for any shared directory, simply select the shared directory, then choose Share As from the Disk menu. You'll see the Shared Directory dialog box, as in Figure 8.25. If the directory has been shared more than once under

FIGURE 8.25:

Shared Directory dialog box

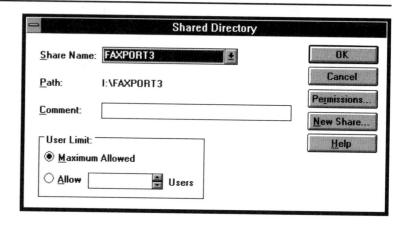

different names, then select the desired name in the Share Name box. From the Shared Directory dialog box, you can:

- Change the number of users allowed access to the shared directory
- Edit the comment box for the shared directory
- Change the shared permissions on the shared directory

Users who are members of the Administrators and Server Operators groups can change the number of users allowed to connect to a shared directory, a shared directory's comment information, or the shared directory's permissions.

Controlling Access to Shares, Directories, and Files

In addition to its file management and directory sharing capabilities, NT Server's File Manager is the basic tool for controlling *who* gets to use *which* data in *what* way. In many ways, it is the companion tool to the User Manager for Domains: While the security features in User Manager for Domains focus on the network's users and their rights to access parts of the system and perform certain tasks, the security features in File Manager focus instead on the files and directories themselves and how users are allowed to access them.

You can control who can (and can't) use a directory via permissions. You really have the finest degree of control over permissions on an NTFS drive, but FAT and HPFS drives still allow you some control.

There are three types of permissions for shared data:

- Share access permissions, which apply to an entire shared directory.

- Directory permissions, which allow you to control which user sees what part of a share—the ability to control who sees subdirectories of a shared directory.

- File permissions, which allow you to control people's access to particular files. Directory and file permissions are only possible on NTFS volumes.

Share permissions can be controlled either from the File Manager on a local machine, or with the Server Manager for any server on the network. You can only control directory and file permissions with the File Manager, whether on the local drives or remotely on network drives.

An Example Drive Structure

Just to make this clearer, let's imagine that we have a server whose hard disk looks like the one in Figure 8.26. On this server's C drive, there are three top-level directories:

- **WINNT35**, which is the directory where the system's files are, and that we don't want *anybody* accessing over the network.

- **Users**, which is the directory that will contain personal directories for all of the users. You see here that I have created subdirectories for three users—Harry, Sue, and Jamal. The important thing to see about the Users directory is that you're going to have to set permissions on its Harry, Sue, and Jamal subdirectories so that Harry can only see Users\Harry and no others, Sue can only see Users\Sue and no others, and Jamal must see Users\Jamal and no others. You don't want Sue being able to mess around in Harry's area. This will provide a nice example of a single share (Users) that contains private areas.

FIGURE 8.26:

Sample directory structure

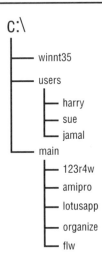

- **Main**, which is a directory that contains things that are communally accessible. In this case, the company uses the Lotus SmartSuite, and so they only have to load one copy of the applications on the server: Amipro is for Ami Pro, 123r4w is for 123 version 4.0, flw is for Freelance 2.0, and organize is for Organizer.

My goal here is to create a share that's accessible by everyone. Every subdirectory in the Main share will be visible to anyone connected to that share. Figure 8.27 summarizes who should receive access to the parts of this hard disk via the network.

Here's a quick preview of what I'll have to do in order to achieve this server disk structure:

1. Create and share Users and Main.

2. Set the share-level permissions for Users to only allow the Administrators group to access it, and set the share-level permissions for Main to let everyone have complete control.

3. Create users\harry, users\sue, and users\jamal, and use *directory-level permissions* to grant sole access for each directory to its new owner Harry, Sue, or Jamal.

FIGURE 8.27:

Example disk structure annotated with desired permissions

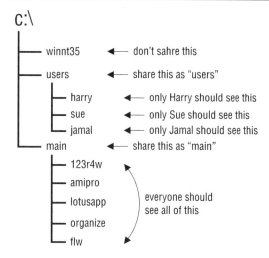

4. Create the subdirectories within Main, but then I won't have to do anything to their permissions because subdirectories inherit the permissions of their main directory unless overridden.

You'll see how to do that in detail, but I just wanted to give you a bit of a road map to what's coming as I first explain each type of permission, then apply it to this example directory structure.

By the way, there's another way to create and share directories to one and only one user—by allowing the User Manager to create a "home directory" for that user. Basically, the User Manager for Domains will create a directory and remove access from everyone *but* the user who owns that directory.

Suppose you already have users name Harry, Sue, and Jamal. How do you create private directories for them and set permissions so that only they can access those directories? Here's how:

1. Open the User Manager for Domains.

2. Select Harry, Sue, and Jamal.

3. Click User, and then Properties....

4. Click the Profile button.

5. Under Home Directory, click Connect…to….

6. In the To field, type *servername***USERS****%USERNAME%**, where *servername* is the name of the server that holds the shared files. For example, on my system I would type \\EISA SERVER\USERS\%USERNAME%.

7. Click OK, then OK again, and NT will create and share the directories.

Controlling Share Access Permissions

Recall that a directory offered to the network for access by network users is called a *directory share*. You can set permissions on shared directories to determine what kind of access users are allowed to have on them.

> **TIP**
>
> Since individual file and directory permissions cannot be set on FAT and HPFS volumes, remember that the *only* way to restrict access to a FAT or HPFS directory is by applying permissions to it when it is shared.

Of course, the network won't allow just *anyone* to change permissions. The only users who can work with shared directory permissions are those logged on as Administrators, Server Operators, or, on NT workstations, Power Users.

To specify share permissions when sharing a directory, select the Permissions… button in the New Share or Shared Directory dialog box. You'll see a dialog box like the one in Figure 8.28. Note the drop-down list box labeled Type of Access; the possible values for Type of Access are summarized in Table 8.2.

These permissions can be set on any shared directory, whether the directory is on a drive formatted using NTFS, FAT, or HPFS. Any share permissions set on a directory apply likewise to that directory's contents, including any directories that may be *inside* that directory.

So far in my directory example, I'd share Users and Main. When I shared them, I'd click the Permissions button and grant Full Control to Everyone for Main, and grant Full Control to the Administrators group for Users, removing anyone else who had any kind of permissions.

FIGURE 8.28:

Share permissions

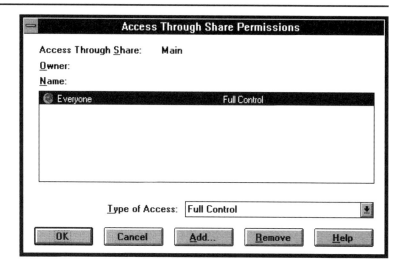

TABLE 8.2: Share Permissions

Share Permission	Level of Access
No Access (None)	Prevents any access to the shared directory, its subdirectories, and its files.
Read	Allows viewing file names and subdirectory names, changing to the shared directory's subdirectories, and viewing data in files and running application files.
Change	Allows viewing file names and subdirectory names, changing to the shared directories' subdirectories, viewing data in files and running applications files, adding files and subdirectories to the shared directory, changing data in files, and deleting subdirectories and files.
Full Control (All)	Allows viewing file names and subdirectory names, changing to the shared directories' subdirectories, viewing data in files and running applications files, adding files and subdirectories to the shared directory, changing data in files, deleting subdirectories and files, changing permission (NTFS files and directories only), and taking ownership (NTFS files and directories only).

TIP

These permissions are really only effective when accessing the directory over the network. Permissions that are set on a shared directory are effective only when the directory is reached via the network, not when accessed locally. In other words, if you log on locally, shared directory permissions don't apply to you, and you can access those now-local directories. If the volume is NTFS, then you can set directory or file permissions, which *can* modify your level of access, but under HPFS and FAT, that's not an option. The bottom line is: To prevent unauthorized access to directories that are not shared (or those that are shared with restrictions), make sure that users cannot log on locally at the server, where the share permissions would not apply.

Ownership and How It Works

Recall that security under NT is all about rights and permissions. Administrators grant rights, but who grants permissions? As you've probably guessed, administrators usually grant permissions, but not always; sometimes a file or directory's permissions are controlled by just a user—*if* the user is the *owner* of that directory or file.

Every single directory, subdirectory, and file on an NTFS volume has an owner; in nearly all cases, the owner of a directory or file is the user who created it. The owner controls access to the directory or file. He or she sets permissions on the directory or file, and can grant certain permissions to others, including permission to take ownership of the directory or file. Ownership allows users to keep private files on a server private, even from the server's administrators.

The way ownership works is like this: Ordinarily, administrators have full control over a directory. So also does the owner of the directory, the user that created it. Now, suppose that user—say it's me—doesn't want the administrators poking around in his directory? Then all I have to do is to run the File Manager from an NT machine, click on my directory, and choose Security/Permissions…, and I might see a dialog box like the one in Figure 8.29.

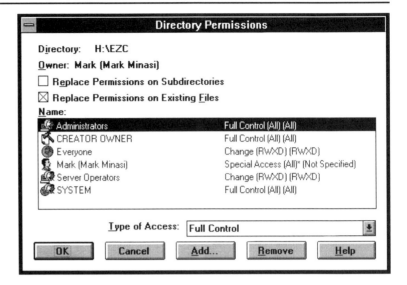

FIGURE 8.29:
Sample Permissions dialog box

Gadzooks! Seems like *everybody* can see and control my directory! Let's change that… Now, as the owner, I have full control—including the ability to change the permissions of *other* users when it comes to my directories. So I just remove everything but CREATOR OWNER from this dialog box, and *voilà*—total control. Now, when an administrator tries to poke around in my directory, all he or she will see is "You do not have access to this directory." (I could have left the administrator with read access, by the way, but I decided to be extreme here.)

What can the nosy administrator do? The administrator can click on my directory in the File Manager, choose Security/Owner, and then be given the ability to seize control of my directory. Assuming that the administrator *does* seize control, he or she then gets access to the directory.

Not very good security, you say? Quite the contrary. First of all, you can't keep stuff from administrators; there's just no way to build a network operating system that could function in the real world without them. But consider now what this administrator has done. By taking ownership of the directory, *the administrator denied me ownership*. The next time I go looking for my directory, I'll be denied access. Sure, the administrator can go poking around in my personal stuff on the server, but not without leaving fingerprints!

How Do I View the Owner of a File?

Select the file in the directory window. From the security menu, choose Owner.

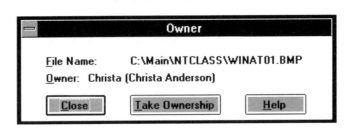

If you are logged on as an administrator and you don't have permission to view the owner, you are presented the option to take ownership of the file.

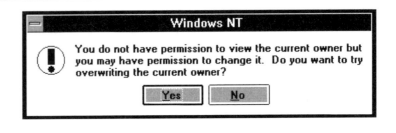

Taking ownership would allow you to view all of the security information for the file. Ownership cannot be transferred back to the file's original owner.

TIP

If you must take control of a directory in order to do something with it—to delete it, for example—then do not be surprised if you can't access it for a few minutes. The change in ownership may not be immediately reflected in the domain's security databases all across the domain. In the worst case, you'll have to wait fifteen minutes for the domain's security databases to re-synchronize.

Directory and File Permissions

If you don't do anything, then by default directories and files inside a share will have the same permissions as the share. But you can zero in further within a share if you like, controlling access to particular directories and even files.

Permissions for directories and files on a server can be granted to:

- Local groups, global groups, and individual users in the server's domain
- Global groups and individual users from domains that this domain trusts
- The special groups Everyone, SYSTEM, INTERACTIVE, and CREATOR OWNER

The type of permissions which are given or denied depend on the type of object—for a directory, subdirectory, or file, possible permissions include Read, Execute, Delete, and Take Ownership. Directories usually inherit their permissions from their parent directories, and files usually inherit their permissions from the directory in which they reside. Directory and file permissions consist of combinations of the individual permissions described in Table 8.3.

TABLE 8.3: Individual Permissions

Individual Permissions	When Applied to a Directory/File
Read	*To a directory:* Allows display of file names within the directory and their attributes; permissions and owner of the directory
	To a file: Allows display of the file's data, attributes, permissions, and owner
Write	*To a directory:* Allows creation of subdirectories and files within the directory and changes to attributes; allows display of permissions and owner
	To a file: Allows changes to the file's data and attributes, and allows display of the file's permissions and owner

TABLE 8.3: Individual Permissions (continued)

Individual Permissions	When Applied to a Directory/File
Execute	*To a directory:* Allows display of attributes, permissions, and owner; allows changing to subdirectories
	To a file: Allows running of program files and display of attributes, permissions, and owner
Delete	*To a directory:* Allows deletion of the directory
	To a file: Allows deletion of the file
Change Permissions	*To a directory:* Allows changes to the directory's permissions
	To a file: Allows changes to the file's permissions
Take Ownership	*To a directory:* Allows changes to the directory's ownership
	To a file: Allows changes to the file's ownership

Setting Directory Permissions

Placing permissions on a directory specifies the access that a group or individual user has to that directory and (by default) the files contained in the directory. Setting permissions on a directory, however, doesn't necessarily grant the same permissions to the directory's subdirectories. Let's take a look at a directory and its permissions. To administer a directory's permissions, either click on the Permissions icon or select the directory in the File Manager window, then choose Permissions (in the Security menu) to get the dialog box shown in Figure 8.30. As you can see, the Directory Permissions dialog box displays the name of the selected directory, the owner, and the current replace options and permissions for the directory.

The default replace option is Replace Permissions on Existing Files. This allows the changes made on permissions to apply to the directory and the files within that directory only (permissions on any subdirectories within the directory will be left unchanged).

To apply the permissions to both the directory, its files, and existing subdirectories (and their files) within that directory, check both Replace Permissions on Existing Files and Replace Permissions on Subdirectories. Clearing both boxes applies the changes in permissions to the directory only, not to any of its files or subdirectories.

FIGURE 8.30:

Directory Permissions dialog box

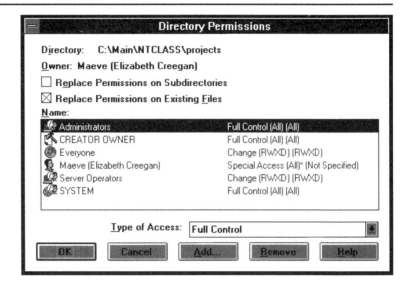

Selecting only Replace Permissions on Subdirectories will apply the desired permission changes to the directory and subdirectories only, but not to the existing files in either.

Following the replace options is an options box displaying a list of the current permissions for the directory. Each of the permissions is followed by two sets of abbreviations for individual permissions, which describe the type of access that the permission grants. The first set is for the directory, while the second applied to the files in the directory. Directory Permissions are summarized in Table 8.4.

You should note that, by default, the Everyone group (which contains all of the domain's members) has Change permission for most of the server's directories and its files (but not its subdirectories). If you *don't* want particular groups or users who can access those directories (through sharing, for example) to be able to change and delete files or directories, you have to change those permissions on them. To modify any of the current permissions, highlight the name of a group or individual user whose access you want to change, then choose a permission from the Type of Access box, as shown in Figure 8.31.

If you want to create a custom set of permissions for a group or user, choose Special Directory Access… or Special File Access… as the type of access; this options lets you pick which individual permissions you want to set on either the directory or the files contained therein. The Special Directory Access dialog box is shown in Figure 8.32. In the Special File Access... dialog box, shown in Figure 8.33, there is an extra option to consider: Access Not Specified. Choosing this option prevents files in the directory from inheriting the directory's permissions.

TABLE 8.4: Description of Directory Permissions

Directory Permission	Individual Permissions on Directory	Individual Permissions on Files in Directory	Access
No Access	(None)	(None)	No access granted at all. Cannot view contents of directory, its subdirectories, or its files.
List	(RX)	(Not specified)	Allows viewing of file names and subdirectory names in a directory; does not give access to files in the directory unless permission is granted by other directories or file permissions.
Read	(RX)	(RX)	Allows viewing file names, subdirectory names, data in files; allows running applications.
Add	(WX)	(Not specified)	Allows adding files and subdirectories to a directory; does not allow access to files in the directory unless granted by other permissions.
Add & Read	(RWX)	(RX)	Allows viewing file names and subdirectory names and changing to the directory's subdirectories, viewing data in files and running applications, adding files and subdirectories to the directory.
Change	(RWXD)	(RWXD)	Allows viewing file names and subdirectory names, changing to the directory's subdirectories, viewing data in files and running applications, adding files and subdirectories to the directory, changing data in files, and deleting the directory and its files.

TABLE 8.4: Description of Directory Permissions (continued)

Directory Permission	Individual Permissions on Directory	Individual Permissions on Files in Directory	Access
Full Control	(All)	(All)	Allows full access, including changing permissions on the directory and its contents and taking ownership of the directory and its contents.
Special Access	*	*	Access depends on which individual permissions have been granted by the creator owner.

* Selected by the directory's owner (i.e., the owner defines the special access).

FIGURE 8.31:

Permission list in the Type of Access box

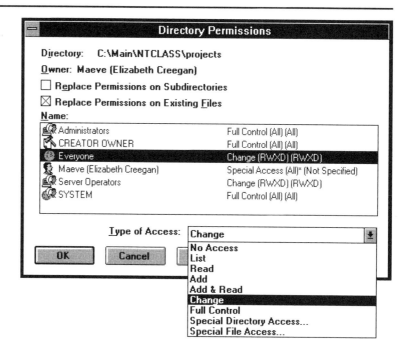

FIGURE 8.32:

Special Directory Access...
dialog box

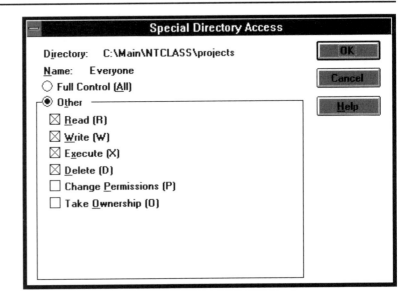

FIGURE 8.33:

Special File Access... dialog box

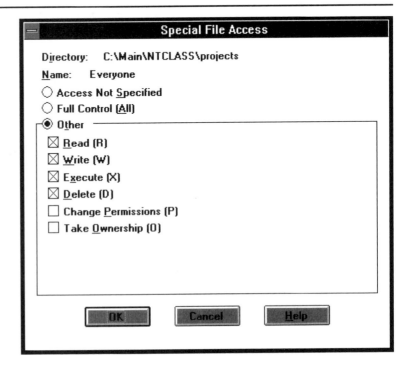

To add users or groups to those with permissions on the directory, use the Add… key to get the Add Users and Groups dialog box shown in Figure 8.34. Let's say we want to deny access to anyone logged on as a Guest in the domain to our example directory. Select the domain, then highlight the Guest group and select the Add button. The group appears below in the Add Names box. Now, choose the type of access for the newly added group. In this case, we select No Access. When done, choose OK. The new group or user will now show up in the permissions list, as in Figure 8.35.

To remove users or groups from the permission list, simply highlight them and click on the Remove button. Click on OK to leave the dialog box and allow the changes to be made.

All permissions are cumulative except for No Access. If a user is a member of two groups, one with Read access to a directory and the other with Change permission, then that user will have Change permission on the directory. However, if the user

FIGURE 8.34:

Adding users and groups to those with permission to access the directory

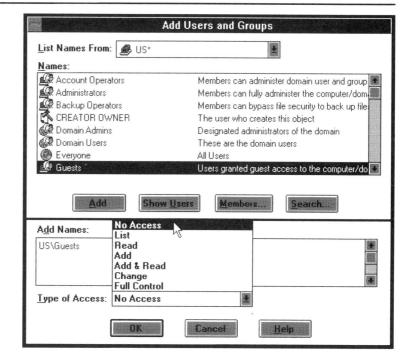

FIGURE 8.35:

A new group added to the
Permissions list of the directory.

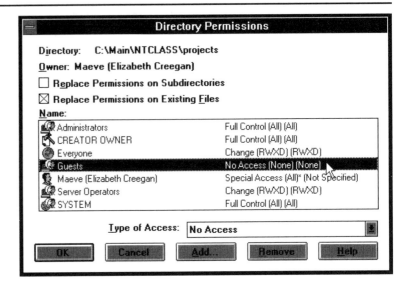

is a member of several groups having Change permission and one group having
No Access, then that user will be unable to access the directory despite the fact that
the other groups the user belongs to have permission to do so. In a similar vein, if
a file within an accessible directory has been specifically designated No Access to a
user, then that user can't access that file by changing the permissions on a directory
and all of its files within, even if the directory grants him permission to do so.

Default Directory Permissions for NT Server Directories

Table 8.5 is a compilation of all of the default directory permissions of NT Server
(and NT) directories. Subdirectories and files created in these directories will inherit the directory permissions unless you set their permissions to something else.
Although several of the system directories seem to give the Everyone group
Change permission, many of these directories are not accessible over the network
unless you are a member of the Administrators or Server Operators groups (see the
earlier section on share permissions and administrative shares).

How Do I Make a Directory Accessible to Only One User (or to Members of Only One Group)?

To make a directory accessible to only one user:

1. Create the directory, if it doesn't exist. Make sure the desired directory is selected in the directory window.

2. From the Security menu, choose Permissions.

3. In the Permissions dialog box, remove all users and groups from the list of those granted permissions on the directory, including Everyone.

4. Add the specific user (or group) back in. Give that user or group Full Control over the directory.

5. If you want all users on the network to have their own personal directory, it's more efficient to specify a home directory in their user accounts under Profiles. If the home directory you specify for the user doesn't already exist on the server, NT Server will create the directory and give it the appropriate permissions to make it accessible only to that user. This feature often, however, does not work in NT, forcing you to create personal user directories by hand.

You can make a directory accessible to only one user or group, but you can't really hide that directory's existence from other users on the network. If you really need to make a hidden, private directory for a user, you can create a hidden share whose share permissions allow only that user to access it, then tell the user the share name so he or she can connect to it (the hidden share won't show up in the Browse list, so its name will have to be typed in). The directory's existence will remain unknown as long as other users don't find out the share name. However, even if they do, other users won't be able to access the directory's contents if all of the permissions on that directory are set appropriately.

TABLE 8.5: Default Directory Permissions in NT Server

Directory	Groups (Permissions)
\root directories of all NTFS volumes	Administrators (Full Control)
	Server Operators (Change)
	Everyone (Change)
	CREATOR OWNER (Full Control)
\SYSTEM32	Administrators (Full Control)
	Server Operators (Change)
	Everyone (Change)
	CREATOR OWNER (Full Control)
\SYSTEM32\CONFIG	Administrators (Full Control)
	Everyone (List)
	CREATOR OWNER (Full Control)
\system32\drivers	Administrators (Full Control)
	Server Operators (Full Control)
	Everyone (Read)
	CREATOR OWNER (Full Control)
\system32\spool	Administrators (Full Control)
	Server Operators (Full Control)
	Print Operators (Full Control)
	Everyone (Read)
	CREATOR OWNER (Full Control)
\system32\repl	Administrators (Full Control)
	Server Operators (Full Control)
	Everyone (Read)
	CREATOR OWNER (Full Control)
\system32\repl\import	Administrators (Full Control)
	Server Operators (Change)
	Everyone (Read)
	CREATOR OWNER (Full Control)

TABLE 8.5: Default Directory Permissions in NT Server (continued)

Directory	Groups (Permissions)
	Replicator (Change)
	NETWORK*
\system32\repl\export	Administrators (Full Control)
	Server Operators (Change)
	CREATOR OWNER (Full Control)
	Replicator (Read)
\users	Administrators (Change)
	Account Operators (Change)
	Everyone (List)
\users\default	Everyone (RWX)
	CREATOR OWNER (Full Control)
\win32\app	Administrators (Full Control)
	Server Operators (Full Control)
	Everyone (Read)
	CREATOR OWNER (Full Control)
\temp	Administrators (Full Control)
	Server Operators (Change)
	Everyone (Change)
	CREATOR OWNER (Full Control)

* No Access, except for Administrators, Server Operators, and Everyone. This is the only case where No Access *does not* override previously granted permissions.

Figure 8.36 summarizes how I used share and directory permissions in my simple server directory layout example.

Share and directory permissions will be sufficient for most purposes, but sometimes you'll need to control access to a lower layer—all the way down to the file level.

FIGURE 8.36:

Which permission types to use in particular situations

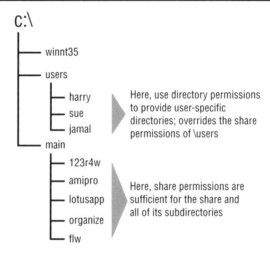

Setting File Permissions

File permissions are set much like the directory permissions. File permissions can similarly be changed only by the owner of the file or by someone else who has been granted permission to change the permissions. To change a file's permissions:

1. In File Manager, select the file.

2. From the Security menu, choose Permissions. You'll see the File Permissions dialog box, as in Figure 8.37.

3. As with the directory permissions, select the name of the group whose permissions you want to change, choose a permission from the Type of Access box, and then click the OK button.

To customize the file's permissions, choose Special Access... in the Type of Access box; this allows you to select from the available individual permissions.

The standard file permissions are the same as the standard directory permissions except that those permissions having to do with viewing a directory's contents

FIGURE 8.37:

File Permissions dialog box

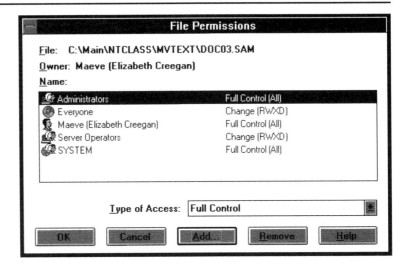

(such as List) do not apply. Adding new groups or users to the permission list is done the same way as described for directory permissions.

When managing access to your files and directories, keep in mind the following security considerations:

- By default, new files and new subdirectories inherit permissions from the directory in which they are created.

- A user who creates a file or directory is the owner of that file or directory, and the owner can always control access to the file or directory by changing the permissions on it (NT workstations only).

- When you change the permissions on an existing directory, you can choose whether or not those changes will apply to all files and subdirectories within the directory.

- Users and groups can be denied access to a file or directory simply by not granting the user or group any permissions for it. You don't have to assign No Access to every user or group that you want to keep out of a file or directory.

- Permissions are cumulative, except for No Access. No Access overrides all other permissions a user might have by virtue of his or her group membership.

How Do I Control Access Rights for a Single File?

Select that file in the directory window. From the Security menu, choose Permissions.

Configure the file's permissions as needed: Change existing permissions, remove users and groups from those that have permissions, and specify permissions for new users and groups.

Keep in mind that providing access by group instead of individual user is more efficient and more manageable. On a server with many users and many files, specifying permissions on each file can be an astronomical chore.

Finally, keep in mind that the share permissions define the highest level of access. In general, on an NTFS volume, it's a good idea to keep the share permissions fairly unrestricted and define user access by specific file and directory permissions.

Let me return for the last time to my directory example, I'd finish up my administration chores by going specifically to \Users\harry in the File Manager, then I'd click Security/Permissions... or click the Permission button on the toolbar. As "harry" was created in \Users, and \Users gave full control to the Administrators group, \Users\harry would also give full control to the Administrators group. I'd remove the Administrators, and then add Harry with full control (click Add, then Show Users, then Harry, Type of Access, Full Control, and then click OK until the dialog boxes go away).

Then I'd do the same for Sue and Jamal. I wouldn't have to do anything with Main, because it's already generally accessible.

Monitoring Access to Files and Directories

In any network there will be times when the administrator needs to monitor user activity, not just to assess network performance, but for security reasons. NT Server provides administrators the opportunity to audit events that occur on the network, and maintains three different types of logs to record information in. These logs are the Applications log, the System log, and the Security log.

In order to record, retrieve, and store log entries of events, auditing must be activated on the server by the administrator. Not surprisingly, file and directory auditing is activated within File Manager.

Auditing for File and Object Access

With NT Server, an administrator can specify which groups or users, as well as which actions, should be audited for any particular directory or file. The information is collected and stored in the Security log and can be viewed in the Event Viewer.

For directories and files to be audited, *you must first* set the security audit policy in User Manager for Domains to allow the auditing of file and object access. To do this, open User Manager for Domains. Under the Policies menu, choose Audit. You'll see the Audit Policy dialog box, as in Figure 8.38.

One of the auditing options available in the list is File and Object Access; make sure you select it. As you can see from the dialog box, you can audit both successful and failed accesses.

FIGURE 8.38:

Choosing File and Object Access event auditing in User Manager for Domains

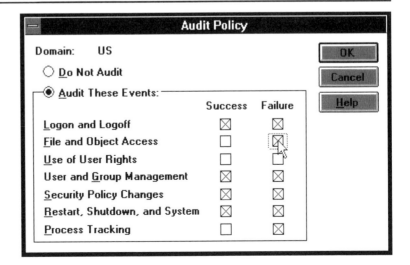

Auditing Directory and File Access

After activating file and object access auditing, you have to choose which files and/or directories, as well as which groups or users who might use the files and directories, you specifically want audited.

To do this, highlight the desired directory or file in the File Manager window. Then, from the Security menu, choose Auditing. If you've selected a file for auditing, you'll see a dialog box like the one in Figure 8.39.

You can choose a specific set of events to audit for each different group or user in the Name list. In this example, everyone's access to the file PRJDATA.TXT is subject to auditing; however, only failed attempts to read, write, execute, and delete (as well as a successful deletion of the file) are actually recorded in the Security log. To add users and groups from those whose access to the file is being audited, choose the Add... options and specify the new users and groups in the resulting dialog

FIGURE 8.39:

Setting up file auditing

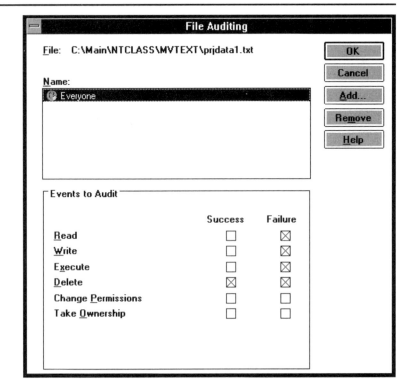

box. Remove a user or group by clicking on one in the current Name list and selecting Remove.

If you are setting up auditing for a directory, there are two additional options to consider, Replace Auditing on Subdirectories and Replace Auditing on Existing Files. Figure 8.40 shows the Directory Auditing dialog box.

The default replace option is Replace Permissions on Existing Files. Selecting this option allows the changes made to auditing to apply to the directory and the files within that directory only, but not to any subdirectories in the directory. To apply auditing changes to the directory and its files as well as existing subdirectories within the directory and their files, check both boxes. Clearing both boxes applies the changes in auditing to the directory only, not to any of the files or subdirectories contained within it. Selecting only Replace Permissions on Subdirectories applies audit changes to the directory and subdirectories only, not to existing files in either.

FIGURE 8.40:

Setting up directory auditing

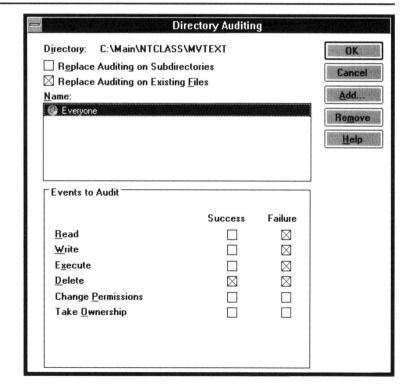

As with file auditing, you can set auditing for each group or user in the list by selecting the name of a group or user in the Names list, then by specifying which events will be audited for that group or user.

To remove file auditing for a group or user, select that group or user and select Remove. To add groups or users to the audit, use the Add option. When you are satisfied with the auditing options, choose OK.

CHAPTER

NINE

Managing Printing Services with NT Server

Print Manager

Printers are essential in any office where computers are used. I mean, you really don't believe that something is true until you see it on paper, right? (If you don't believe me, wouldn't you feel a little unsure about a notice that you got a raise— delivered by e-mail?) Printers convert all those little electronic bits in your computer into hard copy.

But printers cost money, and worse yet, they take up space. Laying equipment and toner costs aside, most offices wouldn't have enough office space to give a laser printer to every employee if they *wanted* to.

Of course, one solution to the printer management and support problem is a network; hence this chapter. In this chapter, you'll learn about

- Creating and fine-tuning printers
- Connecting to existing printers from a variety of operating systems
- Optimizing the printing process
- Controlling access to the printer
- Troubleshooting printing problems

NT Server uses some special vocabulary when discussing printers:

- **Print server** The computer to which the printer is connected and on which the drivers are stored.

- **Printing device** The physical printer, that largish box with the display panel from which you pick up documents.

- **Printer** The *logical* printer as perceived by NT Server and NT. As you'll see in this chapter, the ratio of printers to printing devices is not necessarily one to one—you can have one printer and one printing device, one printer and multiple printing devices, or multiple printers and one printing device, or some combination of any of the above. We'll talk below about the situations in which you might find each of these arrangements useful.

- **Queue** This is a group of documents waiting to be printed. In OS/2, the queue is the primary interface between the application and the printing devices, but in NT Server and NT the printer takes its place.

- **Network-interface printers** Whereas other printers connect to the network through a print server that is hooked into the network, network-interface printers are directly connected to the cabling without requiring an intermediary. These printing devices have built-in network cards.

NT Printer Sharing Features

The unique printer sharing features that NT Server has can make the process of connecting to a networked print device easier than it is with other operating systems.

NT Workstations Don't Need Printer Drivers If you're running an NT workstation with your NT Server, not needing printer drivers will likely be one of your favorite features, as it makes the connection process a lot easier. When you're connecting the workstation to a printer on the server, you don't have to specify what kind of printer you want to connect to, or tell the system where to find the drivers, as you do when connecting a Windows workstation to a networked printing device. Instead, you need only go to the Print Manager, look to see what printers are shared on the network, and double-click on the one that you want. Once you've done that, you're connected.

Direct Support of Printers with Network Interfaces To use a network interface print device (that's one which connects directly to the network, rather than requiring a parallel or serial connection to a print server, remember), you need only load the Data Link Control protocol onto the print server. Although network interface print devices can connect directly to the network without an intervening print server, those network interface print devices still work best with a connection to a computer acting in the role of print server because they have only one incoming data path. With only one path, once the printer had received one print job, it would not be able to queue any others until that job was done. More paths mean more efficient use of printing time, as queuing means that you don't have to keep checking to see if the printer's done, or worry about someone beating you to the printer.

Network interface printers can be useful because, although they still usually connect to a print server, they can be physically distant from it since they don't get jobs through the parallel or serial port. If the network-interface print device is not connected to a print server, the network connection can also speed up the process of downloading documents to the printer, since a network connection is faster than a parallel or serial port. The speed difference isn't great, though, since the printer still has to access the drivers from the print server.

Totally Integrated Printer Support in One Program The Print Manager takes care of all printer maintenance. To connect to, create, fine-tune, or manage a printer, you need only open the Print Manager.

Who Can Be a Print Server?

Like many networks today, your network's workstations and servers are likely to be pretty heterogeneous when it comes to operating systems. Print servers don't necessarily have to be your main file server, or even NT Server machines, but there are limitations on who can share a printer with the rest of the network.

Machines running the following operating systems can be print servers:

- Windows for Workgroups
- Windows 95
- Windows NT
- Windows NT Server
- LAN Manager
- MS-DOS and Windows 3.1 (when running MS Network Client 3.0 for MS-DOS or MS Workgroup DOS Add On)

Machines using these operating systems cannot be print servers:

- DOS (running Workgroup Connection)
- Windows (without running MS Network Client 3.0 or MS Workgroup DOS Add On configured for print sharing)

"Creating" a Printer

The process of setting up a printer to be shared over the network is called "creating" it. You begin creating a printer by choosing Create Printer from the Printers menu in the Print Manager.

You need to create (as opposed to connect to) a printer if you are:

- Physically installing a printer on a computer
- Physically installing a printer that connects directly to the network
- Defining a printer that prints directly to a file (no hard copy)
- Associating multiple printers with diverse properties for the same printing device

When you select Create Printer…, you'll see a screen that looks like Figure 9.1. This dialog box is where you make the following choices:

- **Driver:** Select the printer driver to load. Click on the drop-down arrow to the right of the Driver text box, and you'll see the complete alphabetized list of available printer drivers. Click on the one that your printer requires.

If you don't see your printer's name listed, you may be able to load a driver of a printer very similar to it. Check your printer's documentation for the most compatible drivers.

- **Printer Name:** Choose a printer name (up to 32 characters, including spaces).
- **Description:** Choose a printer description (up to 64 characters, including spaces).

You can use this description to say when the printer is available, how much memory it has, or to name a particular application that it's good for—whatever you like, up to 64 characters. Describing the printer is optional.

- **Print to:** Select the port to which you want to print.

If the printer you are installing is physically connected to the computer, select the parallel or serial port that it's connected to (such as LPT1). If the port you want is

FIGURE 9.1:

Create Printer dialog box

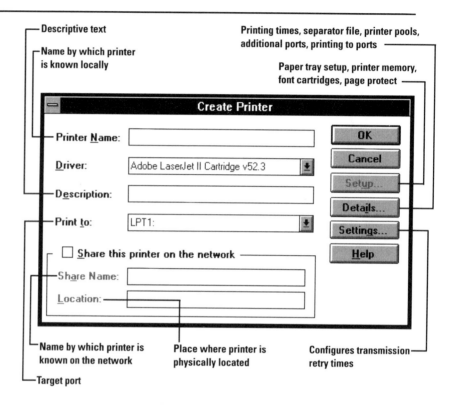

Descriptive text

Name by which printer is known locally

Printing times, separator file, printer pools, additional ports, printing to ports

Paper tray setup, printer memory, font cartridges, page protect

Create Printer

Printer **N**ame:

Driver: Adobe LaserJet II Cartridge v52.3

D**e**scription:

Print **t**o: LPT1:

☐ **S**hare this printer on the network

Sh**a**re Name:

Location:

OK

Cancel

Setup...

Details...

Settings...

Help

Name by which printer is known on the network

Target port

Place where printer is physically located

Configures transmission retry times

not on the list, choose Network Printer. Then, in the Print Destinations dialog box, choose Local Port, and type the name of the new port in the Port Name text box. This port name will then be added to the list of print destinations.

- **Share this printer on the network:** Indicate whether or not the printer will be shared with the network. Oddly enough, for a network server product, a new printer is not shared by default.

- **Share Name:** If shared, select the name by which the printer will be known on the network.

The share name does not have to be the same as the printer name, but it might make it easier to manage the printers if your printer names and share names are the same. The share name can be up to 12 characters long, including spaces. Keep in mind that, if you want MS-DOS machines to be able to use this printer, you need to make sure the name conforms to DOS naming conventions (maximum of eight characters, plus a three-character suffix if you like).

- **Location:** Indicate the physical location of the shared printer, so that people are doubly sure that they're using the right one, and so they can find their print jobs when they're done printing. This is especially critical if you're sharing a printer over a WAN.

When you've made all these selections, your dialog box will look something like Figure 9.2.

TIP   RISC and x86 machines use different printer drivers, so you'll need to install both kinds if you have both kinds of machines on your network.

FIGURE 9.2:
Filled-in Create Printer dialog box

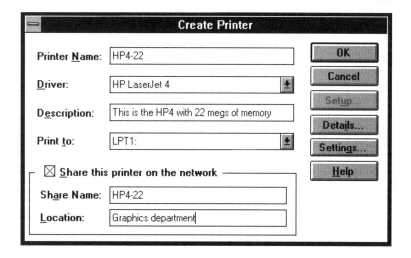

Creating a Second Printer for the Same Print Device

It's often desirable for you to have two (or more) names for the same print device on the network. Having different people access the same device from different names allows you to assign different printing priorities to different users, assign different hours when the printer is available for printing, designate one printer for network use and another for local use, and so forth. Having two or more names allows you to fine-tune the network's access to the printer.

The process of creating a second printer for the same print device is identical to that of creating the first one.

1. Select Create Printer from the Printers menu of the Print Manager.

2. Select a new name for the printer.

3. Choose the same printer driver for the printer that the other printer on this print device uses, and make sure that all other settings are as they should be (Print Manager will send you to the Printer Setup dialog box when you click OK from the Create Printer dialog box). You don't have to share all printers on the network, even if they're attached to the same printing device.

4. Click OK, and you're done. If you shared the new printer with the network, it will now be available for connection.

How Do I Set Up a Printer the First Time for Network Use?

The first time that you're setting up a printer on the network, you need to create it. To do this, go to the Create… option in the Printers menu of the Print Manager. Fill in the appropriate information, including the type of printer, its share name, and whether or not it will be shared with the network.

You can give one physical printer more than one share name, and assign each name to a different group, perhaps with different print privileges. Just repeat the creation process, but assign the printer a different name.

Customizing a Printer's Setup

Once you've done the basic work of creating a printer, you can further customize it. You don't have to customize your printer at the same time that you set it up if you don't want to—you can always adjust the settings at a later date with the Properties... option in the Printers menu.

Using the Details Dialog Box

If you click on the Details... button from either the Properties dialog box or the Create Printer dialog box, you'll see a screen that looks like Figure 9.3. From here, you can:

- List the hours that this printer will print. If you restrict the printing hours, jobs will still spool to the printer during the off-times, but will not print until the hour indicated.

- Choose a separator page file to print before each print job. Separator pages are discussed in detail later in this chapter.

- Choose the ports that you want to print to for printer pooling (more on this below).

FIGURE 9.3:
Printer Details dialog box

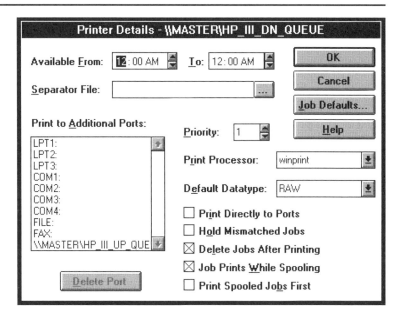

- Select the print processor.

- Determine the printer's priority, if the printer goes by more than one name on the network. For example, if a printer is shared under the name HP4-22 and HP4 and you assign a higher priority to the printer name HP4-22, then print jobs sent to that printer name will be printed first. The default priority is 1, which is the lowest priority. You can set the priority from 1 to 99.

Printer Pooling

Just because you send a print job to a particular print name doesn't mean that your print job has to print at one particular printer. To save time for print jobs, you can use the Details dialog box to pool several *identical* printers into one logical one. If you do this, when you send a print job to that printer name, the first available printer will do the job. This is called *printer pooling,* and it is explained in Figure 9.4. Printer pooling will not work unless the pooled printers are physically identical— the same make and model and the same amount of memory.

FIGURE 9.4:

Printer pooling

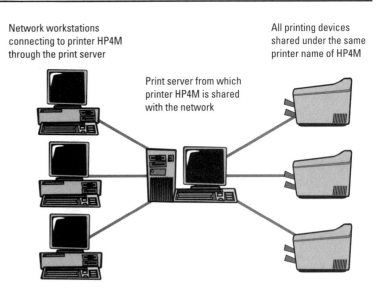

Network workstations connecting to printer HP4M through the print server

Print server from which printer HP4M is shared with the network

All printing devices shared under the same printer name of HP4M

If you have more than one identical printer, you can share them under the same printer name to facilitate speedy printing. This type of sharing is called printer pooling. To the network, it will look as though there is only one printer to connect to, but print jobs will automatically go to whatever pooled printer is available first.

TIP

To set up printer pooling, go to the Details… dialog box that is discussed above. Go to the Additional Ports box and select the ports that correspond to the ports where you've plugged in the other printers. If the ports you need aren't on the list, you can add them from the Printer Properties Box (back out of the Details box to get to it).

1. From the Properties box, select Network Printer in the Print To box.

2. In the Print Destinations box, select Local Port and then click on the OK button.

3. In the Port Name text box, type the name of the port that you want to add in the Enter a Port Name text box, and then click OK.

How Do I Set Up More than One Printer under the Same Name?

To have more than one printer handle print jobs sent to the same print name, you must set up printer pooling. To do this, go to the Properties… item in the Printers menu and click on the Details… button. Go to the Additional Ports box and select the ports that correspond to the ports where you've plugged in the other printers.

On an NT Server machine, you only need one copy of the driver for the type of printer you're pooling, unlike Windows for Workgroups, which requires one copy of the driver for each printer.

Printing Directly to Ports

By default, documents for printing spool to the printer before they are printed. When a document is spooled, it is sent to the print server's hard disk and sent to the printer from there, in an effort to save time and let users get back to what they were doing as soon as possible. This is called "printing in the background."

If you like, however, you can use the Details dialog box to send print jobs directly to the port that a printer is connected to. If you do this, then you won't be able to use your application until the print job is done.

How Do I Print Directly to Ports?

To send print jobs directly to the port to which the printer is connected, rather than spooling normally, go to the Properties… item in the Printers menu and click on the Details button. From this screen, select Print Directly to Ports.

Using Settings

If the printer you are setting up is connected to a parallel port, you can specify the time lapse before the Print Manager decides that the printer is not responding and notifies you (as the user) of an error. Setting the Transmission Retry number higher or lower adjusts the amount of time that the Print Manager will wait for a printer to prepare itself to accept data.

This setting affects not only the printer that you've selected, but also any other local printers that use the same printer driver. Clicking on the Settings button nets you a small dialog box that looks like Figure 9.5. To adjust the time-out, just click on the arrows on the right side of the box, or type in a number by hand. As you can see, the time is measured in seconds.

FIGURE 9.5:
Configure Port dialog box

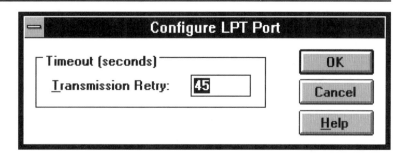

How Do I Set Printer Time-Outs?

To set the number of seconds between the time that you send a print job to the printer and the time that, if the printer doesn't see the job, it tells you that there is a transmission error, choose the Properties… item in the Printers menu and click on the Settings… button. In the dialog box that you'll see, type in the number of seconds that you want for the time-out, or use the arrows to raise or lower the number.

Connecting to a Shared Printer

How you connect a workstation to a printer hooked up to a server running NT Server depends on the operating system that the workstation is using. Windows and Windows for Workgroups machines can connect from the graphical interface, but OS/2 and MS-DOS machines must make connections from the command line. Easiest of all are the Windows NT machines—they don't even require locally loaded printer drivers!

Printing from MS-DOS

All DOS workstations, whether they are running Windows or not, require locally installed printer drivers to share printers on an NT Server network. From a DOS workstation that is not running Windows or Windows for Workgroups, you'll need to install the MS-DOS printer driver file for the laser printer and make sure that it's accessible to all your applications—possibly requiring you to copy the file to all your application directories, depending on how you have your disk set up.

To set up a printing port from MS-DOS, go to the command prompt and type **net use lpt1:** *server**sharename*. For *server* and *sharename*, substitute the name of the print server and the name by which the printer is known on the network. Substitute another port name if LPT1 is already in use. If you want the connection to be made automatically every time that you log onto the network, add the **/persistent:yes** switch to the end of the command. Just typing **/persistent** won't do anything, but if you leave off the persistency switch altogether, it will default to whatever you selected the last time that you used the NET USE command.

For example, suppose you have an MS-DOS workstation that does not have a locally attached printer on any of its parallel ports. Since some older DOS programs don't really give you the chance to select an output port, you'd like the network printer HP4, which is attached to the server BIGSERVER, to intercept any output for LPT1 and print it on HP4. Suppose also that you want this network printer attached every time that you log onto the network. The command for that would be:

```
net use lpt1: \\bigserver\hp4 /persistent:yes
```

TIP

If the print server is using NTFS, workstations may not be able to print from MS-DOS if they have only Read and Execute privileges. The print jobs spool to the print queue, but never print. To resolve this problem, give all users who print from DOS applications or the command prompt full access to the printer.

DOS workstations, whether or not they're running Windows over DOS, will use the locally installed printer driver rather than the one stored on the server. Therefore, if you get an updated version of a printer driver, you'll need to install it at each DOS/Windows workstation individually.

Printing from Windows and Windows for Workgroups

Connecting to an NT Server shared printer from Windows for Workgroups is just like connecting to the same printer on a WfW server. To connect, go first to the Control Panel and select the Printers icon. You'll see a screen that looks like Figure 9.6. This screen shows you the printer connections that you currently have. To connect an existing printer to a new port, click on the Connect button. You'll see a screen that looks like Figure 9.7. If, however, you want to connect to a new printer, you need to click on the Network button in this dialog box. Do so, and you'll see a screen

FIGURE 9.6:

Connecting to an NT Server printer from Windows for Workgroups (screen 1)

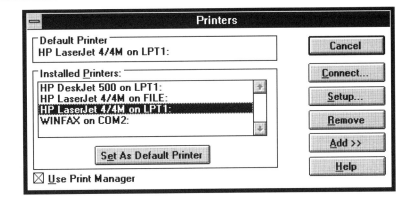

FIGURE 9.7:

Connecting to an NT Server printer from Windows for Workgroups (screen 2)

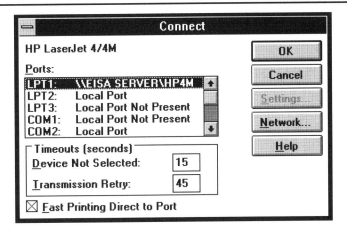

like the one in Figure 9.8, showing you what printers are available for connection. Click on the printer you want, and when its name appears in the Path box, click OK. This will return you to the previous screen, where you can ensure that the printer is connected to the port you want.

That's how you connect to a networked printer *if* the drivers for that printer are already loaded. If they're not loaded, you need to use the Add button in the Printers screen (see Figure 9.6) to add the printer driver to the system. Click on the Add button, and you'll see a list of printers, as in Figure 9.9. Select the printer that you want (for example, the HP LaserJet III), and then click on the Install… button. You'll see

FIGURE 9.8:

Connecting to an NT Server printer from Windows for Workgroups (screen 3)

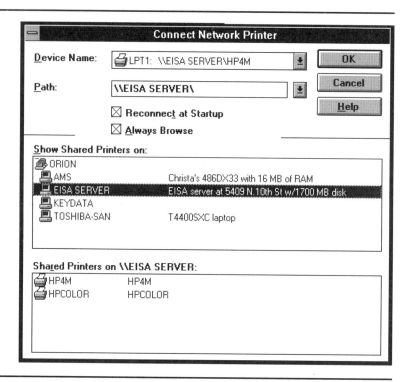

FIGURE 9.9:

Adding a printer driver to the system (step 1)

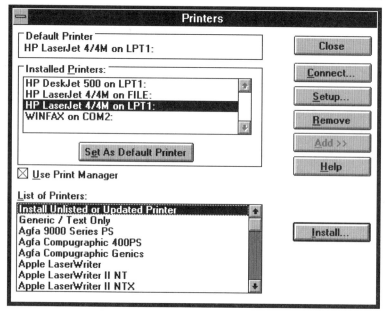

a screen like the one in Figure 9.10. You can use the Browse... button or type in the proper path if you have the driver somewhere on the network; otherwise, you need to insert the appropriate disk. Once you've installed the correct driver, you're ready to connect to the printer.

FIGURE 9.10:

Adding a printer driver to the system (step 2)

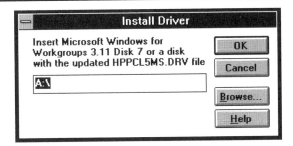

Printing from OS/2

Connecting to an NT Server printer from OS/2 is much like doing it from DOS. To set up a printing port, go to the command prompt (reached from the System folder) and type **net use lpt1:** *server**sharename*. For *server* and *sharename*, substitute the name of the print server and the name by which the printer is known on the network. Substitute another port name if LPT1 is already in use. If you want the connection to be persistent, add the **/persistent:yes** switch to the end of the command.

OS/2, like DOS and Windows, uses local printer drivers when connecting to networking printers rather than drivers stored on the print server. Thus, you need to load the printer drivers locally for the printers you connect to, and if you update the drivers, you need to install the new ones at each workstation.

Printing from Windows NT

If you're using Windows NT, connecting to a shared printer is so easy, you'll be tempted to believe that you didn't do it right until you try to print and it works. Since NT workstations can access the printer drivers located on the print server, you don't need to load them locally. How this works is described in Figure 9.11.

FIGURE 9.11:

Locally loaded printer drivers vs. centrally loaded printer drivers

Printer drivers stored locally at workstation

Printer drivers stored on server, but inaccessible to non-NT workstations

Windows for Workgroups accessing printer through NT Server print server

No printer drivers stored locally

Printer drivers stored on server; accessed by NT workstations

NT workstation accessing printer through NT Server print server

Therefore, rather than define the proper port, find the drivers, or do anything else, all that you need do is go to the Control Panel in the Main group and select the Printers icon. When you do, you'll see a screen that looks like Figure 9.12. When you've reached this screen, click on the Printer drop-down menu and select the

FIGURE 9.12:

First screen in the process of connecting to a shared printer

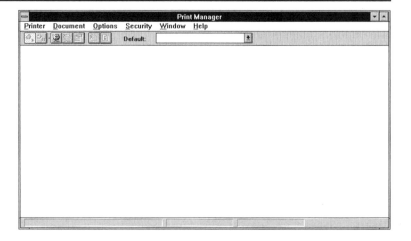

Connect to Printer… option or click on the Connect to Printer button on the toolbar. A screen like the one in Figure 9.13 will appear, showing you the available printers that you can connect to. As you can see from this screen, two printers are currently available on this network.

FIGURE 9.13:

Display of available printers on the network

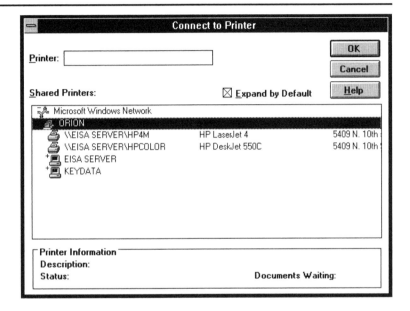

To connect to both HP4M and HPCOLOR, you have to do it one printer at a time. Double-click on HP4M to select it, or click once and then click OK. Once that's done, that's it—you don't have to load drivers, or tell the system the kind of printer that you want to connect to. To connect to HPCOLOR, just repeat the process.

Since NT workstations use the printer drivers stored on the print server, if you install a newer version of a driver on the print server, the NT workstations will use it automatically. You don't need to tweak the workstation connection.

How Do I Connect a Workstation to a Shared Printer?

The process of connecting a workstation to a networked printer varies with the type of operating system that the workstation is using. To connect DOS and OS/2 machines, use the NET USE command from the command prompt. For Windows, Windows for Workgroups, and Windows NT machines, you can use the Print Manager. Printer drivers for each kind of printer must be loaded locally on all kinds of workstations except Windows NT.

Controlling and Monitoring Access to the Printer

Just because you've networked a printer doesn't necessarily mean that you want everyone on its domain to be able to access it. Maybe it's the color printer with the expensive ink that only the graphics people need to use, or you want to reduce the risk of security breaches by limiting the people who can print out company secrets. Either way, you'll want to control access to the printer just as you would any other network device.

By default, only administrators and Power Users have full access to the printer. Only those with full access can pause or resume a printer or set its permissions. Those who just have print access can only administer their own documents.

Setting Printer Permissions

As you'll recall from elsewhere in this book, you secure an NT Server network by setting user rights for what people can *do* on the network, and setting user permissions for what people can *use*. Just as you can with other devices on the network, you are able to restrict printer use by setting the permissions on it.

To set or change printer permissions, first go to the Print Manager and select the printer window or icon for the printer you want. Next, go to the Security drop-down menu, and select Permissions. You'll see a screen that looks like Figure 9.14.

FIGURE 9.14:

Printer Permissions opening screen

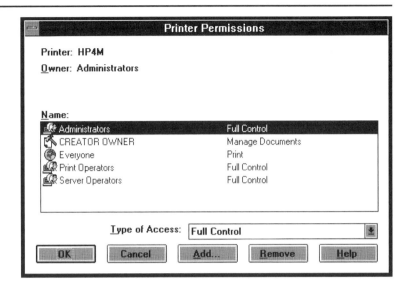

This screen lists the groups for whom some kind of printer access has been set up. From here, you can change the kinds of access that each user group has. The kinds of access are as follows:

- **No Access** No member of that user group can do anything with the printer, including print.

- **Print** Members of that user group can print documents.

- **Manage Documents** Members can control document settings and pause, resume, restart, and delete documents lined up for printing.

- **Full Access** Members can do anything with the printer—print; control document settings; pause, resume, and delete documents and printers; change the printing order of documents; and change printer properties and permissions.

To change a group's type of access, click on the group to highlight it, and then choose the new access type from the Type of Access box at the bottom of the screen. Make very sure that you leave one group with Full Access, or you won't be able to change printer permissions in the future.

To add a user group or user to the printer permissions list, click on the Add button. You'll see a screen that looks like Figure 9.15.

FIGURE 9.15:

Adding users and groups to printer permissions list

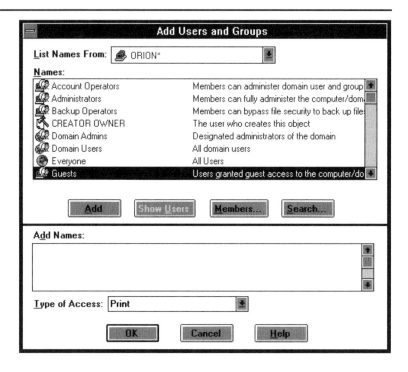

To add a group to the printer permissions list, highlight the kind of permission that you want to give that group, click on the group you want, then click Add and OK. To add only a particular person to the printer permissions list, you have two options:

- You can select a group that the user belongs to, and click on Members. This will give you a list of all the users that belong to that group. Highlight the user that you want.

TIP

Clicking on Members to show the members of the Users group does not get you a list of users; use the Show Users button to do that. If you try to see the members of the Domain Users group, you'll only get a message informing you that the composition of that group is identical to that of the Users group.

- Click on the Show Users button, and then scroll down in the user groups list until you see the entry for Users. Below this entry, you'll see a list of every user on the system. Double-click on the name, just as you would when selecting a user group.

Once you've selected the group or user, the name should appear in the Names box in the top half of the screen. When you're done adding groups or users, click OK.

To remove a group or user from the printer permissions list, go to the first permissions screen, highlight the name of the user or group, and then click Remove.

TIP

If a user is a member of more than one group with different printer permissions, the system always grants the highest-level permission, so that if Jane is a member of one group with Print privileges and one with Full Access privileges, she always has Full Access privileges. The only time that print permissions are *not* cumulative is when one of the groups that a user belongs to has No Access to the printer. In that case, that permission level overrides all higher levels and the user has no access to the printer, regardless of the access level of other user groups she belongs to.

How Do I Set Printer Permissions?

To control which groups or individuals have access to a networked printer, and the kind of access that they have, go to the Security menu in the Print Manager and choose Permissions. Select existing groups and change the kind of printer access that they have, or click on Add… and select new groups to configure. To select individual members of a group, click on the Users button to display membership.

For users in more than one group with different printer permissions, permissions are cumulative except for No Access—if any group of which that user is a member of is forbidden access to the printer, that overrides all other permissions.

Hiding a Printer

You can conceal the fact that a printer even exists, but still share it with the network for a chosen few to access. To do this, attach a dollar sign ($) to the end of the printer share name. This way, the printer name will not show up on the list of networked printers, but if the user types in the name by hand, he or she will be able to connect to the printer.

How Do I Hide a Shared Printer?

To share a printer with the network but keep it from showing up when people browse the network for printers, tack a dollar sign onto the end of its name. That way, users will have to type its name into the printer name box—it won't show up on the list of printers shared with the network.

Setting Print Job Priorities

As discussed earlier, you can set printer priorities from the Details dialog box in the Printer Properties screen (see Figure 9.3). This way, if you want to share your printer with the network but don't want everyone else's print jobs crowding out your own, you can give the printer two names: a name that you use that has a high priority, and a name that everyone else who uses the printer connects to that has a lower one. To further hone print priorities for different user groups, you could give the printer three or more different names, each with its own priority attached, and then assign each group that needed access to the printer a name by which to connect. How this works is illustrated in Figure 9.16.

When you're setting the printer priorities in the Details dialog box, don't forget that higher numbers (up to 99) have a higher priority than lower ones. The default value is 1.

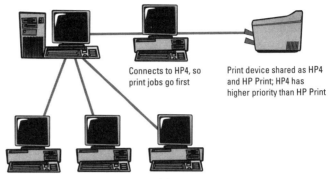

FIGURE 9.16:
Setting print priorities with different printer names

Connects to HP4, so print jobs go first

Print device shared as HP4 and HP Print; HP4 has higher priority than HP Print

Connect to HP Print, so all print jobs have lower priority than HP4 jobs

How Do I Set User Print Priorities?

You can give the print jobs of one person or group priority over those of another person or group. To do this, create another printer for the same print device. Click on the Details button, and you will see a dialog box in which you can set printer priorities. You can set this number from 1 to 99, with 99 being the highest priority. The default is 1.

Setting Printing Hours

Also as discussed in the section on the Details dialog box (see "Using the Details Dialog Box"), you can set the hours during which a printer will produce output. To adjust print times, just click on the ↑ and ↓ arrows of the Available From and To boxes, or type in the times that you want the printer to be available. If a print job is sent to a printer during its "off" hours, that job won't disappear, but will sit there until the printer is authorized to print again.

While you can set user logon hours and printer hours, you can't set printing hours for a particular user or group that are different from those of the others who have access to that printer. For example, you can't restrict the users to using a particular printer only between 9 and 5 if the administrators can access it at any time, unless you adjust the users' logon times and configure their accounts so that the system kicks them off when their time is up. What you *can* do is set up two printer names, one with one time window when it's open for use, and the other with another one. Those who connect to the printer name with the limited hours will only be able to use the printer during those hours. How this works is described in Figure 9.17.

FIGURE 9.17:

Restricting printing hours for a user group

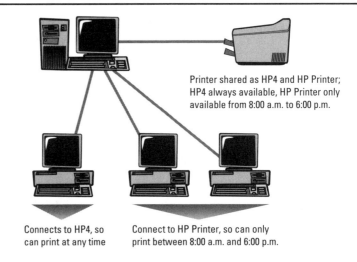

Printer shared as HP4 and HP Printer; HP4 always available, HP Printer only available from 8:00 a.m. to 6:00 p.m.

Connects to HP4, so can print at any time

Connect to HP Printer, so can only print between 8:00 a.m. and 6:00 p.m.

How Do I Set Different Printing Hours for Different Groups?

Although you can't make a printer accessible to one group for one set of hours and to another for a different set, you can customize printer access hours for different sets of users. Simply create more than one printer (remember, printers are logical entities, distinct from the physical printing devices), set the hours for each printer as you require, and then tell each group what printer to connect to.

Receiving Status Messages

One of the auditing functions that you'll use most often is some kind of messenger service to tell you what's happened to print jobs after you've sent them to the server. Printer status messages can tell you when:

- The print job is done
- The printer is out of paper or off-line
- The printer is jammed
- A print job has been deleted

Arranging to receive printer status messages is done a little differently, depending on what operating system the workstation in question is using:

- **NT or NT Server**   Begin the messenger service
- **Windows for Workgroups**   Run WINPOPUP.EXE in the Windows directory
- **DOS and Windows**   Load the messenger service through NET POPUP
- **NetWare**   Begin the CAPTURE program and run the messenger service

Logging and Auditing
Printer Usage

In order to keep an eye on a printer's usage, it's a good idea to audit it. To set up auditing, first go to the User Manager and enable file and object access auditing. Once you've done that, you can set up printer auditing for individuals and groups.

To configure printer auditing, go to the Print Manager and select the Auditing option in the Security menu. When you do, you'll see a screen that looks like Figure 9.18.

Why are all the auditing options grayed out? Before you can audit printer activity, you have to select a group or user to audit. To do this, click on the Add button. You'll see a screen like the one in Figure 9.19. To select a group for auditing, double-click on it or click once and then click on Add. When you've selected a user or group, it should show up in the Add Names box in the bottom half of the screen (as the Users group does in the figure). When you've chosen all the groups that you want to audit, click OK to return to the Printer Auditing screen. It will now look something like Figure 9.20.

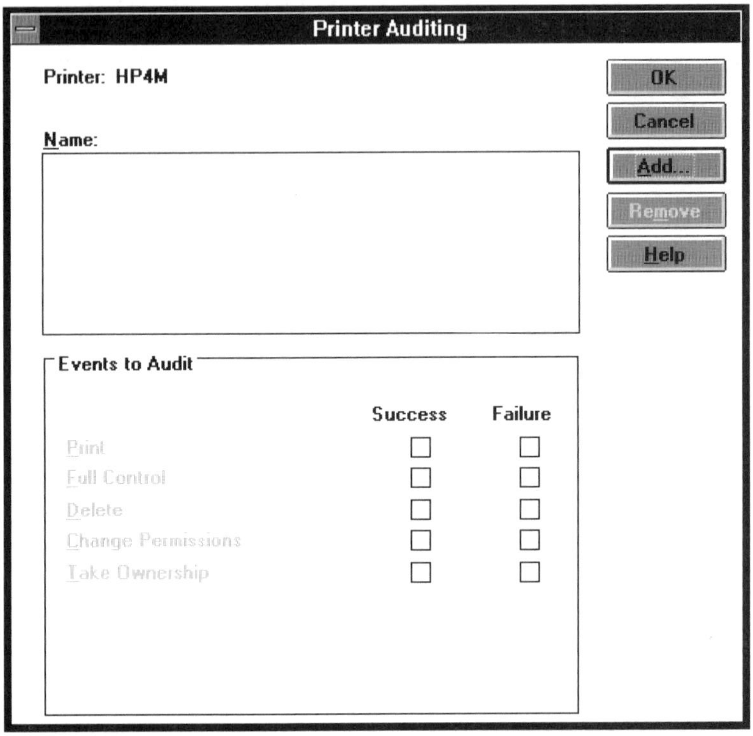

FIGURE 9.18:

Printer Auditing opening screen

Printer Auditing

Printer: HP4M

Name:

OK

Cancel

Add...

Remove

Help

Events to Audit

	Success	Failure
Print	☐	☐
Full Control	☐	☐
Delete	☐	☐
Change Permissions	☐	☐
Take Ownership	☐	☐

How Do I Set Up Event Auditing for a Printer?

To keep track of printer events, go to the Auditing item in the Print Manager's Security menu. By default, no groups are selected for auditing, so you must select a group. Click on the Add button, and a list of possible groups to audit will appear. Select a group, click on the Add button so that the group name appears in the lower box, and then click OK. Once you've selected a group for auditing, you can choose the events that you wish to audit from the list. For each group that you audit, you can set up a special auditing schedule.

FIGURE 9.19:

Add Users and Groups screen for printer auditing

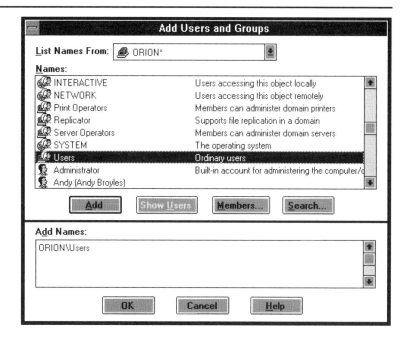

FIGURE 9.20:

Printer Auditing screen with groups chosen for auditing

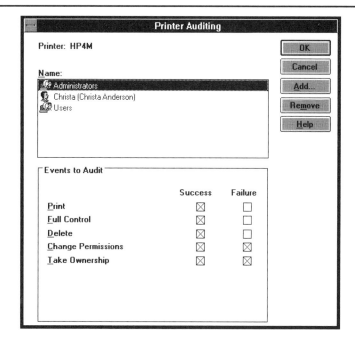

For each group or user that you've chosen to audit, you can select different items to keep track of by checking the appropriate check boxes. When you highlight a group in the Name box here, you'll see the auditing items that you've selected for that particular user or group. There are no defaults attached to auditing a particular group, so you have to set them all by hand. To view the audit information, use the Event Viewer in the Administrative Tools program group.

Separator Pages for Sorting Documents

Separator pages are extra pages printed before the main document. These extra pages are used to identify the owner of a print job, record the print time and date, print a message to users of the printer, and record the job number. They're useful mainly for keeping documents sent to the printer separate from each other. If a number of people are using the same networked printer, you'll probably want to use separator pages to help them keep their documents sorted. Several separator page files are included with NT Server, and you can also create your own by using Notepad.

Creating a Separator Page File

To make your own separator page file, begin a new document in Notepad. On the first line, type a single character and then press Enter. This character will now be the *escape character* that tells the system you're performing a function, not entering text. You should use a character that you don't anticipate needing for anything else, such as a dollar sign ($) or pound sign (#). I've chosen a dollar sign as the escape character.

Now that you've established your escape code, you can customize your separator page with the following variables:

Variable	Use
$N	Prints the user name of the person that submitted the job.
$I	Prints the job number.

Variable	Use
$D	Prints the date the job was printed. The representation of the date is the same as the Date Format in the International section in Control Panel.
$T	Prints the time the job was printed. The representation of the time is the same as the Time Format in the International section in Control Panel.
$L*xxxx*	Prints all the characters (*xxxx*) following it until another escape code is encountered. You can use this code to enter text exhorting people to not waste paper on unnecessary print jobs, to have a nice day, to save the planet, or anything else that you like.
$F*pathname*	Prints the contents of the file specified by path, starting on an empty line. The contents of this file are copied directly to the printer without any processing.
$H*nn*	Sets a printer-specific control sequence, where *nn* is a hexadecimal ASCII code sent directly to the printer. To determine the specific numbers, see your printer manual.
$W*nn*	Sets the width of the separator page. The default width is 80; the maximum width is 256. Any printable characters beyond this width are truncated.
$U	Turns off block character printing.
BS	Prints text in single-width block characters until $U is encountered.

Variable	Use
$E	Ejects a page from the printer. Use this code to start a new separator page or to end the separator page file. If you get an extra blank separator page when you print, remove this code from your separator page file.
$*n*	Skips *n* number of lines (from 0 through 9). Skipping 0 lines moves printing to the next line.
BM	Prints text in double-width block characters until $U is encountered.

For example, consider the following Notepad separator page file:

```
$
$N
$D
$L THIS IS A TEST SEPARATOR FILE. SAVE THE PLANET.
$T
$E
```

It nets you this output:

```
Mark 4/11/1995 THIS IS A TEST SEPARATOR FILE. SAVE THE PLANET.
9:21:22 AM
```

Notice that, even though I pressed Enter after each entry, the output is all on one line. This is because I didn't use the $*n* character to tell the separator page file to skip lines between entries.

How Do I Create a Separator Page?

If you don't want to use any of the default separator pages included with NT Server, you can create your own with the Notepad. Begin a new document, and, on the first line, type a single character to be the escape character—the system's indicator that the next character is a code. Choose an escape character that you won't need for anything else in the file. On the following lines, use the escape character and the variables to make a custom separator page.

Choosing a Separator Page

To specify a particular separator page, choose Printer Properties… from the Printers drop-down menu, and then click on the Details button. You'll see a dialog box that looks like Figure 9.21.

If no separator file is listed, you can select one by typing in the name of the file you want to use or by browsing for the correct file. To browse to a file, either double-click on the three dots to the right of the text box or click on Browse. Once you've selected a separator file, the page with that information in it will print out before every print job. To stop using a separator page, just go to this dialog box and delete the entry in the text box. There is no <None> setting in a drop-down box as there is in some menus. It's a pity that the separator page selection isn't set up like that, but I suppose that it's not because custom separator pages wouldn't necessarily be in the WINNT\SYSTEM32 directory where all the defaults are.

When specifying a separator page, you can type a file name (if you're already in the proper path to find the file) or the file name and path (if you're in another path). You must, however, use a file that is *physically* located on the computer that controls the printer for which you're specifying the separator page. Why can't you use just any file that's accessible from the network? The answer is that the computer that controls the printer stores separator page information in its registry, and so it needs to have that information available locally. If you tell the printer to use a separator

FIGURE 9.21:

Printer Details dialog box

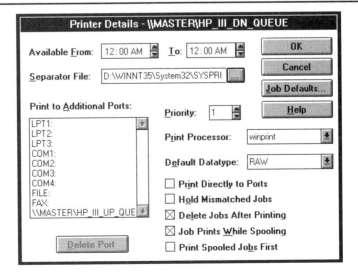

file that is not located on its hard disk, or one that is not in the path that you've indicated, you'll get an error message that says, "Could not set printer: The specified separator file is invalid."

Solving Common Shared Printing Problems

While printing under NT is usually trouble-free, there are a few problems that you may run into. The remainder of this chapter describes some of the most common problems and tells you how to solve them.

Connection Problems

Connection problems appear before you can even use the printer.

Can't Connect to Printer   When connecting to a printer in the Print Manager, you may get an error message that says: "Could not connect to the printer: The remote procedure call failed and did not execute." This isn't really your fault. This problem usually occurs after you've set up and then deleted multiple printers, logging off and on in between removes and setups. Essentially, the registry gets confused. If you see this message, click OK in the dialog box with the error message, then log off and log back on again. When you're back on, you should be able to connect to the printer.

Can't Create Printer   When you go to the Print Manager to remove a printer or create a new one, that option—Create Printer or Remove Printer—may be grayed out, indicating that it's inactive. If you see this, check to make sure that you're logged on as a member of a group with privileges to create or remove printers; only Administrators and Power Users have this privilege.

No Default Printer   If you try to set up a printer from several layers deep in dialog boxes and then select Help while you're still working on the setup, you may get a message that says: "No default printer. Use Print Manager to install and select default printer." You may get this message even though you may already have a default printer installed. To avoid this bug, set up printers before trying to use Help.

Deleted Port   While it is possible to delete a port in the Details part of the Printer Properties dialog box, be warned that it's a lot easier to delete a port than it is to retrieve it. If you blow away a port, you need to use the Registry Editor to replace it.

To retrieve a printer port:

1. Start the Registry Editor (REGEDT32.EXE) and go to the following subkey in the HKEY_LOCAL_MACHINE on Local Machine hive:

   `Software\Microsoft\Windows NT\CurrentVersion\Ports`

2. From the Edit menu, choose Add Value.

3. In the Value Name box, type the printer port that you deleted (for example, COM1: or LPT1:). Keep the default value in the Data box (REG_SZ), and click on OK.

4. In the String box, type the settings that correspond to the port you typed in the Value Name box. For example, you would type 9600,*n*,8,1 for any COM ports. Table 9.1 tells you exactly what the values in each section should be for each port.

5. Exit the Registry Editor. Log off and then log back on, and the port should be back.

If you're doing this fix, see Table 9.1 for a list of the appropriate settings for each port.

TABLE 9.1: Port Settings

Port Name	Data Type	String Value
COM1	REG SZ	9600,n,8,1
COM2	REG SZ	9600,n,8,1
COM3	REG SZ	9600,n,8,1
COM4	REG SZ	9600,n,8,1
FILE	REG SZ	Empty
LPT1	REG SZ	Empty
LPT2	REG SZ	Empty
LPT3	REG SZ	Empty

Be *very careful* when using the Registry Editor! It's very possible to completely screw up your NT Server installation with it. In fact, you could screw it up enough that you have to reinstall the operating system to fix the problem.

General Oddities

General oddity errors don't fall into any particular category. They are described in the following pages.

Print Jobs Remain in the Queue with a JetDirect Connection   I love my JetDirect-connected printers. They let you put a printer just about anywhere you want in your building and they don't require a nearby print server machine, which saves time and cabling. But when you install an HP Series 4 on a JetDirect card, the Print Manager doesn't delete print jobs from the print queue.

The problem stems from HPMON, the routine that controls JetDirect-attached printers. Here's how to fix it (this must be done from the machine that acts as print server for the printer; you can't do this from any other NT machine):

1. Start up the Print Manager.
2. Select the printer that's attached with the JetDirect card.
3. Click Printer/Properties…
4. Click the Settings… button in the Properties dialog box that appears.
5. In the Hewlett-Packard Port Settings dialog box that appears, uncheck Advanced Job Status.

When you're working with a JetDirect card, it's always a good idea to run a self-test on the printer. You'll get a printout with the address of the JetDirect card so you know which card you're dealing with.

Minimized Startup   When you start Windows NT or NT Server, the Print Manager may start minimized, even if you have not set the icon properties to Run Minimized. This will happen if you closed down the Print Manager when it was in a minimized position and you haven't disabled the Save Settings on Exit setting (found under the Options drop-down menu). To stop it from doing this, you have two choices: either make sure that the Print Manager is in the position that you want to see it in when you close (i.e., not minimized), or disable Save Settings on

Exit. If, however, you disable the Save Settings on Exit option, any changes that you make to a printer window will not be saved when you exit Print Manager.

Incorrect "Printer Out of Paper" Message   If you're printing through a *serial* port, you'll get a "Printer Out of Paper" message when any one of the following things is wrong:

- The printing device is out of paper.

- The printing device is off-line.

- The printing device is switched off.

- The cable to the printing device is disconnected.

You get the message because serial connections don't have the status lines available to communicate exactly what the problem is. When something goes wrong, you only know that there's a problem, not what the problem is. The default message is that the printer is out of paper, but you have to check all the other options if you're using a serial connection.

Basic Troubleshooting Tips

The sections above don't cover every possible printing problem and solution, but are instead meant to give you an idea of what *could* go wrong and how to fix it. If your problem isn't dealt with above, this section should give you an idea of how to attack it.

Software

If your print job isn't coming out quite like you expected it to (or at all), make sure that the printer is set up correctly. Have you specified an existing printer port? What about the printer driver—did you install the right one for your printer? If so, you may want to try deleting and reinstalling the printer driver. (Remove the printer from the system and re-create it.)

The problem could also be with the application. Can you print to another printer? Can you print to that printer from another application? If it's a DOS application, try copying the driver file to the application's directory and then try to print again.

Hardware

It's perfectly possible that something has gone wrong with the printer itself, or the cabling, especially if you can't print from DOS. Once you've checked the printer itself to make sure that it's on-line, plugged in, and has paper, check the connection. Will the printer work when attached to another parallel or serial port? You could have a network problem. Try printing the file directly from the print server and see if that works. If nothing else works, try removing extraneous cards from the print server to see if there's a hardware conflict.

NT's ability to network printers is one of its great strengths. With a firm grasp of the Print Manager, you can make sure that all of your users have easy access to printing services.

CHAPTER

TEN

Server Management

10

Server
Manager

NT Server's Server Manager plays two roles in network administration. In its first role, it is a manager of server resources, a companion to the User Manager, which manages user accounts, and the File and Print Managers, which manage directories, files, and printers. In its second role, however, it acts as a minute-by-minute monitoring tool, allowing on-the-spot monitoring and control of both user access to shared resources and relationships between servers.

What You Can Do with Server Manager

When users successfully connect to the server, each begins a *session* with that server. Server Manager monitors session activity and keeps track of all resources and who on the network is accessing them. It displays statistics showing current usage levels on both servers and NT workstations.

With Server Manager, you can view and track:

- All users that currently have sessions on a selected computer
- The resources open during each session
- How long a resource has been open by a user
- How long a session has been idle
- Current information on the number of open file locks, resources, and printers in use

You can also

- Control directory shares on remote servers, removing existing shares or creating new shares
- Add or remove servers from the domain
- Send messages to users
- Receive alerts—messages from the system—at designated computers
- Configure directory replication

You can use the Server Manager to give you minute-by-minute server statistics. By familiarizing yourself with the statistics generated during normal operation, you'll be in a better position to spot abnormal activity. For example, when there's a slow-down in throughput, you might see a number of users trying to download data at the same time. Further investigation into share usage might reveal that the problem is concentrated in a particular spot—an overused resource perhaps.

Server Manager's statistics can only be generated for NT workstations and servers running NT Server or LAN Manager 2.x. You can't monitor or modify attributes of a server with Server Manager unless you are a member of either the Administrators or Account Operators group. Members of the Account Operators group can use Server Manager, but only to add computers to the domain.

Server Manager displays present usage levels and session information; it does not collect statistics over a period of time. To see a computer's cumulative usage statistics since startup, use the commands **net statistics server** at the command prompt, or configure the Performance Monitor to collect statistics.

Who's Who in the Domain

As shown in Figure 10.1, the Server Manager window displays a list of all of the computers that are members of the logon domain, plus computers that the Computer Browser service reports as being active in the domain. This list includes NT

FIGURE 10.1:

Server Manager window

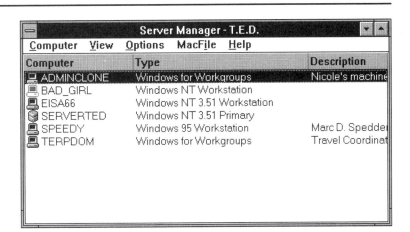

Servers, NT workstations running the Server service, and LAN Manager 2.x servers. Computers running Windows for Workgroups 3.11 and Windows 95 appear in the list, but they can't be remotely administered through Server Manager.

Icons identify the three categories of computers in the Server Manager list:

 Domain controllers, which maintain the domain's security base and authenticate network logons

 Servers, NT Server machines that receive copies of the domain's security base and also authenticate logons

 Workstations, which are any other listed computer

The icons may or may not be dimmed, depending on whether the computer is accessible by the network.

Commands in the View menu allow you to filter the list to show all computers or just the servers, workstations, Macintosh computers, or domain members only. Use the F5 key to refresh the display.

To administer the servers of a different domain or workgroup, choose the Select Domain command from the Computer menu. If the domain or workgroup happens to communicate with your server over a slow link, make sure you choose the Low Speed Connection option.

Server Properties

The properties of any server on the Server Manager list, whether local or remote (provided that remote administration is supported), can be accessed by using these techniques:

- Selecting the computer in the list and choosing Properties from the Computer menu

- Selecting the computer and hitting Enter

- Double-clicking on the selected computer's name in the list.

You'll see the Properties for dialog box, as in Figure 10.2, once you select the server.

FIGURE 10.2:

The Properties for dialog box

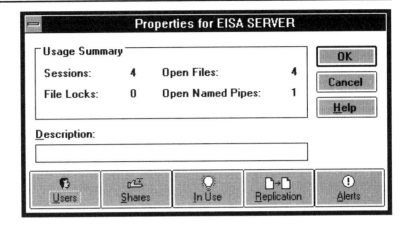

You can also access this dialog box from the Control Panel of the machine for which you want the information. The big value of the Server Manager, however, is that you can access the Properties for dialog box for any server on the network, right from your workstation. In contrast, the Control Panel can only show this dialog box for whatever computer you're currently sitting at.

The Usage Summary box displays:

- The total number of users who have established sessions—in other words, who have remotely connected to the server

- The total number of shared resources currently open on the server

- The total number of file locks held by open resources on the server

- The total number of named pipes currently open on the server

Beneath the Usage Summary box is a box containing the server's optional description. If you want to add or change a server's description, just type in the new information in the box.

At the bottom of the dialog box are five buttons:

Button	Use
Users	Lets you view all users connected to the server, as well as the resources opened by a specific user. Lets you disconnect one or all of the connected users.

Button	Use
Shares	Displays the server's shared resources and those users connected over the network to a selected resource. One or all of the connected users can also be disconnected here.
In Use	Shows the open shared resources on the server and provides the capability to close one or all of the resources.
Replication	Lets you manage directory replication for the server and determine the path for user logon scripts.
Alerts	Allows you to view and manage the list of users and computers that are notified when administrative alerts occur at the server.

User Sessions

To look at and manage user sessions on the server, click on the Users button in the Properties for dialog box. The resulting User Sessions on dialog box, as seen in Figure 10.3, lists all users remotely connected to the server and what resources they are using.

FIGURE 10.3:

User Sessions on dialog box

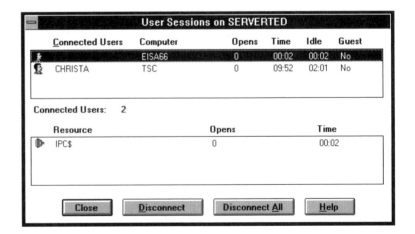

The Connected Users box lists connected users, the name of the computers they are on, the number of resources they have opened, the time since their sessions were established, the length of time since they last initiated an action, and whether or not they are logged on as a guest. Right below the list is a summary of the total number of users remotely connected to the server.

The bottom box displays the resources in use by the currently highlighted user. To view the resources of a different user, simply click on that user in the Connected Users list. Resources in use are graphically identified by the following icons:

 A shared directory

 A remote procedure call

 A shared printer

 A communication-device queue (LAN Manager 2.x servers only)

 An unrecognized resource

Next to the icon is the name of the resource, the number of opens against the resource by the selected user, and the time elapsed since the resource was first opened. Incidentally, a connection to a printer sometimes shows up as a connection to a named pipe instead.

How Do I Disconnect Users from the Server?

To disconnect a single user from the server, select the user name from the Connected Users list, then choose the Disconnect button. Hitting the Disconnect All users button will disconnect everyone from the server. When administering a remote server, your own user account shows up as a user connected to the IPC$ resource, which will not be disconnected.

You should inform users before disconnecting them—use Send Message in the Computer menu to relay your intentions to the connected users.

Available Shares

By choosing the Shares button in the Properties for dialog box, you can view Shared Resources on dialog box, as shown in Figure 10.4. The dialog box lists both the shared resources available on the currently selected server and the users connected to those resources. Shared directories can be managed in either Server Manager or in File Manager. Shared printers are managed in Print Manager.

The top box shows the list of all of the shared resources on the selected computer. For each share, the share name, the number of uses, and its path are given. Once again, icons next to the share name show whether the resource is a directory, named pipe, printer, communication-device queue (LAN Manager 2.x servers only), or an unrecognized resource.

When you click on one of the shared resources in the list, you'll see a list of users connected to that resource (and the time elapsed since the connection was made) in the bottom box. For example, in Figure 10.4, a single user named Christa is connected to the shared directory \Current (the I:\ drive on the selected server). Although she has been connected for over nine hours, the shared directory is currently not in use.

FIGURE 10.4:

Shared Resources on dialog box

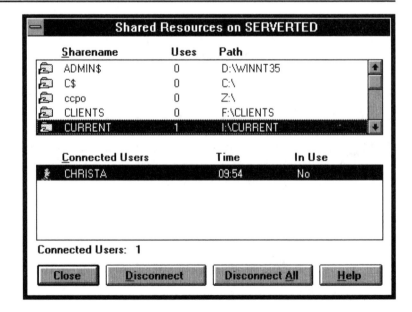

As with User Sessions, you can disconnect one or all users from all shared resources on the server by selecting a user in the Connected Users box and choosing the Disconnect button, or by simply choosing the Disconnect All button. Remember to warn users before disconnecting them from server resources.

Managing Shared Directories in Server Manager

In Server Manager, just as in File Manager, you can

- View shared directories
- Share an unshared directory
- Manage the properties of a shared directory
- Set permissions for a shared directory
- Stop sharing a directory

However, in Server Manager you can create new shares and administer shared directories not only on the local server, but on remote servers in the domain as well.

To view any server's list of shared directories, select the server in the Server Manager window, then choose Shared Directories from the Computer menu. You'll see the Shared Directories dialog box, as in Figure 10.5. The list shows the share names and paths of the shared directories. It includes directories shared by users and administrators, as well as some or all of the following special shares created by the system:

Resource	Description
driveletter$	The root directory of a storage device on the server (can be accessed remotely only by members of the Administrators, Server Operators, and Backup Operators groups).
ADMIN$	The resource used by the system during remote administration of a server. It is always the directory where Windows NT is installed.

FIGURE 10.5:

Shared directories on a selected computer

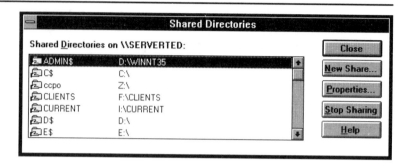

In general, these system shares should not be removed or modified.

Resource	Description
IPC$	This resource shares the named pipes essential for communication between programs. It is used when a computer is being remotely administered, or when viewing a computer's shared resources.
NETLOGON	The resource used by the Net Logon service for processing domain logon requests (exists only on NT Advanced Servers).
PRINT$	The resource that supports shared printers.
REPL$	Required for export replication, this resource is created by the system when a server running NT Server is configured as a replication export server.

In general, these system shares should not be removed or modified.

To modify the properties of any shared directory in the list, select the directory and choose the Properties button. Share access permissions can be set by choosing the Permissions button in the Share Properties dialog box. To stop sharing one of the directories in the list, select the directory and choose the Stop Sharing button. The directory itself is not removed, but it can no longer be accessed by network users. To share an unshared directory on the server, choose the New Share button and type in the share name, path, and other properties, including share permissions.

These procedures are covered in detail in the "Sharing Drives and Directories" section of Chapter 8. Note that you can modify share permissions on a remote computer with Server Manager, but you can't modify directory or file permissions on a remote computer with Server Manager; for that, you just use File Manager. (Use the File Manager to attach to a share over the network—it has to be an NTFS share, or file and directory permissions can't exist. You'll find that the Security menu works just as it always does, assuming that you're logged on as an administrator.)

Active Resources

By choosing the In Use button in the Properties for dialog box (see Figure 10.2), you can see how many resources are currently open on the server, as well as a list of those resources, as in Figure 10.6. Once again, the resources are graphically distinguished by icons:

 A file

 A named pipe

 A print job in a print spooler

 A communication-device queue (LAN Manager 2.x servers only)

 An unrecognized resource

Following the icon is the name of the user who opened the resource, the permission granted when the resource was opened (read, write, execute, etc.),

FIGURE 10.6:

Open Resources dialog box

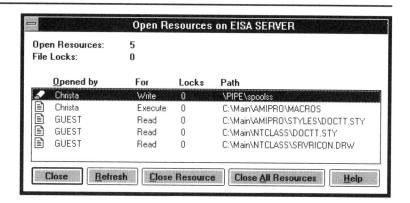

the path of the resource, and the number of locks on the resouce. Print jobs are sometimes represented in this list as open named pipes.

Close an open resource by selecting that resource from the list and choosing the Close Resource button. If you want to close all open resources, hit the Close All Resources button. Make sure you notify the connected users of your intent before you carry it out. To exit, choose Close, then choose OK in the Properties dialog box.

Sending Alerts to a Workstation

When system errors or important events relating to the server or its resources occur, NT Server generates *alerts*. In Server Manager you can specify which users and computers receive these alerts.

TIP

In order to generate an alert, a server must be running the Alerter and Messenger services. On computers that must receive alerts, the Messenger service must be up and running. If the destination computer happens to be turned off, the message eventually times out. In practical terms, this means that the workstation must either be running NT, OS/2, or Windows for Workgroups—all three of which ship with Messenger support—or you'll have to load a DOS- or Windows-based Messenger driver. The "Workgroup Connection" client software from Microsoft, which allows a DOS workstation to connect to an NT network, only requires one diskette, and so that's what I usually recommend you carry around to do quick-and-dirty network installs. The Workgroup Connection, however, does not include messenger service, and so no DOS machine set up with the Workgroup Connection is able to receive alerts.

You can alternatively set up a DOS client with the Microsoft Network Client 3.0 for DOS, a slightly more complex operation that can be accomplished with the Network Client Administrator under NT Server. When you install the Network Client for DOS, you get the option to either "run the Network Client" or "run the Network Client and Load Pop-up." If you load the pop-up, you'll have the messenger service.

To specify the recipient of administrative alerts:

1. Double-click on the server in the Server Manager window to retrieve its Properties dialog box.

2. In the Properties box, choose the Alerts button. You'll see the Alerts on dialog box, as in Figure 10.7.

3. To add a user or computer to the list of those that are receiving alerts, type in the user name or computer name in the New Computer or Username box, and then choose Add.

4. To remove a user or computer from the list of those set to receive alerts, select the user name or computer name in the Send Administrative Alerts To box, and then choose Remove.

The Server and Alerter services both need to be restarted in order for the changes to take effect.

FIGURE 10.7:
Alerts dialog box

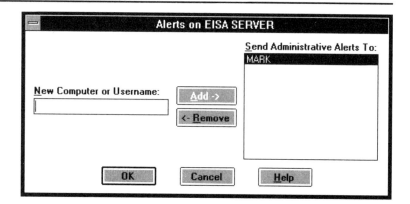

Sending Messages to Users

Prior to administering a server, especially if you have to put certain services or resources on hold while working, you can send a message out to users currently connected to the server. To send a message:

1. Choose the server from the list in the Server Manager window.

2. From the Computer menu, choose Send Message. You'll see the Send Message dialog box shown in Figure 10.8.

3. Type in the message you want to relay to users.

4. Choose OK.

The message is sent to all users currently connected to the selected server, provided that the workstations using NT and NT Server are running the Messenger service, and other workstations (such as those running Windows for Workgroups) are using a message utility such as WinPopup.

FIGURE 10.8:

Send Message dialog box

TIP

If you have an AppleTalk segment on your NT Server network, don't forget to send messages to Macintosh users before taking the server down. From the MacFile menu, choose Send Message. (For more information on supporting Mac clients, read Chapter 18.)

TIP

To send a message to just one user, open a command window and type NET SEND *name message* where *name* is the user name or machine name to send the message to, and *message* is the text of the message you're going to send. For example, to say "hello" to a user named Sally, you would type net send Sally hello

Managing Domain Members

Your network's domains can have one server or many. If a domain has more than one server, which one is in charge? With the Server Manager, you can set up the domain's structure by

- Promoting and demoting primary domain controllers
- Synchronizing servers with the primary domain controller
- Synchronizing all of the domain's servers
- Adding and removing computers from a domain

Specifying the Primary Domain Controller

Every domain must have a primary domain controller (often just called the "domain controller"). The domain controller keeps the master copy of the domain's account and security database, which is automatically updated whenever changes are made. Copies of this database are also automatically received by all other servers in the domain. Every five minutes, the other servers query the domain controller, asking if changes in the database have occurred. If any changes were made within the five minutes, the domain controller sends the changes (not the entire database) to the other servers.

Usually, the domain controller is designated when a new domain is first established. During the installation of NT Server, you can specify whether or not you are creating a new domain (with the computer you're installing NT Server on as the domain controller) in Setup. Inside Server Manager, though, you can change the domain controller status of any server in the domain, depending on your network's needs.

To designate one of the domain's servers as the domain controller, select that computer in the Server Manager window, and choose the command Promote to Domain Controller from the Computer menu. The old domain controller will automatically revert to server status unless it's unavailable to the network—for example, if it's being repaired. If that's the case, you have to manually demote it (in the Computer menu, the command Promote to Domain Controller will change to Demote To Server). If you don't demote it and the old domain controller returns to service, it won't run the Net Logon service or participate in user logon authentication.

In virtually all cases, the domain controller must be a server running NT Server. OS/2 LAN Manager 2.x is the only outside network operating system that can function in NT Server domains, albeit with massively limited capabilities. Take my advice: If you need backup domain controllers, then upgrade those servers to NT Server. If a domain contains servers running both NT Server and LAN Manager 2.x, the domain controller *must* be a server running NT Server that was installed specifically as a "domain controller" rather than a "server." The exception is a domain where all of the servers are running LAN Manager 2.x. In this case, one of the LAN Manager 2.x servers can be designated as the domain controller.

Backup Domain Controllers

As you learned in earlier chapters, the primary domain controller can handle logon validations, but it's a good idea to have another domain controller as a backup. You want the backup for two reasons:

- If the domain controller goes down, the other server can be promoted to domain controller and the domain will continue to function.

- It is a major pain in the neck to reinstall NT Server on the primary domain controller if you have no backup domain controllers, as I explained in Chapter 3. Also, if you have one or more Windows for Workgroups workstations on your network and you are using a router, you must have a backup domain controller.

Since all servers running NT Server in a domain can process logon requests from that domain's user accounts, any one of the domain's servers may authenticate the logon attempts—in essence, all servers in the domain are functioning as backup domain controllers did in LAN Manager 2.x. In addition, having multiple servers spreads the load of logon request processing, which is useful in domains with a large number of user accounts.

In a domain with both NT Server machines and LAN Manager 2.x servers, don't rely solely on LAN Manager servers as your backups. A LAN Manager server can neither validate logon requests from NT workstations nor be promoted to domain controller of an NT Server domain.

Synchronization: Keeping a Uniform Security Database

Synchronizing a domain's servers forces the replication of the domain's security database from the domain controller to all of the servers in the domain. NT Server synchronizes the servers automatically, but in the unlikely case that one server's copy of the security database becomes out of sync with the rest of the domain, you can perform the synchronization manually.

To synchronize a single server with the domain controller, choose that server from the Server Manager list and, from the Computer menu, choose Synchronize with Domain Controller. If you need to synchronize all of the servers with the domain controller instead, choose the domain controller from the Server Manager list. Then, from the Computer menu, choose Synchronize Entire Domain. You'll see the message shown in Figure 10.9. As the messages implies, a manual synchronization can take a significant amount of time to complete if the security database is large.

For a LAN Manager 2.x server, the Synchronize With Domain Controller command reestablishes the computer account password on both the LAN Manager server and the domain controller.

FIGURE 10.9:
The synchronization confirmation message

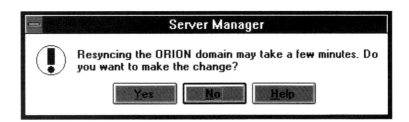

Adding Computers to a Domain

Members of the Administrators, Domain Admins, and Account Operators groups can grant computers membership in a domain. (Note that it's the *computers*, not their users, who are acknowledged as members of the domain.) When a computer is added to a domain, it is given an account in the domain's security database and can participate in domain security. Servers that are granted domain membership also receive copies of the domain's security database.

Adding a computer to a domain is a two-step process. First, the machine account for that computer must be created in the domain. Then, the computer must actually join the domain—a separate step performed at the computer itself during installation of NT or afterwards in its Control Panel.

NT Server Machines

NT SERVER

A new NT Server server can become a member of a domain in either of two ways: during the installation of the NT Server when a new domain is being established, or, also during installation, by designating the machine as a backup domain controller. Alternatively, you can create a machine account for a backup domain controller before installing NT Server on that machine. You do that by performing the following procedure in Server Manager:

1. From the Computer menu, choose Add to Domain. You'll see the Add Computer to Domain dialog box, as in Figure 10.10.

FIGURE 10.10:

Add Computer to Domain dialog box

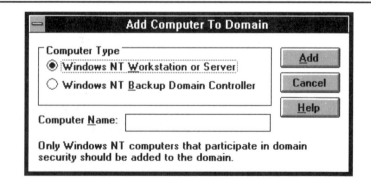

2. Under Computer Type, choose Windows NT Backup Domain Controller.

3. Type in the name of the computer (a maximum of 15 characters), then choose Add.

This action creates the machine account in the domain's security database for a computer of the specified name. The computer, however, doesn't become a member of the domain until it actively joins it. For an NT Server, this can only be done during installation of NT Server on the specified computer.

TIP   It is possible in the short period of time between the "pre-creation" of the machine account and the installation of NT Server on the machine for someone to rename his or her computer to that name and join the domain, masquerading as the intended computer. If this masquerade computer joins the domain as a server, it will gain access to the domain's security database (which is replicated to all domain servers). If you don't want this to happen, don't make any new computer names widely known before the computers actually join the domain, or only use the NT Setup routine to add backup domain controllers to your domain.

NT Workstations

As with NT Servers, domain membership for NT workstations can be granted during the installation of NT on the machine, but only if it's done by an administrator. Once NT has been installed, however, domain membership can be granted in two fashions:

- On the NT workstation itself, by an administrator using the Network option of that workstation's Control Panel.

- Through Server Manager, in which case the administrator or account operator adds a machine account for the computer to the domain's security database, then instructs the computer's user to join the domain under that account (using the Network option in Control Panel).

To create a machine account for the workstation using Server Manager, choose Add to Domain from the Computer menu, select Windows NT Workstation in the Type of Computer box, type in the computer name, then choose Add. You can add a number of computers at once; choose Close when you're finished.

Then, to add the workstation to the domain, log on to that computer. In its Control Panel, choose Network. You'll see the Network Settings dialog box. Select the Change button next to the domain (or workgroup). You'll see the Domain/Workgroup Settings dialog box, as in Figure 10.11. In the Member Of box, select the Domain button and type in the name of the domain that the workstation must join.

NT workstations that are members of a domain don't actually get a copy of the domain's user database and don't participate in domain security, but the workstation still gets the benefits of the domain's user and groups database.

FIGURE 10.11:
Changing the domain membership

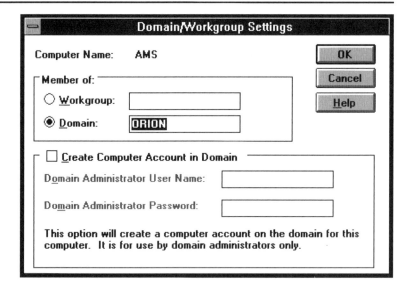

LAN Manager 2.x Servers

LAN Manager 2.x servers are the only servers outside of NT Servers that can be granted membership in a domain. LAN Manager servers can function as supplementary servers in NT Server domains as long as the domain controller is an NT

Server. A LAN Manager server can be designated as a domain controller only in a domain where all of the domain's servers are running LAN Manager 2.x.

As with other NT Servers, LAN Manager servers receive and keep copies of the domain's security database, but they can only validate logon attempts by workstations running Windows for Workgroups or LAN Manager 2.x workstation software (they can't validate logon attempts by NT users).

Because they don't support all types of information contained in NT Server accounts, LAN Manager 2.x servers don't recognize local groups or trust relationships, and are unable to use the users and global groups that are defined in other NT Server domains. Even so, resources in these domains can be accessed by NT workstation users provided that the user has a second account in the LAN Manager domain, or the LAN Manager domain permits guest logons. All in all, LAN Manager servers should be treated as servers, not as domain controllers under NT.

Managing Services

In addition to providing domain membership and shared resource management capabilities, Server Manager also lets you configure the services available on each of your servers. You can start, stop, pause, or continue, as well as provide startup values to specific services. Each of the services in Server Manager are duplicated under the Services option in Control Panel, but unlike Control Panel (which manages services for the local computer only), Server Manager allows you to manage services for remote servers as well as the local computer.

The default services in NT Server are:

Server	Description
Alerter	Notifies selected users and computers of administrative alerts that occur on the server. Used by the Server and other services; requires the Messenger service.
Clipbook Server	Supports the Clipbook Viewer application; allows pages to be seen by remote Clipbooks.

Server	Description
Computer Browser	Maintains a current list of computers and furnishes the list to applications when requested; provides the computer lists shown in the main Server Manager window and in the Select Computer and Select Domain dialog boxes.
Directory Replicator	Replicates directories and their contents between computers.
Event Log	Records system, application, and security events in the event logs.
License logging	Keeps track of used and available licenses.
Messenger	Sends out and receives messages sent by administrators and the Alerter service.
Net Logon	Performs authentications of account logons in NT Server. Keeps the domain's security database synchronized between the domain controller and other servers running NT Server in the domain.
Network DDE	Provides network transport and security for DDE (dynamic data exchange) conversations.
Network DDE DSDM	The DSDM (DDE share database manager) service manages the shared DDE conversations; it is used by the Network DDE service.
Remote Procedure Call (RPC) Locator	Manages the RPC name service database and allows distributed applications to use the RPC name service.
Remote Procedure Call (RPC) Service	This is the RPC subsystem for Windows NT.
Schedule	Permits the use of the AT command to schedule commands and programs to run on a computer at a specific time and date. For some odd reason, this is not started by default, and one of the things that you'll end up doing early on is to set this service to start up automatically.

Server	Description
Server	Provides remote procedure call (RPC) support and allows file, print, and named pipe sharing.
UPS	Manages a UPS (uninterruptible power supply) connected to the server. Should be used in conjunction with Alerter, Messenger, and Event Log services to ensure that events related with the UPS service (such as a power failure) are recorded in the System log and that designated users are notified.
Workstation	Allows network connections and communications.

Additional services will appear in the list based on your network configuration. For example, if you've installed a Macintosh segment of the network, you may see File Server for Macintosh and Print Server for Macintosh listed as services.

To view and manage the services using Server Manager, select the desired server from the main window, open the Computer menu, and select the Services command. You'll see the Services on dialog box shown in Figure 10.12. If the entry in the Status column for a particular service is blank, that indicates that the service has been stopped. You should really only manipulate non-automatic services through this dialog box.

FIGURE 10.12:

Services on dialog box

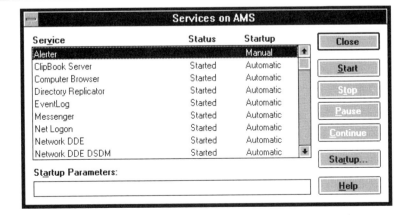

Starting and Stopping Services

You can start, stop, pause, or continue any of the services for a particular computer by following these steps:

1. Select a computer in the Server Manager window.
2. Choose Services from the Computer menu.
3. Select the service from the Services window.
4. Choose the Start, Stop, Pause, or Continue button.

If you need to pass startup parameters to a service, simply type them in the Startup Parameters box at the bottom of the Services on dialog box before choosing the Start button.

TIP Stopping the Server service disconnects all remote users. You should follow this procedure for stopping the Server service:

1. Pause the Server service first; users will thus be prevented from establishing any new connections.
2. With the Send Message command, tell connected users that they will be disconnected after a specified time period.
3. After the specified time period expires, stop the Server services.

When the Server service is stopped, you can't administer it remotely; you must restart it locally.

Configuring Service Startup

Members of the Administrators local groups of the domain can choose whether or not a service is started automatically, manually, or is initially disabled. To do this, select the service in the Services box and choose the Startup button. You'll see the

Schedule Service on dialog box, as in Figure 10.13. Under Startup Type, you can choose:

- Automatic, which starts the service each time the system starts;
- Manual, which allows the service to be started by a user or by a dependent service; or
- Disabled, which prevents the service from being started.

Incidentally, the Server service won't start automatically unless the server has at least 12MB of memory.

FIGURE 10.13:
Schedule Service on dialog box

Beneath the Startup Type box, you can choose which account the service will log on as. Most services log on using the system account. However, a service such as the Schedule service may need more access than that given by the system account, which only provides Guest access. In such a case, you can create a special user account with the required access for the service to log on as. User accounts which are used to log on as a service must have the Password Never Expires option selected.

For the service to log on using the system account, simply select the System Account button. To specify a different account, choose the This Account button and use the browse button (...) to find and select the user account.

When you've acquired the proper account, type in its password in the Password and Confirm Password boxes. Then choose OK to return to the Services dialog box. When you've finished configuring the services, choose Close.

Scheduling Events

When the Schedule service is activated, you can execute programs or commands on the server (or a remote server) to run at a predetermined time. Scheduling these events uses the network command called AT. If you've purchased and installed the NT Server Resource Kit, you can also use WinAT, which is a graphical interface for the AT command.

Note that the Schedule service, by default, logs on under the system account, the same account used by most services. Under these circumstances, the AT command can only access resources that allow Guest access, which may not provide enough access for the desired activity. To gain greater access to network resources when using the AT command, you'll need to create a special user account, give it the appropriate access (if you're scheduling automatic backups, you might want to put the account in the Backup Operators group), then configure the Schedule service to log on using that special account. Make sure you select the Password Never Expires option when you create the account.

Setting Up a Scheduled Event

To set up a scheduled event (a "job") using the AT command, open the Command Prompt and type in the command, using the following syntax:

```
at [\\computername] time [/every:date[,... ] ¦ /next:date[,... ] ]
command
```

where

- *computername* is the computer you are scheduling the event to run on. Leaving it out schedules the event on the local computer.

- The scheduler uses 24-hour time. For 11 a.m., type 11:00; and for 2:30 p.m., type 14:30.

- Any legal command, program, or batch file can be used in the *command* field.

- For the /every: and /next: options, you can either type in the days of the week (Sunday, Monday, etc.), or the number corresponding to the day of the month. Don't leave a space between the colon and the date. (You can abbreviate the days of the week in the /every: and /next: options to M, T, W, Th, F, S, or Su.)

For example, to copy a file at 11:00 a.m. of the current day on a computer named Procyon (a one-time event), you would type:

```
at \\procyon 11:00 "copy c:\users\ellenh\summary.txt c:\users\miked"
```

To run a program named cleanup.exe on the local computer at 5:00 p.m. on the 7, 14, and 21 of every month, you would type:

```
at 17:00 /every:7,14,21 "cleanup"
```

To run a batch file named sayhi.bat on a computer named Rigel at 9:00 a.m. next Thursday, you would type:

```
at \\rigel 9:00 /next:Thursday "sayhi"
```

To view any of the jobs currently scheduled at the local computer, type at, then hit the Enter key (to see the scheduled jobs on another domain server, type at *computername*). Each job is listed with its own ID number. To delete any of the scheduled jobs displayed, type:

```
at \\computername [id number] /delete
```

If you wanted to remove a scheduled job (with the ID number 22) from the local computer, the command would be:

```
at 22 /delete
```

Using WinAT to Schedule Events

WinAT is simply a graphical interface for the at command that comes with the NT Server Resource Kit. But truthfully, there's no "simply" about it; WinAT is a blessing to work with compared to the command-line at command. Opening the WinAT window displays the currently scheduled jobs on the local computer, as shown in Figure 10.14.

FIGURE 10.14:

The WinAT window

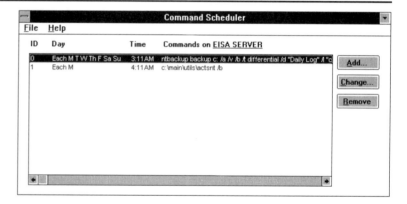

You can view the jobs at a remote server by pulling down the File menu and choosing Computer. To add a new scheduled job, select the Add button. You'll see the Add Command dialog box, as in Figure 10.15. Type in the desired command in the Command box, and choose one of the Today, Tomorrow, Every, and Next buttons. Then, select the days and time the command needs to be run from the Days and Time boxes. When finished, select OK. The new job will appear in the list of scheduled jobs in the main window.

If you need to change an existing job, select that job in the main window, then choose the Change button. You'll see the Change command dialog box. Make the necessary changes, then choose OK. To remove any jobs on the list, simply highlight that job, then select Remove.

FIGURE 10.15:
Add Command dialog box

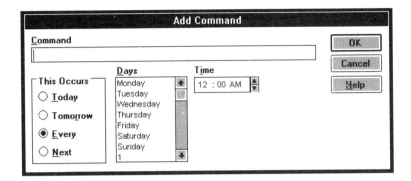

How Do I Set Up a Prescheduled Job at the Local Server?

In this example, we're going to schedule an incremental backup to take place every morning at 3:00 a.m. Type the following command (in an unbroken line):

```
at 3:00 /every:M,T,W,Th,F "ntbackup backup c: /a /v /t
incremental /d ""Daily backup"""
```

The NTBackup command option /a appends to the current backup tape; otherwise, you overwrite the tape's previous backups. The /v option verifies the backup, and the /t followed by *incremental* tells NTBackup to only back things up with the archive bit set, and to reset the archive bit once the backup is done. In the label, two sets of quotes are interpreted as a single set of quotes.

Directory Replication

Directory replication is exactly what it sounds like: the duplication of a master set of directories from a server (called an *export server*) to other NT servers or workstations (called *import computers*). Just like members of a domain, the exporters and importers are not users, but machines (server EISA SERVER exports to workstation AMS, for example, not the domain administrator to user Christa). These duplicate directories are not static copies, but rather remain dynamically linked to the master copy of the directory stored on the export server; if changes or additions are made to that directory, they are automatically reflected in the duplicates on the import computers.

Why would you want to duplicate directories? There are two reasons why having constantly updated, identical copies of directories in more than one place could be a good idea. First of all, replicated directories could help you balance workloads. For example, if a number of workstations need to access a certain directory, you could export that directory to another server and direct some of the workstations to access it from there, rather than from the master copy. This way, you could avoid bottlenecks at the server.

In addition, directory replication also ensures that everybody is working with the same information—something that's important when you're talking about logon scripts or databases that are kept at more than one server. Replication makes the network administrator's job easier, because it doesn't require that the network administrator get a free minute to go around and update all the directories.

Who Can Import? Who Can Export?

Potential exporters on an NT Server network are limited; only NT Server machines can export directories to the rest of the network. Importers are less limited, as NT Server, OS/2 LAN Manager, and Windows NT machines can all import directories from the export servers. The only restriction placed on LAN Manager import computers is that the directories or files being exported must match the naming conventions of the file system of the volume set to which they are exported. For example, if the volume to which the files are exported is formatted to NTFS, the export directory must be set for NTFS.

The commerce between importing computers and export servers does not have to be on an individual basis. If convenient, exporters can export to a domain name rather than to an individual machine, which gives the entire domain access to the replicated directory, or importers can import directories from a domain name. Importing directly eliminates the need for exporters to individually name every machine that needs access to a particular directory. This is demonstrated in Figure 10.16.

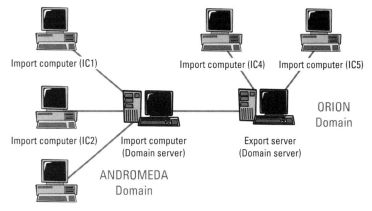

FIGURE 10.16:

Exporting either to domain names or to individual import computers

Import computer (IC1)

Import computer (IC4)   Import computer (IC5)

ORION
Domain

Import computer (IC2)   Import computer
(Domain server)

Export server
(Domain server)

ANDROMEDA
Domain

Import computer (IC3)

ORION's domain server is the export server in this figure. ORION can export either to domain ANDROMEDA and domain ORION, or to individuals (IC1, IC2, IC5, etc.), or perhaps to one entire domain and to individuals in the other one.

The only time that you might have problems exporting to a domain is when some of the domain's import computers are located across a WAN (wide area network) bridge from the export server. In that case, when setting up the list of computers to export to from the export server, you should specify the individual importers by name, and when importing from another domain across the WAN bridge, specify the name of the export server to import from, rather than the domain name. This is illustrated in Figure 10.17.

Setting Up the Directory Replicator Service

Before you can configure an NT Server computer to be an export server, you need to set up a special user account that is part of the Backup Operators group. The Directory Replicator service will use this account to log on, so you need to make sure that:

- The account's password never expires
- The account is accessible 24 hours per day, seven days per week
- The account is assigned to the Backup Operators group

FIGURE 10.17:

Exporting across a WAN bridge

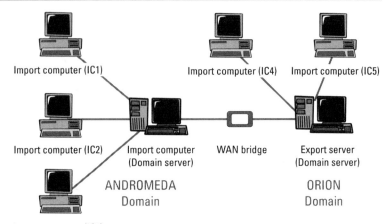

Import computer (IC1)   Import computer (IC4)   Import computer (IC5)

Import computer (IC2)   Import computer   WAN bridge   Export server
                        (Domain server)   (Domain server)

                        ANDROMEDA   ORION
                         Domain   Domain

Import computer (IC3)

ORION's domain server is the export server in this figure. Because it is exporting to computers across a WAN bridge, it must refer to all import computers individually by name (even those in its own domain), rather than exporting to the entire domain and letting the domain server distribute the exported directories.

User accounts are set up under User Manager for Domains (consult Chapter 7 to see how). Don't try to name this account "Replicator"; the system won't let you, as there is already a user group by that name.

Once you've set up this user account, go back to the Server Manager. You now have to configure the Directory Replicator service to start up automatically and to log on using that separate account for each computer in the domain that will participate in replication. To do this, select the computer in the Server Manager window. Then, from the Computer menu, choose Services. You'll see the Services on dialog box. Select the Directory Replicator service, and then click on the Startup... button. You'll see the Directory Replicator Service dialog box, as in Figure 10.18. Select the startup service to begin automatically, select the This Account radio button, and then click the browse button (…) to select the account that you set up for the Directory Replicator service to use. You'll see a screen that looks like Figure 10.19.

Double-click on the name of the account that you want to use (I called mine DR, for "directory replicator") and, when the name of the account shows up in the Add Name text box, click OK. You'll find yourself back in the Directory Replicator Service screen, but now it will have the name of the account you want to use.

FIGURE 10.18:

Configuring startup for the
Directory Replicator service

FIGURE 10.19:

Selecting an account for Replicator
service to use

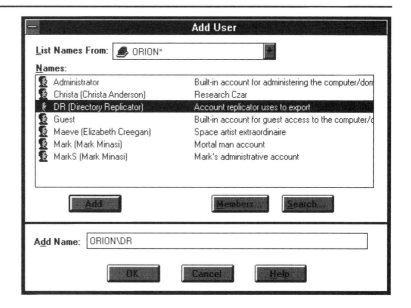

Type in the password that you assigned to the account, and click OK. NT Server will show you a confirmation screen that looks like Figure 10.20. If you like, you can go ahead and manually start the service now, since it won't automatically begin until you've logged off and logged back on again.

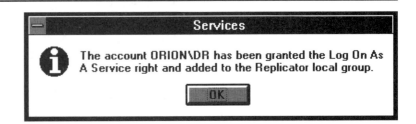

Services

The account ORION\DR has been granted the Log On As A Service right and added to the Replicator local group.

OK

Configuring the Export Server

Once you've set up the Replicator service properly, you're ready to set up the export server for export. As mentioned before, export servers do the following:

- Contain the master set of directories that will be duplicated during replication

- Maintain the list of computers to which the subdirectories are imported

- Export to domain names as well as to individual computers in the domain

NT SERVER

Any NT Server computer can become an export server—but *only* NT Server computers can (NT workstations can't be export servers).

Now, for the directories to export. When NT Server or NT is installed on a machine, the default export and import paths C:\WINNT35\SYSTEM32\REPL\EXPORT and C:\WINNT35\SYSTEM32\REPL\IMPORT are automatically created. (If NT or NT Server is installed in a different location than C:\winnt, these default paths are adjusted accordingly.) Any directories created within the export path are automatically exported, and they and their contents are subsequently placed in the default import path. So, unless you've changed your default directories, you probably want to go to File Manager (or the command prompt) and create the directories that you intend to export within C:\WINNT35\SYSTEM32\REPL\EXPORT. You don't need to put all the files in the directory yet, since any changes that you make to that directory will be dynamically reflected on the import computers, once you have the replication service going.

Once you've created your directories, you can set up directory replication. Directory replication can be configured for the local machine in either Control Panel or in Server Manager. Server Manager, however, lets you configure directory replication remotely for more than one machine at a time.

To set up replication:

1. Do one of the following:

   - In Control Panel, select the Server option; or
   - In Server Manager, select the computer, then choose Properties from the Computer menu (or simply double-click on the computer in the Server Manager window).

2. Choose Replication from the buttons on the bottom of the window. You'll see a screen that looks like Figure 10.21.

3. Select the Export Directories radio button and type the name of the path from which you want to export (you can leave it unchanged if you choose to use the default export path).

FIGURE 10.21:

Initial screen for Directory Replication

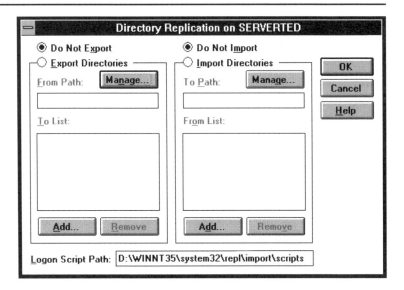

4. Click on the Add... button in the southwest corner of the dialog box, double-click on the domain you want, and select a computer to export to from the list. Your list will look like the one in Figure 10.22.

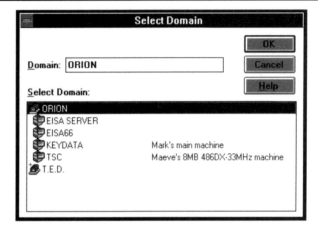

The To List box contains the list of computers that your export directories will be copied to. By default, this list is blank and the local domain automatically receives the exported subdirectories. However, once an entry is made to this list, the local domain is no longer exported to, and must be explicitly added to the list if you want it to receive exported subdirectories.

By the way, permissions for an export directory grant Full Control to members of the Replicator local group. If you change these permissions, files will be copied to the import computers with incorrect permissions, and an "access denied" error will be written in the event log.

If you need to be more specific as to which subdirectories need to be exported, you can choose the Manage button in the Directory Replication window (see Figure 10.21) to manage locks, stabilization, and subtree replication for the subdirectories exported from the server. You'll see a dialog box like the one in Figure 10.23. The Manage Exported Directories dialog box shows the current locks, stabilization status, and subtree replication status for the subdirectories that are to be exported.

FIGURE 10.23:

Managing the export directories

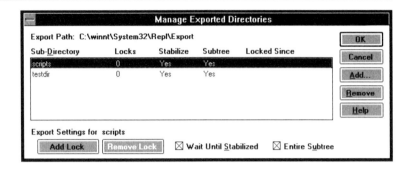

Locks prevent a particular subdirectory from being exported. Subdirectories can have more than one lock applied to them; export will occur only if this column contains a zero. If a subdirectory has been locked, the date and time of the oldest lock is displayed in the Locked Since column. To add a lock to a subdirectory, select it from the list and choose the Add Lock button. To take away a lock, choose the Remove Lock button.

If you choose the Stabilize option by selecting the Wait Until Stabilized box at the bottom, then files in the selected export subdirectory will wait two minutes or more after any changes are made before being exported (this helps eliminate partial replication). Otherwise, files are exported immediately. The default is to *not* wait until stabilization.

Selecting the Entire Subtree option allows all subdirectories and their contents (including additional subdirectories) within the selected subdirectory to be exported. If this option is cleared, only the first-level subdirectories will be exported. Unless you decide to change it, NT Server exports the entire subtree of the directory.

Configuring the Import Computers

Import computers, you recall, are specific servers and computers in the same or other domains that receive the duplicate set of directories from the export server. They maintain a list of export servers from which subdirectories are imported and can import from domain names as well as from individual export servers.

Both NT Server and NT machines can become import computers, but you have to set them up for the service first, just as you did for the export servers. Likewise, you can configure import servers locally using Control Panel, or you can do so remotely with Server Manager. The procedure is the same, except you'll be choosing import options rather than export options in the dialog boxes:

1. Use Administrative powers to create a new user account for the Replication service to use on the import computer, just as you did on the export server.

2. If you're working locally at the workstation, go to the Services icon in the Control Panel and configure the Directory Replicator Service to begin automatically, just as you did on the export server. (If the computer can be remotely administered, you can do this at the server using Server Manager.)

3. Using the Server option in the local computer's Control Panel, or displaying the computer's properties remotely in Server Manager, choose the Replication button and follow the same procedure you would use to export directories, but choose the import directories options instead.

Specifying the Logon Script Path

At the bottom of the Directory Replication dialog box is an edit field containing the logon script path. It is shown in Figure 10.24.

FIGURE 10.24:

Directory Replication dialog box

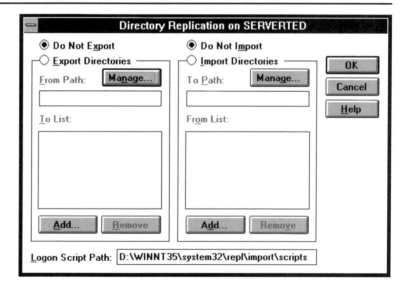

Logon scripts are batch files that can be assigned to specific user accounts so that when a user logs on, the script executes. They are assigned as part of a user's profile (see "User Profiles" in Chapter 7 for more information). When a user logs on, the system looks for the logon script by combining the script's file name (in the user account data) with the logon script path, which is specified in this dialog box.

In NT Server, replication is configured so that servers export logon scripts from the directory C:\WINNT35\SYSTEM32\REPL\EXPORT\SCRIPTS, and import them to the directory C:\WINNT35\SYSTEM32\REPL\IMPORT\SCRIPTS on the import computer. The path for importing logon scripts must be entered in the Logon Script Path box for the domain controller as well as each server that participates in logon authentication for the domain.

How Do I Set the Logon Script Path for a Server?

To configure the logon script path for the selected server, type in a local path in the Logon Scripts Path box of the Directory Replication dialog box (the default, C:\WINNT35\SYSTEM32\REPL\IMPORT\SCRIPTS, is usually sufficient). Entries are required in this edit field, so don't enter a blank space.

Troubleshooting Directory Replication

Setting up the replication service properly can be a bit tricky. If you run into problems, these are some things that you might want to check:

- Have you made the replication service's account a member of the Backup Operators group, or given it the rights accorded to that group?

- Has the Directory Replicator service been started on both the import and export computers?

- Are the import and export computers in the same domain? If not, are the user name and password the same in both domains? Do the domains trust each other?

- For NTFS partitions, have the permissions for the export directory and its contents been altered? Does the Replicator local group have at least Change privileges to these directories?

- Does an account have a file open (on import or export) all the time? This would appear as a sharing violation in the event log.

- When importing or exporting from an NTFS directory, does either directory have file names that differ only in case? The export computer may choose one file while the import computer chooses the other; this can set replication out of sync.

- Are some files with extended attributed (EAs) being replicated from an HPFS volume to an NT Server? NT doesn't support EAs that are written in noncontiguous parts of the disk, which OS/2 sometimes does.

- Are the clocks of the import and export machines synchronized? If they're too far off, the server can't export properly to the import computer.

If you are using OS/2 LAN Manager, be aware of the fact that LAN Manager only allows one set of credentials (i.e., a user name and password) to be used at a time. If someone is logged on locally to one user ID and the Replicator is trying to use another, replication will be delayed until that user logs off.

Errors in the replicator service are entered into the applications log. You can view these entries by opening the Event Viewer in the Administrative Tools group and choosing Application from the Log menu. Make sure you check the logs on both the import and export computers.

Finally, make sure you start the Alerter service and configure alerts so that you can receive messages about the success or failure of directory replication in your system.

PART IV

Managing NTS in the Enterprise Network

CHAPTER

ELEVEN

Cross-Domain Management in NT Networks

11

NT SERVER

By now, you've learned about several pivotal administrative tools in the NT Server world:

- The User Manager for Domains lets you manage users, groups, user rights, and trust relationships with other domains.
- The File Manager lets you control user permissions on files and directories.
- The Print Manager lets you control user permissions on printers and printer pools.
- The Server Manager lets you control user permissions on the files and directories of other machines in your domain and in other domains.

Now let's focus on exactly how to take these tools and manage a multiple-domain enterprise network. The particular tasks that you'll probably most want to perform across domains include:

- Permitting one domain to control another, a concept called *trust relationships*.
- Permitting one domain's users to access directories and files on machines in another domain.
- Making users of one domain users also of another domain.
- Permitting one domain's users to print on printers in another domain.
- Permitting one domain's users to physically log on at computers in another domain.

In this chapter, you'll learn how to do all of those things. And in the process you'll learn about a somewhat thorny concept, *local groups* versus *global groups*.

I find when teaching my classes about NT that cross-domain stuff makes people's heads hurt. ("Now, let's see, domain Personnel trusts domain Finance, but Finance doesn't trust Personnel, so…") In order to make this easier to follow, I've structured this chapter around a simple multiple-domain example—my network. My network is built of two domains: ORION, where my researchers and I do most of our work, and T.E.D., the domain that keeps track of where our seminars and consulting work takes place. (In case you're wondering, T.E.D. stands for "The Engagements Database," a client-server system that we use to maintain schedules for the company's consultants and teachers.)

Getting Acquainted: Trust Relationships

Because high-quality security was one of the most important design principles of NT Server, communications between domains are tightly controlled. Domains can't even *acknowledge* each other unless they are properly introduced, so to speak. That's done with *trust relationships*.

For some reason, trust relationships are controlled with the User Manager for Domains; I guess there's no Domain Security Manager (perhaps there should be one).

Domains are the basic unit of an NT Server network structure. A small network might consist of only one domain, but if your network is large and easily divisible for managerial purposes, you may choose to establish a number of domains. User accounts must be created within a domain (we'll call it the "home domain"), but if the user account belongs to a global group, it can be recognized and have rights and permissions in all of the other domains in the network. In order for this to be possible, however, a *trust relationship* must be established between the user account's home domain and each of those other domains.

What Is a Trust Relationship?

A trust relationship is the first step to cross-domain communication. It's kind of like a treaty between nations, wherein the leader of each nation must initiate the treaty; so also must an administrator from each domain initiate a trust relationship between two domains.

A trust relationship is a link between two domains, allowing one domain (the trusting domain) to recognize all user and global group accounts from another (the trusted domain).

Trust relationships can be one-way or two-way. A two-way trust relationship is just a pair of one-way relationships, where each domain trusts the other. When established correctly, trust relationships allow each user to have only one user account in the network (defined in the user's home domain), yet have access to network resources in other domains.

For example, Figure 11.1 shows a network containing two domains whose names are T.E.D. and ORION. If T.E.D. establishes a trust relationship with ORION, then all user accounts in ORION (the trusted domain) can be used in T.E.D. Now a trust relationship is established, as shown in Figure 11.2.

With the trust relationship established, ORION users can log on at T.E.D.'s workstations, and user accounts created in ORION can be placed in T.E.D.'s local groups and be given permissions and rights within the T.E.D. domain, even though they don't have accounts there. This does *not* mean that T.E.D. users can log on at ORION workstations, or use ORION servers or printers. However, since T.E.D. trusts ORION, T.E.D. gets many benefits, as explained in Figure 11.3.

FIGURE 11.1:

The domains T.E.D. and ORION

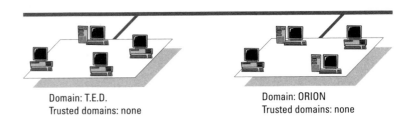

Domain: T.E.D.
Trusted domains: none

Domain: ORION
Trusted domains: none

Two independent domains on the network

FIGURE 11.2:

A trust relationship is established.

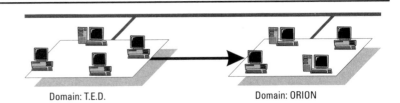

Domain: T.E.D.

Domain: ORION

Domain T.E.D. establishes a trust relationship with ORION.

FIGURE 11.3:

The benefits of a trust relationship

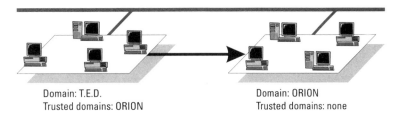

Domain: T.E.D.
Trusted domains: ORION

Domain: ORION
Trusted domains: none

T.E.D. trusts ORION

All ORION users can log on at T.E.D. workstations.
ORION user accounts and global groups can be placed in T.E.D. local groups.
ORION users can be given rights and permissions in the T.E.D. domain.

Unless the ORION domain in turn establishes a trust relationship with T.E.D., accounts in the T.E.D. domain can't be used in ORION. In other words, T.E.D. may trust ORION, but that doesn't make ORION automatically trust T.E.D.

Trust between different domains is likewise not transferred. If T.E.D. trusts Orion, and Orion trusts a domain named Andromeda, then T.E.D. does not automatically trust Andromeda, as shown in Figure 11.4. If the network administrator wanted to be able to use Andromeda's accounts in the T.E.D. domain, he or she would have to set up an additional trust relationship between those two domains.

Bear in mind that trust relationships can only be established between NT Server domains. The Trust Relationships command isn't available when administering LAN Manager 2.x domains or NT workstations.

FIGURE 11.4:

Trust is not transferred through
trusted domains.

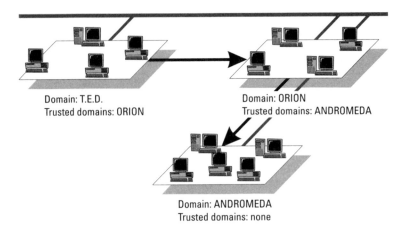

Domain: T.E.D.
Trusted domains: ORION

Domain: ORION
Trusted domains: ANDROMEDA

Domain: ANDROMEDA
Trusted domains: none

Although ORION trusts ANDROMEDA and T.E.D. trusts ORION,
T.E.D. does not automatically trust ANDROMEDA.

When to Establish Trust Relationships

Establishing trust relationships between domains on a network enables user accounts and global groups to be used in domains other than the domain where they are located. Administration becomes easier this way, since a user account only needs to be created once on the entire network, yet can be given access to any computer on the network (not simply the computers in its home domain).

Microsoft describes four domain models for structuring a network:

Domain Model	Description
Single domain	For networks that don't have too many users and don't need to be logically divided for effective management, one single large domain may suffice. Obviously, no trust relationships are required.

Domain Model	Description
Master domain	All user accounts and global groups are created in one domain, the master domain, whose main purpose is to manage the network's accounts. All other domains trust this master domain, and users in the master domain can use the user accounts and global groups defined within the user domains.
Multiple master domain	Suitable for larger networks, this network type contains several master domains; all user accounts on the network are created in one or another of the master domains. Each master domain has a two-way trust relationship with all other domains. All other domains trust each master domain, but may or may not trust each other, depending on the needs of the network.
Complete trust	Each domain on the network has a two-way trust relationship with every other domain. Every domain administrator can manage his or her own domain and define its own users and global groups, yet because of the multiple trust relationships, these users and global groups can be used on all domains in the network.

I find that the "master domain" approach works well for most organizations, since most companies just can't afford a whole pile of network administrators. With the master domain approach, you just create one MIS domain, put the administrators there, and give them control of the user domains.

Establishing Trust Relationships

Establishing a trust relationship with another domain is a two-step process and is performed in two domains. First, your domain must permit a second domain to trust it, then the second domain must be set to trust your domain. It is important to note that if you wish to establish a two-way trust relationship between domains, then you have to do *both* of these steps in *each* domain.

The two steps can be performed in any order, but if you follow the order below, the new trust relationship takes effect immediately. You can reverse the order of the steps and still establish the trust relationship, but you won't receive any confirmation that the trust was established, and the process can be delayed for up to fifteen minutes.

Step 1: Permitting the T.E.D. Domain to Trust ORION

You do this step at the ORION workstation. But before we do it, let's look at the domains T.E.D. and ORION again. If you want the outside domain T.E.D. to trust your domain ORION, you must first *permit* T.E.D. to trust ORION. To do this:

1. Log onto the ORION domain as an ORION administrator.

2. Open User Manager for Domains in the ORION domain.

3. From the Policies menu, choose Trust Relationships. You'll see the Trust Relationships dialog box shown in Figure 11.5.

The Trust Relationships dialog box shows which domains ORION is currently permitted to trust, as well as those which are already trusted. In this case, there are none.

4. Select the Add button next to the Permitted to Trust this Domain box. The Permit Domains to Trust box appears.

FIGURE 11.5:

Trust Relationships dialog box

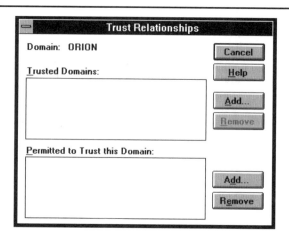

5. Type in the name of the domain you want to permit to trust, T.E.D. in our sample case.

6. Type a password in both the Initial Password and Confirm Password boxes, as in Figure 11.6. Passwords are case-sensitive and can be blank.

FIGURE 11.6:

Permit Domain to Trust dialog box

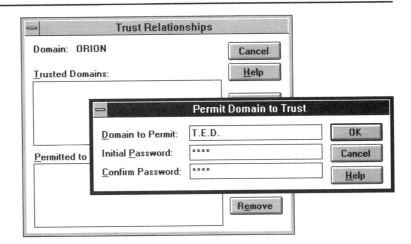

7. Choose OK. T.E.D., the added domain, now appears in the Permitted to Trust this Domain section of the Trust Relationships dialog box.

8. Close the Trust Relationships dialog box by double-clicking the top-left corner.

You've basically given one domain (the domain T.E.D.) permission to trust your domain (ORION), but the trust relationship isn't complete until the other domain actually takes the action of trusting your domain.

Step 2: Trusting ORION (Performed at T.E.D.)

Now that you've permitted T.E.D. to trust ORION, you must give the password you entered in the Permit Domain to Trust dialog box to the administrator of the T.E.D. domain. He or she should then do the following:

1. Log onto the T.E.D. domain as a T.E.D. administrator.

2. Open User Manager for Domains for the T.E.D. domain.

3. From the Policies menu, choose Trust Relationships.

4. Select the Add button next to the Trusted Domains list. The Add Trusted Domain dialog box appears, as in Figure 11.7.

5. In the Domain and Password boxes, the T.E.D. administrator should type in ORION and the password you provided, then choose OK.

FIGURE 11.7:

The Add Trusted Domain dialog box

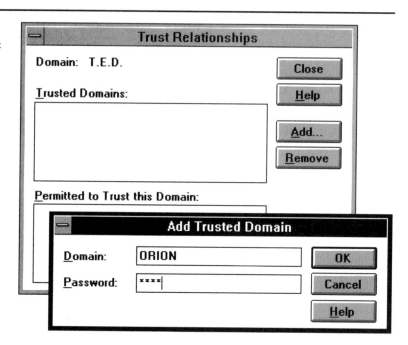

The added domain name, ORION, should now appear in the Trusted Domains list of the Trust Relationships dialog box—the domain T.E.D. now trusts ORION. To exit the Trust Relationships dialog box, close by double-clicking the Control button in the upper-left corner.

Once a domain is trusted, its users can access the domain that trusts it. Note the following about trusted domains:

- The trusted domain shows up as an option in the logon box, which means that users from the trusted domain can log on at workstations in the domain that trusts it.

- The trusted domains' users and groups appear in browse lists.
- Network connections can be made to shared directories on the trusting domain's servers.

Terminating a Trust Relationship

Just like establishing a trust relationship, terminating a trust relationship is another two-step process, done in two different domains. First, one domain has to stop trusting the other domain, then the other domain has to take away the permission of the first domain to trust it.

To stop trusting another domain, open User Manager for Domains and choose Trust Relationships from the Policies menu. Highlight the name of the domain in the Trusted Domains box that will no longer trust your domain, then choose Remove. The explicit message shown in Figure 11.8 appears to remind you about the two-step process. Choose Yes, then close the Trust Relationships dialog box.

Now, still following our "T.E.D. trusts ORION" example, the administrator in ORION has to stop permitting the T.E.D. domain to trust it. This is done by opening User Manager for Domains in ORION, selecting Trust Relationships on the Policies menu, highlighting T.E.D. in the Permitted to Trust this Domain box, and once again selecting Remove. When finished, close the Trust Relationships dialog box.

FIGURE 11.8:
Removing a domain from the
Trusted Domains list

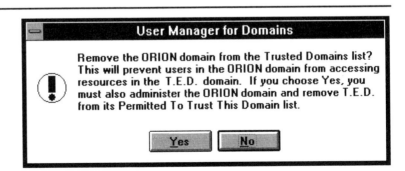

Keep in mind that both of these steps must be performed to properly terminate the trust relationship between domains. Let's summarize this whole process with a "How Do I?"

How Do I Get One Domain to Trust Another?

Let's say that you have a domain named TRUSTING and you want it to trust the main administrative domain (named TRUSTED) so that its administrator can manage TRUSTING's accounts.

TRUSTED's administrator must perform the following:

1. In the User Manager for Domains, choose Trust Relationships in the Policies menu.
2. Choose the Add button next to the Permitted to Trust this Domain list.
3. Type in TRUSTING in the Add box, then type in a password (it can be a blank password). Choose OK.

TRUSTING is now *permitted* to trust TRUSTED, but the trust relationship isn't complete until TRUSTING actually takes the action of trusting TRUSTED. To do this, TRUSTING's administrator must:

1. Open User Manager for Domains in the TRUSTING domain and choose Trust Relationships in the Policies menu.
2. Next to the Trusted Domains box, choose Add.
3. In the Add Trusted Domain box, type in TRUSTED and the password provided by TRUSTED's administrator.

This establishes the trust relationship between the two domains—TRUSTING now trusts TRUSTED.

When you trust another domain, you are giving it the potential to control your domain. Users from TRUSTED can log on at TRUSTING's workstations, and TRUSTED's local groups can now contain TRUSTING's global groups.

Extending File Permissions across Domains

Now that the two domains have some trust, let's put it to use. As I told you before, my network includes two domains, ORION and T.E.D. I'm a member of ORION, which is to say I have a user account on ORION. How could I get access to files on machines in T.E.D.? There are actually *four* ways for the administrators of both domains to give me access to T.E.D. files and directories:

- A T.E.D. administrator can log onto one of T.E.D.'s servers physically, and give user ORION\Mark permission to access a file or directory.

- Someone with both ORION and T.E.D. administrative status can log onto an NT workstation in ORION and use the Server Manager to give ORION\Mark access to a T.E.D. directory share. (The system name for the user Mark in the domain ORION is ORION\Mark.)

- A T.E.D. administrator can put my ORION\Mark account into T.E.D.'s Users group.

- A T.E.D. administrator could make *all* of ORION's users T.E.D. users.

Understanding each method brings you one step closer to being the Lord of all Domains, so let's take a look at each method. Along the way, I'll also promise to make clear one of the great confusing issues in NT management (well, confusing to *me* at first, anyway): local and global groups.

Providing Cross-Domain Access with File Manager

Let me restate my goal in order to clarify what I'm trying to accomplish here. I'm a user in the ORION domain named Mark. There is a directory on a server in the T.E.D. domain that I want my Mark account to be able to read and write. Let's also say for this example that the particular server on T.E.D. that contains the directories that I want to get into are on a machine named SERVERTED. (Okay, so we're not so original in naming our servers.)

Now, if this directory were in ORION, then giving me access to the directory would be a piece of cake; you've already seen how to use the Security item on the File Manager menu to extend file and directory permissions to a particular user. So let's use File Manager to give Mark access to the directory on SERVERTED.

Unfortunately, in order to run the File Manager on a directory in T.E.D., someone—someone with T.E.D. administrative powers—has to physically walk over to the machine SERVERTED and log on. From there, the steps that a T.E.D. administrator would go through to get me the access that I need are as follows:

1. Start up the File Manager, select the directory that Mark (that's me, remember) wants access to, click Security, and then click Permissions…

Looking over that administrator's shoulder, you would see a dialog box that gives file permissions. It would probably show that Everyone has read/write access. That "Everyone," however, means Everyone who's a member of the T.E.D. domain; I'm *not* a member of T.E.D.

By the way, the correct answer to getting me onto T.E.D. resources is *not* giving me a T.E.D. account. That would allow me to log onto T.E.D., but at the expense of losing my ORION rights and permissions.

But getting back to our administrator, here are the rest of the steps he or she would take to give me access to the directory on T.E.D.:

2. To find me to add, click the Add… button.

A large dialog box appears, offering users to add to file permissions. At the top of the dialog box is a single-selection drop-down list box labeled List Names From, and a list of the domains that our enterprise network sees.

3. Choose ORION. After a pause, the ORION groups appear.
4. Click the Show Users… button. The ORION users appear, including me.
5. Click on Mark and then press OK until all the dialog boxes are gone.

Once all that's done, my Mark account would be able to access the directory on T.E.D.

Providing Cross-Domain Access with the Server Manager

If you paid close attention in Chapter 10, the Server Manager chapter, you may have been saying in the previous section, "Wait! There's another way…" and indeed there is. The Server Manager allows remote control of servers, even servers in other domains.

To give me (an ORION user) access to a T.E.D. directory, someone with T.E.D. administrative powers would have to log on at T.E.D. and add my name to the share permissions for a given directory. Here's how.

1. A T.E.D. administrator logs on inside T.E.D., and starts the Server Manager. The Server Manager's screen then looks like the dialog box in Figure 11.9.

2. Server Manager will then show all the machines in T.E.D. As SERVERTED has the directory that I want access to, the T.E.D. administrator would click on that machine, and then click on Computer, and Shared Directories…; a dialog box like one in Figure 11.10 appears.

3. This is a list of all the shares, administrative and otherwise, on SERVERTED. If the T.E.D. administrator clicks on one of them, and then clicks on the Properties… button, he sees a dialog box like the one in Figure 11.11.

4. To control who can use the share, the administrator would click on Permissions… and see a dialog box labeled Access Through Share Permissions, as in Figure 11.12.

FIGURE 11.9:

Opening screen of Server Manager

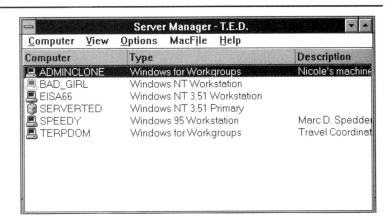

437

FIGURE 11.10:

Shared Directories screen in Server Manager

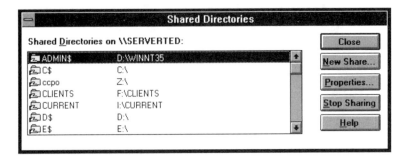

FIGURE 11.11:

Properties of a share

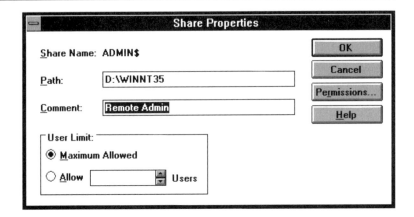

FIGURE 11.12:

Access to a share

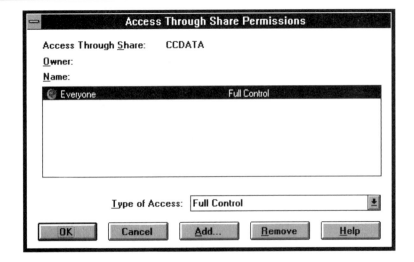

5. He can now add me to the list of people with access to this directory, with the Add… button. The process from here is basically the same as for File Manager. The T.E.D. administrator just chooses the ORION domain, clicks the Show Users… button, picks my name, and then clicks OK until he's out of the dialog boxes.

Become a User of a Foreign Domain

Wouldn't this whole thing be simpler if I just became a T.E.D. user? Well, I said before that if I got an account named Mark in T.E.D., I'd have to choose whether I was going to log onto T.E.D.—which would deny me access to ORION facilities—or log onto ORION, which would deny me access to T.E.D. facilities (unless I went through the rigmarole that we've gone through so far). There would be two separate Mark personas, each with certain abilities. I don't want that; I want *one* Mark, with dual-domain powers.

TIP

There is a kind of sneaky way to do this. Create a Mark account in T.E.D. *and* a Mark account in ORION, and assign them both the same password. Then Mark can log on from either domain and see the other one. It works, but it's an administrative nightmare.

A better solution is simply to take my ORION account and tuck it into the T.E.D. "Users" group. Here's how. (Again, all of this requires someone with administrative powers for T.E.D., the foreign domain.)

1. This administrator starts up the User Manager for Domains, as shown in Figure 11.13. It shows the T.E.D. users; notice that I'm not in there.

2. Notice that, as with virtually all domains, there's a group called Users. The T.E.D. administrator would double-click on that, and she'd see a dialog box labeled Local Group Properties, showing who's in T.E.D.'s Users group; the dialog box looks like Figure 11.14.

3. The administrator would next click Add. At this point a dialog box labeled Add Users and Groups should appear, like the one in Figure 11.15.

FIGURE 11.13:

Opening screen of User Manager for Domains on T.E.D.

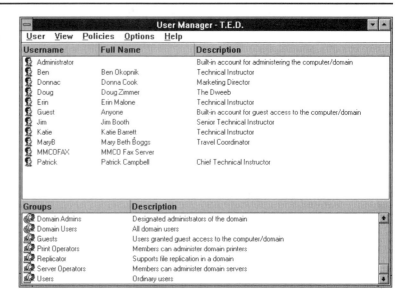

FIGURE 11.14:

Display of T.E.D.'s Users group membership

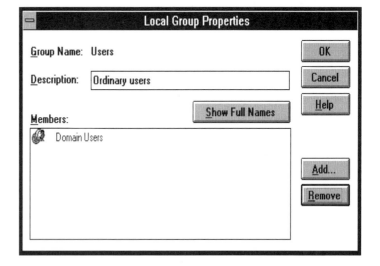

FIGURE 11.15:

Adding members to a group

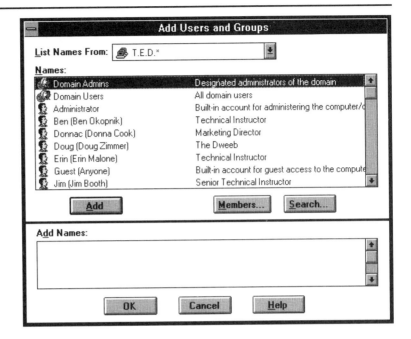

4. I want her to add user Mark, but Mark's in ORION, not T.E.D., so she pulls down the List Names From list box, chooses ORION, and sees the ORION users. She selects my account, clicks Add and OK, and now the list of the members of the T.E.D. Users group looks like Figure 11.16.

Now I can access anything that *any* user of T.E.D. can access.

Why Not Put All the Local Domain Users into the Foreign Domain's?

That was a fair amount of work. Why make the T.E.D. administrators do all that work for *all* the ORION users? I mean, it would be a real pain to have to put all the ORION users in the T.E.D. Users group, person by person. It would seem that the logical thing to do, since T.E.D. trusts ORION anyway, would be to put the ORION Users group into the T.E.D. Users group.

A good idea, but it can't be done. Why? Understanding that requires understanding local and global groups.

FIGURE 11.16:

The ORION user Mark added to T.E.D.'s Users group

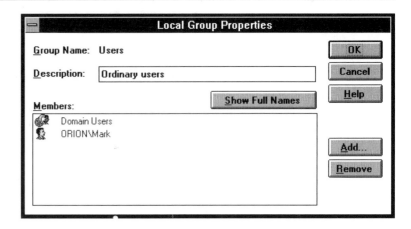

Local and Global Groups Explained

If you peruse the NT Server manuals, you'll notice that they are rife with references to "local" groups versus "global" groups. Although the manuals make a valiant effort to explain the difference, the explanation is a bit rough to follow unless you understand *why* there are local and global groups. And, truthfully, there isn't all that much "local" about a "local group," nor "global" about a "global group." Just suspend for a moment your existing notions about what "local" and "global" mean, and I'll try to make this make sense.

The difference is best explained with an example. Once again, we'll use my company's two domains, ORION and T.E.D. The people in the ORION domain need access to some of the information on T.E.D., so suppose I decide to put ORION's Users group into T.E.D.'s Users group; that would let the ORION people log onto T.E.D. and get the same kind of access that normal T.E.D. users get—in fact, they'd *be* normal T.E.D. users. So the answer seems to be to put the ORION group named "Users" into the T.E.D. group named "Users." That ought to do the trick.

Unfortunately, you can't do it. NT won't let you.

What if, at some future point, my replacement read a book like this, and decided that T.E.D.'s Users group should become part of ORION's Users group? The result would be a circular trap, in which ORION's Users group would be part of T.E.D.'s Users group, which would be part of ORION's Users group, which would be… You get the idea. (Ever see the M.C. Escher work "Drawing Hands," where two hands draw each other? It's kind of the same idea.) Because of this possibility, NT will not let you put one domain's Users group inside that of another domain.

Kinds of Groups

Microsoft chose to avoid that pitfall by creating two kinds of user groups: those which could *contain* other groups and those which could *be contained* within those groups. For the sake of example, let's begin by calling these types Group Type One and Group Type Two.

Type One groups have three characteristics:

- They can contain individual users as members.

- They can contain Type Two groups.

- They cannot be contained by any other group.

Type Two groups also have three characteristics:

- They can only contain individual users as members.

- They can be contained *inside* a Type One group.

- They cannot contain any other groups, even groups of Type Two.

Essentially, this structure creates a situation in which the nesting can only go in one direction:

- Type One groups can contain Type Two groups but not other Type One groups.

- Type Two groups cannot contain either kind of group.

To repeat: Type Ones can contain Type Twos. No other combinations are allowed. Ready for the real names now? What I've been calling "Type One" groups are called "local" groups in NT. The "Type Two" groups are called "global" groups in NT.

How does this setup apply to cross-domain membership management? Let's look at our T.E.D. and ORION domains again. T.E.D. and ORION will each require a "Local Users" group and a "Global Users" group. Their user groups' membership starts out looking like Table 11.1.

TABLE 11.1 : Beginning composition of ORION and T.E.D. domains

ORION	T.E.D.
Local Users group	**Local Users Group**
Gloria	Tom
Betty	Dick
Camille	Harry
Global Users group	**Global Users group**
Gloria	Tom
Betty	Dick
Camille	Harry

We want to make Gloria, Betty, and Camille members of T.E.D.'s local Users group. To do so, we would open T.E.D.'s User Manager for Domains and make ORION's Global Users group a member of T.E.D.'s Users group, so that the new group memberships look like Table 11.2.

TABLE 11.2 : ORION and T.E.D. domains after making ORION's global users local T.E.D. users

ORION	T.E.D.
Local Users group	**Local Users Group**
Gloria	Tom
Betty	Dick
Camille	Harry
	Global Users (ORION)

TABLE 11.2 : ORION and T.E.D. domains after making ORION's global users local T.E.D. users (continued)

ORION	T.E.D.
Global Users group	**Global Users group**
Gloria	Tom
Betty	Dick
Camille	Harry

This is a good beginning, but it's not a complete solution. What happens when the membership of ORION's Users group changes? It's a pain to have to make new members part of both the Local Users and Global Users groups. How can you solve this? Well, remember: global groups go into local groups.

Why not put ORION's Global Users group into ORION's Local Users group? (You could also do it with T.E.D.) Then ORION's and T.E.D.'s group memberships would look like Table 11.3.

TABLE 11.3 : Domain membership organized to update nested groups automatically

ORION	T.E.D.
Local Users group	**Local Users Group**
Global Users (ORION)	Global Users (T.E.D.)
	Global Users (ORION)
Global Users group	**Global Users group**
Gloria	Tom
Betty	Dick
Camille	Harry

Notice that the membership of the Local Users groups no longer includes individuals; the local groups are now composed entirely of global groups. This way, any time you change the membership of a global group, the membership of the local group of which *it* is a member is automatically updated.

This is basically what Microsoft did.

Ever notice that you've got a pre-built group named Users? It's the "Local Users" group. Similarly, you've probably noticed that you have a group named Domain Users. It's what I've been calling "Global Users." The same thing applies to the "Administrators" and "Domain Administrators" groups.

One way to underscore the difference between a global group and a local group is to look at the dialog box that lets you add members to a local group, and compare it to the dialog box that lets you add members to a global group. A local group's Local Group Properties dialog box looks like Figure 11.17.

FIGURE 11.17:

Members of Users local group

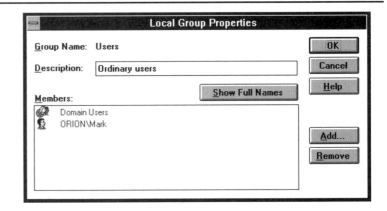

The Add... button produces the dialog box that you see in Figure 11.18.

Notice that you can't add any *local* groups—just global groups and individual users. You can also add people and groups *from other domains*.

In contrast, consider the dialog box that lets you add members to a *global* group. That's the Properties dialog box that you'd see in the User Manager for Domains when you've selected a global group. You see that dialog box in Figure 11.19.

Notice that not only is the Add... button grayed out; there's also no chance to choose another domain, and no groups are offered to add.

FIGURE 11.18:

Adding members to a local group

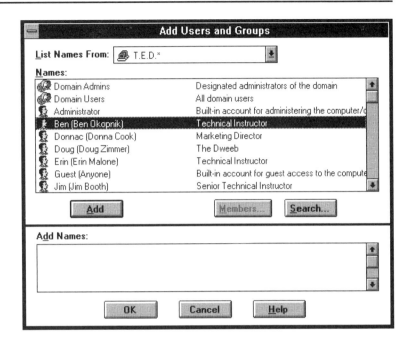

FIGURE 11.19:

Adding members to a global group

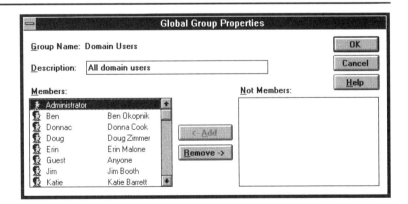

To review, the big points to understand about local and global groups are:

- In a single-domain NT Server network, global groups are basically irrelevant.
- Local groups can contain both individuals and global groups.
- Global groups can *only* contain individuals.

Following are some suggestions concerning group management.

A Group Needing Rights and Permissions in One Domain   If you require a group whose members need rights and permissions in one domain only, your group must be local. Local groups can contain users and global groups from other domains (in addition to those from the local domain) that need rights and permissions in the local domain, but can only be used in the local domain.

A Group that Can Contain Others Groups and User Accounts   If you want a group that can contain other groups as well as user accounts, your group must be local. Local groups can contain global groups and individual user accounts; no group can contain other local groups.

A Group that Can Have Users from Multiple Domains   If you need a group that can include users from multiple domains, your group must be local. Local groups can only be used in the domain in which they are created. If you need to grant this local group permissions in more than one domain, you will have to manually create the local group (and define its permissions and rights) in every domain in which you need it.

Grouping Users of One Domain into a Unit for Use in Other Domains   If you want to group users of one domain into a single unit for use in other domains, your group must be global. Global groups can be put into other domains' local groups and can be given rights and permissions directly in other domains.

A Group that Can Be Granted Permissions on NT Workstations   If you need a group that can be granted permissions on NT workstations, your group must be global. A domain's global groups can be given permissions on Windows NT workstations, but a domain's local groups cannot, as they are relevant only within the local domain.

Using Local and Global Groups

Now let's get back to my original question from a few pages back: How do I get all the users of ORION to be part of T.E.D.\Users?

Well, the Users group is a local group, so I can't put ORION's Users group into T.E.D.'s Users group: globals go into locals, not the other way around. (I had to repeat that to myself about fifty times before I remembered it: "Globals go into locals, globals go into locals,…") What I need is a kind of analog to the Users group, only a global group. Sort of a "Global Users" group.

I could create an ORION group called Global Users and then copy all of the users into that. *Then* I could put the ORION\Global Users group into the T.E.D.\Users group—that's a global into a local, so I'd be okay. And from that point on, anyone in ORION\Global Users would be instantly given user privileges in T.E.D. By always adding new users to the ORION\Global Users group, I'd make sure that all new ORION users could get to T.E.D. resources.

That's a good solution, but it's a bit cumbersome, as it requires that I keep ORION's *local* users group, ORION\Users, *and* the ORION\Global Users group in sync. But NT Server has an answer for that.

First of all, I needn't create ORION\Global Users; it has already been created. Its name is ORION\Domain Users. Second, the way that we keep ORION\Users and ORION\Domain Users in sync is simple. Hint: Recall that globals go into locals. Just put any users into the global ORION\Domain Users group, and then put just one entry into ORION\Users—the ORION\Domain Users group. Elegant, eh? If I put ORION\Domain Users into both T.E.D.\Users *and* ORION\Users, then adding a new user to both domains is simple—just put the user in ORION\Domain Users. Since ORION\Domain Users is in both T.E.D.\Users and ORION\Users, then the new user shows up in both domains.

Rules for Building and Using Groups

If you have a multiple-domain enterprise network to administer, consider the following rules when building and using groups.

Rule 1 If you have a group that needs to be in more than one domain, then create *two* groups: the local and the global. The one sort of "shadows" the other. Example: the built-in Administrators (local) and Domain Admins (global), and the built-in Users (local), and Domain Users (global).

Rule 2 Make user accounts members of the *global* domain, not the local. Put people with administrative privileges in Domain Admins, not Administrators. Put new users into Domain Users, not Users.

Rule 3 Put the global account into the local account. If you have no members of your Users group from outside of your domain, for example, then the only member of your Users group should be your Domain Users group.

An Example: Making All the ORION Users T.E.D. Users

Just to cement this, let's take a look at an example. I'll give all the ORION users privileges in T.E.D. as users. The steps are as follows:

1. Start up the User Manager for Domains.
2. Tell it to work on the T.E.D. domain.
3. Add an item to the (local group) T.E.D.\Administrators, the ORION\Domain Admins.

This is a particularly useful example, so let's make it a "How Do I" sidebar.

How Do I Administer the User Accounts on a Different Domain from My Own Domain?

First of all, before you can administer another domain's accounts, that domain must trust your domain. Let's go back to the domain T.E.D., which trusts the domain ORION. How can we administer T.E.D. while logged on in the ORION domain?

Members of T.E.D.'s local group Administrators are the only ones capable of administering the T.E.D. domain. Local groups, as you recall, can contain not only local users and groups, but also global groups and users from other trusted domains. Therefore, in order for the administrator of ORION to manage T.E.D.'s accounts, ORION's global group Domain Admins must be placed into T.E.D.'s local Administrators group. Equally, if the administrator of ORION didn't want all of its domain administrators to be able to administer T.E.D., he or she could simply add a single ORION administrator to T.E.D.'s local Administrator group.

This is done in the following fashion by the administrator of ORION:

1. In ORION, open User Manager for Domains. Under the User menu, choose Select Domain to display the home domain and any domain that trusts it:

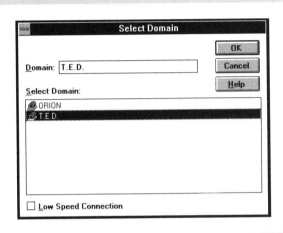

2. Choose the T.E.D. domain. You'll now see T.E.D.'s users and groups.

3. In the Groups segment of the window, double-click on the Administrators local group to display its properties:

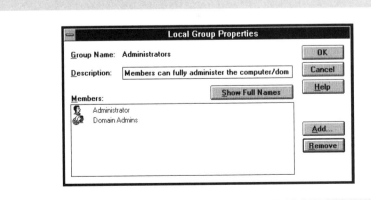

4. Select the Add button to get the Add Users and Groups list. Under the List Names From box at the top, choose the domain ORION.

5. Out of ORION's list of groups, select the global group Domain Admins. Choose Add, then choose OK.

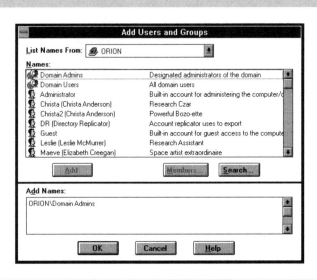

6. In the Properties box, the group ORION\Domain Admins will now appear in the membership list of T.E.D.'s local Administrators group:

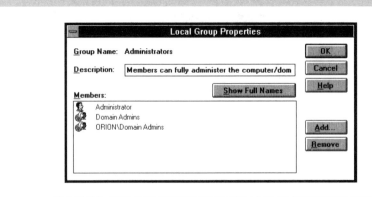

7. Choose OK.

With T.E.D.'s local Administrators group now containing the global group ORION\Domain Admins, any administrator in ORION who is a member of its Domain Admins group can manage the T.E.D. domain as well.

Granting User Rights and Printer Permissions across Domains

Thus far, I've discussed granting file permissions, which is probably of more concern to you more often than are user rights or even printer permissions.

By now, you've seen that the Add... button that appears in many dialog boxes opens up the door, when clicked, to other domains. By using those dialog boxes, you can assign user rights and printer permissions to users from other domains, just as you've seen how to assign file permissions to "alien" users.

Logging on from Foreign Domains

Many companies adopt a model wherein user departments are organized into domains, and the MIS group has its own domain from which all other domains are managed.

In that model, the trust relationships look like Figure 11.20. All the user departments trust the MIS domain, but the MIS domain doesn't trust any of them. A LAN administrator, who is probably a member of the MIS domain, may find him- or herself at a server in *any* domain, wanting to log onto that server and do some kind of maintenance. How should the accounts be arranged so that this LAN administrator can log onto any server?

FIGURE 11.20:

Special trust relationship model

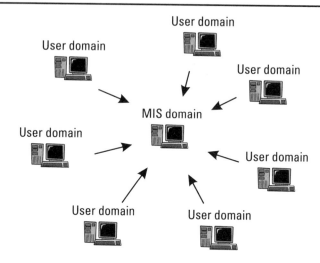

Well, logging onto a server requires two things, a recognized account on a trusted domain, and the user right to log onto a server (ordinary users can't just sit down to the server and start working). As you've seen, it doesn't make sense to give this central administrator an account on every single domain and, besides, that makes for some cumbersome administrative nightmares.

The LAN administrator in this example can get onto any machine via a two-step process.

First, make sure that the MIS domain's Domain Admins group is in every user department domain's Administrators group. That assures Administrator status for any MIS administrators. It also gives MIS administrators the user right to log on at a server. Up to now, the phrase "global group" hasn't had much meaning, but consider that this MIS domain's global group "Domain Admins" appears in each of the user domain's local Administrators group; in that context, it makes a bit more sense.

Second, when logging onto an NT Server machine, log on as the normal user name, but enter MIS or whatever the name of the MIS domain is in the From field. This way, MIS administrators can get on from anywhere.

Getting Domain Resources even though You're Not a Domain Member

Here's an oddity that you may come across. Suppose you were a normal user in the MIS domain, not an administrator. Could you sit down at a Windows for Workgroups machine in a user department's domain and get to your machine? You could, because you can specify from Windows for Workgroups which domain you wish to log onto. Suppose you're at the desk of a member of the Personnel domain, and you go to log onto the MIS domain. You log on okay, but then you notice that the machine that you've logged onto has persistent connections that hook it up to some resources in the Personnel domain. After a moment, it dawns on you: *I shouldn't be able to get to Personnel resources*. And yet you can. What's going on?

The Guest account, that's what's going on. If the Guest account doesn't have a password, and if you haven't restricted its access to domain resources, then someone who logs on whom the domain doesn't recognize gets logged onto the local domain's resources as a guest. This is true even if the user logging on is from a trusted domain. If the Guest account had been disabled, then you would have been prompted for a password before you could go any further, as the Windows for Workgroups machine would want to finish establishing persistent connections.

The thing that separates NT from many other network systems, including earlier Microsoft offerings, is its enterprise-wide structure. By using global groups, by having a good knowledge of cross-domain techniques, you can build a network that is easy to administer, even from miles away.

CHAPTER

TWELVE

Novell NetWare in an NT Server Environment

Novell NetWare commands somewhere between 60 and 70 percent of the PC-based server market, between its three offerings in versions 2.2, 3.12, and 4.*x*. For that reason, many NT networks incorporate some kind of NetWare connectivity. Similarly, many NetWare networks out there find themselves having to deal with NT Server and NT workstations, as networks these days just aren't homogenous.

In this chapter, you'll learn how to integrate NT- and NetWare-based networks, so that you can enjoy the best of both worlds. There are several integration options, but the best (in my opinion) is the Client and Gateway Services for NetWare that ships with NT Server.

How NT and NetWare Interact

There are three main ways in which NT networks and NetWare networks interact.

NT Workstations on Novell NetWare First, a Novell NetWare network may incorporate NT machines solely as workstations. This is fairly simple, as it requires no work on the server side at all. All you need do is to obtain NT NetWare client software from Novell to accomplish this.

This solution is really only relevant to NT *workstations*, however. Users of an NT Server network would not be able to access resources on the Novell network with this solution.

NT Server in a Novell NetWare Network If your current network is a Novell NetWare-based one, then your workstations all run NetWare client software. If you add an NT Server machine to an existing Novell NetWare network, then you'll have to load *dual* network client software on the workstations. The aspects of this solution include:

- It requires dual network client software, which can be hard to manage and requires more memory.

- It *does* provide for access to both Novell NetWare and NT Server resources, but security and programming interfaces are not integrated.

- Remote access and backup processes could not be shared under this system.

- It involves no special software installation on the *servers*, and so may be attractive to some network administrators. In a sense, it even may be a slightly more reliable solution, as it's the older one.

This second option is, unfortunately, the one that most of us use. But many could benefit from the third option, Novell NetWare in an NT Server Network.

Novell NetWare in an NT Server Network   Starting with NT 3.5, a third solution—the Gateway Service—has been available. With the Gateway Service, all NetWare resources become NT Server resources. Yes, you read that right: All access to NetWare resources occurs through the NT servers. Aspects of this solution include:

- You need only run one set of network software, the NDIS and NetBIOS software, on the client in order to access the NetWare servers.
- Backup and remote access services can be integrated.
- Security can be integrated.
- As a side bonus, Novell NetWare server/user limitations can be bypassed.

It's quite an attractive solution, but how does it work? I'll cover that in most of the remainder of the chapter, but first let's take a quick look at Novell's answer.

Netware Client Software for NT

The NetWare Client for NT (NCNT) software was released by Novell in late June of 1994. It has the following features:

- It replaces the NDIS-based network stack on an NT workstation with an ODI-based stack.
- The Open Data-link Interface (ODI) standard is the Novell analog to NDIS, which is troublesome, because there are likely to be fewer NT-compatible ODI drivers around.
- The NT services that require NDIS get NDIS-like service from ODI via an on-the-fly translation program called ODINSUP.

Overall, it's an answer more appropriate for a few lone NT workstations in a NetWare environment than it is for an NT Server-based environment.

Using NWLink without the Gateway Service

Using NWLink without the Gateway Service is not really a NetWare connectivity solution, but one thing that ships with NT is NWLink, a transport protocol that is IPX/SPX-compatible. (IPX/SPX stands for *internetworking packet exchange/sequenced packet exchange*.) NWLink is another STREAMS and TDI-integrated transport protocol, a "plug-and-play" option like TCP/IP. You could, if you wanted, install it in place of (or in addition to) NetBEUI or TCP/IP as your domain's transport protocol.

Why would you do that? Well, NWLink supports the "sockets" application program interface (API). Since some NetWare-based applications servers, or NetWare Loadable Modules (NLMs), use sockets to communicate with client computers, your NT machines could act as clients in a NetWare-based client/server environment. NWLink is relatively useless all by itself, however, because it does not include a NetWare-compatible redirector. In English, that means that you could not access NetWare file servers or shared printers solely with NWLink.

NWLink mimics Novell's IPX/SPX stack, but many Novell users also load a Novell version of NetBIOS. To maintain compatibility with that NetBIOS, Microsoft also ships NWBLink, a transport stack that runs alongside NWLink, providing NetBIOS support much like that provided by Novell. (Novell's NetBIOS is a bit different from the Microsoft version, as you've probably figured out if you've ever tried to install something on your Novell network that required NetBIOS.)

If you're installing NWBLink on an Ethernet, you may run up against a common situation that appears under Novell with Ethernets: frame type. In the Ethernet world, you can configure your network to work with either the IEEE 802.3 (CSMA/CD) or IEEE 802.2 (Logical Link Control) frame formats. If you are communicating with a Netware 2.2 or 3.11 server, then the frame format is usually 802.3. Netware 4.x servers generally use frame type 802.2.

Running NetWare and NT Server in Parallel

The idea here is simple: Your office has both NT servers and a NetWare server or servers. The NT servers talk NetBIOS/NetBEUI and perhaps TCP/IP, and the Novell servers talk IPX/SPX. Getting the two server families (NetWare and NT) to talk to one another is a mite tricky, goes the reasoning, *so don't bother*. Instead, load both IPX/SPX and NetBIOS/NetBEUI stacks on your workstations.

Many of you have probably already chosen this solution if you're running Windows for Workgroups. Windows for Workgroups ships with an IPX/SPX stack that runs in combination with NetBIOS/NetBEUI, making it possible to carry on conversations with both servers. Here are some features of the NetWare and NT Server in parallel solution:

- Simplicity, kind of, in that you needn't install any software on the servers. You needn't put NWLink on your NT machines, nor some kind of odd NLM on your NetWare servers.

- Lack of drivers. To date, Windows for Workgroups does not ship with a NetWare redirector. The IPX/SPX protocol is in place, but the redirector is not, requiring you to run the redirector that came with Windows for Workgroups version 3.1. Microsoft gives you no warning of this until you're partway through the installation of Windows for Workgroups version 3.11 (Nice touch, boys and girls!). In addition, the combination of 3.11 and the old 3.1 driver is a bit wobbly.

- Lack of drivers II: If you're running NetWare 4.x servers, there's just no way that you can make the old Windows for Workgroups 3.1 NetWare drivers work reliably. You have to download a bunch of drivers from Novell. They seem to talk fairly well to the NetWare servers, but tend to eliminate some of the benefits of Workgroups. Besides, they cut off your connections to NT Server machines periodically.

- Memory management becomes a problem in that you're loading a *lot* of stuff on the workstation.

- Because you're still running two different server environments, they don't share anything. You have to create separate user accounts on the NT side of the house from the NetWare side. Remote access services aren't shared, requiring twice as many modems. Backup services aren't shared, so you have to keep track of twice as many tapes.

Windows 95 greatly simplifies matters, as Microsoft has written complete protocol stacks and client software for both NT and Novell networks, use all Microsoft client software, and you'll only be dealing with one vendor.

Microsoft Gateway Service

The Microsoft Gateway Service could get to be a real candidate for "the" NT-to-NetWare answer.

In mid-June 1994, Microsoft released the first version of its complete NetWare-to-NT solution. It came in two parts: the NetWare Client Service and the NetWare Gateway Service. You'll be most interested in the Gateway Service.

The Client Service is a complete NT-based, 32-bit NetWare redirector. It allows you to sit at an NT machine and use all the resources of your NetWare network, just as you've been able to do for years from your DOS workstations. The Client Service is just software like TCP/IP or NWLink that you install via the Add Software option on the Control Panel. No changes are required on the NetWare servers except, of course, the NT user must have a valid account. You must install NWLink before installing the Client Service.

Where things get really strange is when you install the Gateway Service. After you install it, *any workstation that is connected to your NT Server machine can also see the Net-Ware drives*. Pretty spooky, but the NT Server machine becomes a gateway to the NetWare services. All the NetWare server sees is the one logical connection between NetWare and the NT machine, so actually dozens of people can use a single NetWare connection!

The characteristics of the Gateway Service are:

- It allows shared remote access services.
- Ditto for backups.
- Accounts become integrated because the NT Server machine is the "front end" to the NetWare network, and so the NT Server machine handles login validation and permissions as if they were just other resources in the NT domain.
- An NT Server machine must serve as the gateway.
- This only works with 4.x servers that are running bindery emulation; there's no support for NetWare directory services so far.

The Gateway Service answer is the newest one to the "How do I integrate NetWare and NT?" question, and it could be the best one.

Installing the NetWare Gateway

When you install the NetWare Gateway Service, you also install NWLink. As with all NT network software modules, you install the Gateway Service by starting up the Control Panel, then clicking on the Networks icon. You see the dialog box shown in Figure 12.1. Click on the Add Software button, and you'll see options for other add-ons to NT. Choose Gateway Service for NetWare, and click Continue. You'll then have to provide the path where NT can find the setup files (the CD-ROM for most of us), and once again click Continue.

Installing the Gateway Service

If you have RAS running, you'll receive the following setup message: "Setup has discovered that you have Remote Access Services installed. Do you want to configure RAS to support NWLink protocol?" If you want to have remote access configured for using the IPX protocol, click OK. Click Cancel if you don't want to install the IPX protocol for use with RAS.

FIGURE 12.1:
Network Settings dialog box

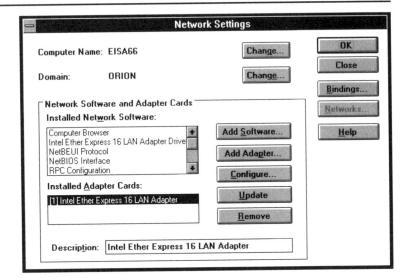

After some grinding of disks, you'll then be back at the Network Settings dialog box (see Figure 12.1). Click OK. The system will then start asking you for configuration information on the Gateway Services. The first dialog box describes the NWLink service, and it looks like Figure 12.2.

You can select Auto Frame Type Detection, but if you're running a Novell network with Ethernet hardware, it's a good idea to talk to your Novell administrator to figure out what frame type your NetWare servers use.

Because it sees that my system has an Ethernet card, the NWLink software must guess whether I use the 802.3 frame type (common to NetWare 2.x and 3.x) or the 802.2 frame type (common to NetWare 4.x). My preferred server is going to be a NetWare 4.x machine, so I'll change the frame type to 802.2. If you get it wrong, don't worry; you can always fire up the Control Panel, click on the Network icon, choose the NWLink IPX/SPX Compatible Transport, and click the Configure button. When you click OK, the server will reset itself.

FIGURE 12.2:
NWLink IPX/SPX Protocol
Configuration dialog box

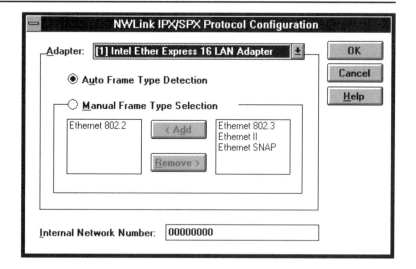

Creating the User

As the server boots, move over to a NetWare-attached workstation and run SYSCON, NWADMIN, or its equivalent. You have to get the NetWare servers ready for the NT client with the following steps:

1. Create a user whose name is the same as the user that will log onto the NT machine. In my example, I'm hooking up an NT Server machine to NetWare, so the user name that I use to log onto the NT Server machine is Administrator. Create a *Novell* user named Administrator.
2. Create a NetWare group called NTGATEWAY.
3. Put your user—Administrator in my case—into that NTGATEWAY group.
4. Set the password of Administrator to the same value as the password of the NT user named "Administrator." (This isn't necessary for the simple Client Services setup, but it will prove essential for the Gateway Services later.)

Now, back to the NT side of the setup.

TIP

If you are going to run the Gateway Service (in contrast to the Client Service), be aware that if you log onto the machine running the Gateway Service, then you may be unable to access the Novell drives unless you supply the gateway name and password. For example, I've been using a user named Administrator for my examples. If I log onto EISA66, the NT machine that's running the Gateway Service, and use the name "Mark," I'll get a password verification the first time that I try to use the Novell drives locally. All I'd have to do would be to supply the user name "Administrator" and the password for that account.

The Gateway Service Setup, Part 2

When the server comes back up, it prompts you for a preferred NetWare server, but don't pick one yet. Just choose Cancel for now, and when the server asks you if you want to continue, tell it Yes. Start up the Control Panel, and you'll see that it has a new icon labeled GSNW. Click on GSNW, and you'll see the Gateway Service for Netware dialog box, as in Figure 12.3.

FIGURE 12.3:

Gateway Service for NetWare dailog box

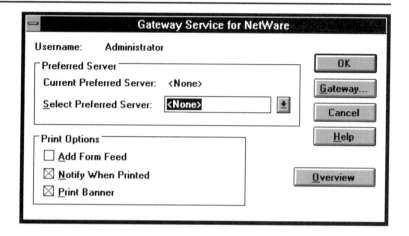

The important field in this dialog box is Select Preferred Server; your system should be able to list the available NetWare servers without any trouble. I haven't chosen one yet, but the server that I want to log onto is called Master, so I chose that server. Your server will no doubt have a different name.

Note that the dialog box says "Username: Administrator" at the top. That's the name that the *Novell* network sees. Click OK and close the Control Panel. Try starting up the File Manager, and choose Connect Network Drive. You'll see a new set of networks, as shown in Figure 12.4.

Notice that there is now a reference to NetWare Network in the Shared Directories box. This NT machine can see the Novell servers, but *only* this machine can see the Novell servers; none of the clients of the NT machine can see the Novell resources. This is the *client* part of the NetWare connectivity software. To activate gateway services, go back to the GSNW icon in the Control Panel and click the Gateway… button. You'll see a dialog box like the one in Figure 12.5.

Notice that the buttons in the lower-right corner of the dialog box have grayed text on them; don't worry, they'll be enabled in a minute. Get this going with the following steps:

1. Enable the gateway by checking the Enable Gateway check box.

2. In Gateway Account, enter the user name that you've created on your Novell network. Again, in my example it's Administrator. You could, if you wanted, create a special account just to be the gateway's name.

FIGURE 12.4:

Connect Network Drive dialog box

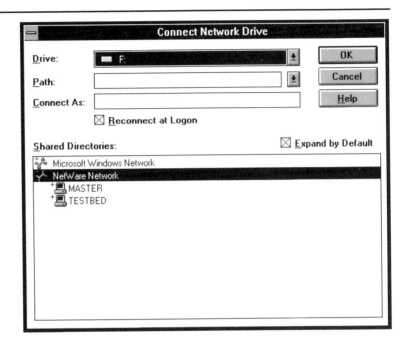

FIGURE 12.5:

Configure Gateway dialog box

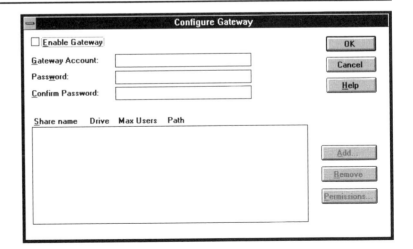

3. Enter the password, which should be both the NT password and the Novell password.

Now you're ready to start making NetWare volumes available for sharing. You're used to using the File Manager to share drives, but you share NetWare volumes right here in the Configure Gateway dialog box. (Not very obvious, but after all, this is relatively new software.) The Add... button will be enabled by now. Click it, and you'll see a dialog box like Figure 12.6.

FIGURE 12.6:

New Share dialog box

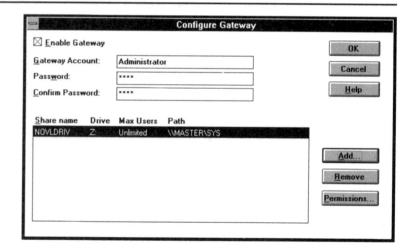

To make NetWare volumes available for sharing:

1. In the Share Name field, enter the share name that you want a workstation to see, as you would do with normal NT shared directories.

2. In the Network Path field, enter the name of the Novell volume. Its name should be a UNC-type name, just as you've used so far: *machinename* *volumename*. For example, on my network the NetWare 4.x server's name is MASTER, and its volume is SYS. The UNC name is \\MASTER\SYS.

3. Add a comment if you like, and assign a drive letter in the Use Drive box.

4. Click OK to get out of the New Share dialog box, and click OK in the Configure Gateway dialog box.

Now the gateway is ready, as you can see in Figure 12.7. Click OK, and you're done.

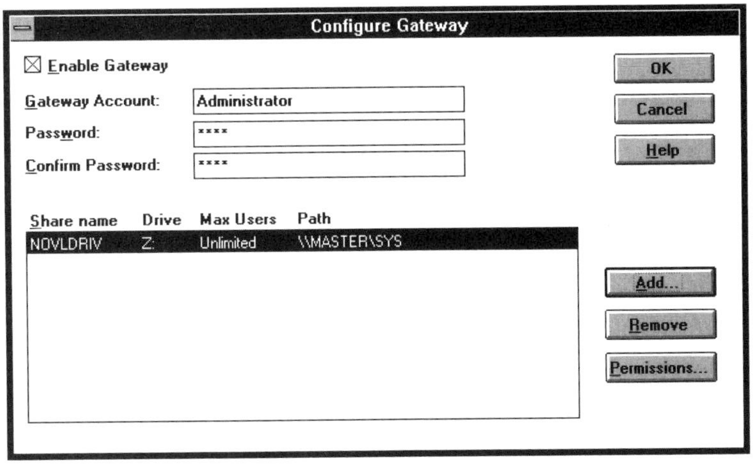

FIGURE 12.7:

Configure Gateway dialog box with a NetWare volume ready to be shared

FIGURE 12.7:

Configure Gateway dialog box with a NetWare volume ready to be shared

---

Trying It Out

Now, it's time to go see if it works. Just go to any client machine and try to attach to the share name. For instance, on my example network, I'd go to a DOS workstation and type

```
net use * \\EISA66\novldriv
```

Notice that EISA66 is the machine name of the NT server, rather than "master," the machine name of the Novell server. If I were connecting from inside Windows for Workgroups, then I could, as usual, just use the File Manager to connect (Drives/Connect Network Drive…).

Security for Novell Volumes:
The Bad News

Volumes shared through the gateway are subject to permissions *not* through the File Manager, as you're accustomed to, but rather through the GSNW icon in the

Control Panel. The Configure Gateway dialog box (see Figure 12.7) includes a button labeled Permissions that you use to control access to the Novell volume.

What this means is that the Gateway Service only provides *share-level* permissions. You can share a particular Novell volume on the NT network, but all Gateway Service users on the NT network will have identical permissions for the data on the Novell volume. If you try to set file or directory permissions with the File Manager, you'll see the message "This is an invalid device name."

The downside of this should be obvious. It is customary to give all users on a network their own "private" directories that only they can access. That's impossible here. The only alternative would be to create different shares and give them different drive letters. For example, you saw that I shared the volume SYS, which was on the server MASTER. Within MASTER\SYS was a subdirectory called MARK. I could add a new share just called \\MASTER\SYS\MARK, and only give myself access to that share. That would give me my own home directory, but that Novell share would get a drive letter on my NT gateway server—and there are only 26 letters in the alphabet.

In case that's not clear, here's an example. Before NT existed, suppose I had a NetWare 3.12 server with 50 users on it. Each of the 50 users had his or her own private "home" directory, and I would have owned a 50-user license for NetWare 3.12. Could I use the NT/Novell Gateway Service to get around that 50-user limit?

At first glance, it might seem possible to buy a 5-user license for NetWare 3.12, install the NT Gateway Service, and then just hook up the 50 users as NT users. They would all then have access to the NetWare volumes via the Gateway. But that wouldn't work, because my NT server probably has four drives already (A through D, including a CD-ROM) and I can only create a maximum of 22 new NetWare shares, drives E through Z. That means that I couldn't serve more than 22 users with home drives on the NetWare server.

(In case you're wondering, I'm told that it *is* legal to put those 22 users onto Novell via NT because the Novell licenses are not per *user*, they're per *connection*. Novell sees just one connection, so it's legal. In fact, I imagine that the legality question will boil down to which of the two companies can afford better lawyers.)

The Gateway Service seems the best solution when you want to share a directory both on the Novell and the NT sides of the house. However, I don't want to have to load IPX/SPX and a NetWare redirector on all of the machines on the NT side just to get to this particular directory on this NetWare volume.

Providing Print Gateway Services

The Gateway Service not only allows NT clients access to NetWare volumes, it also provides access to NetWare print queues. The printer gateway software is activated at the same time as the volume gateway software, but you have to complete one step before the clients can get to the printer—you have to connect your NT Server machine to the Novell printer queues.

Just as you can provide access to NetWare drives via a bogus drive on your NT server, so also can you provide access to NetWare print queues by claiming that your NT servers are physically connected to printers that are actually NetWare printers. That sounds complex, but it's not. Here's how to do it:

1. On the NT Server machine, start up the Print Manager.

2. Choose Printer, and then Connect to Printer…. The Connect to Printer dialog box appears, as in Figure 12.8.

FIGURE 12.8:

Connect to Printer dialog box

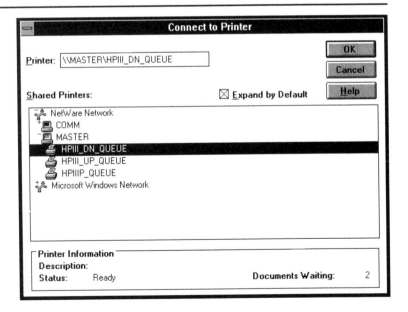

Notice that the Shared Printers box shows two network types, NetWare Network and Microsoft Windows Network.

3. Click on NetWare Network to open up that network, and you'll see your Net-Ware servers. Open them up, and you'll see the NetWare print queues, as in Figure 12.8.

4. Choose a printer. You'll probably get a message box like the one in Figure 12.9.

FIGURE 12.9:

Connect to Printer message box

This message just means, "There is no Windows printer driver on that Novell machine." It's not terribly important, as your DOS and Windows clients use their own local drivers anyway.

5. Click OK.

6. You'll be asked what kind of printer is on the Novell print queue. The driver of the printer you choose will then be grabbed off the NT installation CD-ROM.

The Novell printer will then appear on the Print Manager as if it were a locally attached printer. You can view its queue, delete documents, and so on.

Before the rest of your NT network can see the printer, however, you have got to share it, just as you always do, in the Printer Properties dialog box.

7. From the Print Manager, choose a printer, then click Printer and Printer Properties. Check the box labeled Share this printer on the network and your printer will be available to all NT clients.

How Do I Share a Novell Printer with an NT Network?

To share a Novell printer with an NT network:

1. On the NT Server machine, start up the Print Manager.

2. Choose Printer and then Connect to Printer…. The Connect to Printer dialog box will appear.

3. Click on the NetWare Network option to open up that network, and you'll see your NetWare servers. Open them up, and you'll see the NetWare print queues.

4. Choose a printer.

Even though you'll probably get a nastygram telling you that there is no Windows printer driver on that Novell machine, it's not terribly important, since your DOS and Windows clients use their own local drivers anyway. Click OK.

5. Click OK.

6. You'll be asked what kind of printer is on the Novell print queue, and that printer's driver will then be taken off the NT installation CD-ROM. The Novell printer will then appear on the Print Manager just as if it were a locally attached printer. You can view its queue, delete documents, and so on.

Before the rest of your NT network can see the printer, you have to share it from the Printer Properties dialog box.

7. From the Print Manager, choose a printer, then click Printer and Printer Properties. Check the box labeled Share this printer on the network.

The printer is now available to all NT clients.

Novell Commands Available from NT

At the NT server, you can open up a command line and run a number of Novell commands, including the ones in Table 12.1. You can also run NetWare-aware applications (some of them, anyway) with some support programs. Windows-based, NetWare-aware applications may require files NETWARE.386, NWCALLS.DLL, and NWNETAPI.DLL. They can be found in your system32 directory.

Novell supplies a file called NWIPXSPX.DLL that some client-server applications depend upon; Gupta SQLBase and Lotus Notes are two examples.

TABLE 12.1: Novell Commands at the NT Command Line

chkvol	help	rconsole	settts
colorpal	listdir	remove	slist
dspace	map	revoke	syscon
flag	ncopy	rights	tlist
flagdir	ndir	security	userlist
fconsole	pconsole	send	volinfo
filer	psc	session	whoami
grant	pstat	setpass	

Potential Problems with the Gateway Service

The Gateway Service is terrific, but it still has a few wrinkles. Following is a discussion of the problems you may encounter with the Gateway Service.

Slower than NetWare The gateway overhead of going through NT slows the data transfer process a bit. That's normal, and it's an outgrowth of the "1.0" nature of the Gateway Service. You can monitor the performance of the IPX/SPX module with the Performance Monitor. You'll see a new object called NWLink NetBIOS,

NWLink IPX, and NWLink SPX that contain a number of counters. The Bytes/second counter of NWLink IPX gives some idea of the NetWare traffic being generated.

You May be Prompted for a Password   When the Gateway is first loading, you may get a message from it asking for a NetWare password. This happens if you've set a different NT password than a Novell password. Just use the Novell *setpass* command to change your password so that the two passwords match.

"This is an invalid device name."   Try to share a part of a Novell volume, or set its permissions, and you'll get the following message: "This is an invalid device name." That's perfectly normal, and it reflects the fact that you do *not* control shared Novell volumes through the File Manager. Instead, you use the GSNW icon in the Control Panel.

Migrating Users from Novell to NT

Migration Tool
for NetWare

The fundamental reason why Microsoft offers the Gateway Service is to make it simple for people to gradually move from being primarily Novell-based to becoming primarily NT-based. Now, suppose you had a Novell-based network, and you wanted to become NT-based. What kinds of things would you have to do? Basically, you would have to

- Rebuild all of your Novell users on your NT server

- Move information from the hard disks of the Novell servers to the hard disks of the NT servers

The first concern isn't a small one. Running a parallel NetWare/NT network means that every time you create a user in the NetWare side of the network, you have to duplicate your efforts on the NT side. It would be nice if there were a simple way to essentially "lock together" the NetWare user administration tools and the User Manager for Domains, so that a change in the roster of NT users would be immediately reflected in the roster of NetWare users.

Unfortunately, there isn't a tool like that, at least not yet (it's a lucrative third-party opportunity for some enterprising software author). Instead, Microsoft includes a tool with NT called the Migration Tool for NetWare. (Its beta name was called "Visine," as in "gets the red out." Get it? Yuk. Yuk.) Start up Migration Tool for NetWare (double-click the icon in the Control Panel or run WINNT35\SYSTEM32\NWCONV.EXE) and it looks like Figure 12.10.

FIGURE 12.10:

Migration Tool for NetWare opening screen

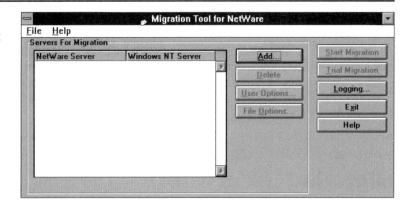

Now, I'm not going to discuss this very much for an important reason: I think it's a niche product with a fairly limited use. If Microsoft had taken the time to create a product that locks together the user accounts of Novell and NT, this application would be exciting. But it is really only of interest to someone *abandoning* Novell for NT.

You start off using this program by selecting which servers you'd like to migrate *from* (the Novell ones) and which servers you'd like migrate *to* (the NT servers). Do that by clicking Add…. You'll see a dialog box like Figure 12.11. Click the browser buttons (…) to the side of From NetWare Server and To Windows NT Server boxes to choose which server will soon be abandoned and which will soon be flush with users. In my case, I've chosen to migrate users from my NetWare 4.01 server MAS-TER to my NT server EISA66. The Migration Tool then looks like Figure 12.12.

FIGURE 12.11:

Specifying source and destination servers for NetWare migration

FIGURE 12.12:

Migration Tool after selecting servers

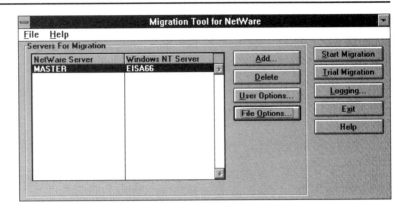

Now that the buttons are enabled, you can see what you can do with this tool. Following is an overview of what each of the buttons do.

Add..., Delete, Exit, and Help Buttons

The Add… button is the one that you press to specify which servers you'll be working with. I clicked it to specify MASTER and EISA66. Delete would undo that selection. Exit and Help pretty much do what you expect them to do.

User Options...

The User Options… button controls how the migration will happen. When you select it, you see the dialog box in Figure 12.13. Odd looking NT dialog box, isn't it? You'll probably recognize it as the user interface used in Windows 95. You click the Passwords, Usernames, Group Names, or Defaults tabs to bring up "index cards." The aim of Passwords is to ask, "What passwords should I assign to the newly created NT users?" My first thought was, "Well, why not keep their old Novell passwords?" But then I realized (I'm a little slow some days) that *there is no way for the Migration Tool to get the passwords; Novell won't give them up.* So you have the options that you see in the figure—no password at all, a password that matches the user name, or a fixed password.

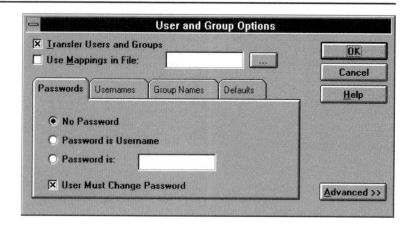

The Names and Group Names file cards are concerned with the question, "What should the Migration Tool do if it finds a Novell user named, say, Jack, and it tries to create an NT user named Jack, but there's *already* a user named Jack?" Your options are as follows:

- To not create a user when there's a conflict, and then either log the problem or ignore it;

- To simply create the new user, overwriting the old user; or

- To take the user name and prefix it with some fixed text.

You have the same options for group names.

The Defaults file card controls first how to handle account policies (minimum password lengths and the like) and how to treat Novell users with supervisor privileges. You can opt to automatically put any user with supervisor privileges into the Administrators group.

File Options...

The Migration Tool will blast a whole server's worth of files from a NetWare server to an NT server, kind of like a monster XCOPY command. The File Options... button lets you control which files to copy. When you select this button, you see a dialog box that lets you restrict which files or directories get copied to the NT server.

Logging...

The Logging... button brings up the dialog box that you see in Figure 12.14. The Popup on errors check box will make the Migration Tool stop and notify you about every single error—*and* warning. I'd recommend against it. Verbose User/Group Logging is essential, as it records any problems that arise when converting users from Novell to NT. Verbose File Logging just gives you an exhaustive list of all the files transferred from one server to another.

FIGURE 12.14:

Logging dialog box

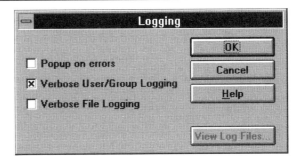

Trial Migration

A server migration is a pretty drastic step, so Microsoft included a "dry run" option, Trial Migration. Click this and you'll see what the results of the migration process will be *before* you've committed yourself. This can take *quite* a while, so don't expect immediate results.

The big advantage that I found with a trial migration was that it identified my potential user name and group name conflicts nice and early. I was then able to change the NT names or delete the redundant users, preparing for a smoother migration.

Following is an example of the output from the migration process:

```
[ALEX]              (Added)
Original Account Info:
Name:
Account disabled: No
Account expires: (Never)
Password expires: (Never)
Grace Logins: (Unlimited)
Initial Grace Logins: (Unlimited)
```

```
Minimum Password Length: 0
# days to Password Expiration: (Never)
Maximum Number of Connections: (Unlimited)
Restrictions:
Anyone who knows password can change it
Unique passwords required: No
Number of login failures: 0
Max Disk Blocks: (Unlimited)

Login Times:
Midnight            AM                    Noon                  PM
12 1  2  3  4  5  6  7  8  9  10 11 12 1  2  3  4  5  6  7  8  9  10 11
+---------------------------------------------------------------------+
Sun ** ** ** ** ** ** ** ** ** ** ** ** ** ** ** ** ** ** ** ** ** ** ** **
Mon ** ** ** ** ** ** ** ** ** ** ** ** ** ** ** ** ** ** ** ** ** ** ** **
Tue ** ** ** ** ** ** ** ** ** ** ** ** ** ** ** ** ** ** ** ** ** ** ** **
Wed ** ** ** ** ** ** ** ** ** ** ** ** ** ** ** ** ** ** ** ** ** ** ** **
Thu ** ** ** ** ** ** ** ** ** ** ** ** ** ** ** ** ** ** ** ** ** ** ** **
Fri ** ** ** ** ** ** ** ** ** ** ** ** ** ** ** ** ** ** ** ** ** ** ** **
Sat ** ** ** ** ** ** ** ** ** ** ** ** ** ** ** ** ** ** ** ** ** ** ** **
```

The bottom line on the Migration Tool is, again, that it can help you if you're abandoning Novell, or if you want to set up an NT system with users whose NT accounts mirror their Novell accounts. The Migration Tool will only create NT users and groups that mirror the status of the Novell users and groups *at that moment*, and that's the problem with it. What we need is a *dynamic* Migration Tool.

Between the Client Service, the Gateway Service, and the Migration Tool, Microsoft has assembled a nice set of capabilities for those contemplating a dual Novell/NT network. Get to know them, and you can simplify your life as a schizophrenic network administrator.

CHAPTER

THIRTEEN

TCP/IP on Windows NT

In the last few years, the term TCP/IP (Transport Control Protocol/Interface Program) has moved from obscurity to a "must-know" concept. TCP/IP has become the *lingua franca* of networks, a network language ("transport protocol" is the more accurate term) like NetBIOS, SNA, IPX/SPX, or X.25, with one very important difference: Most of the above-mentioned transport protocols are designed to work well either in a LAN environment *or* in a WAN environment, but not in both. In contrast, TCP/IP can fill both needs, and that's one of its greatest strengths, as you'll see in this chapter.

This is a *big* chapter. In this chapter, I do several things:

- First, I explain what TCP/IP and the Internet are.

- Second, I look at the "innards" of IP, the part of TCP/IP that you have to worry about if you're doing TCP/IP on NT.

- Third, I show you the options you have for setting up IP addresses and computer names. I'll show you an older method that requires a bit more work but is more compatible with other computers doing TCP/IP, and a newer method incorporating two relatively new protocols called the Dynamic Host Configuration Protocol (DHCP) and the Windows Internet Naming System (WINS). I'll go over how to build an NT-based internet both ways.

- Finally, I'll introduce you to the "big three" of TCP/IP applications—Telnet, FTP, and Internet mail.

When you're done, you'll be at least *dangerous* in TCP/IP administration. As Microsoft says, "On the internet, no one knows you're running NT."

A Brief History of TCP/IP

TCP/IP is a collection of software created over the years, much of it with the help of large infusions of government research money. Originally, TCP/IP was intended for the Department of Defense. You see, DoD tends to buy a *lot* of equipment, and much of that equipment is incompatible with other equipment. For example, back in the late 70s, when the work that led to TCP/IP was first begun, it was nearly impossible to get an IBM mainframe to talk to a Burroughs mainframe. That was because the two computers were designed with entirely different *protocols:*

To get some idea of what the DoD was facing, imagine that you pick up the phone in the U.S. and call someone in Mexico. You have a perfectly good hardware connection, as the Mexican phone system is compatible with the American phone system. But despite the *hardware* compatibility, you face a *software* incompatibility. The person on the other end of the phone is looking for a different protocol, a different language. It's not that one language is better or worse than the other, but the English speaker cannot understand the Spanish speaker, and vice versa. Rather than force the Spanish speaker to learn English or the English speaker to learn Spanish, we can teach them both a "universal" language such as Esperanto, the "universal language" designed in 1888. If Esperanto were used in my telephone example, neither speaker would use it at home, but they would use it to communicate with each other.

That was how TCP/IP began—as a simple *alternative* communications language. As time went on, however, TCP/IP evolved into a mature, well-understood, robust set of protocols, and many sites adopted it as their *main* communications language.

The Origins of TCP/IP

The original DoD network wouldn't just hook up military sites, although that was an important goal of the first defense internetwork. Much of the basic research in the U.S. was funded by an arm of the Defense Department called the Advanced Research Projects Agency, or ARPA. ARPA gave, and still gives, a lot of money to university researchers to study all kinds of things. ARPA thought it would be useful for these researchers to be able to communicate with one another, as well as with the Pentagon. In Figure 13.1, you can see how it was for researchers after ARPANET.

The new network, dubbed ARPANET, was designed and put in place by a private contractor called Bolt, Barenek and Newman. For the first time, it linked university

FIGURE 13.1:

Researchers after ARPANET

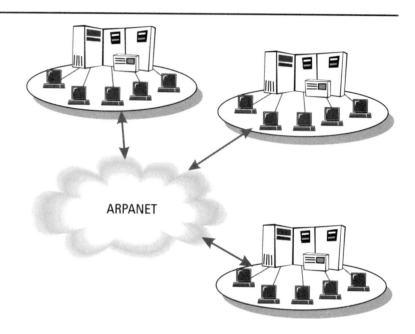

ARPANET

professors both to each other and to military and civilian project leaders around the country. Because ARPANET linked the separate private university networks and the separate military networks, ARPANET was considered a "network of networks." For a while, people bandied about the term "hypernet" for this phenomenon, but the term "internet" was the one that stuck. ARPANET lived for a while, but eventually its underlying protocols were redesigned, and the result was the TCP/IP suite.

Goals of TCP/IP's Design

When DoD started building this set of network protocols, it had a few design goals. Understanding those design goals will help you understand why it's worth making the effort to use TCP/IP in the first place. The original design goals included:

- Good failure recovery
- Ability to plug in new subnetworks without disrupting services
- Ability to handle high error rates

- Independence from a particular vendor or type of network
- Very little data overhead

I'm sure no one had any idea how central those design goals would be to the amazing success of TCP/IP both in private internets and in *the* Internet. Let's take a look at those design goals in more detail.

Good Failure Recovery   Remember, this was to be a *defense* network, so it had to work even if portions of the network hardware suddenly and without warning went off-line. That's kind of a nice way of saying that the network had to work even if big pieces of it got nuked.

You see, for many networks, the only way to work on problems is to take the network down, fix the problem, and restart it—to essentially "reboot the network." Today, that's just not acceptable not only in defense matters, but in the business world. To me, being able to fix problems without taking the network off-line is TCP's greatest strength. When major software upgrades are introduced into the Internet, it just keeps on running while the changes take place.

Is this possible? Has this resilient nature of TCP/IP ever been tested? In 1990, during the Persian Gulf War, the allied forces bombed strategic Iraqi targets with the goal of knocking out Iraq's communications, command and control system. That goal was eventually realized, but it took a *lot* longer than anyone expected. After the brief war, an analysis of the Iraqi military network showed that they, not surprisingly, used the same public domain programs to run *their* network as are used on the Internet. This wasn't exactly the field test that the United States Department of Defense planned for TCP/IP, but it proved TCP's robustness nevertheless.

The Ability to Plug in New Subnetworks "On the Fly"   This second goal, being able to plug in new subnetworks without disrupting services, is related to the first one. It says that it should be possible to bring entire new networks into an internet—and here, again, "internet" can mean your company's private internet or *the* Internet—without interrupting existing network service.

The Ability to Handle High Error Rates   An internet should be able to tolerate high or unpredictable error rates and still provide a 100-percent reliable end-to-end service. If you're transferring data from Washington, DC, to Portland, Oregon, and the links that you're using through Texas get destroyed by a tornado, data lost in the storm should be resent and rerouted via different lines.

Independence from a Particular Vendor or Network Type   The new network architecture should work with any kind of network, and not be dedicated or tied to any one vendor. This is essential in the 90s. The days of "we're just an IBM shop" or "we only buy Novell stuff" are gone for many, and going fast for others. Companies must be able to live in a multivendor world.

Very Little Data Overhead   The last goal was for the network protocols to have as little overhead as is possible. To understand this, let's compare TCP/IP to other protocols. While no one knows what protocol will end up being *the* world protocol twenty years from now—if any protocol *ever* gets that much acceptance—one of TCP/IP's rivals is a set of protocols built by the International Standards Organization, or ISO. ISO has some standards that are very similar to the kinds of things that TCP/IP does, standards named X.25 and TP4. But every protocol packages its data with an extra set of bytes, kind of like an envelope. The vast majority of data packets using the IP protocol have a simple, fixed-size, 20-byte header. The maximum size that the header can be is 60 bytes, if all possible options are enabled. The fixed 20 bytes always appear as the first 20 bytes of the packet. In contrast, X.25 uses dozens of possible headers, with no appreciable fixed portion to it. (I promise to explain soon why TCP and IP are actually two very different protocols and what those protocols are.)

But why should *you* be concerned about overhead bytes? Really for one reason only: performance. Simpler protocols mean faster transmission and packet switching (we'll take up packet switching a little later).

How ARPANET Became the Internet

The ARPANET became the Internet through a few evolutions that were prompted by the design goals that you just read about. Probably the first major development step occurred in 1974, when Vinton Cerf and Robert Kahn proposed the protocols that would become TCP and IP. Over its more than twenty-year history, the Internet and its predecessors have gone through several stages of growth and adjustment. Ten years ago, the Internet could only claim a few thousand users. When last I heard, there were three *million* computers and twenty million users on the Internet—and the Internet appears to double in size about every year. It can't do that indefinitely, but it's certainly a time of change for this huge network of networks.

Originally, the Internet protocols were intended to support connection of mainframe-based networks, which were basically the only ones that existed through most of the 70s. But the 80s saw the growth of UNIX workstations, microcomputers, and minicomputers. The Berkeley version of UNIX was built largely with government money, and the government said, "Put the TCP/IP protocol in that thing." There was some resistance at first, but adding IP as a built-in part of Berkeley UNIX has helped the growth of both UNIX and internetworking. The IP protocol was used on many of the UNIX-based Ethernet networks that appeared in the 80s and exist to this day.

As a matter of fact, you'll probably have to learn at least a smidgen of UNIX to get around the Internet, but don't let that put you off. In this chapter, I'll teach you all the UNIX you'll need.

In the mid-80s, the National Science Foundation created five supercomputing centers and put them on the internet. This served two purposes: It made supercomputers available to NSF grantees around the country, and it also ended up serving as a major "backbone" of the Internet. The backbone portion of the network, called NSFNET, was for a long time the largest part of the Internet. It is now being superseded by the National Research and Education Network, or NREN.

For many years, commercial users were pretty much kept off the Internet, as most of the funding was governmental. But those restrictions have been relaxed, and now a large amount of the Internet's traffic is routed over commercially run lines rather than government-run lines. There's a kind of uneasy accommodation that says, "Well, the commercial traffic shouldn't be going over government lines, but if the commercial providers allow government traffic over the commercial lines, then the government providers will accept the commercial traffic." But the commercial traffic is growing and growing, so *something* is going to change in the Internet soon. There is talk of privatizing the Internet and letting commercial providers manage it, just as private companies provide phone service today. No matter what changes occur, however, there's no getting around it: The Internet is the "data superhighway" for the U.S. and, increasingly, for more and more of the world. If your company isn't on the Internet now, it will be soon. Remember when fax machines became popular in the early 80s? Overnight people stopped saying, "Do you have a fax?" and just started asking, "What's your fax number?" It's getting so that if you don't have an Internet address, you're just not a person.

But enough about the Internet for now. Let's get to the question of what TCP and IP are. Originally, TCP/IP was just a set of programs that could hook up dissimilar computers and transfer information between them. But that set of programs grew into a large number of programs that are now collectively known as the *TCP/IP suite*.

The Internet Protocol (IP)

The most basic part of the internet is the *Internet Protocol,* or IP. If you want to send data over an internet, then that data must be packaged in an IP packet. The packet is then *routed* from one part of the internet to another.

A Sample Internet

IP is supposed to allow messages to travel from one part of a network to another. How does it do this?

An internet is built of at least two *subnets.* The notion of a subnet is built upon the fact that most popular LAN architectures (Ethernet, token-ring, and ARCnet) are based on broadcasts. Everyone on the same Ethernet segment hears all of the traffic on their segment, just as each device on a given ring in a token-ring network must examine every message that goes around the network.

That means that in a single Ethernet segment or a single token-ring ring that there is *no routing*. There are no routing decisions to make; everything is heard by everybody. (Your network adapter filters out any traffic not destined for you, in case you're wondering.) Figure 13.2 shows how a broadcast-based network operates.

FIGURE 13.2:

A broadcast-based network

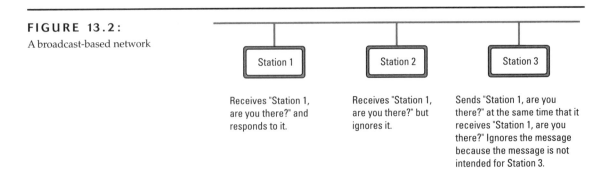

Station 1	Station 2	Station 3
Receives "Station 1, are you there?" and responds to it.	Receives "Station 1, are you there?" but ignores it.	Sends "Station 1, are you there?" at the same time that it receives "Station 1, are you there?" Ignores the message because the message is not intended for Station 3.

But now suppose you've got two separate Ethernets connected to each other, as you see in Figure 13.3.

In this figure, you see two Ethernet segments, Rome and Carthage. (I was getting tired of "shipping" and "finance," the examples that everyone uses.) Three computers—A, B, and C—reside solely in Rome. Three more computers reside in Carthage, labeled F, G, and H.

FIGURE 13.3:

A multisegment internet

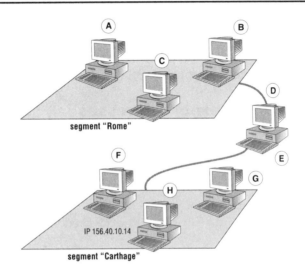

segment "Rome"

IP 156.40.10.14

segment "Carthage"

IP Addresses and Ethernet Addresses

Before going on, let's briefly discuss the labels A, B, C, and so on, and how those labels actually are manifest in an internet. Each computer on this net is attached to the net via an Ethernet board, and each Ethernet board on an internet has two addresses: an *IP address* and an *Ethernet address*. (There are, of course, other ways to get onto an internet besides via Ethernet, but let's stay with the Ethernet example, since it's the most common one on TCP/IP internets.)

Subnets and Routers

Much of the architecture for internets is built around the observation that PCs A, B, and C can communicate directly with each other, and PCs F, G, and H can communicate directly with each other, but A, B, and C *cannot* communicate with F, G, and H without some help from the machine containing Ethernet cards D and E. That D/E machine will serve in the function of a *router*, a machine that allows communication between different network segments. A, B, and C could be said to be in each other's "broadcast range," as could F, G, and H. What I've just called a "broadcast range" is called more correctly in internetworking terminology a "subnet." Let's set that definition out a bit:

Subnet: a collection of machines that can communicate with each other without the need for routing.

Ethernet Addresses

Each Ethernet board's Ethernet address is a unique 48-bit identification code, unique in the world. If it seems unlikely that every Ethernet board in the world can have a unique address, consider that 48 bits offer 280,000,000,000,000 identification codes. Ethernet itself only uses about one quarter of those possibilities, but that's still a lot of possible addresses. In any case, the important thing to get here is that a board's Ethernet address is predetermined and is hard-coded into the board.

IP Addresses and Quad Format

In contrast, an IP address is a 32-bit value. IP addresses are numbers set at a workstation (or server) by a network administrator—unlike Ethernet addresses, they're not a hard-coded hardware kind of address. Now, telling someone that your IP address is "10101110100101010010101100010111" doesn't sound like much fun, so for simplicity's sake, IP addresses are usually represented like *w.x.y.z*, where *w*, *x*, *y*, and *z* are all decimal values between 0 and 255. For example, the IP address of the machine that I'm currently writing this at is 199.34.57.10. This method of writing IP addresses as four numbers separated by periods is sometimes called the *dotted quad* format.

Each of the numbers in the dotted quad corresponds to eight bits of an internet address. ("IP address" and "internet address" are synonymous.) As the value for eight bits can range from 0 to 255, each value in a dotted quad can range from 0 to 255. For example, to convert an IP address of 11001010000011111010101000000001 into dotted quad format, it would be first be broken up into eight bit groups:

11001010   00001111   10101010   00000001

And each of those eight-bit numbers would be converted to a decimal equivalent. (If you're not comfortable with binary-to-decimal conversion, don't worry about it: just load the NT calculator, click View, click Scientific, and then press the F8 key to put the Calculator in binary mode. Enter the binary number, press F6, and the number will be converted to decimal for you.) Our number converts like so:

11001010   00001111   10101010   00000001
   202   15   170   1

Which results in a dotted quad address of 202.15.170.1.

To review, each of these computers has at least one Ethernet card in it, and that Ethernet card has an predefined address. The network administrator of this network has gone around and installed IP software on these PCs, and, in the process, has assigned IP addresses to each of them. (Note, by the way, that the phrase "has assigned IP addresses to each of them" may not be true if you are using the Dynamic Host Configuration Protocol, or DHCP. For the first part of this chapter, however, I'm going to assume that you're not using DHCP, which can assign addresses automatically.)

Figure 13.4 shows the internet from Figure 13.3, but now totally arbitrary IP addresses and Ethernet addresses have been added.

IP Routers

Now let's return to the computer in the middle. It is part of *both* segments. How do I get one computer to be part of two networks? By putting two Ethernet cards in it. In this example, one of the Ethernet cards is on the Rome subnet, and the other is on the Carthage subnet. (By the way, each computer on an internet is called a *host*.)

Now, each Ethernet card must get a separate IP address, so as a result, the computer in the middle has *two* IP addresses, D and E. Think of this computer as suffering from multiple personality disorder: if a message is broadcast around Rome, then adapter D hears it, and E doesn't. Likewise, if a message is broadcast around Carthage, then adapter E hears it, but D doesn't.

FIGURE 13.4:

Example two-subnet internet with
Ethernet and IP addresses

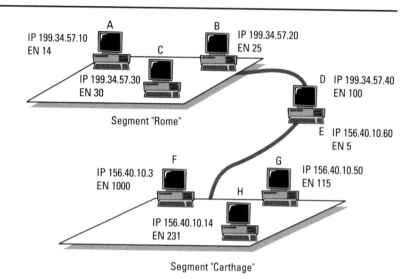

How would we build an internetwork from these two subnets? How can station A, for example, send a message to station G? Obviously, the only way the message will get from A to G is if it is received on the Ethernet adapter with address D, and then sent out again over the Ethernet adapter with address E. Once E resends the message, G will hear it, as it is on the same network as E. A computer that can perform this resending function is called an *IP router*. It is possible with Windows NT to use an NT computer—any NT computer, not just an NT Server computer—to act as an IP router, as you'll learn later.

Under IP, the sending station, A in this case, examines the address of the destination, G in this case, and realizes that it does not know how to get to G. (I'll explain exactly *how* it knows that in a minute.) Now, if A has to send something to an address that it doesn't understand, then it uses a kind of "catch-all" address called *the default router* address. A's network administrator has already configured A's default router as D, so A sends the message to D. Once D gets the message, it sees that the message is not destined for itself, but rather for G, so it resends the message from board E.

Routing in More Detail

Now let's look a little closer at how that message gets from segment A to G. Each computer, as you've already seen, has one *or more* IP addresses. Notice that there is no relationship whatsoever between an Ethernet card's address and the IP address associated with it. Notice also that the two nets have different-looking IP addresses. In Figure 13.4, Rome's addresses all look like 199.34.57.*x*, where *x* is some number; and Carthage's addresses all look like 156.40.10.*x*, where, again, *x* can be any number. The Ethernet addresses, however, follow no rhyme or reason, and are really grouped by the board's manufacturer.

Let's reexamine how the message gets from segment A to G:

1. The IP software in A first says, "How do I get this message to G? Can I just broadcast it, or must it be routed?"

In order to make that decision, it has to find out whether G is on the same *subnet* as A. A subnet is simply a "broadcast area." Host A is asking, "Is G part of Rome, like I am?"

2. Station A determines that it is on a different subnet from station G by examining their addresses.

In our example from Figure 13.4, A knows that it has address 199.34.57.10 and that it must send its message to 156.40.10.50. A has a simple rule for this: If the destination address looks like 199.34.57.*x*, where *x* can be any value, then the destination is in the same subnet, and so no routing is required. 156.40.10.50 is *not* in the same subnet.

If, on the other hand, G *had* been on the same subnet, then A would have sent the IP packet straight to G, referring specifically to its IP and Ethernet address.

3. Station A can't directly send its IP packets to G. It then looks for another way.

When A's network administrator set up A's IP software, he or she told A the IP address of A's *default router*. The default router is basically the address that says, "If you can't get directly to somewhere, send it to me, and I'll try to get it there." A's default router is D.

4. Station A then sends an Ethernet frame from itself to D. The Ethernet frame contains this information:
   - Source Ethernet address: 14
   - Destination Ethernet address: 100

- Source IP address: 199.34.57.10
- Destination IP address: 156.40.10.50

5. Ethernet card D receives the frame, and hands it to the IP software running in its PC.

The PC sees that the IP destination address is not *its* IP address, so the PC knows that it must route this IP packet.

6. Examining the subnet, the PC sees that the destination lies on the subnet that Ethernet adapter E is on, so it sends out a frame from Ethernet adapter E, with this information:

- Source Ethernet address: 100
- Destination Ethernet address: 115
- Source IP address: 199.34.57.10
- Destination IP address: 156.40.10.50

That's a simple example of how IP routes, but its algorithms are powerful enough to serve as the backbone for a network as large as the Internet.

TIP

There are different kinds of routing algorithms in TCP/IP. Windows NT does not support the most-used, robust protocols, like the Routing Internet Protocol (RIP) or OSPF. You need either third-party software or a dedicated router to build large, complex internets with NT.

A, B, and C Networks, and Subnetting

Before leaving IP routing, let's take a more specific look at subnets and IP addresses. The whole idea behind 32-bit IP addresses is to make it relatively simple to segment the task of managing *the* Internet or, for that matter, *any* internet.

To become part of the Internet, contact the Network Information Center, or NIC. Its e-mail address is hostmaster@rs.internic.net, or you can call (703) 742-4777 7 a.m. through 7 p.m. Eastern Standard Time.

A-, B-, and C-Class Networks

The NIC assigns each company a block of IP addresses according to the company's size. Big companies get A-class networks (but none are left—they've all been given out), medium-sized companies get B-class networks (we're out of those, too), and others get C-class networks (they're still available). Although there are three network classes, there are five kinds of IP addresses, as you see in Figure 13.5.

Because it seemed, in the early days of the Internet, that four billion addresses left plenty of space for growth, the original designers were a bit sloppy with their use

FIGURE 13.5:

Internet network classes and reserved addresses

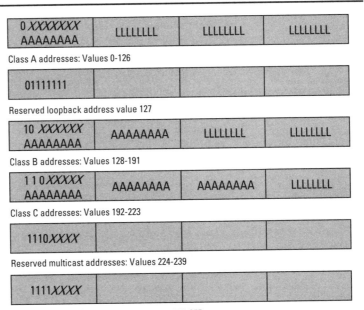

| 0 *XXXXXXX*
AAAAAAAA | LLLLLLLL | LLLLLLLL | LLLLLLLL |

Class A addresses: Values 0-126

| 01111111 | | | |

Reserved loopback address value 127

| 10 *XXXXXX*
AAAAAAAA | AAAAAAAA | LLLLLLLL | LLLLLLLL |

Class B addresses: Values 128-191

| 1 1 0 *XXXXX*
AAAAAAAA | AAAAAAAA | AAAAAAAA | LLLLLLLL |

Class C addresses: Values 192-223

| 1110*XXXX* | | | |

Reserved multicast addresses: Values 224-239

| 1111*XXXX* | | | |

Reserved experimental addresses: Values 240-255

A=Assigned by NIC
L=Locally administered

of addresses. They defined three classes of networks for the Internet: large networks, medium-sized networks, and small networks. The creators of the Internet used 8-bit sections of the 32-bit addresses to delineate the difference between different classes of networks.

- **A-class networks** A large network would have its first 8 bits set by the NIC, and the network's internal administrators could set the remaining 24 bits. The leftmost 8 bits could have values between 0 and 126, allowing for 127 class A networks. Companies like IBM get these, and there are only 127 of these addresses. As only 8 bits have been taken, 24 remain; that means that class A networks can contain up to 2^{24}, or 16 million, hosts.

- **B-class networks** Medium-sized networks have the leftmost *16* bits preassigned to them, leaving 16 bits for local use. Class B addresses always have the values 128 through 191 in their first quad, then a value between 0 and 255 in their second quad. There are 16,384 possible class B networks. Each of them can have up to 65,535 hosts.

- **C-class networks** Small networks have the leftmost *24* bits preassigned to them, leaving only 8 bits for local administration (which is bad, as it means that class C networks can't have more than 254 hosts). However, because the NIC has 24 bits to work with, it can easily give out class C network addresses (which is good). Class C addresses start off with a value between 192 and 223. As the second and third quads can be any value between 0 and 255, that means that there can potentially be 2,097,152 class C networks. (That's what our network, mmco.com, is.)

- **Reserved experimental addresses** A number of addresses are reserved for multicast purposes and for experimental purposes, so they can't be assigned for networks.

If you're just going to build your own internet and you don't want to connect to *the* Internet, you don't have to call up the NIC to get addresses. If you ever want to connect to the outside world, however, get a NIC-approved address before going very far into TCP/IP. You can always get an address and use it just internally until you're ready to "go public."

You Can't Use All of the Numbers

There are some special rules to internet names:

- You can't use .0, .1, or .255 for the last quad. They're used for the network number, the broadcast address, and the default gateway, as I'll explain in a few pages.

- Sometimes you can't even use .2. The second address is typically reserved for the subnet's default router. That address is usually .1. Some Internet providers use a *half-bridge* approach to connecting your network to the Internet; in that case, you'd use the .2 address. And, yes, it *is* always .2, as the half-bridge standard is defined for C-class networks interfacing to the Internet.

- The address 127.0.0.1 is reserved as a loopback. If you send a message to 127.0.0.1, it should get to you, unless there's something wrong on the network. And so no network has an address 127.*xxxxxxxx.xxxxxxxx.xxxxxxxx*, an unfortunate waste of 24 million addresses.

Once you get a range of addresses from the NIC, you are said to have an *IP domain*. (*Domain* in Internet talk has nothing to do with *domain* in the NT security sense.) For example, my IP domain (it's named mmco.com, but we'll cover names in a minute) uses addresses that look like 199.34.57.*x*, where *x* is some value from 2 to 254.

If you've got a small internet, many of the devices in your network probably broadcast to one another, and so no routing is required. On the other hand, you may have a domain so large that using broadcasting to communicate within it would be unworkable, requiring you to subnet your domain further. Consider IBM's situation, with an A class network that can theoretically support 16 million hosts. Managing *that* network cries out for routers. For this reason, it may be necessary for the IP software on your PC to route data over a router even if it's staying within your company. Let's ask again, and in more detail this time, "How does a machine know whether to route or not?"

Subnet Masks

That's where subnets are important. Subnets make it possible, as you've seen, for a host (a PC) to determine whether it can just lob a message straight over to another host or must go through routers. You tell a host's IP software how to distinguish whether or not another host is in the same subnet through the *subnet mask*.

Recall from Figure 13.4 that all of the IP addresses in Rome looked like 199.34.57.*x*, where *x* was a number between 1 and 255. You could then say that all members of the Rome subnet are defined as the hosts whose first three quads match. Now, on some subnets, the only requirement for membership in the same subnet might be that the first *two* quads be the same—a company that decided for some reason to make its entire B-class network a single subnet would be an example. (Yes, they *do* exist; I've seen firms that make a single subnet out of a B-class, with the help of some bizarre smart bridges. No, I don't recommend it.)

When a computer is trying to figure out whether the IP address that it owns is on the same subnet as the place it's trying to communicate with, a subnet mask answers the question, "Which bits must match for us to be on the same subnet?"

The easiest way to express that for computers is by using a *mask*, a combination of ones and zeroes like so:

11111111 11111111 11111111 00000000

Here's how a host would use this mask. The host with IP address 199.34.57.10 (station A in Figure 13.4) wants to know if it is on the same subnet as the host with IP address (station B). The address 199.34.57.10 expressed in binary is 11000111 00100010 00111001 00001010, and 199.34.57.20 is 11000111 00100010 00111001 00010100. The IP software in A compares the subnet mask to its own address. Comparing each bit of its own address to the mask, it copies any bits where the mask specifies a 1, and zeroes out any bits where the mask specifies a zero. (This is called a *logical AND* operation.)

11111111 11111111 11111111 00000000 *the subnet mask*

11000111 00100010 00111001 00001010 *A's IP address*

11000111 00100010 00111001 00000000 *the result*

Next, the IP software in A does the same thing on B's address:

11111111 11111111 11111111 00000000 *the subnet mask*

11000111 00100010 00111001 00010100 *B's address*

11000111 00100010 00111001 00000000 *the result*

The results of the two AND operations match, and so host A knows that host B is on the same subnet.

How do you set a subnet mask? Well, if you've got a class C number, and all of your workstations are on a single subnet, then you have a case like we just saw, a subnet mask of 11111111 11111111 11111111 00000000 which, in dotted quad terminology, is 255.255.255.0. In contrast, you might decide to break your C-class network into two subnets. You might decide that all the numbers from 1 to 127—00000001 to 01111111—are subnet 1, and the numbers from 128 to 255—10000000 to 11111111—are subnet 2. In that case, the values within your subnets will vary only in the last seven bits, rather than (as in the previous example) in the last eight bits. The subnet mask would be, then, 11111111 11111111 11111111 10000000, or 255.255.255.128.

Reserved Addresses: Network Numbers, Routers, and Broadcast Addresses

In planning your subnets, you must understand that there are some addresses that look like regular old IP addresses, but they're not, and trying to use them like regular old IP addresses will usually make something not work. Those addresses are the network number, the broadcast address, and the router address.

Network Number

Sometimes you need to refer to an entire subnet with a single number. For example, to tell a router, "To get this message to the subnet that ranges from 100.100.100.0 through 100.100.100.255, first route to the router at 99.98.97.103," you've got to have some way to designate the range of addresses 100.100.100.0–100.100.100.255. We could have just used two addresses with a hyphen between them, but that's a bit cumbersome. Instead, the address that ends in all binary zeroes is reserved as the *network number*, the TCP/IP name for the range of addresses in a subnet. In my 100.100.100.*x* example, you would never use the address 100.100.100.0—you never give that IP address to a machine under TCP/IP.

For example, to tell the router, "To get this message to the subnet that ranges from 100.100.100.0 through 100.100.100.255, first route to the router at 99.98.97.103," you would type (on very simple routers)

```
route add 100.100.100.0 99.98.97.103
```

The ROUTE ADD command expects to see a network number as the first parameter and the specific address of an IP router as the second number.

IP Broadcast Address

Another reserved address is the TCP/IP broadcast address. It looks like the address of one machine, but it isn't; it's the address you'd use to broadcast to each machine on a subnet. That address is all binary ones.

For example, on a simple C-class subnet, the broadcast address would be $x.y.z.255$. When would you need to know this? Some IP software needs this address when you configure it; most routers require the broadcast address (as well as the network number).

Default Router Address

The default address for the router is 1; for example, on a simple C-class network, the address of the router should be $x.y.z.1$.

There's an exception to this. If your C-class network is your only Internet network, and an external Internet service provider is handling your routing, your router should be the .2 address. For example, my network's router is at 199.34.57.2.

If you're going to break down your subnets smaller than C-class, all of this can get kind of confusing. Table 13.1 summarizes how you can break a C-class network down into one, two, four, or eight smaller subnets, with the attendant subnet masks, network numbers, broadcast addresses, and router addresses. I've assumed that you are starting from a C-class address, so you'll only be working with the fourth quad. The first three quads I have simply designated $x.y.z$.

For example, suppose you want to chop up a C-class network, $200.211.192.x$, into two subnets. As you see in the table, you'd use a subnet mask of 255.255.255.128 for each subnet. The first subnet would have network number 200.211.192.0, router address 200.211.192.1, and broadcast address 200.211.192.127. You could assign IP addresses 200.211.192.2 through 200.211.192.126, 125 different IP addresses. (Notice that heavily subnetting a network leads to losing a greater and greater percentage of addresses to the network number, broadcast address, and router address.) The second subnet would have network number 200.211.192.128, router address 200.211.192.129, and broadcast address 200.211.192.255.

TABLE 13.1: Breaking a C-Class Network into Subnets

Number of desired subnets	Subnet mask	Network number	Router address	Broadcast address	Remaining number of IP addresses
1	255.255.255.0	*x.y.z.*0	*x.y.z.*1	*x.y.z.*255	253
2	255.255.255.128	*x.y.z.*0	*x.y.z.*1	*x.y.z.*127	125
		*x.y.z.*128	*x.y.z.*129	*x.y.z.*255	125
4	255.255.255.192	*x.y.z.*0	*x.y.z.*1	*x.y.z.*63	61
		*x.y.z.*64	*x.y.z.*65	*x.y.z.*127	61
		*x.y.z.*128	*x.y.z.*129	*x.y.z.*191	61
		*x.y.z.*192	*x.y.z.*193	*x.y.z.*255	61
8	255.255.255.224	*x.y.z.*0	*x.y.z.*1	*x.y.z.*31	29
		*x.y.z.*32	*x.y.z.*33	*x.y.z.*63	29
		*x.y.z.*64	*x.y.z.*65	*x.y.z.*95	29
		*x.y.z.*96	*x.y.z.*97	*x.y.z.*127	29
		*x.y.z.*128	*x.y.z.*129	*x.y.z.*159	29
		*x.y.z.*160	*x.y.z.*161	*x.y.z.*191	29
		*x.y.z.*192	*x.y.z.*193	*x.y.z.*223	29
		*x.y.z.*224	*x.y.z.*225	*x.y.z.*255	29

In case you're wondering, it is entirely possible to subnet further, into 16 subnets of 13 hosts apiece (remember you always lose three numbers) or 32 subnets of 5 hosts apiece, but at that point, you're losing an awful lot of addresses to IP overhead.

Internet Host Names

All that discussion of IP addresses may have you wondering, "When I send e-mail to my friends, I don't send it to 199.45.23.17. I send it to something like robbie@ somefirm.com. What's IP got to do with it?"

IP addresses are useful because they're precise and because they're easy to subnet. But they're tough to remember, since people like more English-sounding names. So TCP/IP allows us to give domains names, like the name of my domain (mmco.com), or Microsoft's domain (microsoft.com), or Exxon's domain (exxon.com), or the White House's domain (whitehouse.gov). Particular machines within a domain can have names that include the domain name. For example, within my mmco.com domain I have machines named tcpgw.mmco.com, keydata.mmco.com, toshiba-san.mmco.com, eisa66.mmco.com, and serverted.mmco.com. The specific machine names are called *host names*.

How does TCP/IP connect the English names—the "host" names—to the IP addresses? And how can I sit at my PC in mmco.com and get the information needed to be able to find another host called archie.au, when archie's all the way on the other side of the world in Australia? Simple—with HOSTS, DNS, and, later in this chapter, WINS. Read on.

Simple Naming Systems (HOSTS)

When you set up your subnet, you don't want to have to explicitly use IP addresses every time you want to run some TCP/IP utility and hook up with another computer in your subnet. That's why you create a file called HOSTS that looks like this:

```
199.34.57.50 keydata.mmco.com
199.34.57.129 serverted.mmco.com
```

This is just a simple ASCII text file. Each host goes on one line, and the line starts off with the host's IP address. Enter at least one space and the host's English name. Do this for each host.

Ah, but now comes the really rotten part: You have to put one of these HOSTS files on *every single workstation*. That means that every single time you change anyone's HOSTS file, you have to go around and change *everybody's* HOSTS file. Every workstation must contain a copy of this file, which is basically a "telephone directory" of every machine in your subnet. It's a pain, yes, but it's simple. If you're thinking, "Why can't I just put a central HOSTS file on a server and do all my administration with *that* file?" The answer is that you can, but only with newer TCP/IP protocols, called DHCP and WINS, which I will discuss later in this chapter.

You put HOSTS in \WINNT35\system32\drivers\etc on an NT system, in the Windows directory on a Windows for Workgroups machine, and wherever the network software is installed in other kinds of machines (DOS or OS/2).

Domain Naming System (DNS)

HOSTS is a pain, but it's a necessary pain if you want to communicate within your subnet. How does IP find a name outside of your subnet, or outside of your domain?

Suppose someone at exxon.com wanted to send a file to mmco.com? Surely the exxon.com HOSTS files don't contain the IP address of my company, and vice versa? To take a fictitious example, how would TCP/IP find a machine at some software company named "Macrosoft"? How would IP figure out that a host named, say, database.macrosoft.com really has an IP address of, say, 181.50.47.22?

Within an organization, name resolution can clearly be accomplished by the HOSTS file. Between domains, however, name resolution is handled by the Domain Naming Service, or DNS. A central naming clearinghouse called the InterNIC Registration Services exists for the Internet, but, with 20 million Internet users, can you imagine having to call the NIC every single time you put a new user on one of your networks? That's why the NIC created the Domain Naming System, of which you see only a small portion. The NIC started off with six initial naming domains: EDU was for educational institutions, NET for network providers, COM for commercial users, MIL for military users, ORG for organizations, and GOV for civilian government.

In order to get onto the Internet, Macrosoft registers its entire company with the name macrosoft.com, placing itself in the commercial domain. From there, Macrosoft dubs someone in the organization the "name administrator." That person can then create subsets of the Macrosoft domain. In Figure 13.6, you see a possible arrangement. The Macrosoft name administrator has subdivided the macrosoft.com domain into two subdomains called wp.macrosoft.com and database.macrosoft.com. The administrator has the right to do this, as the rest of the Internet doesn't care what goes on inside macrosoft.com. Control of names extends from macrosoft.com *down* the naming hierarchy.

The Macrosoft name administrator maintains a database of host names within macrosoft.com by running a *name server* program on one of the Macrosoft computers. *Name servers* are computers whose main job is simply to answer the question, "What's the IP address of the machine somefirm.com?" Sending data from one host (machine) in database.macrosoft.com to another host in database.macrosoft.com

FIGURE 13.6:

Name hierarchy in the internet

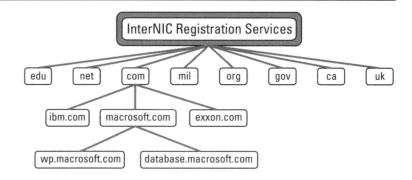

would only involve asking the local name server about the receiver's machine's name. In contrast, if someone were to transfer data from some host in database.macrosoft.com to some host in exxon.com, the request would get bumped up even further, to one of the main Internet name servers. There are eight Internet name servers in the world, and they reload their massive name databases from the NIC at regular intervals.

> **TIP**
>
> Unfortunately, there is no DNS router software shipped with NT, so an NT machine cannot serve as a name server with the software that's right in the NT box. Instead, Microsoft has built something called the Windows Internet Naming Service (WINS), which is a dynamic name resolver but is not compatible with the widely used DNS found on the Internet. You'll need someone else's DNS software to build your own name routers that will work with non-Microsoft clients, or you can use a DNS server that Microsoft offers as unsupported beta software; it's on the CD-ROM shipped with the Resource Kit, or you can find it on ftp.microsoft.com. (The latest information says that the software was scheduled to be released in late 1995, but as of this writing it's still in beta.)

E-mail Names: a Note

If you've previously messed around with e-mail under TCP/IP, then you may be wondering something about these addresses. After all, you don't send mail to mmco.com, you'd send it to a name like mark@mmco.com, which is an e-mail address. The way it works is this: a group of users in a TCP/IP domain decide to implement mail. (Remember that a Windows NT domain is a different concept than a domain on the Internet.)

In order to receive mail, a machine must be up and running, ready to accept mail from the outside world (that is, some other subnet or domain). Now, mail can arrive at any time of day, so this machine must be up and running all of the time. As you can see, it would be a dumb idea to get mail delivered straight to your desktop. So, instead, TCP mail dedicates a machine to the "mail router" tasks:

- receiving mail from the outside world,
- holding that mail until you want to see your mail, and
- taking mail addressed to some location in the outside world and routing it to the appropriate mail router.

The name of the most common TCP/IP mail router program is *sendmail*. The name of the protocol used most commonly for routing e-mail on the Internet, by the way, is the Simple Mail Transfer Protocol, or SMTP.

Unfortunately, Microsoft did not include an SMTP router program in either the workstation or the server version of NT, so you'll either have to connect to an existing mail router in order to get Internet mail, or you'll have to buy a third-party mail product to work under NT, like the Internet mail gateways available for cc:Mail, MHS, and Microsoft Mail.

You can see how mail works in Figure 13.7. In this small domain, we've got two users, mark and christa. (The great thing about the Internet is that you don't need that pesky Shift key on your keyboard.) Mark works on keydata.mmco.com, and Christa works on ams.mmco.com. Now, suppose Christa wants to send some mail to her friend Corky, executive director of Surfers of America; Corky's address is corky@surferdudes.org. She fires up a program on her workstation, which is called

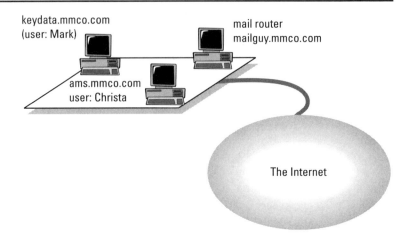

FIGURE 13.7:

Relationship of host names, e-mail names, and the Internet

a *mail client*. The mail client allows her to create and send new messages, as well as receive incoming messages. She sends the message, and closes her mail client. Notice that her mail client software doesn't do routing—it just lets her create, send, and receive messages.

The mail client has been configured to send messages to the program *sendmail*, which is running in this subnet on mailguy.mmco.com. Mailguy is kind of the "post office" (in Internet lingo, a "mail router") for this group of users. Sendmail on mailguy.mmco.com stores the message, and it then sends the message off to the machine with the DNS name surferdudes.org, trusting IP to route the message without trouble to surferdudes.

Additionally, sendmail knows the names "christa" and "mark." It is the workstation that is the interface to the outside world *vis a vis* mail. Note, by the way, that *DNS* has no idea who mark or christa are; DNS is concerned with *host* names, not *e-mail* names. It's DNS that worries about how to find mailguy.mmco.com.

A bit later, Corky gets the message, and sends a reply to Christa. The reply does *not* go to Christa's machine ams.mmco.com; instead, it goes to mailguy.mmco.com, because Corky sent mail to christa@mmco.com. The mail system sends the messages to mmco.com, but what machine has the address mmco.com? Simple: we give mailguy.mmco.com an alias, and mail goes to it.

Eventually, Christa starts up the mail client program once again. The mail program sends a query to the local mail router mailguy.mmco.com, asking "any new mail for christa?" There *is* mail, and Christa sees it.

Error Checking on Internets

Whether you're on *an* internet or *the* Internet, it looks like your data gets bounced around quite a bit. How do we keep it from becoming damaged? Let's look briefly at that topic, which will lead us to a short talk on TCP.

The IP block also has something called a *checksum header*, indicating whether the header information was damaged on the way from sender to receiver. Most protocols use checksums as shown in Figure 13.8.

FIGURE 13.8:
Simple error checking and response

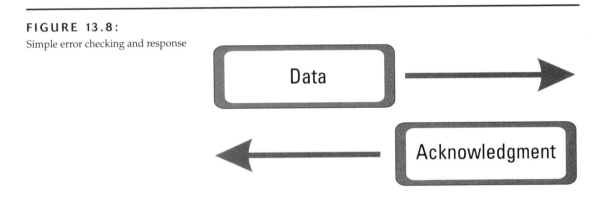

The way it usually works is something like this: I send you some data. You use the checksum to make sure that the data wasn't damaged in transit, perhaps by line noise. Once you're satisfied that the data was not damaged, then you send me a message that says, "OK—I got it." If the checksum indicates that it did *not* get to you undamaged, then you send me a message that says, "That data was damaged—please resend it," and I resend it.

Such a protocol is said to provide *reliable* service. *But IP does not provide reliable service.* If an IP receiver gets a damaged packet, it just discards the packet, and says nothing to the receiver. Surprised? I won't keep you in suspense: it's TCP that provides the reliability. The IP header checksum is used to see if a header is valid; if it isn't, then the datagram is discarded.

By now, you may be wondering what IP's job is in the first place, if it doesn't help keep the transmitted data clean. IP's job is simply to do its best to get a packet to its destination.

The Transmission Control Protocol (TCP)

I said earlier that IP handled routing, and really didn't concern itself that much with whether the message got to its final destination or not. If there are seven IP "hops" from one point to the next, then each hop is an independent action—there's no coordination, no notion of whether a particular hop is hop number three out of seven. Each IP hop is totally unaware of the others. How, then, could we use IP to provide reliable service?

TCP Error Detection/Correction

Recall the discussion a few paragraphs back about reliable service. I used a generic example of how computers send data between themselves error-free. Notice that whenever sending a block of data, at least *two* blocks are generated: the original data block, and the block that acknowledges the receipt of the data. Now, again, IP does not do those sorts of things, but a programmer could *use* IP to get the same effect. The process would work roughly like this:

1. Send data
2. Wait for ack
3. No ack, resend

First, you might send an IP packet that was just an instruction that said, "some IP packets are on their way, expect X number of them; I expect an acknowledgment." You'd wait for an acknowledgment of the original message. If you didn't get it, then you'd assume that it had been lost, and you'd send another. Eventually, you'd get an acknowledgment that yes, indeed, the other side was awake and ready and willing to receive data. You'd send the first block as an IP packet, and wait for an IP packet responding to the block. If it did not respond, you'd resend the packet, and so on. It would certainly take a lot of IP packets to get the job done, but it could be done reliably. This is essentially what TCP does.

Connecting a program in one machine to another program in another machine is kind of like placing a telephone call. The sender must know the phone number of the receiver, and the receiver must be around his phone, waiting to pick it up. In the TCP world, a "phone number" is called a "socket." A socket is composed of two parts: the IP address of the receiver, which we've already discussed, and the receiving program's *port number*, which we haven't yet discussed.

TCP/IP Port Numbers

Suppose the PC on your desk running Windows wants to talk to a PC on *my* desk running Windows. Obviously, for this to happen, we've got to know each other's IP addresses. But that's not all; after all, in my PC I've got a whole bunch of programs running (my network connection, my word processor, my operating system, my personal organizer, and so on). So if TCP says, "hey, Mark's machine, I want to talk to you," then my machine would say, "which *one* of us—the word processor, the e-mail program, or what?" So the TCP/IP world assigns a 16-bit number to each program that wants to send or receive TCP information, a number called the *port* of that program.

How Sockets Work

Suppose, for instance, that I've written a TCP/IP-based "chat" program that allows me to type messages to you and receive typed messages from you. This fictitious *chat* program might get port number 1500. Anyone running *chat*, then, would install it on port 1500. Then, to *chat* with my computer, which has an imaginary IP address of 123.124.55.67, your *chat* program would essentially "place a phone call"—that is, set up a TCP session—with port 1500 at address 123.124.55.67. The combination of port 1500 with IP address 123.124.55.67 is a *socket address*.

In order for your computer to *chat* with my computer, my computer must be *ready* to *chat*. So I've got to run my *chat* program. It would probably say something like, "Do you want to chat anyone, or do you just want to wait to be called?" I tell it that I just want to wait to be called, so it sits quietly in my PC's memory, but first it tells the PC, "if anyone calls for me, wake me up—I'm willing to take calls at port 1500." That's called a *passive open* on TCP.

Then, when your computer wants to *chat* my computer, it sends an *active open* request to my computer, saying "want to talk?". It also says, "I can accept up to X bytes of data in my buffers." My computer responds by saying, "sure, I'll talk, and I can accept up to Y bytes of data in my buffers."

The two computers then blast data back and forth, being careful not to overflow the other computer's buffers. When a buffer's worth of information is sent by your computer, then your computer doesn't send my computer any more data until my computer acknowledges that it received the data.

Once the *chat* is over, both sides politely say "good-bye," and hang up. My computer can choose to continue to wait for incoming calls, as before.

TCP Protocol Features

That's basically the idea behind TCP. Its main job is the orderly transmission of data from one host on an internet to another. Its main features include

- Handshaking
- Packet sequencing
- Flow control
- Error handling

Handshake

Whereas IP has no manners—it just shoves data at a computer whether that computer is ready for it or not—TCP makes sure that each side is properly introduced before trying to transfer. TCP sets up the connection.

Sequencing

As IP does not use a virtual circuit, different data packets may end up arriving at different times, and in fact in different order. In Figure 13.9, you see a simple internet transferring four segments of data across a network with multiple possible pathways. The first segment "takes the high road," so to speak, and is delayed. The second through the fourth do not, and so get to the destination more quickly. TCP's job on the receiving side is then to reassemble things in order.

FIGURE 13.9:

How sequencing works

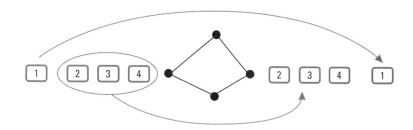

Flow Control

Along with sequencing is flow control. What if fifty segments of data had been sent, and they all arrived out of order? The receiver would have to hold them all in memory before sorting them out and writing them to disk. Part of what TCP worries about is *pacing* the data—not sending it to the receiver until the receiver is ready for it.

Error Detection/Correction

And finally, TCP handles error detection and correction, as I've already said. TCP is very efficient in the way that it does error handling. Some protocols acknowledge each and every block, generating a large overhead of blocks. TCP, in contrast, tells the other side, "I am capable of accepting and buffering some number of blocks. Don't expect an acknowledgment until I've gotten that number of blocks. And if a block is received incorrectly, I will not acknowledge it, so if I don't acknowledge as quickly as you expect me to do, then just go ahead and resend the block."

Getting on an Internet

So far, I've talked quite a bit about how an internet works, and what kinds of things there are that you can do with an internet. But I haven't told you enough yet to actually get *on* an internet, whether it's your company's private internet or *the* Internet. There are three basic options for an individual computer or workstation:

- You can connect to a multiuser system, and appear to the Internet as a dumb terminal.

- You can connect to an Internet provider via a serial port and a protocol called either the Serial Line Interface Protocol (SLIP) or the Point to Point Protocol (PPP), and appear to the Internet as a host.

- You can be part of a local area network that is an Internet subnet, and then load TCP/IP software on your system, and appear to the Internet as a host.

Each of these options has pros and cons, as you'll see. The general rule is that in order to access an internet, all you basically have to do is to connect up to a computer that is already on that internet.

Dumb Terminal Connection

This is a common way for someone to get an account that allows access to *the* Internet. For example, you can get an account with Performance Systems Inc. (PSI), Delphi, or Digital Express, to name a few Internet access providers.

Delphi, for example, has computers all around the U.S., so to get onto the Internet all you need to do is run a terminal emulation package on your system and dial up to their terminal servers. This kind of access is often quite cheap, at least in the U.S.: $25/month is common. If you wanted to do this with NT, then you needn't even run TCP/IP on your NT machine, either server or workstation. Instead, all you'd have to do would be to put a modem on your system and use Terminal to dial up to your Internet access provider.

Now, understand: this is just a *terminal* access capability that I've gotten, so it's kind of limited. Suppose, for example, that I live in Virginia (which is true) and I connect to the Internet via a host in Maine (which is not true). From the Internet's point of view, I'm not in my office in Virginia: I'm wherever the host that I'm connected to is. I work in Virginia, but if I were dialing a host in Maine, then from the Internet's point of view I'd be in Maine. Any requests that I make for file transfers, for example, wouldn't go to Virginia—they'd go to my host in Maine.

Now, that can be a bit of a hassle. Say I'm at my Virginia location logged onto the Internet via the Maine host. I get onto Microsoft's FTP site—I'll cover FTP later in this chapter, but basically FTP is just a means of providing a library of files to the outside world—and I grab a few files, perhaps an updated video driver. My FTP program says, "I got the file," but the file is now on the host in Maine. That means that I'm only half done, as I now have to run some other kind of file transfer program to move the file from the host in Maine to my computer in Virginia.

SLIP/PPP Serial Connection

A somewhat better way to connect to a TCP/IP-based network—that is, an internet—is by a direct serial connection to an existing internet host. If you use PCs, then you may know of a program called LapLink that allows two PCs to share each other's hard disks via their RS232 serial ports; SLIP and PPP are similar ideas, used on internets. A SLIP/PPP connection needn't be a serial port, but it often is. SLIP is the Serial Line Interface Protocol, an older protocol that I sometimes think of as the *simple* line interface protocol. There's really nothing to SLIP—no error checking, no security, no flow control. It's the simplest protocol imaginable: just send the data, then send a special byte that means, "This is the end of the data." PPP, in contrast, was designed to retain the low overhead of SLIP, and yet to include some extra information required so that more intelligent parts of an internet—items like routers—could use it effectively. The Point to Point Protocol works by establishing an explicit link between one side and another, then uses a checksum (as discussed earlier) to monitor noise on the line.

Which protocol should you use? The basic rule I use is that SLIP doesn't provide error checking, but also uses less overhead, and PPP provides error checking, and uses more overhead. Therefore, when I'm using error-correcting modems, I use SLIP. On noisy lines and without error-correcting modems, I use PPP.

NT supports both PPP and SLIP via Remote Access Services, discussed in Chapter 17.

LAN Connection

The most common way to connect to an internet is simply by being a LAN workstation on a local area network that is an internet subnetwork. Again, this needn't be *the* Internet—almost any LAN can use the TCP/IP protocol suite.

This is the connection that most NT Servers will use to provide TCP/IP services to workstations. Microsoft's main reason for implementing TCP/IP on NT is to provide an alternative to NetBEUI, as NetBEUI is quick and applicable to small networks, but really inappropriate for large corporate networks. In contrast, TCP/IP has always been good for internetworking, but (historically) suffered tremendously in speed. That's not true any more, however; for example, a quick test of TCP/IP versus NetBEUI on one of my workstations showed network read rates of 1250 Kbytes/sec for NetBEUI and 833 Kbytes/sec for TCP/IP, and write rates of 312 Kbytes/sec for NetBEUI and 250 KBytes/sec for TCP/IP. Again, TCP's slower, but not by a lot.

Terminal Connections versus Other Connections

Before moving on to the next topic, I'd like to return to the difference between a terminal connection and a SLIP, PPP, or LAN connection. In Figure 13.10, you see three PCs on an Ethernet attached to two minicomputers, which in turn serve four dumb terminals.

The minicomputer-to-minicomputer link might be SLIP or PPP, or then again they might be LANned together. Notice that only the *computers* in this scenario have internetwork protocol (IP) addresses. Whenever you send mail to one of the people on the PCs at the top of the picture, it goes directly to that person's PC. If you were to scrutinize the IP addresses—and most of the time, you will not—then you'd see that everyone had the same IP address. In contrast, the people at the *bottom* of the picture get their mail sent to one of the minicomputers, and so, in this example, each pair of terminals shares an IP address. If Shelly and George in your office access your company's internet through terminals connected to the same computer, then a close look at mail from them would show that they have the same IP address.

FIGURE 13.10:
When internet connections involve
IP numbers and when they don't

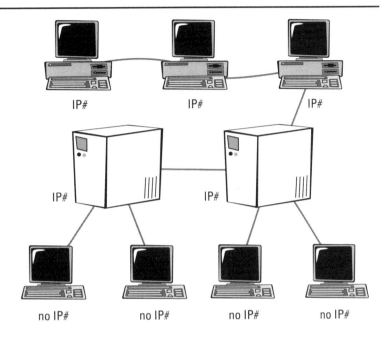

So, in summary: if you want to get onto *the* Internet from a remote location, then your best bet is to sign up with a service that will bill you monthly for connect charges, like Delphi. To attach to a private internet, you'll need to dial up to a multiuser computer on that internet, or you'll need a SLIP or PPP connection, or you'll have to be on a workstation on a LAN that's part of that internet. As the administrator of an NT Server network, you have the tools available to set up your users' workstations to speak TCP/IP, so that they can be part of your internet—and *the* Internet.

Setting up TCP/IP on NT with Fixed IP Addresses

Enough talking about internetting; let's do it.

Traditionally, one of the burdens of an IP administrator has been that she must assign separate IP numbers to each machine, a bit of bookkeeping hassle. You can adopt this "fixed IP address" approach, and in fact there are some good reasons to do it, as it's compatible with more TCP/IP software and systems. It is also possible, however, to have a server assign IP addresses "on the fly" with the DHCP system that I've mentioned earlier.

Some of you will set up your internet with fixed IP addresses, and some will use dynamic addresses. For that reason, I first want to start the discussion of setting up TCP/IP with just fixed addresses. Then I'll take on dynamic addressing.

Here's basically how to set up TCP/IP on an NT system:

1. Load the TCP/IP protocol.

2. Set the IP address and subnet.

3. Prepare the HOSTS file.

4. Connect to a default router.

5. Connect to a DNS server.

Let's look at those steps, one by one.

Installing TCP/IP Software

You install the TCP/IP protocol (if you didn't choose it when you first installed NT) by opening up the Control Panel, and then choosing the Network icon. You'll see a dialog box like the one in Figure 13.11.

Choose Add Software…, and select TCP/IP Protocol and Related Components. You'll then see a dialog box like the one in Figure 13.12.

Click Continue, and, as usual whenever you install new software, you'll get the "where are the NT files?" dialog box, as in Figure 13.13.

Once you click Continue, you'll see some files load, and then you'll return to the previous dialog box. Click OK, and the Control Panel will start configuring the new software. As this new software is TCP/IP, the Control Panel will see that it must get a bit of information from *you* before it goes any further. That's when you'll see the

FIGURE 13.11:

Initial Control Panel dialog for installing network software

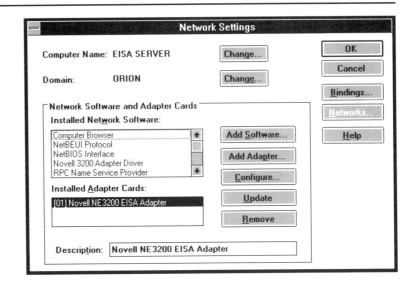

FIGURE 13.12:

Choosing TCP/IP Protocol setup

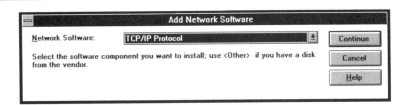

FIGURE 13.13:

Looking for setup files

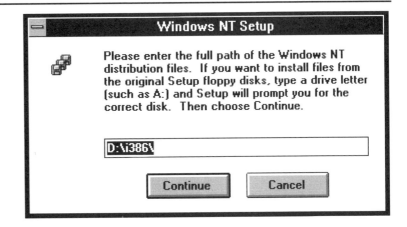

dialog box shown in Figure 13.14. Here, I've already filled in some numbers. Let's review what you'll have to do to set up this dialog box.

First, you'll put your IP address into the IP Address: field. Using the first quad of your address, NT will guess a subnet mask based on your network class—255.0.0.0 for class A, 255.255.0.0 for class B, and 255.255.255.0 for class C.

If your network uses subnetting *within* its Internet domain, then you'll have to change the subnet mask. For example, suppose you've got a class C net, which can theoretically support 254 hosts—*x.y.z.*1 through *x.y.z.*254. But within your company—that is, your class C network—you've got four separate Ethernet segments, which will be TCP/IP subnets. You've separated the four segments like so:

- Host numbers 1 through 63 (binary 00000001 to 00111111) are the first subnet. (Note that "host numbers" refers solely to the last quad number, as the first three will always be the same throughout your network, assuming a class C network.)

- Host numbers 64 through 127 (binary 01000000 to 01111111) are the second subnet.

FIGURE 13.14:
Basic TCP/IP setup

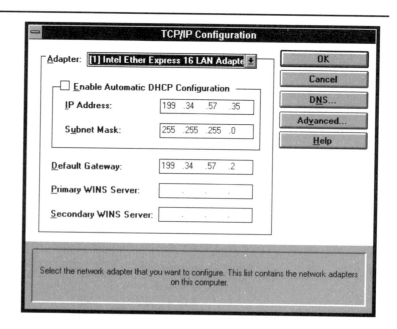

- Host numbers 128 through 191 (binary 10000000 to 10111111) are the third subnet.

- Host numbers 192 through 254 (binary 11000000 to 11111110) are the fourth subnet.

TCP/IP can distinguish which subnet a given host belongs to by looking at the left-most two bits of that host's number. Everything in the first subnet has an address like 00xxxxxx, the second subnet looks like 01xxxxxx, the third 10xxxxxx, and the fourth 11xxxxxx. Because the leftmost two bits are the bits that determine which subnet an IP address is in, they get a 1 on their subnet mask, and the other six bits get zeroes. The first three quads get ones on their subnet masks, making an entire subnet mask that looks like

11111111 11111111 11111111 11000000

Rendered in decimal, that becomes 255.255.255.192. In the case of my TCP/IP network, I put all of my machines on the same subnet, so my mask is the standard C-class mask 255.255.255.0.

Finally, you should enter the IP address of your default gateway, the machine on your Ethernet segment that connects to the outside world either via a router, a SLIP, or a PPP connection. To clarify that, Figure 13.15 shows an example Internet connection.

FIGURE 13.15:

Example of a connection to the Internet

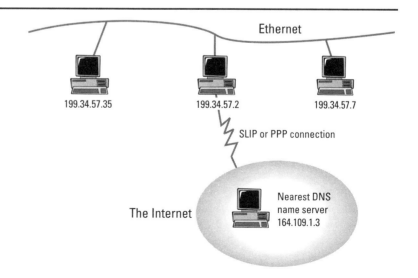

Suppose you're configuring the machine in the upper-left corner of the diagram. You enter its IP address into the TCP/IP Configuration dialog box that you saw in Figure 13.14, entering the value 199.34.57.35. Presuming that your class C net-work—since the first quad is 199, it must be a class C network—is not further sub-netted, the subnet mask would be 255.255.255.0, and the default gateway would be the machine with the SLIP connection to the Internet, so you'd enter 199.34.57.2 for the address of the default gateway. Notice the DNS router is at 164.109.1.3. You haven't had a chance to incorporate that information into the TCP/IP setup yet, but you will soon.

Next, click the DNS... button. You'll see a dialog box like the one in Figure 13.16.

The important parts of this screen are the host name, the TCP domain name, the name resolution, and the DNS search order.

The TCP domain name is your company's domain name, like exxon.com, or, if your company is further divided beyond the domain level, perhaps refining exxon.com to damgctrl.exxon.com or something similar. The host name is your computer's name—marks-computer, printserver, or the like.

FIGURE 13.16:

DNS Configuration screen

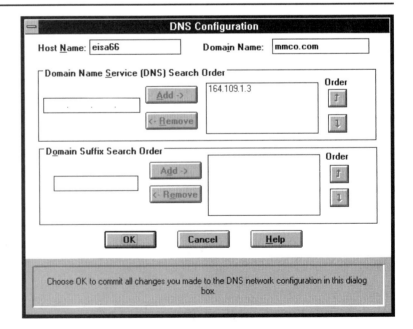

Next, you tell NT where to find a DNS server. You can use just a HOSTS file, or DNS name servers, or a combination. If you use a DNS name server or servers, however, you've got to tell NT where the nearest DNS name server is. You can specify one, two, or three DNS servers, and the order in which to search them, in the DNS Name Service Search Order field. In general, you'll only include the name of one or two DNS name servers, a primary and a secondary for use in case the primary name server is down.

Next, you'll click OK to return to the main TCP/IP configuration screen, and click the Advanced button. You'll then see a dialog box like the screen in Figure 13.17.

FIGURE 13.17:
Advanced TCP/IP configuration screen

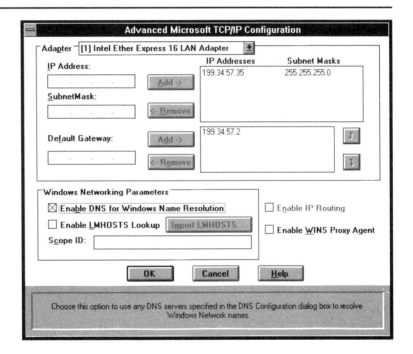

If you've got more than one network adapter in your system, then you'd enter the IP addresses of the extra adapters here. You'd also click the Enable DNS for Windows Name Resolution box. I'll discuss multiple adapters, IP Routing, and WINS Proxy Agents later.

Click enough OKs to get back to the Control Panel, and the Control Panel will tell you that you'll have to reboot for the changes to take effect. Do that.

Just to get started, create your HOSTS file; remember that it goes in winnt35\system32\drivers\etc. The file is reread every time a name must be resolved, so you needn't reboot every time you change the contents of HOSTS.

Testing Your TCP/IP Installation

Your TCP/IP software should now be ready to go, so let's test it.

TCP/IP has a very handy little tool for finding out whether or not your TCP/IP software is up and running, and whether or not you've got a connection to another point—*ping*.

Ping is a program that lets you send a short message to another TCP/IP node, asking it, "are you there?" If the other node is there, then it says, "yes," to ping, and ping tells you that. You can see an example ping in Figure 13.18.

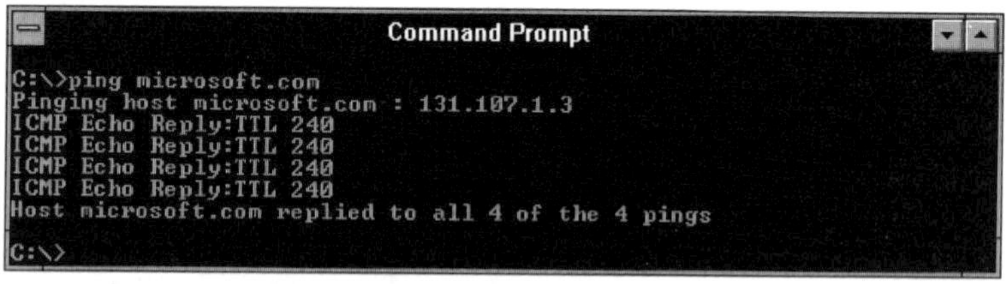

FIGURE 13.18:

Sample Ping output

```
Command Prompt
C:\>ping microsoft.com
Pinging host microsoft.com : 131.107.1.3
ICMP Echo Reply:TTL 240
ICMP Echo Reply:TTL 240
ICMP Echo Reply:TTL 240
ICMP Echo Reply:TTL 240
Host microsoft.com replied to all 4 of the 4 pings
C:\>
```

In this figure, I pinged Microsoft or, rather, whatever network Microsoft exposes to the outside world. (Notice it's a class B network—those Microsoft guys really rate.) The ping was successful, which is all that matters. But *don't* ping Microsoft for your first test; actually, their system no longer responds to ping requests anyway. (I guess they couldn't figure out a way to charge for them.) Instead, use ping to gradually test first your IP software, then your connection to the network, your name resolution, and finally your gateway to the rest of your internet.

How Do I Make Sure TCP/IP Is Set Up Properly?

Follow these steps to make sure TCP/IP is set up properly:

1. First, test that you've installed the IP software by pinging the built-in IP "loopback" address. Type `ping 127.0.0.1`.

If that fails, you know that you've done something wrong in the initial installation, so recheck that the software's installed on your system.

2. Next, ping your specific IP address. You can do this by typing `ping` *w.x.y.z*, where *w.x.y.z* is the dotted quad notation for your IP address— the one you entered when you configured TCP/IP on your system. You should get a reply. For example, on my system, I'd type `ping 199.34.57.35`.

If that fails, your TCP/IP stack probably isn't installed correctly, or perhaps you mistyped the IP number, or perhaps you gave the *same* IP number to another workstation.

3. Ping your gateway to see that you can get to the gateway, which should be on your subnet. In my case, the gateway is at 199.34.57.2, so I type `ping 199.34.57.2` and all should be well.

If you can't get to the gateway, check that the gateway is up, and that your network connection is all right. There's nothing more embarrassing than calling in outside network support, only to find that your LAN cable fell out of the back of your computer.

4. Ping something on the other side of your gateway, like an external DNS server.

If you can't get there, it's likely that your gateway isn't working properly.

5. Next, test the name resolution on your system. Ping yourself *by name*. Instead of saying `ping 199.34.57.35`, I'd say `ping eisa66.mmco.com` (the machine I'm on at the moment). That tests HOSTS and/or DNS.

6. Then, ping someone else on your subnet. Again, try using a host name, like mizar.ursamajor.edu, but if that doesn't work, use the IP address.

If the IP address works, but the host name doesn't, double-check the HOSTS file or DNS.

7. Finally, ping someone outside your domain, like house.gov (the U.S. House of Representatives).

If that doesn't work, but all the pings inside your network work, then you've probably got a problem with your Internet provider.

If you're successful on all of these tests, it should be set up properly.

Setting Up NT Routers

Up to now, I've assumed that you had your NT network connected to the Internet, or to your enterprise internet, via some third-party (Cisco, Bay Networks, or whomever) router. But you can also use NT machines as routers, albeit low-power ones. In general NT servers are not very efficient in the role of IP router.

Look back to the Advanced TCP/IP Configuration screen (Figure 13.17), and you'll see a grayed-out option called Enable IP Routing. That's how you turn on NT's routing capability.

Let's see how to set up this router. Imagine you've got an internet that looks like Figure 13.19.

We're going to use the machine that's on both Rome and Carthage as the router. (Actually, there's no choice here, as it's the *only* machine in both TCP/IP domains, and any router between two domains must be a member of both domains.) All you've got to do is to go to the machine with two Ethernet cards and set up both cards with an IP address. The Enable IP Routing box will no longer be grayed out, and you can then check the box.

A sample internet

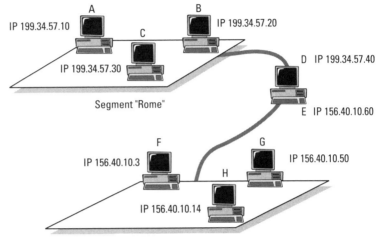

Segment "Rome"

Segment "Carthage"

How Do I Build an IP Router with NT?

To build an IP router with NT:

1. Install two network cards (let's use Ethernet for this example) in an NT machine. The NT machine *need not be* an NT Server machine; an NT workstation is okay.

2. Configure the Ethernet card on the Rome subnet with an IP address for the Rome subnet. When you are working in the TCP/IP Configuration dialog box, you'll notice a single-selection drop-down list box labeled Adapter. You can use that to control which Ethernet card you are assigning to what IP address.

3. Click the Advanced... button.

4. Check the Enable IP Routing option.

5. Click OK until you get out of the Control Panel.

The system will reboot, and your router will be active.

This will allow an IP router to move traffic from one subnet to another. It will *not*, however, route traffic between three or more subnets.

Using an NT Server Machine as an Internet Gateway

Consider this. Your company has purchased a full-time SLIP connection from some Internet provider. You've got your LAN all running TCP/IP, with NIC-approved IP numbers. (NIC stands for Network Information Center, an organization that assigns Domain names and IP addresses to Internet hosts.) All you need is a machine that will route your local traffic over the Internet when you want to FTP, use e-mail, or whatever. How do you hook up your internet to *the* Internet?

Look back to Figure 13.15. It showed both a small internet and a machine acting as an Internet gateway. It served as an Internet gateway by containing both an Ethernet card and a serial port, with a SLIP connection. That machine was essentially doing the job of TCP/IP routing. How do you do that in NT?

Well, according to Microsoft, you can't. I spent an entire day trying to get it to work with an early 3.5 beta, so finally I filed a bug report asking for help. Microsoft responded two days later (very politely and somewhat apologetically) that I had misunderstood.

"NT's TCP/IP support," they explained to me, "either lets you route between two LANs running TCP/IP, *or* it lets you use a stand-alone PC to connect to an internet via SLIP. The SLIP software can't be used in combination with routing. Sorry to be the one to break the bad news."

Now, I would have been frustrated, save for the fact that I'd figured out how to do it before I got the message from Microsoft!

Looking back at the Advanced TCP/IP Setup dialog box, it seemed obvious that I needed to check the Enable IP Routing box. But I couldn't do that—it was grayed out—unless I had two Ethernet cards in a system. SLIP just didn't count.

Now, I had an Ethernet card in my system, which I'd given the IP address 199.34.57.4. And my Internet provider expected me to dial into 199.34.57.2. That meant to me that the IP address that I'd assign to my SLIP line was 199.34.57.2. Again, though, *how do I get the system to recognize my 199.34.57.2 SLIP address so that I can enable routing*?

Simple. I lied.

I told my system that my Ethernet card had more than one IP address. Not only did it have address 199.34.57.4, which it also knew about, but it also had address 199.34.57.2. With the second address, the Enable IP Routing box became enabled, and I checked it.

Then I used RAS to dial up to my Internet provider. When you get a SLIP connection, you see a SLIP logon screen that looks like Figure 13.20.

FIGURE 13.20:

SLIP login screen

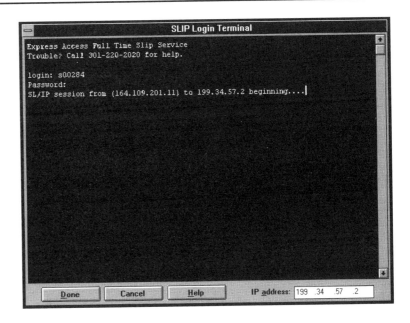

Notice that in the lower right-hand corner is an edit field labeled IP address:; you can put any address in there that you like. I put in the address that my Internet provider wanted. (By the way, Internet providers will generally assume that any C class license will be dialing in on the ".2" address.)

Once that was done, my connection worked like a charm. Let's review the whole thing, sort of as an "Internet link cookbook."

1. With the usual TCP/IP installation software, specify the IP address of your local Ethernet card. Set its default gateway to whatever "default router" or "default gateway" address your Internet provider told you to use. This address will *not* be on your subnet. For example, my 199.34.57.x net has as a gateway a machine at 164.109.203.3, which is an address in my *provider's* domain. (Again, don't confuse Internet domains with NT Server domains.)

2. Click the Advanced button, and add the address *X.Y.Z.2*, where *X.Y.Z* is your first three quads.

3. You now have two addresses on your Ethernet (or token-ring or ARCNet) card. The Enable IP Routing box is now enabled; check it.

4. Close up the TCP/IP configuration screen. Don't reboot yet.

5. If you haven't installed RAS yet, install it.

6. Set up an entry in your RAS dialing directory for a SLIP (or PPP, if you use that) dialup.

7. When you first dial up via SLIP, enter the *X.Y.Z.2* address in the IP Address: field of the SLIP logon terminal.

You are then connected to the Internet.

Routing More than Two Subnets

The IP router software in NT isn't too sophisticated. Take, for example, the internet displayed in Figure 13.21.

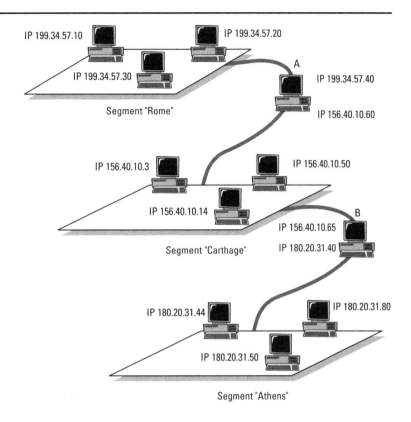

FIGURE 13.21:
Three-subnet router

IP 199.34.57.10

IP 199.34.57.20

IP 199.34.57.30

Segment "Rome"

A

IP 199.34.57.40

IP 156.40.10.60

IP 156.40.10.3

IP 156.40.10.50

IP 156.40.10.14

Segment "Carthage"

B

IP 156.40.10.65

IP 180.20.31.40

IP 180.20.31.44

IP 180.20.31.80

IP 180.20.31.50

Segment "Athens"

The two routers, now labeled A and B, should be configured as you just learned. But the job isn't done, as none of the IP packets from the 199.34.57.*x* network can get to the 180.20.31.*x* network. The A router can move things from 199.34.57.*x* to the 156.40.10.*x* network, but not from 199.34.57.*x* to 180.20.31.*x*—unless you tell it how to.

You tell a router how to get to far-off (well, more than one hop away) places with the NT *route* command. With this command, you tell a router, "if you see an address starting with this partial dotted quad, send it to this router for further routing." Now, the network that A and B have in common is the 156.40.10.*x* network. So, to tell the A router how to get messages to 180.20.31.*x* via 156.40.10.*x*, we just give it the address of the adapter in B that's part of 150.40.10.*x*. Do that like so:

```
route add 180.20.31 156.40.10.65
```

The command `route add` adds information to A's routing table. (This is a command-line command, so you'll have to open a command line in order to enter route commands.) 180.20.31 is the first part of the target network, and 156.40.10.65 is the IP address to send any packets destined for 180.20.31.*x*.

You've got to do the same thing for the B router, as it does not know how to get to 199.34.57.*x*. The corresponding command is

```
route add 199.34.57 156.40.10.60
```

The address 156.40.10.60 refers to the Ethernet adapter on router A that is "visible" to router B.

Using Multiple Gateways

Thus far, the internets you've seen provide only one router—"default gateway"— for each workstation. But now consider the case of an internet with multiple pathways from one point to another, as in Figure 13.22.

Notice that now Rome, Carthage, and Athens have a third router, router C, which is a member of both Rome and Athens. Before router C was added, it was possible to get messages from anywhere on this internet to anywhere else on this internet— but there was only *one* way to do it. Now there's more than one path. Previously, all of the Athens computers would specify a default gateway of 180.20.31.40. Now, however, they can specify both that address, and the address 180.20.31.70, router C. How do you specify multiple gateways? With the Advanced TCP/IP screen.

Well, by now, you're on an internet in the "traditional" way. Microsoft adds two possible options to this setup, the Dynamic Host Configuration Protocol (DHCP) and the Windows Internet Naming Service (WINS).

FIGURE 13.22:

Internet with more than one pathway

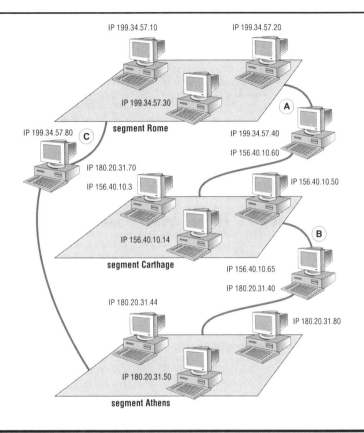

How Do I Enter Multiple TCP/IP Gateways?

To enter multiple TCP/IP gateways:

1. In the TCP/IP Configuration dialog box (choose Control Panel, then the Network applet, then click on TCP/IP and then on Configure...), click the Advanced... button. Look back at Figure 13.17 for an example screen shot of the Advanced TCP/IP options.

2. In the Default Gateway: field, enter the IP address or host name of the gateway. Click on Add.

3. In the example illustrated in Figure 13.22, you would do this for *every machine* in the Athens subnet. You might make 180.20.31.40 the default gateway (which you can, of course, enter in via the Control Panel), and 180.20.31.70 as the additional gateway.

You must shut down your system and restart for the changes to take effect.

Installing TCP/IP with DHCP

Everything that you've learned so far is just about all you would need to set up an internet. But you can see that this business of assigning IP addresses can be something of a pain. In particular, consider these problems:

- What if you run out of IP addresses?

- Wouldn't it be nice not to have to keep track of which IP addresses you've used, and which ones remain?

Looking at these problems—and a possible solution—leads us to seeing what DHCP (Dynamic Host Configuration Protocol) is, and how to install it. Note, by the way, that this discussion assumes that you've already read this chapter up to this point; don't think that if you decided from the start to go with DHCP, you could skip the previous sections.

The "Not Enough Addresses" Problem

Suppose your company has 500 computers, but only a class C network. That implies you can only support about 250 IP addresses; what should you do? One approach would be to get a number of C-class addresses, and route between the different C-class subnets within the company.

Another is DHCP. Under DHCP, you take about 240 of those addresses, put them in a pool of unassigned IP addresses, and designate a computer (the DHCP server) that is authorized to give out those addresses.

Then, when a PC logs onto the network, it doesn't have a hard-wired IP address. Instead, it goes to the DHCP server (which *must* have a hard-wired address) and requests an IP address. The DHCP server then picks an IP address from the pool of available addresses and gives the workstation PC a *lease* on that IP address. When the workstation PC logs off the network, the IP address is freed up, and can be recycled to another PC.

In the example of the company with 500 PCs, DHCP could let them share, say, two hundred IP addresses among 500 machines, just as long as no more than two hundred (or their maximum number of IP addresses) PCs are on the network at any moment in time.

Simplifying TCP/IP Administration

I keep a little list of PCs and IP addresses. It serves as a "master directory" of which IP addresses have been used so far. Obviously, I've got to consult it when I put TCP/IP on each new computer.

That's *obvious*, but what's *unfortunate* is that I never seem to have the notebook with me when I need it. So I started keeping this list of computers and IP addresses on one of my servers, in a kind of common HOSTS file. It served two purposes: first, it told me what IP addresses were already used, and second, it gave me a HOSTS file to copy to the local computer's hard disk.

When it comes right down to it, however, this whole thing seems kind of stupid. Why am I doing what is clearly a rote, mechanical job—you know, the kind of thing that computers are good at?

The Internet world agreed, and invented a TCP/IP protocol called BOOTP; BOOTP became DHCP, and I no longer have to keep my paper list.

With DHCP, you only have to hard-wire the IP addresses of a few machines, like your BOOTP/DHCP server and your default gateway.

Installing and Configuring DHCP Servers

DHCP servers are the machines that provide IP addresses to machines that request access to the LAN. DHCP only works if the TCP/IP software on the workstations is *built* to work with DHCP—if the TCP/IP software includes a "DHCP client." NT includes TCP/IP software with DHCP clients for Windows for Workgroups, Windows, and DOS. Windows 95 ships with an integrated DHCP client.

To get ready for DHCP configuration,

- Have an IP address ready for your DHCP server—this is one computer on your network that *must* have a hard-wired IP address.

- Know which IP addresses are free to assign. You'll use these available IP addresses to create a "pool" of IP addresses.

To begin the installation, open the Control Panel and the Network applet, and click the Install software... button. In the available options, pick TCP/IP and Related Components, and click Continue. You'll see a screen like the one in Figure 13.23.

Check DHCP Server Service, and click the Continue button. You'll be prompted, as always, for the location of the files, and the DHCP software will install. Back at the Network Settings dialog, click OK and the system will reboot.

Once the system has rebooted, you'll find a new icon in the Network Administration group, the DHCP Manager. Start it up, and you'll see a screen like the one in Figure 13.24. Not much to look at now, as there are no scopes set up yet. Scopes? What's a scope?

DHCP Scopes

In order for DHCP to give out IP addresses, it must know what IP addresses it can give out. You tell it with a *scope*. A scope is just a range of IP addresses, a pool from which they can be drawn. You use scopes for one of two reasons. First, you assign at least one scope to each subnet serviced by your DHCP servers (yes, it *is* possible for one DHCP server to handle multiple subnets). Second, you might want to

FIGURE 13.23:

Windows TCP/IP Installation
Options dialog box

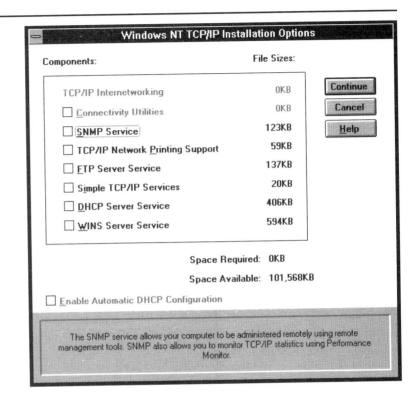

FIGURE 13.24:

DHCP opening screen

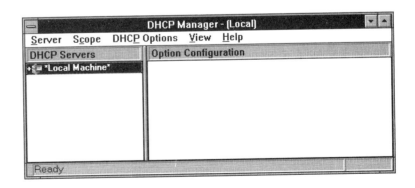

divide up a subnet's IP addresses for fault tolerance. I give the majority of my IP addresses to my "main" scope. I leave a few for a "backup" scope; I'll discuss bulletproofing DHCP in a minute.

You've got to create a scope for your DHCP server. Do that by clicking on Scope, and Create...; you'll see a screen like the one in Figure 13.25.

FIGURE 13.25:

Create Scope dialog box

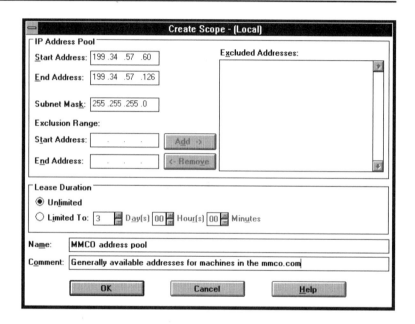

Note that the dialog box's title is Create Scope (Local). That's because you can control a DHCP server from another NT machine, as is the case with so many NT network functions.

You should also note that I've filled in the Start Address, End Address, Lease Duration, Name, and Comment fields. The start and end addresses specify a range of possible IP addresses to give out. Here, I've offered the addresses from my ".60" address through my ".126" address for the IP pool. That's 67 addresses, which are sufficient for my network. I *could* have offered all 250-odd addresses, and then excluded particular addresses with the Exclusion Range field; that's just as valid an option.

The Name and Comment field are used mainly for administering scopes later. Click OK, and you'll see a dialog box like the one in Figure 13.26.

Click Yes, and it'll be immediately available. The DHCP manager will then look something like Figure 13.27.

FIGURE 13.26:

Activating a new scope

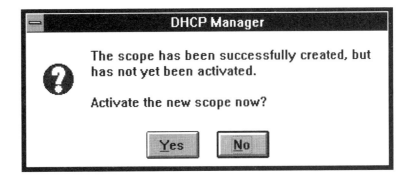

FIGURE 13.27:

DHCP Manager with an active scope

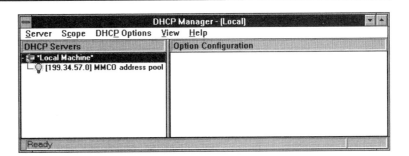

Notice the lighted light bulb; that indicates an *active* scope. But you're not done yet. DHCP can provide default values for a whole host of TCP/IP parameters, including these basic items:

- default gateway
- domain name
- DNS server
- WINS server (DHCP calls it a "WINS/NBT server")

Remember that you had to punch all that stuff in when you assigned fixed IP addresses? Well, DHCP lets you specify some defaults, making it an even more attractive addressing alternative. Just click DHCP Options, and you'll see the options Global, Local, and Default.

Click Global to modify options that don't change from subnet to subnet, like the domain name or the DNS and WINS server addresses. Click Local to modify options that are relevant to particular subnets, like the address of the default gateway (which DHCP, for some perverse reason, calls the "Router").

Most of the settings are global, so click Global, and you'll see a dialog box like Figure 13.28.

FIGURE 13.28:

Setting DHCP global options

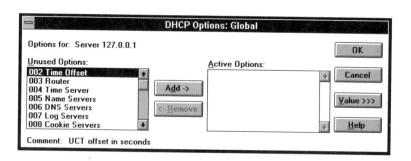

Just as there are piles of NetBEUI parameters that you'll never end up touching, most of the TCP/IP options in this dialog box can also be safely ignored. The five that I adjusted were:

- DNS Servers; here I named our two DNS servers.

- Domain Name, which is mmco.com.

- WINS/NBT Server, with the addresses of my WINS servers (which I'll cover soon). Setting this requires that you also set…

- WINS/NBT Node Type, a cryptic setting that you needn't worry about, except to set it to 0x8; that makes WINS run best.

- Then going over to the Local settings, I set Router, which is, again, the DHCP equivalent of the Default Gateway option in the TCP/IP setup screen.

I set these by highlighting the option that I want to use, and then clicking Add. Then I clicked Value and edited the value. For example, say I want to make my default gateway 199.34.57.2. I click on Router, then Add, and then Value; I then get a dialog box that looks like Figure 13.29.

FIGURE 13.29:

Setting the default router address

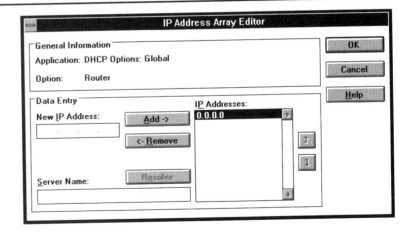

Notice that the original default value is 0.0.0.0, which is a meaningless address in this context. I enter 199.34.57.2 and click Add, but I don't stop there; next, I click on 0.0.0.0 and click on Remove. *Then* I click OK.

I do the same things with the domain name and the DNS router, and I'm set. The DHCP Manager then looks something like Figure 13.30. Notice the different icons for the global settings and the local settings. Close up the DHCP Manager, and your server is set up; you needn't even reboot.

FIGURE 13.30:

Configured DHCP server

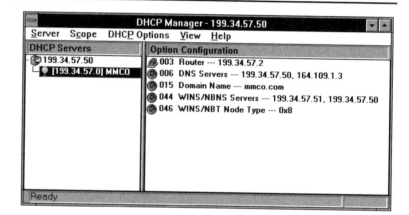

DHCP on the Client Side

Now that you've set up DHCP on a server, how do you tell clients to use that DHCP? Simple. The Windows for Workgroups TCP/IP-32 bit software has DHCP configuration as an installation option, as does the latest Microsoft Client software for DOS and Windows. If you want to find out what IP address a client machine has, go to that machine, open up a command line, and type `ipconfig /all`.

DHCP in Detail

You've seen how to set up DHCP. But how does it work and, unfortunately, how does it sometimes *not* work?

DHCP supplies IP addresses based on the idea of *client leases*. When a machine (a DHCP client) needs an IP address, it asks a DHCP server for that address. (*How it does that is important, and I'll get to it in a minute.*) A DHCP server then gives an IP address to the client, *but only for a temporary period of time*—hence the term "IP lease." You might have noticed that you can set the term of an IP lease from DHCP; it's one of the settings in Scope/Properties.

The client then knows how long it's got the lease. Even if you reboot or reset your computer, it'll remember what lease is active for it, and how much longer it's got to go on the lease.

TIP On a Windows 3.*x* machine, that information is kept in DHCP.BIN in the Windows directory. On a Windows 95 machine, it's in HKEY_LOCAL_MACHINE\System\CurrentControlSet\Services\VxD\DHCP\Dhcpinfo*xx*, where "*xx*" is two digits.

So, if your PC had a four-day lease on some address, and you rebooted two days into its lease, then the PC wouldn't just blindly ask for an IP address; instead, it would go back to the DHCP server that it got its IP address from, and request the particular IP address that it had before. If the DHCP server were still up, it would acknowledge the request, letting the workstation use the IP address. If, on the other hand, the DHCP server has had its lease information wiped out through some disaster, then it will either give the IP address to the machine (if no one else is using the address), or it will send a "negative acknowledgment," or "NACK" to the machine, and the DHCP server will make a note of that NACK in the Event Log.

By the way, if you're wondering how DHCP remembers which IP address went with which machine, DHCP matches IP addresses with the 48-bit Ethernet or token-ring addresses, usually called the "MAC" addresses (not after the Macintosh; it stands for Media Access Control layer).

This leads me to the following tip.

TIP   Do *not* set the leases to Infinite. I used to think that this was a cool way to easily assign fixed IP addresses. The first time a system logged on, it would get an IP address, and all would be good, right? There are two problems with this. First, a minor problem. What if you have to reinstall your DHCP server, but did not back up the Registry (where the DHCP database lives)? Then your system spends a lot of time NACKing innocent PCs. Second, what if you want to reconfigure your network? Suppose you have 200 people in two departments on the same subnet. You decide to divide them up into two subnets. Half of the users of the old subnet will now be on a new subnet, requiring a whole new set of IP addresses. Obviously you've got to create a new scope, but creating the new scope is easy. The *problem* is, how do you force a new IP address on the people in the new subnet? Their leases never expire, so they never really give the DHCP server a chance to assign them new addresses. (Well, it will, but only after lots of NACKing and plenty of systems that will randomly refuse to communicate with anything.) Set the lease to a few days, and then you can enforce changes to your subnet structure automatically through the DHCP servers.

Let me expand upon that a bit. Suppose you know that on November 1 you're going to take your 200.1.1.*x* subnet and break it up into 200.1.1.*x* and 200.1.2.*x*. Now, with old static IP addresses, you'd be faced with the prospect of having to go to every single workstation and change its IP address by hand. With DHCP, however, you don't have to do that.

Instead, here's the process. Suppose you give out ten-day leases. Nine days before November 1, reduce the lease length to nine days. The next day, reduce the leases to eight days, and so on. On October 31, reduce lease length to just a few hours. Then, after hours, do the physical partitioning of your subnets—install the routers and isolate the machines for the new subnet on the 200.1.2.*x* side—and create the new 200.1.2.*x* scope on your DHCP server. Then your work is done.

Getting an IP address from DHCP

A DHCP client gets an IP address from a DHCP server with a few steps.

Initial DHCP Request

First, a DHCP client sends out a message saying, in effect, "are there any DHCP servers out there? If so, I want an IP address." You might ask, "how can a machine communicate if it doesn't have an address?" Through a different protocol than TCP—UDP, or the User Datagram Protocol. It's not a NetBIOS or NetBEUI creature; it's all TCP/IP-suite stuff.

DHCP grew out of an older TCP/IP protocol called BOOTP. BOOTP wasn't built for PCs; it was developed with UNIX systems in mind. Microsoft and some other vendors worked to get DHCP accepted within the suite of Internet standards, and they were able to do that by largely building DHCP out of BOOTP.

DHCP Offers Addresses from Near and Far

Any DHCP servers within "earshot"—that is, any that receive the UDP datagram—respond to the client with an offer, a proposed IP address. Again, this is an offer, not the final IP address.

This offering part of the DHCP process is essential because, as I just hinted, it's possible for more than one DHCP server to hear the original client request. If every DHCP server just thrust an IP address at the hapless client, then it would end up with multiple IP addresses, addresses wasted in the sense that the DHCP servers would consider them all taken, and so they couldn't give those addresses out to other machines.

Worse yet, what if a DHCP server from another subnet gave an IP address to our client? Wouldn't that put the client in the wrong subnet? DHCP keeps that from happening via BOOTP forwarding. The original UDP message, "are there any DHCP servers out there?" is a broadcast. Most routers, as you know, do not forward broadcasts. This reduces network traffic congestion, and it's a positive side-effect of routers. But if DHCP requests don't go over routers, then that would imply that you've got to have a DHCP server on every subnet, a rather expensive proposition.

The BOOTP standard got around this by defining an RFC 1542, a specification whereby routers would recognize BOOTP broadcasts, and would forward them to other subnets. The feature must be implemented in your routers' software, and it's commonly known as *BOOTP forwarding*. Of course, when an NT machine acts as an IP router, it implements BOOTP forwarding.

Assuming you've got routers that implement BOOTP forwarding, then the original DHCP request gets out to all of them. But how do we keep a DHCP server in subnet 200.1.2.*x* from giving an address in 200.1.2.*x* to a PC sitting in 200.1.1.*x*? Simple. When the router forwards the BOOTP request, it attaches a little note to it that says, "this came from 200.1.1.*x*." The DHCP server then sees that information, and so it only responds if it has a scope within 200.1.1.*x*.

Picking from the Offers

The DHCP client then looks through the offers that it has, and picks the one that's best for it. If there are multiple offers that look equally good, it picks the one that arrived first. Then it sends another UDP datagram, but not a broadcast this time. Instead, it makes a request like the first one that it sent, but this one is directed at the IP address of the DHCP server with the most desirable DHCP offer.

The Lease is Signed

Finally, the DHCP server responds with the shiny brand-new IP address. It also tells the client its new subnet mask, lease period, and whatever else you specified (gateway, WINS server, DNS server, and the like).

You can find out what your IP configuration looks like after DHCP by typing IPCONFIG /ALL. It may run off the screen, so you may need to add " | more" to the line. This works on DOS, Windows for Workgroups, and NT machines. You can see a sample run of IPCONFIG /ALL in Figure 13.31.

Windows 95 machines have a graphical version of IPCONFIG.

Lost Our Lease! Must Sell!

What happens when the lease runs out? Well, when that happens, you're supposed to stop using the IP address. But that's not likely to happen. When the lease is half

FIGURE 13.31:
Run of IPCONFIG

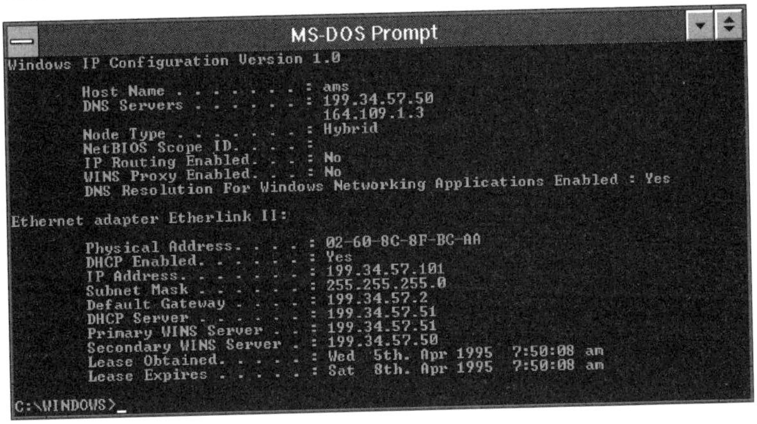

```
                            MS-DOS Prompt
Windows IP Configuration Version 1.0

        Host Name . . . . . . . : ams
        DNS Servers . . . . . . : 199.34.57.50
                                  164.109.1.3
        Node Type . . . . . . . : Hybrid
        NetBIOS Scope ID. . . . :
        IP Routing Enabled. . . : No
        WINS Proxy Enabled. . . : No
        DNS Resolution For Windows Networking Applications Enabled : Yes

Ethernet adapter Etherlink II:

        Physical Address. . . . : 02-60-8C-8F-BC-AA
        DHCP Enabled. . . . . . : Yes
        IP Address. . . . . . . : 199.34.57.101
        Subnet Mask . . . . . . : 255.255.255.0
        Default Gateway . . . . : 199.34.57.2
        DHCP Server . . . . . . : 199.34.57.51
        Primary WINS Server . . : 199.34.57.51
        Secondary WINS Server . : 199.34.57.50
        Lease Obtained. . . . . : Wed  5th. Apr 1995  7:50:08 am
        Lease Expires . . . . . : Sat  8th. Apr 1995  7:50:08 am

C:\WINDOWS>_
```

over, the DHCP client begins renegotiating the IP lease with directed UDP messages to its original DHCP server. Once the lease is renewed, all is well until it's half over again, and so on. If the client doesn't get a response from the DHCP server by the time the lease is 87.5 percent over (wonder how they figured out that one!), then it returns to the UDP broadcast mode.

Installing TCP/IP with WINS

DHCP made IP addressing simpler, but ignored the newly created problem of keeping track of the newly assigned IP numbers and the hosts attached to them. Suppose you were sitting at a TCP/IP-connected workstation with a host name like, for example, t1000.skynet.com, and this host had received its IP address from a DHCP server. You were trying to "ping" t1000.skynet.com. What would happen? You'd get a "timed out" message. Your system wouldn't know its own name, because no DNS server knows what's going on with its dynamic IP address, and no one's updated a HOSTS file. What we need is a kind of dynamic name resolver, a sort of "dynamic DNS." (Recall that "name resolution" is the term for looking up that t1000.skynet.com is really 122.44.23.3.)

That dynamic DNS is the Windows Internet Naming Service, or WINS. While DHCP is part of a wider group of BOOTP-related protocols, WINS is mainly Microsoft's, and that's a problem. WINS, a name resolution service, is pretty much only recognized by Microsoft clients (NT, Windows for Workgroups, DOS, Windows machines, and presumably OS/2 clients eventually). WINS is *not* DNS-compatible, meaning that machines running WINS clients *inside* your network will be able to resolve your Microsoft client's TCP/IP names, but non-WINS clients inside your network, as well as *everyone* outside of your domain, will be unable to resolve names.

That implies that you probably have to find some kind of DNS server software in order to use the outside world's name resolution within your subnet. One such software is the bind utility that's included in Chameleon32/NFS from NetManage (the company's address is 10725 N. DeAnza Blvd., Cupertino, CA 95014; telephone (408) 973-7171; fax 257-6405). Within that DNS server software, you'd only include the hard-coded IP addresses of the few machines that you wanted the outside world to see, such as:

- Your gateway
- Your mail router
- Any FTP or Telnet servers

Microsoft also claims that using WINS name resolution services will reduce traffic on IP networks.

How WINS Administers NetBEUI Networks over Routers

What WINS is *really* good for is administering NetBEUI networks over routers. Huh? NetBEUI is fast and easy to understand. Its main problem, however, is that it is very heavily dependent on broadcasts. For example, if my workstation is to be called LEGACY, then we can't have any other LEGACY workstations around. So my workstation starts out the conversation by saying, "Anybody here named LEGACY?" If no one responds, my workstation feels justified in taking that name. (This is the NetBEUI equivalent of name resolution.) That question, "Anybody here named LEGACY?" is a broadcast. Broadcasts don't get passed over routers, however, so NetBEUI doesn't work in a network based on routers.

Microsoft's TCP/IP includes a very important feature called NBT, or NetBIOS over TCP/IP. Microsoft's redirector on the workstation, and its network file mounter on the server, both respond to NetBIOS commands. (Reread Chapter 2 if you've forgotten this stuff.) Recall that NetBIOS is the Application Program Interface (API) that is used with the NetBEUI transport protocol.

Until Microsoft embraced TCP/IP, it sold networks whose transport layers were NetBEUI and whose redirectors and network file mounters were built atop the NetBIOS API and relied upon the NetBIOS API. Traditionally, people who use TCP/IP for file serving also use the TCP/IP API—that is, TCP/IP sockets—instead of NetBIOS. That would mean that the Microsoft network file mounter would not work, as it assumes the existence of a transport layer speaking NetBIOS.

Cleverly, Microsoft implemented a version of the NetBIOS API—but on top of the TCP/IP transport stack. That means that the redirectors and the network file mounters work fine even though the transport protocols are completely different.

Another reason why that's clever is that it largely removes the need for DNS and WINS and HOSTS in small Microsoft TCP/IP networks. Since Microsoft TCP/IP supports NetBIOS, the system can use the simple NetBEUI/NetBIOS approach to name resolution. Recall that under TCP/IP, you have to figure out how a name relates to an IP address so that you can look at the IP address and the subnet mask, and from there you can figure out whether you can broadcast a message or route a message. In NetBIOS/NetBEUI, in contrast, you never make the "broadcast or route?" decision—you always broadcast. For that reason, as long as every workstation is on the same network segment, TCP/IP can act pretty much like NetBEUI because everything is broadcast.

The problem comes in going across routers with NetBIOS requests, and that's where WINS comes in. By putting a WINS server on every subnet, you restrict the "Who are you? Can I use this name?" stuff to point-to-point WINS messages rather than general broadcasts that can't move across routers. Each WINS server in each subnet already knows what the other WINS servers know about hosts on the other subnets. There is no need for broadcasts blitzes from one subnet to another to find names.

You actually do not even need a WINS server on each subnet. All you really need is one WINS server, and then in each subnet you should have one workstation with the WINS Proxy enabled. (It's a feature of the WINS client software, and I'll cover it in a minute.)

Installing WINS

Installing WINS is much like installing all the other software that we've installed elsewhere in this chapter and in the book:

1. Open the Control Panel.
2. Within the Control Panel, open the Networks applet.
3. Click on Add Software…
4. Choose TCP/IP Protocol and Related Components, then choose the Continue button.
5. In the Windows NT TCP/IP Installation Options dialog box, check WINS Server Service and click the Continue button.
6. Tell the program where to find the files on your CD-ROM or whatever drive you used to install NT. The files will load, and you'll return to the Network Settings dialog box.
7. Click OK.
8. The system will want to restart; let it. Once you've rebooted, you'll find a new icon in the Network Administration group, the WINS Manager.
9. Start it up. You'll see a screen like the one in Figure 13.32.

The first thing you should do on your WINS server is to tell it which machines on your subnet have hard-coded IP addresses. You do that by clicking the Mappings menu and then clicking Static Mappings…. You'll see a dialog box like the one in Figure 13.33.

In the figure, you see that I've added the IP addresses for two devices with predefined IP addresses. Just click Add Mappings, and you get a dialog box that lets you add IP addresses and host names as static values. If you have an existing HOSTS file, you can click Import Mappings… and the program will take that information to build a static mapping database.

FIGURE 13.32:

Initial WINS Manager screen

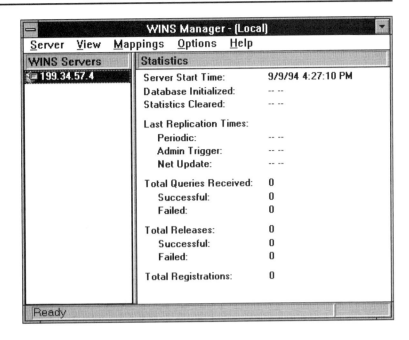

FIGURE 13.33:

Static Mappings table

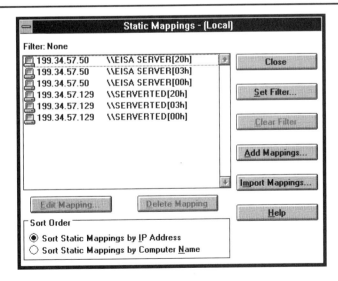

WINS Proxy Agent

WINS can significantly reduce your network's traffic. Ordinarily, the NetBIOS API directs its underlying protocol to do a lot of broadcasts; NetBIOS pretty much relies upon broadcasts to do name discoveries. ("Name discoveries" is a techie way of saying, "I've got a message for HUGH776. Anybody here named HUGH776?") Broadcasts can slow down *all* of the computers on the network, because they're all forced to stop what they're doing and listen (and perhaps respond) to the broadcast.

WINS is, as you've seen, a centralized naming service, and so the NetBIOS broadcasts become largely unnecessary. A module called the IP Helper on a WINS-enabled workstation intercepts any attempts to do NetBIOS broadcasts, translating them where possible into directed TCP or UDP messages to the WINS server.

WINS seems to do a number of great things; it fixes the NetBIOS name resolution over routers problem and it reduces network traffic. But, again, it lacks the all-important ability to talk to systems other than PCs with WINS-aware client software. What do we do about other systems?

Well, for PCs with older client software that cannot be upgraded to WINS-awareness, you can install a WINS proxy agent.

Imagine a TCP/IP network with two PCs in different subnets. Call them PC1 and PCSERVER. They're running a NetBIOS application (like file serving), and so PC1 sends a "give me some data" request to PCSERVER. How does the name resolver in PC1 find PCSERVER, given that a broadcast won't work since they're on different subnets? Well, if PC1 is running a WINS client, there's no trouble. But if it isn't, then PC1 either needs an LMHOSTS file (don't ask; they're no fun to set up), or it needs a hand.

If PC1's subnet has a WINS proxy agent in it, then it's in luck. The WINS proxy agent is a kind of "good Samaritan" for systems like PC1. It sees that PC1 is trying (via a broadcast) to find PCSERVER. But the WINS proxy agent knows that PCSERVER will not hear the broadcast, as the broadcast doesn't jump the routers between PC1 and PCSERVER, so the WINS proxy agent responds *for* PCSERVER. PC1 gets a response, so it's happy.

 Make sure there is only *one* WINS proxy agent per subnet! Otherwise, two PCs will respond to PC1, causing—how do the manuals put it? ah, yes—"unpredictable results."

DNS under WINS

If you need DNS, Microsoft has a version of DNS that links dynamically to WINS. It's in the Resource Kit, or you can find it on Microsoft's FTP site ftp.microsoft.com in the dnsbeta directory.

That's really all there is to installing and using WINS. The NT manual discusses some of the more esoteric options that you may use in special cases, but this is basically all you have to ever worry about. Just find one machine that will be up all the time, probably a file server, hard-code its IP address, and make it the DHCP and WINS server. In each subnet, designate a machine that's up all the time to be the WINS proxy agent.

Now you know the ins and outs of installing and configuring TCP/IP. It's time to learn how to use the oldest TCP/IP tool—the Telnet remote login program.

Using Telnet for Remote Login

In the early days of TCP/IP and internetting, people's first concern was getting onto other people's computers. For instance, suppose I worked at the John Von Neumann Supercomputing Center and I had written a fantastic celestial motion simulator—a program that could compute the locations of thousands of planets, planetoids, and comets in the Solar System. Suppose also that I had developed my simulator with government money, and the Feds wanted to offer it to everyone. Well, how does one get to this simulator?

In all likelihood, in order to get to this program you'd have to come to the Von Neumann Center. That's true for two reasons. First, I developed it on a supercomputer for a good reason—it's too darn big to fit anywhere else. Stick it on a normal computer and it would take weeks to get an answer to a simple question like, "When will Jupiter and Mars next be near to each other and high in the night sky?" The second reason is that we're back in the early days of internetting, recall, and in those days programs tended to be very specific to the machines that they were built on. Moving this program to another computer would be a pain in the neck, even if I were willing to put up with the slower speed.

The most likely way to offer this service to everyone would be to put some modems on the Von Neumann system and allow anyone to dial into the system and access the program. In fact, things like that have been done—but they end up generating awfully large phone bills for the people on the other side of the country.

Telnet solves this problem. It lets me work on the terminal or computer on my desk and access other hosts just as if I were there on site. In the case of the Von Neumann Center, I could access it just as if I were right in Princeton, New Jersey, where the Center is located. Now, no publicly available astronomical simulator is located at Von Neumann, at least as far as I know, so I can't show you anything like that. What I *can* show you is "Archie," an essential Internet tool.

Seeing What's on the Internet: Using Archie

As we'll discuss later, the Internet is a very big source of information, with everything from recipes to rutabaga farming tips to religion. And that leads to the question, "How do I know what's available on the Internet?"

The main way to find out what's on the internet is to use archie. A large number of computers on the Internet—called "hosts"—hold files available for public downloading and use. For example, something called Project Gutenberg puts the text of some well-known books on servers for anyone to download. But, again, how would you find out about the existence of these things? Ask Archie at the following Internet locations:

- archie.rutgers.edu NE US
- archie.sura.net SE US
- archie.unl.edu Western US
- archie.ans.net The Internet backbone

- archie.mcgill.ca Canada
- archie.funet.fi Europe
- archie.doc.ic.ac.uk United Kingdom
- archie.au Australia and Pacific Rim

Archie is available on several servers around the world. It's best to hook up to the Archie server closest to you so as to minimize network traffic. For example, data transfer capability to England is limited, so internetting from the U.S. to England, while it might seem cosmopolitan, is inconsiderate and ties up the Internet. I hook up to Archie at Rutgers.

I'll do the Telnet login from the command line. Once the session is active, however, I am shifted automatically to the NT Terminal program. I remotely log onto Archie in New Jersey by typing

```
telnet archie.rutgers.edu
```

After some introductory things, I get a prompt that says "login?" I respond by entering **archie**. Not every Telnet site requires a login. Some drop you right into the middle of the application and others require you to have an account to use the service and may even charge you for using whatever service they're purveying over the net—that's fair game. Expect to see more and more for-pay services on the Internet. The Net is slowly going commercial.

Anyway, I get a prompt that says archie>. This tells me that when I type something, when I make a request for information, my request will not be processed by the computer in Connecticut, but by the computer running Archie at Rutgers University in New Jersey.

When I ask it for a file name, I want Archie not to show me only the files whose names match exactly—I want *anything* that contains what I type. To tell Archie this, I type **set sub**. When you use the set sub command, be very careful what you ask for. If you search for "e," for example, and you'll get every file that has an *e* in its name! I'm looking for a server with the text of *Alice in Wonderland* on it, so I'll look for files that contain the word *Alice*. I do that by typing the command **prog**, which asks for a search of programs, and then the word **alice**, like so:

```
prog alice
```

The search shows me the following:

```
login: archie
Last login: Thu Oct 7 06:06:29 from bix.com
SunOS Release 4.1.3 (TDSERVER-SUN4C) #2: Mon Jul 19 18:37:02 EDT 1993


# Bunyip Information Systems, 1993

# Terminal type set to 'vt100 24 80'.
# 'erase' character is '^?'.
# 'search' (type string) has the value 'sub'.
archie> prog alice
# Search type: sub.
# Your queue position: 1
working...

Host cair.kaist.ac.kr  (143.248.11.170)
Last updated 10:29 4 Oct 1993

Host uceng.uc.edu  (129.137.189.1)
Last updated 20:43 3 Oct 1993

    Location: /pub/wuarchive/doc/misc/if-archive/games/source/gags
      FILE    -r--r--r--   16681 bytes  01:00 18 Mar 1993  alice.zip


Host ftp.sunet.se   (130.238.127.3)
Last updated 11:48  6 Oct 1993

    Location: /pub/etext/gutenberg/etext91
      FILE    -r--r--r--  162153 bytes  22:00 17 Sep 2000  alice29.txt


Host roxette.mty.itesm.mx   (131.178.17.100)
Last updated 21:26  2 Oct 1993

    Location: /pub/next/Literature/Gutenberg/etext91
      FILE    -r--r--r--   64809 bytes  00:00  1 May 1992  alice29.zip


Host ftp.wustl.edu   (128.252.135.4)
Last updated 20:43  2 Oct 1993
```

```
     Location: /mirrors/misc/books
        FILE    -rw-r--r--   64809 bytes  00:00 15 Jun 1992  alice29.zip

Host ftp.wustl.edu    (128.252.135.4)
Last updated 20:43  2 Oct 1993

     Location: /systems/amiga/aminet/text/tex
        FILE    -rw-rw-r--    5593 bytes  05:13 27 Sep 1993  decalice.lha
        FILE    -rw-rw-r--     254 bytes  05:13 27 Sep 1993  decalice.readme

     Location: /systems/amiga/boing/video/pics/gif
        FILE    -rw-rw-r--  109870 bytes  01:00  8 Feb 1993  palice.jpg
archie> bye
# Bye.
Connection closed by foreign host.
```

Notice that every group of information starts off with "Host." That's important, because "Host" is the name of the place that we'd have to go in order to get *Alice.* After the host is a file name. The parts in front of it are exactly *where* the file is. If you're a PC user, you may at first glance think that you recognize the subdirectory usage, but look again! Instead of backslashes (\), which DOS uses to separate subdirectory levels, UNIX uses *forward* slashes (/).

Anyway, now we've found *Alice.* We'll quit Archie by typing **quit**. The message "Connection closed by foreign host" is a message from my computer to me. It says that the Archie computer at Rutgers—which it calls the "foreign host," has stopped talking to me.

Nonstandardization Problems

In general, Telnet works fine with computers of all kinds. But some host computers just plain won't talk to you unless you're an IBM 3270-type dumb terminal, so there is another program, tn3270. tn3270 is a variation of Telnet that emulates an IBM 3270 full-screen terminal. The main things to know about tn3270 are that 3270-type terminals have a *lot* of functions about them. Not all implementations of tn3270 are equal, so don't be totally shocked if you Telnet to an IBM site using tn3270, work for a while, and get a message that says "Unexpected command sequence—program terminated." It means that your tn3270 couldn't handle a command that the IBM host sent it.

IBM terminal emulation can be a real pain in the neck when it comes to key mapping. On the IBM terminal are a set of function keys labeled PF1, PF2, and so on. As there are no such keys on a PC or a Mac, what key should you press to get PF4, for instance? Well, it's Esc-4 on some implementations of tn3270 and F4 on others, and there doesn't seem to be any real agreement on what the key is or what the key should be. Make sure that you have the documentation for your tn3270 nearby before you start telnetting to an IBM host.

TIP   No TN3270 is shipped with NT.

Why Use Telnet?

Summing up this section, what is Telnet good for, anyway? Several things. First, it is the best way to access a number of specialized basic information services. For instance, many large libraries put their entire card catalog on Telnet servers. University researchers can look for an item and request it through an interlibrary loan. The University of Michigan's "geographic server" is another specialized information service. It offers geographic information. Just type the following and you're in:

```
telnet martini.eecs.umich.edu
```

Then you'll see:

```
access% telnet martini.eecs.umich.edu 3000
Trying 141.212.99.9 ...
Connected to martini.eecs.umich.edu.
Escape character is '^]'.
# Geographic Name Server, Copyright 1992 Regents of the Univer-
sity of Michigan.
# Version 8/19/92. Use "help" or "?" for assistance, "info" for
hints.
.
arlington, va 22205
0 Arlington
1 51013 Arlington
2 VA Virginia
3 US United States
R county seat
F 45 Populated place
```

```
L 38 52 15 N 77 06 05 W
E 250
Z 22200 22201 22202 22203 22204 22205 22206 22207 22209 22210
Z 22212 22213 22214 22215 22216 22217 22222 22223 22225 22226
```

Ask the U of M for information about the weather by typing:

```
telnet madlab.sprl.umich.edu 3000
```

and find out whether or not it's raining in Dallas.

A second reason for using Telnet is that some commercial firms offer an online ordering services. You just log on, browse through the descriptions of the items available, and place an order electronically.

A third, somewhat technical, reason for using Telnet is that it can be used as a debugging tool. Using Telnet, I can essentially "impersonate" different applications, like FTP and Mail (you'll meet them soon). That's a bit beyond the scope of this book, but I mention it in passing.

The final reason for Telnet is simply its original reason for existence—remote login to a service on a distant host. That has become a feature of much less value than it was when it first appeared, largely because of the way that we now use computers. Twenty years ago, you would have had a dumb terminal on your desk. Today, you are likely to have a computer on your desk, a computer with more computing power than a mainframe from twenty years ago. We are less interested today in borrowing someone else's computing power than we are in borrowing their information—with their permission, of course. Specifically, we often seek to transfer files to and from other computers over an internet. For that reason, we'll consider another TCP/IP application— FTP, the file transfer protocol—next.

Using FTP for File Transfers

If you have a PC or Macintosh on your desk, think for a moment about how you use your computer in a network situation. You may have a computer elsewhere in your building that acts as a *file server*, a computer that holds the files shared in your facility or your department. How do you ask that server to transfer a file from itself to your computer? You may say, "I don't do that," but you *do*. Whenever you attach to a shared network resource, you ask the system to provide your computer with shared files. How you actually *ask* for them is very simple: You just connect to a server, which looks like an extra folder on your desktop if you're a Mac user, or an extra drive letter, like X or E if you are a PC user.

The Internet world has a facility like that, a facility that lets you attach a distant computer to your computer as if the distant computer were a local drive; it is called NFS, the Network File System. But NFS is relatively recent in the TCP/IP world. It's much more common to attach to a host, browse the files that the host contains, and selectively transfer files to your local host. You do that with FTP, the File Transfer Protocol.

The essentials of FTP include, first of all, how to start it up, then how to navigate around the directories of the FTP server, then how to actually get a file from an FTP server. After that, we'll look at a special kind of FTP called *anonymous* FTP. Let's get started by looking at how the files on an FTP server are organized.

FTP Organization

The first time that you get on an FTP server, you're likely to want to just get right off. FTP, like much of the TCP/IP world, was built with the idea that software should be *functional* and not necessarily pretty or, to use an overused phrase, user-friendly. If you're a PC user, the UNIX file structure of FTP will be somewhat familiar, as the DOS file structure was stolen—I mean, *borrowed*—from UNIX. Mac users will have a bit more trouble.

I just referred to the "UNIX file structure." That's because FTP servers *usually* use UNIX. But some don't, so you may come across FTP servers that seem not to make sense. For the purposes of this discussion, I'll assume that the FTP servers here are UNIX, but again, be aware that you may run into non-UNIX FTP servers. The occasional FTP server runs on a DEC VAX, and such servers usually run the VMS operating system; other servers run on an IBM mainframe, and may be running either MVS or VM. Very rarely, an FTP server runs under DOS, OS/2, NT, or some other PC operating system.

As shown in Figure 13.34, FTP uses a tree-structured directory represented in the UNIX fashion. The top of the directory is called ourfiles and it has two *sub*directories below called ourfiles/bin and ourfiles/text. In the UNIX world, *bin* refers to executable files. We might call these files "program files" in other operating systems; EXE or COM files in the PC world; or "load modules" in the IBM mainframe world.

FIGURE 13.34:

FTP's tree-structured directory

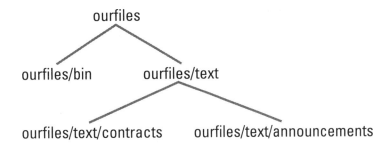

The /text directory contains two directories below it, one called contracts and one called announcements.

A couple of notes here. PC users may think that things look a bit familiar, but there *are* a couple of differences. First, notice the subdirectory named /announcements. That name is more than eight characters long, which is quite acceptable, even though it *isn't acceptable* in the PC world. UNIX accepts file names hundreds of characters long. Second, notice that there are not backslashes (\) between the different levels, but only *forward* slashes (/); that's also a UNIX feature. What complicates matters for users of non-UNIX systems is that FTP pretty much assumes that *your* system uses the UNIX file system as well. That means that you have to get comfortable with traversing *two* directory structures—the one on the remote FTP server, and the one on your local hard disk.

File Navigation

You'll get an FTP command line—I'll demonstrate it in a minute—that expects you to tell it where to get files *from, and* where to put files *to,* using these two commands:

- remote—cd
- local—lcd

You use these commands because there's a tree structure on both the remote system—the one that you're getting the files from—and the local system. Let's look at a few examples to nail down exactly how all this cd-ing works.

Moving in FTP

When I enter an FTP site, I start out at the top of the directory structure, as shown in Figure 13.35. This top is called the "root" of the directory. In the figure, the root is called ourfiles. To move down one level, to ourfiles/text, I could type **cd files**. That says to FTP, "Move down one level relative to the current location." Alternatively, I could skip the relative reference and say absolutely, "Go to ourfiles/text." I would do that by typing **cd /ourfiles/text**. The fact that the entry *starts* with a slash tells cd that your command is not a relative one, but an absolute one.

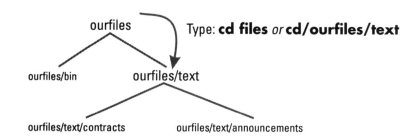

FIGURE 13.35:
Navigating directories

Now let's try moving back up a level. As shown in Figure 13.36, at any point you can back up one level either by typing the command **cdup** or by typing **cd ..** The two periods (..) mean "one level upward" to both DOS and UNIX. You can also do an absolute reference by typing **cd /ourfiles**.

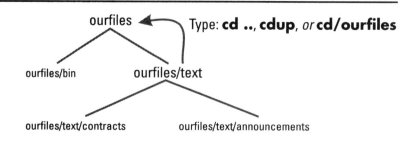

FIGURE 13.36:
Moving back up a level

Suppose I'm all the way at the bottom of this structure. It's a simple three-level directory, and you'll often see directory structures that are a good bit more complex than this one. As shown in Figure 13.37, to move back up from ourfiles/text/announcements to ourfiles/text, you can do as before, and either type **cdup** or **cd ...** Or you could do an absolute reference, as in **cd /ourfiles/text**. To go back *two* levels, you can either issue two separate **cdup** or **cd ..** commands, or use an absolute reference, as in **cd /ourfiles**. To type two **cdup** or **cd ..** commands, you type the command, then press Enter, then type the second command. Do not try to issue two commands on the same line.

FIGURE 13.37:

Moving up more than one level at a time

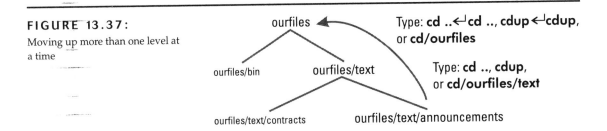

Example Navigation: Go Get Alice

Now that you can navigate the twisty passages of FTP directories, it's a good time to get *Alice*. We found earlier that we could get the *Alice in Wonderland* text at a number of sites. One of those sites was roxette.mty.itesm.mx in the directory pub/next/Literature/Gutenberg/etext91. Let me FTP to that site and get the file. I type **ftp roxette.mty.itesm.mx** at the command prompt, and then I get a Name? prompt. This site doesn't know me, so I can't log on with a local name and password.

And this is where the idea of the *anonymous* FTP becomes useful. You see, you can often log onto an FTP site and download data that's been put there specifically for public use. Anonymous FTP is the same as regular FTP, except that you log in with the name "anonymous." The FTP site responds that a "guest" login is OK, but an e-mail address is needed for a password. I put in my e-mail address and I'm in.

Now, it might be that there are places on this server that I *cannot* get to because I signed on as anonymous, but that doesn't matter—*Alice* is in the public area. Next, I can do a dir command and see what's on this directory. Here's what I see:

```
ftp> dir
200 PORT command successful.
150 Opening ASCII mode data connection for /bin/ls.
total 2009
drwxr-xr-x 2 root     wheel      1024 Jun 2 02:48 .NeXT
drwxr-xr-x 3 ftpadmin daemon     1024 Apr 5 1993 .NextTrash
drwx------ 2 ftpadmin other      1024 May 20 22:46 .elm
-rw------- 1 ftpadmin other      1706 Sep 21 08:04 .history
-rwxr-x--- 1 ftpadmin wheel       186 Jul 21 1992 .login
-rwxr-x--- 1 ftpadmin wheel       238 Feb 25 1991 .profile
-rw-r--r-- 1 ftpadmin wheel        27 May 20 22:53 .rhosts
-rw-r----- 1 ftpadmin wheel       589 Jun 9 1992 .tcshrc
-rw-r--r-- 1 ftpadmin wheel   2027520 Oct 2 22:17 IRC.tar
drwx------ 2 ftpadmin other      1024 May 20 22:46 Mail
drwxr-xr-x 2 ftpadmin wheel      1024 May 29 1992 bin
drwxr-xr-x 3 ftpadmin wheel      1024 Nov 11 1992 etc
drwxr-x--- 2 ftpadmin wheel      1024 May 19 01:31 mirror
drwxr-xr-x 6 root     wheel      4096 Jul 15 00:36 pub
226 Transfer complete.
863 bytes received in 0.6 seconds (1.4 Kbytes/s)
ftp> cd pub
250 CWD command successful.
ftp> dir
200 PORT command successful.
150 Opening ASCII mode data connection for /bin/ls.
total 20
drwxrwxrwt 6 root     daemon     4096 Jun 10 15:58 .NextTrash
-rw-r----- 1 jleon    wheel       205 May 29 02:42 .dir3_0.wmd
drwxr-xr-x 5 ftpadmin other      4096 May 19 01:47 X11R5
drwxrwxrwt 3 ftpadmin other      4096 Sep 26 03:04 incoming
drwxr-xr-x 20 ftpadmin other     4096 Oct 6 02:29 next
```

It's not a very pretty sight, but let's see what we can see. Notice all the *r*'s, *x*'s, *w*'s, and *d*'s to the left of each entry. They represent the privilege levels of access to this file. One of the important things is whether or not the leftmost letter is a *d*. If it is, then that's not a file, it's a directory. Notice that entry *pub*; it's a directory, but we already knew that, because archie told us that we'd find *Alice* in the directory pub/next/Literature/Gutenberg/etext91.

I have to move to that directory to ftp it, so I type:

```
cd pub/next/Literature/Gutenberg/etext91
```

Notice that there are no spaces except between the *cd* and the directory name. Notice also that, in general, you must be careful about capitalization—if the directory's name is Literature with a capital *L*, trying to change to a directory whose name is literature with a lowercase *l* will probably fail. Why? It's another UNIX thing; the UNIX file system is case-sensitive. In contrast, if you found yourself talking to an OS/2-based TCP/IP host, case would be irrelevant. How do you know what your host runs? Well, it is sometimes announced in the sign-on message, but not always. The best bet is to always assume that case is important.

Anyway, once I get to the directory, another dir command shows me what's in it:

```
ftp> dir
200 PORT command successful.
150 Opening ASCII mode data connection for /bin/ls.
total 7940
-r--r--r--  1 ftpadmin wheel       885 May 1 1992 AAINDEX.NEW.Z
-r--r--r--  1 ftpadmin wheel       885 May 1 1992 INDEX.NEW.Z
-r--r--r--  1 ftpadmin wheel       876 May 1 1992 INDEX91.Z
-r--r--r--  1 ftpadmin wheel      1170 Oct 2 07:01 Index
-r--r--r--  1 ftpadmin wheel      8575 May 1 1992 LIST.COM.Z
-r--r--r--  1 ftpadmin wheel      8917 May 1 1992 README.Z
-r--r--r--  1 ftpadmin wheel     98605 May 1 1992 aesop10.txt.Z
-r--r--r--  1 ftpadmin wheel    101607 May 1 1992 aesop10.zip
-r--r--r--  1 ftpadmin wheel     67597 May 1 1992 alice29.txt.Z
-r--r--r--  1 ftpadmin wheel     64809 May 1 1992 alice29.zip
-r--r--r--  1 ftpadmin wheel    435039 May 1 1992 feder11.txt.Z
-r--r--r--  1 ftpadmin wheel    463269 May 1 1992 feder11.zip
-r--r--r--  1 ftpadmin wheel     14841 May 1 1992 highways.apl.Z
-r--r--r--  1 ftpadmin wheel     79801 May 1 1992 hisong10.txt.Z
-r--r--r--  1 ftpadmin wheel     75310 May 1 1992 hisong10.zip
-r--r--r--  1 ftpadmin wheel     75541 May 1 1992 lglass16.txt.Z
-r--r--r--  1 ftpadmin wheel     73128 May 1 1992 lglass16.zip
-r--r--r--  1 ftpadmin wheel    606033 May 1 1992 moby.zip
-r--r--r--  1 ftpadmin wheel    530686 May 1 1992 mormon12.txt.Z
-r--r--r--  1 ftpadmin wheel    529476 May 1 1992 mormon12.zip
-r--r--r--  1 ftpadmin wheel    129601 May 1 1992 opion10.txt.Z
-r--r--r--  1 ftpadmin wheel    138296 May 1 1992 opion10.zip
-r--r--r--  1 ftpadmin wheel    203785 May 1 1992 plboss10.txt.Z
-r--r--r--  1 ftpadmin wheel    219257 May 1 1992 plboss10.zip
-r--r--r--  1 ftpadmin wheel    206661 May 1 1992 plrabn10.txt.Z
```

```
-r--r--r-- 1 ftpadmin wheel   221387 May 1 1992 plrabn10.zip
-r--r--r-- 1 ftpadmin wheel   621855 May 1 1992 roget11.txt.Z
-r--r--r-- 1 ftpadmin wheel   592247 May 1 1992 roget11.zip
-r--r--r-- 1 ftpadmin wheel   657390 May 1 1992 roget12.zip
-r--r--r-- 1 ftpadmin wheel    19790 May 1 1992 snark12.txt.Z
-r--r--r-- 1 ftpadmin wheel    17184 May 1 1992 snark12.zip
-r--r--r-- 1 ftpadmin wheel   789836 May 1 1992 world11.txt.Z
-r--r--r-- 1 ftpadmin wheel   825269 May 1 1992 world11.zip
226 Transfer complete.
2214 bytes received in 1.4 seconds (1.5 Kbytes/s)
```

These are the files from Project Gutenberg. They include *Moby Dick, Alice in Wonderland, The Book of Mormon, The Hunting of the Snark, Roget's Thesaurus,* and more. Notice the *Alice in Wonderland* file is offered in two ways, as alice29.zip and alice29.txt.z. The zip extension usually means that it has been compressed using the PKZIP algorithm on an MS-DOS system. The UNIX counterpart to that is a file ending simply in z, as in alice29.txt.z. It can be uncompressed with the gzip program that you can find on many libraries.

More specifically, suppose you download alice29.zip to a PC. If you tried to look at the file, it would look like gibberish. That's because the file is compressed and must be uncompressed before it can be viewed. It was compressed so that there would be fewer bytes to transfer around the network; after all, this *is* a book, and you don't want to clog up the network with millions of bytes when thousands can do the job. You'd transfer this to your PC, and then you'd use an unzip program to uncompress the file. But the file that ends with z, the one done with gzip, can be unzipped *while it's being transferred*! Suppose you don't have a copy of either pkunzip or gzip and you don't want to have to mess around with finding an unzip program. All you would need do is to request the file not as alice29.txt.z, but as alice29.txt. The ftp program is smart enough to know that it should uncompress the file as it transfers it to your machine! A pretty neat feature, I'd say.

Before we get the *Alice in Wonderland* file, there's one more thing that I should point out. Years ago, most files were transferred as plain ASCII text. Nowadays, many files are *not* ASCII—even data files created by spreadsheets and word processors contain data other than simple text. Such files are, as you probably know, called *binary* files. ftp must be alerted if you want to transfer binary files. You do that by just typing **binary** at the ftp> prompt. FTP responds by saying:

```
Type set to I
```

That is FTP's inimitable way of saying that it's now ready to do a binary file transfer, or, as FTP calls it, an "image" file transfer.

Transferring a File

Now let's get the file. Here is how you do it:

```
access% ftp roxette.mty.itesm.mx
Connected to roxette.mty.itesm.mx.
220 roxette FTP server (Version 5.20 (NeXT 1.0) Sun Nov 11, 1990)
ready.
Name (roxette.mty.itesm.mx:mminasi): anonymous
331 Guest login ok, send ident as password.
Password:
230 Guest login ok, access restrictions apply.
ftp> cd pub/next/Literature/Gutenberg/etext91
250 CWD command successful.
ftp> binary
200 Type set to I.
ftp> get alice29.zip
200 PORT command successful.
150 Opening BINARY mode data connection for alice29.zip (64809
bytes).
226 Transfer complete.
local: alice29.zip remote: alice29.zip
64809 bytes received in 16 seconds (4 Kbytes/s)
ftp> bye
221 Goodbye.
access%
```

Notice that once I got the file, the system reported some throughput statistics.

It takes some time to transfer a file. And no nice bar graphic or anything like it appears to clue us about how far the transfer has proceeded. There *is* a command called hash, however, that gives you *some* idea about how the transfer is progressing. Type **hash** and, from that point on, the system prints a pound sign (#) for each 2K that is transferred. For example, say I'm on a Gutenberg system and I want to download the *Bible*, bible10.zip. (Is it sacrilegious to compress the *Bible*? Interesting theological question.) The file is about 1600K in size, so I'll see 800 pound signs. Along the way, the screen may look like Figure 13.38.

```
total 7904
-r--r--r--  1 24      wheel          885 May  1 1992 AAINDEX.NEW.Z
-r--r--r--  1 24      wheel          972 Jun 15 07:01 Index
-r--r--r--  1 24      wheel          486 May  9 1992 Index.Z
-r--r--r--  1 24      wheel         8575 May  1 1992 LIST.COM.Z
-r--r--r--  1 24      wheel        34991 May  1 1992 aesopa10.txt.Z
-r--r--r--  1 24      wheel        32091 May  1 1992 aesopa10.zip
-r--r--r--  1 24      wheel      1647999 May  1 1992 bible10.txt.Z
-r--r--r--  1 24      wheel      1636512 May  1 1992 bible10.zip
-r--r--r--  1 24      wheel        13831 May  1 1992 census00.txt.Z
-r--r--r--  1 24      wheel       337341 May  1 1992 crowd10.txt.Z
-r--r--r--  1 24      wheel       359641 May  1 1992 crowd10.zip
-r--r--r--  1 24      wheel       333327 May  1 1992 crowd13.txt.Z
-r--r--r--  1 24      wheel       358371 May  1 1992 crowd13.zip
-r--r--r--  1 24      wheel       101227 May  1 1992 duglas10.txt.Z
-r--r--r--  1 24      wheel       102886 May  1 1992 duglas10.zip
-r--r--r--  1 24      wheel       132013 May 11 1992 hrlnd10.txt.Z
-r--r--r--  1 24      wheel       136293 May 11 1992 hrlnd10.zip
-r--r--r--  1 24      wheel        99063 May  1 1992 oedip10.txt.Z
-r--r--r--  1 24      wheel       103284 May  1 1992 oedip10.zip
-r--r--r--  1 24      wheel       129601 May  1 1992 opion10.txt.Z
-r--r--r--  1 24      wheel       138296 May  1 1992 opion10.zip
-r--r--r--  1 24      wheel       206661 May  1 1992 plrabn10.txt.Z
-r--r--r--  1 24      wheel       221387 May  1 1992 plrabn10.zip
-r--r--r--  1 24      wheel        59233 May  1 1992 uscen90.txt.Z
-r--r--r--  1 24      wheel        38665 May  1 1992 uscen90.zip
-r--r--r--  1 24      wheel       880992 May  1 1992 world91a.txt.Z
-r--r--r--  1 24      wheel       912325 May  1 1992 world91a.zip

226 Transfer complete.
1790 bytes received in 2.87 seconds (0.62 Kbytes/sec)
ftp> get bible10.zip
200 PORT command successful.
150 Opening BINARY mode data connection for bible10.zip (1636512 bytes).
#################################################################
```

Each line shows me 80 characters, so each line of pound sign characters means 160K of data has been transferred. It will take ten lines of pound characters (*ten lines!*) before the entire file is transferred. (Why does this take so long on my system? Well, the Internet is pretty fast, but my connection to it is just a simple v.32 bis modem. My company is part of the information superhighway, but we're kind of an unimproved country road.)

FTP: A Quick Review

Let's review what we've seen so far. First, you use the FTP program to log onto a remote system, in a manner similar to telnetting onto a remote system. In fact, some people have trouble understanding why there's a difference between Telnet and FTP. Telnet is for terminal emulation into another facility's computing power; FTP is for transferring files to and from another facility's computers. Once you FTP to another site, you'll usually find files organized into a set of directories in a tree structure. You move FTP's attention from one directory to another with the cd command. You may have a tree-structured directory on your system; if you wish to tell FTP to transfer to or from a particular directory, you use the "local" cd command, or lcd. You use the "binary" command to tell FTP that you want to transfer files with their program-related code intact. The get command requests that the remote system give you a file, and, although I haven't mentioned it yet, the put command requests that the remote system *accept* a file from you. And that's the basics of FTP, the File Transfer Protocol.

To get more information about FTP commands, double-click on the Windows NT Help icon in the Main program group. Click on the Command Reference Help button, click the FTP command's name, and choose the FTP command name for which you want more information.

Downloading to the Screen

Let's go to *another* Gutenberg site to illustrate another helpful tip. Earlier when I was using Archie I noticed a location that had an *Alice* called ftp.wustl.edu. Let's see what *they've* got—maybe a newer version, perhaps? Now, I know that you're thinking: "A newer version of *Alice in Wonderland*? Isn't Lewis Carroll dead?" Well, yes, Mr. Dodson is long gone, but the text is typed in by volunteers, and mistakes creep in.

First we get off this current FTP site by typing **BYE**. That command may vary, but it seems pretty standard for most of the FTP and Telnet world. Again, it informs me that I'm disconnected from the roxette site. I'll FTP to ftp.wustl.edu now. Again, I'm doing an *anonymous* FTP, so I type in the user name **anonymous**—in lowercase, remember—and use my e-mail address mminasi@access.digex.net as the password. You don't see that because the password doesn't echo. I get the usual chatter, and then I'm in.

Now, Archie told me that *Alice* was in mirrors/misc/books, so I cd over there by typing **cd mirrors/misc/books** and type **dir** to see what's there:

```
ftp> dir
200 PORT command successful.
150 Opening ASCII mode data connection for /bin/ls.
total 12060
-rw-r--r--  1 root     archive      3110 May  1  18:00 00-index.txt
-rw-r--r--  1 root     archive    552711 Apr 16  18:00 2sqrt10.zip
-rw-r--r--  1 root     archive    102164 Jun 15  1992 aesop11.zip
-rw-r--r--  1 root     archive     32091 Jun 18  1992 aesopa10.zip
-rw-r--r--  1 root     archive     15768 Apr 16  18:00 alad10.zip
-rw-r--r--  1 root     archive     64809 Jun 15  1992 alice29.zip
-rw-r--r--  1 root     archive    244863 Dec  2  1992 anne10.zip
-rw-r--r--  1 root     archive   1636512 Jun 18  1992 bible10.zip
```

```
-rw-r--r--   1 root     archive   358371 Jun 18 1992 crowd13.zip
-rw-r--r--   1 root     archive    50736 Apr 16 18:00 dcart10.zip
-rw-r--r--   1 root     archive   102460 Jun 18 1992 duglas11.zip
-rw-r--r--   1 root     archive   467260 Jun 15 1992 feder15.zip
-rw-r--r--   1 root     archive    78337 Jun 15 1992 hisong12.zip
-rw-r--r--   1 root     archive   136293 Jun 18 1992 hrlnd10.zip
-rw-r--r--   1 root     archive    70714 Oct 23 1992 hyde10.zip
-rw-r--r--   1 root     archive    69860 Oct 23 1992 hyde10a.zip
-rw-r--r--   1 root     archive   176408 Apr 16 18:00 iland10.zip
-rw-r--r--   1 root     archive    73128 Jun 15 1992 lglass16.zip
-rw-r--r--   1 root     archive   149481 Apr 16 18:00 locet10.zip
-rw-r--r--   1 root     archive   606033 Jun 15 1992 moby.zip
-rw-r--r--   1 root     archive   513720 Jun 15 1992 mormon13.zip
-rw-r--r--   1 root     archive    11579 Apr 16 18:00 nren210.zip
-rw-r--r--   1 root     archive   103284 Jun 18 1992 oedip10.zip
-rw-r--r--   1 root     archive    95167 Apr 16 18:00 ozland10.zip
-rw-r--r--   1 root     archive   692080 Apr 16 18:00 pimil10.zip
-rw-r--r--   1 root     archive   217770 Jun 15 1992 plboss11.zip
-rw-r--r--   1 root     archive   214541 Jun 18 1992 plrabn11.zip
-rw-r--r--   1 root     archive    44204 Apr 16 18:00 rgain10.zip
-rw-r--r--   1 root     archive   580335 Jun 15 1992 roget13.zip
-rw-r--r--   1 root     archive   643011 Jun 15 1992 roget13a.zip
-rw-r--r--   1 root     archive   222695 Jun 30 1992 scrlt10.zip
-rw-r--r--   1 root     archive    35695 Oct 23 1992 sleep10.zip
-rw-r--r--   1 root     archive    17184 Jun 15 1992 snark12.zip
-rw-r--r--   1 root     archive    26009 Apr 16 18:00 surf10.zip
-rw-r--r--   1 root     archive    84641 Jul 31 1992 timem10.zip
-rw-r--r--   1 root     archive    38665 Jun 18 1992 uscen90.zip
-rw-r--r--   1 root     archive    63270 Aug 24 1992 uscen902.zip
-rw-r--r--   1 root     archive   161767 Jul 31 1992 warw10.zip
-rw-r--r--   1 root     archive    79409 Apr 16 18:00 wizoz10.zip
-rw-r--r--   1 root     archive   798086 Jun 15 1992 world12.zip
-rw-r--r--   1 root     archive   724062 Apr 16 18:00 world192.zip
-rw-r--r--   1 root     archive   912325 Jun 18 1992 world91a.zip
-rw-r--r--   1 root     archive   712389 Apr 16 18:00 world92.zip
-rw-r--r--   1 root     archive    71459 Jun 30 1992 zen10.zip
226 Transfer complete.
3008 bytes received in 0.34 seconds (8.6 Kbytes/s)
```

What's there? A whole bunch of things! There's a file up top called 00-index.txt that looks like it could tell me what's going on. I *could* just "get" this file, but think what a pain that would be. After I get the file, I disconnect from ftp.wustl.edu. Then I examine the file with a text editor. A lot of work just to find out what's in a readme file.

Here's a trick you can use to see a file—just "get" it, but get it to your screen! You do that by typing:

```
get filename -
```

and pressing Enter, as I'll do here: **get 00-index.txt -**. The file zips by, so it's a good thing that I have the ability to scroll text back.

But what if I *didn't* have the ability to scroll text back? Then I could make the remote FTP program *pause* by adding

```
"¦ more"
```

You need quotes around the vertical bar and the *more*, so in my case I'd type:

```
get 00-index.txt - "¦more"
```

You can usually freeze a screen temporarily by pressing Ctrl-S for stop; start it up again with Ctrl-Q.

A lot depends on the system that you're working with, but it may only be possible to do this "get" and "more" if your FTP session is set for ASCII transfers rather than binary transfers. You change that by just typing **ascii** at the command line. You'll see the response:

```
type set to A
```

That's about all that I'll say here about FTP. There is lots and lots more that FTP can do, but I've given you the basics that you can use to get started and get some work done in the TCP/IP world. If this all looks ugly, user-unfriendly, and hard to re-member—well it *is*, at least to someone used to a Macintosh or Windows. But there's no reason why a graphical FTP program couldn't exist, and indeed some are appearing. FTP is two things: the FTP protocol, which is the set of rules that the computers on an Internet use to communicate, and the program *called* FTP that you start up in order to do file transfers. The FTP *protocol* doesn't change, and probably won't change. But the FTP *program*, which is usually known as the FTP *client*, can be as easy-to-use as its designer wants. So go on out, learn to spell *anonymous*, and have some fun on those FTP sites! But there's more to an internet than files, which is why we'll next look at electronic mail.

E-Mail on TCP/IP

Computers all by themselves are little more than glorified calculators. Hooking up computers via networks is what has really made computers useful, and of course networks are a big part of communications. But networks are of no value unless people use them—and people won't use them without a reason.

This brings me to electronic mail. E-mail is often the "gateway" application for people, the first computer application that they ever use; for some people, it's the *only* application that they ever use. And e-mail is probably the most important thing running on the Internet.

Even though mail is probably the single most important application on the Internet, I actually don't have too much to say about it here, because Microsoft doesn't ship much in the way of mail tools. Mail on the Internet is implemented in two pieces. First, there's the mail transfer unit, or MTU. Then, there's the mail client.

The most common MTU is a program called sendmail. Again, there is no NT version of sendmail, so you'll have to route mail with either a third-party product or a mail router run on top of another operating system. The same is true of mail clients, although Microsoft offers an Internet mail-compatible module for their Microsoft Mail product.

How E-Mail Works

The Internet mail system, like other parts of the Internet, uses a hop-by-hop approach to transferring data from one place to another. You learned earlier that IP transfers data via packet switching, a method that allows the Internet to move data from one point to another in under a second, even if the data is being transferred from one side of the globe to the other. With mail, in contrast, entire messages get sent from one node to the next, and are *stored* at each intermediate node until received by the next node. The hops may take minutes or even hours, but usually don't take more than a day.

You've met Telnet and FTP so far; they are the older protocols in the Internet. In the case of both Telnet and FTP, there are two meanings for the words. There is a Telnet *protocol*, as well as a program called the *Telnet client* that allows you to use the Telnet protocol to do remote logins. Similarly, FTP is both a protocol that describes how to transfer a file and a program called an *FTP client* that uses the FTP protocol to transfer files.

By the time that mail arrived, it was clear that tightly matching protocols and clients wasn't such a good idea, as it robbed the system of flexibility. So the mail protocol was developed, and a mail client appeared, but these aren't the only mail clients used. In fact, there is probably no one mail client that is used by most people. The mail protocol, by the way, is called SMTP, the Simple Mail Transfer Protocol. Clients vary widely in that they can be graphical, textual, very easy to work with, and sometimes extremely primitive.

E-Mail Security Concerns

As the Internet grows, more and more gateways will be built to other e-mail systems. You can't get everywhere, but in time you'll be able to reach anyone from the Internet. That's a good thing, but as e-mail becomes more important, it is essential to keep your mind on the fact that e-mail is *not secure*. Your mail packets get bounced all around the Internet, as you know. Think about what that means. When you send a message to someone on the Internet, your mail can sit in intermediate computers like mine, *on the hard disk*, for seconds, minutes, or hours at a time. It's a simple matter for any number of utility programs to peek into the mail queue on the mail that's "just passing through." *Never* say anything on mail that you don't want to be public knowledge. Even if no one peeks at your mail, if you mail is backed up to a disk, it may sit on magnetic media for years in some archive.

I sometimes imagine that in the middle of the twenty-first century we'll see "the unpublished letters of Douglas Adams"—e-mail notes that someone stumbles across while picking through some 70-year-old backups. It will be the latter-day equivalent of going through some dead celebrity's trash. Anyway, the bottom line is: Don't write anything that you wouldn't want your boss, your spouse, your parents, or your kids to read.

In this chapter, you've been introduced to internets and the Internet, the underlying whys and wherefores, and you have a little insight into why using the TCP/IP protocol suite in your business is an efficient, intelligent, money-saving thing. You should also now be equipped to go out and Telnet to foreign lands, to FTP megabytes of data treasures, and to talk to friends and associates far and near with mail. Internet vets call Internet exploration "surfing the net"—the surf's never been up like this, even if your company's internet doesn't connect to *the* Internet.

CHAPTER

FOURTEEN

Tuning and Monitoring Your NT Server Network

Even without any tuning, NT Server usually offers better performance than LAN Manager. But a little adjustment can increase the responsiveness of your NT server. All networks are built out of components from many vendors. Only with a systematic approach (and a few tools) can you hope to track down network failures. This chapter offers a simple, down-to-earth approach to network troubleshooting that will get you the fewest network problems for the least money.

Using the Performance Monitor

NT comes with a quick-and-easy way to keep track of what's happening on your servers—the Performance Monitor. Learning to use the Performance Monitor correctly is useful if you want to reduce the amount of work you have to do to maintain the network.

The Performance Monitor can:

- Log minima, maxima, and averages of critical system values
- Send alerts to you (or any other network member) when important events occur on the network
- Provide a simple, visual view of your network's "vital signs"

Start up the Performance Monitor and you'll see a screen like the one in Figure 14.1. The Performance Monitor comes up by default in Chart mode. There is also a Report mode, an Alert mode, and a Log mode.

Charting with the Performance Monitor

Start out in the Performance Monitor with the Chart mode. Click Edit and then Add to Chart…, and you'll get a multitude of things that you can monitor. Let's pick an easy one to start with. How many bytes per second is the server processing? Once you click Edit and Add to Chart…, you'll see a dialog box like Figure 14.2.

FIGURE 14.1:
Performance Monitor dialog box

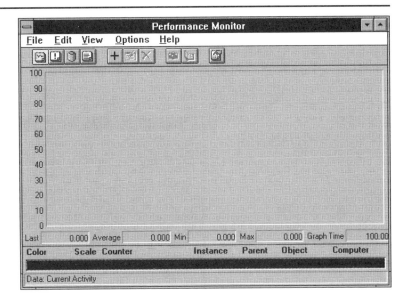

FIGURE 14.2:
Add to Chart dialog box

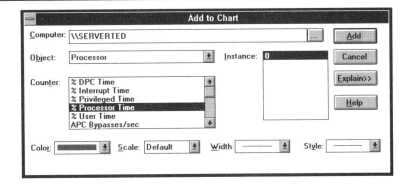

The Object drop-down list box lets you select the general area of items to monitor. The first one, which you can see in the dialog box, is the object Processor, a collection of information about your server's processor. Information is categorized as %Privileged Time, %Processor Time, %User Time, or Interrupts/sec. Each of these particular pieces of information is called a *counter* and is listed in the Counter box. For example, the piece of information that reports how many interrupts per second the system experiences (Interrupts/sec.) is a counter.

Pull down the Object list box and choose the Server object. Now the Counter box shows the Bytes Total/sec counter. Click on the Add button. The Cancel button will be renamed "Done." Click the Done button and you'll see a screen like the one in Figure 14.3. This will give you some idea of how busy your server is.

FIGURE 14.3:

Performance Monitor–Bytes Total/sec on EISA Server

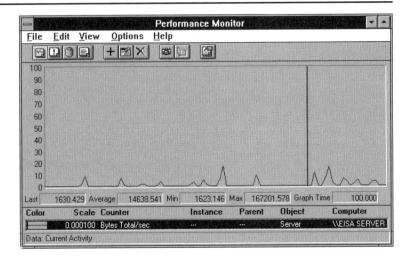

Notice that this server isn't terribly busy. But minimize the Performance Monitor, do some things, and come back to it later—after all, NT *is* a multitasking system, and it can do several things at once. Return to it after a while and you'll see Last (most recent bytes/second value), Average, Min (minimum value over the sampling period), and Max.

Server bytes/second is one of the basic counters that tells you how busy your server is. Other counters include:

- Percentage of processor utilization (object Processor, counter %Processor Time), which tell you how CPU-bound the server is.

- Pages swapped in and out (object Memory, counter Pages/sec), which shows you how frequently the server is swapping information from memory to disk. If this happens a lot, you know that you're running short of RAM and you might want to add more to your server.

Additionally, you can monitor *several* servers at the same time. In Figure 14.4, I'm monitoring processor utilization on both EISA SERVER and SERVERTED, two servers on our network. A quick look at this figure shows that EISA SERVER is doing a lot more work than is SERVERTED, at least at the moment. But keep the monitor running for a while and you can get the averages and extremes that you need to be able to say that with certainty.

What if SERVERTED is a relative layabout compared to EISA SERVER? Then you might improve performance for EISA SERVER users by moving a few of them over to SERVERTED. ("Moving a few of them" means move the directories that they use. As their data moves, they'll follow it.)

FIGURE 14.4:
Performance Monitor—EISA
SERVER and SERVERTED

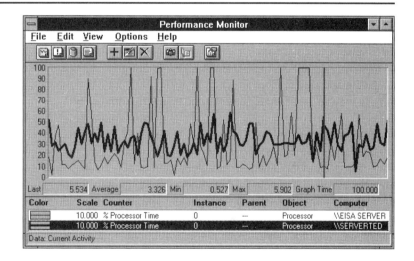

Tracking CPU Hogs with a Histogram

Suppose you find that your CPU is being driven to high-percentage utilization levels. Wouldn't it be nice to find out *what program* on the CPU is doing all the CPU hogging? You can do that with the Performance Monitor.

First, switch the Chart mode to a histogram. Click Options, then Chart…. You'll see a dialog box like the one in Figure 14.5. Under Gallery, click the Histogram radio button, then click OK to return to the main Performance Monitor window. Next,

FIGURE 14.5:

Chart Options dialog box

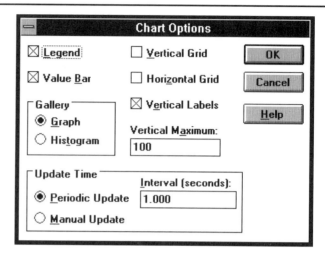

insert the counters for each process in the system. Just click Edit and then Add to Chart..., and choose the Process object. You'll see the Add to Chart dialog box again (see Figure 14.2).

Notice that the Instance list box now names all of the processes active on your computer. One by one, you can click on a process's name in the Instance list box and click Add to add that process to the list of things being monitored.

For example, my server shows the screen in Figure 14.6 when I conduct a complete search of its hard disk. In this particular case, the process named 92 (whatever that is) grabs about 50 percent of the CPU. Where could I use this? Suppose I used an NT Server in a client-server network, and the network bogged down. The machine acting as an application server might have more than one application server program running on it, and I could use this tool to find out which of the server programs was grabbing most of the CPU.

Building Alerts with the Performance Monitor

Another neat thing to be able to keep track of on a server is the amount of free space left on it. If free space gets too low, a LAN disaster may follow. (The counter for free space on the server is part of the object LogicalDisk, with the counter Free Megabytes.)

FIGURE 14.6:

Search for hard disk

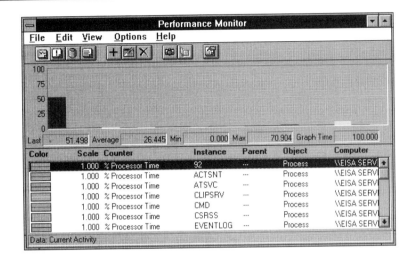

When it comes right down to it, however, you probably don't want to have to *watch* the Performance Monitor to keep an eye on free server space. It would be nice if the server just came and tapped you on the shoulder when its free disk space dropped below some critical value. You control that with Alerts. Click View, then Alert, and the screen will change. Again, you'll have to add Free Megabytes to the list of observed counters, just as you did for the Chart view. The dialog box that you see when you try to add Free Megabytes to the Alert view, however, looks a bit different, as you see in Figure 14.7.

Now there are two new fields—Alert If and Run Program on Alert. I can tell it to alert me if the disk shows less than, say, 87MB free by putting 87 in the text field in the Alert If field and clicking on Under.

What does the system do when it sees less than 87MB free? You control that by clicking Options and then Alert.... You'll see a dialog box that gives you the option of either putting an entry in the system log or of sending a message to either a machine name (like KEYDATA) or a user name (like Mark). Unfortunately, you can specify only one recipient.

Note that alerts are NetBIOS messages, so the Messenger service and the NetBIOS interface must be active on both the alerting machine and the receiving machine.

FIGURE 14.7:

Add to Alert dialog box

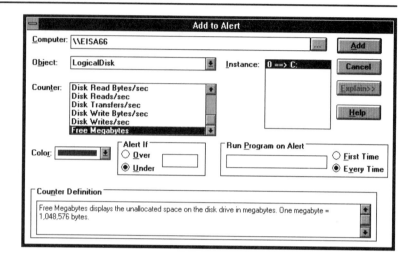

Logging Data for Statistical Reports

Few things that a network administrator can do impress quite as much as those nifty utilization graphs. (Well, better network performance *is* more impressive, but that's why you're reading this book.) By logging statistical information, you can later export the data to a graphing program or spreadsheet for reporting purposes. You can log your counters to disk with the Log View command. The log can then be read into the Performance Viewer later (by choosing Options and Data From…) and examined.

First, choose Log from the View menu. You'll see that you can add items to the log, as with the other views, but you can only specify entire objects to add. That means that if you wanted to view the number of interrupts per minute, for example, you couldn't tell the log to just keep that counter—you'd have to log the entire Processor object.

Then you click Log on the Options menu and give your log file a name. You also tell the Performance Monitor how often to update the log. Finally, you click the Start Log button. (It then becomes a Stop Log button so you can stop the logging process whenever you want. After all, there are lots of spotted owls in the Northwest… Sorry, couldn't resist that logging joke.)

To play back the log, click Options and Data From…. In the dialog box that appears, you can also tell the Performance Monitor to return to displaying real-time data.

Tuning Your System: the Big Four

So your server seems like it's getting a bit slow. Well, the obvious thing to do is to throw money at it, right? Go buy more memory, an extra processor if it's an SMP (Symmetric Multiprocessor) PC; get a faster network card, or a faster disk.

Doing those things will probably get you a faster server. But it's also a good way to throw money down a rat-hole. If your server is spending all of its time waiting for the disk drive, then getting a faster CPU may indeed speed it up—but by a tiny percentage. In that case, your money's better spent on (logically) a faster disk controller.

The big four sources of performance bottlenecks are

- the disk subsystem
- the network card and software
- the CPU
- the memory, which includes the RAM and the disk

People use NT servers either as file servers or as application servers. File servers tend to respond well to speedups in disk and network boards. Application servers tend to respond well to speedups in CPU and memory.

You can use the Performance Monitor to locate the source of your bottlenecks; I'll show you what to do about those bottlenecks.

Solving Disk Bottlenecks

The disk drive has the dubious honor of being a source of bottlenecks both for file servers and for application servers. For file servers, the bottleneck is obvious; grabbing data and slapping it onto the network is what file servers do. For application servers, the problem with the disk subsystem typically stems from the tremendous amount of memory needed to run application server programs; for example, Microsoft recommends 64 MB of RAM for a computer running their Server Management System (SMS). It's simple with SQL Server or Exchange to start banging hard up against the amount of memory that your system has—and when that happens, the system goes after your disk drive for virtual memory.

You can recognize a disk bottleneck in a few ways. Look in the Performance Monitor and watch the object Physical Disk, and the counters Percent Disk Time and Disk Queue Length. If the percent of disk time is getting up over 90 percent, there's a problem. Similarly, if the disk queue length exceeds the value 2, then the disk is a bottleneck.

What can you do about it? First, you can buy some new hardware. Let's see what to buy.

Fast Seek Times

The faster the disk can find data, the less time we spend waiting for it. Drives nowadays have seek times in the single digits; buy them.

Better Data Transfer Rate

Data transfer rate is the province of the disk controller or host adapter. Here are a few features to keep in mind:

- Buy 32-bit SCSI host adapters. Putting a 16-bit host adapter on your server chokes the server's ability to zap data out onto the network.

- Use bus mastering host adapters. There are three methods of getting the data from the host adapter to the computer's memory: programmed input/output (PIO), direct memory access (DMA), and bus mastering. Bus mastering is the fastest of the three. You can only bus master on MCA, EISA, or PCI buses.

- Get host adapters that support asynchronous input/output. Many SCSI-II or SCSI-III host adapters allow multiple drives to work independently. That means you can buy a bunch of drives, hang them off a host adapter, and have all of the drives seeking at the same time. Note that most host adapters don't support this, so getting multiple drives doesn't do anything for your system's speed.

- Create stripe sets with multiple drives. Because a stripe set distributes a disk's data over several drives, reading the data can be quite fast, as all of the physical drives on the stripe set can work in parallel—assuming, of course, that you've got an asynchronous host adapter.

Tuning Network Boards and Drivers

Making your network boards work better is partly accomplished by making the software run better as well. In the Performance Monitor, look in the object Server to ferret out bottlenecks. Look at "Sessions errored out," "work item shortages," "errors system," "pool non-paged failures," "pool paged failures," and "blocking requests rejected."

Rearrange Your Redirectors

If you're running the NetWare redirector in combination with the Microsoft redirector, then you'll see a button in the Network dialog box of the Control Panel. (Actually, it's always there, but it's grayed out unless you've got more than one redirector.) Click it, and you will see both redirectors. You can then use buttons with "up" or "down" arrows on them to highlight a redirector and make it less or more relatively important.

Simplify Protocols

If you're using the TCP/IP stack, you'll find that it sometimes receives short shrift from the network, as the more frenetic IPX and NetBEUI protocols grab more processor attention. As a result, the TCP/IP stack may end up dropping more messages than it would if the other protocols didn't exist; one other symptom is an incomplete browse list. If you can, remove extraneous protocols. If possible, just trim down to TCP/IP.

You can also click on the Bindings… button, select NetBIOS, and choose the order in which the transport protocols are bound to NetBIOS. Basically, you're saying to NetBIOS (which is, recall, a network API, not a protocol), "when you've got a message to send, send it with TCP/IP first; if that doesn't work, use IPX, and then NetBEUI." That's just one example; you can arrange them in any way that you like. If you are using TCP/IP and WINS, then binding NetBIOS to TCP/IP first will greatly reduce broadcasts in your system.

Raise Server Priority

By default, the file server actually has a lower priority than does the print server, causing printing to slow down the server. Printing priority is set by default to 2, and file server priority is set to 1; larger numbers are better. Change that by modifying the Registry. In the current control set, in Services\Lanman\Server\Parameters, add a value entry ThreadPriority, type **DWORD**, and set it to 2.

Modify How Often BDCs Update

All of the chatter between the PDC and the BDCs takes up processor time and network bandwidth. In NT 3.5 and later, you can alter how often the PDC updates the BDCs. By default, that time period is 300 seconds (five minutes), but you can change that in the current control set in Hkey_local_machine\system\CurrentControlSet\Services\Netlogon\pulse. It's of type DWORD, and you can set the value from 60 to 3600 seconds.

Use Interrupt 10

IRQ10 has a slightly higher system priority than does the more commonly used IRQ5, so employ it for your boards when possible.

Enable shared RAM with TCP/IP

While there is no generally accepted benchmark for network performance that is both generic (runs on all networks) and nontrivial, my tests with TCP/IP drivers on Ethernet and Token Ring cards show that if you've got an option to enable shared RAM on your network cards, then you should do it, and use as much as possible.

This does not apply for bus master EISA, PCI, and Micro Channel cards; shared RAM doesn't seem to improve their performance.

Get 32-Bit, Bus Master Network Cards

Get these if you can afford them. You should be *sure* to afford them for your servers. But be sure that NT drivers exist for them.

Watching the CPU

I've already shown you how to build a histogram of the processes running on your server. That will help pinpoint any CPU hogs. You can also look under the object Processor, and watch "percent processor time;" if that's up over 90 percent, you may need more CPU horsepower.

Also, you might keep an eye on Interrupts/Second. If it gets into four digits, then more than likely something's going wrong, either a buggy program or a board spewing out spurious interrupts. And here's a way to sniff out badly designed device drivers: check that Context Switches in the System object stays under 500. If it's higher than that, then the writer of some device driver has built in parts of the driver's code called *critical sections* that are too long.

Remember that there are two ways to make your system faster CPU-wise: either buy a faster CPU, or add another CPU to an existing multiprocessor computer. Think seriously about buying SMP systems for your big servers.

Oh, and by the way—don't run one of the complex screen savers on your server. 3DPipes can chew up over 90 percent of the CPU power of a server. It's doing some heavy-duty calculations.

Managing Memory

NT and NT apps are memory-hungry. Microsoft suggests 32 MB of RAM for a SQL Server machine, and 64 MB for an SMS machine. Even a lowly file server needs 16-plus megabytes. You can literally throw memory at your system for as long as you like, and it will probably find some way to use it. How?

Checking Memory Status

Well, for one thing, NT uses an enormous amount of its memory—up to half of it, in some cases—as a disk cache. Take a look at memory status in the Performance Monitor by looking at the Memory object, committed bytes and pages/second. And make sure that Available Bytes is at least a megabyte.

Committed bytes should be less than actual physical memory, on average. Pages/second should be 5 or under. As you learned in Chapter 6, there is a memory load index in WinMSD; use that to get an indication of how hard your disk is working.

The disk performance counters under NT, by the way, are shipped disabled. To enable them, go to a command line, type `diskperf -y` and press Enter. From that point on, you'll be able to monitor disk usage.

Controlling Virtual Memory

Why am I talking about disk usage in a section on memory? Because NT relies so heavily on virtual memory. If you've supported Windows 3.x, then you probably learned about the paging capability of Windows, a method whereby Windows solves an "out of memory" problem on a computer by using extra *disk* space as if it were RAM space.

If you were a real Windows expert, you knew that Windows had a particularly inefficient virtual memory algorithm, and that your best bet for Windows performance was to just increase your workstation's memory to 16 MB and disable Windows virtual memory altogether.

If you tried to use that logic under Windows NT, you found that Windows NT is quite different: it seems to require at least *some* virtual memory, no matter how much RAM you have. Oddly enough, that's because of the way NT does disk caching—NT will often allocate half of the system's RAM to a disk cache. As a result, NT is often in need of physical memory to allow it to run some program. So it starts paging.

You can adjust memory needs a bit under NT; open the Control Panel and open the Network icon, then double-click on Server, and you'll see a dialog box like Figure 14.8.

Use the following guidelines to set this dialog box:

- If the number of users will be under ten, choose Minimize Memory Used.
- If the number of users will between 10 and 64, choose Balance.
- For more than 64 users, choose Maximize Throughput for File Sharing.
- On a client-server application server machine, choose Maximize Throughput for Network Application.

The most time-consuming part about the paging process is going out and finding a place to put the data on the disk. So NT preallocates a large block of disk into an area that it gives a file name, pagefile.sys. This is a contiguous area of disk. You see, having a contiguous area of disk to work with allows NT to bypass the file system and do direct hardware disk reads and writes. (Remember, this is the kernel—ring 0—so it can do direct hardware access.)

You control the amount of preallocated space on disk via the Control Panel; just click System/Virtual Memory, and you'll see a dialog box like Figure 14.9.

FIGURE 14.8:

Configuring Server memory usage

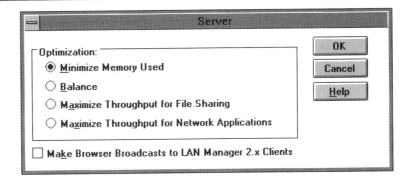

FIGURE 14.9:

Establishing Virtual Memory settings

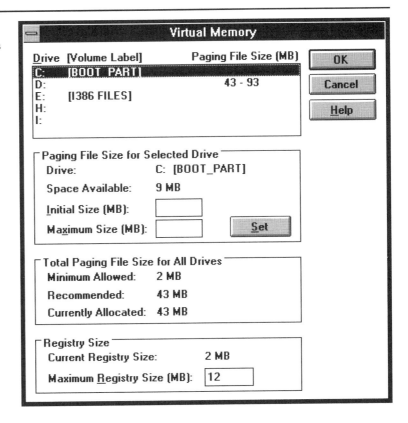

The pagefile.sys file starts out on a 16 MB machine at 27 MB. NT knows that it can get to up to 27 MB of disk space with direct hardware reads and writes.

NT also has, of course, physical memory that it can access. But how much? Despite all the grumbling that I (and many others) have done about NT's memory requirements, it's really not bad. NT 3.5x can run on a machine in about 5.5 MB. That's the part of NT that cannot be paged out to disk.

> **TIP** You can find out how much memory on an application can't be paged with an application called PMON, which ships with the Resource Kit.

Now, if I've got a 16 MB machine, that leaves 10.5 MB of free RAM for NT to play with. Add the 10.5 (let's call it 11 for simplicity's sake) to the 27 MB of pagefile.sys space, and NT's got 38 MB of working room, or, as the Performance Monitor would refer to it, we'd say that NT on my machine has a 38 MB "commit limit." If the sum of the programs that NT is running (called the "working set") remains at about 38 MB or less, then NT need not enlarge the paging file.

If, on the other hand, NT must get to more memory, then it can expand the paging file, albeit at a cost of time. The paging file can grow up to 77 MB on my system, meaning that NT can run up to 77 plus 11 or 88 MB of programs on this system before it runs out of memory.

Once NT starts enlarging the paging file, it may not enlarge it *enough*. That leads to a kind of "sawtooth" size of the paging file, as NT continues to "go back to the well" for more space until it finally runs out of space.

You can avoid this by keeping an eye on the commit limit on your machine. Add the counters Commit Limit and Committed Bytes to the Performance Monitor, and watch the difference between them. When the committed bytes exceed the commit limit, NT must increase the page file size. If you're interested in seeing the size of the things that won't be paged, add the counter Pool Nonpaged Bytes.

One suggestion would be to log the committed bytes over a period of a few weeks with the Performance Monitor, then note the maximum value that the Performance Monitor reports. Increase that by some small amount—10 or 20 percent—and make your NT system's minimum pagefile that size.

Speeding Up Memory

You can't speed up RAM, but you can speed up the disks that virtual memory sits on. As with disks, just get fast drives and drive controllers. Get multiple drives and spread the pagefile out across drives—but *don't* put the pagefile on a stripe set; you won't get any performance improvement like that.

Defragment the drive that the pagefile sits on, run NTFS, and you'll just squeeze the maximum out of your virtual memory.

Reducing Memory Requirements

Unfortunately, the best way to improve NT's memory hunger is to cut down on the features that you use. Optional memory-hungry features include

- RAS
- TCP/IP support
- RAID

The other things that really chew up memory are the applications that you may run on your NT Server as applications servers, like SQL Server: that's got a recommended memory amount of *32 MB* of RAM on the server.

One thing to look at, however, is the list of services. NT starts up a lot of services that you may not need. If your server doesn't have a printer, then the Spooler service is unnecessary. If all of your storage devices are SCSI, check to see if the ATDISK—the IDE interface—is active. In both cases, you can shut down a service or device. Even better, get rid of any protocols you're not using any more; they can be memory-hungry.

Tuning the Kernel

NT is an operating system and, like all multitasking operating systems, it offers a number of tuning options. This section discusses multitasking, virtual memory, and reducing memory requirements.

Multitasking

Go to the Control Panel and open the System icon. Click Tasking... and you'll see the dialog box shown in Figure 14.10. On an NT Server, you definitely do *not* want to check the Best Foreground Application Response Time option. No one's going to run applications on your NT server anyway, and if someone does, it's probably just the administrator fooling around with the network so there is no need to slow everybody else down. Check the Foreground and Background Applications Equally Responsive box. Essentially, it says, "Don't give any special treatment to the foreground applications."

Understanding and Troubleshooting Browsers

Back in Chapter 2, I introduced the concept of browsers and browsing. Browsing is significant in that it can slow down your workstation's response time and clog your network with unnecessary traffic.

In case you've forgotten, browsing is a method whereby servers on the network tell a computer called the master browser who they are and what they offer to the users

---

FIGURE 14.10:

Tasking dialog box

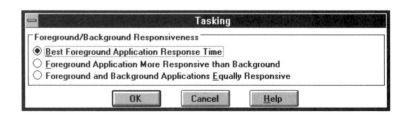

of the network. The browsing service in Microsoft enterprise networks makes it possible for a workstation to see what the network has to offer. A few specifics about browsing:

- The master browser designates one backup browser for about every fifteen computers.
- If you run multiple transport protocols, each transport protocol needs its own set of browsers.
- Backup browsers re-verify their database with the master browser every 15 minutes.
- Servers first announce their existence to the master browser, then they reannounce their existence periodically. Eventually they "settle down" to announcing themselves only once every 12 minutes.

Electing a Master Browser

If there is no master browser, an *election* is held to determine what computer would be the best master browser. Elections are held when the master browser is powered down gracefully; consequently, if the master browser is just turned off, it may take a while (almost an hour in some cases) before another one becomes active.

If you're not a master browser, you're either a backup browser or a potential browser, or else you've opted out of the whole election process. (I'll show you how to do that in a minute.) Backup browse servers also help remove some of the load from the master browser, since they can respond to browse requests.

When an election occurs, the master browser is chosen with a scoring system that works like this:

- NT Servers beat NT workstations 3.5 and 3.1, which beat everything else (Windows for Workgroups clients or LAN Manager servers).
- If there is a tie, the election goes to the *primary domain controller*. I haven't yet introduced the primary domain controller, but it's the computer that keeps all the account records for your network.
- If there still is a tie, the election goes to a Preferred Master (a setting you can make on a computer running NT).

- If there is still a tie but one of the candidates is a workstation that has its MaintainServerList (explained in a few paragraphs) parameter set to Yes, the election goes to the workstation.

- If after all this there still is a tie, the election goes to the present backup browser.

If you want to find out which computer is the master browser on your NT Server-based network, use the BROWMON.EXE program that comes with the Windows NT Resource Kit. When I start it up, I get an opening screen like the partial screen shot in Figure 14.11. This screen shows that the master browser is \\SERVERTED. Transport in the dialog box refers to the transport layer used—NetBEUI, TCP/IP, or IPX/SPX. (DLC can't be used for anything other than printing services, and it doesn't work peer-to-peer, so there is no DLC browse master.) Essentially, this dialog box says, "\\SERVERTED is the browser for everyone speaking English on the network." This network could simultaneously support people speaking Greek, Spanish, or Urdu, but the people speaking Urdu wouldn't be able to understand the browser broadcasts of the English speakers. For that reason, NT supports browsers for each network protocol, each language.

If I double-click on the highlighted line, I get a screen like the one in Figure 14.12. This shows me that there are two machines (EISA66 and SERVERTED) acting as browsers on the network, and six machines (ADMINCLONE, BUDDY, EISA66, SERVERTED, SPEEDY, and TERPDOM) acting as servers of some type. I can find

FIGURE 14.11:

Browser Monitor dialog box

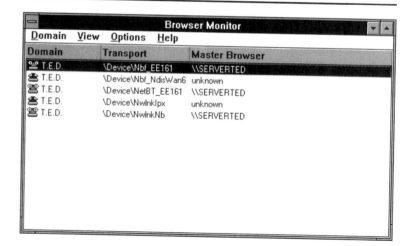

FIGURE 14.12:

Browser status on ORION dialog box

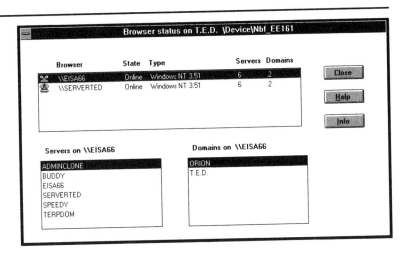

out more details about SERVERTED's browsing by double-clicking on its line in the Browsers list box. I then see a dialog box like the one in Figure 14.13.

The Browser Info dialog box shows a number of things that, frankly, we aren't interested in, but a few interesting statistics are worth noticing. First, look at the Details line. It says that this machine acts as both a workstation and a server, is the domain controller, and, among other things, is a backup browser and a master browser. Confusing as that may sound, it's normal: The master browser is *always* on the backup browser list. The Details line is very descriptive of a computer; for example, if I double-clicked on EISA66 instead of SERVERTED, I would see Workstation | Server | Windows NT | Potential Browser | Backup Browser on the Details line.

The Browser Info dialog box says that these are the statistics for the browser since 8:00 on 9/13/95, when I last rebooted the server. I ran BROWMON at about 10:00 on 9/15, so these are statistics for about 50 hours' worth of network browse mastering.

For example, Server Announcements, the first item in the box, are messages received by the browser master from machines on the network that are available to be servers. There are so many of those announcements because each "server"—that is, every Windows for Workgroups workstation, every NT workstation, and every NT Server machine—broadcasts its presence regularly.

FIGURE 14.13:

Browser Info dialog box

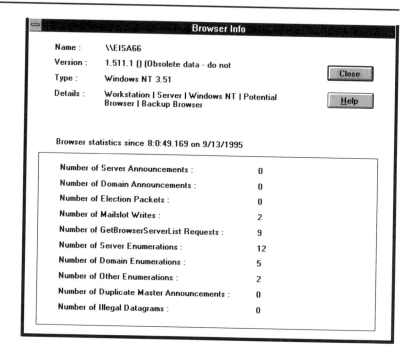

Preventing Computers from Being Browser Masters

Elections can take a lot of time on a network. You can simplify the election process and cut down on the number of elections by forcing a Windows for Workgroups computer to never be the master browser. Do this by adding the following line to the [network] section of SYSTEM.INI:

```
MaintainServerList=No
```

You would add this line if you didn't want to accept the performance hit that being master browser entails, or if you're running a mixed NT/Windows network. You see, it's possible to end up with an NT master browser and a Windows for Workgroups browse backup. The problem arises because the Windows workstation must talk to the NT machine to exchange services information. The NT machine isn't allowed to talk to the Windows machine *for any reason at all* unless the Windows machine either has an account on the that machine and is logged in, or the NT machine has a Guest account that is enabled. If neither of those things is the case, the newly elected backup browser finds itself without any information, and the master browser essentially "keeps it in the dark." If the master browser goes down, then the browser can end up taking its place in a fairly ignorant state, which leads to empty browse lists.

You can make Windows 95 machines ineligible for being browse masters either from the Control Panel (easiest) or, if you're feeling arcane, from the Registry. From the Control Panel, click Networks, then select File and Printer Sharing for Microsoft Networks from the list of installed network components. Click the Properties… button to move to the next screen, and set the value of the Browse Master property to Disabled. To change the setting from the Registry, run REGEDIT.EXE, and find the entry MaintainServerList. (It's in HKEY_LOCAL_MACHINE\System\CurrentControlSet\Services\VxD\VNetSeup, but it's probably easier to press F3 to use the Find utility.) Set the value of MaintainServerList to 0 if it isn't already, and the Windows 95 machine will not serve as a master browser.

The default value of MaintainServerList is auto, which means "Make me a master browser if needed." You can alternately use a value of Yes, which means, "If there's a tie when electing browse masters, make me master browser." For NT workstations, there is a corresponding Registry entry, MaintainServerList, which goes in HKEY_LOCAL_MACHINE\System\CurrentControlSet\Services\Browser\ Parameters. It is of type REG_SZ and its value can be TRUE or FALSE.

If your primary protocol is TCP/IP, one way to avoid elections is to simply make one machine very attractive, so attractive that elections needn't take place. You can do that by going to the NT Server that is your primary domain controller and declaring one machine the browse master. You can do that with an NT Server machine by adding a new value, IsDomainMasterBrowser equal to TRUE, to that machine's registry in the key HKEY_LOCAL_MACHINE\SYSTEM\CurrentControlSet\Services\Browser\Parameters. Its data type is REG_SZ. By making this machine a browse master, you essentially revert to a fixed name server scenario, but that's not so bad if you have machines you are pretty sure will stay up all the time—like servers. Note: This only works on TCP/IP browsers.

Refreshing a Browse List

In general, browse requests are resolved by either the master browser or a backup browser, so you never know who's provided your browse list. But you can force the system to browse you via the Browse Master with the following command-line command:

```
net view
```

Browsing with LAN Manager

Browse problems can also appear if you have LAN Manager 2.2 servers on the network. LAN Manager used a SAP-like approach, broadcasting data within network segments and making browsing across routers impossible.

Because NT and NT Server don't broadcast, they don't produce browser information that LAN Manager can understand. You can change that by enabling LAN Manager broadcasts in your NT machines, both server and workstation. Read the "How Do I" sidebar to find out how.

Why Isn't My Resource on the Browse List?

You can experience browsing trouble (i.e., the browse list isn't available or the list is incorrect) if computers do not exit Windows gracefully—that is, if they just get shut off without first exiting Windows. Such a computer may appear on the master browser list for up to 45 minutes. Even worse, if a *browser* terminates unexpectedly, it may become impossible to browse for over an hour.

Remember that if you can't see something on the browser, that's no big deal. If you know the universal naming convention for the resource—a name like \\markspc\c—then you can always just punch that value in and be connected with no trouble, even if the browsers are all confused.

Let's look in a bit more detail at how the browse service works. It can take up to 51 minutes for the browser to notice that a resource has disappeared, and in that time the browser may erroneously report that something is available when it is not. Why does that happen?

When a server (the computer offering the shared resource) is running, it announces itself to the master browser every 12 minutes. When a server stops running, the master browser won't assume it has gone away for three announce periods, or 36 minutes. This makes it sound as if the longest you need ever wait for the browse list to work properly and eradicate a "no longer available" resource is 36 minutes.

How Do I Enable LAN Manager to Understand Broadcasts?

To make LAN Manager understand broadcasts:

1. Open the Control Panel and double-click on the Network applet.

2. Under Installed Network Software, choose Server, double-click Server, or click Configure.

3. In the Server Configuration window, select the Make Browser Broadcasts to LAN Manager 2.x Clients check box.

In a similar vein, if you have a LAN Manager domain that is on the same LAN segment as an NT domain but does not contain any NT workstations, then the LAN Manager servers will not show up on the browse lists unless you go into the Control Panel and, in the Computer Browser, set the LAN Manager domains to be "other domains."

And if you're using Windows for Workgroups workstations with LAN Manager servers but the Windows for Workgroups machines don't see the LAN Manager servers, then add the following line to the [networks] section of SYSTEM.INI:

```
LMAnnounce=yes
```

But what if your browser is a *backup browser*? The backup browser polls the master every 15 minutes. The longest possible time for a backup browser to query the master is 15 minutes later, which means that the worst-case time for a server to disappear from the browse list is 51 minutes.

New services, in contrast, are announced to the master browser immediately, and, again, the backup browsers may hear of them as much as 15 minutes later, so the longest that it should take for a new service to appear on the browse list is 15 minutes.

By the way, when I said that servers reannounce themselves to the master browser every 12 minutes, I simplified the truth a bit. The whole truth is that when a service first starts up, it announces itself more frequently. New services announce at intervals of 1, 4, 8, and 12 minutes after they are started. After they reach 12 minutes, they announce at 12-minute intervals.

Another reason why you may not see a resource is that its server may be using a different protocol from your workstation. You see, services offered by NetBEUI-using machines are maintained on a different browse list than services offered by TCP/IP-using machines. There is a different master browser for each transport protocol except DLC.

By the way, how does the network know to hold an election if someone just pulls the plug on the master browser, and the master browser doesn't get a chance to force an election? The next time another computer asks for browse information and doesn't get a response, that computer forces an election.

If you are running TCP/IP, resources may not appear on the TCP/IP browse list because the IPX and/or NetBEUI protocols are hogging the network's attention. If you can, remove the other protocols, and the TCP/IP browser will work more smoothly. (If you take the other protocols off the PDC, be sure to re-enable MaintainServerList on some other machine, or NetBEUI and IPX will be without browsers.)

Why Is My Browser So Slow?

Set up Windows for Workgroups, accept all the defaults, and try to connect to a network drive with the File Manager, (Disk/Connect Network Drive...), and you'll wait for a couple of minutes. Why?

By default, WfW loads two protocols: NetBEUI and "IPX/SPX with NetBIOS." Recall that a network-aware program communicates with the network via the Application Program Interface, or API. The API used by NetBEUI is NetBIOS, and the typical API for IPX/SPX is Novell Sockets. But Microsoft has implemented a version of IPX/SPX that has a NetBIOS API on it. (Novell did the same thing long ago.)

Now, the Browser is just a network-aware application that depends on NetBIOS. So the Browser sees *two* NetBIOSes, the one atop NetBEUI and the one atop the IPX/SPX protocol stack. For some reason, that confuses it. Result: the long wait.

You can solve this problem simply. Just go to the Network Setup program in WfW and remove the IPX/SPX with NetBIOS item, replacing it with just IPX/SPX. The system will browse almost instantaneously. In general, getting rid of superfluous protocols will almost always improve performance.

Tuning the Machine

NT SERVER

Some of these things are obvious, but you can improve your server—you can "tune the hardware"—with a few simple changes.

Use an Advanced Bus   I hope that all servers are equipped with a bus better than the basic ISA bus. PCI and EISA are both quite attractive and cost-effective alternatives. Avoid VESA, as it is fast but limited in its functions.

High-Performance Video Is Unnecessary   Here's a way to save money: Just get a simple generic video card and a fixed-frequency VGA monitor. The lower resolution of a VGA card means less CPU time is spent on screen housekeeping.

Get 20+ MB of RAM   If you're supporting RAID, CSNW, and/or TCP/IP, then your server needs at least 20MB to really run well. More users also requires getting more RAM.

Do RAID   Hard disks are cheap these days. RAIDing a bunch of drives will cost you some disk space (RAIDing together three 1GB drives will only give you 2GB of storage), but you'll often see improved throughput. You'll also get the peace of mind that comes from knowing that if a drive just rolls over, kicks up its legs, and shows x's across its eyes, you still have all of your data. (I'm talking here about RAID level 5.) For more information about RAID, see Chapter 4.

Monitoring the Network with the Event Viewer

NT Server defines an *event* as any significant occurrence in the system or in an application that users should be aware of and perhaps notified about. If the event is critical, such as an interrupted power supply or a full disk on a server, messages are sent to the screens of all of the workstations. Noncritical event information, however, can be fed into a log file once event auditing has been configured. Both successful and unsuccessful events can be audited.

In order to record, retrieve, and store logs of events on an NT Server, the administrator must activate and configure event auditing. File and directory access, printer access, and security events can all be audited. File and directory auditing is activated within File Manager, printer auditing is set within Print Manager, and security auditing is configured in User Manager for Domains.

NT Server maintains three types of logs: the *System log*, the *Security log*, and the *Applications log*:

- **System log**   The System log records events logged by the Windows NT system components, such as the failure of a driver or other system component to load during startup. As shown in Figure 14.14, this log is displayed the first time you start up the Event Viewer.

- **Security log**   The Security log records security events (changes in security policy, attempts to log on or access a file or directory, etc.) based on the security auditing policy options specified by the administrator under Auditing in User Manager for Domains. Incidentally, this log can only be accessed by members of the Administrators group. It is shown in Figure 14.15.

- **Applications log**   The Applications log records events logged by applications on the system. For example, it records file errors that occur in database programs. The Applications log is shown in Figure 14.16.

To view a log, open the Event Viewer. Under the Log menu, choose System, Security, or Applications, depending on which log you want to see. Events in the log are listed in sequence by date and time of occurrence, with the default being newest first; you can change this to oldest first in the View menu. Note that the event logs are not automatically updated during the time they are in view. To see any new events that may have been logged after opening the Event Viewer, choose the Refresh command under the View menu (or simply hit the F5 key).

FIGURE 14.14:
The System log

Event Viewer - System Log on \\EISA SERVER

Log View Options Help

Date	Time	Source	Category	Event	User	Computer
10/22/94	11:37:08 AM	Print	None	17	SYSTEM	EISA S
10/22/94	11:36:35 AM	Print	None	17	SYSTEM	EISA S
10/22/94	11:18:15 AM	Print	None	13	Mark	EISA S
10/22/94	11:18:15 AM	Print	None	10	Mark	EISA S
10/22/94	11:18:15 AM	Print	None	17	SYSTEM	EISA S
10/22/94	11:18:10 AM	Print	None	17	Administrator	EISA S
10/22/94	11:18:08 AM	Print	None	17	SYSTEM	EISA S
10/22/94	11:13:20 AM	NETLOGON	None	5722	N/A	EISA S
10/22/94	11:13:20 AM	NETLOGON	None	5722	N/A	EISA S
10/22/94	11:12:50 AM	Rdr	None	3013	N/A	EISA S
10/22/94	11:07:58 AM	Print	None	13	Mark	EISA S
10/22/94	11:07:58 AM	Print	None	10	Mark	EISA S

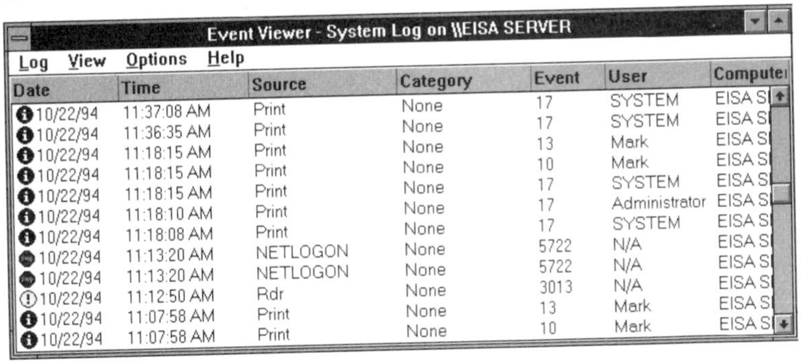

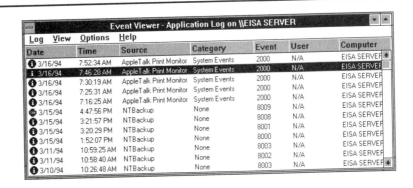

FIGURE 14.15:
The Security log

Event Viewer - Security Log on \\EISA SERVER

Log View Options Help

Date	Time	Source	Category	Event	User	Computer
3/18/94	11:35:30 AM	Security	Object Access	560	Administrator	EISA SERVER
3/18/94	10:00:25 AM	Security	Logon/Logoff	528	Administrator	EISA SERVER
3/18/94	10:00:12 AM	Security	Logon/Logoff	538	Maeve	EISA SERVER
3/18/94	9:59:34 AM	Security	Object Access	560	Maeve	EISA SERVER
3/18/94	9:58:44 AM	Security	Logon/Logoff	528	Maeve	EISA SERVER
3/18/94	9:54:06 AM	Security	Account Management	642	Maeve	EISA SERVER
3/18/94	9:54:06 AM	Security	Logon/Logoff	528	Maeve	EISA SERVER
3/18/94	9:30:34 AM	Security	Logon/Logoff	528	Christa	EISA SERVER
3/18/94	9:00:57 AM	Security	Account Management	642	ANONYMOUS LC	EISA SERVER
3/18/94	9:00:55 AM	Security	Logon/Logoff	537	SYSTEM	EISA SERVER
3/18/94	8:59:00 AM	Security	Logon/Logoff	538	Christa	EISA SERVER
3/17/94	10:37:03 PM	Security	Logon/Logoff	538	Andy	EISA SERVER

FIGURE 14.16:
The Applications log

Event Viewer - Application Log on \\EISA SERVER

Log View Options Help

Date	Time	Source	Category	Event	User	Computer
3/16/94	7:52:34 AM	AppleTalk Print Monitor	System Events	2000	N/A	EISA SERVER
3/16/94	7:46:28 AM	AppleTalk Print Monitor	System Events	2000	N/A	EISA SERVER
3/16/94	7:30:19 AM	AppleTalk Print Monitor	System Events	2000	N/A	EISA SERVER
3/16/94	7:25:31 AM	AppleTalk Print Monitor	System Events	2000	N/A	EISA SERVER
3/16/94	7:16:25 AM	AppleTalk Print Monitor	System Events	2000	N/A	EISA SERVER
3/15/94	4:47:56 PM	NTBackup	None	8009	N/A	EISA SERVER
3/15/94	3:21:57 PM	NTBackup	None	8008	N/A	EISA SERVER
3/15/94	3:20:29 PM	NTBackup	None	8001	N/A	EISA SERVER
3/15/94	1:52:07 PM	NTBackup	None	8000	N/A	EISA SERVER
3/11/94	10:59:25 AM	NTBackup	None	8003	N/A	EISA SERVER
3/11/94	10:58:40 AM	NTBackup	None	8002	N/A	EISA SERVER
3/10/94	10:26:48 AM	NTBackup	None	8003	N/A	EISA SERVER

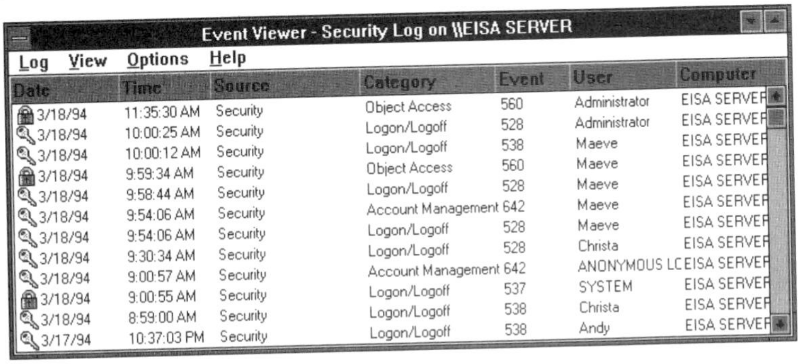

When the Event Viewer is opened, it displays the logs for the local computer by default. To view logs for another computer, choose Select Computer from the Log menu. NT Server allows you to view logs for NT workstations, NT Server servers and domain controllers, and servers using LAN Manager 2.x. Select the Low Speed Connection box if the computer you want is across a link with slow transmission rates; when this box is checked, NT Server doesn't list all of the computers in the default domain, thereby minimizing network traffic across the link.

Reading Log Information

Log entries are classified into one of five categories. These categories are marked by an event type icon at the beginning of the entry:

- The Information icon indicates an event that describes the successful operation of a major server service.

- The Warning icon indicates that the event wasn't necessarily significant but might point to possible future problems.

- The Error icon indicates that the event resulted in a loss of data or a loss of functions.

- The Success Audit icon indicates an audited security access event which was successful.

- The Failure Audit icon indicates an audited security access event that failed.

Following the event-type icon is a list of data pertinent to the event:

- The date and time the event occurred.
- The source of the event (typically the software that logged the event, which can be either an application name or a component of the system or of a large application, such as a driver name).
- The category of the event by the event source. Not all events are categorized (these events fall in the None category). Application events can be listed as System events or Administrative events. Security events fall into a number of

categories, including Logon/Logoff, Privilege Use, System Event, Policy Change, Account Management, Object Access, and Detailed Tracking.

- An event number unique to each kind of event. Event numbers can be used to identify the event. For example, in the Security log, events in the Logon/Logoff categories are identified by event number, as shown in Table 14.1. The numbers are used primarily by product support representatives to track precisely which event occurred within the system. You can check what a specific event ID number indicates by looking at the Event Details (more on that shortly) for any log entry having that particular event ID.

- The user name of the user who was logged on and was working when the event occurred is recorded in the event log (the entry N/A indicates that the log entry didn't specify a user).

- The computer name for the computer where the event occurred.

TABLE 14.1: Event ID Numbers for Selected Logon/Logoff Events

Logon/Logoff Event ID Number	Meaning
528	Successful logon
529	Unknown user name or bad password
531	Account currently disabled
535	The specified user's password has expired
537	Unexpected error occurred during logon
538	User logoff

Event Display

The default display layout for all of the event logs is to show every entry, with the most recent entries at the top. However, you can filter these details to see only what you need to see by selecting the Filter Events… option in the View menu. Filtering merely affects the view and has no effect on the Event log as a whole; events specified in the auditing policies are logged all the time, whether or not the filter is active.

If you select Save Settings On Exit from the Options menu, then the choices you made for filtering will remain in effect every time you start the Event Viewer.

To filter the log events, choose Filter Events... in the View menu. You'll see the Filter dialog box, as in Figure 14.17. The options available in the Filter dialog box are as follows:

Option	Filters Log For
View From	Events after a specific date and time; the default is the date of the first event in the log.
View Through	Events up to (and including) a specific date and time; the default is the date of the last event in the log.
Information	Information events (not available for LAN Manager 2.x servers).
Warning	Warning events (not available for LAN Manager 2.x servers).
Error	Error events (not available for LAN Manager 2.x servers).
Success Audit	Audited security access attempts that were successful (not available for LAN Manager 2.x servers).
Failure Audit	Audited security access attempts that failed (not available for LAN Manager 2.x servers).
Source	Events logged by a specific source, such as an application, a system component, or a device driver (not available for audit logs on LAN Manager 2.x servers).
Category	All events of a particular classification (for example, security event categories include Logon and Logoff, Policy Change, Privilege Use, System Event, Object Access, Detailed Tracking, and Account Management). This option is not available for error logs on LAN Manager 2.x servers.

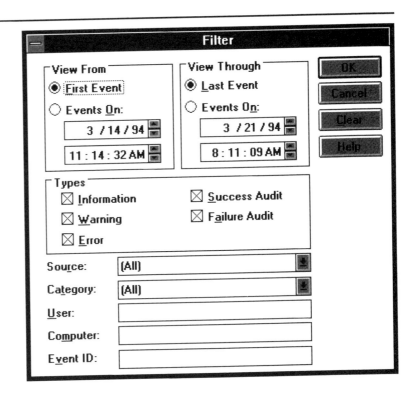

FIGURE 14.17:
The Filter dialog box

Option	Filters Log For
User	Events that occurred while a specified user was logged on and working. Note that not all events have a user associated with them. This field is not case-sensitive. It is not available for error logs on LAN Manager 2.x servers.
Computer	Events that occurred for a particular computer by the specified name. This field is not case-sensitive. It is not available for error logs on LAN Manager 2.x servers.
Event ID	Events of a particular type in a category, identified by a specific event ID number. Not available for audit logs on LAN Manager 2.x servers.

If you need to, you can also use the Find option to locate a particular type of entry in any of the logs. Under the View menu, choose Find (or hit the F3 key). You'll be asked for the same type of information as required by the Filter option. Use the Up or Down buttons in the Direction box to determine which direction to make the search.

Interpreting Event Details in Log Entries

By double-clicking on any event in a log (or by choosing Details in the View menu), you can call up a more detailed record of that event. Event details contain additional information about the event in question. For example, the details of a System log entry might look like Figure 14.18. Here, the details confirm that the entry was a rather straightforward information event—printing a document. An Applications log entry might look like Figure 14.19. Security log event details can be relatively straightforward as well, but usually contain a greater amount of information, as shown in Figure 14.20. Understanding the meaning of these details requires some basic knowledge of how NT Server handles system security.

System Security in NT Server

In NT Server, all named objects (as well as some unnamed objects) can be secured. The security attributes for an object are described by a *security descriptor*. The security descriptor is made of the following four parts:

- An owner security ID, which indicates the user or group who owns the object (the owner of the object, you may recall, can change all access permissions for that object).

- A group security ID, which is used only by the POSIX subsystem and ignored by the rest of NT.

- A discretionary *access control list* (ACL), which identifies which users and groups are granted or denied which access permissions (discretionary ACLs are controlled by the owner of the object).

- A system ACL, which controls which auditing messages the system will generate. System ACLs are controlled by the security administrators.

FIGURE 14.18:

Event details for a System log entry

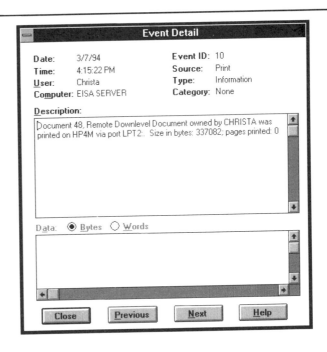

FIGURE 14.19:

Event details for an Application log entry

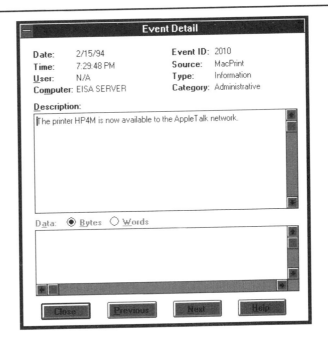

FIGURE 14.20:

Event details from a Security
log entry

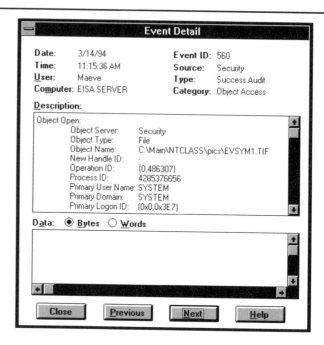

Whenever an owner of an object assigns permissions to other users and groups, he
or she is building the discretionary ACL for that object. Likewise, an administrator's choices about which events to audit determine the system ACL for the object.

Each of the ACLs in turn is made up of *access control entries* (ACEs). The ACEs for
an object specify access or auditing permissions to that object for one user or group.
ACEs include a security ID and a set of access rights for each group or user that can
access (or is denied access to) the object. Any process with a matching security ID
is either allowed access rights, denied rights, or allowed rights with auditing,
depending on the contents of the ACE. There are three ACE types: two of them,
AccessAllowed and AccessDenied, are discretionary ACEs that explicitly grant or
deny access to a user or group. The other, SystemAudit, is the system security ACE
that is used to keep a log of security events involving object access and to create and
record security audit messages.

By the way, the NT Permissions Editor places any AccessDenied ACEs first in the list of ACEs to check and, once it finds one, disregards any other AccessAllowed ACEs that follow. This way, if someone is a member of two groups, one that has access to a file and another to which access has been denied, that person will not be able to access the file despite his or her multiple group membership.

Included in each object's ACEs is an *access mask*, which is basically a menu from which granted and denied permissions are chosen. The access mask defines all possible actions for a particular directory, file, device, or other object. Access masks contain *access types*, of which there are standard types and specific types.

Standard access types apply to all objects and consist of the access permissions listed in Table 14.2. Specific types vary, depending on the type of object. For example, the specific access types for NT files are ReadData, WriteData, AppendData, ReadEA (Extended Attribute), WriteEA (Extended Attribute), Execute, ReadAttributes, and WriteAttributes.

TABLE 14.2: Standard Access Types

Access Type	Function
SYNCHRONIZE	Used to synchronize access and to allow a process to wait for an object to enter the signaled state
WRITE_OWNER	Used to assign the write owner
WRITE_DAC	Used to grant or deny write access to the discretionary ACL
READ_CONTROL	Used to grant or deny read access to the security descriptor and owner
DELETE	Used to grant or deny delete access

Specific and standard access types appear in the event details for entries in the Security log. Each type of object (i.e., file, file and directory, device, etc.) can have up to 16 specific access types. If you've enabled auditing of process tracking, you can follow a user's (or the system's) activity as it accesses an object by examining the specific and standard accesses shown in the event details.

Let's take a closer look at the example event detail for the Security log entry shown back in Figure 14.20. This particular event is a successful object access event involving a file for which security auditing has been activated. If we read through the entire event detail's description, we'll see the information shown in Figure 14.21. The

FIGURE 14.21:

Event detail description for Security log entry

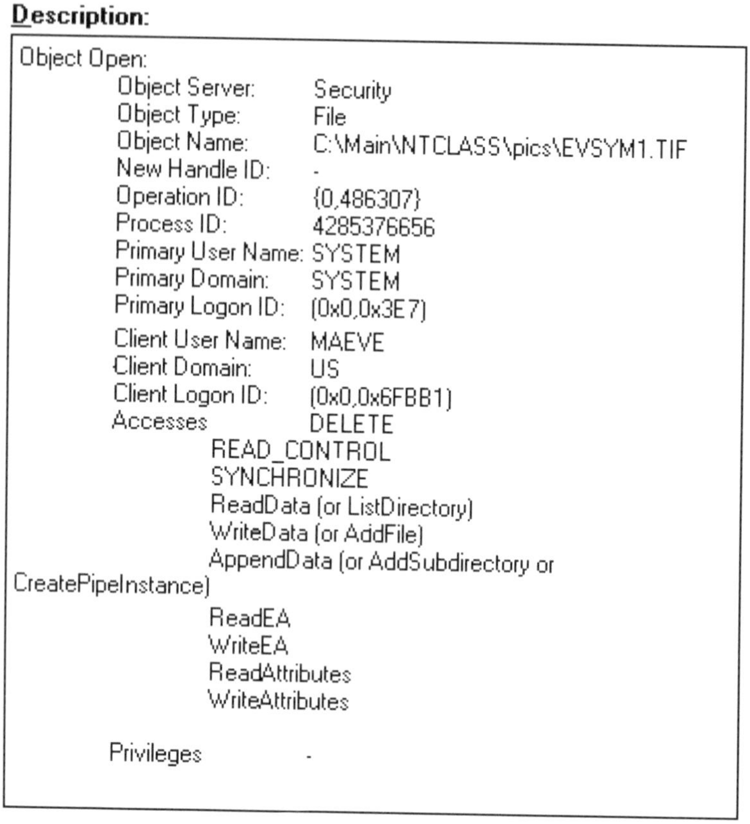

Description:

```
Object Open:
            Object Server:      Security
            Object Type:        File
            Object Name:        C:\Main\NTCLASS\pics\EVSYM1.TIF
            New Handle ID:      -
            Operation ID:       {0,486307}
            Process ID:         4285376656
            Primary User Name: SYSTEM
            Primary Domain:     SYSTEM
            Primary Logon ID:   (0x0,0x3E7)
            Client User Name:   MAEVE
            Client Domain:      US
            Client Logon ID:    (0x0,0x6FBB1)
            Accesses            DELETE
                    READ_CONTROL
                    SYNCHRONIZE
                    ReadData (or ListDirectory)
                    WriteData (or AddFile)
                    AppendData (or AddSubdirectory or
CreatePipeInstance)
                    ReadEA
                    WriteEA
                    ReadAttributes
                    WriteAttributes

            Privileges          -
```

first thing to note in the description is that an object was opened, that the object server, in this case, was Security, and that the object is a file, namely EVSYM1.TIF.

We see that no new handle ID is associated with this particular event. Handle IDs are assigned (and an audit event generated) when a file is first opened; when the file is closed, another audit event with the same handle ID is created. This information can be used to see how long a file remained open, but bear in mind that many applications open a file only long enough to read its contents into memory; a handle may be open only for a very short time.

The Operation ID and Process ID numbers are unique numbers assigned to any particular operations within a process and to the process as a whole, respectively. For example, when an application is started, it is assigned a Process ID, and all events involving that application will have that same ID. Individual operations within the application, such as opening a particular file, are assigned an Operation ID.

Continuing through the list, we note the Primary User Name, Primary Domain, and Primary Logon ID, as well as the Client User Name, Client Domain, and Client Logon ID. To ensure that the programs a user runs have no more access to objects than the user does, NT allows processes to take on the security attributes of another process or user through a technique called *impersonation*. Impersonation allows a program or process to run on the user's behalf with the same accesses that the user has been granted, or to put it another way, to run in the user's *security context*. We can see in our example that the primary user for this event was the system, but the client user, whose security context the process is running under, is also identified. The Client Logon ID is a number assigned to a logon session whenever a user logs on, and, if Logon/Logoff events are being audited, it can be used to search the logon entries to find out when the particular user logged on prior to the event in question.

The last collection of information in the description consists of lists of Accesses and Privileges that have been used (and thus audited). Since this particular event was a successful one, the Accesses list indicates which actions actually took place. The first three accesses are standard accesses for deleting a file, granting or denying read access to the file's security attributes, and for synchronizing access. The next three, ReadData (or ListDirectory), WriteData (or AddFile), and AppendData (or AddSubdirectory or CreatePipeInstance), are specific access types for files and directories. The last four accesses are specific types for files. Since nothing is indicated under Privileges, we can tell that no particular user rights were invoked for this event.

From this particular list of accesses, you can deduce what the event involving the file EVSYM1.TIF actually was: The file was successfully replaced with an edited version of itself. In the case of a failure audit entry, the list of accesses displayed usually represents those which were attempted but failed due to lack of access.

Changing Size and Overwrite Options for an Event Log

The default size for all three event logs is 512K, and events older than seven days are overwritten as needed when the log becomes full. To change this, open the

Event Viewer, and select Settings under the Log menu. You'll see the Event Log Settings dialog box shown in Figure 14.22. In addition to changing the log size, you can specify how the event log is overwritten by choosing one of three options in this dialog box:

- **Overwrite Events as Needed** New events will continue to be written into the log. When the log is full, each additional new event will replace the oldest event in the log.

- **Overwrite Events Older than [ ] Days** Logged events will be retained for the number of days specified (the default is 7) before being overwritten. This is a handy choice if you are archiving logs on a weekly basis.

- **Do Not Overwrite Events (Clear Log Manually)** With this option, the log is never overwritten. When full, events are no longer logged. When that situation occurs, a message appears on the screen saying that the log is full. Select this particular option only if it is important not to miss any events, and make sure that someone is able to manually clear the log when needed. (You might select this option for Security logs where all of the log info is vital.)

As mentioned earlier, choose carefully the events to be audited and consider the amount of disk space you are willing to devote to the logs when you set up auditing. You cannot make the system add more entries to a full log by simply increasing the log size under Log Settings.

FIGURE 14.22:

The Log Settings dialog box

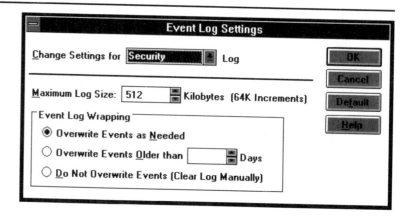

Archiving Event Logs

The event logs shown in NT Server's Event Viewer can be archived for future inspection and use. The log information can be stored three ways:

- As .evt files, a format that allows the data (and all of its details) to be viewed in the Event Viewer whenever desired

- As text files (.txt)

- As comma-delimited text files

The latter two formats allow the log information to be used in other applications.

Archiving the event log saves the entire log, regardless of the currently selected filtering options. Event logs saved as text or comma-delimited text, however, are saved in the current sort order. The data is stored in the following sequence: date, time, source, type, category, event, user, computer, and description. Any binary data in the event records is dropped.

Event logs can be archived in two ways, but no matter which method you use, the log that is currently displayed in the Event Viewer is the one that gets archived. To choose the desired log, open the Log menu and select System, Security, or Application.

The first method merely saves the event log as a file without clearing the log. With the desired log displayed, open the Log menu and choose Save As. By writing in a name for the file and picking a file format in the Save As dialog box, you can save the current log information to disk.

If you need to archive the current log and clear it from the Event Viewer too, then select the Clear All Events option under the Log menu. The Clear Event Log dialog box appears, as in Figure 14.23. It gives you the option to save before clearing.

FIGURE 14.23:
Clear Event Log dialog box

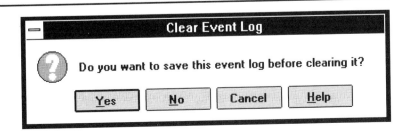

Selecting Yes will trigger the Save As dialog box. Choose the file format option desired and enter a file name for the archived log.

Upon selecting OK, you will get the message in Figure 14.24 (in this case, for the Security log). Since you've just saved the current information to a file, those events won't be lost (contrary to what this message implies). Selecting Yes will clear the log of the just-archived information. New event information will be added to the log according to the criteria set under Log Settings. If, in the Log Settings option, you've specified Overwrite Events Older Than 7 Days (see Figure 14.22), you can archive weekly without necessarily clearing the event log, since the older events are overwritten in the week after archiving the log.

FIGURE 14.24:

Clearing an event log

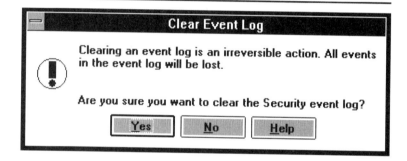

It is important to check, archive, and clear event logs regularly if you selected the Do Not Overwrite Events (Clear Log Manually) option in the Event Log Settings dialog box (see Figure 14.22). If an event log is full, no more information can be stored, and what might be vital information will not get recorded. When a log is full, the administrator is notified by a message on the screen. If the option Restart, Shutdown, or System was selected for auditing under the Audit policy in User Manager for Domains, then a log entry, indicating that a log is full, will be recorded.

Viewing Previously Archived Logs

To view a previously archived log, select the Open option in the Log menu of the Event Viewer, and choose which previously archived log you wish to see. After selecting a file, you will be prompted as to which type of log it is, as shown in Figure 14.25. Make sure you choose the type of log that the file happens to be correctly, or else the event description shown in the log details will be incorrect.

FIGURE 14.25:

Selecting a previously archived file to view

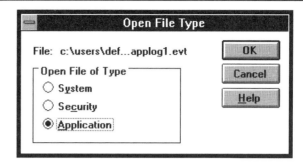

If you need a printed copy of the log, use the Save As option to save the log as a comma-delimited text file. As mentioned earlier, all information will be saved in the current sort order, and any binary data associated with a log entry will be discarded. You can print a comma-delimited text file for future reference or scrutiny. The example below shows part of a Security log stored as a comma-delimited text file:

```
3/10/94,9:27:31 AM,Security,Success Audit,Logon/Logoff,528,
Administrator,EISA SERVER,Successful Logon:
        User Name:        Administrator
        Domain:                           US
        Logon ID:                         (0x0,0x50D65)
        Logon Type:       2
        Logon Process:    User32
        Authentication Package:
        MICROSOFT_AUTHENTICATION_PACKAGE_V1_0

3/10/94,9:27:19 AM,Security,Success Audit,Logon/Logoff ,538,
Maeve,EISA SERVER,User Logoff:
        User Name:        Maeve
        Domain:                           US
        Logon ID:         (0x0,0x501BC)
        Logon Type:       2

3/10/94,9:27:03 AM,Security,Failure Audit,Object Access ,560,
Maeve,EISA SERVER,Object Open:
        Object Server:    Security
        Object Type:      File
        Object Name:      C:\Main\NTCLASS\MVTEXT\prjdata1.txt
        New Handle ID:    —
        Operation ID:     {0,330786}
        Process ID:       4285798960
```

```
Primary User Name:Maeve
Primary Domain:  US
Primary Logon ID:(0x0,0x501BC)
Client User Name:-
Client Domain:   -
Client Logon ID: -
Accesses                              SYNCHRONIZE
                    ReadAttributes

Privileges                            -
```

The first two entries reveal a successful logon by the Administrator and a user log-off. The third entry is a failure audit for a user's attempt to change a file (in this example, PRJDATA.TXT) for which he or she only had read access.

CHAPTER

FIFTEEN

15

Recovering from Disaster

Y ou can set up fault tolerance all you want to, but sooner or later a fault that you can't tolerate will hit your system. It could be something as simple as a bug in NT Server or an incorrect configuration, or something as dramatic as your server falling down a crack in an earthquake. RAID's nice, but disk mirroring and disk striping cannot help you here. What you need now is a way to rebuild your server's operating system and data, from the bottom up if need be.

Read This and You Can Skip the Rest of the Chapter

Well, not really. But an ounce of prevention is worth a pound of cure, right?

One of the main concerns in computer security, and the one that this section mainly addresses, is *physical security*. Physical security is a blanket term for the ways in which you *physically* protect your server and network from harm—from stupid accidents, espionage, and theft.

Preventing Environmental Problems

It would be terrible if you went to all the trouble of protecting your server from theft or tampering and then lost it to a cup of coffee spilled into its air intake vents.

Electrical Protection

The first source of environmental problems that should never be ignored is the wall socket.

- Use a UPS/power conditioner on your servers to protect them from dirty power and power surges. If you don't want to buy a UPS for every workstation (and I don't blame you if you don't, since that could get expensive), buy a *power conditioner*. This roughly $150 device cleans up noisy power and compensates for low voltage.

- While nothing can guarantee 100-percent protection from lightning damage, you can reduce lightning damage with this odd trick: tie five knots in each workstation's power cord, as close to the wall as you can. That way, if lightning strikes the wiring, it will kill the cord rather than travel through the cord to kill the computer.

Does this really work? Well, Washington, DC, where I live, was hit by a terrible lightning storm in 1990. I tied knots in the cords of all the computers in my house beforehand, but hadn't thought to do it to the television. During the storm, a huge power surge hit my wiring when one of my neighbors took a direct lightning hit. The cords of all the computers were warmed up a bit, but the power surge never touched the computers themselves. The television was another matter—the surge traveled straight through the cord to the TV's innards, rendering the television DOA. I couldn't have asked for a better test, though at the time I wasn't in a mood to appreciate the benefits of having had an unknotted control group to compare the knotted cords with.

- Don't plug any computers into the same plug as a power hog like a refrigerator, copier, or laser printer. Laser printers periodically draw as much power as an entire kitchen full of appliances.

- If your computers are all in one room and you ground it, don't just ground that room; ground the entire office. Otherwise, it's kind of like putting a giant "KICK ME" sign on your computers, as they'll be the easiest thing around for lightning to reach.

There is more to know about power and PCs, but so ends the quick overview.

Know Your Building

When you're positioning servers and workstations, know what's in the building that could affect them. For example, are there old (or new) leaks in the building? Putting a server or workstation underneath a suspicious brown stain in the ceiling is a bad idea, even if the leak was "fixed" years ago and the building manager claims that "it can't possibly still be a problem."

Excessive heat and moisture are bad for equipment. Is any heat-producing equipment mounted in the ceiling? How about equipment that produces water condensation? One company moved into a new building and discovered that the air-conditioning equipment was mounted in the ceiling over the server room. Not only did the AC generate copious amounts of heat in exactly the place where it was least wanted, but the water condensation that the units generated began raining down onto the servers one morning. Luckily, the servers recovered nicely, but it could have been an ugly scene.

If the servers are locked in their own room, is that room staying cool enough for safety? The regular air conditioning that the rest of the office uses might not be enough, due to the restricted ventilation in a closed room and all the heat that computers generate.

Obviously, you shouldn't position *any* computer, whether it's a workstation or a server, in direct sunlight.

Keep Contaminants away from the Servers

It is hard to keep people from eating or drinking near their workstations, but this should not be true of the server room. A strict no food, no beverage policy is necessary for that room to keep someone from pouring a Coke into the file server. The proliferation of nonsmoking offices makes the next comment almost unnecessary, but even if employees can smoke in the office, the one place they should *not* smoke is around the servers or workstations. Smoke particles in a hard disk are a *very* bad idea.

Preventing Theft and Tampering

Although the lion's share of physical security problems stems from accidents, theft and tampering are also things to watch out for if the information on your system might be valuable to someone else. To keep unauthorized people from gaining access to the network's information, do the following.

Keep the Server Room Locked   Most people using the network will never have any valid reason for going into the server room, so you can keep it locked. If people can't get into the server room, they can't:

- Reboot the server. If you are using the FAT file system, an intruder could reboot the server from a floppy (assuming that there are floppy drives on your server) and copy or delete valuable data. This, by the way, is one of the main reasons for using the NTFS file system—NTFS files and directories are invisible to anyone using the FAT file system.

- Steal the hard drive(s). This might sound improbable, but someone who has the tools and the experience can simply remove the hard drive and take it elsewhere to crack into it at leisure, rather than try to work with it on site. Stealing a hard drive is less awkward than stealing an entire server, but locking the file server room can also prevent server theft.

- Reinstall NT Server. While this sounds like a lot of trouble to go through, it's perfectly possible. Reinstalling the operating system doesn't harm the data already on the drive (unless you repartition it), so someone with the knowledge and the time could reinstall NT Server and change all the passwords, giving themselves access to your data.

Limit Access to the Server   Even if you can't lock up the server for space or administrative reasons, you can still limit people's physical access to it with the following tactics:

- Disable the server's A drive. Without an A drive, no one can reboot the system from a floppy unless they reconnect the A drive first. Admittedly, this means you can't reboot either, but this could buy you some time if someone broke in intending to reboot the server.

  Also, without an A drive, it's impossible to reinstall NT Server, even with the system disks or the CD-ROM, since you must boot from Install Disk #1 before beginning the installation process. If you can't reinstall the system or access the Administrative account, you can't change the system passwords. Use the floplock service that comes with the Windows NT Resource Kit. When the floplock service is running, only members of the Administrators group can access the floppy drives.

- Disable the reset button and on/off switch. Most of the time, if you need to reboot the server, you do it from the Shutdown… option in the Program Manager. Without a Big Red Switch or reset button, no one can boot the server unless they use the Shutdown option.

These are extreme measures, and truthfully I don't have a great enough need for security to implement them on my network. Some of my clients, however (I live in Washington, remember?), have found these suggestions to be quite implementable.

Using Passwords Well

Well-chosen passwords are an important part of the security process. When selecting them, strike a balance between passwords that are too easy to guess and in service too long, and passwords that are complicated and changed so frequently that users write them down to remember them. An eight-letter minimum and a 30-day change policy (with the user unable to use the same password more often than once every three changes), is probably about right. Experimentation and experience will help you choose a combination that fits your needs. When choosing passwords, keep the following advice in mind.

NT Server passwords are case-sensitive, so you can make them more difficult to guess by capitalizing them in unexpected places (like pAssword). Don't get too creative, however, or your users will never be able to type them in right.

There are programs that can guess passwords. These programs feed a dictionary to the system until the system accepts a word. To eliminate this path into your system, use words not found in the dictionary, such as names (picard), misspelled words (phantum), foreign words (mejor), or made-up words (aooga). At password-changing time in one government installation, the users are presented with a two-column list of four-letter words (not obscenities, just words with four letters in them). The users pick one word from column A and one from column B, and then they combine them to form the new password, leading to such combinations as PINKFEET or BOATHEAD. These passwords are easy to remember and can't be found in the dictionary.

Most names are not found in the dictionary, but that doesn't mean you should let your users use the names of their spouses, children, pets, or anything else as passwords. One branch security manager at the Pentagon tells me that he had to go in and change all of his users' passwords when he discovered that a number of them had chosen the names of Japanese WWII battleships for their passwords—a subject related to their mission and therefore not impossible to guess.

While the password-generating programs that randomly select a number-letter combination will create nearly invulnerable passwords, these passwords may not be the most effective protection. They're too hard for most people to remember, and will end up being written down.

Remove old user accounts from the system if the person using the account no longer needs it. If the user may need the account again (a summer intern, for example, could return the following summer), you can just disable it rather than wiping it out altogether, but don't keep active accounts on the system unless someone is using them.

Finally, even if someone figures out a password and breaks into the system, you can reduce the possible damage by only giving users minimum access to the system and to files that they need. There's more about this in Chapter 8.

Controlling Access to the Printer

The printer might seem like a harmless part of your network, but think again: If you have company secrets, they can leave your network as printouts even if you've adopted diskless workstations. To avoid this, try taking these steps:

- Restrict printer access to those who need it. (You can also restrict access to keep people from playing with an expensive color printer.)

- Audit printer use in the Print Manager so that you know who is printing what. If you discover someone who prints more output than their work justifies, that person might not be stealing company secrets—but he or she might be wasting company time and resources on personal projects. Be aware, however, that auditing server activity will slow down the server.

- Restrict printer access time to normal working hours.

- Don't give out Power User rights to just anyone. Power users can create and connect to network devices, thereby negating all that you've done to control access to the devices.

Preventing Portable Penetration

Say that you have an Ethernet bus network. What happens if someone comes in with a portable and plugs in? What rights does that person have on the network?

Potentially disastrous as this sounds, if you've set up the network as a domain and the person with the portable does not know the administrator's password, plugging in the portable won't get that person anywhere. This is because the administrator is the only one who can add a computer to the domain, and a non-member of the domain is shut out of the domain.

If, however, your network is set up on a peer-to-peer basis, a plugged-in portable can do a lot more damage, due to the Guest Account on all machines. Many people never bother to change the Guest Account password from the default, so using the Guest Account is one of the easiest ways of accessing the network. While Guest access is not as powerful as that of the Administrator, Guests can still view, copy, and delete files to which they have not been expressly refused access.

623

Therefore, to protect your network best, institute a domain controller so that no one can log on to the system from a new computer. If you *must* have a peer-to-peer setup, eliminate the Guest Account on all the network's workstations or, at the very least, change the password on a regular basis.

How Much Protection Is Too Much?

Protecting your system is a never-ending process; for every means you use to safeguard it, there's another means to get past those safeguards. Therefore, when protecting your network, come up with a balance between how much the data is worth and how much the protection costs. If protecting your data costs more than the data is worth, then it's time to relax a little. The cost of perfect protection is infinite amounts of money and eternal vigilance. If you hope to ever get anything done or to have money to spend on anything else, weigh your protection costs against what you're protecting and plan accordingly. There's little point in spending the money for more drives so that you can do RAID fault tolerance, for example, if all that you're protecting is some applications for which you have the original disks and backups.

When something goes wrong with your system, think *non-invasive*. Three of your most valuable troubleshooting implements are:

- An NT-bootable disk.

- The Emergency Repair Disk for the machine in trouble (don't forget, they're specific to the machine on which they were made).

- Your notebook, in which you record every change you make to the servers and workstations, so that when something goes wrong, you can figure out what's changed between now and the last time it worked.

Restoring a Configuration

Sometimes, no matter how vigilant you've been, mistakes happen or something just goes wrong, and you need to fix your system. These fixes range from easy to horrific.

We'll start with a relatively easy one. What happens if you successfully install NT Server and try to adjust your system configuration, but in so doing render your server unusable, or even unbootable? Something as simple as changing the video driver to something that your system can't handle will do that, and it's hard to restore the original driver if you can't read what's on your screen. If you've messed up your system's configuration, what do you do?

One thing that you *could* do is reinstall NT Server. Personally, I would try to avoid this; I've installed NT Server a number of times while experimenting with it, and the installation process doesn't get any more fun. Not only do you have to complete the installation process itself, but you have to set up all services and user accounts again, and this gets very boring and/or frustrating very quickly. Luckily, there are other ways to fix your setup when something's gone wrong.

The Last Known Good Menu

If you've changed your system so that it can't boot NT Server, one of these better solutions to this problem can be seen while you're rebooting. If you watch while your machine's booting up, you'll see a message on a black screen that says, "Press spacebar NOW to evoke the Last Known Good Configuration." If you press the spacebar, you'll see a menu asking you whether you want to

- Use the current configuration,
- Use the *last known good configuration*—the configuration that was used the last time the machine booted successfully, or
- Restart the computer.

If your machine won't boot, you probably don't want to use the current configuration, so go instead to the Last Known Good Configuration. This should make your machine bootable.

When Does (and Doesn't) It Work?

What are the criteria for a configuration being the Last Known Good? To qualify, a configuration must not have produced any system-critical errors involving a driver or a system file, and a user must have been able to log onto the system at least once.

The Last Known Good Configuration can't always help you. If any of the following things are true, you'll have to use another solution to restore things as you want them:

- You made a change more than one successful boot ago and want to restore things as they were before the change.

- The information that you want to change is not related to control set information—user profiles and file permissions fall into the category of information that can't be changed with the Last Known Good menu.

- The system boots, a user logs on, and then the system hangs.

- You change your video driver to an incompatible driver, restart the system, and then log on with the bad driver (you can still type, even if you can't see).

Using the Emergency Repair Disk

If you've screwed up your operating system setup in a way that using the Last Known Good Configuration can't help you, you still have another option before (groan) reinstalling the operating system. Every time you make a successful change to your system's configuration, you should back it up (you'll see how to do that in just a minute). The backup disk, where your system's configuration information is stored, is your Emergency Repair Disk.

To use the Emergency Repair Disk, put Disk #1 of the operating system Setup Disks into the A drive as though you planned to reinstall Windows NT, and reboot. You'll come to the setup screen after inserting Setup Disk #2, where the installation program will appear and prompt you to learn more about setup, set up now, repair a damaged installation, or quit setup. Press R to repair your system. You'll see some drive activity, and then a message will appear prompting you to insert the Emergency Repair Disk into drive A. Do so, and you'll see a message along the status bar in the bottom of the screen that Setup is reading REPAIR.INF. When it's done that, it will prompt you again for the Setup disk.

After you insert Disk #1, Setup will ask you if you want to do the following:

- Inspect registry files
- Inspect startup environment
- Verify Windows NT system files
- Inspect boot sector

By default, all of these options will be checked. To deselect them, use the ↑ and ↓ arrows to select an option, and then press Enter to select or deselect that option. When you've finished, select Continue (perform selected tasks). Press Enter to detect your adapters and you will be asked to insert Setup Disk #3 to load various device drivers. When that's done, you'll be prompted to insert the Emergency Repair Disk. You'll see messages along the status bar in the bottom of the screen telling you that Setup is checking and then examining drive C (or whatever your system drive is). You'll see a screen saying Setup has completed repairs. Press Enter to restart your computer.

What if you *didn't* create an Emergency Repair Disk (shame on you)? NT 3.5x creates a REPAIR directory in the WINNT35 directory; you can just refer the repair program to that directory, and it will get the same information it would get from the Repair Disk.

The Repair Disk contains a registry based on your *initial* setup. There are no users save for the Administrator and the Guest. None of the permissions that you've established are on the Repair Disk. You can, however, update your Repair Disk (or create a completely new disk) with a program called RDISK.EXE in the SYSTEM32 directory. Just run it and follow the instructions.

Backing Up Your Configuration

In addition to the Emergency Repair Disk, you can save your partition information so that you can replace it if you do something that you didn't want to do. Here's how:

1. Go to the Disk Administrator.

2. From the Partition Menu, choose Configuration, and then Save. You'll see a screen that looks like Figure 15.1.

3. Insert the disk and press OK. The system will save the information, and then you'll see a message, as in Figure 15.2, confirming that the configuration was saved.

4. Click OK, and you're done. Remove the disk from the drive, label it with the date, and put it somewhere safe. You now have a backup of your hardware configuration on your Emergency Repair Disk.

FIGURE 15.1:

Insert Disk dialog box

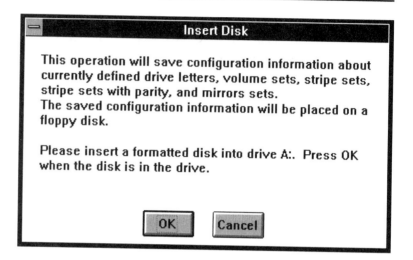

FIGURE 15.2:

Disk Administrator confirmation of
your configuration change

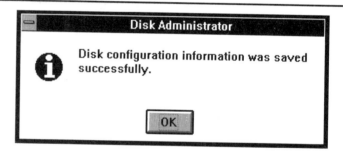

TIP   If you blast a partition and your data, restoring the partition won't restore
the data.

Recovering from Bad Video Drivers

You may recall from the earlier discussion of the Last Known Good Configuration
that if you change the video drivers to something your system can't handle, you

reboot, and then you log on with the bad drivers (you can still type a password even if the screen is messed up), the Last Known Good solution can no longer help you. You have, after all, successfully rebooted and logged on to the system; the fact that you can't *see* anything is immaterial.

Under NT 3.1, this was something of a rigmarole. But NT 3.5x builds into the operating system picker an option called NT Server 3.5 (VGA drivers). All you have to do is shut down the server, restart it, and choose the setup with VGA drivers. Then, once you have the system back up, just select Display from the Control Panel and take a second shot at choosing a video driver. Even better, there is a Test button in the Control Panel that you can use to find out *before* you commit yourself whether or not the video drivers work.

Diagnosing Server Boot Failures

Last Known Good restores are of no value if you can't get to the "Press a key now to restore Last Known Good..." message. In this section, I'll explain the steps that the server goes through in order to boot, and I'll tell you what outward signs those steps display, so that you can figure out what went wrong when your server won't boot.

Before the Boot: The Hardware Must Work

Before anything else can happen, your server must be free of hardware problems. You may not be able to boot if:

- Your boot drive or boot drive's controller is malfunctioning or is not set up correctly.

- You have an interrupt conflict.

- The CPU or some other vital circuitry is failing.

Too often, the fan on the server's power supply stops working. The result is that the temperature inside of your server rises to over 130°F (55°C), slowly roasting your components.

A company in Bonsall, California, by the name of PC Power and Cooling Systems makes a temperature sensor that fits inside a PC case and squawks when the PC's internal temperature rises above 100 degrees. It's not cheap (it cost $100 the last time I looked), but buying a sensor is cheaper than replacing the server.

Another problem I've run into that can make a machine not boot is an EISA misconfiguration. Of course, the fact that EISA allows for software configuration of machines is wonderful. EISA is a real dream for those of us who have spent too much of our lives flipping DIP switches and wrestling jumpers out of hard-to-get-to spaces. But the EISA setup routines on some EISA machines have a quirk: If they don't understand *something*, then they respond by knowing *nothing*.

To show what I mean, suppose you have an EISA disk controller in your server. You shut down the server and replace your old ISA LAN board with an EISA LAN board. You put the cover on your system and try to boot, only to get the message "EISA CMOS failure" and a stopped computer. What happened was this: The system knew to expect the EISA disk controller, but it *didn't* know to expect the EISA LAN board. Just to play it safe, the computer refused to use the EISA disk controller. Result: You can't boot your system from the hard disk. The system will continue to do this until you run the EISA configuration program.

To make matters worse, most people's floppy disk controller is on the hard disk controller card, which makes it impossible to boot from the floppy. If you can't run the EISA configuration program from either the hard disk *or* the floppy disk, what can you do?

I've found that the best bet in this case is to run the EISA configuration program *before* you install the board. Load the EISA configuration file for the new board, and configure the board even before it's in your system. The configuration program will complain a bit about the fact that the board is not actually *in* the system, but it will all work in the end. Then shut down the computer and install the new board.

Step One: NTLDR

The first thing that your NT server loads is the file NTLDR, a small program in the root directory. NTLDR announces itself by clearing the screen and displaying:

```
Windows NT
Portable Boot Loader
```

NTLDR looks for these files:

File	Description
BOOT.INI	A text file that tells the NT multiboot loader which operating systems are available.
NTDETECT.COM	A program that detects the hardware on your NT system.
BOOTSECT.DOS	This file is present on your root directory if you dual-boot with DOS, something unlikely on an NT Server machine.
NTBOOTDD.SYS	This file is present if you boot from a SCSI drive. It's a kind of micro-SCSI driver.

At this point, I've seen messages such as "Unable to open NTDETECT.COM," followed by an error code. That means that something has damaged data in your root directory, making it impossible for NTDETECT.COM to load. The answer to this problem is to use the NT Repair Disk; I've found that it can reconstruct most root structures.

NTLDR then does these things:

1. Shifts your processor to 386 mode (iapx86 systems).
2. Starts the very simple file system based either on a standard disk interface (known as INT13 for non-SCSI systems) or uses NTBOOTDD.SYS to boot from the SCSI drive.
3. Reads BOOT.INI to find out if there are other operating systems to offer, and shows those options on the screen.
4. Accepts the user's decision on which OS to load.

Assuming that you pick NT, then NTDETECT runs.

Step Two: NTDETECT

Next, NTDETECT.COM runs to figure out what kind of hardware you have. NTDETECT finds:

- Your PC's machine ID byte
- Its bus type
- Its video board
- Its keyboard type
- The serial ports attached to your computer
- Any parallel ports on the PC
- Floppy drives on the computer
- A mouse, if present

As mentioned in Chapter 3, a special version of NTDETECT on the NT installation CD-ROM gives a blow-by-blow account of how the hardware detection is proceeding if you find that your system is locking up at this point.

Step Three: NTOSKRNL

Next, the NT kernel loads, along with the hardware abstraction layer (HAL), the part of NT that allows the operating system to be hardware-independent. The kernel loads in four phases:

- The kernel load phase
- The kernel initialization phase
- The services load phase
- The Windows subsystem start phase

Kernel Load Phase   The first part of a kernel load is the HAL load. Then the system hive, which lives normally in HKEY_LOCAL_MACHINE\SYSTEM\ CurrentControlSet\Services, is loaded, and the system scans for device drivers to load. A look at Services will show names like 8514a, Abiosdisk, Atd, Aha1542x, etc.

Some of those drivers should be loaded *before* the kernel, and that's indicated by a value Start, which has the value 0 if that driver is supposed to load before the kernel. (One example you can usually find is Atdisk.)

Kernel Initialization Phase   You know you're here because the screen turns blue and goes to a 50-line mode. The kernel's internal variables are initialized, and once that's done, the kernel again scans the current control set for drivers with a start value of 1. Those drivers get loaded and initialized. A new current control set gets built in anticipation of the boot being successful, but it's not saved yet, as NT doesn't know whether or not this will be a LastKnownGood set.

A program called AUTOCHK.EXE, a CHKDSK-like program, runs to make sure that the file system is intact. The virtual memory page files are also set up.

Services Load Phase   The session manager, a program called SMSS.EXE, loads at this point, and loads the Win32 subsystem. The Current Control Set gets written to the system hive.

Windows Subsystem Start Phase   The Win32 subsystem initializes and starts any services that are supposed to start upon boot. This is the last step before the logon dialog box appears. At the same time, the CloneControlSet (a copy of the currently running system configuration) is copied to the LastKnownGood configuration.

Win32 starts up WINLOGON.EXE, which looks in HKEY_LOCAL_MACHINE\Software\Microsoft\Windows NT\Current Version\Winlogin for the value System, where it finds the names of necessary subsystems. For example, mine contains lsass.exe, the name of the local security authority.

Finally, the logon process happens. This process puts the Press Ctrl-Alt-Del to logon to Windows NT window on your screen. If you get this far, your configuration is good.

Disaster Recovery

Sometimes using the Last Known Good Configuration or the Repair disk doesn't fix your problems. Hard disk failures or natural disasters require a bit more in the way of hard-core disaster recovery.

What does "disaster recovery" mean? Essentially, it's exactly what it sounds like: A way of recovering from disaster—at best, turning a potential disaster into a minor inconvenience. Disaster can mean anything: theft, flood, an earthquake, a virus, or anything that could keep you from accessing your data. After all, it's not really the server that's important. While servers may be expensive, they are replaceable. Your data, on the other hand, is either difficult or impossible to recover. Could you re-produce your client mailing list from memory? What about the corporate accounts?

Creating a Disaster Recovery Plan

When creating a disaster recovery plan, the most important part of the plan lies in identifying what "disaster" means to you and your company. Obviously, perma-nently losing all of your company's data would be a disaster, but what else would? How about your installation becoming inaccessible for a week or longer? When planning for disaster, think about all the conditions that could render your data or your workplace unreachable, and plan accordingly.

Implementing Disaster Recovery

Okay, it's 2:00 p.m. on Thursday, and you get a report that the network has died. What do you do?

1. **Write things down.** Immediately write down everything that everyone tells you: what happened, when it happened, who gave you the information, and anything else that happened at the same time that might possibly be related.

2. **Check the event logs.** If you can get to them, look at the Security and Event logs on the server to see if you can tell what happened right before the server crashed. If you're using directory replication to maintain a "hot fix" server, the log information may be on the replicated server even if you can't get to the original.

3. **Ascertain the cause of the failure and fix it.** "Easy for you to say," I hear someone muttering. It can be done, however. Once you know what events happened, it becomes easier to find out what they happened to.

If It's a Software Problem   Is it a software problem? If it is, have you changed the configuration? If you've changed something, rebooted, and been unable to boot, it's time to use the Last Known Good Configuration discussed earlier. If you can boot but the operating system won't function properly, use the Emergency Repair Disk that you've made to restore the hardware configuration.

If you have another server with NT Server already installed identically to the server that failed, switch servers and see if the backup server works before you reinstall the operating system. If the "hot start" server doesn't work, you could be facing a network problem.

If It's a Hardware Problem   Is it a hardware problem? If you have a physically identical file server (also known as a "hot start" server, since it's ready to go whenever you need it) around the office, put it in place of the failed server and see if you can bring the network back up. If so, the problem lies with the dead server, and you can fix or replace it while you have the other one in place. If not, check the network's cabling.

If one drive from a stripe set or mirror set has died, the system should still be fine (if the drive that died is not the one with the system partition on it), but you should still fix the set anyway. Striping and mirroring give you access to your data while the missing data is being regenerated, but if something else happens to the set before you regenerate the missing data, you're sunk because the set can only deal with one error at a time.

If necessary, reload the backups.

Making Sure the Plan Works

The most crucial part of any disaster recovery plan lies in making sure it works down to the last detail. Don't just check the hardware, check everything. When a server crashes, backups will do you no good at all if they're locked in a cabinet and the business manager who has the keys is on vacation in Tahiti.

In the interests of having your plan actually work, following are some questions to which you need to know the answers.

Who Has the Keys?   Who has the keys to the backups and/or the file server case? The example mentioned above of the business manager having the only set of keys is not an acceptable situation, for reasons that should be painfully obvious. At any given time, someone *must* have access to the backups.

You could set up a rotating schedule of duty, wherein one person who has the keys is always on call and the keys are passed to the next person when a shift is up. However, that solution is not foolproof. If there's an emergency, the person on call could forget to hand the keys off to the next person, or the person on call could be rendered inaccessible through a dead beeper battery or downed telephone line. It's better to have two trusted people with keys to the backups and server, so that if the person on call can't be reached, you have a backup key person.

Is Special Software Required for the Backups?   Must any special software be loaded for the backups to work? I nearly gave myself heart failure when, after repartitioning a hard disk and reinstalling an operating system, I attempted to restore the backups that I'd made before wiping out all the data on the file server's hard disk. The backups wouldn't work. After much frustration, I figured out that Service Pack 2 had been installed on the server before. I reinstalled the Service Pack from my copy on another computer, and the backups worked. I just wish that I'd figured that out several hours earlier…

Do the Backups Work and Can You Restore Them?   Do the backups work, and do you know how to restore them? Verifying backups takes a little longer than just backing them up; but if you verify, you know that what's on the tape matches what is on the drive. As far as restoring goes, practice restoring files *before* you have a problem. Learning to do it right is a lot easier when you don't have to learn under pressure, and if you restore files periodically, you'll know that the files backed up okay.

Have Users Backed Up Their Own Work?   In the interests of preventing your operating system from coming to a complete halt while you're fixing the downed network, it might not be a bad idea to have people store a copy of whatever they're working on, and the application needed to run it, on their workstations. This way, people who only work on one or two things at a time could work while you get the server back on line.

Backup Strategies

Backup

Backups are like exercises—they're necessary, but they often don't get done unless they're easy to do. NT Server does a lot toward making sure that backups get done by providing a tape backup program that is fast and easy to use.

Performing Backups

You can find the Backup icon in the Administrative Tools program group. When you double-click on the icon, you'll see a screen that looks like Figure 15.3.

FIGURE 15.3:
Opening screen for Backup

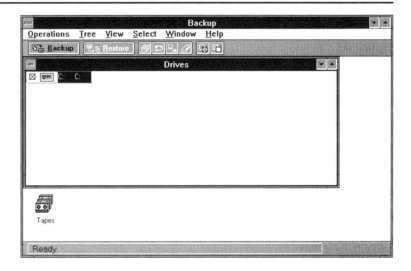

When you want to back up a drive, you need to select the drive first, even if you only have one on your server. To do so, click in the check box next to the drive until it has an X in it. If for some reason you open the Backup screen and the drives window is not open but is an icon similar to the Tapes icon at the bottom of Figure 15.3, just double-click on it to open it.

Once you've selected the drive that you want to back up and you have a tape in the drive, you're ready to go. Click on the Backup button in the upper-left corner or select the Backup option from the Operations drop-down menu. You'll see a screen that looks like Figure 15.4.

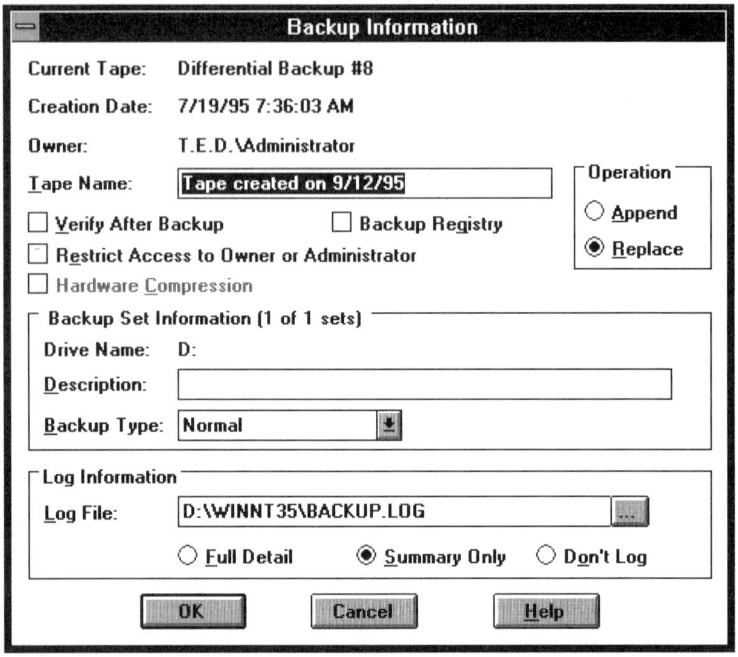

FIGURE 15.4:

Backup Information dialog box

```
┌─────────────────────────────────────────────────────────────┐
│ ━                    Backup Information                      │
├─────────────────────────────────────────────────────────────┤
│  Current Tape:    Differential Backup #8                     │
│  Creation Date:   7/19/95 7:36:03 AM                         │
│  Owner:           T.E.D.\Administrator                       │
│                                             ┌─ Operation ──┐ │
│  Tape Name:    [Tape created on 9/12/95  ]  │ ○ Append     │ │
│   □ Verify After Backup      □ Backup Registry │ ◉ Replace  │ │
│   □ Restrict Access to Owner or Administrator  └───────────┘ │
│   □ Hardware Compression                                     │
│   ┌─ Backup Set Information (1 of 1 sets) ─────────────────┐ │
│   │ Drive Name:   D:                                       │ │
│   │ Description:  [                                       ] │ │
│   │ Backup Type:  [Normal              ▼]                  │ │
│   └───────────────────────────────────────────────────────┘ │
│   ┌─ Log Information ──────────────────────────────────────┐ │
│   │ Log File:    [D:\WINNT35\BACKUP.LOG            ] [...]  │ │
│   │     ○ Full Detail    ◉ Summary Only    ○ Don't Log     │ │
│   └───────────────────────────────────────────────────────┘ │
│        [   OK   ]      [  Cancel  ]      [  Help  ]          │
└─────────────────────────────────────────────────────────────┘
```

The Backup Information Dialog Box

The Backup Information dialog box gives you information about the tape you have in the drive and lets you make decisions about how you want the backup to be conducted. Let's look at each part of this dialog box in order:

Field	Description
Current Tape	As you might guess, this is the tape that you have in the drive. I'm reusing an old backup, so the Backup program reads and gives me the tape name, which is the tape's creation date. This is good, because if I use this tape for my backup, I'll lose the data from the 2/23 backup, and this reminder of when the tape was made could save me from mistakenly overwriting my data.
Creation Date	If you'd named the tape something other than the date it was created, this tells you when the current tape was created.

Field	Description
Owner	This is the domain and user name of the person who made the backup. As you can see in Figure 15.4, in this case the owner is the Administrator of domain T.E.D.
Tape Name	This is the name that you give the new information on this tape. You can call it the default name of "Tape created on [date]" if you like, or you can call it something like "Backup before installing OS/2 do not erase" to give your memory a little extra jog. The tape name can be up to 50 characters long, including spaces, but if it's longer than 32 characters you won't be able to see the entire name without scrolling down the line.
Verify After Backup	If you select this option, the backup program will check to make sure that, after it's done, the backup matches the original data on the disk. Verification takes a little longer, but it's a good way to double-check that your backups will actually be complete and accurate when you need them.
Backup Registry	Check this box to include a copy of the local registry files in the backup set. The local registry files are your disk configuration information, and in the case of disaster, having this information might not be a bad idea.
Operation	Selecting Append or Replace makes a decision about what happens to the data already on the tape, if there is any. Select Append to add the new backup to the backup already on the tape and not lose anything. Make sure that you have enough room on the tape for both the old data and the new. Select Replace to have the new backup overwrite the old one. Be sure that you no longer need an old backup before selecting Replace, because you can't get back the data once you overwrite it.

Field	Description
Restrict Access to Owner or Administrator	Restricting access to the owner or administrator is probably a good idea for a number of reasons. First, no one but the owner or administrator should have any need to access backed-up files. If someone else needs an old copy of a file, they can ask the people authorized to give it to them. Second, making everyone responsible for their own backups can avoid recrimination when a backup is missing or corrupted. If no one can use a backup other than its owner and something happens to the backup, it's clear who did it.
Drive Name	The drive name is the name of the drive you selected for backup before you got to this dialog box. You can't change it here, so if you selected the wrong drive, cancel out of this box and change your selection.
Description	You can fill in a description of the backup in addition to its name. If you wanted to record both the date and the contents of the drive, you could name the tape "Backup from 03/09/96" and *describe* it as "Pre-OS/2 installation backup—keep," or some such thing.
Backup Type	If you click on the ↓ on the right side of this box, you'll see that you have a number of different backup types to chose from:

Normal A full backup—everything selected gets backed up, whether or not the archive bit is set. (The archive bit is attached to a file when it's changed and removed when it's backed up, allowing selective backups of the files that have changed since the last backup.) This is the default option. Even if you normally do incremental backups (described below), periodically doing a normal backup to make sure that you have everything on the disk backed up is a good idea.

Copy A full backup of all the selected files on the disk. In this case, however, the archive bit is not reset after the files have been backed up—from looking at the File Manager, you couldn't tell that anything was backed up.

Differential Backs up only those files with the archive bit set, but doesn't reset it afterwards. This is useful for interim backups between full backups, because restoring the data only requires restoring the last full backup and the most recent differential.

Incremental Like a differential backup, this option backs up only those files with the archive bit set, but the incremental backup then resets the bit.

Daily Backs up only those files that have been modified *that day* (as opposed to since the last backup), and does not reset the archive bit. If you want to take home the files that you've worked on during a given day, this can be a good way of getting them all.

Log Information	Backup log records how the backup went: how many files were backed up, how many skipped (if any), how many errors there were (if any), and how long the backup took. You might as well keep the backup logs in the default directory unless you have a good reason to move them elsewhere, just so you don't forget where they are.
	On the bottom of the dialog box, you can see that you have a choice of two kinds of backup log records: *Full Detail* and *Summary Only* (or no log). A full log records the name of every file backed up, in addition to the other information about major events that's described above. A summary merely records major events. For most purposes, a summary log is fine. The only time that I can think of when you might need a full log is if you were doing a differential backup and wanted to have some record of what files you'd backed up.

Now that you've filled out the Backup Information dialog box, you're ready to do the backup. Click OK, and, if you're using an old backup tape and you selected the Replace option, you'll see a screen that looks like Figure 15.5. Once again, if you're sure that you want to overwrite the data, click on Yes. You'll move to the screen in Figure 15.6, which keeps you informed of the backup's progress.

FIGURE 15.5:

Warning that data will be overwritten

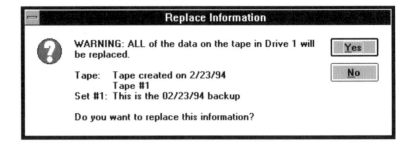

FIGURE 15.6:

Backup Status screen

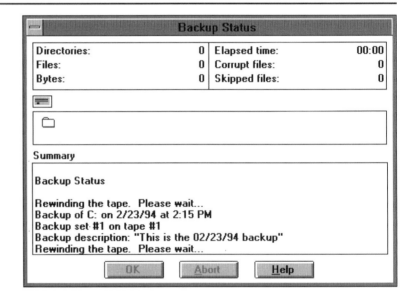

Normally, when you see this screen, the Abort button will not be grayed out unless you had to abort the backup, and OK won't be a viable choice from the time you begin the backup until it's finished. As the backup progresses, you'll be able to keep track of it by looking at this screen.

How Do I Back Up Data?

With a tape in the drive, start the Backups program in the Administrative Tools program group. Select the drive that you want to back up, and then click on the Backup button in the upper-left of the screen. Fill in the Backup Information dialog box as appropriate, and click OK.

The backup should proceed normally.

Important Note: You cannot read or restore tapes backed up in NT Server 3.51 on a server running a previous version of NT Server.

Performing Automatic Backups

To be safest, you should back up your drive every day, since that way you'll never lose more than one day's worth of work. Unfortunately, running even an easy-to-use backup program like NT Server's takes away from your day—the task-switching involved takes time from your real work, and you might forget to back up altogether if you get caught up in something else.

Fortunately, you don't have to rely on your memory or your schedule to do daily backups. NT Server provides two ways to run backups on a regular schedule: the command prompt and the WINAT.EXE GUI program.

Backing Up from the Command Prompt

Elsewhere in this book, we talked about how to use the net schedule and at commands to schedule batch commands to run at a certain time. Among the other programs that you can run with the at command is the DOS version of NT Server's backup program, called ntbackup. The parameters this command uses provide you with almost the same flexibility that the GUI backup program does—it's just a little trickier to use.

To run ntbackup, type the following:

```
ntbackup backup path options
```

where *path* is the drive (and directory, if you're only backing up part of a drive) that you want to back up and *options* is one of the switches shown in Table 15.1. You can select more than one drive at a time—just type the drive letters with colons after them. In the path, you can also specify individual files to back up, or specify all the files of a certain type with the asterisk wildcard (*).

TABLE 15.1: Switches for Use with NTBACKUP

Switch	Description
/a	Makes the mode of backup append, so that the backed up files will be added to those already on the tape. If this switch is omitted, the new files will overwrite any files now on the tape.
/v	Verifies that the backup was done correctly by comparing the data on the tape with the original data on the drive after the backup's done. Backups take a little longer with verification, but they let you know that the data was written correctly.
/r	Restricts access to the tape's owner and the network administrator.
/d	Lets you describe the backup. Enclose your text in quotation marks after the /d switch.
/b	Backs up the local registry.
/t	Lets you select the backup type. You can choose to do a Normal, Copy, Incremental, Differential, or Daily backup; /t incremental gives you an incremental backup. If you don't use this switch, you'll perform a normal backup.
/l	Writes a log of the backup. You must specify a location for the log to be written, like this: /l "c:\log\log.txt". As shown, you enclose the log's destination in quotation marks.

Let's start with a simple example. To do a full backup of all the files on a C\wpfiles directory that ends with the extension .doc, you would type:

```
ntbackup backup c:\wpfiles\*.doc
```

Finally, suppose you wanted to perform a differential backup of all the files in both drives C and D, verify backup, describe the backup as "The monster drives on the server," perform a backup of the local registry, restrict access to the owner and network administrator, and record a backup log under the name C:\LOG\LOG.TXT. You would type the following on one line:

```
ntbackup backup c: d: /v/r/b/d "The monster drives on the server"
/l "c:\log\log.txt"
```

Now that you're familiar with the DOS parameters for the backup program, you can use it to do timed backups. Start the scheduler service by typing **net schedule**, and then use the at command to set up the automatic backup. For instance, to do an incremental backup every day of the \wpfiles directory on drive c, verify backup, append the files to the ones already on the disk, describe the backup as "My wordprocessing files," and record the log in c:\log\log.txt, you'd type this on one line:

```
at ntbackup backup c:\wpfiles /t incremental /v/a/d "My wordproc-
essing files" /l"c:\log\log.txt"
```

For another example, to back up your C drive at 11:00 every Wednesday, first you'd start the scheduling service by typing **net schedule**, and then you'd type:

```
at 11:00 every:wednesday ntbackup backup c:
```

These commands would then be entered on the jobs list, which you can view by typing **at** from the command prompt. You don't have to set up the command as you see it in the example; you can use the switches to configure your backup procedure as you see fit. No matter what combination of switches you use to customize your automatic backups, however, using the /a switch to append the new backups to the ones already on your tape is probably a good idea. You're using this daily incremental backup to keep your backups current between weekly full backups, so you'll want to keep a complete record of all changes made between those full backups.

Using the Scheduler (WINAT) Program

Unless you're really fond of working from the command prompt, the WINAT GUI program is probably easier to use, even though you still need to know MS-DOS syntax. WINAT is one of a number of handy applications that come with the Windows NT Resource Kit. Once you load the Resource Kit, you need to use the Program Manager's New... option to add it manually to one of the program groups. You can put the program item wherever you like; I put mine in the Administrative Tools program group.

When you've added WINAT to a program group, you're ready to go. Double-click on the program icon, pull down the File menu, choose Select Computer, type in your computer name if it's not already there, click OK, and then choose the Add... button. You'll see a screen like the one in Figure 15.7.

FIGURE 15.7:

Add Command dialog box

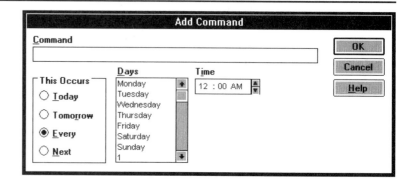

In the Command text box, type in the command syntax, following the rules in the previous section on using the command prompt. Once you've typed in the command, use the radio buttons to determine how often you want the event to occur (since we're configuring a daily incremental backup, choose Every). Next, Ctrl-click on all the days of the week on which you want the backup to run. For our installation, we selected every day for those times when someone's working over the weekend, but you may want to choose different days. Finally, choose the time when you want the backup to run. It's best to choose a time very late at night or early in the morning when there's likely to be little network activity and people should be done changing files. Once you've set up the command and the times, click OK to return to the original screen. It should look like Figure 15.8.

If you need to adjust the settings of your job, click the Change... button. You'll see the Change Command dialog box, which looks much like the Add Command

FIGURE 15.8:

Command Scheduler dialog box

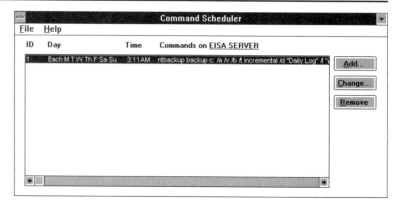

dialog box (see Figure 15.9). From this screen, you can adjust your backup (or any other scheduled service) as necessary, using the same procedures that you used to add it.

If you need to remove your backup command, select it in the Command Scheduler screen and click Remove. When you do, the system will prompt you for confirmation. Click Yes and the command will be removed. Don't remove an event unless you're sure that you want to, however—there's no Cancel function in that screen. Every time you add a job to this list, it will be assigned a job identification number. When you remove a job, the numbers assigned to the other jobs in the list do not change, and future jobs take the next highest number available. If you erase job 0, leaving job 1 intact, and then add job 0 back, it will become job 2.

What about the Scheduler service? Yes, it still needs to be running for WINAT to work, just as it does for the AT command in the command prompt. You can start it from the Services icon in the Control Panel, or you can just go ahead and start WINAT. A message box will tell you that the Scheduler is not running and ask you if you want to start running it. When you say Yes, the service will begin.

Special Backup Operations

We've just discussed how to do a normal, vanilla-flavored backup that hits every file on your hard disk, only requires one tape, backs up a local disk, and doesn't need to be aborted. Special circumstances may require you to do the job a bit differently, however, and that's what this section covers.

Backing Up Only Selected Files

At some point, you may want to back up only certain directories or files on your hard disk; not necessarily the ones with the archive bit set, but an assortment. To do this, you must select the directories or files to be copied, and deselect everything else.

The process begins as though you were backing up the entire disk. Go to the initial Backup screen (see Figure 15.3) and select the drive that you want to back up. Rather than now clicking on the Backup button, however, double-click on the gray drive icon. You'll see a screen that looks like Figure 15.9.

When I opened this screen, every directory had a filled check box next to it. Since I only wanted to back up files from some of the directories, I clicked the check box next to the C drive and deselected it so that I could individually select the directory

FIGURE 15.9:

Selection of directories to back up

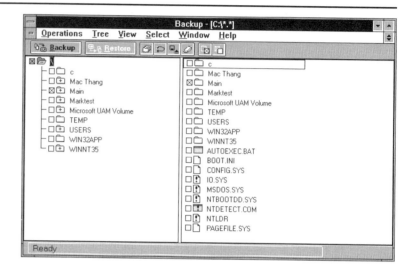

that I wanted. From here, I chose as many directories as I liked. When I double-clicked on NTCLASS, I got a list of its files and subdirectories, as shown in Figure 15.10.

Once again, to keep from selecting every file and subdirectory in the NTCLASS directory, I clicked on the check box for that directory to deselect it. Now, only the files

FIGURE 15.10:

Selection of files and subdirectories to back up

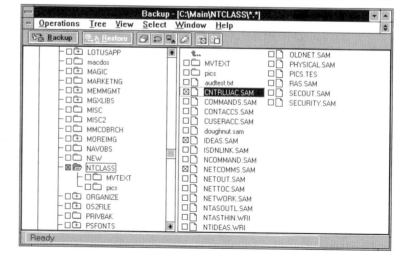

that I selected would be backed up. As you can see in the figure, I chose three files for backup.

Now I'm ready to complete the backup. From here, you'd click on the Backup button, as you did earlier to back up the entire drive. You'd be returned to the initial Backup Information dialog box (see Figure 15.4). The rest of the operation is exactly like backing up an entire directory.

By the way, please note that, although I only selected one directory to draw files from for this example, you can do this with as many directories and subdirectories as you like. Just make sure that you deselect everything before you select anything, or else you'll end up backing up more files than you intended.

Using More Than One Tape

Using more than one tape for backup isn't difficult to do. If you choose Append from the Backup Information dialog box or you have an absolutely huge hard drive, you may run out of space on your tape before the backup is done. If this happens, the Backup program will prompt you for a new tape with a dialog box. Just insert the new tape and press OK.

Aborting a Backup

If you realize that you don't want to back up your data once you've started, you can click on the Abort button, and the process will stop. If the program was in the middle of backing up a file and there was less than 1MB to go, that file will be completed; otherwise a message box will appear asking if you really want to stop now and have the file be corrupted on the tape.

Clicking on Abort does not cancel the backup; it only stops it at the point at which you aborted. Whatever files had backed up before you aborted the process will be on the tape.

Backing Up to Floppy Disks

If you don't have a tape drive, you can still back up your most important files to floppy disks. To do so, go to the command prompt and use either the xcopy or the backup command. The backup command is perhaps a little simpler.

When using the backup command, you can specify drives (although that's not likely if you're backing up to floppies), directories, or individual files. The syntax looks like this:

```
backup source destination drive: options
```

where *source* specifies the source files, directories, or drive. You can use wildcards to specify all the files of a certain type, or spell out all the file names. For example, to back up all of directory C:\WPFILES, you'd type **c:\wpfiles**. To back up all the files in that directory with the .doc suffix, you'd type **c:\wpfiles*.doc**. For *destination drive:*, substitute the name of the drive (such as A) where you want the backups to be stored. For *options*, include one or more of the switches shown in Table 15.2.

Alternatively, you can use xcopy to back up your files or put files on disk to take them on a trip. Use xcopy rather than copy, because COPY doesn't use the archive

TABLE 15.2: Switches for Use in Backing Up to Floppy Disks

Switch	Description
/s	Tells the backup program to search all subdirectories for files. If you don't select this option, the backup program will only back up the files in the directory that you're actually in. For example, if you specify C:*.DOC for the source directory and don't use the /s switch, only .doc files in the root directory will be backed up.
/m	Backs up only the files with the archive bit set—the ones that have changed since the last backup.
/a	Appends the current backup to the files already on the destination disk. Omitting this switch will cause the destination disk to be overwritten.
/f: [size]	Specifies the size of the disk to be formatted, if you want the destination disk to be formatted before you write to it. Put the *size* of the disk (1.44MB, for example) after the colon.
/d: [date]	Backs up only the files that have changed after the *date* you place after the colon, whether or not they have the archive bit set.
/t: [time]	Backs up only the files that have changed after the *time* you specify, whether or not they have the archive bit set.
/l [drive:path]	Creates a log file in the drive and path you specify.

bit and is not as customizable. While XCOPY has many switches, these are some of the most relevant when it comes to backing up NTFS files:

Switch	Description
/a	Copies files with the archive attribute set, but doesn't change the attribute. This switch is good for when you're copying the files that you've worked with on a given day but don't want them to get skipped by the daily incremental backup.
/m	Copies with the archive bit set and then removes the bit.
/d: [date]	Copies only the files changed on or after the date you specify.
/h	Copies hidden and system files, as well as normal ones.
/u	Updates the files in the destination.
/n	Copies NTFS files, using shorter names created for use with FAT file system. Only works on NTFS files.

If you want more help with XCOPY, type the following from the command prompt (there's more than one screen of options):

```
xcopy /? |more
```

Backing Up Removable Media

If you want to back up the data in a removable media drive (such as a Bernoulli or a Floptical), it may seem impossible at first because NT Server's backup program doesn't recognize removable drives as available for backup. You can, however, get around this fairly easily. To see how, read the "How Do I" sidebar.

Backing up a Network Drive

Even if you're using an internal tape drive on your server, you can still use that drive to back up other hard disks on your system. The process is quite straightforward:

1. Go to the computer that you want to back up and share the drive or directory for backup with the network.

2. From the server's File Manager, connect to the shared directory.

Now, when you start the backup program, you'll notice a new icon for a network drive in the list of available drives for backup. From here, the backup process is identical to that of backing up a local drive.

How Do I Back Up a Removable Drive?

To back up a removable drive:

1. Go to the File Manager or the command prompt and share the drive that you want to back up.

2. Connect to the shared drive from the File Manager or command prompt.

3. The backup program will now be able to see the drive under the letter assigned it, so long as you have a disk in the drive.

You're now set. Back it up as you would any other drive.

Backing Up Open Files

NT's Backup program has one distinct failure: it can't back up open files. If you normally schedule backups for 2 AM when no one's working, this wouldn't seem to be a problem. However, on many of our networks, there are some files that will be open at 2 AM and *must* stay open: the files that control the internal naming services, and the files for the DHCP server that allocates IP addresses.

Luckily, there's an easy way around this. To make sure that the WINS and DHCP files get backed up, make this simple batch file part of your regularly scheduled backup:

```
C:
CD \USERS
CACLS DHCP /T /E /G EVERYONE:F
CACLS WINS /T /E /G EVERYONE:F
```

```
net stop "Microsoft DHCP Server"
net stop "Windows internet name service"
xcopy c:\winnt35\system32\dhcp c:\users\sysjunk\dhcp >>C:\USERS\DBAK.LOG
xcopy c:\winnt35\system32\wins c:\users\sysjunk\wins >>C:\USERS\DBAK.LOG
net start "Windows internet name service"
net start "Microsoft DHCP Server"
```

It's not hard to tell what's going on here: the files that run the DHCP server and WINS are getting copied from the \system32 directory to an (unopened) log file in the \users directory so that they can be backed up. This batch file stops the DHCP Server and the Windows Internet Service before it copies the files, restarting the services after the files are copied, but since the whole batch file takes only a few seconds to execute, the services are not shut down long enough to present a problem.

If you don't recognize the CACLS command, that's because it's not documented. It's a useful NT command that allows you to change the ownership and control of a file or directory from the command line. In our version of this batch file, we had to include a command giving the Everyone group full control of the WINS and DHCP directories because these directories were owned by the System and thus even Administrators could not copy them. You could give only Administrators or Backup Operators full control if you liked; in our case, it didn't matter if Everyone could control the directories.

If you're using the AT command to schedule backups, you can make this batch file part of your weekly backup: just add it to the scheduler to run a few minutes before the backup job.

Protecting Backups

Backing up your system is a vital part of any decent security program. However, it's quite easy for an intruder to access confidential files on the tapes that you back up to. If you don't keep an eye on the tapes, they can be rendered useless when you try to restore them. Any user can back up files that he or she has access to, and any Administrator or Backup Operator can back up the entire drive (even if, for example, your Backup Operator cannot normally access the files that he or she's backing up). Be very careful about who you assign backup rights to.

Once you have your backup tapes, you need to protect them from damage, as well as protect them from theft. To this end, here are some things to consider when it comes to tape storage:

- Tapes are comfortable under approximately the same conditions that you are. Excessive heat or dampness will do your backups no good. *Never* store tapes on a windowsill.

- While you want your backups to be fairly convenient, so that you can restore information if you blast your hard drive, it won't do you any good to have backups if your office burns down and takes the originals and the backups of all your data with it. For best protection, store all of your backups but the most recent in a safe location (locked, fireproof, waterproof) off-site.

- Enable the Restrict Access to Owner or Administrator option when backing up files. For extra protection, keep server backups locked up, and only allow the network administrator or the security manager access to them. If workstations get backed up, the tapes and their usability should be the responsibility of the workstation's user.

- Label your tapes clearly and completely (on both their paper labels and their electronic volume labels), so that you don't erase a vital tape by thinking that it's something else. In NT Server, you can be very explicit about the volume label on a tape, so use this capability to identify tapes that you don't want to reuse.

Restoring Files

Your backups are useless unless you can restore them to your machine in good order. Restoring files is much like backing them up. First, click open the Backups item in the Administrative Tools program group. You'll see the Backup screen that you saw when you backed up originally (see Figure 15.3). But this time, select the Tapes window instead of a drive. You'll see a screen that looks like Figure 15.11.

To begin the restoration process, select the tape by clicking in the check box next to it. If you want to restore an entire tape, the selection process is done, but you probably want to restore selected files from a tape, not the whole thing, so we'll go through the selection process now.

FIGURE 15.11:

Opening Restore screen

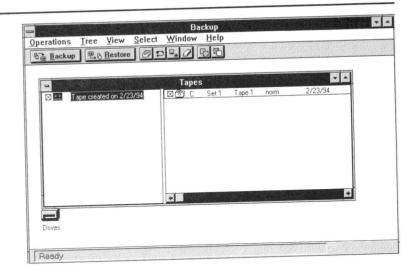

Double-click on the tape icon, and the restore program will load the tape's catalog, so that it can find files on the tape. This process will take a couple of minutes, and while it's doing this, you'll see a screen that looks like Figure 15.12.

When the cataloging process is finished, you can click on the yellow files icon on the other side of the initial screen. When you do, you'll see a screen like the one in Figure 15.13. This screen shows you all the available directories on the tape.

As you can see, everything is currently deselected. I didn't want to restore every file, so I unchecked the drive's check box. From there, I expanded the Main directory, and then the AMIPRO directory, and from there the STYLES directory, by double-clicking on their yellow file icons. You don't have to check the check boxes

FIGURE 15.12:

Catalog Status message

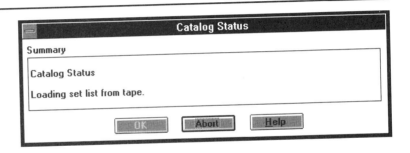

FIGURE 15.13:

Available directories for restoration

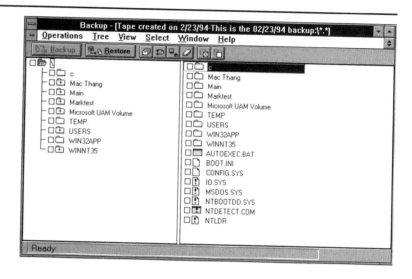

to select a drive or a directory before expanding it, and it's safer not to, if you're doing a selective restore as I am in this example. If you select a drive or directory, everything in it will be restored.

Once you've progressed to the directory that you want, click on the file or files that you want to restore, just as you did when you were backing up. Your screen should look something like Figure 15.14.

Now you're ready to restore. Go ahead and click on the Restore button. A dialog box similar to the Backup Information box will open, as in Figure 15.15.

The Restore Information dialog box is much simpler than the Backup Information one. Essentially, all that you must do here is decide whether or not you want to verify that the information was written correctly (a good idea, even though it adds time to the restoration process), restore the local registry if you backed it up, and restore the file permissions that were in place for the file when you backed it up. If you like, you can choose to restore the data to a different drive than the one you backed it up from, although you cannot restore registry information to a drive other than the one from which you backed it up. You can also choose what kind of log file you want and where you'd like it stored.

FIGURE 15.14:

Files selected for restoration

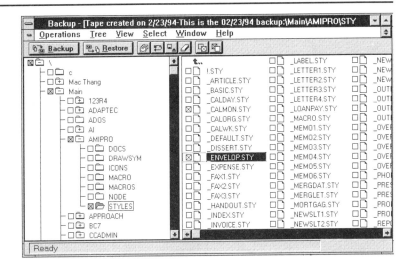

FIGURE 15.15:

Restore Information dialog box

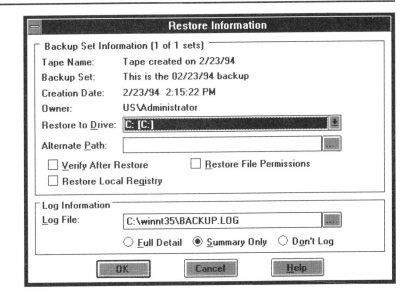

When you're done, click OK, and the restoration progress will begin. You can watch the process onscreen, as in Figure 15.16.

If you're restoring individual files to your drive because the originals were corrupted somehow, the Restore program will ask you if you're sure that you want to replace the file on disk with the file on the tape. You'll see a dialog box like the one in Figure 15.17. Your files are now restored to your hard disk.

FIGURE 15.16:

File restoration progress screen

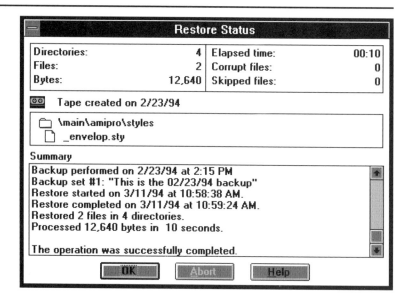

FIGURE 15.17:

Confirm File Replace dialog box

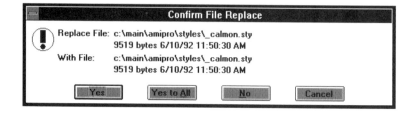

Side Note: Restoring Data after Reinstalling NT Server

When writing this book, there were some things that I could not experiment with without reinstalling NT Server. Given that the operating system really isn't difficult to install (just time-consuming), this wasn't much of a problem, but one instance of reinstalling the operating system and trying to restore my data nearly gave me heart failure.

I was experimenting with the Disk Administrator and needed to repartition the drive with the NT Server installation on it. I prepared to back up my data and reinstall the server. I did everything by the book: backed up the hard disk to tape, verified the backup, restored a couple of files from the backup (just to make sure that the files could be read). I was ready to go. I installed NT Server, blowing away my old disk partition in the process so that *none* of the data was left, and then, two hours later when the installation was done, prepared to restore the data.

When I tried to catalog the tape, all I got was a cryptic Dr. Watson message advising me that the system had generated an application error, and then the backup program closed. When I reopened it, I could see the icon for the tape catalog tantalizingly sitting there, but when I tried to double-click on it to open it, I got the same Dr. Watson message.

In desperation, I selected the catalog and attempted to restore without being able to access it, but all that got me was the data thrown back on the hard disk any which way, not in its original directories but in strange directories with names that the system seemed to have made up from truncated file names. I checked a couple of the files after this strange restoration and they seemed okay, but I knew that I couldn't count on the data's integrity, and I'd never be able to find anything anyway. Restoring the data without the catalog was useless.

If the situation I was in isn't quite clear, let me just explain that the tape that I couldn't read contained all the data on the hard drive: all my books, all the company's manuals, all of *everything* except the mailing list. I had the backup—I was clutching it, white-knuckled, in my hand—but I couldn't read it.

I reinstalled NT Server, just to see if there was a problem with the installation that prevented me from reading my tape. Then I did it again. And again. I scoured the documentation, looking for clues. Finally, I got desperate (well, more desperate), decided that it was time to call in the Marines, and called Microsoft's $150-per-question Tech Support line with my problem. Even at $150 per question, however, they didn't know the answer. (That didn't keep them from charging me, however.)

Finally, many hours and several installations later, I decided to try installing all the system software and *then* restoring the data. I reinstalled everything that I'd had on the system before, including the Service Pack 2 patches—this was under NT 3.1— that I'd had on the system before, on the theory that it might affect how the backup worked. *This* time, I could restore the data.

The moral of this story? Before trying to restore data after a complete reinstallation of NT Server, install all your system software first. It seems obvious now, but it wasn't at the time, and that mistake nearly killed me. (End of digression.)

How Do I Restore Data from Backups?

With the tape from which you want to restore in the drive, begin the Backup program in the Administrative Tools program group. Double-click on the tape icon to catalog it. Once it's cataloged, select the item(s) that you wish to restore, or select the entire catalog, and then click on the Restore button. A dialog box will appear; fill it in as appropriate. The restoration process should take place normally. If you don't have a tape drive, the programs REGBACK and REGREST, available with the NT Resource Kit, will save and restore registries to and from floppies.

Special Restoration Operations

Sometimes, you can't restore files in the traditional way described above. A backup set is spread over more than one tape, or you've blasted the disk registry and need to restore it. When you need special restoration techniques, this is how to do them.

Restoring from a Tape Set with a Missing Tape

To restore data from a backup set that extends over more than one tape, you'll need to insert the last tape in the set and load the backup catalog from there.

If that tape has been lost or destroyed, you can still load the backup catalogs from the tapes that you have, but it's a more arduous process. In this case, you must build a partial tape catalog by inserting the available tapes and loading their individual catalogs. Once you've done that, you can restore the data. If you're restoring the data from the command prompt, run NTBACKUP with the /missingtape switch.

Restoring Data to a Networked Drive

The process of restoring data to a networked drive is pretty much as you'd expect. Connect to the drive or directory through the File Manager, and then choose to restore to that drive letter when you're setting up the Restore options. From here, the process is identical to restoring locally.

Restoring a Disk Registry

If you blast your hard disk or its registry gets corrupted and you lose your system volume, you can restore it and get your data back if you backed up the registry earlier. To restore it from the GUI interface, click on the Restore Registry check box. From the command line, the process works as described in the "How Do I" sidebar.

How Do I Restore a Disk Registry?

To restore a disk registry:

1. From Windows NT Backup, restore the CONFIG directory in the System32 directory.

2. Reboot your machine.

3. Restore the entire backup set *except* for the Registry files.

4. Reboot your machine again.

The volume should be back to its original state.

> **TIP** You cannot restore a disk registry to any disk except the one from which you backed it up. In other words, you can't apply the disk registry from drive C to drive E. This is so that you can't sneak around NT's security system.

Disasters shouldn't happen, but they sometimes do. With the proper preventive planning beforehand, disasters can become entertaining war stories rather than sources of battle fatigue.

CHAPTER

SIXTEEN

16

NET-ing Results: Using the Command Prompt

Just as you could with LAN Manager, you can control your network's settings from the MS-DOS command prompt in NT Server. In this section, we'll discuss these commands, their switches, and how to use them.

In this chapter, we'll discuss how to use the command prompt, but first there are a few things that you should know before beginning:

- Those of you who have used LAN Manager will notice that some of the commands look familiar (but not quite as you remember them) and that some are missing altogether. This is because the way that NT Server works affected the way that some commands worked in LAN Manager, and made other commands totally useless (like NET LOGON, for example, since logging onto the network is inherent to NT Server).

- A single entry from the command prompt is limited to 1,024 characters. This limit will probably not restrict you, but if you are sending a long message with NET SEND (discussed later in this chapter) and you suddenly can't enter any more characters, you've exceeded the 1,024 limit.

NT SERVER

- Most of the commands in this chapter work on both NT workstations and NT Server servers, but a few only work under NT Server. When a command applies only to a server, you'll see the Server margin icon shown here.

What You Can Do with the NET Commands

What can you do with the NET commands? You can adjust your system, manipulating accounts and connections much the same way you can from the graphical interface. There are six categories of things that you can do from the command prompt.

Manipulate User Accounts   From the command line, you can add or delete users from user groups, view group memberships, and adjust the configuration of user accounts.

View and Change Domain Memberships   As you'll no doubt remember from elsewhere in this book, users are members of groups, while computers are members of domains. From the command prompt, you can add or delete computers to and from domains, or view the membership of domains.

Connect to Shared Resources and Share Resources   The biggest advantage to networking is the ability it gives you to connect to other computers' drives and peripheral devices, such as printers. From the command prompt, you can connect to others' devices and share your own, setting whatever passwords you like.

Start and Stop Services   The services that you can begin from the Server Manager or Control Panel can also be reached from the command prompt. From here, you can start, stop, pause, and continue network services.

Send and Receive Messages   Although the messaging capabilities of NT Server are no substitute for an e-mail package, you can use NT to send messages on the network and alert people to situations. For example, you could send this message: "The server is going down in five minutes—save whatever you're working on."

Set or View Time   If you have a time server on your network, you can set workstation clocks to synchronize with it. You can also check the time on workstations and servers.

Getting Help

This section comes first because, if you get completely stuck while trying to use a NET command, the two commands discussed here may be able to help you. NET HELP and NET HELPMSG are not universal panaceas, and sometimes they're downright unhelpful, but they come in useful at times.

NET HELP: Getting Help from the Command Prompt

You'll probably use the NET HELP command most when you're first learning how to use the rest of the network commands. When you enter this command, you see the screen like the one in Figure 16.1. For example, if you need help with the command NET PRINT, you can simply type

```
net help net print ¦more
```

to get all the help file information attached to that command. The ¦ more switch is necessary for commands that have more than one screen of information.

If you prefer, you can get the same information shown in the figure by typing

```
net print /help
```

instead of NET HELP NET PRINT. Just typing NET PRINT/? to get command information, as you might under MS-DOS, doesn't net much information (no pun intended) under NT Server—it merely gives you the proper syntax for the command. To view an explanation of all of the command syntax symbols, just type

```
net help syntax
```

By the way, regardless of what the NET HELP SERVICES command tells you, no online help is available for the following services from the command prompt:

- Client Service for Netware
- DHCP Client

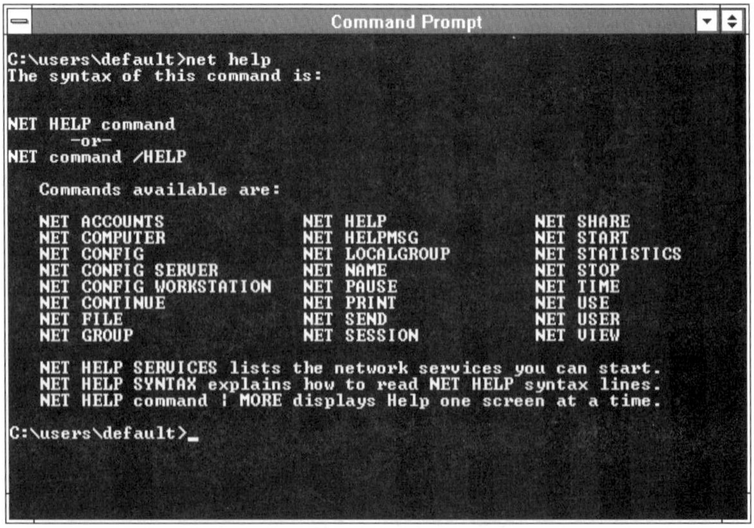

FIGURE 16.1:

The NET HELP command

```
                              Command Prompt                         ▼ ◆

C:\users\default>net help
The syntax of this command is:

NET HELP command
       -or-
NET command /HELP

   Commands available are:

   NET ACCOUNTS              NET HELP            NET SHARE
   NET COMPUTER              NET HELPMSG         NET START
   NET CONFIG                NET LOCALGROUP      NET STATISTICS
   NET CONFIG SERVER         NET NAME            NET STOP
   NET CONFIG WORKSTATION    NET PAUSE           NET TIME
   NET CONTINUE              NET PRINT           NET USE
   NET FILE                  NET SEND            NET USER
   NET GROUP                 NET SESSION         NET VIEW

   NET HELP SERVICES lists the network services you can start.
   NET HELP SYNTAX explains how to read NET HELP syntax lines.
   NET HELP command ¦ MORE displays Help one screen at a time.

C:\users\default>_
```

- File Server for the Macintosh
- Gateway Service for Netware
- LPDSVC
- Microsoft DHCP Server
- Network DDE DSDM
- Network Monitoring Agent
- NT LM Security Support Provider
- OLE
- Print Server for Macintosh
- Remote Procedure Call (RPC) Locator
- Remote Access Connection Manager
- Remote Access Server
- Remote Access ISNSAP Service
- Remote Procedure Call (RPC) Service
- Remote Boot
- Simple TCP/IP Services
- Spooler
- TCPIP NETBIOS Helper
- Windows Internet Name Service

How Do I Get Help from the Command Prompt?

If you need help with the syntax or other particulars of a command, type

`net help command`

where *command* is a command name. The command's help file will be displayed. If the file takes up more than one screen, add the |more switch to the end of the help request.

NET HELPMSG: Decoding Error, Warning, and Alert Messages

NET HELPMSG works as a decoder for NT error, warning, and alert messages. For example, if you see a message such as "Error 2223" that doesn't tell you much, you can type NET HELPMSG 2223 and see a screen like the one in Figure 16.2.

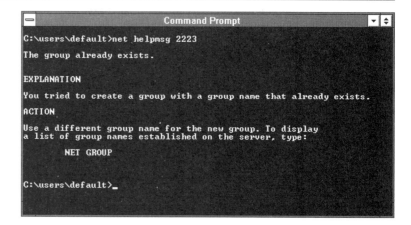

This command is not always terribly helpful. When you're trying out commands and aren't sure of their syntax, you can't always get the command to work right. NET HELPMSG may only tell you that you misspelled a user's name and refer you to the regular help file for the command.

How Do I Decipher Help Message Numbers?

When you get an error message with a number attached, type

`net helpmsg number`

to see the help file attached to that error message.

Manipulating User Accounts

When it comes to user accounts, you can do just about everything from the command prompt that you can from NT Server's GUI programs: adding and deleting accounts, viewing and changing group membership, and configuring user accounts. Here's how.

NET USER: Creating User Accounts

You can use the NET USER command from the server to control user accounts—to add them, delete them, and change them. If you type this command without parameters, you get a list of the user accounts for that server. You can use switches and parameters to manipulate accounts.

To view the existing account of a user on your domain named, for example, Christa, you would type

```
net user christa
```

The case, even of user names, doesn't matter. You don't need to include any passwords to view account information. Once you enter the NET USER command, you'll see a screen that looks like Figure 16.3.

Most of the information should be pretty self-explanatory. Essentially, you see a description of the account, its name, its limitations, and when it was last accessed. To actually *change* anything, you need to use the switches and parameters included in the command. For example, to add a user named Frank to your home domain, you could type

```
net user frank /add
```

That was simple enough: Frank now has an account. At this point, however, he can't use it—primarily because no password was specified. If, instead, you type

```
net user frank * /add
```

with an asterisk to create the new account, you'll be prompted for a password to assign to the account, and once you do, Frank will be able to log on (provided you give him the password).

FIGURE 16.3:

A sample NET USER screen

```
                              Command Prompt
C:\users\default>net user christa ¦more
User name                       Christa
Full Name                       Christa Anderson
Comment                         Research Czar
User's comment
Parameters
Country code                    000 (System Default)
Account active                  Yes
Account expires                 Never

Password last set               3/2/94 8:57AM
Password expires                Never
Password changeable             3/2/94 8:57AM
Password required               Yes
User may change password        No

Workstations allowed            All
Logon script
User profile
Home directory
Last logon                      3/2/94 3:56PM

Logon hours allowed             All

Local Group Memberships         *Account Operators    *Backup Operators
                                *Print Operators
Global Group memberships        *Domain Users
The command completed successfully.


C:\users\default>_
```

At this point, Frank's account exists, but all parameters have been given the default values, and the account information doesn't even include his real name, as you can see in the listing from the command NET USER FRANK in Figure 16.4. Now you need to configure the account with the options available to this command. Table 16.1 shows these options.

Following are some examples of setting up user accounts to give you an idea of how it's done. To add an option to a user's account, type

```
net user frank /option
```

substituting whatever option you want to adjust for *option*. The options and their syntax are listed in Table 16.1. You can include more than one option when configuring an account.

To delete Frank's account, you would just type

```
net user frank /delete
```

Finally, if you're performing this operation on a workstation that does not have NT Server loaded, add the switch /domain to the end of the command to make the command apply to the domain controller of the domain you're in.

FIGURE 16.4:

Frank's new account

How Do I Set Up a User Account from the Command Prompt?

To create and customize a user account, first create the user account by typing

net user *name* /add

where *name* is the user name for the new account. Once you've created the account, customize it with the options in Table 16.1 by typing

net user *name* /*option*

where *option* is the option that you want to add to the account.

TABLE 16.1: User Account Options for the NET USER Command

Option	Description
*	An asterisk after the user's name prompts you to enter and confirm a new password for the user account.
/ACTIVE:{YES | NO}	Determines whether the account is active or inactive. If it is inactive, the user cannot log onto it. Deactivating an account is not the same thing as deleting it. A deactivated account can be reinstated simply by reactivating it, but a deleted account is *dead*; its parameters are lost, and even if you create a new account with the same name and password, you'll need to rebuild the user rights and other account information. The default for this option is YES.
/COMMENT:"*text*"	You don't have to put a comment on an account, but it could be useful if you have a large number of users and you can't recall which account belongs to which user. Enclose the text (no more than 48 characters long, including spaces) in quotation marks.
/COUNTRYCODE:*nnn*	The operating system's country code so that the operating system knows what language to use for help and error messages. The default for this option is 0.
/EXPIRES:{*date* | NEVER}	If you enter a date after the colon, the account will expire on that date; NEVER sets no time limit on the account. Depending on the country code, type the expiration date in *mm,dd,yy* or *dd,mm,yy* format (the format in the US is *mm,dd,yy*). You can enter the year as four characters or two, and months as a number, as two letters, or spelled out. Use commas or forward slashes (/) to separate the parts of the date, not spaces.
/FULLNAME:"*name*"	The user's full name, as opposed to the user name. Enclose this name in quotation marks, as it has a space in it.
/HOMEDIR:*pathname*	If you've set up a home directory for the user, this is where you include the pointers to that directory. You have to set up the home directory before you set up this part of the account.
/HOMEDIRREQ:{YES | NO}	If the user is required to use a home directory, say so here. You must have already created the directory and used the /HOMEDIR switch to specify where it is.
/PASSWORDCHG:{YES | NO}	Specify whether or not users can change their own passwords. The default is YES.
/PASSWORDREQ: {YES | NO}	This determines whether or not a password is required on the user account. The default is YES.

TABLE 16.1: User Account Options for the NET USER Command (continued)

Option	Description
/PROFILEPATH:*path*	Selects a path for the user's logon profile, if there is one for the account.
/SCRIPTPATH:*pathname*	Tells where the user's logon script is located.
/TIMES:(*times* | ALL)	You determine the user's logon hours here. Unless you specify ALL, you must spell out the permitted logon times for every day of the week. Days can be spelled out or be two-letter abbreviations; hours can be in either 12- or 24-hour notation. Separate day and time entries with a comma and days with a semicolon. Don't leave this option blank: if you do, the user will never be able to log on.

NET ACCOUNTS: Making Adjustments to the Entire User Database

To make individual adjustments to user accounts, you'd use the NET USER command. To make adjustments concerning such things as forcible logoffs and password ages to the *entire user account database*, you'd use the NET ACCOUNTS command. When used without switches, NET ACCOUNTS displays the current account information in a screen that looks something like Figure 16.5.

FIGURE 16.5:

A sample NET ACCOUNTS screen

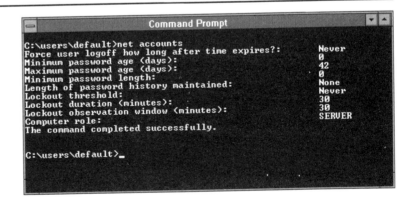

In the screen, you can see that users will be forcibly logged off two minutes after their logon hours expire, that they must change their passwords every 42 days but may do so at any time before that point, and that there is no limit to how long their passwords must be.

So much for looking at the status quo... How do you amend this information? That's where the switches come in. With the switches listed below, you can change all the information that you see on a screen like the one in Figure 16.5.

NET ACCOUNTS Switches

Although I've listed the switches here individually for the sake of clarity, you can, of course, include more than one switch in the NET ACCOUNTS command if you want to change more than one part of a user account.

net accounts /sync   This switch updates the user account database immediately, rather than waiting for a logoff/logon action.

net accounts /forcelogoff:{number} or {no}   This switch sets the number of minutes a user has between the time that the account expires or the logon period ends and the time that the server forcibly disconnects the user. The default is no, but if you've arranged for a user's account to expire or decided that the user has only certain hours in which to log on, you might want to activate this option so that the user has to log off when he or she is supposed to.

net accounts /minpwlen   This switch specifies the minimum number of characters that a user's account must have, from 0 to 14. The default is 6. Clearly, the more letters that a password has, the harder it is to guess and the more random combinations a random password-guessing program has to cycle through. This switch is a bit of a tradeoff, however. You must choose between higher security and the possibility that users will forget their passwords all the time because they can't remember all 14 characters.

net accounts /maxpwage: or /minpwage   These switches specify the minimum and maximum number of days that must pass before the user modifies his or her password. The possible range for /maxpwage is 0 to 49,710 days (a little more than 136 years, which makes you wonder how Microsoft decided on that maximum value), with a default value of 90 days. You can set the value to UNLIMITED if you want the password never to expire.

The /minpwage switch can also be set from 0 to 49,710 days, but its default value is 0 days, meaning that the user can change the password whenever he or she wants to, even more than once a day.

Setting a maximum password age is a good security measure. It will foil an intruder who gets a user account name and password because the information will only be useful to the intruder until the next time the user changes the password. There is a tradeoff between changing passwords often enough that they don't become common knowledge and changing them so often that the person needs to write them down.

net accounts /uniquepw   Determines the number of unique passwords a user must cycle through before repeating one. The highest value that you can assign to this variable is 8. Since people are likely to use old passwords over and over again because they're easier to remember, activating this option might not be a bad idea lest an intruder get an old password. The /uniquepw switch doesn't prevent users from reusing passwords, but it puts a longer stretch between repeats than might otherwise be the case.

net accounts /domain   You'd use the net accounts /domain switch if you were performing the net accounts command on a domain machine that does not have NT Server loaded. If the machine has NT Server on board, the information automatically passes to the domain controller.

How Do I Make Changes to the Entire User Account Database?

To change settings on the entire user account database concerning such matters as forcible logoff times and password ages, type

```
net accounts /option
```

where *option* is a NET ACCOUNTS switch. These switches are shown in the list above.

NET GROUP: Changing Global Group Membership

NT SERVER

The NET GROUP command provides you with information on global groups on a server and gives you the ability to modify this information. Typed without parameters, NET GROUP just gives you a list of the global groups on your server, but you can use the options to modify the membership of global groups, check on their membership, add comments to the group names, or add or delete global groups on the server.

To view the membership of a local group, such as the domain users, type

```
net group "domain users"
```

(If you're not working right at the domain controller, then add the /domain switch at the end of the command.) Notice that, since the group name has a blank space in it, you have to enclose it in quotation marks. If the group name had no blank spaces in it—for example, if the group name was a single word like *administrators*—you wouldn't need the quotation marks. The NET GROUP command gets you a screen like the one in Figure 16.6. The names that end with a dollar sign ($) are domain-controllers.

To add a new global group to a domain, list the group's name in quotation marks. For example, if the new global group is named "mail administrators," you would type

```
net group "mail administrators" /add
```

FIGURE 16.6:

A sample NET GROUP screen

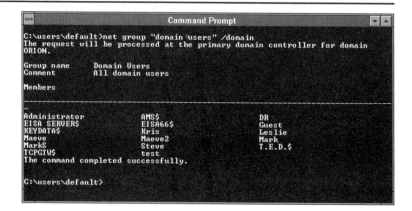

To delete a group with this name, you'd substitute the /delete switch for the /add switch. Once again, note that, if the group name has no blank spaces in it, you don't need to enclose it in quotation marks.

To add a descriptive comment to a new or existing group, add the /comment switch and enclose the comment in quotation marks at the end of the command, like so:

```
/comment:"These are the mail administrators"
```

To add a user to a group, you would type

```
net group "mail administrators"
```

If you are executing the NET GROUP command from a workstation that does not have NT Server installed, add the /domain switch to the end of the statement to make the command apply to the domain controller. Otherwise, you'll only perform the action that you requested at the workstation you are working from. If you're working on a server with NT Server installed, the /domain switch isn't necessary.

How Do I Change Global Group Settings?

To change anything about a global group (that is, a group that extends across a domain), type the following from the command prompt:

```
net group /option
```

where *option* is the name of a switch.

NET LOCALGROUP: Changing Local Group Membership

The NET LOCALGROUP command is very similar to NET GROUP, which is discussed above. The only difference is that NET LOCALGROUP refers to local user groups, and NET GROUP refers to global, or domain-wide, groups. It would probably have been helpful had NET GROUP been called NET GLOBALGROUP instead, so as to avoid confusion. Unlike NET GROUP, this command can be used on NT workstations as well as NT Server servers.

Typed without parameters, NET LOCALGROUP just gives you a list of the local groups on your server, but you can use options to modify the membership of local groups, check on their membership, add comments to the group names, or add or delete global groups on the server.

Checking Membership   To view the membership of a local user group, such as one named "backup operators," you type

```
net localgroup "backup operators"
```

Notice that, since the user group name has a blank space in it, you have to enclose it in quotation marks. If the name had no blank spaces in it you wouldn't need the quotation marks.

Adding Groups   To add a new local group to the server, such as one named "relief administrators," you type

```
net group "relief administrators" /add
```

To delete a group with this name, you'd substitute the /delete for the /add switch. Once again, note that if the group name has no blank spaces in it, you don't need to enclose it in quotation marks.

Describing Groups   To add a descriptive comment to a new or existing group, add the word /comment: and then the text in quotation marks at the end of the command, like so:

```
/comment:"These are the relief administrators"
```

Adding Users to Groups   To add a user named Paul to a group, you would type

```
net group "relief administrators" paul /add
```

If Paul were from another domain, such as Engineering, you would type

```
net group "relief administrators" engineering\paul /add
```

To remove Paul from the group, you'd substitute the /delete for /add switch.

You can add either local users or global groups to local groups, but you cannot add one entire local group to another one. Just put the name of the group or user that you want to add after the name of the group you want to add to. If you add users or groups to a local group, you must set up an account for them on that server or workstation.

Updating the Domain Controller   If you are executing this command from a computer other than the domain controller, add the /domain switch to the end of the statement to make the command apply to the domain controller. Otherwise, you'll only perform the action that you requested at the workstation you are working from. If you're working at the domain controller, the /domain switch isn't necessary.

How Do I Change Local Group Settings?

To change anything about a local group (a group particular to the computer on which it exists, not to the entire domain), type

```
net localgroup /option
```

where *option* is one of the switches explained above.

Computer and Session Information

You can get a variety of computer, domain, and session information from the command prompt. Using the commands found in this section, you can:

- View computer information
- Add computers to or delete them from a domain
- Get information about sessions between workstations and the server

NET COMPUTER: Adding or Deleting Computers from a Domain

The NET COMPUTER command adds or deletes computers (not users) from a domain. Since domains are administrative units, you might use this command, for example, if a workstation that was used by a person in the Personnel domain began to be used by a person in the Accounting domain. As long as it's attached to the network, the workstation does not need to physically move—it's just logically reassigned. The syntax for NET COMPUTER looks like this:

```
net computer \\computername\ /add
```

(or /delete if you want to remove the computer from the domain). *Computername* is the name of the computer to be added to the local domain. This command works only on computers running NT Server, and can only be applied to the local domain—I can't assign a computer to a domain other than the one that I am logged onto. If, however, my domain and another have a trust relationship, I can log onto that domain and add or delete computers on that domain that way.

Note, by the way, that NET COMPUTER applies to computers, not to users. Users are not members of domains, only computers are. (I know, I know, I keep harping on that, but it's important to understand the difference when you're configuring your network, and it's not always an easy distinction to grasp.)

How Do I Change the Domain that a Computer Is In?

To add a computer to the local domain, type

```
net computer \\computername /add
```

To delete it, substitute the /delete for the /add switch. You can only add computers to the domain that you are currently logged onto.

NET CONFIG: Learning About and Changing Configurations

You can use the NET CONFIG command to see how a machine is configured to behave on the network and, to a limited extent, change that configuration.

Viewing Current Server and Workstation Settings

Used without switches, NET CONFIG names the configurable services (namely, the server and the workstation). If you include one of the configurable services in the command. For example, if you type NET CONFIG SERVER, you'll see a screen something like Figure 16.7. This screen tells you:

- The name of the computer (EISA SERVER in the case of the figure).

- The software version, Windows NT 3.5x (yes, it says the same thing whether you run this on an NT Workstation or NT Server machine—it's always Windows NT 3.5x).

- The network card's name and address, which are listed below the software version.

- That the server is visible to the network, there is no limit on the number of users that can log on, and the maximum number of files that can be open per session with another computer is 2048—a restriction that isn't likely to cause most users much grief.

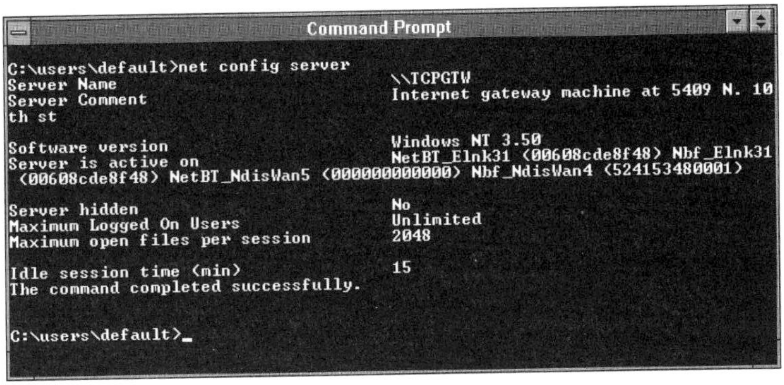

FIGURE 16.7:

A sample NET CONFIG server screen

```
                              Command Prompt
C:\users\default>net config server
Server Name                        \\TCPGTW
Server Comment                     Internet gateway machine at 5409 N. 10
th st
Software version                   Windows NT 3.50
Server is active on                NetBT_Elnk31 (00608cde8f48) Nbf_Elnk31
 (00608cde8f48) NetBT_NdisWan5 (000000000000) Nbf_NdisWan4 (524153480001)

Server hidden                      No
Maximum Logged On Users            Unlimited
Maximum open files per session     2048

Idle session time (min)            15
The command completed successfully.


C:\users\default>_
```

• The idle session time is 15 minutes.

Although you can run this command on any NT workstation or any NT Server (NET CONFIG means something different in other operating systems, and the command NET CONFIG SERVER or NET CONFIG WORKSTATION won't work) it doesn't mean that the NT workstations are set up to be servers.

Suppose you type the following command on the machine from Figure 16.7:

```
net config workstation
```

You'll see a screen like the one in Figure 16.8. This screen gives you information about how this computer is configured for use as a network workstation. You see the computer and user names, the network card address, the domain, and so forth. Why run NET CONFIG WORKSTATION on a server? Bear in mind that there is no *physical* reason why an NT Server machine can't be a workstation. It's possible, if not likely, that you could be using the NT Server machine for a workstation, especially if you're short of machines and don't have a dedicated server.

To get basic information about a computer, such as its domain, name, the name of its current user and so forth, type either of these commands:

```
net config server
net config workstation
```

depending on whether you want information about its setup as a server or workstation.

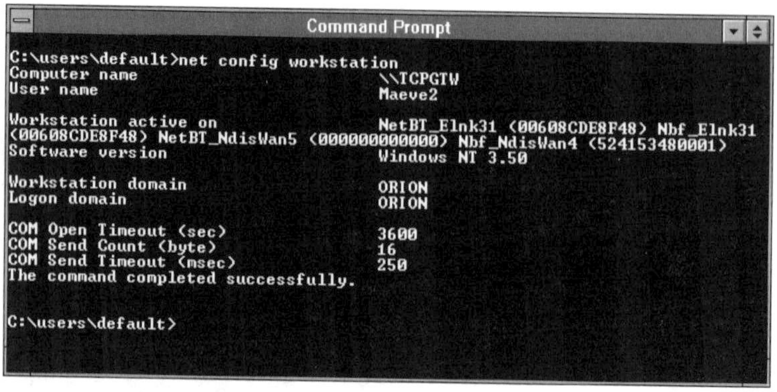

FIGURE 16.8:

A sample NET CONFIG WORKSTATION screen

```
                          Command Prompt
C:\users\default>net config workstation
Computer name                          \\TCPGTW
User name                              Maeve2

Workstation active on                  NetBT_Elnk31 (00608CDE8F48) Nbf_Elnk31
(00608CDE8F48) NetBT_NdisWan5 (000000000000) Nbf_NdisWan4 (524153480001)
Software version                       Windows NT 3.50

Workstation domain                     ORION
Logon domain                           ORION

COM Open Timeout (sec)                 3600
COM Send Count (byte)                  16
COM Send Timeout (msec)                250
The command completed successfully.

C:\users\default>
```

Changing Server and Workstation Settings

You can use the NET CONFIG commands for more than just information; within a limited scope, you can use them to adjust the way that a machine works on the network. If you type

```
net help net config server
```

you'll see that this command has three suboptions that you can adjust:

Suboption	Description
/autodisconnect:*time*	Sets the number of minutes a user's session with that computer can be inactive before it's disconnected. If you specify −1 (the default), the session will never disconnect. The upper limit is 65,535 minutes (don't use commas when using the command), a little more than 45 hours.
/srvcomment:"*text*"	Adds a comment to a server (here, that means any machine that's sharing resources with the network) that people can see when they view network resources with NET VIEW. Your comment, which can be up to 48 characters long including spaces, should be enclosed in quotation marks.
/hidden:*yes* or *no*	Allows you the option of not displaying that server on the list of network resources. Hiding a server doesn't change people's ability to access it, but only keeps people who don't need to know about it from accessing it. The default is no.

The workstation settings are a little different; they have to do with how the machine collects data from and sends it to communication devices. You probably won't have much need for these commands, but if you type

```
net help net config workstation
```

you'll see that this command also has three options:

Option	Description
/charcount:*bytes*	Sets the amount of data that NT collects before sending the data to a communication device. The range is 0 to 65,535 bytes (don't use commas in the number), and the default is 16.
/chartime:*msec*	Sets the amount of time during which the machine collects data for transmittal before forwarding it to the communication device. If the /charcount/*bytes* option is also used, the specification satisfied first will be the one that NT acts on. You can set the *msec* value from 0 to 655,350,000; the default is 250 milliseconds.
/charwait:*sec*	Sets the number of seconds that NT waits for a communication device to become available. The range is 0 to 65,535 seconds, and the default is 3,600.

NET SESSION: Accessing Connection Information

Used on servers, the NET SESSION command displays information about sessions between the server and other computers on the network. If you type the command without switches, you get a screen showing all the computers that are logged onto that server.

If you include NET SESSION switches, you can get more detailed information about a session with a particular computer, or delete a session (that is, disconnect a computer from the server). For example, to get more information about a session with computer TSC, you'd type

```
net session \\tsc
```

You'd see a screen that looks like Figure 16.9. This screen tells you:

- The user logged into computer TSC is called Maeve.

- The user is not logged in as a guest.

- This machine is not running Windows NT, but is working in a DOS environment. This doesn't necessarily mean that the user is using DOS programs (in fact, Maeve is logged on under Windows for Workgroups), but that DOS is the basic operating system. Don't forget—unlike NT or NT Server, Windows is not a true operating system, but an operating environment.

- Maeve has been logged on for two minutes and fourteen seconds. Her machine has been idle for one minute forty-five seconds.

- TSC is connected to drive C of the server and printers HP4M and HPCOLOR. Maeve has no current print jobs, but has two files open from the server.

FIGURE 16.9:

A sample NET SESSION screen

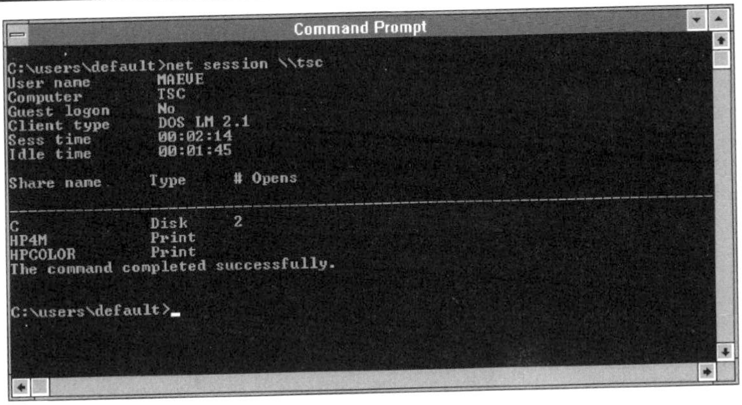

```
C:\users\default>net session \\tsc
User name       MAEVE
Computer        TSC
Guest logon     No
Client type     DOS LM 2.1
Sess time       00:02:14
Idle time       00:01:45

Share name      Type      # Opens

C               Disk      2
HP4M            Print
HPCOLOR         Print
The command completed successfully.

C:\users\default>_
```

How do I get information about current sessions? To view the current sessions open between a computer and the rest of the network, type

```
net session
```

on the computer for which you want the information. To remove the connection between the server and TSC, you'd type

```
net session \\tsc /delete
```

Be *careful* when using the /delete switch! If you neglect to include the computer name in the command, you'll end all current sessions and everyone will have to reconnect to the server.

In case you were wondering, you cannot use this command to initiate sessions between the server and networked computers. Each user does that when he or she logs on.

How Do I Forcibly Break a Connection between Computers?

To end a connection between two networked computers, go to one of the two computers and type

```
net session \\computername /delete
```

where *computername* is the name of the computer you wish to disconnect. If you don't specify a specific computer, you will break all connections between the computer you're typing on and the rest of the network.

NET STATISTICS: Getting a Report on a Computer

The NET STATISTICS command gives you a report on the computer on which you run it. If you type just the following command, you get a list of the services for which statistics are available (server and/or workstation, depending on whether you use the command on an NT or NT Server machine):

```
net statistics
```

But if you type either of the following two commands, you'll get, respectively, a server report like the one in Figure 16.10, and a workstation report like the one in Figure 16.11:

```
net statistics server
net statistics workstation
```

FIGURE 16.10:

A sample NET STATISTICS SERVER screen

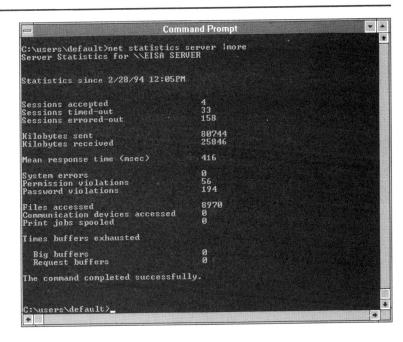

FIGURE 16.11:

A sample NET STATISTICS WORKSTATION screen

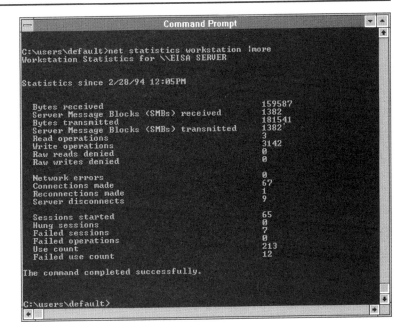

You can use either NET STATISTICS SERVER or NET STATISTICS WORKSTATION from any NT or NT Server machine, but the command can only give information about the machine on which you run it. You can't use this command to get information about computer AMS, for example, if you type the command from computer TSC.

What's Out There? Connecting to Networked Devices

Since the main point of a network is to allow users to access devices that belong to computers other than their own, you would expect to be able to make these connections from the command prompt, just as you can from the graphical interface. You would be right. With the NET commands, you can connect to drives and printers on the network with the same flexibility that you can when using the icons. In this section, we'll talk about how to see what's available on the network, how to connect to it, and (if you're using this command from a server), who's using what.

If you're working from the command prompt, before you can use any of the commands listed in this section, you must make sure that the workstation service is started. To do this from the command prompt, type

```
net start workstation
```

NET VIEW: Seeing the Resources Being Shared

You can't change anything with the NET VIEW command; you can only use it to see the resources being shared on the servers and domains on the network.

- If you type the following command on its own, you get a list of the local servers on the domain—that is, the services shared by the computer upon which you're typing:

```
net view
```

- If you can amend the name of the server you want to look at to the command and see a list of the resources that server is sharing with the network. For example, if the server is named TED, you would type

```
net view \\ted
```

You can check this for any server on the network.

- If you want to look at a server in another domain (perhaps server BIGDOG in domain ENGINEERING), type

```
net view \\bigdog /domain:engineering
```

If you omit the domain name from the command, you'll see a list of all domains on the network.

How Do I View Available Resources on the Network?

To see what servers are available in your domain, type

```
net view
```

To see the resources that a particular server is sharing with the domain, type

```
net view \\servername
```

where *servername* is the name of the server that you want to view. (Incidentally, if the server name contains spaces, put quotation marks around the server name like so: "*servername*".)

If you want to see a server in another domain, type

```
net view /domain
```

To see the domains available, type

```
net view /domain:domainname
```

to see the list of available servers on a particular domain and then type

```
net view \\servername /domain:domainname
```

when you've selected the server that you want.

TIP

Although this takes a pretty specific set of circumstances, if your network has both servers running NT Server *and* servers running Windows for Workgroups, you may see the error message "There are no entries in the list" when you enter the NET VIEW command. This happens when a Windows for Workgroups machine is the backup master browser for the workgroup, and the Guest account is disabled on the NT Server that is the usual master browser. This error occurs because a workgroup (unlike a domain) has no centralized account database. The Workgroups server must use the database maintained on the NT Server to obtain the list of resources shared with the network, and if the Guest account on the NT Server is disabled, the Workgroups server may not be able to access the list of servers. Therefore, to avoid this potential problem, just keep the Guest account on the master browser enabled.

NET USE: Connecting to Other Drives and Printer Ports

Once you've browsed the network with NET VIEW, you can connect to all the available goodies (or disconnect from those you don't want) with the NET USE command. Use this command to connect to drives D through Z and printer ports LPT1 through LPT9. (If you get help on this command, you'll notice that it claims that you can only use printer names LPT1 through LPT3. Technically, this isn't true, but the help file probably puts it this way because some MS-DOS applications are not able to access printer ports with numbers higher than 3.)

To get information about the workstation's current connections, type

```
net use
```

without options. To actually *make* connections, use the command's switches, as described below.

Connecting to a Resource in the Local Domain

To connect to a shared resource, such as a the printer shared as HP4M on server TED, type

```
net use lpt1: \\ted\hp4m
```

In this case, if you wanted to connect to a directory called WPFILES on that server and make that your E drive, you'd substitute *e:* for *lpt1* and *wpfiles* for *hp4m* in the example above. You get to specify the port name or drive letter that you want to connect a resource to, but you're restricted to drive letters D through Z and ports LPT1 through LPT9. (Remember, although the help file will say that LPT3 is the highest port that you can specify, this is not true.) Also, if the computer that you're getting the resource from has a blank character in its name (that is, has two words in it), you must put the name in quotation marks, as in "\\eisa server".

If there is a password (let's say it's "artuser") attached to the resource that you're trying to connect to, you need to include the password in your connection command, like this:

```
net use lpt1: \\ted\hp4m artuser
```

Or, if you want the computer to prompt you for the password so that it isn't displayed on the screen, append an asterisk:

```
net use lpt1: \\ted\hp4m *
```

To connect to your home directory (the directory on the server that has been assigned to you, assuming that there is one), type

```
net use /home
```

with the password on the end as explained above if one is attached.

If you want to make the connection for another user rather than for yourself, add the user's name (let's say it's Frank) to the end of the line, like this:

```
net use lpt1: \\ted\hp4m user:frank
```

Passwords go before the user's name in the statement. If the user for whom you are making the connection is in another domain, the user part of the statement looks like this:

```
user:domainname/frank
```

where *domainname* is the name of that user's home domain.

How Do I Connect to a Shared Resource?

To access a shared resource on the network, type

```
net use devicename: \\servername\sharename
```

where *devicename* is what you intend to call the connection (such as D: or LPT1), *servername* is the name of the server sharing the resource, and *sharename* is the name by which the server is sharing the resource.

Connecting to a Resource in Another Domain

In order to connect to a resource in a different domain from your usual one, you must first log onto that domain. If your domain and the other one don't have a trust relationship with each other, you need to create a user account for yourself on that domain. Once you've logged onto the proper domain, the process is the same as described above.

Other Switches for Making Connections

No matter what kind of connection you make, you can make it persistent (that is, remake it every time you connect to the network). To do this, add the switch /persistent:yes to the end of the line. If you don't want it to be persistent, type /persistent: no instead.

If you don't specify one or the other, the default is whatever you chose last. If you want to make all future connections persistent, type

```
net use /persistent:yes
```

(or type *:no* if you want all future connections to be temporary). Typing /persistent by itself at the end of the line won't do anything.

To disconnect from a resource, type

```
net use devicename /delete
```

where *devicename* is the connection (such as D: or LPT1). You don't have to provide a password or say anything about persistency to disconnect from a resource.

NET SHARE: Creating and Deleting Shared Resources

If you're administering a server, you probably spend more time making resources available to the resource than in connecting yourself to those belonging to other machines. The NET SHARE command applies to resources that the server is sharing with the network. Used alone, it gives you a list of all resources currently being shared with the network. With its switches, you can create and delete shared resources.

The NET SHARE command provides you with information about a particular shared resource:

```
net share sharename
```

For example, if one of the printers on a server is called HP4M (the share name), you could type NET SHARE hp4m and see a screen like the one in Figure 16.12. From this screen, you can tell what a resource's share name and path are, see descriptive remarks attached to the shared resource, and see how many users may use the device at one time and how many are currently using it.

FIGURE 16.12:

A sample NET SHARE screen

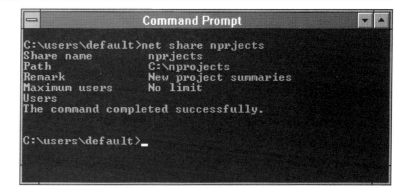

```
C:\users\default>net share nprjects
Share name            nprjects
Path                  C:\nprojects
Remark                New project summaries
Maximum users         No limit
Users
The command completed successfully.


C:\users\default>_
```

NET SHARE is a useful command not only for viewing the setup of existing shared devices, but also for creating new ones and configuring existing shares. You must be using an account with administrative rights to use this command; ordinary user accounts can't take advantage of it.

Specifying Absolute Path   To share a device or drive, you must tell the system where to find it. Thus, to share the directory C:\MAIN as drive C, you would type

```
net share C=c:\main
```

Limiting User Access   To specify the number of users who can use a particular device at the same time, add the parameter /users:*number*, where *number* is the number of users that you want to be able to use the device at once. To place no limit on the number of users, substitute the parameter /unlimited. From the example above, you would type

```
net share C=c:\main /users:5
```

if you wanted, at any given time, five users to be able to access the \MAIN directory on the server's C drive. If you don't use the /users switch, an unlimited number of users can access the device.

Describing Shared Devices   You can add a descriptive comment to a shared device to give network users a better idea of exactly what device it is they are reaching. Do this by using the /remark switch and adding a comment to the end of the NET SHARE statement, like so:

```
/remark:"This is the main data storage directory"
```

Note that there are no spaces between the colon and the text, and that the text must be enclosed in quotation marks.

Stop Sharing   To stop sharing a device, type NET SHARE, the share name, device name, or drive and path, and then add the /delete switch.

When using the NET SHARE command, keep in mind that if the guest account is enabled, any devices that you share with the network are automatically available to the entire network; you can't set individual or group permissions with this command. If you want to restrict access to devices or drives, you must set the permissions on the pertinent device or drive from the File Manager or Print Manager.

How Do I Share a Device with the Network?

To share a device with the network, type

```
net share sharename= directory
```

where *sharename* is the name by which the device will be known on the network, and *directory* is the location where the device is found. For example, to share the directory c:\public on the network as Public, you'd type

```
net share Public=c:\public
```

NET FILE: Finding Out What's Open and Who's Using It

NT SERVER

Without switches, the NET FILE command is used on servers to display the open files. If you type the command from a server, you'll see a screen something like Figure 16.13. This screen lets you know what's open and who (users, not computers)

FIGURE 16.13:

A sample NET FILE screen

is using it. If you add the switches, you can identify that file to the server and shut it down, removing all file locks. For example, in this situation you might want to shut down FLPERMS.TIF. To do so, you'd type

```
net file 3381 /close
```

because 3381 is that file's ID number. Notice that more than one person can access a file at a time (PSP.EXE), but that each access has its own ID number.

NET PRINT: Controlling Print Jobs

You can use the command prompt not only to connect to networked devices, but, in some cases, to control them. With the NET PRINT command, you can control print jobs, just as you can with the Print Manager.

If you type the following command, you'll get a list of all the jobs currently printing or waiting on that printer:

```
net print \\computername\sharename
```

where *sharename* is the name by which the printer is shared on the network. You'll see that each job is assigned a job number. To delete a print job, refer to that number and type

```
net print \\computername job# /delete
```

substituting the job number for *job#*. If you want to hold a print job (keep it in the print queue but let other jobs print ahead of it) or release it (free a held job to print), substitute the /hold or /release switch for /delete.

While it is possible to control print jobs from the command line, it's much easier to do it from the Print Manager. If you're trying to delete a print job, it could be done printing by the time you've typed the server name and queue incorrectly, noticed the problem, and reentered the data.

TIP
If you have configured your default printer to print directly to ports, you won't be able to print to a local port from the command prompt. Currently, there isn't anything that you can do about this except go into the Print Manager, remove the Print Directly to Ports option, and resend the job.

How Do I Control a Print Job from the Command Prompt?

To pause, continue, or delete a print job from the command prompt, first type

```
net print \\computername\sharename
```

where *computername**sharename* is the name of the computer and printer with the print job that you wish to control. This command will give you a list of the pending print jobs for that printer and their job numbers. Find the number that corresponds to the print job that you want to control, and, to delete a job, type

```
net print \\computername job# /delete
```

To hold or release the job instead of deleting it, substitute the /hold or /release switch for the /delete switch. You don't need to specify the share name with this command.

Using Network Services

The NET START *servicename* command is not capable of starting all the services that are available from the Services icon in the Control Panel, but only the network-related ones. In this section, we'll talk about what those commands are and how to start, pause, continue, and stop them.

NET START: Starting a Service

The NET START command encompasses a long list of network services that can be started. On its own, it doesn't do anything except list the services that have already been started. Be warned: The list that you see when you type **net start** is not a complete list of all the available network services. To view the available services, type either of these commands:

```
net start /help |more
net help net start |more
```

How Do I Start a Network Service?

To start a network service from the command prompt, type

`net start servicename`

where *servicename* is the name of the service to start. This command works only for the network services described in this section.

All two-word commands, such as "clipbook server" and "computer browser," must be enclosed within quotation marks for the NET START commands to work.

The default services in Windows NT Server are described below.

NET START ALERTER The alerter service sends messages about the network to users. You select the events for which you want to trigger alerts in the Performance Monitor. For these alerts to be sent, both the alerter and messenger services must be running on the computer originating the alerts, and the messenger service must be running on the computer receiving them.

NET START "CLIPBOOK SERVER" The clipbook viewer is a temporary or permanent storage place for text or graphics that you want to cut and paste between applications. From the command line, start this service by typing

`net start "clipbook server"`

You'll see either a message that says the service has been started, or, if you've already started it from NT Server, a message that the service was already started.

NET START "COMPUTER BROWSER" The computer browser service allows your computer to browse and be browsed on the network. When you start it from the command prompt, however, you get no further information than that the service has started.

NET START "DIRECTORY REPLICATOR" You can type this command in either of two ways:

```
net start "directory replicator"
net start replicator
```

It begins a service that allows you to dynamically update files between servers. You must have replication rights to use this command, which means you have to set up a user account with replication rights before you start this service. (There is a default user group with those rights that comes with NT Server, so you can just assign an account to that group.) For more information on the Directory Replication service, see Chapter 10.

NET START EVENTLOG   This command begins the event log, which audits selected events on the network, such as file access, user logons and logoffs, and the starting of programs. You can select which events you want to log, and also whether you want the log to consist of both successful and failed attempts, just failures, or just successes (although just recording successes doesn't sound terribly useful if you're trying to monitor the system).

NET START MESSENGER   A command called NET SEND allows you to send brief messages over the network when working from the command prompt. For this command to work, however, the messenger service must first be running on both the machine sending the message and the one(s) receiving it. To begin the messenger service, type

```
net start messenger
```

If you're running the alerter service to keep yourself informed of what's going on at the server, the messenger service must also be running on both the server and the workstation where you want to receive the messages.

NET START "NET LOGON"   This command starts the netlogon service, which verifies logon requests and controls replication of the user accounts database (see NET START DIRECTORY REPLICATOR). The netlogon service isn't used for logging onto your computer, but for logging onto the domain that your computer is part of; if you log on just to a computer, you can use anything there that isn't dependent on domain membership (such as directory replication). Even if you don't log onto the domain, you can still access resources shared with the network if you have rights and permissions to use them. The process of logging onto the domain, as opposed to just the workstation, is called *pass-through validation*.

NET START "NETWORK DDE"   This service provides a network transport for dynamic data exchange (DDE) conversations and provides security for them.

NET START "NETWORK DDE DSDM"   Used by the DDE service described above, the DDE share database manager (DSDM) manages the DDE conversations.

NET START "NT LM SECURITY SUPPORT PROVIDER"   This service provides Windows NT security to RPC applications that use transports other than LAN Manager named pipes.

NET START "REMOTE PROCEDURE CALL (RPC) SERVICE"   The Remote Procedure Call (RPC) Service is a mechanism that makes it easier for programmers to develop distributed applications by providing pointers to direct the applications. Before you can use RPC, you need to configure it by specifying the Name Service Interface (NSI) that it will use. You have to know what NSI provider that it will use and, if you'll be using the DCE Cell Directory Service, the network address of the provider. The default name service is the Windows NT Locator.

NET START "REMOTE PROCEDURE CALL (RPC) LOCATOR"   This service allows distributed applications to use the RPC-provided pointer by directing the applications to those pointers. This service manages the RPC NSI database.

NET START SCHEDULE   This command starts the scheduling service, which must be running to use the AT command. The AT command can be used to schedule commands and programs (like the backup program, for instance) to run on a certain computer at a specific time and date. By default, the scheduling service is configured to log on under the system account, but if it logs on under that account, the AT command can only be used for programs to which the Guest users have access. Thus, to run a restricted program (like the backup operation), you'd need to configure the scheduling service to log on under an account with rights to the programs you want to run.

To start a program at a certain time, you would specify

- The computer on which you wanted the program to run (if you don't specify one, the default is the computer at which you execute the at command).

- The time and date when you want the program to begin running. (If you don't specify a date, the program will run on the day that you execute the command, at the appointed time.) You can also schedule an event for the next date (such as a Thursday), or make the event a repeating event scheduled to run on every occasion of a date.

- The command that you want to run (typed in quotation marks).

For example, to change the name of a file from JUNK.SAM to JUNKER.SAM on the local computer at 10:52 today, you would type

```
at 10:52 "rename c:\ntclass\junk.sam junker.sam"
```

If you wanted to perform a similar action on a networked computer named AMS, and set the "alarm clock" for 11:00 next Wednesday, you'd type

```
at \\ams 11:00 /next:wednesday "rename c:\ntclass\junk.sam
junker.sam"
```

Of course, this line would be unbroken. To make this command happen every Wednesday, you'd substitute *every:wednesday* for *next:wednesday*. For every 7, 14, and 21 of the month, you'd type *every:7,14,21* (make sure no blanks appear between the colon and the numbers). By the way, you can abbreviate day names like this: M, T, W, Th, F, Sa, Su.

NET START SERVER   To control access to network resources from the command line, type

```
net start server
```

This service must be running before you can perform these actions:

- Directory sharing
- Printer sharing
- Remote procedure call (rpc) access
- Named pipe sharing

When you stop the server service, you disconnect all users attached to your machine, so before doing so you should follow these steps:

1. From the command line, type

   ```
   net pause server
   ```

   to pause the server service. This keeps any new users from connecting to the server, but does not disrupt any current connections.

2. Notify people who are connected that you're going to shut it down, and that they need to log off before a certain time. You can use the NET SEND command to do this. To see the NET SEND message, NT machines must be running the messenger service; Windows, Windows for Workgroups, and Windows 95 machines must be running WinPopUp.

3. After that time has passed, type

```
net stop server
```

to end the service without messing anyone up.

When you end the server service, you take the computer browser and netlogon with it, so if you stop the server service and then restart it, you need to restart those programs as well.

NET START SPOOLER   As its name implies, this service provides print spooler capabilities.

NET START UPS   One of the best things about Windows NT is its built-in preparedness to contend with disaster, as you've seen with features like the backup program, disk mirroring, duplexing, and striping. The UPS (uninterrupted power supply) service links your workstation or server with a UPS to protect your computer from dirty power, power surges, and power failures. You still have to buy the UPS, but this service makes the hardware even more useful than it already is.

Before you run the UPS service for the first time from the command prompt (by typing NET START UPS), you must configure the service. When configuring, you make a number of choices about how the service will function, including

- The serial port to which the UPS is connected.

- Whether or not the UPS signals you when the following events occur: power supply interruption and low battery power (UPS's run from batteries when normal power fails).

- How the computer will shut down.

- How long the battery life is and how long it will take to recharge.

- How frequently you will see warning messages.

Obviously, you need to check with your UPS's documentation before configuring the UPS service. Once it's up and running, the UPS service protects your machine from power problems and keeps you as notified of what's going on as you want to be.

NET START WORKSTATION   As you'd guess from the name, this command is intended for workstations. It enables them to connect to and use shared network resources. Once you start this service, you can see what's on the network and connect to it.

NT Server also has a number of special services that can be started using the NET START command. These include:

- Client Server For NetWare
- DHCP Client
- File Server for Macintosh
- FTP Server
- Gateway Service for NetWare
- NLPDSVC
- Microsoft DHCP Server
- Network Monitoring Agent
- OLE
- Print Server for Macintosh
- Remote Access Server
- Remote Access Connection Manager
- Remote Access ISNSAP Service
- Remoteboot
- Simple TCP/IP Services
- SNMP
- TCP/IP NetBIOS Helper
- Windows Internet Name Service

NET PAUSE and NET CONTINUE: Halting a Service Temporarily

If you need to temporarily halt a service, you can use the NET PAUSE command to do it. Just type

```
net pause service
```

and the service will be temporarily suspended. To restart the paused service, type

```
net continue service
```

The NET PAUSE and NET CONTINUE commands affect the following default services:

- NET LOGON
- SERVER
- SCHEDULE
- NETWORK DDE
- NETWORK DDE DSDM
- WORKSTATION

NET STOP: Stopping a Service

NET STOP works in the same way that NET START does. On its own, it can't do anything, but when you add the name of a service that you want to stop, it stops it. See the NET START section preceding for more details on what each of the services does.

Be careful when stopping a service! Some services are dependent on others (such as NET START, NET LOGON, and NET START WORKSTATION), so if you shut down one, you may shut down another without meaning to. If you just need to stop a service temporarily, use NET START PAUSE instead. You need administrative rights to stop a service.

How Do I Stop, Pause, and Continue a Service?

Once you've started a service, you can stop, pause, or continue it in much the same way that you started it in the first place. Just type

```
net action servicename
```

where *action* is what you want to do (stop, pause, or continue) and *servicename* is the name of the service that you want to control.

Sending Messages

You're not dependent on e-mail to send messages across the network. From the command prompt, you can send messages and arrange to have your own forwarded so that they catch up with you wherever you are. As long as your computer and the computer to which you direct the messages are running the message service, you can reach anywhere on the network.

NET NAME: Adding or Deleting a Messaging Name

The NET NAME command adds or deletes a messaging name (also known as an *alias*) at a workstation. The messaging name is the name that receives messages at that station; any messages sent over the network will go to where the messaging name is. Although this command comes with two switches, /add and /delete, the /add switch is not necessary to add a messaging name to a workstation; instead, you need only type

```
net name username
```

to add that messaging name to the appropriate workstation.

For example, to add the messaging name "Paul" to the computer in Figure 16.14, I only had to type

```
net name Paul
```

FIGURE 16.14:

A sample NET NAME screen

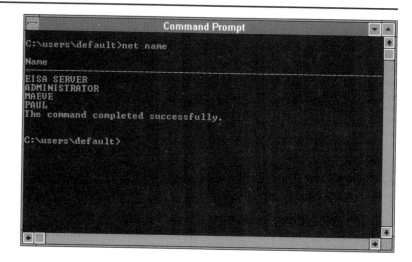

But if I wanted to remove him, I'd have to type

```
net name Paul /delete
```

The difference between messaging names and user names may not be immediately clear. The user name is the name of the person who is logged onto a particular machine. It can be deleted from the messaging name list; that is, messages can be rerouted from the machine at which a user is working to another machine if you use the NET NAME command to add the name to that machine. While you can delete both the user name and any messaging names from a computer, you cannot delete the computer's name from the list. In Figure 16.14, the name of the computer is EISA SERVER, Administrator is the user name, and Maeve and Paul are messaging names.

NET SEND: Sending Messages

NET SEND is a messaging service for sending a message to one person, to all the people in your group, to all the people in your domain, to all the people on the network, or to all the users connected to the server. NET SEND does not work without

How Do I Forward My Messages to Another Machine?

If you're working at a machine other than the one that you're accustomed to using, you can make sure that your messages follow you there. Just type

`net name username`

(or *machinename*) on the machine where you'll be working. All messages addressed to that user name or machine name will show up at that location. Messaging names cannot be already in use anywhere else on the network. If you try to add a name that's already in use to a messaging name list, it won't work.

its parameters, as you need to tell it what to send and where to send it. The basic parameters are as follows:

`net send name message text`

where

- *name* is the name (user name, messaging name, or computer name) that you want to send the message to.

TIP   According to the help file, substituting an asterisk (*) in place of a name sends the message to everyone in your user group. However, when I used it the Messenger Service sent the message to everyone connected to the domain controller, rather than to the user group of the account that did the sending.

- *message text* is whatever text you wish to include in your message. The text doesn't have to be enclosed in quotation marks. Even though NET SEND isn't meant to be a substitute for an e-mail program, you can send fairly hefty messages with it. If you try to send too long a message, the system refuses to let you type any more characters, but in a test message it took thirteen full lines to reach that point. If you want to send a message longer than thirteen lines, it's probably easier to use e-mail.

NET SEND Options

Sometimes you'll need more than the basic parameters to get your message where it needs to go. In that case, you can use whichever of these options is necessary (only one at a time):

Option	Description
/domain	Sends the message to everyone in your domain. Just substitute your domain's name for the word domain. If you include a name of a domain or workgroup like this:
	/domain:domainname
	where domainname is the name of the domain or workgroup that you wish to receive the message, then the message will be sent to all users in the domain or workgroup. If you don't include a name with this switch, the message will be sent to the local domain.
/broadcast	Sends the message to all users on the network—not the domain, not the user group, but the network.
/users	Sends the message to all users connected to the server.

Using NET SEND

Even if you understand the parameters, getting NET SEND to work can be a little confusing. This would probably be a good time for some real-life examples.

To send a message saying, "This is a test message" to Paula, who is part of your domain, you would type

```
net send paula This is a test message
```

If you wanted to send a message saying, "This is a test message" to Sam, who is part of the Engineering domain, you would type

```
net send sam \engineering This is a test message
```

If you wanted to send a message saying, "This is a test message" to everyone in your domain, you would type:

```
net send * This is a test message
```

Once you've successfully sent a message, everyone who meets these criteria will see a message like the one in Figure 16.15:

- The message is directed to them
- They are logged on as of the time of transmittal
- They have the messenger service running on their machines

Which is better, e-mail or messaging? Each has its time and place. E-mail works better for messages attached to files, since it's not limited to text transmittal. But e-mail does have one disadvantage: it's ignorable. Even if you've arranged to be notified when mail is waiting, you can ignore the notification or not hear it at all if you're away from your machine.

Therefore, if you have a question for someone and you need an answer *right now*, the messenger service is probably the way to go. When you send a message to someone at an NT workstation, the dialog box in Figure 16.15 appears on their screen and does not disappear until they click the OK button.

FIGURE 16.15:

A sample Messenger Service pop-up window

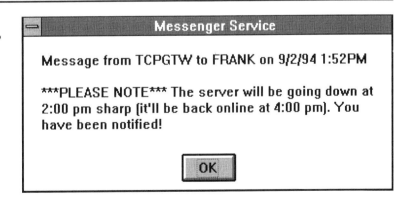

How Do I Send Messages?

To send messages from the command prompt, use the NET SEND command. Using the parameters described above, you can send messages to individuals or groups, within a domain or across domains. Again, NT machines need to be running the messenger service to see NET SEND messages; Windows, Windows for Workgroups, and Windows 95 machines must be running WinPopUp.

Getting Synched: Viewing and Setting the Time

For some services, such as directory replication, to work correctly, the server's clock and the workstations' clocks must be set to the same time. To automate this process, you can use the NET TIME command.

NET TIME: Coordinating Server and Workstation Clocks

The NET TIME command works differently depending on whether you execute it from a server or a workstation. If you run it from a server, it displays the current time; if you run it from a workstation, you can synchronize your computer's clock with that of the time server, and you can even select a server from another domain if there is a trusted relationship between your domain and the other one. Ordinary users cannot set the server time from a workstation—only members of the Administrators or Server Manager groups, logged onto the server (logically if not physically) can set the system time.

To coordinate the clocks from a workstation:

1. Check the time on a time server. For example, on a server named EISA SERVER, you would type

   ```
   net time \\eisa server
   ```

If you typed only `net time`, by default you'd get the current time on the server that serves as your time server. (If there is no time server on your domain, you'll get a message saying that the system could not locate a time server.)

To check the time on a time server in another domain (called TED, for instance), you would type

```
net time /domain:ted
```

2. Set the time from the time server. In our example, you would type

```
net time \\eisa server /set
```

If there is no time server set up for your domain but you want to synchronize a workstation's clock with that of the domain controller for domain named TED, for example, you would type

```
net time /domain:ted /set
```

Set the time from a time server in another domain (here called OTHERS) by typing

```
net time /domain:others /set
```

From a server, you use the same commands to check the time on another server or set the time to correspond with that on another domain, but if you type NET TIME without switches, the screen will show the time on the time server for that domain, if one exists.

How Do I Synchronize a Workstation's Time with the Server's?

To coordinate a workstation's time with the server's, type

```
net time \\servername /set
```

where *servername* is the name of the server with which you want to coordinate.

Why Use the Command Prompt?

Most of the time I hope you won't have to use the command prompt. By now you have a pretty good idea of how to do just about anything from the command prompt that you can do in a normal session, but typing commands correctly is a lot harder than pointing and clicking. The only advantage I can see to using the command prompt over the graphical interface is that you don't have to remember where anything is. If you can remember the command name, you can do everything from the same place.

In general, the people who need the command prompt to connect are the network's OS/2 and DOS clients. If you're administering the server, you probably won't have much occasion to use the command prompt, except when making adjustments to DOS and OS/2 workstations.

CHAPTER
SEVENTEEN

Using the Remote Access Server

Remote
Access

Less and less of our "office work" actually takes place *in* the office. Many of us travel, and when we travel we often need what's on the server back at the office. If I had a nickel for every time on the road that I discovered—too late—that I was missing some data or an application... For greater numbers of us, "the office" is a place we visit a couple of times a week, with most work being done at home. "Tele-commuting" is a good idea for more and more businesses.

An old technology that's finally coming into its own is the Integrated Services Digital Network, or ISDN. ISDN is a telecommunications standard that can integrate data, voice, and video signals over a digital telephone line. Narrowband ISDN provides two 64 kbps (or 56 kbps, depending on the area) channels per phone line, which can be combined to achieve one 128 (or 112) kbps channel. RAS can use either narrowband or broadband ISDN with the right drivers. But getting software that supports ISDN has been difficult because it's a new technology in the eyes of most software designers. NT, in contrast, has ISDN support built right in.

The idea of remote access to a local area network is by no means a new one. People quite commonly use a program like Carbon Copy or PC/Anywhere to accomplish remote LAN access. These programs work by allowing you to take remote control of a PC that is physically on the office premises, a PC that's a workstation on your network's LAN. By taking remote control of a workstation PC, you can access the LAN, as it is local to the remotely controlled PC. This sounds like a perfectly reasonable approach, and it is, save for the fact that you end up transferring lots of screenfuls of data back and forth over the phone line; every mouse-click can potentially change the whole screen, which could result in having to transfer a megabyte of information. At the common modem speeds of roughly 20,000 bps with compression (don't tell me about the 28,800 bps modems, as they only work at top speed with preternaturally clear phone lines), transferring that megabyte could take 50 seconds. Waiting 50 seconds for each mouse-click requires a bit more patience than I have, which is why I prefer the NT approach.

An Overview of RAS

The whole idea of the Remote Access Service (RAS) is that it basically runs the NetBEUI transport stack over the phone line and converts your serial ports into

Ethernet cards. Furthermore, RAS will "tunnel" IPX/SPX or TCP/IP through Net-BEUI, making it possible to gain access to servers *not* running NetBEUI. Additionally, RAS supports two popular TCP/IP protocols, SLIP (Serial Line Interface Protocol) and PPP (Point to Point Protocol), so you can connect an NT machine to the Internet.

RAS won't just be interesting to network *users*; network administrators can use RAS too. You can do any administrative work over the remote connection that doesn't require you to actually touch the remote workstation.

Why use RAS rather than another remote-access package? Well, for starters, you've already paid for it—you got it free with NT Server. Even if you have DOS and Windows clients and so can't use the normal RAS client software, you can get the supplemental disks free from Microsoft. Just fill out the form in the back of your System Guide, send it in, and the software shows up in about a week.

Using RAS is simple for both users and administrators. Remote clients can access files and network devices just as though they were using the network from inside the office, and administer their accounts as if they were administering any other user account. Another advantage to using RAS over using other remote-access software is that RAS has the same built-in security measures that other NT Server user accounts have, with a few more for good measure. A RAS link does not provide the same access to your network that other kinds of remote access connections can. Finally, RAS is flexible. Running from an NT Server machine, it can support up to 64 simultaneous connections. Simple NT workstations can only support two RAS connections.

Connection Types

You're not limited to one method of connecting your RAS server and its clients. You can link them by modem, over an ISDN connection, or even use RAS to eliminate the need for a network card in a workstation. In this section, we'll talk about your connection options, how they work, and what you need for them.

Modem Support

Most RAS servers will connect to their clients through a modem (modulator/demodulator). On the sending end, modems convert digital computer signals into analog signals that can be transferred over ordinary telephone lines. On the receiving end, another modem takes the analog signals and reverts them to the original digital signal. For this modulation/demodulation process to work, the modems must be compatible.

Modem Compatibility Issues

Not all modems work with RAS. In the NT Server Hardware Compatibility List, Microsoft provides a list of modems with which it has successfully tested RAS. If you're buying a modem specifically for RAS, make sure that you choose one from this list. Alternatively, you can venture into the depths of a file called MODEMS.INF and "program" NT to support your modem. (I'm not going to cover that in this book, but it's explained in the NT RAS documentation.)

Even if you choose modems from the "approved" list, not all modems can work together in all modes. It's best to use the same model of modem on both the sending and receiving end of the RAS connection. It's not vital that you do this, if both modems conform to industry standards like V.32 *bis* or V.34 (the 14,400 and 19,200 bps standards). But getting the same modem model can prevent compatibility problems that arise even in machines conforming to the same standard. The higher the speed, the more likely compatibility problems are, since modems use different methods to achieve high speeds. Another answer is to use Hayes modems, as modem designers seem to use Hayes modems to test *their* modems' compatibility; everything seems to talk to a Hayes.

Hardware Requirements for Using RAS

In addition to the software, you need the following to use RAS over a modem connection:

- Two compatible modems, one for the server and one for the client
- A telephone line

Pooling Modems

Just as you can connect more than one physical printer to a logical printer name (see Chapter 9 to see how to do this), you can pool identical modems so that more than one modem is connected to the same number. The modems must be the same manufacture and model. If you pool modems, you can avoid some traffic problems when a number of RAS clients are trying to connect to the same server at once.

ISDN Support

Running RAS over a modem is inexpensive, but it's also slow; a good modem connection runs over an analog voice channel at about 28,800 bps. If you want a faster remote connection, you need a point-to-point service like ISDN. Basic Rate Interface (BRI) ISDN runs over a digital line at either 64 or 128 kilobits (*thousands* of bits) per second. Given the startup costs (not huge, but more than buying a modem and getting another telephone line), this connection may not be worth it if your transmission needs are small and mostly text-based, but if a good deal of data will be traveling between the RAS server and client, ISDN could save you transmittal time for nonmobile clients.

If BRI ISDN doesn't provide as much throughput as you need, you can subscribe to its faster sibling, Primary Rate Interface (PRI) ISDN. Rather than the copper wire that BRI uses, PRI uses T-1 (fiber optic) cables with 23 data-carrying channels. These channels can handle data transfers up to 1.544 mbps.

Hardware Requirements

To use RAS over an ISDN connection, you need the following hardware:

- Two ISDN cards, one in each computer at either end of the connection.
- A digital-grade cable connecting the cards (either copper or fiber).
- A network termination (NT) device that connects the cards to the cable. Inside the U.S., the telephone company owns the NT; outside, the customer owns it. This NT device can have up to eight ports for multiple ISDN connections.

Basically, if you're thinking of going ISDN, contact your local telephone company to see if it offers ISDN (not all locations have it yet). Next, look to either Digiboard or Intel for ISDN interface hardware.

Differences in Transmission Speed

As noted above, BRI ISDN transmits at either 64 or 128 kbps. Where does the difference in transmittal speed come from? A BRI ISDN line comes with three channels: two bearer (B) channels for data, which transmit at 64 kbps; and one D channel for signaling to the other ISDN card, which transmits at 16 kbps. When you're setting up the connection, you can either configure each B channel to be its own port, or logically combine the two into a single port, get twice the bandwidth, and thus double your transmission speed.

What merits does each approach have? Two channels are better for RAS servers that have a number of clients, because more clients will be able to get through at one time. For most people, this will be the most efficient use of bandwidth. If, however, your RAS configuration has only one client, you don't need more than one port and you can combine the bandwidth.

X.25 Connection

X.25 is a protocol that coordinates communication between two machines. It routes information through a packet-switched public data network. Operating at the two lowest levels of the OSI protocol model (Physical and Data-Link), X.25 operates at a top speed of 64 kpbs. Even though this isn't terribly fast by modern standards, it can run more slowly if the type of line that it's using requires it.

If you're familiar with some of the new wide area network (WAN) technologies for connecting point A to point B, X.25 may seem slow to you. Truthfully, it is slow; X.25 was developed at a time when telephone lines were not as reliable as they are now, so it includes extensive error-checking at every node in its path to ensure that the data arrives at its destination in the same condition in which it left. Error-checking takes time, so X.25 is slower than other WAN protocols that don't use it, like frame relay.

If it's slower than other protocols, why use X.25? First of all, it's available. No matter where in the world you go, you can be almost certain that the country you're in offers X.25 services. Even countries with unreliable telephone systems can use it because of its error-checking capabilities. For international applications, X.25 may be the only way for one country to connect to another.

Even within the U.S., X.25 has the advantage of being offered by most carriers. You could even build a private X.25 network with on-site switching equipment and lease lines connecting the sites.

You can set up RAS to work with X.25 lines without too much difficulty. Like setting up the system for ISDN, it's mostly a matter of making sure that things are coordinated with the telephone company and that your connections are made properly. We'll discuss configuring your system for X.25 shortly.

There are two main ways in which you can arrange RAS to work with X.25, either with a dial-up asynchronous packet assembler-disassembler (PAD) or via a direct connection to the X.25 service provider.

Packet Assembler-Disassembler   A *packet assembler-disassembler*, or PAD, is in charge of taking nonpacket data streams, such as the start and stop bits that begin and end a transmission, and converting them to packets that can be transported over the X.25 network. Once the converted packets reach their destinations, another PAD reverts the packets to their original form.

With a PAD hookup, a dial-up connection connects the remote workstation and the server through PAD services offered by a public network, such as Sprintnet. The client's software has a "conversation" with the PAD, and then the PAD has a "conversation" with the server that gets the data to the server.

PAD configurations include the client external PAD and the server external PAD layouts. In the client external PAD configuration, an RS-232 cable attached to the client's serial port connects the client and the PAD. In the PAD.INF file, you must have a script telling the client how to connect to the server. In the server external PAD configuration, it must be configured to receive incoming calls. (Given that you're using the server to connect your LAN to remote clients, this is probably what you wanted to do anyway.)

Direct Connection   The other approach to X.25 connection is a direct connection. Connecting directly from the remote workstation to the server requires a device called a *smart card*. This device acts like a modem, in both the server and the client. (Clients not using the direct X.25 connection don't need smart cards.) A smart card is a piece of hardware with a PAD embedded in it. It fools the computer into thinking that its communications ports are already attached to PADs.

Hardware Requirements for Using RAS with X.25

To use RAS with X.25, you need the following:

- A modem (for dial-up connections)
- A "smart" X.25 direct interface card (for direct connections)
- A leased line (for direct connections)

We'll discuss the mechanics of how to set up RAS to work with X.25 in the section on installation and configuration.

Direct Serial Connection

The final way that you can use RAS is to avoid having to get a network card. Using a null modem cable, you can connect the server and client directly through the serial port. Although this setup eliminates the need for a network card in either machine (assuming the server is not connected to any other clients), serial connections are much slower than networks, and performance suffers.

To use RAS through a serial connection, you need the following:

- One client and one server machine
- A 9-pin or 25-pin (depending on your serial connector) null-modem cable

Now, there are null modem cables, and there are null modem cables. Many computer null modem applications work fine with simple null modem cables, but RAS is pretty exacting in its requirements. Table 17.1 summarizes the requirements for constructing a RAS-ready null modem cable. The table covers both 25-pin connectors and 9-pin connectors.

SLIP and PPP Dial-Up Utilities

Most of the Remote Access Service is devoted to allowing you to attach remotely to NT servers. But Microsoft added a pair of irrelevant—but very useful nonetheless—connection types to NT as of version 3.5. They are TCP/IP dial-up utilities SLIP and PPP.

TABLE 17.1: Requirements for Constructing RAS-Ready Null Modem Cable

Host[1]	Pin No.\ 9-pin	Pin No.\ 25-pin	Workstation[2]	Pin No.\ 9-pin	Pin No.\ 25-pin
Transmit data	3	2	Receive data	2	3
Receive data	2	3	Transmit data	3	2
Request to send	7	4	Clear to send	8	5
Clear to send	8	5	Request to send	7	4
Data set ready and data carrier detect	6,1	6,8	Data terminal ready	4	20
Data terminal ready	4	20	Data set ready and data carrier detect	6,1	6,8
Signal ground	5	7	Signal ground	5	7

1. This column lists the NT Server machine serial port signal name.

2. This column lists the workstation serial port signal name.

As explained in Chapter 13, SLIP and PPP allow a machine to dial into a TCP/IP network—most commonly *the* TCP/IP network, the Internet—and become a member of that network. That's a different kind of dial-up service than the more common dumb terminal hookup (also explained in Chapter 13), because the "local host" is your computer under SLIP or PPP. SLIP has an undocumented value under NT, however: it can act as a TCP/IP router for your entire network, a router that lets you connect your entire network into the Internet. Chapter 13 documents how to do this.

NT and NT Server Installation

Although the Remote Access Service comes with NT Server, it is not automatically installed when you install the operating system. Therefore, don't look for it on the hard disk—you need to go to the Control Panel to install it. Once it's installed, you can customize it for your needs from the RAS Administrator program, which you'll find in a newly created Remote Access Service program group.

If you are installing RAS on an NT or NT Server machine, follow these steps:

1. Go to the Control Panel and choose the Network icon. You'll see a screen that looks like Figure 17.1. Click on the Add Software button, and you'll see a screen like the one in Figure 17.2.

2. Click on the ↓ arrow next to the text box to see your choices and select Remote Access Service. Next, select Continue.

FIGURE 17.1:

Network Settings screen

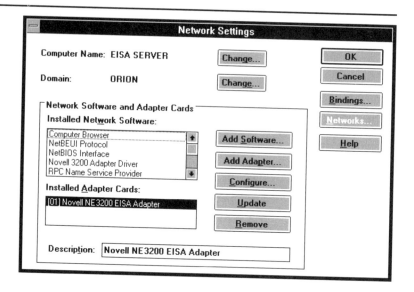

FIGURE 17.2:

Add Network Software screen

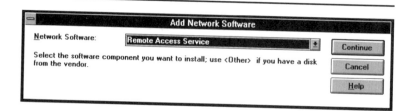

Once you've clicked on the Continue button, NT Server will either prompt you for the correct disk, if you installed NT Server from floppies, or will list the CD-ROM drive with the proper directory. If you're using the CD-ROM, make sure that NT Server is looking for the proper drive letter. If you've set up another drive with the Disk Administrator and your CD-ROM's drive letter changed, NT Server will still keep looking for the same drive letter that it used when installing the system, and you'll be trying to figure out why a perfectly functional CD-ROM won't work.

You'll next see a dialog box like Figure 17.3.

FIGURE 17.3:

Choosing a modem port

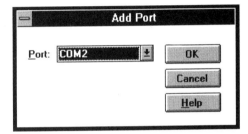

3. Choose the port that your modem (or other communications device) is attached to and click OK. You'll see the box in Figure 17.4.

4. Click OK.

Your modem lights will flash for a few minutes. Once NT figures out what kind of modem you have, it will ask for confirmation that it has guessed right.

FIGURE 17.4:

Modem auto-detect

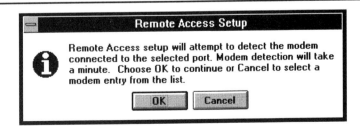

5. Choose the correct modem, click OK, and you'll see a screen like the one in Figure 17.5.

6. Select whether the modem will call out, receive, or call and receive calls.

7. Adjust the modem settings. While you're setting up the modem, you can adjust how it works as well as how the users can use the modem. To do this, click on the Settings… button, and you'll see a screen that looks like the one in Figure 17.6.

FIGURE 17.5:

Configuring the modem and port

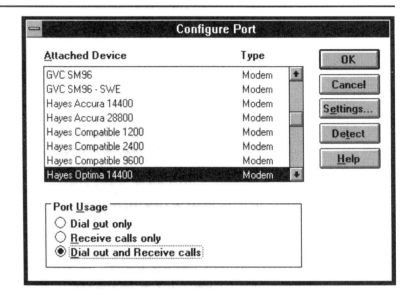

FIGURE 17.6:

The Settings screen

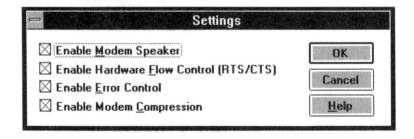

The options on this screen are as follows:

- **Enable Modem Speaker**   This is pretty self-explanatory. With a check in the box, every squeal and grunt from the modem is broadcast through its speaker; unchecked, the modem works silently.

- **Enable Hardware Flow Control**   Checking this option enables handshaking between the modem and the computer, so that if the modem falls behind in receiving, it can halt the flow of data rather than just registering an overflow error. In short, enabling this option allows the modem to slow its eating speed rather than choke.

- **Enable Error Control**   Checking this option enables error checking through cyclical redundancy checks (CRCs). Enabling this option increases modem efficiency, as it eliminates the need for start and stop bits (bits that signal the beginning and end of data transmission).

- **Enable Modem Compression**   This option is not checked by default, but I recommend checking it. It allows your modem to compress the data stream using the V.42 *bis* compression algorithm. Not all modems support compression, which is probably why this is disabled by default. Most high-speed modems *do* support compression nowadays, however, so it's probably a safe bet to enable compression. Just as data compression programs like Stacker work better on some kinds of files than others, the amount of compression that takes place depends on how much redundancy is in the data transmission. This will vary with the type of transmission.

If you realize after you've finished that you didn't set up the modem correctly, click on the Configure button in the Network Settings screen (see Figure 17.1), and you'll be able to change the settings and configurations that you assigned.

8. Click OK to close the Settings dialog box.

Once you've selected the modem, you'll see the main Remote Access Services setup screen, as in Figure 17.7.

9. Click Network, and you'll see a dialog box like the one in Figure 17.8.

10. Choose which protocols you use when dialing out.

FIGURE 17.7:

RAS Setup screen

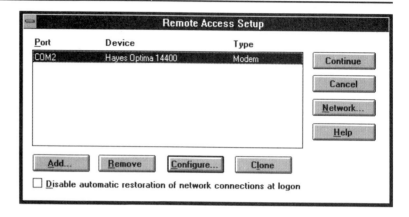

FIGURE 17.8:

RAS Network Configuration screen

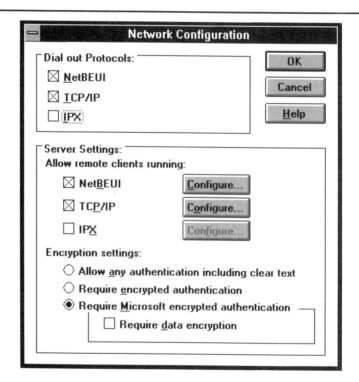

To find out which protocols you need, contact the person who set up the RAS server that you'll be calling. If you are setting up a RAS server, you'll choose the Server Settings protocol(s) (NetBEUI, TCP/IP, or IPX, depending on which protocol you use to talk to your servers) that you want to service the RAS clients dialing in. Choose TCP/IP and/or NetBEUI depending on which transport protocol you use to talk to your Microsoft enterprise network servers. Choose IPX only if the clients calling in are NT machines running the NWLink protocol and the Client Services for NetWare software, and if they intend to connect to NetWare servers.

11. Choose Encryption settings.

The Encryption settings that you need will vary depending on the kinds of network clients that will be dialing in. Only Windows NT 3.5x clients can provide encrypted passwords, so using DOS or Windows for Workgroups workstations implies that you should check Allow any identification... in the Encryption Settings area.

12. When you are done with the Network dialog box, click OK and then click Continue in the RAS Setup dialog box.

The RAS software and the RAS group in the Program Manager will install. You get a reminder that you have to use the RAS Admin program to allow particular users to call in to the server—merely being a user on this network is not sufficient to be able to call in on a RAS server.

13. Using the Advanced Configuration button, determine whether callers will be restricted to this computer or will be able to access the entire network. By default, all users can use the entire network through RAS. You can see this in the dialog box in Figure 17.9.

You have now installed the Remote Access Service. RAS will appear in the list of installed software in the initial Network screen, and the network will be automatically configured. Although you must shut down the system in order for the changes to take effect (you'll see a dialog box prompting you to this effect), you have the option of restarting the system at a later time, if you've installed RAS at a time when you can't shut down. Once you shut down the system and restart, the Program Manager will have a new program group containing the RAS icons.

FIGURE 17.9:

Advanced Configuration dialog box

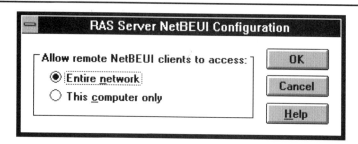

How Do I Set Up RAS for NT or NT Server Machines?

To set up RAS for NT or NT Server machines:

1. Click on the Networks icon in the Control Panel. When it's open, choose the Add Software button.

2. Select Remote Access Service from the list of software and click Continue. The system will prompt you for the file's location. Make sure that it's correct, and click OK.

3. Once the service has been installed, you'll be able to add ports for RAS's use. Click on the Add... button and choose the correct port and modem.

4. Click the Settings button to enable or disable the modem options.

5. Use the Advanced Configuration button to either permit all callers to access the entire network, or restrict them to the RAS server.

Connecting over ISDN

If you're using an ISDN connection rather than a modem, you need to do just a little more tweaking to make sure that it's set up properly. If you're making an ISDN connection from an old modem, you don't need to trash the old one and start over. Just select the entry in the Phone Book and edit it to use ISDN. If you're using BRI ISDN, tell the system that you'll be using two channels.

In addition to the tweaking you do in the office, you need to do some tweaking with the telephone company. When setting up your ISDN connection, be sure to have the connection set up in the following way:

- **Switch protocols** AT&T 5ESS switch—proprietary or N11 (if it is available) protocol; Northern Telecom DMS100 switch—Functional or N11 protocol; National ISDN 1 compatible switch—N11.

- **Terminal type** The terminal type is A, or D if A is not available or already being used by other equipment on the box.

- **TEL assignment** The TEL assignment should be Auto.

- **Multipoint** Multipoint should be set to Yes, meaning that each B channel (those are the ones the data travels on, remember) can be used for separate purposes by the machine. One B channel could be used for inbound traffic, and one could be used for outbound traffic. You might have to explain this one to the telephone company, since "multipoint" may mean something different to them, depending on what part of the country you live in.

- **SPIDs** If you want to be able to use the two high-speed channels independently, you *must* make sure that the telephone company sets the number of SPIDs (logical terminals) to 2. This will give you two telephone numbers on the same ISDN line. If you don't have two logical terminals, you won't be able to use the channels independently, as the SPID controlling the transmission will be unavailable once the channel is in use.

- **EKTS** Set EKTS to No.

TIP

ISDN is a new technology, and, as such, can be a bit finicky at times. If you're having connection problems, try switching the IMAC off and back on again, and make sure the NT1 is functioning. If the problems persist, check with the telephone company or the company who installed ISDN for you. There could be problems with the telephone company's connection, or the ISDN setup could be configured incorrectly.

Connecting via X.25

Setting up RAS to work with X.25 isn't much different from setting it up to work with ISDN:

1. Go to the RAS Phone Book and click the Add, Edit, or Clone button, depending on whether you're making a new entry, changing an existing one, or copying an existing one.

2. On the Phone Book entry dialog box, click the Advanced button.

3. Choose Any X.25 port from the list of available ports and then click on the X.25 button. You'll see a dialog box that looks like Figure 17.10.

FIGURE 17.10:
X.25 Settings screen

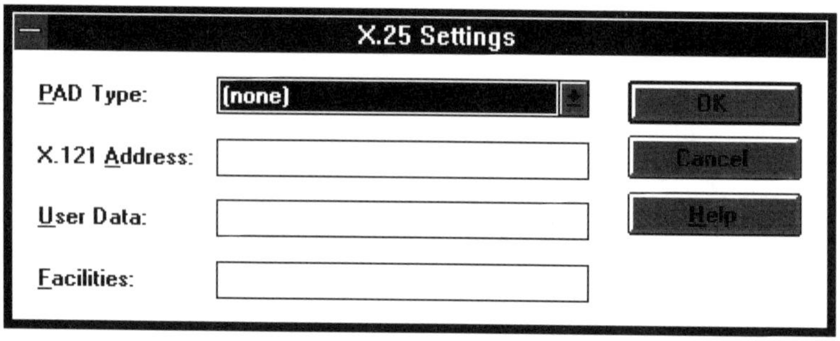

The settings in this dialog box are as follows:

- **PAD Type:** The type of X.25 packet assembler/dissembler that you'll be using. If you're using a dial-up PAD, select the name of your provider.

- **X.121 Address:** The X.25 equivalent of a telephone number. Enter the one associated with the machine that you want to call.

- **User Data Box:** Any additional information that the X.25 host computer needs to make the connection is placed in the User Data box. Typically, nothing is entered here.

- **Facilities:** In the Facilities box, put any additional parameters that your X.25 provider supplies, such as reverse charging. If you're not sure what options you have, check with your provider and your documentation.

Once you've filled in the boxes here, you should be ready to use RAS over X.25. The connection process, which is discussed below, doesn't change with the kind of connection that's in place.

> **TIP** X.25 has one drawback: You can't use the Callback security feature with it.

RAS Installation on DOS and Windows Clients

To set up RAS on a machine that is running DOS or Windows rather than NT or NT Server, you need the Remote Access Service 1.1a client that comes on the NT Server 3.5x CD. If the machine that you're installing it on uses DOS or Windows, LAN Manager 2.2c or MS Network Client 3.0 must be installed first. Windows for Workgroups, since it already has networking capabilities, needs no special software. If you haven't already loaded the operating environment or network software that you need, reboot between the time that you finish loading it and the time that you try to load RAS.

Customizing Your RAS Setup

Remote
Access Admin

Now that the service is installed, you need to set it up so that each user has only the type of access that he or she needs. To do this, go to the Remote Access Service Administrator in the RAS program group. Open it, and you'll see a screen that looks like Figure 17.11.

To determine which users can access the server through RAS, and what kind of access they have, click on the Users menu and choose Permissions. You'll see a screen that looks like Figure 17.12.

By default, no users can dial into the RAS server. To grant permission, either select the user you want and check in the Grant dialin [sic] permission to user box, or click on the Grant All button to grant every user account RAS access.

How Do I Install RAS on Non-NT Machines?

To install RAS on non-NT machines:

1. From the command prompt, type **setup**. The system will count down the files to copy.

2. When it's done, you'll be prompted for the COM port name. If you don't know what COM port your modem uses, check with your documentation. Internal modems frequently use COM2.

3. You'll see the configuration screen. Use the Tab key to move to the selection that you need. Since you've already added a port, move to Select Modem and choose the kind of modem that you have. If you selected the wrong COM port, you can remove it here with the Remove Port button and create a new one with the Add Port button.

4. When you've finished, restart your computer. RAS is now installed.

If you're setting up RAS on a computer running Windows for Workgroups or the DOS Workgroup connection, the process is the same except that you'll type wfwsetup in step 1 instead of setup.

FIGURE 17.11:

Opening screen for RAS Administrator

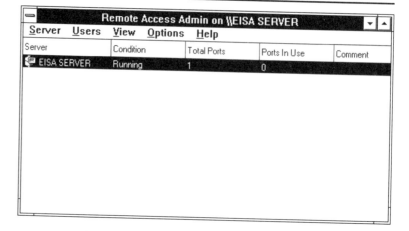

FIGURE 17.12:

FIGURE 17.12:

RAS Administrator Permissions
screen

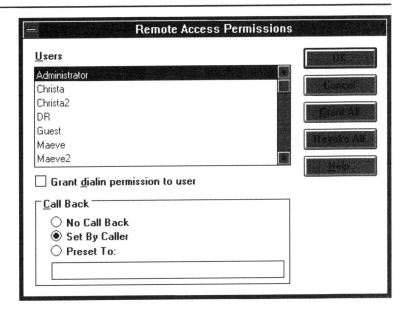

TIP

Microsoft does not recommend granting the Guest account RAS access. Microsoft suggests, if you must grant it access, putting a password on the account. You can probably see why: A Guest account that can dial into the server from an outside location is a security breach waiting to happen. If you do grant the Guest account dial-in permission, be sure to give the account a password—and don't make it *password*.

For every account that has permission to dial in, you must choose how it is to be done with the Call Back options at the bottom of the dialog box:

- **No Call Back:** This option offers no extra system security. With it checked, the user dials in directly from wherever he or she is. This is the default option.

- **Set By Caller:** Although it doesn't offer any system security either, this option allows on-the-road users to avoid big telephone bills. With this option checked, the RAS server calls the user back at the number the user indicates once the user's account has been validated.

- **Preset To:** This is the most secure option. For users that routinely call in from the same location, you can preset a telephone number from which they must always call. After the user dials in and is validated, the RAS server breaks the connection and then calls the user back at the preset telephone number. If the user is calling from a different number than the one in the RAS database, he or she won't be able to make the connection.

If you mess up when establishing who can dial in and how, you can always start over by clicking the Revoke All button and eliminating all dial-in permissions.

How Do I Set User Access through the RAS Server?

To set user access through the RAS Server:

1. Open the RAS Administrator and select the connection that you want to customize.

2. Click Server/Choose Domain or Server...

3. When the list of domains appears, click on the domain's name *once*, then click OK. You'll see the list of users for that domain.

4. Choose Permissions from the Users menu.

5. Click on the name of a user to whom you want to extend RAS privileges.

6. Check the Grant login privilege check box for that user.

7. Repeat steps 4 through 6 for all users to whom you want to grant login privileges.

Alternatively, you can use the Grant All button to allow everyone to log on to the RAS server. If you do that, go back and de-select the Guest account; don't let it log in on RAS.

Connecting to RAS Servers from Clients

Once you've set up the service and have it running on both the server and the workstation from which you want to access the server, you're ready to make the remote connection. How you make the connection varies depending on whether you're running NT's RAS or the special version used with DOS, Windows, and Windows for Workgroups.

Connecting from an NT or NT Server Machine

To make the remote connection from an NT or NT Server machine:

1. Go to the RAS icon and open it.

Since this is the first time that you've used the program, there will be no entries in the Phone Book, but RAS will automatically dump you to a screen for creating Phone Book entries, as in Figure 17.13.

2. To create an entry, fill in this screen with the name, the telephone number, and a description of the RAS server you want to connect to.

The name and description of the connection are up to you; they're for identification purposes only. Also, when entering the number, it's okay to just type the numbers—you don't need spaces or hyphens. If you need to change the type of modem or the COM port to which you are connected, click on the Advanced>> button. You'll be

---

Add Phone Book Entry

Entry Name:

Phone Number:

Description:

☒ Authenticate using current user name and password

OK

Cancel

Advanced >>

Help

able to change modem types of the COM port from the screen shown in Figure 17.14.

If you click OK before filling in the boxes completely, don't worry; you can change the connection information at any time by clicking on the Edit button in the RAS dialout program. The only time that this option is not available is when the connection is in use.

FIGURE 17.14:

The screen for changing modem types and COM ports

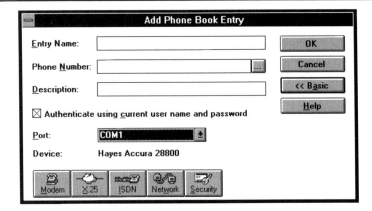

Once you've filled in your entry, you're ready to dial:

3. Choose the line for the connection that you want to make, and click on the Dial button. As you see in Figure 17.15, the system will ask you for your password and may also need the name of the domain to which you wish to connect.

4. Fill in the information as appropriate and click OK.

RAS then dials the number, verifies your name and password, and registers your computer as part of the domain. It also sets the connection speed. When it's done, you'll see the dialog box in Figure 17.16. This dialog box tells you that the connection is made, asks if you'd like to minimize the RAS icon while the remote connection is in place, and asks if you want the notice to appear in the future.

If you look at the RAS window now, you will notice that the card icon next to the name of the selection you made has changed to a telephone icon, as you can see in Figure 17.17. This means that the connection is in service.

FIGURE 17.15:

Authentication dialog box

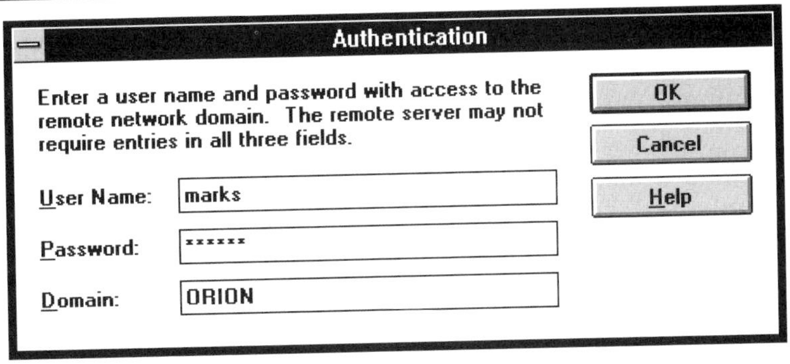

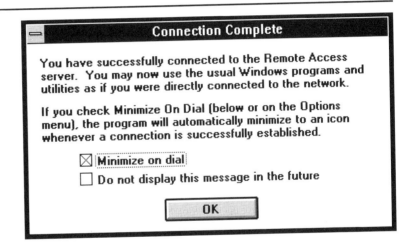

FIGURE 17.16:

Connection Complete dialog box

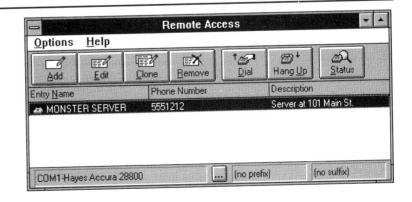

FIGURE 17.17:

Remote Access dialog box with a telephone icon to show the connection is in service

Notice also that a new drive is available in the File Manager. You can now connect to the RAS server's drive just as you could if you were connected over a cabled network. To disconnect from the RAS server, select the connection that you wish to break and click on the Hang Up button. A dialog box will ask you to confirm the action. If you click Yes, the connection will be severed until you restart it.

By the way, if you're opening RAS on a server that never calls out, it's possible that you'll never need any entries in your Phone Book. As long as there are no entries, however, you'll get dumped into the Add Phone Book Entry dialog box (see Figure 17.13) every time you start RAS. To avoid this, you can create a null entry to fool the system into not skipping to the Add Phone Book Entry dialog box. For me, it's worth the couple of minutes it takes to make a null entry rather than the extra step of canceling out of the dialog box every time I start RAS.

How Do I Call a RAS Server or Workstation from an NT Machine?

To call a RAS server or workstation from an NT Machine:

1. Create a Phone Book entry.

2. Open the RAS service and select the entry that you want.

3. Click on the Dial button. RAS will prompt you for the password to that connection. Enter your user password. You may also have to enter the domain to which the RAS server belongs. Click OK.

Assuming that you are authorized for this service, your RAS service will now call the other one. If the other server is working properly, it will make the connection and inform you when it's done.

Connecting from a Windows for Workgroups Station

The process of connecting from a Windows for Workgroups station is identical to that of connecting from an NT workstation. RAS comes with WfW just as it does with NT, so all that you must do is use the WFWSETUP.EXE program found on the disk that you use for non-NT installations. Once you've done that, a RAS icon will appear in your Network program group. From there, the process is identical to that described in the preceding section.

Connecting from Other Operating Systems

The process of connecting to a RAS server from an operating system other than NT varies, depending on which system you're using. The basic steps are the same, but you don't need to include all of them when you're working with certain systems.

Connecting to a Netware Server

ENTERPRISE
NETWORKING

Due to the large market share that Novell has, you will likely need to connect an NT client to a NetWare server through RAS. One approach is to run the Client Services for NetWare on the client machine and then call the RAS server for the initial connection to the network, and let CSNW do the rest. Another approach is to install the Gateway Services for NetWare on the NT network; the NetWare drives then look like normal NT shared drives to any user of the network.

As long as the drive connection between the servers is maintained, the NT Server server will reshare the NetWare drive connection with any Microsoft client to which it is linked, either locally or remotely.

Keeping Dial-In Intruders Off the Network

No doubt, RAS offers increased flexibility and the opportunity to increase output. With this increased flexibility comes new security risks, however. How do you keep just anyone from dialing into your server, if some of your employees can? Once employees log onto the server from their home or hotel, how do you restrict them to files that they need? To answer these concerns, Microsoft included security measures that permit authorized remote users to use files that they need, but keep unauthorized people off the network.

How Do I Connect a Non-NT Workstation to a RAS Server?

If you are running DOS and LAN Manager Enhanced on a dual-role computer, start at step 1. If you are running DOS and any other configuration (except Windows for Workgroups), start at step 2. If you are running OS/2, start at step 3.

1. From the command prompt, type **unload protocol**.

2. Type **rasload** to load the RAS drivers.

3. Type **rasphone** to open the RAS Phone Book.

4. Create and save a Phone Book entry. To do so, click on the File menu and choose Create. Fill in the blanks for the connection name (this is up to you—the name is for your identification purposes only), the domain, and the telephone number.

5. Type **Alt-D** to reach the Dial menu, and choose Connect. You will be prompted for your password, but, if you've selected an entry, the other information should be filled in. Type in your password and press Enter.

6. You will see a dialog box telling you that the system is trying to make the connection and asking you to wait. If you need to stop before the connection is made, press Enter to cancel.

Once the connection is complete, you will see a message telling you that you can now access the network as though you were connected to the LAN.

Modem Security

Along with the special security features that NT Server offers, you can take other measures to reduce your network's vulnerability to dial-in intruders:

- Keep unauthorized users away from your modem and telephone lines. This could mean burying the cables and/or encasing them in some kind of protection like a concrete pipe, just as you might with data cables connecting one office to another.

- Don't publicize your server's telephone number. People who don't need to know it shouldn't be able to get it from your business card.

- If you use a callback modem (discussed below), don't use call forwarding, as that could let an intruder forward calls from an authorized client machine to his or her own (unauthorized) machine.

Types of Secure Modems

Secure modems fall into four categories—callback, password, encryption, and silent. Each is discussed below.

Callback Modems   Callback modems give you the same capabilities as the Preset To option described above. There's not much point in using a callback modem on an NT Server system, because the modems work the same way the software does: They hang up and call the client back at the authorized number preset in the user database.

Password Modems   Password modems build in an extra layer of security by requiring the user to provide a password before the server will connect the client to itself.

Encryption Modems   Encryption modems can be used in conjunction with NT Server. NT Server encrypts the password as the client logs in, but then does not encrypt the rest of the data as the client accesses the server. An encryption modem would encode all data that passes between the server and client computers, thus dissuading wiretaps. This method of protection requires an encryption modem at each end of the connection so that the data can be decrypted once it gets to the server or the client. This also keeps unauthorized people from dialing into the server, as they won't have the proper kind of encryption, and any information that they download will be gibberish.

Silent Modems   Silent modems don't signal that a connection has been made until you have begun the login process. This keeps intruders who are randomly dialing telephone numbers looking for a modem from realizing that they've found a computer.

Enabling and Disabling Bindings

Once remote users have logged on, it still might be necessary to restrict them to only a part of the network, even if they can normally access all or most of it. You do this by disabling *bindings*. Bindings are the virtual circuits that link computers in a network together. By default, remote users can access the entire network.

Troubleshooting RAS

Just as with any other network connection, RAS won't work at times. If you happen across one of those times, here are some ways in which you can find out and maybe fix what's wrong.

If the Connection Has Never Worked Before...

If you're trying to use RAS for the first time after you've set it up and it doesn't work, there may be gremlins in the system. Probably the problem has to do with an incorrect configuration, your modem, or ISDN problems.

Incorrect Configuration   Have you used the RAS Administrator to give all the proper users dial-in permission? Have you configured the server so that it is able to receive calls? Is the preset number at which the server is trying to call a user the correct one?

Modem Problems   If you're using a new modem, the problem could be found there. It could be a compatibility problem, or the modem simply might not work.

If you're not sure that a modem works, check it with the Terminal program found in the Accessories program group:

1. Double-click on the Terminal icon to open it.
2. Choose Communications... from the Settings menu. You'll see a screen that looks like the one in Figure 17.18.

FIGURE 17.18:

Communications screen

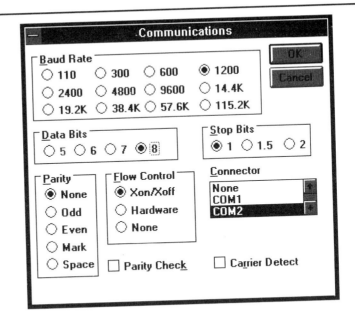

3. Select the speed at which your modem transmits and the COM port to which it is connected, and click OK.

4. Type **ATT** on the Terminal screen and press Enter.

If it is working properly, the modem will reply OK or 0, depending on its result code settings. If this doesn't work and you've got the modem set up properly, call its manufacturer.

What if your Terminal test was successful and the modem still doesn't seem to work? Modems from different manufacturers, and even different models from the same manufacturer, are not always fully compatible with each other. In addition, compatibility problems are exacerbated at high speeds, so that modems running at 9600 bps or faster may not always be able to talk to each other and may fall back to 2400 bps (sort of negating the reason why you get fast modems in the first place). Even modems that claim to follow the Hayes AT standard may not be able to communicate under every circumstance.

ISDN Problems If you're running RAS over ISDN, is the ISDN connection set up properly?

If the Connection Has Worked Before...

If the connection *used* to run but doesn't now, pinpointing the problem is generally a matter of establishing what's different. What changed between the last time the service worked and now? Sometimes the problem is an internal one you can control, and sometimes you can't do much about the problem and you have, for example, a downed telephone line.

If the problem is an internal one, ask yourself these questions. Is the service running on both the server and client machines? Has a user with a preset callback number changed his or her telephone number? Have you reinstalled the operating system and forgotten to reinstall RAS? Is the modem running?

If the problem is external, ask yourself if the telephone lines between the RAS server and client are working. If you're using an ISDN connection, is the telephone company's hub working?

Checking the Audit Records

You don't have to rely merely on intuition and problem-solving ability when it comes to troubleshooting RAS. You can either monitor connection attempts as they occur, using the RAS Administrator, or you can check the record of all audits and error messages that is stored in the Event Viewer.

Real-Time Auditing with the RAS Administrator

If you suspect that one of your ports is not working, you can check it from the RAS Administrator's initial screen. When you open the Administrator, you'll see a display of all the ports that the service can determine. If you don't see a port and you expected it to be there, probably something is wrong with the connection.

Suppose a user can't connect to the server. You can monitor the attempt as it's happening. Open the RAS Administrator and choose Communication Ports... from the Server menu. A screen appears showing all the possible ports for the server. Select the one on which the user is trying to dial in, and click the Port Status button. You'll see a screen that looks like Figure 17.19.

FIGURE 17.19:

Port Status dialog box (at rest)

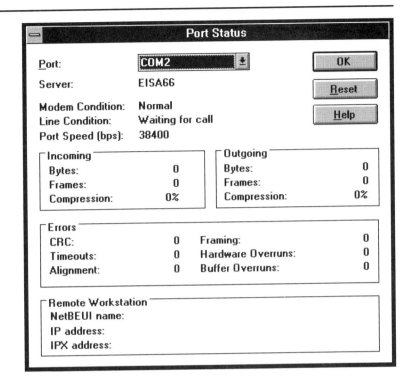

This is a modem at rest, with no incoming calls. When a call is coming in, this screen displays current information about the transaction: the number of bytes and frames coming in/going out, the degree of data compression, and the number and type of errors. It will look something like Figure 17.20.

The information on this screen changes during the connection. It registers the level of compression, the amount of data traveling between the server and client, any errors that take place, and so forth. If things go well, the values in the Errors section remain at 0. Errors aren't the end of the world, however; a few of them won't hurt anything.

Click the Reset button if you want to reset all the values back to 0. This doesn't break the connection—the counting just starts over. Resetting to 0 is useful if you're trying to determine, for example, the number of line errors that take place in a ten-minute period.

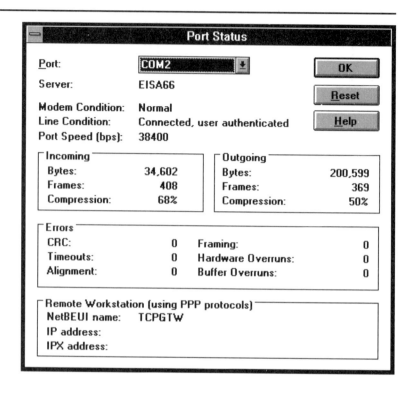

Using the Event Viewer to Monitor Problems

To monitor past problems, you can check the Event Viewer to see what it has to say about a situation. Make sure that auditing is enabled (it is by default). Three kinds of events are recorded in the Event Viewer—audits, warnings, and errors:

- **Audit** A normal event recorded for administrative reasons. A normal connection would be recorded as an audit. You can choose to audit only successful events, failed events, or both.

- **Warning** An irregular event that doesn't affect how the system functions.

- **Error** A failed event or network error.

Examining Logged Information

If you're having trouble with the connection, connection information about each RAS session is saved in a file called DEVICE.LOG in the SYSTEM32 directory. DEVICE.LOG contains the strings that are sent to and received from the serial device (modem or X.25 PAD) that transmits the information between client and server. When looking at this file, be sure to use a text editor that can handle both regular characters and hexadecimal output, because if you don't some of the information will turn into gibberish. You can track the entire progress of a session with this file. It contains the command string sent to the serial device, the echo of the command, the device's response and, for modems, the rate of transmittal.

Before you can use DEVICE.LOG, you must create it. How to do this is explained in the "How Do I" sidebar.

How Do I Create Device.LOG?

To create the DEVICE.LOG file:

1. Hang up any remote connections currently in place, and exit RAS.

2. Open the Registry by running REGEDIT32. You can also access the Registry from inside WINMSD.

3. Go to HKEY_LOCAL_MACHINE and access this key:

   `\SYSTEM\CurrentControlSet\Services\RasMan\Parameters`

4. Change the value of the logging parameter to 1, so that it looks like this:

   `Logging:REG_DWORD:0x1`

Logging begins whenever you open the Remote Access icon or restart the service. You don't need to shut down the system or log off and on first. To view the log, open it in Write or some other text editor. Be sure to use an editor that can handle hexadecimal information, or else part of the log will end up as gibberish. Also, when looking at this file, you can disregard the h0D and h0A characters at the end of each line. Those are, respectively, carriage-return and linefeed bytes and don't have any other significance.

TIP
As always, before editing the Registry you should make a copy of it. Messing up the Registry can affect your system badly enough that you need to reinstall the operating system. See Chapter 5 for information on that.

For DEVICE.LOG to work, you need to make sure that your modem is configured to return the data terminal equipment speed—that is, how fast the modem is transmitting. If you also configure it to return the carrier (Data Communication Equipment) speed, DEVICE.LOG will record it and display it for you, but without DTE, RAS can't reset the port to go with the modem speed and you'll get transmission errors.

DEVICE.LOG only records information about dial-up connections. If you're having trouble with a direct connection, this file won't be able to help you.

Running Applications Remotely

This is a short topic: I don't recommend running applications remotely. Accessing files over a RAS connection is one thing, but using a remote *application* is something else altogether. Assuming your permissions allow it, nothing stops you from putting an icon in your Program Manager for a remote executable file. But loading that program will take forever, and doing anything with that program will take just as long. The problem is that every time you access the program file, all of it must travel to you, since the program stays stored on the computer where it resides. Most programs aren't set up to be client-server packages in which the client takes only the parts of the programs that it needs.

CHAPTER

EIGHTEEN

Making the Mac Connection

18

Attaching a Macintosh computer to a PC-based network has never been easier thanks to NT Server. All the software you need to support Mac clients, called Services for Macintosh, is included right in the NT Server box. There's nothing else to buy.

NT's support for Macintosh clients is significant, since Apple represents a sizable proportion of corporate networked computers. Mac users are beginning to demand access to the same shared services that PC users enjoy. In fact, Mac users and PC users often work together on shared projects and *require* access to shared information and resources. Bridging requirements are growing, and until now, Mac to DOS connections have been less than easy.

At the same time, supporting Mac clients is a challenge. Perhaps the biggest challenge lies in working with the filing systems of both Macintoshes and DOS-based computers. The Macintosh file system is significantly different from the DOS file system, and any DOS-based server must be able to accommodate these differences. NT Server uses NTFS to provide what looks to a Mac like native file space, while making the same space available to NT, DOS, Windows, and OS/2 clients.

The following list summarizes some of the other features and benefits of Services for Macintosh:

Feature	Benefit
A file server that is fully compliant with AppleShare Filing Protocol	Mac users access the NT server in the usual way. They may not know that the server is not a Macintosh computer.
Support of Macintosh file name attributes, such as resource forks and data forks (stored as a single NT file), 32-character file names, icons, and access privileges	Mac users don't have to change their file names or learn a new file naming convention (although this may be desirable if files are to be *shared* with PC users).
Native support for AppleTalk protocols	A protocol converter (gateway) is not required.
PostScript emulation for non-PostScript printers	Allows Mac users to access PC printers without converting documents.

Feature	Benefit
Access to LaserWriter printers by Windows, NT, DOS, and OS/2 clients	Allows PC users to access Mac printers without converting documents.
255 simultaneous connections to an NT server, using approximately 15K per session	Relatively low overhead for a large number of potential users.
Support for LocalTalk, Ethernet, TokenRing, and FDDI	Macintosh computers can use any Data Link mechanism to connect to the network.
Extension mapping for PC data files	Enables PC files to be recognized by Mac-based applications, for those apps which are not cross-platform.

Mac Connection in a Nutshell

In this chapter I'll cover all of the things you need to do to get Macs to talk to NT Server, but here's an overview. First, you'll have to get the server ready for Mac support. That means loading the NT software that enables NT to create Mac-accessible volumes. Then you create the directories that will hold Mac data.

Next, you have to load the NT network software on each Mac workstation. Now, Microsoft could have enclosed a Mac-readable diskette with the drivers to allow a Mac to get onto an NT network, but they instead adopted (in my opinion) a more elegant plan. You see, all Macs have networking capabilities built right into their operating system. That networking capability isn't really compatible with NT, however, because it doesn't enforce the kind of security that NT requires. So NT lets the Mac into the domain solely as a guest who can access one file and one file only—the Macintosh NT client software. Your Mac logs onto the NT Server machine, grabs the NT client software, reboots with the new client drivers, and it is then able to conduct itself as an NT-compatible workstation. Very easy, and very clean. Following are the details.

Preparing the Server to Support Your Mac

All of the software to support Services for Macintosh is included in every box of NT Server, although it is not enabled by default. Before installing the components to support Mac clients, you must prepare the NT server.

The Physical Connection

AppleTalk is Apple's built-in networking system. LocalTalk is the physical component of AppleTalk—the port, software driver, and cable used to connect Macs. Apple-Talk is not a high-performance network like Ethernet; in fact, it's quite a bit slower, at one-fortieth the speed of the average Ethernet.

Macintosh computers can be connected together via a number of data-link mechanisms. LocalTalk is the most inexpensive method since just about everything needed to connect this type of network is included with every Mac computer. If the Macs are connected on a LocalTalk network, a LocalTalk card is needed for the server. A router knows AppleTalk must exist somewhere on the network; NT Server itself can act as a router, if necessary.

Macintosh computers can also be connected via Ethernet, Token Ring, or FDDI. In this case, just connect the existing PC network to the Mac network—no additional hardware or routing is needed on the NT server.

Unfortunately, NT Server does not support RAS for Mac clients. Remote or dial-in access is not available.

Preparing the NT Server Hard Disk

Two requirements need to be met before Services for Macintosh can be installed on the server drive:

- Services for Macintosh requires an additional 2MB of space on the server drive.
- Directories for Mac clients must exist on an NTFS partition of the server hard disk, or on a CD-ROM drive. You need an NTFS partition to load Services for Macintosh.

Getting Services for Macintosh Up and Running

Installing Services for Macintosh is straightforward except for the few diversions you'll encounter along the way. These diversions are not very well documented. After a few false starts, here is what seems to be the best procedure for the installation:

1. Install the Services for Macintosh module. This activates the software required for Mac file sharing, print sharing, and application extension mapping. The installation adds some additional tools to your Control Panel, as well as additional selections to your File Manager menus.

2. Set attributes for Mac-accessible volumes. Here you can create a logon message and set security and connection limitations.

3. Prepare Microsoft UAM Volume for use by Mac clients. This volume is created during the above installation. It contains software for Mac clients that enables user authentication (a fancy word for encrypted passwords). You can connect Mac users at this point and enable user authentication, or continue on with the process and create Mac-accessible volumes, as described here.

4. Create Mac-accessible volumes. These are directories of the NTFS partition to which Mac users have access. Mac users won't have access to any other directories or partitions on the server.

Each step is discussed in this section.

Installing Services for Macintosh

Search through the pile of books that came with your copy of NT Server and you'll find one called *Services for Macintosh*. Just follow the book for this part of the installation. Here's a recap of the procedure, in case you can't find the book:

1. Open Control Panel and double-click Network. You'll see the Network Settings screen shown in Figure 18.1.

2. Select Add Software… You'll see a dialog box that says something like Add Network Software, as in Figure 18.2.

3. Click the pop-up list, then scroll down the list until you find Services for Macintosh. Select that, then click Continue.

FIGURE 18.1:

Network Settings dialog box

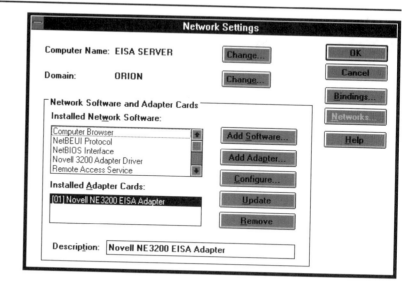

FIGURE 18.2:

Adding Services for Macintosh to the network software

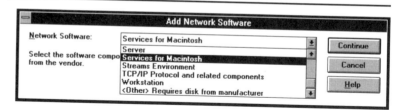

4. Enter the path where the NT Server software is located (probably the drive containing the CD that NT Server was originally installed from).

The files to support Mac services are copied to the server drive. When finished, the installation returns to the Network Settings screen (see Figure 18.1).

5. Highlight Services for Macintosh, then click Configure...

You'll see the window shown in Figure 18.3. If you have multiple zones in your network (a "zone" to a Mac is like a "domain" to NT Server), their names will appear in the Zone drop-down.

6. Select the zone you want to be the default zone for the Mac clients. If the Macs on your network are connected via LocalTalk and there is a LocalTalk

FIGURE 18.3:

Configuring Services for Macintosh

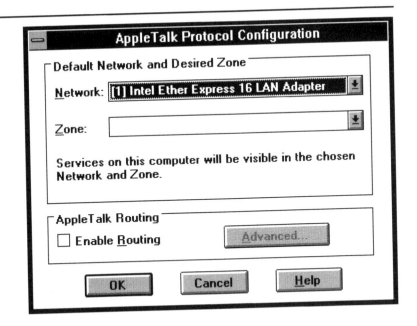

card in the server, check Enable Routing if you want NT Server to act as a router for LocalTalk. Just click OK if you have a single-zone network or you don't need routing.

7. You'll get a message that Services for Macintosh is configured. Click Close.

8. Click OK in the last dialog box.

The installation is now complete. You need to reboot the NT server for the changes to take effect (you'll get a dialog box telling you this).

Setting Attributes for Mac-Accessible Volumes

Next, set up access attributes for all of the Macintosh volumes that you'll create. Go to Control Panel and select MacFile (this appears as part of the above installation). You'll see the MacFile Properties dialog box, as in Figure 18.4. Click the Attributes button. You'll see the MacFile Attributes dialog box, as in Figure 18.5.

FIGURE 18.4:

MacFile Properties dialog box

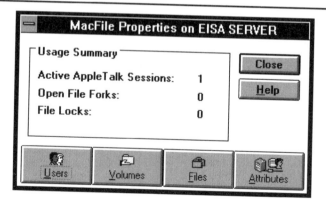

FIGURE 18.5:

The MacFile Attributes dialog box

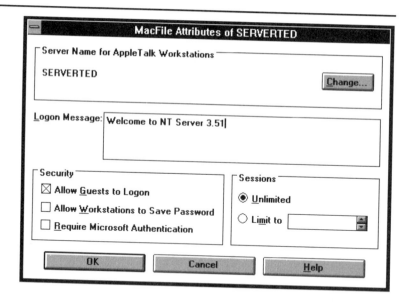

There's really nothing to change or set in this dialog box, unless you want to create a logon message or change the name of the NT server (the name that you use here is the name that appears in the Mac user's Chooser). At some point, you should come back to this section and check the Require Microsoft Authentication box (it may already be checked on your system—if so, just leave it). This check box enables additional security for Mac clients.

Setting Up Microsoft Authentication

Any time after restarting the server (this step could be done before the previous step), go to the File Manager. You'll see that the volume Microsoft UAM Volume was added to the NTFS partition, as in Figure 18.6. This volume contains the software needed to enable Microsoft Authentication for the Mac clients. Microsoft Authentication enables password encryption for Mac clients. The Mac operating system only supports "clear text" passwords, which can be intercepted by a "sniffer" device. Clear text passwords violate NT Server's C2-level security.

Don't try to get to the volume from the Mac yet. Highlight the volume, then go to the File Manager's MacFile item (which magically appeared when you rebooted with Mac services), highlight the Mac volume, and click View/Modify Volumes... You'll see the View/Modify dialog box with the volume highlighted, as in Figure 18.7. Click the button labeled Properties.... You'll see the Properties dialog box, as in Figure 18.8.

FIGURE 18.6:

The Microsoft UAM volume, now visible in File Manager

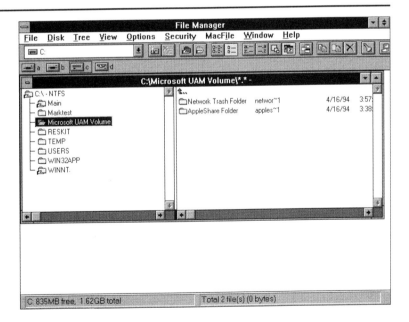

FIGURE 18.7:

Configuring the Mac-accessible volume

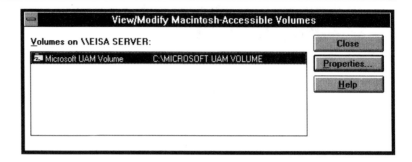

FIGURE 18.8:

Properties of the Mac-accessible volume

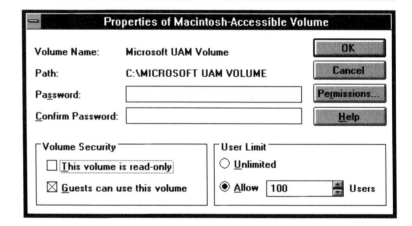

You needn't change this dialog box at all; I bring it to your attention so that you'll know where to go to control permissions on the volume. (Don't change permissions on *this* volume, as it doesn't contain anything except the Microsoft Authentication software. But other Mac-accessible volumes may require permissions.)

Creating Mac-Accessible Volumes

The final step in the server setup process involves setting up shared directories for Mac clients (called "Mac-accessible volumes"). This is done in much the same way shared directories are set up for PC clients. Only permissions are handled differently.

TIP Mac-accessible volumes can be CD-ROMs. Just mark the volume read-only.

First, create a volume as usual by using the File Manager. Then follow these steps:

1. Share the volume by selecting it, choosing Disk, choosing Share As…, and clicking OK.

2. From the File Manager, select MacFile, select Create Volume, and then click Properties.

3. Click Permissions. You'll see the Macintosh View of Directory Permissions dialog box, as in Figure 18.9.

You've probably seen a screen like this before. Here, the permissions look a little different. Table 18.1 explains what these permissions mean.

There's one other main difference between this screen and the others you've seen. With NT Server, permissions for a user or group override those for "everyone." This is a major difference between NT Server and Macintosh file servers, where permissions for "everyone" override permissions for an individual or group.

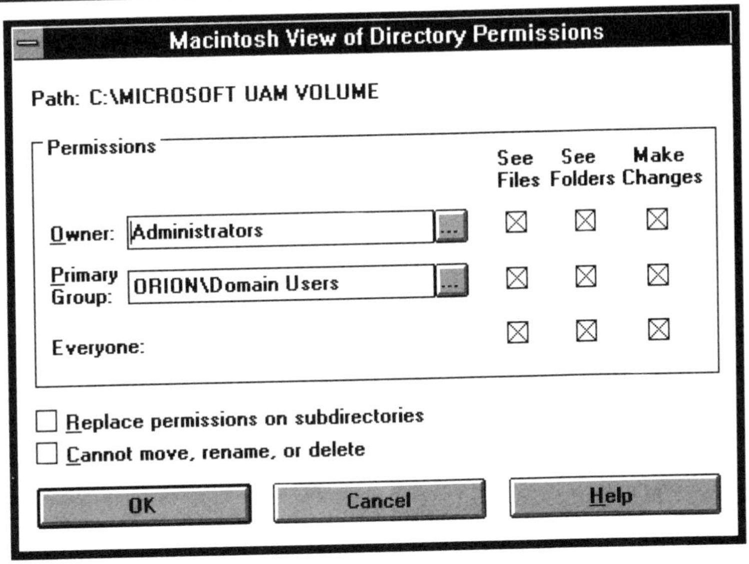

FIGURE 18.9:

Directory Permissions dialog box

Macintosh View of Directory Permissions

Path: C:\MICROSOFT UAM VOLUME

Permissions

	See Files	See Folders	Make Changes
Owner: Administrators	☒	☒	☒
Primary Group: ORION\Domain Users	☒	☒	☒
Everyone:	☒	☒	☒

☐ Replace permissions on subdirectories
☐ Cannot move, rename, or delete

OK   Cancel   Help

TABLE 18.1 : Mac vs. NT Server Permissions

Mac Permission	NT Equivalent
See Files Allows the owner, primary group, or everyone to see and open the files that are contained within this folder.	Read
See Folders Allows the owner, primary group, or everyone to see and open any folders contained within this folder.	Read
Make Changes Allows the owner, primary group, or everyone to add or delete files and folders, and save changes to files in this folder.	Write, Delete
Replace permissions on subdirectories Copies the permissions you just set to all folders within this volume or folder. (This is the same as "Make all enclosed folders like this one" on Mac file servers.)	*Same*
Cannot move, rename, or delete Prevents the volume or folder from being moved, renamed, or deleted by Mac users.	*Same*

Create additional volumes if you wish, or exit from File Manager. That's all that needs to be done on the NT server.

Setting Up the Mac for NT Connection

NT Server is an *AFP-compliant* server, which means NT Server directly supports the AppleShare Filing Protocols (AFP) required by Macintosh clients. There's nothing to do from the Mac except log on to the NT server in exactly the same way as you log on to a Macintosh server. NT Server's Mac-accessible volumes and shared printers are directly available through the Apple Chooser. To access them, click AppleShare for the file server(s) or LaserWriter for the printer(s).

Mac clients that connect to NT require System 6.0.7 or higher. NT Server fully supports System 7 clients. PowerPC Macintosh computers can be clients on an NT server.

No additional software is required for the Mac, although you are advised to enable Microsoft authentication to maintain NT Server's C2 security. The software for accomplishing this is included with NT Server and needs to be installed at each Mac workstation.

First Time Logon

Before Mac users can log on to an NT server as a registered user, they have to log on as a guest and fetch the software to enable Microsoft authentication. Here's how that's done:

1. From the Mac's Apple menu, select Chooser.

2. From the Chooser, click AppleShare. A list of available servers appears.

3. From the list, select the NT server, and then click OK.

You'll get the option to log on as a guest or a registered user. However, the option to log on as a registered user isn't currently available—it's grayed out.

4. Log on as a guest, as in Figure 18.10.

You'll see the list of shared volumes, as in Figure 18.11. The first time around you may see only one, the Microsoft UAM Volume.

5. Click on Microsoft UAM Volume, then on OK.

If a logon message was enabled from MacFile Attributes, you'll see a screen similar to Figure 18.12.

6. Click OK, then close the Chooser. An icon for Microsoft UAM Volume appears on the Mac desktop, as in Figure 18.13.

FIGURE 18.10:
Logging on to the NT server

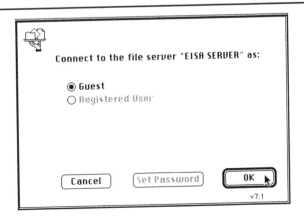

FIGURE 18.11:

Selecting the volume

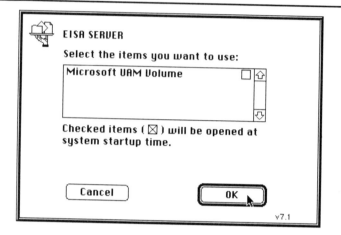

FIGURE 18.12:

Logon message from the NT server

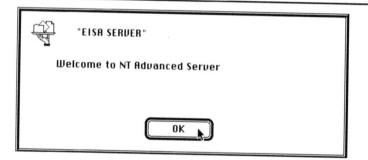

FIGURE 18.13:

Microsoft UAM icon

7. Open the Microsoft UAM Volume. It contains a folder called AppleShare folder. You can see this folder in Figure 18.14. Drag that folder into your System folder.

8. Restart the Mac. From now on, when you log on to a server, your password will be encrypted for additional security.

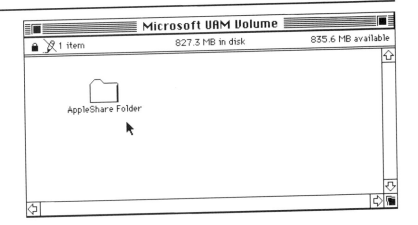

TIP

Before dragging the AppleShare folder into your System folder, check to see if there is already a folder with that name. If there is, take the contents from this folder and drag them into your existing AppleShare folder.

Next Time Logon

The next time you log on from the Mac, select the NT server through the Chooser as usual. You'll get a dialog box asking you to select a logon method. Choose Microsoft Authentication. Then you'll see a logon dialog box similar to the one in Figure 18.15 for entering your user name and password. This dialog box looks slightly different from the one you would see if this were a Mac-based server because you installed Microsoft authentication support in the previous step.

Click Registered User, enter your user name and password, and click OK. A list of available Mac-accessible volumes appears, as in Figure 18.16. If a volume name is grayed out, it means that you are either already logged on to that volume or you don't have the correct privileges to access it. Select a volume.

FIGURE 18.15:

Logon dialog box after Microsoft authentication support is installed

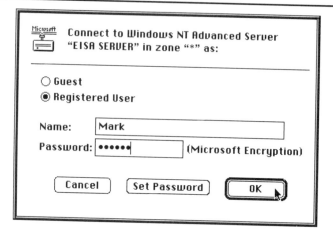

FIGURE 18.16:

Selecting an accessible volume

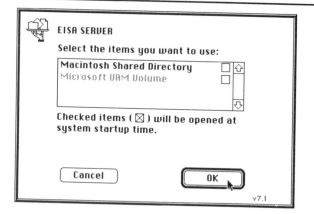

Services for Macintosh Printer Support

Services for Macintosh provides printer support in two different ways: Mac users can use non-PostScript printers connected to an NT Server network, and PC users can use Mac printers connected to an AppleTalk network.

Mac clients access non-PostScript printers via PostScript emulation. PostScript emulation is provided as part of Services for Macintosh and is invisible to Mac users. They won't need to change anything about their documents or change the way they access the printer. Mac clients work through the Chooser, as usual.

Mac printers may be made available to PCs by using NT Server's Print Manager (and the associated print spooler) along with "capturing" the Mac printers. Macintosh printers (we're talking about laser printers here) are usually connected to AppleTalk networks and are network-ready devices. When a Mac user sends a print job to a Mac printer, the Macintosh computer spools the print job to the user's local hard disk and prints it in the background. This often slows response time for the Mac.

Capturing a Mac printer causes a print spool to be created; print jobs are sent to the server and stored in a print queue.

Avoiding "LaserPrep Wars"

LaserPrep is a part of the Mac's built in laser printer driver. The LaserPrep driver is downloaded to the printer at the beginning of each printer session. If several users share the same printer, the first LaserPrep driver is retained in the printer's memory and does not need to be downloaded each time. This saves time when printing.

There are many different versions of LaserPrep, and a network administrator is often faced with the task of making sure that all versions of this driver are the same for every Mac on a network. If they are not the same, users complain of slow printing because the LaserPrep driver is downloaded at the beginning of each print job and the printer must reset itself.

By capturing the printer, LaserPrep wars are avoided. NT sends it's own LaserPrep code with each print job—this takes a little time, but not as much as keeping the driver resident in the printer and replacing it each time.

Installing Services for Macintosh Printing

The procedure to install print services for Mac clients is described in detail in the NT Server documentation. Here you'll find a summary for reference purposes.

Start the Print Manager and select Printer/Create Printer. Type in a name for the printer, select a driver from the available list, and provide a description for the printer if you like. Select a Print to destination. If the printer is connected directly to the server, the destination will be a port such as LPT1. If the printer is a networked Macintosh printer, the destination is Network printer… If you select Network printer, you'll see the Printer Properties dialog box, as in Figure 18.17. This dialog box lists possible print destinations. Select AppleTalk printing devices. Check the Share this printer on the network box.

FIGURE 18.17:
Printer Properties dialog box

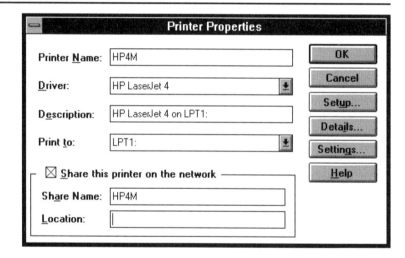

The printer is now available to PC users as usual. For Mac users, you need to create a user account. Start Control Panel/Services, select Print Server for Macintosh, and click the Startup button. A dialog box like the one in Figure 18.18 appears. Under the Log On As section, click System Account to enable all Mac users to access the printer. Click This Account and enter a user name to enable a single Mac user to access the printer. Macs should now have print access. They'll access the printer as usual, through the Chooser.

FIGURE 18.18:

Print Server for Macintosh Service
screen

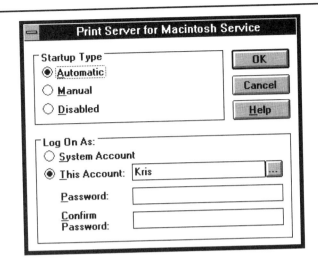

Transferring Data between Macs and PCs with NT Server

Now that you have the data from the Mac on the NT server, what can you do with it? Well, that depends…

If all you want to do is use the NT server as a place to *store* files, all you have to do is copy them from the Mac local hard drive to the NT shared volume. But before getting into that, it's good to understand a few things about the Mac file system. Then you can consider the problems of file formats, extensions, filtering, and document translation.

Forks, Forks Everywhere—and Nothing to Eat

Mac files are created in two distinct pieces—a *data fork* and a *resource fork*. The data fork contains the data for the file, while the resource fork contains information needed by the application that created the file, such as fonts, formatting information, and the like. A data file has a big data fork and a small resource fork, while an application program has a large resource fork and a small data fork.

PC-based file systems don't understand forks, since PC files are stored as one distinct entity (albeit that entity may be in fragments on the disk). Forks are okay with NT, though. NT stores the data fork and the resource fork together on the server in a single file.

Those Pesky File Names

First, the rules for naming files on DOS, Mac, and NT. Then, let's see what happens to the file names when files are moved around. Here is the lowdown on file names:

- **DOS names** DOS file names are limited to an 8-character file name, followed by an optional period and a 3-character extension. DOS file names can't contain spaces, and shouldn't contain any special characters. This is the FAT convention.

- **Mac names** Mac file names are limited to 32 characters, and can include any character on the keyboard with the exception of the colon (:). The colon is used to distinguish levels of folders, kind of like a backslash (\) distinguishes levels of directories in DOS and NT.

- **NT names** NT file names are limited to 256 characters, and can include upper- and lowercase characters, spaces, and some special characters. This is the NTFS convention, and it is available only to users of Windows NT workstations (and the server, of course).

Now, using those rules, let's see what happens when you move files around:

- A file created using the FAT convention (8+3) displays as created to NTFS users and Mac users.

- A file created using the 32-character Mac limit displays as created to NTFS users. DOS users see the name truncated to 8+3 format. This can have some very unusual (not to mention unwanted) results.

- A file created using the NTFS 256-character limit displays as created to Mac users if it is 32 characters or less. Otherwise, it is truncated to the 8+3 format.

Mac users should use 8+3 filenames if they are going to *share* the files with DOS users. While this may seem limiting to Mac users, it avoids a lot of confusion down the line.

Which Application Does the Data File Belong To?

The DOS world has something of a convention when it comes to naming files. Many applications attach a particular extension to their data files—.SAM to Ami-Pro documents, .WK4 to Lotus 1-2-3 worksheets, .DBF to dBASE databases, and so forth. Users can generally change these extensions if they like, although most don't, since application programs are written to display data files using their default extensions.

Mac files don't follow these rules; they have their own. Every Mac file is assigned a *type* and *creator* code that defines which application created it. The type and creator code are embedded in the file's resource fork, and enable the file to be displayed on the Mac desktop with an icon that is unique and recognizable for each application program. The type and creator code enable Mac users to double-click documents to launch their associated applications.

When a Mac file is placed on the NT server, the Mac user loses the ability to determine what type of file it is. Worse yet, any PC file that the Mac user copies to a Mac doesn't have a type and creator code; it appears as a blank document.

The first problem, determining the type of file, is easy to overcome if Mac users name files using the same conventions that DOS users employ—a three-character extension that indicates the file type. The second problem, that of making the Mac understand a PC file type, is overcome by using something called extension mapping.

Extension Mapping

Extension mapping is a process whereby a file that contains a specific extension, such as .WK4, is mapped to a particular Mac application, such as Excel. Users can determine which data files they want to be associated with which applications. Then, when the data files are copied to the Mac hard disk, a type and creator code is assigned to them for that application.

Extension mapping is a good idea in theory, but in practice it doesn't ensure that a data file is compatible with a particular application. The data file may need to be *translated*.

NT Server's Services for Macintosh is already set up to conduct extension mapping with popular application programs. A listing of available extension maps can be found on pages 98 to 100 in the *Services for Macintosh* booklet. You can create additional maps using NT Server's File Manager Associations.

To add additional associations, open the File Manager and select MacFile. From the MacFile menu, select Associate. You'll see a screen similar to the one in Figure 18.19. Add the MS-DOS file extension you want to be associated with a Mac application in the appropriate field, and then select the Macintosh application you want to be associated with files having that extension.

FIGURE 18.19:

Associate dialog box

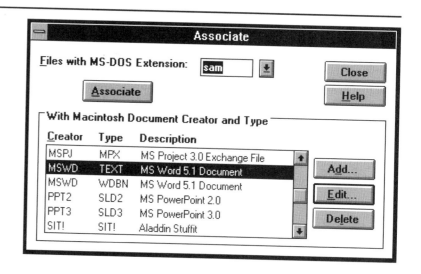

If a Mac application program's name isn't included on the list, you can add it, but you need to know its creator code and the type codes for the documents it supports. If you don't know this information, you can usually find it in the application program's documentation, or you can get it by calling the manufacturer of the application program.

Let's say you want to add the Mac application Teach Text to the list:

1. Open the File Manager and select MacFile.
2. From the MacFile menu, select Associate.

3. Click the Add button and you see the Add Document Type dialog box, as in Figure 18.20.

4. Type in the four-letter creator code and the four-character type code for the application you want to add.

5. In the Description field, type in the name of the Mac application program. The name will be added to the list that you used in the previous step.

6. Click Close when you're done.

TIP
Type and Creator codes are four-character codes that are assigned to application programs by Apple. They are not made up by programmers or by users. Be careful when adding type and creator codes. If you don't know an application's codes, check the documentation, call the program's manufacturer, or call Apple.

File Filters and Translations

Many application programs have built-in *file filters*, the programs that convert one kind of data file to another. Perhaps the best example of this is a program like Microsoft Excel. Excel can read data files created from Lotus 1-2-3 and several other spreadsheet programs and convert them to Excel format. Other programs have optional filters that must be installed. Word processors and graphics programs, for example, often support a number of file formats.

Be careful when using filters. Just because a program has a translator built in to it doesn't mean everything translates properly.

FIGURE 18.20:
Add Document Type dialog box

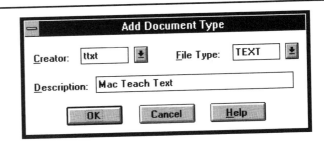

If a particular application program doesn't have translators built in or included as options, usually third-party programs are available to do the job. Conversions Plus and Mac-In-DOS are two such programs that come to mind. For the Mac, try MacLink Plus, Access PC, or PC Exchange.

Using Cross-Platform Applications

Just about the cleanest way to get applications to understand data files in a shared environment is to use *cross-platform applications*. These applications include both a PC version and a Mac version, and the data files are fully transportable across the two platforms.

Examples of cross-platform applications include:

- Microsoft Word, Excel, PowerPoint, and Mail
- Lotus 1-2-3
- WordPerfect
- PageMaker
- Quark Xpress
- FileMaker Pro
- cc:Mail
- QuickMail
- First Class Mail

Be careful with cross-platform applications. Just because an application is cross-platform doesn't necessarily mean that documents convert entirely correctly. Also, if a document contains embedded graphics (as is the case with PageMaker), the graphics need to be removed from the original, converted separately, and reinserted in the cross-platform document.

Bad Dates

A word of caution about dates: Mac and DOS files are date-stamped differently. At Microsoft, time started on January 1, 1980. At Apple, time began on January 1, 1904. All file dates are internally converted to a Julian dating system, which calls day 1 whatever the day 1 is for the particular company and numbers each day from there. The difference in date-stamping methods causes enormous problems when data files contain date functions. Suppose you have a spreadsheet with a formula such as (*today*)+30. If this is a Mac file, *today* means something completely different when this file is used by a PC application.

The Downside (and You Knew There'd Be One)

While all of this Mac connectivity stuff sounds good, there are a few limitations to what Mac clients can do in the NT world:

- RAS doesn't support AppleTalk, since AppleTalk doesn't send NetBIOS packets.

- MS-Mail is supported, but Mac client support is not provided unless you buy it separately (buy the upgrade kit—Mac clients aren't compatible with Workgroup mail).

- Mac clients do not execute logon scripts and can't take advantage of user profiles.

- Mac clients can't participate in inter-domain trust relationships or see resources from other NT Server domains, unless Services for Macintosh has been enabled in those domains and they are on the *same* network.

That's all that I had to say in this book. If you made it this far, thanks! It's nice to know that someone did as much reading as I did writing.

NT is an example of a "next generation" server. Not only does it include enterprise features, it is priced reasonably. Although I wrote the book for those with "enterprise" networks, I'm sure that plenty of people will install NT for small office networks as well—the system is certainly cheap enough.

But this isn't the end of the story, for two reasons. First, NT 3.51 isn't Microsoft's final goal, nor *has* it been. Years ago, Bill Gates outlined a strategy called "information at your fingertips," and this strategy will be realized in the next version of NT. Code-named "Cairo," this new NT will be as much of a leap from NT 3.51 as NT was from LAN Manager. We won't see it until at least 1996, but it will no doubt be interesting.

The second reason why this isn't the end of the story is the most important. This book was written for *you*, the support person. I don't know the answers to all NT questions, but I'd like to. If you come across a tidbit of information or a tough question, feel free to send it to me at the e-mail addresses listed in the Introduction. I can't guarantee that I'll be able to help you, but I'll try. And if you give me a terrific tip for the next edition of the book, then I'll give you credit. Good luck and happy networking!

INDEX

Note to the Reader: Throughout this index **boldface** page numbers indicate primary discussions of a topic. *Italic* page numbers indicate illustrations.

D

F

G

I

N

O

P

Q

R

S

T

W

X

Z

FOR EVERY COMPUTER QUESTION,
THERE IS A SYBEX BOOK THAT HAS THE ANSWER

Each computer user learns in a different way. Some need thorough, methodical explanations, while others are too busy for details. At Sybex we bring nearly 20 years of experience to developing the book that's right for you. Whatever your needs, we can help you get the most from your software and hardware, at a pace that's comfortable for you.

We start beginners out right. You will learn by seeing and doing with our **Quick & Easy** series: friendly, colorful guidebooks with screen-by-screen illustrations. For hardware novices, the **Your First** series offers valuable purchasing advice and installation support.

Often recognized for excellence in national book reviews, our **Mastering** titles are designed for the intermediate to advanced user, without leaving the beginner behind. A **Mastering** book provides the most detailed reference available. Add our pocket-sized **Instant Reference** titles for a complete guidance system. Programmers will find that the new **Developer's Handbook** series provides a more advanced perspective on developing innovative and original code.

With the breathtaking advances common in computing today comes an ever increasing demand to remain technologically up-to-date. In many of our books, we provide the added value of software, on disks or CDs. Sybex remains your source for information on software development, operating systems, networking, and every kind of desktop application. We even have books for kids. Sybex can help smooth your travels on the **Internet** and provide **Strategies and Secrets** to your favorite computer games.

As you read this book, take note of its quality. Sybex publishes books written by experts—authors chosen for their extensive topical knowledge. In fact, many are professionals working in the computer software field. In addition, each manuscript is thoroughly reviewed by our technical, editorial, and production personnel for accuracy and ease-of-use before you ever see it—our guarantee that you'll buy a quality Sybex book every time.

To manage your hardware headaches and optimize your software potential, ask for a Sybex book.

FOR MORE INFORMATION, PLEASE CONTACT:

Sybex Inc.
2021 Challenger Drive
Alameda, CA 94501
Tel: (510) 523-8233 • (800) 227-2346
Fax: (510) 523-2373

Sybex is committed to using natural resources wisely to preserve and improve our environment. As a leader in the computer books publishing industry, we are aware that over 40% of America's solid waste is paper. This is why we have been printing our books on recycled paper since 1982.

This year our use of recycled paper will result in the saving of more than 153,000 trees. We will lower air pollution effluents by 54,000 pounds, save 6,300,000 gallons of water, and reduce landfill by 27,000 cubic yards.

In choosing a Sybex book you are not only making a choice for the best in skills and information, you are also choosing to enhance the quality of life for all of us.

GET A FREE CATALOG JUST FOR EXPRESSING YOUR OPINION.

Help us improve our books and get a **FREE** full-color catalog in the bargain. Please complete this form, pull out this page and send it in today. The address is on the reverse side.

Name _____   Company _____

Address _____   City _____ State ____ Zip _____

Phone (____) _____

1. How would you rate the overall quality of this book?

❑ Excellent
❑ Very Good
❑ Good
❑ Fair
❑ Below Average
❑ Poor

2. What were the things you liked most about the book? (Check all that apply)

❑ Pace
❑ Format
❑ Writing Style
❑ Examples
❑ Table of Contents
❑ Index
❑ Price
❑ Illustrations
❑ Type Style
❑ Cover
❑ Depth of Coverage
❑ Fast Track Notes

3. What were the things you liked *least* about the book? (Check all that apply)

❑ Pace
❑ Format
❑ Writing Style
❑ Examples
❑ Table of Contents
❑ Index
❑ Price
❑ Illustrations
❑ Type Style
❑ Cover
❑ Depth of Coverage
❑ Fast Track Notes

4. Where did you buy this book?

❑ Bookstore chain
❑ Small independent bookstore
❑ Computer store
❑ Wholesale club
❑ College bookstore
❑ Technical bookstore
❑ Other _____

5. How did you decide to buy this particular book?

❑ Recommended by friend
❑ Recommended by store personnel
❑ Author's reputation
❑ Sybex's reputation
❑ Read book review in _____
❑ Other _____

6. How did you pay for this book?

❑ Used own funds
❑ Reimbursed by company
❑ Received book as a gift

7. What is your level of experience with the subject covered in this book?

❑ Beginner
❑ Intermediate
❑ Advanced

8. How long have you been using a computer?

years _____
months _____

9. Where do you most often use your computer?

❑ Home
❑ Work

❑ Both
❑ Other _____

10. What kind of computer equipment do you have? (Check all that apply)

❑ PC Compatible Desktop Computer
❑ PC Compatible Laptop Computer
❑ Apple/Mac Computer
❑ Apple/Mac Laptop Computer
❑ CD ROM
❑ Fax Modem
❑ Data Modem
❑ Scanner
❑ Sound Card
❑ Other _____

11. What other kinds of software packages do you ordinarily use?

❑ Accounting
❑ Databases
❑ Networks
❑ Apple/Mac
❑ Desktop Publishing
❑ Spreadsheets
❑ CAD
❑ Games
❑ Word Processing
❑ Communications
❑ Money Management
❑ Other _____

12. What operating systems do you ordinarily use?

❑ DOS
❑ OS/2
❑ Windows
❑ Apple/Mac
❑ Windows NT
❑ Other _____

13. On what computer-related subject(s) would you like to see more books?

_____

_____

_____

_____

14. Do you have any other comments about this book? (Please feel free to use a separate piece of paper if you need more room)

_____

_____

_____

_____

_____

PLEASE FOLD, SEAL, AND MAIL TO SYBEX

SYBEX INC.
Department M
2021 Challenger Drive
Alameda, CA
94501

Let us hear from you.

 Talk to SYBEX authors, editors and fellow forum members.

 Get tips, hints and advice online.

 Download magazine articles, book art, and shareware.

How Do I?